THE ESSENTIAL RUSSELL KIRK

Russell Amos Kirk (1918–94)

THE ESSENTIAL RUSSELL KIRK

❖

Selected Essays

EDITED BY
GEORGE A. PANICHAS

ISI BOOKS
2007

Kirk, Russell.

The essential Russell Kirk : selected essays / edited by George A. Panichas. — 1st ed. — Wilmington, DE : ISI Books, 2007.

p. ; cm.

ISBN-13: 978-1-933859-01-9
ISBN-13: 978-1-933859-02-6 (PBK.)
ISBN-10: 1-933859-01-6
ISBN-10: 1-933859-02-4 (PBK.)

1. Conservatism. 2. Politics. 3. Essays. I. Panichas, George A. II. Title.

JC573 .K57 2007 2006929182
320.52—dc22 0701

ISI BOOKS
INTERCOLLEGIATE STUDIES INSTITUTE
POST OFFICE BOX 4431
WILMINGTON, DELAWARE 19807

I offer perpetual congratulation to the scholar; he has drawn the white lot in life. The very disadvantages of his condition point at superiorities. He is too good for the world; he is in advance of his race; his function is prophetic.

—Ralph Waldo Emerson

"The Man of Letters"
Lectures and Biographical Sketches (1895)

There is nothing more wholesome than to dip into the strong and steady current of wise judgment.

—Paul Elmer More

"The Centenary of Sainte-Beuve"
Shelburne Essays, Volume III (1905)

I.

THE IDEA OF CONSERVATISM

II.

OUR SACRED PATRIMONY

III.

PRINCIPLES OF ORDER

IV.

THE MORAL IMAGINATION

V.

PLACES AND PEOPLE

VI.

THE DRUG OF IDEOLOGY

VII.

DECADENCE AND RENEWAL IN EDUCATION

VIII.

THE AMERICAN REPUBLIC

IX.

CONSERVATORS OF CIVILIZATION

Preface

I

The Essential Russell Kirk has as its chief purpose the task of offering to a new generation of readers representative writings of a distinguished American man of letters of the twentieth century. The crises of modern civilization that Kirk confronted head-on in his lifetime have not abated and now continue into the twenty-first century in forms and with a force and thrust perhaps different from but surely no less threatening than in the preceding century.

To the office of the man of letters Kirk brought considerable distinction, and for which he will be principally remembered and honored. He exemplifies "the supreme importance of the Man of Letters in modern Society," about which the nineteenth-century Scots social prophet and historian, Thomas Carlyle, has valuable things to say. The man of letters, he states, is a "heroic seeker" who proclaims that "life must be pitched on a higher plane." Above all, he struggles against the ravages of "spiritual paralysis" in a world in which "the battle of Belief against Unbelief is the never-ending battle." These pregnant words of his famous Scots forefather help us to gauge Kirk's calling as a modern man of letters who discharges his function as "a guardian of old truths and old rights," and who strains to push things up to their first principles.

For more than forty years and in more than thirty books, and in countless articles, Kirk fought on the front line in the war of ideas. The nine major categories and the selected essays contained in this book present a map of the terrain on which Kirk fought. They identify the particular locales of the battles in which he was engaged, and they also encompass the strategies and tactics of the general warfare which demanded from him the utmost effort, tenacity, courage, belief.

"The Idea of Conservatism"; "Our Sacred Patrimony"; "Principles of Order"; "The Moral Imagination"; "Places and People"; "The Drug of Ideology"; "Decadence and Renewal in Education"; "The American Republic"; "Conservators of Civilization": these are the respective titles of the nine categories around which *The Essential Russell Kirk* is organized and developed. They are arranged so as to aid the reader not only in reflecting on the primary questions that Kirk's major critical texts pose, but also in measuring the significance of his mission, his work in life. It should also be remarked at this point that a succinct interpretive summary, or overview, introduces each category, and a descriptive headnote precedes each essay. The object of these editorial inclusions is to supply the reader with pertinent background material, as well as to facilitate a more cogent comprehension of the book's content in its discrete parts.

The selections featured in this work are indicative of Kirk's gifts as an essayist, critic, and lecturer. (He was also an accomplished writer of fiction whose three novels and three collections of ghostly tales constitute a body of work that stands on its own and deserves separate critical comment.) Full-scale essays, reviews, review-essays, prefatory pieces, whether in the form of a foreword or an introduction, public addresses, and entire chapters from his books disclose Kirk's range of interests and the nature of his criteria and opinions as a man of letters. Seen in their completeness, these selections disclose his extraordinary breadth and thought as a social critic and an ethical teacher. Whether one studies these writings selectively or systematically, one is bound to respond to the issues they present and to the challenge of Kirk's interpretations. And one becomes not a mere spectator to but rather a foot-soldier in what Kirk himself was to experience in "a half-century of literary conflict" in the modern age.

From these nine categories there emerges a graphic picture of the struggle in which Kirk was involved and in which he displayed unusual perseverance. These categories are closely interconnected and interdependent, as they should be in establishing the main lines of Kirk's achievement as a major American thinker and critic in the twentieth century. The organization of this anthology is a thematic one, with the aim of assisting a reader to respond to Kirk's fundamental preoccupations, to fathom his critical disquisitions, to hear his distinct voice speaking in each of the selections published here. Additionally, a reader will be enabled to enter the assiduous process of Kirk's arguments, to ponder the circumstances that inspired their exposition, and to assess the social, political, intellectual, philosophical, literary, and religious conditions that characterize the historical setting of Kirk's commentaries. Although Kirk is examining the prevailing state of American consciousness, his findings and judgments travel beyond regional and temporal frontiers and are founded in universal history and mankind.

In a large sense, then, these categories seek to outline the intellectual and moral struggles in which Kirk took part without interruption, from beginning to end, when only death itself finally intervened. The scope of these epochal struggles is specified here, and is to be seen in its magnitude, its urgency, its significance. It is hoped that the nine categories, and the particular essays found in each, will provide a detailed index to Kirk's multiple efforts to expose the profane dialectics of a modern cosmology and to defend the values and principles of a humane civilization. It is hoped, too, that they will substantiate his unfolding vision of order and virtue, which he steadfastly avowed as a moral historian, a political philosopher, a conservative humanist, and a social and cultural critic.

The pressing needs of the American community and the condition of the American soul are pivotal concerns which Kirk addresses in essay after essay with fierce independence of thought. His prose writings, as they are arranged here, are further designed to involve the reader as an active player in American social and cultural history in a time of swift transition and change in the years following World War II. A discriminate reading of these writings will help pinpoint the consequences of these changes as they continue to affect the present-day situation. Even for those who harbor doubts about or objections to the traditions and the institutions of Western society, the pervasive seriousness of these writings will prove compelling and will illustrate the truth expressed by the ancients, that "the greater joy comes from seriousness."

II

Russell Amos Kirk was born on October 19, 1918, in Plymouth, Michigan, the year that saw the ending of the Great War and the beginning of huge and shattering changes in Western civilization, when, as the poet William Butler Yeats wrote in his "Second Coming"(1919), "Things fall apart; the centre cannot hold; / Mere anarchy is loosed upon the world." Giving steady witness to Yeats's prophetic words, Kirk was to demonstrate in his long career that the War did not in fact end on Armistice Day of 1918, but continued throughout the century. His writings attest not only to the broken world in the post-1918 era, with its increasing disillusionment, fragmentation, dehumanization, confusion, but also to the very nature of the human predicament that the philosopher Karl Jaspers captured in these words: "Every truth we may think complete will prove itself untruth at the moment of shipwreck."

For Kirk, however, truth endures despite the exigencies of time and place and of the losses that civilization was to suffer. Indeed, his writings measure the cruel losses in the immediate context of the disorder and decadence that Kirk diagnoses as the most severe symptoms of a collapsing of civilization in the twentieth century. And again and again he weighs the motives and methods of modern social engineers: those utopian reformers who, as T. S. Eliot writes, are ever "dreaming of systems so perfect that no one will need be good"—in short, those who continue to deepen and broaden the gulf of disinheritance on which we find ourselves stranded at the start of the third millennium. By no means does Kirk try either to evade or to underestimate the gravity of the forces and abnormities that besiege modern life. He examines them in all their intricate forms and excesses, and he does so with a profound sense of the reality and the lessons of history. What he sees and finds in the visible world around him, and in the soul of man, elicits his most serious concerns in "a time of troubles."

His testimony is laced with honesty and conviction. He makes no attempt to cover up difficulties or to soften their effects. And he writes about these matters in a crisp, straightforward, civilized style that on occasion rises to the level of prose poetry. Clarity and simplicity, classical virtues that Kirk much valued, infuse his vocabulary and syntax. He is never laborious to read. His prose is distinctly one of temperateness: vigorous, sophisticated, eloquent, lucid, at times humorous and even whimsical. Its rhythm is one of order and measure; its tone, balanced. His language is never obscure or abstract; the diction is that of an educated, urbane thinker. His reverence for language is implicit. Autobiographical elements are selectedly employed to humanize prose and meaning. Aphorisms abound in memorable ways. The qualities of robustness and sanity and good reason are in constant evidence, and there is always a note of hope and unwavering belief in individual and cultural rebirth. "Yet cheerfulness will keep breaking in," Kirk assures us.

Although Kirk's is a learned style, anchored in extraordinarily wide reading in ancient and modern literature, in history, in economics, in politics, in philosophy, in theology, in law, it is not one that intimidates the reader. It is a style that emerges from his high regard for paradigms of intellect and character and culture, for the need for roots and order, for the idea of limit, of measure, of proportion, and above all humility. Invariably he discloses a deep awareness of the moral responsibility of the writer. The non-centered, non-discriminating content of many modern writers embodies for Kirk a negative symptom of the modern temper, to which he refuses to bend.

For Kirk the power of words and the responsibility of the writer have a conjoining ethical and moral connection ultimately informing and unifying vision and style. To direct readers to the principles of style in Kirk's writings is still another important aspect of this collection of selected essays. His style, in effect, has the added value of involving a reader in a verbal process bespeaking the ultimate morality of mind. Communicating both the sincerity and the beneficences of Kirk's style is one of the larger and impelling intentions of *The Essential Russell Kirk.*

Some of Kirk's readers will perhaps notice a certain repetitive pattern of phrase and argument in his writings, when language and ideas over the years tend to take on circular, or rotative, motions. One's immediate reaction may even be that key terms, sentences, and paragraphs are restated, thus re-echoing by expanding their first appearance and meaning. This rotative quality is neither a flaw nor an infelicity in Kirk's train of thought and expression. Rather, it reveals an intrinsic attribute of his reflections in direct proportion to the constantly widening rhythms and circles of his critical concentration and analysis that are an inevitable part of the influx of re-apprehending, re-thinking, re-writing, re-conceptualizing.

The fact is that there is no single terminal point, no fixture, in Kirk's expository concerns and aspirations; there is only the constant and living necessity to press and press the essences of an idea or a thought, to wrestle ceaselessly with words and meaning, and to proceed towards a deeper recognition of the nexus of the old and the new, of cause and effect, of human and divine truths. These words from an earlier master essayist, Ralph Waldo Emerson, go a long way in allowing a reader to recognize the pattern and movement of Kirk's style and vision: "Our life is an apprenticeship to the truth that around every circle another can be drawn; that there is no end in nature, but every end is a beginning; that there is always another dawn risen on mid-noon, and under every deep a lower deep opens."

Kirk's first loyalty is to first principles; defending and preserving and passing them on anew in their incorruptible substance demands that he focus and re-focus on them in the shifting stages of history. If anything, Kirk is sharply aware of the realities of change, of adapting to their volatility and passion without at the same time yielding in his fundamental loyalty to universal values, to normative truths and standards. To unmask the changing faces and lexicon of relativism, as well as the simultaneous need to give allegiance to reverent principles of order, are needs that, for Kirk, test the ability of "one who combines with a disposition to preserve an ability to reform"—or, as he wrote early on in his career, "to lead the waters of novelty into the canals of custom." His words here help to elucidate the recurring configurations that one encounters in his style and content.

For Kirk there could be no neutral ground where one hides from others and from one's self. In effect he was always under arms. To reclaim a sacred patrimony is a battle that requires unflinching commitment. In his writings he articulates the full nature and extent of his many skirmishes with radical ideologies that reject principles of order and universal absolutes. Throughout his lifetime he placed himself in direct opposition to the mainstream of liberal and radical intellectuals. Within the academy, in particular, he focused on a free-wheeling professoriate sowing the seeds of "vulgarized pragmatism." There was no doubt in his mind that those who are now known as postmodern intellectuals were held fast in "the clutch of ideology." He was in constant readiness, then, to resist the spirit of relativism which one academic ideologue proudly sums up in these words: "Postmodernism maintains only that there can be no independent standard for determining which of many rival interpretations of an event is the true one." Such a view, Kirk held, abrogates all standards of historical, ethical, moral, and religious truth.

III

The following selected essays establish Kirk's grounding in the heritage of Western civilization: in the classical and the biblical tradition; in Judeo-Christian spiritual thought; in Eurocentric literary and intellectual values; and in British-American political and legal institutions. His worldview is centrally defined and shaped by his loyalty to this venerable inheritance; and his works as a whole seek to defend and guard its bounty. His efforts, as such, are indefatigable, and one will find in any perusal of his writings that, whatever their diversity of subject matter and approach, first principles are their mainstay. As a man of letters, Kirk assays the multiform problems of our civilization in their many offshoots, paradoxes, antinomies. Yet his writings unfailingly return to a moral center. The centripetal quality of Kirk's ideas and judgments exerts total control in his works, and acts as a great unifier. As this book will disclose, his essays take different paths and directions, but there is always a prescriptive position, a seat of judgment, a central creed and identity, to which he comes back again and again for support and ratification.

Repeatedly, as Kirk discloses in his writings, modern secular society subordinates and even betrays standards of judgment to ideological dogmas and to quantitative reductionisms that promote "the abolition of man" through the abolition of history and logic and religious certitude. He reminds us of

Plato's contention that the improvement of the life of the soul must be the ultimate purpose of discourse. Indeed, Kirk's words can be described as discourses of reason in which moral insight helps to engender moral prudence ("the soul's stern sacristan," as one poet expresses it). He was quintessentially aware that in our time social and personal disintegration mirrors the Evil Spirit. For Kirk this is a process of disorder that destroys our great inheritance of Western tradition and, in turn, dilutes what he calls "the springs of American metaphysics and American morality, as they are of European metaphysics and morality."

Inevitably this is also a destructive process that abolishes the message of the Hebrew Prophets, the words of Christ and His Disciples, the writings of the Holy Fathers and Angelic Doctors of the Church, the witness of the Christian martyrs and Saints, the treatises of the Schoolmen, the discourses of the great divines of Reformation and Counter-Reformation. In this respect, *The Essential Russell Kirk* records the multiform and tensive labors of an American sage and critic in his pursuit of virtue in a frenzied era of spiritual and intellectual devolution.

What gives unity and harmony to Kirk's critical dynamic and outlook, what gives it distinct character and discipline, is the constant interaction and interdependence between its parts and its whole. Each selection found in this volume has its own intellectual authority and voice, appropriate to the particular subject under discussion. It can, of course, stand completely on its own, yet at the same time the selection is no mere fugitive piece of writing, or simply a discrete part of a miscellany. Thus, though a selection can be read for its own internal value and pertinence, it also has a distinctly proportionate and relational place in Kirk's acute apprehension of human destiny. Kirk's writings, then, must be considered in their oneness and continuity.

Completely free from malice, Kirk's critiques are sobering but illuminating. His relation to the reader is, in this respect, based on trust, refreshingly free of the superciliousness and the ostentation of many academic critics and liberal oracles. His candor is especially disarming, touching, as when he simply announces that he has a "Gothic mind, medieval in its temper and structure"; that he seeks for "a complex of variety, mystery, tradition, the venerable, the awful"; that he is "groping for faith, honor, and prescriptive loyalties"; that he would give "any number of neoclassical pediments for one poor battered gargoyle." His aim, he makes unmistakably clear, is to improve the life of the mind and of the spirit and to foster discriminations and judgments. He does not necessarily seek to make friends or even allies of his readers, but instead to appeal to their right reason and sense of justice—and to beckon them to join him on the path to truth. He does not shout or shove or strut as he strives to make readers aware of "a world split apart." For him, schism of the soul and schism of the community have a distinctly mutual relationship, which to refuse to acknowledge diminishes any hope of "redeeming the time."

As a conservative social critic Kirk is particularly adept in examining acute dimensions of the American experience, past and present. At the same time his critiques, often found in the form of dissents, move beyond national boundaries and biases, and are ultimately anchored in transcendent standards and universal referents. It is the separation of political order from moral order that especially disturbs Kirk as he measures the costs of this separation at all levels of democracy and leadership, and of life and letters, on both the national and the international scene. Above all, he reminds us of the need to see the world as an organic whole. The failure to do so constricts a proper understanding of mankind by imposing false and fragmentary schemes.

During the last decade of his life Kirk was to sound a more anxious note in his social criticism. Although his usual temperate tone remained steady, there was an added urgency ignited by his growing awareness of a host of changes affecting the direction of a nation entering a fateful era. Sentiments and not reflections, he believed, were becoming more infectious and dominant among the citizenry, reflecting the impact of the electronic media in altering civilized discourse and in conducing a "servile intellect." He was strongly critical, for example, of federal and state courts for failing to restrain merchants of indecency freely marketing pornography, obscenity, salacity. He was equally critical of "the curious sect of multiculturalists" who, in the name of "relevance" and "inclusion," were actually contributing to educational decay and a false sense of equality.

Always wary of politically legislated programs, Kirk viewed them as instruments of ideology leading to the larger decline of general culture. In particular, Kirk expressed his fears for the safety and continuation of English language and literature transmitted to America from Britain, and carrying with them "certain assumptions about the human condition, 'of moral evil and of good.'" For Kirk, too, an expanding culture of greed further menaced the ethical basis of a humane economy and magnified the dilemma of capitalism and collectivism. The increasing disintegration of urban areas, in which social boredom and violence were spreading like a cancer, was also prompting additional worry.

Not one to shun the hard realities of the human situation, Kirk unfailingly alerts us to moral and spiritual afflictions that besiege humankind and that deepen modern man's vacuum of disinheritance. In especial he seeks to remind us of antinomian and abnormative lures and practices that lead to skepticism, disorder, restlessness, alienation, and the perversions issuing from "the diabolic imagination." And he is profoundly cognizant of what takes place when moral virtues are extinct in a profane secular society, as "the flight from God" becomes an irreversible process in which the search "after strange gods" constitutes in itself an *ersatz* religion, with all the entailing consequences. Indeed, his work, in its astonishing continuity, exposes the power of "the antagonist world" and its cumulative vices and demons. To permit indifference, or apathy, or failure of nerve deters us from challenging the "enemies of the permanent things," he warns, solidifies the tendencies and terrors that set in with the coming of the French Revolution in 1789.

Again and again, Kirk calls us back to Plato's belief that the elevation of the life of the soul must be the ultimate goal of discourse. For only when we acknowledge the needs of the soul, he keeps saying, will we be able to resist the intrusions of imperious ideologies on human existence. No ideological scheme can possibly be complete, or authentic, that ignores spiritual questions—or worse, that strives to suffocate the soul. In the clearest of terms, Kirk also shows how the life of the soul, in conjunction with the life of the community, remains in a technosecular social system a largely unacknowledged subject of concern. Almost alone among modern writers and thinkers Kirk chose to explain, patiently and diligently, just how insidious were the preachers of "armed doctrines," which acquired so much dominion in modern political thought.

As Kirk was often to emphasize, "the errors of ideology" would not be reversed until a clearcut willingness was demonstrated, yes, even among conservative thinkers, to defend "prudential politics as opposed to ideologized politics." Political order and spiritual order, he never tired of asserting, are contiguous: the refusal to accept this fact inevitably undermines any apprehension of higher reality. Unlike many of his contemporaries in the American intelligentsia, unwilling to grapple with moral and spiritual problems, and unyielding in their empirico-critical habits of thought, Kirk refused to put divine things, as the Gospel writer would have it, "under a bushel, or under a bed."

IV

Despite the chaos that Kirk sees in so much of modern existence, he speaks for life. Identifying opportunities for moral discovery and reformation is an unflagging impulse. His warnings and strictures must not be approached as instances of pessimism or of irresolution. As long as we can appeal to paradigms of character, and of intellectual and moral integrity, the possibilities of spiritual renewal are never exhausted. Enduring faith, patience, hope are ingredients that cohere in the dynamic of Kirk's acceptances and affirmations. The men and women whose lives and works he asks us to ponder share in a moral vision that conduces understanding of our humanity and our divinity. In an age that has watered down the genuine meaning of heroism, Kirk strove to turn our attention to "conservators of civilization" whose insight and wisdom have for us the further value of restoring order to the commonwealth and to the soul. These exemplars convey foundational thought that is not the hostage of the spirit of the age or that fluctuates and drifts with the opinions of democratic majorities and with the fashions and trends and fads of the times.

With the "keen-sighted few" who compose the great moralist tradition of English-speaking men of letters in the twentieth century—Irving Babbitt, Paul Elmer More, T. S. Eliot, Richard M. Weaver—and also of great European thinkers like Eric Voegelin, Werner Jaeger, Simone Weil, Max Picard, Joseph Pieper, Kirk sought to teach wisdom rather than illusory opinions and vain hopes. Not surprisingly he was a strong champion of Joseph Conrad's moral vision of genius rendered in such novels as *Under Western Eyes* (1911), *The Secret Agent* (1907), and *Nostromo* (1904), which he viewed as entertaining absolutely no illusions about socio-political revisionist schemes and systems that too often lead to dead-ends like nihilism and anarchy.

Kirk refused to endorse "philodoxers" of opinions and doctrines who would require us in the end to "be utterly demythologized, disenchanted, desacralized, and deconsecrated." In their ideology of a "new morality" he detected the potential for human degradation and corruption. It is with especial approbation, hence, that Kirk quotes these choice words of Gustave Thibon, the late French religious philosopher: "The decline of moral habit produces, in its first stage, a rigid and exalted moralism; and in its second, an immoralism raised to the level of doctrine; sooner or later, it invariably gives birth to the lowest level of immorality."

For Kirk neither disorder nor decadence can be the last word on the condition of modern human existence. The same Christian virtue of patience that he so much admired in T. S. Eliot is fully evident in Kirk's outlook. "Renewal" and "restoration" are words that have a visible and viable place in his conservatism of reflection. We have the "instruments for the recovery of moral order," he insists, even as we must affirm faith in "the possibility of a conservative renewal of society" as we actively reject the intrusions and anomalies of modern society—what Pope John Paul II has aptly labeled as "the noisy propaganda of liberalism, of freedom without truth or responsibility."

Elsewhere, in signaling his acceptance of the rule of measure, as inspired by the classical Greek and Roman ways of thinking, he asserts that "our best efforts succeed only in making a temporarily tolerable society, not one that is perfect." Clearly Kirk maintained in his writings that, whether directly or indirectly, transfiguration and salvation are not absent from the human scene, and embody possibilities that can influence the course of human history and destiny. There are, he believes, neglected beneficences that can be rediscovered and restored to human experience and can make an enormous difference in the human equation. Particularly in the area of education, which he scrutinized regularly, he specifically identified the array of problems that originated with the pragmatism and instrumentalism preached by the philosopher John Dewey and his disciples. In this respect his essays and books were not only diagnostic but also corrective in suggesting ways of both teaching humane literature and revitalizing the educational system.

As a critic and teacher, Kirk presented his conservative worldview in concrete terms, always supporting his theoretical theses and general ideas with a specificity of example and analysis and of text and context. Even a perusal of the selections featured in this anthology will readily confirm the critical power of his capacity to reconcile the abstract and the concrete, and to heed what Irving Babbitt, the renowned American critic and teacher who had permanent influence on Kirk, calls "the actual data of experience." He does not allow the shadow to pass between idea and reality. And though Kirk can be described as a generalist, he does not fall into the traps of generalization. There is nothing hazy about his writings, in which life, literature, and thought remain in continuous dialogue and enjoy a parity of reason and esteem. For Kirk, pedantic no less than romantic attitudes and practices, especially as found in literature and society, were murky and dilatory in value and principle. One must, he stresses, get "to the point."

To be sure, the essays found here underline, both implicitly and explicitly, the conservative origins and ethos of Kirk's work and thought, and the truth that he is one of the most prominent purveyors of American conservative ideas and considered as a pioneer of intellectual conservatism in the United States. Since the amazing publication in 1953 of his book *The Conservative Mind*, he has achieved fame, reputation, and influence as the founder of the American conservative movement in post–World War II political history. But as these essays demonstrate, in terms of his place in American life and letters,

Kirk moves beyond the exclusive designation of his conservative instincts and loyalties. Back in 1994, the historian John Lukacs quite rightly observed: "Even now when he is the Old Sage (preferable to Older Statesman) among the conservatives he is independent of most of them, and not at all by striking, or preserving, a pose."

Kirk's conservatism is much greater in both its significance and its inclusiveness. In short, his conservatism is essentially a part, even a stage, of a larger intellectual and spiritual search for the higher civilizational values. This search can more accurately be identified as a conservatorship, and Kirk himself as a conservator who keeps modifying, refining, and advancing his conservative views and affirmations in discrete and discriminating ways. The conservative thinker as conservator is still another way of defining and clarifying what Kirk is, what he seeks, what he does. His office and faculty as a conservator are what guide and shape his calling to preserve and protect the sound principles of things, no less than to understand the universal end of all things. For him, the "two principles of conservation and correction," which Burke espoused, were of cardinal importance.

A cautionary note, then, must be sounded in any estimate of Kirk's conservatism, if he is to be saved from the nets of political partisanship and party loyalty. To repeat, his is a conservatism of reflection: a conservatism that is first, last, and always ratiocinative and contemplative in its constitution and in its aspiration. And unless the uniqueness of this feature of his achievement is fully grasped and assimilated, not only the true value of his vision but also the moral properties of his mission will be misunderstood or misinterpreted. A formidable critical intention of *The Essential Russell Kirk* is to present his thought and achievement in their unalloyed prudence, and in their fullness of critical intelligence and maturity.

What is finally inescapable in Kirk's outlook is the quality of hopefulness, and the absence of crippling bitterness and despair. "Be strong, and of good courage," the Psalmist's injunction, are words that undergird Kirk's perseverance even in the midst of adversity and tragedy itself. His heroes and leaders, those whom he admires most and who are exemplary in word and work, are "God-fearing" men and women intensely dedicated to their normative labors of teaching and defending principles of moral order. Kirk's achievement is thus best defined by its emphasis on the possibility of ascent, and on human worth and greatness. The overwhelming question, "Is life worth living?" is one that Kirk is not afraid to ask. Nor is it a question that he shirks to answer by submitting it to the inveterate advocates of Efficiency, Progress, and Equality.

V

Some readers and auditors may complain that Kirk fails to provide viable solutions to the problems to which he is responding. Such complaints inevitably mirror the age in which we live, addicted to the modern titanism that holds that there is a solution to any human problem that arises, that we have all the requisite aptitude and machinery, all the technology and material resources, the science, the industry, the know-how, the force of arms, to make absolutely no difficulty, no obstacle insurmountable. "The totalists say," Kirk declares, "that the old order is a corpse, and that man and society must be fashioned afresh, in grim fashion, upon a grim plan."The man-God of earlier centuries has now been replaced by technosecular potentates restrained by no other power except their own Promethean self-assertion. For them the old metaphysics, the old beliefs, the old criticism are dead, and have been replaced by King Demos, or by the grand artificers of a new social and moral order, by those named Legion, by those principalities and powers that have defeated the past, rule the present, and control the future: in short, those who have the means to make the invisible visible and the visible invisible at any time and at the slightest whim or opportunity, as it happens to be needed—or not needed; when eternity itself is annexed by the Kingdom of Chronos, the Empire of Might, and the incumbent Ethnarch of Solution.

The faculty of reflection, as Kirk makes plain in his work and thought, precedes solution and at its highest point of maturation is solution. The flow of reflection transforms into principles of action; it is a meditative sequence that leads up to conclusions, as the mind proceeds through illation to penetrate mysteries and discover enduring truths. What John Henry Newman called "the illative sense" deeply influenced Kirk and stamped his point of view and his grasp of first principles. Indeed, the process of reflection is at the very heart not only of Kirk's reasoning but also of his moral certainties. The principle of the illative sense suffuses his reflections and in turn his solutions—the selfsame solutions that some of Kirk's critics find wanting in his work and thought. It is a dynamic principle that gathers judgmental strength based on intuitions, inferences, tacit understandings, apprehensions, assents, as the intellect and imagination converse in the presence of a moral disposition.

Reflection and solution are inseparable, as Kirk's writings reveal. He has the faculty to make value judgments that go beyond immediate and conditional considerations, and that are rooted in the moral sense and in belief. Thus it is necessary to understand Kirk's conservative worldview in terms of his basic acceptations and affirmations as these set in motion his remedies for social and individual problems. His is a long-range view of the world in the sense that, as Confucius states, "the man who does not take far views, will have near troubles." Kirk crafted his intellectual character and his religious faith through careful reflection on the final causes.

For Kirk the individualizing efforts to attain both a sapiential and a sacramental vision of human existence and meaning constituted an earnest struggle against the powerful pull of modern infidelity. During World War II (1942–46), Kirk was in the United States Army, serving as a staff sergeant in the Chemical Warfare Service and stationed at Dugway Proving Ground, near the heart of the Great Salt Lake Desert in the state of Utah. Here he was a recorder and custodian of classified documents. And it was here that a reflective Kirk began to overcome his early admiration of the Enlightenment mind, the positivism of his teens, and the skepticism of his twenties, as well as to transmute the principles of Stoicism that he always revered. It can perhaps be said that these were conversionary years that contained the seeds of the faith of a Christian man of letters who would come to discern his vision and develop and continuously refine his own grammar of assent until the hour of his death, at the age of seventy-five, on October 29, 1994, in his ancestral home at Piety Hill, in Mecosta, Michigan.

An "encourager unto all good labours," as well as "encourager of letters and the arts," Kirk graced the office of man of letters with dignity and with style. In his ministry, so to speak, he manifested the gift of perception, which is essentially diagnostic. Perhaps the greatest gift apportioned to him was what Saint Paul speaks of as "the discerning of spirits." Kirk possessed the discriminating sense, the ability to make exact distinctions after careful observation and reflection. This ability is itself a sign of one who has copiously meditated and measured. His censorial inspection of the modern situation was always conducted in the spirit of affirmation, in the belief that adversity "frequently opens the way for the impulse toward virtue"—and, too, in the expectation that "there endures a wise man of the stamp of Pascal or Samuel Johnson, abiding in a tradition, still employing the power of the Word to scourge the follies of the time."

There are no entries for "man of letters" in the major encyclopedias. Rather perfunctorily, *Webster's Third New International Dictionary* defines the man of letters as "1. a learned man: scholar; 2. a literary man." Any judicious estimate of Kirk's achievement should considerably expand our view of what exactly a man of letters signifies. Those same marks of greatness that one finds in the poets, the novelists, the seers, as Kirk's style of thinking and writing shows with abundance, can be equally present in the man of letters, who has the prophetic ability to make us see things in ways we have never seen before. Thus, Kirk has also helped change Americans' conception of the conservative mind and of the moral imagination. Only an independent, creative man of thought can bring about this propitious happening, particularly in a time of history hostile to what Burke calls "the ancient permanent sense of mankind."

As a man of letters Kirk was far more than one who possesses much learning and full intellectual authority. He addressed himself to the total human situation, and to the need to "speak to the condition," to quote the Quaker phrase. To the office of the man of letters he gave the added moral dimension of one who, in the ancient Greek context, is both a *spoudaios*, a man of character, of excellence, of moral probity, and an *hierophylax*, a keeper of the holy things.

Beyond the combative facets of Kirk's immediate engagement in the war of ideas, there is the visionary and sapiential legacy of his message and meaning. The ultimate aim of this anthology is to portray and to transmit the full power and truth of this legacy and what it says to us about ourselves, about conditions in our time of history, about our sociopolitical and cultural institutions, needs, expectations, possibilities. *The Essential Russell Kirk* honors the worthiness of this legacy and proffers its intellectual and spiritual treasures to a rising generation of readers for safekeeping.

—Russell Amos Kirk—

1918–94

A Composite Chronicle of His Life and Work in His Own Words

Shortly before his death on April 29, 1994, Russell Kirk completed The Sword of Imagination: Memoirs of a Half-Century of Literary Conflict, *which was published on June 5, 1995, by William B. Eerdmans of Grand Rapids, Michigan. Throughout his memoirs Kirk chose to refer to himself in the third person, in effect borrowing a literary device that he found to be consonant with the belief of another renowned Scots man of letters, James Boswell, that "every man's life may be best written by himself." The composite chronicle of Kirk's life and work that follows is presented in his own words, selectively and sequentially excerpted from* The Sword of Imagination. *For purposes of clarification and amplification, and only when required, biographical, bibliographical, and factual information has been added by the editor to Kirk's text in brackets.*

1918 Russell Amos Kirk was born on October 19, 1918, when already the old shell of the social and moral order had been cracked, a few weeks before the Armistice with Germany that concluded the War expected to end all wars. The Bolsheviki had held power in Russia for nearly a year; the Habsburg system was collapsing as the baby was born; the crash of empires would resound throughout his life.

His strong father, Russell Andrew Kirk, had left school before the sixth grade; he was a railroad engineman, soft-spoken and kindly, who would have preferred to work with horses, being the son of a drayman. His little mother, tender and romantic, a reader of good poetry, had been a waitress at her father's railroad restaurant, which stood between their house and the railway line.

A good town to be born into, Plymouth was as old as civilization goes in Michigan, founded by New Englanders in the 1820s. Plymouth in 1918—and indeed until the Second World War—remained a tranquil place with handsome old houses (nearly all of them vanished today), tree-shaded streets, and a square on the New England model.

1922–35 For thirteen years, beginning in 1922, the boy was sent to the public schools of Plymouth, where some of the teachers were very good, indeed, and nearly all were competent. He learned a great deal of history, geography, and humane letters, although his progress in mathematics and the sciences was undistinguished.

1925 During those months before the birth of his sister, Carolyn, Marjorie Pierce tried to fix in her boy's memory everything they did together: it was the close of their isolated intimacy, mother and child, first child. Her tenderness was very great. But, usually, like his father, the boy kept his emotions to himself, tight locked except in some desperate hour.

In fine, Russell's was a childhood of wonder and love, mystery and familial memories. He never knew the tyranny of the "age-peer group," having always the counsel and companionship of family—especially of his grandfather. They two, on their long walks, a conscience speaking to a conscience, had talked. . . . Yet it was by example rather than through discourse that the old gentleman taught the boy charity and fortitude.

1936 As graduation day approached, young Russell had no prospects of employment. To his chagrin, he won a scholarship. In September 1936, seventeen years of age, Russell Kirk arrived at Michigan State College of Agriculture and Applied Science (later to become Michigan State University).

Little could be said for MSC's architecture, however, except for three or four smallish neo-romanesque survivals of red sandstone. One of them, the Old Music Building, Kirk would save from demolition during his undergraduate years there—the one achievement for which he would be mentioned in the official history of Michigan State.

The department of history, in those years, was surprisingly thorough, if somewhat dull; Kirk majored in history.

1937 And during 1936–37, he commenced to write for the serious quarterlies. *College English* accepted and published his essay "Tragedy and the Moderns," unaware that it was submitted by an undergraduate, not a professor; the *South Atlantic Quarterly* printed his first political essay, "Jefferson and the Faithless."

Summers, beginning in 1937, he worked for Mr. Henry Ford. Although Ford's interest lay in technology rather than humane disciplines, the liberal education of young Russell Kirk was much advanced by his being employed at Greenfield Village as a guide during his summer vacations from college.

1940 Upon being graduated from the cow college, whither might he turn? He took an assistantship (for which, as it turned out, he never was required to perform any duties) at Duke; he was well satisfied to be granted a waiving of tuition (then a modest sum) and a stipend of two hundred dollars—for him, wealth beyond the dreams of avarice.

It behooved Kirk to acclimate himself by studying Southern history and Southern literature. At Duke, in 1940–41, were two leading professors in those fields, both of them much published and nationally known: Charles Sydnor in history, Jay Hubbell (the founder of the quarterly *American Literature*) in the latter discipline.

Kirk, as was his way, saying little in their seminars, Dr. Sydnor and Dr. Hubbell were considerably surprised by the papers he submitted to them; and Sydnor would express his astonishment at the master's thesis Kirk produced.

Without anybody's advice, Kirk had chosen for the subject of his thesis the politics of John Randolph of Roanoke, the most interesting and unusual man ever to be a power in the Congress of the United States.

1941 At the end of the academic year, in 1941, Kirk's study of Randolph's thought, his master's thesis, was accepted by the University. Perhaps no other master's thesis in American history, written in a space of eight months, has enjoyed such long life in print, even unto this very day.

In the South, then and later, he learned that some of the more oppressive "problems" in life never are solved, unless by Time and Providence. He read deeply about the South and poked into its ashes. In Richmond and Charleston he found communities that had not surrendered unconditionally to the new order of American life.

But back to Michigan he rode. Later he was told that Dr. Sydnor and Dr. Hubbell had expected him to return to Duke for doctoral studies and would have provided for him. But, a war intervening, Kirk never again saw the faces of those men of learning and manners.

For some months he was employed again at Greenfield Village. On December 7, 1941, he was in his friend Warren Fleischauer's rooms in East Lansing when over the radio came the news of the bombing of the fleet at Pearl Harbor.

Greenfield Village then closing its doors for the duration of the war, Kirk was transferred to the payroll department of the new aircraft engine building at the Rouge Plant. Here he was set to work at an electromatic typewriter, recording payroll statistics.

In Plymouth, twenty miles distant, his mother was beginning to die of cancer, she still young and still hopeful for the twentieth century.

His mother's decline, and the listlessness that afflicts a good many people who turn the great wheel of circulation of modern industry, sat heavy upon him. During those months Kirk read nothing but the letters of Charles Lamb, endeavoring to ignore the future, being weighed down by the bent condition of the world generally as well as by his own troubles.

In company with a friend from Duke, he made a day's expedition to Ontario, with some notion of enlisting in the Essex Scottish regiment. It was well for the two Americans that they did not enlist, for the Essex Scottish would be blotted out in a desperate British commando raid across the Channel. Kirk applied to the United States Army Air Corps, but his eyesight would not pass muster.

Kirk was twenty-two years of age now—though fancying himself much older—and a master of arts, without the slightest expectation of ever accomplishing anything here below.

1942 From these circumstances the United States Army rescued him in the summer of 1942. With other conscripts, euphemistically styled inductees, a high-school band playing, he was marched down to the Plymouth railway station, across the alley from his own birthplace, and put aboard a train for Camp Custer, Michigan.

Russell Kirk, M.A., was not permitted to linger at Camp Custer. With a hundred other neophytes, he was handed orders to proceed to Fort Douglas, Utah.

The conscripts ascertained that they would end at a mysterious installation called Dugway (some said Dogway) Proving Ground, some ninety miles distant from Salt Lake City. Of Kirk's four years in the army, three would be spent here near the heart of the Great Salt Lake Desert.

Late in 1942, word came from Plymouth that Marjorie Rachel Kirk had not long to live: the operation for intestinal cancer had failed.

While still young, Kirk had lost the two created beings—his grandfather and now his mother—that he loved passionately.

1946 In 1946, at San Pedro, he was presented with his discharge papers.

Kirk found himself back at Plymouth and Mecosta, himself little altered outwardly, but his Plymouth household broken up, his father remarried, his sister off to college, his high-school friends scattered, the fields he used to walk with his grandfather now covered by factories, and his fortune at a stay.

Circumstances at Michigan State in 1946 were unfriendly to the higher learning. Kirk taught the history of civilization, in the newly founded Basic College [teaching there one semester per year as an assistant professor until 1953].

In partnership with his friend Adrian Smith, Kirk found a basement in East Lansing's business district where they might install their Red Cedar Bookshop. Kirk's sister, Carolyn, then an undergraduate at Michigan State, was installed as clerk of the shop.

What other practical prospect had Kirk? American graduate schools, pedantic, bureaucratic, and given to excessive supervision, seemed repellent. He came upon a slim book by Sir D'Arcy Thompson, professor of natural science at St. Andrews University, in Scotland.

A very brief form was sent to him; he filled it out, and was admitted as a candidate for St. Andrews' highest arts degree, doctor of letters.

St. Andrews was the oldest university in Scotland, the third oldest in Britain, and the smallest in the British Isles except for Aberdeen. Samuel Johnson, on his Scottish tour, had remarked that St.

Andrews seemed eminently suited for study, from the cheapness of living and the cloistered quiet. It was so still in Kirk's time.

1948 Kirk reached St. Andrews in September 1948, aged nearly thirty years, owning nothing but the contents of the suitcases he brought with him, his portable typewriter, and a few books he had left at Plymouth or Mecosta.

Lodged in Victorian rooms in the genteel street of Queens Gardens, and later in the picturesque old suburb of Argyle outside the medieval West Port, from the autumn of 1948 until the spring of 1952—except for occasional sessions of teaching at Michigan State—Kirk was writing the chapters of the book that was to become *The Conservative Mind*.

Strolling the byways—sometimes wintry—of several lands from 1948 to 1963, Russell Kirk thought often of ultimate things. Sleeping usually at the oldest inns, contriving to subsist pleasantly on a few dollars daily in Scotland, England, Ireland, Wales, France, Germany, Switzerland, Austria, Italy, Sicily, Spain, Mallorca, Tunisia, and Morocco, he had become one of that dying breed, the peregrine seekers after knowledge.

1951 In 1951, when Kirk was thirty-two years old, the University of Chicago Press published his first book, *Randolph of Roanoke: A Study in Conservative Thought*. (Later, in 1962, an enlarged edition would appear, with some of Randolph's speeches and letters appended; and in 1978, a third and still larger edition.)

1952 In the spring of 1952, three learned men read Kirk's fat dissertation on conservative thought in the line of Burke: T. M. Knox, the distinguished professor of philosophy, later vice chancellor of St. Andrews; W. L. Burn, the Durham University historian; and J. W. Williams, the professor of history at St. Andrews—he having consented to read it in typescript after all, once the dissertation was bound. They found it good.

Within a few months it would be published in America under the title *The Conservative Mind* [Chicago: Regnery, 1953]. Over the next three decades, *The Conservative Mind* would go through six revised editions (including the London edition by Faber and Faber, which T. S. Eliot brought out), many printings, various paperback printings by two different houses, a Spanish translation, and a German one.

Early in July 1952, Russell Kirk was granted the degree of *litteratum doctorem*, the highest arts degree of the senior Scottish university.

Kirk returned to his huge classes at Michigan State.

1953 By March 1953, it became clear that the College was committed to the educational degradation of the democratic dogma. Growthmanship!

The question for Kirk was whether he should continue, well enough paid, in this academic barbarism, or whether he should fold his tent like the Arab, and as silently steal away.

Kirk went to Scotland in the summer of 1953, while all this compost was steaming. There he lived in the eighteenth-century cottage at Kellie, the grieve's cottage where Archibald Constable, the Napoleon of booksellers, had been born; he wrote essays and short stories in solitude, and enjoyed leisure enough to think of what he ought to do about Michigan State.

T. S. Eliot and Kirk met face to face in a little private hotel in Edinburgh, during the Edinburgh Festival of 1953, at which Eliot's play *The Confidential Clerk* first was performed.

Kirk was to review for the *Month* that comedy; and Eliot, of the firm of Faber and Faber, was planning to publish the London edition of *The Conservative Mind*. At that first encounter Kirk was moved by Eliot's kindness.

From Kellie, he sent to the head of his department his letter of resignation. The chairman replied, very tardily, that Kirk's views considered, it was honorable for him to resign; but he would be needed for the fall. Kirk went back.

Having arrived at MSC, he was informed that he would not be needed after all. Although he had no money and no immediate prospects, Kirk was not discomposed; he would go north to Mecosta.

1954 His polemical work *A Program for Conservatives* appeared, published by Regnery in Chicago. Very widely reviewed, it obtained a book-club adoption, and over the years would appear in three later editions, two of which would bear the revised title *Prospects for Conservatives*.

An abundance of information about university and town was incorporated in an illustrated book, *St. Andrews*, that the London firm of Batsford would publish in 1954. Some of the photographs therein had been taken by Kirk. The book made Kirk a celebrity in the old gray town for decades to come.

1955 In 1955, Regnery published his *Academic Freedom: An Essay in Definition*, in which Kirk argued that of the many difficulties in the academy after the Second World War, the worst was the deliberate lowering of academic standards to create the mass campus.

At the house then called Cold Chimneys, in Smyrna, Tennessee, where Brainard and Fanny Cheney lived, Flannery O'Connor and Kirk met—for the first time and the last, here below. This occurred in October 1955.

Back at Mecosta, Kirk resumed his meditations about a conservative journal of ideas. Journals of that character, among them the *Bookman* and the *American Review*, had gone down to Avernus during the Thirties.

It was not without irony that Kirk clapped the name *Modern Age* upon a new quarterly of ideas. At first it had been his intention to entitle the magazine the *Conservative Review*, but friends had dissuaded him, fancying that the Tower of Siloam might tumble upon editor and publisher should they be so tememarious as to proclaim openly their attachment to the permanent things.

Next he had inclined toward the *Federal Review*, but Henry Regnery suggested that people would think of the Federal Reserve Board. *Modern Age* the periodical became, in sardonic defiance of the fads and foibles of the twentieth century.

One of the purposes of *Modern Age*, as of Eliot's *Criterion*, had been to establish some communion among the better minds of Europe and America. Such a temperate magazine *Modern Age* was intended to become; and not an ideological publication seeking to indoctrinate in secular dogmata.

1956 Kirk's *Beyond the Dreams of Avarice: Essays of a Social Critic* was published by Regnery in 1956.

1957 The first number of *Modern Age* appeared in [Summer] 1957.

The American Cause, a slim volume about American moral, political, and economic institutions and principles, was written because of the ignorance of such matters that afflicted many American soldiers during the Korean War. It was published by Regnery in 1957; later there appeared a paperback edition, with an introduction by John Dos Passos.

Originally written as a series of pamphlets for use by Republican Women's clubs, Kirk's slender book *The Intelligent Woman's Guide to Conservatism* was published by Devin Adair [New York] in 1957. A paperback edition was brought out several years later.

1958 Kirk would publish no books from 1958 to 1960: editing the infant *Modern Age* and serving as research professor of politics at C. W. Post College—and presently university professor of Long Island University—kept him too busy.

1959 Kirk resigned the editorship [of *Modern Age*] at the end of 1959. He and David Collier (the managing editor, in Chicago) had disagreements in policy; that being so, it would have been next to impossible to direct the magazine from Mecosta, two hundred miles to the north.

Besides, as an impecunious but travel-fond bachelor, Kirk would have been unwilling to settle down to full-time editorial labors.

Surviving vicissitudes, *Modern Age* remained a principal medium for the discussion of large questions, down through the Eighties, when Kirk returned to that journal as a contributor, and indeed its most frequent contributor. The quarterly endures to the present under the able guidance of George Panichas.

During the Fifties he spoke on some two hundred campuses. There would be more debates, and fiercer, in the Sixties.

Also there were published during the Fifties some nine of his short stories, chiefly uncanny or mystical tales.

1960 In February 1960, Kirk had been invited by AWARE, an organization opposing Communism in the theater arts, to speak at the Hotel Wellington (then elegant) near Columbus Circle, in Manhattan. This was a meeting of young people, undergraduates chiefly, of a conservative bent, or at least opposed to Communist ideology.

Entering the ballroom, Kirk glanced at the program, finding to his surprise that someone was to speak on his recent book *The American Cause* before he was to speak on educational standards, and that the person talking about his book was Miss Annette Courtemanche, elder daughter of the lady he had met a moment before.

Kirk assumed the presidency of The Educational Reviewer, Inc., a non-profit educational corporation; he began editing its quarterly, the *University Bookman*.

1961 His solitary evenings gave him opportunity to write mostly for his own entertainment, a Gothick romance, conforming to the canons of Ann Radcliffe as described by Walter Scott: an antique genre, forgotten.

The tone of the narrative, which Kirk entitled *Old House of Fear*, was more nearly that of Stevenson than of Radcliffe or Scott. The story was set (under other island names) in the Small Isles of the Hebrides, which Kirk knew well. The new firm of Fleet published it in New York in 1961. The romance's popular success astonished the publisher. *Time* reviewed it lengthily, with a photograph of a rather sinister Kirk emerging from the doocot at Durie House (Kirk being in Scotland when the book was published).

[He begins a term as Justice of the Peace for Morton Township, Mecosta County, serving until April 1965.]

1962–63 In April 1962, a good many daily papers began publishing "To the Point" by Russell Kirk. This was to be a "general" column—about subjects of widespread interest, rather than concerning politics merely (although partisan politics are meat and drink to most newspaper editors).

A Kirk-Courtemanche correspondence had commenced. Even when lecturing at Post College, in Long Island, Kirk had no way of seeing Annette, public transportation to Springfield Gardens [in Long Island] being most difficult, and he possessing no automobile.

Most of the time he was back at Mecosta, seven hundred miles distant; he was long accustomed to the art of writing interesting letters; his epistles were welcome at Springfield Gardens. Thus 1962 and much of 1963 passed away, the exchange of letters steadily becoming more frequent.

In 1963, Fleet [New York] published a collection of his *National Review* essays and syndicated newspaper columns, *Confessions of a Bohemian Tory: Episodes and Reflections of a Vagrant Career*.

1964 Annette, on March 19, 1964—thereafter known to them as the Letter Day—sent to Russell Amos Kirk a letter which declared to dear Russell, "I have decided that our marriage is inevitable."

Formally engaged on May 20, Annette's twenty-fourth birthday, they began making plans. He was to be baptized in the Catholic Church before their wedding: only indolence, the press of business, and lack of guidance had impeded his arranging to be received earlier into the Church.

By August, at Mecosta, Annette and Russell would be of one mind: only after the wedding would Annette go abroad, and then of course with Russell. The sacrament of marriage was to join them at Our Lady of the Skies, Idlewild (Kennedy) Airport's Catholic Chapel—since demolished, not even one brick being obtained as a memento—on the nineteenth of September, 1964.

In September, their wedding was pleasantly simple, Annette's high loveliness and air of exaltation being grander than any ceremonial ostentation. Three priest-friends said mass and administered the sacrament of matrimony. Russell Kirk was half dazed at his good fortune.

1965 By February 1965, the Kirks were back at Mecosta. They had moved from their cottage on Lake Mecosta to the Old House of Piety Hill, sharing it with Russell's surviving great-aunt, Norma Johnson.

Fleet brought out the first collection of his occult and mystical stories, in 1965—*The Surly Sullen Bell: Ten Stories or Sketches, Uncanny or Uncomfortable, with a Note on the Ghostly Tale*. This was very well received by the review media; presently a London paperback edition appeared; also an American paperback edition, under the title *Lost Lake*—which was the title of one of the Mecosta vignettes within the volume.

In 1965 there appeared also his book *The Intemperate Professor and Other Cultural Splenetics,* published by Louisiana State University Press [Baton Rouge], a collection of his essays on colleges and culture; religion, morals, and culture; wealth and culture; and beauty, community, and culture. (A revised edition would be brought out by Sherwood Sugden [Sauk City, Wis.] in 1988.)

It may be worth noting that from 1958 through 1966 he published no book dealing with political theory or practice. Despite his activity in the Goldwater campaign, there had echoed in his mind Gissing's aphorism: politics is the preoccupation of the quarter-educated.

1966 During this period of the late Sixties and early Seventies, Kirk produced one novel or romance, *A Creature of the Twilight: His Memorials* published by Fleet in 1966.

1967 Monica Rachel [the Kirks' first daughter], born in 1967, would justify her name by soon growing very much attached to matters of the hearth and the heart.

In 1967 Arlington House [New Rochelle, N.Y.] published his *Edmund Burke: A Genius Reconsidered,* which for some years was the only biography of Burke in print; Sherwood Sugden [Peru, Ill.] would publish a paperback edition, revised, in 1988.

In collaboration with his friend James McClellan, in 1967, Kirk brought out *The Political Principles of Robert A. Taft*, published by Fleet.

More of Kirk's uncanny tales were published. "Balgrummo's Hell," set in a decayed great house in Scotland (suggested in part by Melville House), was published in 1967; some thought it the most alarming of Kirk's tales of the supernatural.

1968 Cecilia Abigail [the Kirks' second daughter], born in 1968, would become intelligent, independent, often piquant.

1969 In 1969 there appeared a collection of Kirk's essays, *Enemies of the Permanent Things: Observations of Abnormity in Literature and Politics*, published by Arlington House. Kirk thought it in some ways his most nearly original and imaginative book. A paperback edition, first released by Sherwood Sugden in 1984, soon went through two printings.

He had his work cut out for him, in the late Sixties and the early Seventies, for the radicals were out in force, in the Academy and in the street. They were mastering the quarterly journals of the learned societies; they were marching on Washington.

His essays appeared in more periodicals than ever, in those turbulent years: *Kenyon Review, Sewanee Review, Center Magazine,* the *New York Times Magazine, Book Week, Triumph*, and others—even in *Cosmopolitan,* the contribution to this last entitled "You Can't Trust Perpetual Adolescents."

His *National Review* pages—mostly concerned with education at various levels, but occasionally touching on his travels and general reflections—attracted a great deal of attention and thrust upon him a burden of correspondence.

Kirk conducted a good many college classes during the Sixties and Seventies and Eighties, as distinguished visiting professor of something or other at a diversity of institutions—Los Angeles State College, Pepperdine University, Central Michigan University, Hillsdale College, Olivet College, Albion College, Troy State University, Indiana University, the University of Colorado, Grand Valley State University.

Also twelve honorary doctorates were conferred upon him, in addition to his earned doctorate of letters. Though much bedoctored, Kirk settled on no campus.

1970 Felicia Annette [the Kirks' third daughter], born in 1970, would develop into a gentle and shy beauty.

Piety Hill's increase of population made necessary the house's enlargement. In 1970 there was added a huge wing of brick, a tail wagging its dog, four stories high, connected with the original house by a passage: the New House in the Italianate style of the Old House, with a grand drawing room and thirteen other chambers. A prudent steel sliding door parted New House from Old.

1971–72 A really major book, *Eliot and His Age: T. S. Eliot's Moral Imagination in the Twentieth Century*, was published by Random House [New York] in 1971. Allen Tate, in his *Britannica* article on Eliot, named Kirk's lengthy study as one of the two books about Eliot recommended for a general survey of Eliot's life and writings.

Interestingly, the most cordial reviews of *Eliot and His Age* appeared in weeklies of the Left, the *Nation* and the *Progressive*; Malcolm Muggeridge reviewed it approvingly in *Esquire.* Sherwood Sugden brought out a revised paperback edition in 1984, and another printing in 1988. Kirk was given a Christopher Award for the book [in 1972].

1973 Early in the Seventies there had commenced the Piety Hill seminars, sponsored by the Intercollegiate Studies Institute (ISI). In the Eighties the frequency of these gatherings increased to three, four, or even five a year. Between 1973 and 1993, more than two thousand students, from all over the land—and some from abroad—would participate in ISI seminars.

1974 *The Roots of American Order* was published by Open Court [La Salle, I11.] in 1974. This had been written at the request of Pepperdine University. This historical, political, and moral study continues to be used in university and college classes. The Open Court edition was succeeded by a Pepperdine University edition, in both cloth and paperback; in 1991, a third edition would be brought out.

1975 In February 1975, Kirk was visiting professor at Olivet College. On Ash Wednesday, he attended a Congregational service early in the morning at the college chapel, and in the afternoon he read Eliot's *Ash-Wednesday,* in part, to his students, and played a record of Eliot reading that mysterious poem himself. That night he was roused from bed by the news that his house, a hundred miles to the north, was burning; and the Old House already was beyond saving.

Andrea Seton [the Kirks' fourth daughter], born in 1975 soon after the Kirks' Great Fire of Piety Hill, the self-styled Fire Baby, would be of good cheer, dancing and drawing, affectionate, imaginative.

Kirk had ceased to write his syndicated column a few months after the Great Fire of Ash Wednesday, 1975; even had he desired to linger as a newspaperman, he had become too busy rebuilding Piety Hill to bother with daily scribbling.

Gradually a new-old Piety Hill took form. Their friend James Nachtegall, a Grand Rapids architect, drew up designs for an Italianate house more striking than the old one had been. Once Michigan had been rich in Italianate houses; doubtless the restored Piety Hill would be the last ever constructed in that archaic but very practical style.

1976–78 "There's a Long, Long Trail a-Winding" became the most widely anthologized of all Kirk's tales, and for it he received the award for short fiction from the Third World Fantasy Convention [in 1977]; it was published in 1976.

He completed *Decadence and Renewal in the Higher Learning: An Episodic History of American University and College Since 1953*, the chapters of which each discussed, consecutively, one year of decay. Gateway Editions (the new name of Henry Regnery's publishing firm, then managed by the younger Henry Regnery, with Kirk's former student, the cheerful and rather martial Dennis Connell, as sales manager) published the book in 1978.

[Russell Kirk was named a Heritage Distinguished Scholar in 1978; over the next fifteen years he delivered four lectures annually for a total of sixty lectures at the Heritage Foundation, established in 1973 as one of the country's leading public policy research institutes, in Washington, D.C.]

1979 In 1979, Kirk's mystical fiction emerged again in two volumes: a collection of his uncanny tales, *The Princess of All Lands*, published by Arkham House [Sauk City, Wis.]; and *Lord of the Hollow Dark*, published by St. Martin's Press [New York], in form a Gothick romance, by intent a symbolic representation of the corrupting cults that had come up from underground in the latter half of the twentieth century.

Princess received many cordial reviews; the first printing soon was sold out, and the second printing did not last long. "Sorworth Place," the first story in the book, Rod Serling adapted for his television series of occult and uncanny films; it was shown on the networks many times.

[Russell Kirk becomes president of the Marguerite Eyer Wilbur Foundation and director of the Educational Research Council of America's social science program.]

1980–81 For a quarter of a century, commencing in 1955, he had written for *National Review* his page "From the Academy." But if "From the Academy" resulted in any improvements at any level of American education, over the years, Kirk was unable to discern such reforms; he longed to spend his time at writing of a more enduring sort. So he gave up "From the Academy" shortly after Mr. Reagan's election in 1980.

Charles Brown, who had known Kirk for a good many years, compiled a bibliography of Kirk's writings, which the Clarke Historical Library [Mount Pleasant, Mich.] was to publish in 1981. Through the year 1980, his bibliographer found, Kirk had published sixteen volumes of history, politics, literary and educational criticism, and biography; five volumes of fiction; seven hundred and thirteen periodical essays; fourteen articles in works of reference; twenty-two introductions or forewords to books; forty-three published addresses, pamphlets, and miscellanea; one hundred and fifty major book reviews; seventeen short stories; and nineteen articles or essays first published in, or reprinted in, anthologies.

His father [died] blind, sick, and old [in 1981]. The elder Russell Kirk accepted his tribulations uncomplainingly, though he never had read the Stoics, or for that matter the Book of Job.

1982 *Reclaiming a Patrimony* a collection of his formal lectures, sponsored [and published] by the Heritage Foundation, appeared in 1982; among the subjects discussed were "Church and State in Conflict"; "The Perversity of Recent Fiction"; "Criminal Character and Mercy"; "The Architecture of Servitude and Boredom"; "Regaining Historical Consciousness"; and "Audacity, Rhetoric, and Poetry in Politics."

The editors of the big publishing firm of Viking Penguin [New York] asked him to draw up an anthology of conservative thought, which was published in 1982 under the title *The Portable Conservative Reader.*

1983 In 1983 he was invited to give the keynote address to the International Congress on the Family, meeting that year in Rome. Fourteen members of the Congress, the Kirks among them, were admitted to an audience with Pope John Paul II.

1984 *Watchers at the Strait Gate,* another collection of Kirk's mystical tales, appeared in 1984, published by Arkham House.

He received the Richard Weaver Award (for scholarly writing) of the Ingersoll Prizes—no empty honor, for there went with it fifteen thousand tax-free dollars, at once flung into the chasm of Kirk's debts.

1986 He was able to bring out, in 1986, through the National Humanities Institute, a handsome new edition of Irving Babbitt's *Literature and the American College* [originally published in 1908], with a learned introduction nearly so long as the book itself, from Kirk's typewriter.

1987 *The Wise Men Know What Wicked Things Are Written on the Sky* (a line borrowed from Chesterton's long poem *The Ballad of the White Horse*) was published by Regnery in 1987; it was fairly widely reviewed and read. This was a second collection of Heritage Lectures: it included several formal lectures on aspects of education, and others on prospects for the United States.

He was appointed Fulbright lecturer at St. Andrews University, and during the same season he lectured at the University of Trier, the University of Groningen, and elsewhere in the Continent.

1988 His *Work and Prosperity,* a textbook in economics for high-school students, was published by the Christian textbook firm of Beta Books [Pensacola, Fla.] in 1988 [1989]. This manual was the final production of the Educational Research Council of America, with offices in Cleveland.

At the request of Irving Louis Horowitz, of Transaction Publishers [New Brunswick, N.J.], Russell Kirk began editing a series entitled The Library of Conservative Thought; nearly all volumes would have introductions or forewords by Kirk. Among the volumes published in 1988, 1989, 1990, and 1991 were *Collected Letters of John Randolph of Roanoke to John Brockenbrough,* Mallock's *A Critical Examination of Socialism*, Scott-Moncrieff's *Burke Street*, Wilson's *The Case for Conservatism, Selected Political Essays of Orestes Brownson,* Davidson's *The Attack on Leviathan*, a collection of Stanlis's essays on Burke, and a collection of critical essays on Burke edited by Daniel Ritchie.

1989 During his last week in office, President Reagan presented to Kirk and some thirty-five others the Presidential Citizens Medal for Distinguished Service to the United States; Kirk was the only man of letters so recognized.

1990 A fellowship from the National Endowment for the Humanities, in 1985, gave him time to commence the writing of a series of essays and lectures on the Constitution of the United States—published by Regnery as a book in 1990. He particularly emphasized in his study the neglected influence of Edmund Burke on the framers and the interpreters of the Constitution. *The Conservative Constitution* undid the claim of the disciples of Leo Strauss that somehow the Declaration of Independence and the Constitution had conformed slavishly to the doctrines of John Locke.

1991 [Russell Kirk gave his daughter Monica in marriage to Brian Scott Carman in July at St. Anne's Church, Mackinac Island.]

[He was awarded the Salvatori Prize for historical writing, in December.]

1993 Russell Kirk in 1993, on the eve of his seventy-fifth birthday, published two more books: *America's British Culture* (Transaction), a counter-buffet to Demon Multiculturalism; and *The Politics of Prudence* (Intercollegiate Studies Institute [Bryn Mawr, Pa.]), addressed to the rising generation in search of principles.

Kirk was overwhelmed by a whole series of celebrations in honor of the fortieth anniversary of the publication of *The Conservative Mind* and the seventy-fifth anniversary of that book's author.

Jeffrey O. Nelson, publications director of ISI, marrying Miss Cecilia Abigail Kirk just before Christmas 1993, might carry on Russell Kirk's literary raids against the enemies of the Permanent Things.

1994 [Exhausted by the lecture tour that had extended until late November 1993, after which he was confined to bed by his doctor for a month, Kirk's physical vitality began to wane; he had little appetite and was noticeably thin and frail.]

[On the eve of Ash Wednesday (February 16, 1994), his doctor informed him that, succumbing to congestive heart failure, he had but a few months to live.]

[Undaunted, he completed the final chapter of *The Sword of Imagination*, "Is Life Worth Living?" reaffirming his belief "that man is made for eternity."]

[As Easter approached, Kirk, although bedridden, indexed *Redeeming the Time* (Wilmington, Del.: Intercollegiate Studies Institute, 1996)].

[On the morning of April 29th, shortly after 10:00 a.m., in the presence of members of his family, Russell Kirk passed away, quietly and serenely, having now come to the end of his life's labors.]

"Then," said he, "I am going to my Father's. . . . My Sword I give to him that shall succeed me in my Pilgrimage, and my Courage and Skill to him that can get it. My Marks and Scars I carry with me, to be a witness for me that I have fought His battles who now will be my Rewarder."

—John Bunyan, *The Pilgrim's Progress* (1678)

A Note on the Text

Throughout the following selections from Russell Kirk's writings I have striven to employ his own texts in style and format. In some few cases, I have quietly corrected typographical errors, as well as names, dates, and book titles. For the sake of consistency I have added to book titles mentioned in the text the year of publication in parentheses. In several instances, I have slightly altered Kirk's original title in order to identify more precisely for the reader the subject of a particular selection. In this respect, the alteration is explained in its full bibliographical citation found within brackets at the very end of each selection.

For ellipsis within a sentence three spaced periods (. . .) are used; for ellipsis after the conclusion of a complete sentence, three spaced periods in addition to the sentence period (. . . .) are used. Elisions in the text are restricted to materials that are redundant or of a purely perfunctory or transitional nature. In a few rare instances, the omission of one or more extraneous paragraphs is indicated by three spaced asterisks (* * *). Notes have been added by the editor to the following essays: "T. S. Eliot's Permanent Things," "Eric Voegelin's Normative Labor," "Normative Art and Modern Vices," "Criminal Character and Mercy," "The Conservative Purpose of a Liberal Education," and "Orestes Brownson and the Just Society." All notes are assembled in the section titled "Notes" (see pp. 575–85), and are cited under the titles of the individual essays.

The index has been carefully prepared so as to include names, authors, titles of books, ideas, places, and any cursory references included in the text that are deserving of explanation. No less than the bracketed bibliographical citations and information, the index seeks to help a reader locate and also clarify textual sources in expeditious ways. I bear full responsibility for all changes and interpolations found in the entire text.

I.

THE IDEA OF CONSERVATISM

What Is Conservatism? ❖ The Dissolution of Liberalism ❖ Ten Exemplary Conservatives ❖ Why I Am a Conservative

No other figure surpasses Russell Kirk in his exposition of fundamental conservative ideas in the twentieth century. In defining and evaluating the intellectual history of English and American conservatism during the past two hundred years, Kirk discloses a scholarly grasp and critical understanding that he communicates with vigor and insight. Conservatism is not some reductivist political or economic system but, as he shows, a discriminating faith, temper, impulse, to be carefully distinguished not only from doctrinaire ideology but also from modern liberal and radical reformers who advance their collectivist social engineering and agenda of change. It speaks to the total human condition, to both community and soul, without a fanatical and strident tone and always with a distinct and sympathetic awareness of human and social limitations.

Kirk's appraisal of conservatism is anchored in reverence, in humility, in moderation, and is shaped by both the religious sense and the moral sense. As such, Kirk's conception of conservatism revolves around higher paradigms of character and culture. It exposes sociopolitical extremisms that build empires of might that rule by force and writ. As Kirk writes: "[C]onservatism is the negation of ideology . . . a state of mind, a type of character, a way of looking at the civil social order. The attitude we call conservatism is sustained by a body of sentiments, rather than by a system of ideological dogmata."

Perhaps another way of pinpointing Kirk's conservatism is to see it as a conservatism of reflection, one that is essentially meditative in nature and aspiration, and also one that transforms into a discipline of mind and thought in the contemplation of religious, ethical, and moral truths that promote the dignity and the sacredness of human existence. The sources of conservative order, he insists, are not found in theoretical writings, but rather in custom, convention, continuity.

In writing about conservatism—its canons, principles, assumptions—Kirk readily admits to incremental differences and changes reflecting the emphases occurring over time. But for him "the diversity of ways in which conservative views may find expression is itself proof that conservatism is no fixed ideology." To be conservative ultimately means, for Kirk, to be a conservator, that is, a preserver, a guardian, a custodian, a keeper—one who keeps the world safe.

❖

What Is Conservatism?

This essay is excerpted from Russell Kirk's introduction to The Portable Conservative Reader *(1982), an anthology of English and American conservative thought. Here he focuses on conservative attitudes in a modern context, beginning with the age of Edmund Burke in the last quarter of the eighteenth century. Kirk sets down general principles that reinforce the "canons of conservative thought" found in* The Conservative Mind *(1953), which established Kirk as a seminal thinker in the conservative movement in the United States. Conservatism, he asserts, is not an ideology with pretensions to universality and infallibility. It is a way "of looking at the civic social order," and centers around basic beliefs in a transcendent order, in social continuity, in "things established by immemorial usage," in the virtue of prudence, in human variety, and in human imperfectibility. For anyone who wants to know what conservatism is, this essay is indispensable as a descriptive overview.*

1. Succinct Description

"What is conservatism?" Abraham Lincoln inquired rhetorically, as he campaigned for the presidency of the United States. "Is it not adherence to the old and tried, against the new and untried?" By that test, the candidate told his audience, Abraham Lincoln was a conservative.

Other definitions have been offered. In Ambrose Bierce's *Devil's Dictionary* one encounters this: "Conservative, *n.* A statesman who is enamored of existing evils, as distinguished from the Liberal, who wishes to replace them with others." . . .

As a coherent body of political thought, what we call conservatism is a modern development. It is approximately as old as the different body of opinions called liberalism, and some decades older than the ideologies called socialism, communism, and anarchism. The roots of conservative thought, for all that, extend deep into the history of ideas and of social institutions.

In various medieval cities, particularly in Italy, the title of "conservator" was given to guardians of the laws. English justices of the peace originally were styled *custodes pacis*—conservators of the peace. Chaucer, in "The House of Fame," uses the word "conservatif" in its sense of protection and preservation. Jeremy Taylor, in the seventeenth century, wrote that "the Holy Spirit is the great conservative of the new life." The word, in short, implied security—a commendatory word. But not until the third decade of the nineteenth century was the word incorporated into the English lexicon of political controversy.

True, one might trace a continuity of conservative political thought (though not of the word itself) back into the seventeenth century. Lord Falkland, during the English Civil Wars, touched upon the essence of conservative convictions in declaring, "When it is not necessary to change, it is necessary not to change." A rudimentary conservatism may be discerned in colonial America, too, assuming definite form just after the American Revolution in the most successful conservative device, the Constitution of the United States.

For that matter, conservative impulses and interests have existed ever since a civil social order came into being. By analogy, it is possible to speak of Aristophanes as a conservative, or Plato, or Cicero. . . .

So we commence with the age of Edmund Burke—the last quarter of the eighteenth century. Modern use of the word "conservatism" implies those principles of social thought and action that are set against radical innovation after the pattern of the French Revolution. Edmund Burke opposed his "moral imagination" to what has been called the "idyllic imagination" of Jean-Jacques Rousseau. From that contest arose what Walter Bagehot called "the conservatism of reflection." Almost by definition, ever since Burke published his *Reflections on the Revolution in France*, the principal conservatives in the Western world have been conscious or unconscious disciples of Burke.

Burke himself did not employ the word "conservative," speaking rather of "preservation"—as in his aphorism "Change is the means of our preservation," or his remark that the able statesman is one who combines with a disposition to preserve an ability to reform. During Burke's own lifetime there existed no sharp demarcation between the words "conservative" and "liberal."

As a term of politics, the word "conservative" arose in France during and just after the Napoleonic era. Philosophical statesmen as varied in opinion and faction as Guizot, Bonald, Maistre, Chateaubriand, and Tocqueville all were influenced by Burke's writings. Seeking for a word to describe a policy of moderation, intended to reconcile the best in the old order with the necessities of the nineteenth century, French political writers hit upon the concept of the *conservateur*, the guardian of the heritage of civilization and of the principles of justice.

From France, this concept passed into England. The editors of *The Quarterly Review*, in 1830, approved "conservative" over "Tory" to describe the British party of order. By the 1840s, the word "conservative" had attained popularity in the United States, being employed with approbation by John C. Calhoun, Daniel Webster, and Orestes Brownson.

Burke's political concepts spread rapidly across Europe, especially in the Germanys and the Austrian system. The European revolutionary movements of 1829–30 and of 1848 caused greater emphasis to be placed upon distinctions among conservatives, liberals, and radicals. Throughout Europe, conservatism came to mean hostility toward the principles of the French Revolution, with its violent leveling innovations; while liberalism increasingly signified sympathy with the revolutionary ideals of liberty, equality, fraternity, and material progress.

Conservatives, especially in Britain, soon found themselves opposing another radicalism than the theories of Rousseau: that is, the radical utilitarianism of Jeremy Bentham, called by John Stuart Mill "the great subversive." Thus the intellectual heirs of Burke, and the conservative interest generally, did battle on two fronts: against the successors of the Jacobins, with their "armed doctrine"; and against the economists of Manchester, with their reliance upon the nexus of cash payment.

Our first necessity here, then, is to endeavor to describe (rather than to define) the conservatives' understanding of society. In recent years the term "conservatism" often has been employed to mean "reactionary" or "obscurantist" or "oldfangled"; it has even been confounded with the economic dogmas of the Manchester School. What does the word really signify?

Strictly speaking, conservatism is not a political system, and certainly not an ideology. In the phrase of H. Stuart Hughes, "Conservatism is the negation of ideology." Instead, conservatism is a way of looking at the civil social order. Although certain general principles held by most conservatives may be described, there exists wide variety in application of these ideas from age to age and country to country. Thus conservative views and parties have existed under monarchical, aristocratic, despotic, and democratic regimes, and in a considerable range of economic systems. The conservatives of Peru, for instance, differ much from those of Australia, say; they may share a preference for the established order of society, these conservatives of the Spanish and the English heritages; yet the institutions and customs which these conservative factions respectively wish to preserve are by no means identical.

Unlike socialism, anarchism, and even liberalism, then, conservatism offers no universal pattern of politics for adoption everywhere. On the contrary, conservatives reason that social institutions always must differ considerably from nation to nation, since any land's politics must be the product of that country's dominant religion, ancient customs, and historic experience.

Although it is no ideology, conservatism may be apprehended reasonably well by attention to what leading writers and politicians, generally called conservative, have said and done. . . . "Conservatism," to put the matter another way, amounts to the consensus of the leading conservative thinkers and actors over the past two centuries. For our present purpose, however, we may set down below several general principles upon which most eminent conservatives in some degree may be said to have agreed implicitly. The following first principles are best discerned in the theoretical and practical politics of British and American conservatives.

First, conservatives generally believe that there exists a transcendent moral order, to which we ought to try to conform the ways of society. A divine tactic, however dimly descried, is at work in human society. Such convictions may take the form of belief in "natural law" or may assume some other expression; but with few exceptions conservatives recognize the need for enduring moral authority. This conviction contrasts strongly with the liberals' utilitarian view of the state (most consistently expressed by Bentham's disciples), and with the radicals' detestation of theological postulates.

Second, conservatives uphold the principle of social continuity. They prefer the devil they know to the devil they don't know. Order and justice and freedom, they believe, are the artificial products of a long and painful social experience, the results of centuries of trial and reflection and sacrifice. Thus the body social is a kind of spiritual corporation, comparable to the church; it may even be called a community of souls. Human society is no machine, to be treated mechanically. The continuity, the lifeblood, of a society must not be interrupted. Burke's reminder of the social necessity for prudent change is in the minds of conservatives. But necessary change, they argue, ought to be gradual and discriminatory, never "unfixing old interests at once." Revolution slices through the arteries of a culture, a cure that kills.

Third, conservatives believe in what may be called the principle of prescription. "The wisdom of our ancestors" is one of the more important phrases in the writings of Burke; presumably Burke derived it from Richard Hooker. Conservatives sense that modern men and women are dwarfs on the shoulders of giants, able to see farther than their ancestors only because of the great stature of those who have preceded us in time. Therefore conservatives very frequently emphasize the importance of "prescription"—that is, of things established by immemorial usage, so "that the mind of man runneth not to the contrary." There exist rights of which the chief sanction is their antiquity—including rights in property, often. Similarly, our morals are prescriptive in great part. Conservatives argue that we are unlikely, we moderns, to make any brave new discoveries in morals or politics or taste. It is perilous to weigh every passing issue on the basis of private judgment and private rationality. "The individual is foolish, but the species is wise," Burke declared. In politics we do well to abide by precedent and precept and even prejudice, for "the great mysterious incorporation of the human race" has acquired habits, customs, and conventions of remote origin which are woven into the fabric of our social being; the innovator, in Santayana's phrase, never knows how near to the taproot of the tree he is hacking.

Fourth, conservatives are guided by their principle of prudence. Burke agrees with Plato that in the statesman, prudence is chief among virtues. Any public measure ought to be judged by its probable long-run consequences, not merely by temporary advantage or popularity. Liberals and radicals, the conservative holds, are imprudent: for they dash at their objectives without giving much heed to the risk of new abuses worse than the evils they hope to sweep away. Human society being complex, remedies cannot be simple if they are to be effective. The conservative declares that he acts only after sufficient reflection, having weighed the consequences. Sudden and slashing reforms are perilous as sudden and slashing surgery. The march of providence is slow; it is the devil who always hurries.

Fifth, conservatives pay attention to the principle of variety. They feel affection for the proliferating intricacy of long-established social institutions and modes of life, as distinguished from the narrowing uniformity and deadening egalitarianism of radical systems. For the preservation of a healthy diversity in any civilization, there must survive orders and classes, differences in material condition, and many sorts of inequality. The only true forms of equality are equality in the Last Judgment and equality before a just court of law; all other attempts at leveling lead, at best, to social stagnation. Society longs for honest and able leadership; and if natural and institutional differences among people are destroyed, presently some tyrant or host of squalid oligarchs will create new forms of inequality. Similarly, conservatives uphold the institution of private property as productive of human variety: without private property, liberty is reduced and culture is impoverished.

Sixth, conservatives are chastened by their principle of imperfectibility. Human nature suffers irremediably from certain faults, the conservatives know. Man being imperfect, no perfect social order ever can be created. Because of human restlessness, mankind would grow rebellious under any utopian domination, and would break out once more in violent discontent—or else expire of boredom. To aim for utopia is to end in disaster, the conservative says: we are not made for perfect things. All that we reasonably can expect is a tolerably ordered, just, and free society, in which some evils, maladjustments, and suffering continue to lurk. By proper attention to prudent reform, we may preserve and improve this tolerable order. But if the old institutional and moral safeguards of a nation are forgotten, then the anarchic impulses in man break loose: "the ceremony of innocence is drowned."

Such are six of the major premises of what Walter Bagehot, a century ago, called "reflective conservatism." To have set down some principal convictions of conservative thinkers, in the fashion above, may be misleading: for conservative thought is not a body of immutable secular dogmas. Our purpose here has been broad description, not fixed definition. If one requires a single sentence—why, let it be said that for the conservative, politics is the art of the possible, not the art of the ideal.

Edmund Burke turned to first principles in politics only with reluctance, believing that "metaphysical" politicians let loose dreadful mischief by attempting to govern nations according to abstract notions. Conservatives have believed, following Burke, that general principles always must be tempered, in any particular circumstances, by what Burke called expedience, or prudence; for particular circumstances vary infinitely, and every nation must observe its own traditions and historical experience—which should take precedence over universal notions drawn up in some quiet study. Yet Burke did not abjure general ideas; he distinguished between "abstraction" (or *a priori* notions divorced from a nation's history and necessities) and "principle" (or sound general ideas derived from a knowledge of human nature and of the past). Principles are necessary to a statesman, but they must be applied discreetly and with infinite caution to the workaday world. The preceding six conservative principles, therefore, are to be taken as a rough catalog of the general assumptions of conservatives, and not as a tidy system of doctrines for governing a state.

So much, just now, for our attempt at honest description of the character of conservative writing. Let us turn for a moment to some account of what this conservatism is not.

2. Misapprehensions of Conservatism

Misunderstandings of the conservative mentality and of conservative arguments may be divided into two categories: first, the errors of scholars; second, popular confusions. Turn we to the blunders of the learned.

A failure to grasp Burke's distinction between abstraction and principle has led to considerable error as to the theoretical basis of conservatism, from the day of rationalistic historians such as Henry Buckle down to the present day. This controversy takes four principal forms, all at loggerheads with one another. They may be summarized thus: (1) conservatism is metaphysically mystical; (2) conservatism has no philosophical foundation; (3) conservatism is empirical; (4) conservatism is pragmatic. These views require reasoned examination.

(1) Conservatism by its nature is not "mystical," "abstract," or "doctrinaire." Burke and his school, as practical statesmen, did not think that political and metaphysical schemes should be created out of whole cloth. Rather than enveloping politics in mysterious theories of a General Will or of Thesis and Antithesis, Burke and his followers accepted as given the political institutions of their country and their age; as for moral postulates, they took those from the King James Version and the Book of Common Prayer. It is true that some Continental men of the Right, and some English scholars toward the end of the nineteenth century, came under the influence of Hegel's idealism. But (as Alexis de Tocqueville foresaw) Hegel's influence came to be far stronger upon socialist theorists than upon conservative writers and politicians.

(2) Conservatism, despite Burke's contempt for desiccated rationality and abstract speculation, does not lack some theoretical basis. Burke proclaimed that he knew nothing more wicked than the heart of an abstract metaphysician—that is, of some coffeehouse philosopher who would presume to write a new constitution for the human race on the basis of arid intellectual abstractions. The intellectual foundation which Burke and his associates took for granted was what since has been called the Great Tradition—that is, the classical and Christian intellectual patrimony which then still formed the curriculum of schools. Burke referred to "the Schoolmen of the fourteenth century" and other Christian philosophers. In the view of the eighteenth-century conservatives, a man is afflicted by *hubris*, overweening presumption, if he

tries to cast aside the wisdom of his ancestors and to create out of his tiny private stock of reason some brand-new structure of metaphysical doctrines. Burke's metaphysics, in short, were the philosophical postulates of Richard Hooker, John Bramhall, and other English divines.

(3) Conservatism is empirical only in the sense that conservatives respect the wisdom of the species and think that history, the recorded experience of mankind, should be constantly consulted by the statesman. Yet mere practical experience, "empiricism" in the sense of being guided simply by yesterday's pains or pleasures, is not enough for the conservative, who believes that we can apply our knowledge of the remote or the immediate past with prudence only if we are guided by some general principles, which have been laid down for us over the centuries by prophets and philosophers. Burke broke with Locke's empiricism.

(4) Conservatism is pragmatic only in the sense that it disavows utopian speculation and experiment, putting its faith instead in prudence and moderation. Modern pragmatism is intent upon experiment—that is, groping forward with scant respect for the past; conservatism, on the contrary, relies upon tradition and the bank and capital of the ages. Conservatives think that mere change may as easily be retrogression as progress, and that to tamper experimentally with great states and human nature, out of a vague faith in Progress and Process, is infinitely perilous.

Some doctors of the schools notwithstanding, then, the conservative school of politics cannot be thrust into any mystical, empirical, pragmatic, or nondescript pigeonhole. Recent studies by Peter Stanlis, Francis Canavan, Charles Parkin, and other scholars have sufficiently undone earlier notions about Burke's first principles. Yet even today a good many professors of politics or of history remain afflicted by rather a muddy notion of the intellectual sources of conservative belief.

Such a confusion is more readily pardoned among the mass of men and women, as the twentieth century nears its end, two hundred years after the events that brought forth conservative politics. The word "conservative," at this writing, enjoys a renewed popularity in both the United States and Britain. Whether those who exalt "conservative" to the condition of a god-term, or those who condemn it to the condition of a devil-term, actually know what the word has meant—why, that's another matter. . . .

It is not surprising that in some quarters (especially in America) there lingers an impression that the conservative is "some sort of radical"—a paradox no more startling than many other paradoxes of popular opinion. For decades popular jounalists often have used the word "conservative" in a sense considerably different from the intellectual conservatism described earlier. . . . Among many people unfamiliar with the writings of Burke or of the Adamses there does flourish, after all, a set of opinions which Walter Bagehot once unflatteringly described as "the ignorant Democratic Conservatism of the masses." There endures also "shop-and-till conservatism," or mere attachment to one's little property, out of fear that radical political measures would injure or destroy the material interests of anyone possessing property. This "party of order," as it was called in France and elsewhere in Europe during the nineteenth century, is animated by fear, Bagehot wrote: "dread that their shop, their house, their life—not so much their physical life as their whole mode and sources of existence—will be destroyed and cast away." Just so; precisely that has happened in half the world since Bagehot wrote; so the high-spirited conservatism of Burke has been reinforced by the shop-and-till victims of twentieth-century ideological fanaticism.

So it is that some conservatives are learned, and some ignorant; some rich, and some poor. It is not easy to show a close correspondence between political conservatism and personal prosperity. At several general elections, the Conservative party in Britain has won the votes of millions of trade-union members; while in the United States hard-pressed small farmers generally are a bulwark of the conservative interest on many issues, and so increasingly is a large proportion of the "blue-collar" vote.

Between religious convictions and conservative political views, there is a nearer alliance, despite the radicalism of many modern clergy (very like the English clergy of Burke's day). Because ideology is by essence antireligious, Christians tend to be attracted to ideology's negation, conservatism.

Do most of the men and women who vote for conservative candidates and conservative policies thoroughly apprehend the six conservative principles sketched earlier in this introductory essay? No, of course not—no more than the typical liberal or the typical radical voter can set up as a political philosopher.

Most conservatives, like their liberal and radical adversaries, are not metaphysicians; they hold their convictions somewhat vaguely, as prejudices rather than reasoned conclusions. Even more than liberals and radicals, typical conservatives (sensing that politics is not the whole of life) remain indifferent to political action so long as possible; there are more interesting things to do. It was for this reason that John Stuart Mill called conservatives "the stupid party." The conservative scholar F. J. C. Hearnshaw wrote in this century that "It is commonly sufficient for practical purposes if conservatives, without saying anything, just sit and think, or even if they merely sit." The conservative has on his side the mighty power of inertia; the radical has on his side the grim power of love of change. In the modern world, the love of change has been gaining at the expense of the love of things established, with a consequent weakening of the conservative interest—at least until very late in the day.

Conservatives, it should be understood, are neither angels nor devils. Conservatism has its vice, and that vice is selfishness. Self-centered conservatives mutter, with Fafnir, "Let me rest: I lie in possession." Radicalism, too, has its vice, and that vice is envy. Such radicals growl, as in *Dr. Faustus*, "Why shouldst thou sit, and I stand?" (As for the liberals, nowadays they seem in the sere and yellow leaf, so that it would be cruel to tax them with vices.) Most conservatives hold by their particular social convictions because of early prejudices and experiences; their minds are not susceptible to temperate argument, nor can they express with much lucidity the postulates from which they draw their professed opinions. That, however, is true of the majority of political partisans of whatever persuasion; indeed, probably it is less true of conservatives than of their adversaries, conservatism being no ideology—and therefore not so overwhelmed by the passions of political religion. And it must be kept in mind that in any country, in any age, there exists more than one sort of conservative.

Walter Bagehot, in his brief essay "Intellectual Conservatism," distinguishes three types of conservatives: the conservatives of enjoyment, loyal to old ways, like the Cavaliers; the conservatives of fear, like the French middle classes in the nineteenth century; and the conservatives of reflection. These last always are relatively few in number, and yet they leaven the whole of the conservative interest. . . .

3. The Course of Conservative Politics in America

Although American conservatism did not become self-aware, so to speak, until the close of the Revolution, nevertheless strongly conservative influences and factions may be discerned in the colonial era. The planter societies of Virginia, Maryland, and South Carolina, especially, were governed for the most part by constitutions (written or unwritten) which we should call conservative. New York, with its great landed estates and its established mercantile interests, was socially conservative; so was New Jersey. Even the colonies founded upon dissent, the New England settlements and Pennsylvania, became relatively conservative shortly after they acquired wealth and population: only a few years after the landing at Plymouth, for instance, Governor

Bradford was writing of the mischievous illusion that property should be held in common, and laying emphasis on the necessity for order, authority, and true community.

Yet a Tory party in the old English sense scarcely existed in America. Political debates in the colonies usually occurred between two factions of Whigs, both attached to the Whig idea of liberty, but differing as to means and the relationship with the Crown. Neither of these Whig factions was radical essentially, although some leveling elements were to be found among the Patriots. The triumph of the Patriots in the Revolution expelled from the Thirteen Colonies what little Toryism had existed there, and along with it many of the moderate Whigs. For all that, recent scholarship inclines toward the view that the American Revolution was no revolution truly, but simply a War of Independence—a revolution (in Burke's phrase concerning the Glorious Revolution of 1688) "not made, but prevented."

The intellectual leaders of the Americans during the troubled period of Confederation were men, most of them, of conservative tendency—John Adams, Gouverneur Morris, John Jay, Hamilton, Madison. Even Jefferson, despite certain French influences upon his mind, was no frantic innovator. Most other Southern leaders, such as Pinckney or Mason, differed more about means than about the ends of society: their view of the state was conservative—viewed, that is, from a twentieth-century vantage point. Even some eminent radicals of the time, notably Patrick Henry, grew steadily more conservative as responsibility settled upon them.

Out of the discussions and compromises of these masterful politicians grew the Federal Constitution, which Sir Henry Maine called the most successful conservative device in the history of government. And the *Federalist Papers,* written to obtain acceptance of the Constitution, reflect the conservative concepts of moderation, balance, order, and prudence—together with those conservative guarantees of prescriptive usage, arrangement of political checks, restrictions upon power, protection for private property, and restraints upon popular impulses.

During the early years of the United States, the chief political contests may be regarded as a long acrimonious debate between two powerful conservative interests—the mercantile interest of the North, the agricultural interest of the South—confused by lesser issues and personalities. At first, the two types of conservatism were represented respectively by John Adams and James Madison. As the slavery question began to divide the country, John Randolph and John C. Calhoun came to speak for the conservative impulse of the South, and Daniel Webster for that of the North. On the eve of the Civil War, the two most interesting conservative thinkers were men of letters, rather than politicians: Nathaniel Hawthorne and Orestes Brownson; but they could not prevail against Abolitionists and Fire-Eaters.

The catastrophe of the Civil War dealt a grim blow to reflective conservatism, North or South. In the Gilded Age, little political principle of any kind could be distinguished. In the writings of Henry Adams lingered something of the old New England conservatism; in the books of John W. Burgess was expressed a new sort of conservative liberalism, heavily influenced by German thought. Yet amidst the material aggrandizement of America during the concluding third of the nineteenth century, the better public men in both parties retained conservative attitudes: Grover Cleveland and Theodore Roosevelt, for examples.

As the United States grew into the greatest power in the world, with corresponding duties and hard choices, conservative concepts were discussed again, notably by such writers as Paul Elmer More, Irving Babbitt, and George Santayana. The Great Depression and the ascendancy of Franklin Roosevelt seemed to quash this renewal of conservative thought. Until the first administration of Franklin Roosevelt, the term "liberal" had not been popular among American politicians; but Rooseveltian liberalism swept everything before it during the 1930s and 1940s. Not until the early 1950s did there appear, or reappear, a strong body of conservative thought, expressed in books and periodical literature, to challenge the dominant liberalism. . . .

America has known many conservative politicians and men of ideas, but no national Conservative party—or, for that matter, a national Liberal party, let alone a powerful Radical party. The United States ordinarily has been spared ideological passions in its great parties. In the past, the absence of a distinct aristocracy and the numerous opportunities for personal advancement tended to discourage the formation of class parties or ideological parties.

The triumph of merciless ideologies in half of the world, nevertheless, and the national interest of the United States in restraining the ambitions of Hitlerian Germany, the Soviet Union, and Communist China, have been important causes of the revival of political thought in America. Ideology of any sort being radical, a consequence of America's opposition to the totalist powers has been the stimulating of conservative ideas. . . .

In America, as in other countries, the particular forms assumed by the conservative impulse tend to be shaped by the nation's established social and political modes. Thus an American political conservative, at least as the term is employed popularly, is a person who believes strongly that the old pattern of American society ought not to be much altered. Typically, such a person holds by the Constitution, maintaining that it should be strictly interpreted; he endeavors to oppose the drift toward political centralization; he dislikes organizations on the grand scale, in government, in business and industry, in organized labor; he is a defender of private property; he resents the heavy increase of taxation and many of the "transfer payments" of the welfare state; he is unalterably opposed to the Communist ideology and the aspirations of the Soviet Union; he sighs, or perhaps shouts, *O tempora! O mores!* at the decay of private and public morality. In former years this typical conservative was a Protestant; but from the early 1940s, for a number of reasons, more and more American Catholics have moved toward conservative political attitudes, and often have taken the lead in conservative causes.

We never step in the same river twice. This representative conservative American of the 1980s is not identical with a Federalist of the 1780s. Yet some continuity of belief and institution connects those two figures; and it seems probable that the literature of American conservative thought and character may endure as long as the Republic.

4. English Conservatism

Under various names, political parties founded on conservative concepts appeared throughout Europe early in the nineteenth century. Of these, only Britain's Conservative party—now the oldest political party of any sort, anywhere in the world—has remained powerful right down to the present day.

The history of conservative parties and movements in Germany and France is an important and lively subject which cannot be examined here. Until the Bolshevik Revolution and Soviet imperialism extirpated the old social order in Eastern Europe, every European country had some political party or faction which deserved to be classified as conservative—the aims and complexion of the party varying from one state to another. In Northern Europe, these parties were sustained particularly by the landed gentry; they also enjoyed a good deal of support from peasants and from a part of the middle classes. In the Austrian system and in Southern Europe, links between the conservative parties and the Catholic Church existed. But throughout the Continent, in the face of vigorous liberal parties and of armed risings against the established order, the conservatives gradually lost ground; and after the revolutions of 1848, with the flight of Metternich from Austria and of Louis Philippe from France, conservative regimes surrendered power to liberals and nationalists or else clung to influence only in coalition with other political groups.

The coming of modern industrialism, too, hastened the decline of old-style conservatism, transferring wealth and power to new hands and breaking what Bagehot called "the cake of custom." Industrialism undermined the habitual acceptance of things long established that is bound up with the conservative understanding of community. Between 1830 and 1880, roughly speaking, liberalism beat down the conservative ascendancy in much of Europe. Even in Russia and Prussia, liberal assumptions and measures were adopted by the reigning monarchs.

Only in Britain did a party—and a climate of opinion—unabashedly conservative maintain ascendancy much of time throughout the whole of the nineteenth century, obtaining the support of at least half the electorate. Originally taking form as a coalition of Tories and Portland Whigs in William Pitt's ministry during the war with revolutionary France, the English conservatives began to use the word "conservative" as early as 1824, implying by that word their discipleship to Burke; and gradually "Conservative" became the name of their party.

The English people's marked aversion to change made the Conservative party palatable to a great part of the public. (Had most of Britain's electors belonged to the "Celtic fringe" of Scotland, Wales, and Ireland, the Conservative party would have found itself in a permanent minority.) When the French socialist speculator Saint-Simon visited Britain during the formative years of the Conservative party, he predicted that British society, already industrialized, soon would be overwhelmed by a rising of the proletariat. Nothing of the sort occurred, in that time or later in the century. After the passing of a century and a half, indeed, the British Conservative party still can win general elections.

Although shaken by the Whig Reform Bill of 1832 and by the passage of other Whig and Liberal measures that undermined the agricultural interest, the Conservatives were rescued by the fertile imagination and astute management of Benjamin Disraeli. From the time of the French Revolution to the Reform Bill of 1867, the backbone of the Conservative party was formed by the landed proprietors—the squirearchy. Disraeli's reform of 1867 attached to the Conservatives a considerable part of the artisan classes. As the Liberals turned their attention toward egalitarian measures and humanitarian projects, successive segments of the middle classes and of the surviving Whig interest went over to the Conservatives—most notably, the Liberal Unionists, in 1886. At the end of the nineteenth century, under the leadership of Lord Salisbury, the conservatives stood seemingly at the summit of their popularity.

An overwhelming Liberal victory in the general election of 1906 terminated this ascendancy—but only temporarily, for the rise of socialism was pressing the Liberals hard, and the Labour victory of 1924 meant the end of the Liberal party as an effective force. During the following four decades, conservatives formed the government most of the time. Since the Second World War, Labour and Conservative governments have alternated in power.

In absorbing much of the former Liberal interest, the British Conservative party has adopted also some elements of Liberal policy, so that the Conservative party has become a union of old Tory and Liberal factions, combined against Labour. Although the Conservatives yielded much ground to their opponents as the decades passed, what they have succeeded in retaining is more remarkable. The monarchy remains so popular as to be quite unchallenged; an aristocratic element survives both *de jure* and *de facto*; parliamentary government is not menaced; most property remains in private possession; the welfare state is being modified by the Conservatives; there is still a church by law established; intellectually, the conservative interest has recovered from the shaken state in which it lay after the Second World War. . . .

5. Prospects for Conservative Thought and Policy

Despite the persistence, or perhaps recrudescence, of the conservative impulse in America and Britain, can conservative views and interests long endure in an age of ideology, when two of the three great powers in the world are ruled by Marxist doctrinaires, and while technological and economic and cultural change continue to tear apart the cake of custom everywhere? The English-speaking peoples aside, in what it has become fashionable to call "the Post-Modern Age" or "the Post-Christian Era" indeed it seems as if (fulfilling Burke's vaticinations) "generation will not link with generation, and men will be as the flies of a summer." Brooks Adams wrote that "With conservative populations, slaughter is nature's remedy." The conservative populations of Vietnam, Cambodia, and Laos have been butchered very recently. Will people after people be devoted to the Savage God of ideology?

Consider the European continent. After suffering suppression under the dictatorial regimes of the 1930s and during the Second World War, European conservative groups began to regain vigor about 1946. Soviet power had extirpated effectual conservatism in Poland, Hungary, Czechoslovakia, Rumania, Bulgaria, and lesser states; but to the chagrin of the Communists, and indeed of the socialist parties of Western Europe, conservative parties—or, more commonly, Christian Democratic parties in which various conservative and liberal elements were leagued—won national elections in several countries; elsewhere, except under Marxist governments, they exercised a moderating influence.

Yet this revived conservatism was shorn of many of its old associations and had come to terms, in most countries, with old-fashioned economic liberalism. Paradoxically, the conservatives' partial success was brought about by the menace of Marxism: after the failure of the Nazi and Fascist regimes, and the ineffectuality of postwar "democratic" socialism, many Europeans turned once more to quasi-conservative policies as the only alternatives to a totalist order. "Conservative" governments in France, Germany, Italy, Austria, and some other European states today may be conservative in the broader and comparative sense of the term, but they differ markedly from the conservative parties and their views before 1914. It may be argued that in truth these recent "conservative" governments have been substantially liberal governments in the nineteenth-century sense, with some admixture of conservative elements and conservative rhetoric. How long such regimes might stand, were they shorn of American protection, nobody knows.

Turn to Latin America. Ever since their wars of independence, the Latin American states have striven to establish stable political orders. They have not succeeded. Their formal constitutions, usually imitating European or North American models, rarely have reflected the real social circumstances of their peoples; and so have not exerted a conservative influence like that of the Constitution of the United States. Except for relatively long periods in the history of Chile and Colombia, and shorter periods in the history of Venezuela, Argentina, Costa Rica, and El Salvador, dictatorship or oligarchy ordinarily has triumphed over the representative institutions that characterize Anglo-American and most European states. Social and racial conflicts have swept away many of the bulwarks of conservatism. Struggles with the Catholic Church in several countries have weakened the religious foundations of the conservative interest. The triumph of a Marxist regime in Cuba illustrated the feebleness of conservative elements in much of Latin America. Joseph Conrad's novel *Nostromo* remains as accurate a picture of Latin American social instability as it was at its publication in 1904. One cannot look to Latin America for signs of conservative imagination and hope.

In Asia, Western ideology and Western technology, both blending with a new ferocious nationalism in some countries, have so thoroughly broken up the old order of things that it scarcely is possible to speak of conservative politics anywhere except in Japan and some of the Muslim states. Japanese conservatism, now recovering from the injuries inflicted by war and military occupation, is an interesting development, arising out of old Japanese concepts of piety, duty, and honor. This subtle conservatism gradually may reassert itself: as Lafcadio Hearn wrote, Japan wears successively, and perhaps sincerely, a series of Western masks; but these are discarded in turn, for beneath the masks the old Japanese character lives. The present mask of Western materialism and technocracy will not endure forever; but it does not follow that it must be succeeded by the mask of proletarian dictatorship.

In India, Western socialist and liberal ideas are dominant, though yielding perhaps to Marxist influences. Western conservatism on the English pattern, never deep-rooted in India, has become negligible. A powerfully conservative body of Hindu culture does provide some check upon Western ideology. A somewhat similar struggle between Western progressivism and conservative Muslim tradition continues in Pakistan, Indonesia, and elsewhere.

In short, it is not to be expected that there can be brought to pass any concert of conservative political regimes, throughout the world, with the intention of withstanding Marxist ideology. Conservatism on the American or the British model would be an impossible exotic in central Africa or in other regions where nothing comparable to the British or the American historical experience ever has occurred. As Daniel Boorstin puts it, "The American Constitution is not for export." If sovereign states cooperate to resist Soviet imperialism, that will be on the ground of the national interest of each state, not because of a general political consensus. Conservatism not being an ideology with pretensions to universality and infallibility, there can be no Capitalist Manifesto to set against the Communist Manifesto. For that matter, not many conservatives would be happy to enlist under the banner of one abstraction, Capitalism, against another abstraction, Communism—or to die, absurdly, for "a higher standard of living."

And yet, transcending the differences of culture and history and race and national frontiers, something that we may call the conservative impulse or the conservative yearning does exist among all peoples. Without this instinct, any society would fall to pieces. Coleridge wrote that in any state there must be its Permanence, or elements of stability and continuity; and its Progression, or elements of growth and experiment. If the restraining conservative influence were destroyed, any society would fly apart from the vertiginous speed of change.

In that sense, a kind of universal conservatism may be glimpsed. It has not been stamped out even in Soviet Russia. Under tribulation, it is nurtured by an instinct for veneration almost inextinguishable in some people; by an insight best expressed by Richard Hooker: "The reason first why we do admire those things which are greatest, and second those things which are ancientest, is because the one are the least distant from the infinite substance, the other from the infinite continuance, of God."

At bottom, then, conservatism is not a matter of economic interests and economic theories; not a matter of political advantages and political systems; not a matter of power or preferment. If we penetrate to the root, we discover that "conservatism" is a way of looking at the human condition. As a conservative Polish proverb puts it, "Old truths, old laws, old boots, old books, and old friends are the best." The conservative impulse is a man's desire to walk in the paths that his father followed; it is a woman's desire for the sureties of hearth and home.

In every culture, what does the imaginative conservative aspire to conserve? Why, to conserve order: both order in the soul and order in the state. With Luke, the man of conservative impulses says to himself, "No man having drunk old wine straightway desireth new; for he saith, The old is better." Out of the deep well of the past comes order, and as Simone Weil reminds us, "Order is the first need of all."

From relevation, from right reason, from poetic vision, from much study, from the experience of the species—so the conservative argues—we humans have learned certain ways and principles of order. Were we lacking these, we would lie at the mercy of will and appetite—in private life, in public concerns. It is this order, this old safeguard against private and public anarchy, which the conservative refuses to surrender to the evangels of Progress. . . .

Were there no ordering of the soul and the state, no human society could survive; indeed, no civilized individual could endure. That being so, conservative beliefs will not cease to be unless the civil social order ceases to be. Many voices nowadays tell us that the Liberal Era is far gone in senescence; the Marxist Era, already repudiated by men of letters and false to its own promises, may not endure long; so there may come round again a time for the restoration of old standards. . . .

6. The Literature of Conservatism

In practical affairs, during the past two centuries, the rearguard actions of conservatives very often have fallen into routs. In the realm of letters, nevertheless, often conservative writers have won the day, from the triumph of Burke's rhetoric to the ascendancy of Eliot's poetry and criticism. Liberals have become painfully aware of this seeming paradox.

"[I]magination governs the human race." Who said that? No poet: instead, Napoleon, master of the big battalions. He knew that in the long run, the power of the moral imagination exceeds the power of a whiff of grapeshot. If the world is entering upon the Post-Modern Age (John Lukacs setting AD 1945 as the Year Zero of this Post-Modern Age), new-seeming ideas and new-seeming sentiments and new-seeming modes of statecraft may grow popular during the next few decades. The Post-Modern imagination stands ready to be captured. And the seemingly novel ideas and sentiments and modes may turn out, after all, to be revived truths and institutions, well known to surviving conservatives. Lionel Trilling, more than thirty years ago, found the liberal imagination nearly bankrupt; that kind of imagination has not prospered since then. It may be the conservative imagination which is to guide the Post-Modern Age, particularly in America. The aim of Burke, says Paul Elmer More, was "to use the imagination as a force for order and self-restraint and political health." It is just conceivable that such conservative imagination may attain its fullness in the twenty-first century.

["What Is Conservatism?" The Portable Conservative Reader *(New York: Viking Penguin, 1982), xi–xl.]*

❖

The Dissolution of Liberalism

"The Dissolution of Liberalism," which first appeared in Commonweal, *January 7, 1955, inspects the system of thought called liberalism that came into existence in the nineteenth century and that, Kirk reckons, is dying. He links liberalism to the myth of individual free will and self-sufficiency, severed from tradition and religion. The marks of this severance are evident when one looks at the twentieth-century liberals who have surrendered the values of variety, individuality, and moral improvement to equalitarian stability, uniformity, and what Kirk calls "uninspired collectivism." The task of filling the vacuum created by liberal reformers belongs to the conservator. As Kirk declares: "The liberal imagination has run out; the liberal myth, feeble in its beginnings, is now exhausted; and what is best in our society will have to be saved . . . by the advocates of some older and more stalwart system of thought."*

All great systems, ethical or political, attain their ascendancy over the minds of men by virtue of their appeal to the imagination; and when they cease to touch the chords of wonder and mystery and hope, their power is lost, and men look elsewhere for some set of principles by which they may be guided.

We live by myth. "Myth" is not falsehood; on the contrary, the great and ancient myths are profoundly true. The myth of Prometheus will always be a high poetic representation of an ineluctable truth, and so will the myth of Pandora. A myth may grow out of an actual event almost lost in the remote past, but it comes to transcend the particular circumstances of its origin, assuming a significance universal and abiding.

Nor is a myth simply a work of fancy: true myth is only represented, never created, by a poet. Prometheus and Pandora were not invented by the solitary imagination of Hesiod. Real myths are the product of the moral experience of a people, groping toward divine love and wisdom—implanted in a people's consciousness, before the dawn of history, by a power and a means we never have been able to describe in terms of mundane knowledge.

A recent writer in *Partisan Review*, expatiating upon a concept of Thomas Mann's, endeavored to argue that all myths are deceptive and dangerous, because a hypothetical "myth" created out of whole cloth by a Mann character was deceptive and dangerous. The trouble with this notion is that true myth cannot be invented by Thomas Mann's character, or by Thomas Mann, or by anyone else. All that the poet or projector can create is romance, fiction, a work of fancy.

A "myth" got up by a single ingenious romancer to suit his ends is no real myth at all. One might as well argue that all the books of the Bible are so many hoaxes because Joseph Smith turned up the Book of Mormon under rather curious circumstances. The fallacy in this contention is that the Book of Mormon is not part of the Bible.

Just so the "myths" of Nietzsche, or of Mann, are not really myths at all; they are not the collective expression of a people's moral experience, but only the fancies of ingenious individuals. Myth, properly understood, is not a delusion or a hoax: it is an expression of wisdom transcending the private reason.

I repeat that no great ethical or political movement comes to master the minds of men without some sanction of myth. The quality and power of that myth may vary, and the particular system may represent myth badly or deliberately distort it, but the rudiment of myth must be there. So it has been even with the system of thought called liberalism, which came into being early in the nineteenth century, and is now fading out of the world. As great ethical and political systems go, liberalism has been short-lived. And I believe that the ephemeral character of the liberal movement is in consequence of the fact that liberalism's mythical roots always were feeble, and now are nearly dead. Liberalism is expiring under our very eyes for lack of the higher imagination.

❖

Mr. Christopher Dawson recently described the origins and historical weaknesses of liberalism better than I can; yet I venture to suggest that the power of liberalism, so far as it came to influence the masses of men, came from a kind of residual store of myth, however much doctrinaire liberals might disavow myth in general. The arch-liberal, Jeremy Bentham, was contemptuously hostile to all myth, and yet the liberal parties of the past century and a half attained political power through an implicit appeal to a myth of strong popular appeal, however misunderstood or distorted. That myth is what Lord Percy of Newcastle calls "the heresy of democracy"—literally a heresy, the belief that political power and political wisdom emanate from an abstract People, rather than from divine Providence.

Orestes Brownson, more than a century ago, penetratingly exposed this fallacy in liberalism, and went on to describe socialism as a "Christian heresy"—and that in the very year of the Communist Manifesto. (He is echoed nowadays by Professor Toynbee and a great many others.) Liberalism, in short, found its popular support in myth, but in myth distorted: the myth of individual free will, but a free will stripped of divine guidance and of grace; the myth of popular sovereignty, but a myth deprived of the saving phrase "under God"; the myth of natural rights, but a myth shorn of the Providential order which gives such rights their sanction.

The liberal system attained popularity because it promised progress without the onerous duties exacted by tradition and religion. It is now in the process of dissolution because, founded on an imperfect and distorted myth, it has been unable to fulfill its promise, and because it no longer appeals in any degree to the higher imagination. It has been undone by social disillusion. Before long, no one will be able to take shelter under the ruinous fabric of liberalism. I see three alternatives to the liberal system: some iron discipline like that of Communism, founded upon a gross heresy from Christian principle; some Machiavellian scheme founded upon self-interest and creature-comforts; or a reinvigorated adherence to religious doctrine and traditional rights, which system we call, in politics, "conservatism."

❖

The abstract system called liberalism has brought into disrepute the good old word "liberal," which nowadays retains its original meaning almost solely in conjunction with "education"; and liberal education, we all know, has harder sledding every year that passes. "Liberal," properly understood, means those qualities possessed by truly free men, cognizant of their rights and their corresponding duties. It often implied, once upon a time, a far-ranging tolerance—but a tolerance based upon firm belief in enduring principles.

It was in this sense that Burke praised "a liberal understanding." It was in this sense that Newman took up the cause of liberal education against the Utilitarians. But Liberalism as a secular dogmatism, as a presumptuous system with an overweening confidence in Rationality, early became a force hostile to the liberality of mind that was Burke's and Newman's.

It is significant that the Utilitarian educational zealots against whom Newman contended were the leaders of English liberalism. Newman first heard the word "liberalism" in connection with the opinions of Byron and his admirers. "Afterwards," Newman writes, "Liberalism was the badge of a theological school, not very dangerous in itself, though dangerous as opening the door to evils which it did not itself either anticipate or comprehend. At present it is nothing else than that deep, plausible skepticism, . . . the development of human reason, as practically exercised by the natural man."

I have written that liberalism is founded upon a distortion of the myth of free will. Free will is mythical; it is also true. All evidence is against it, and all necessity for it. The story of the Fall is the myth of the terrible and yet liberating reality of free will. The historical narrative of the Coming is the completion of that myth. I repeat that myths may be in history, though they transcend history. Well, the great and true myth of free will was distorted by the school of liberalism into the cult of the omnicompetence of private judgment.

The doctrinaire liberal, from the beginning, repudiated authority, tradition, and the wisdom of our ancestors, intending to supplant these checks upon the natural man by Rationality with a capital R. Enlightened self interest, the English and Continental liberals assumed, joined to an all-sufficing enlightened private rationality, henceforth would emancipate mankind from obedience to tradition, authority, and the past experience of humanity. This assumption led the liberals into a deadly sin, pride of spirit, the arrogant rationality of the man who believes he has the right to judge all things in heaven and earth according to his petty private taste. It led to the enormity of Utilitarian moral calculus, the pleasure-pain equation. Bentham, the enemy of myth, himself carried the myth of free will to absurdity by making the individual the arbiter of all.

As the liberal ideology (for it has been an ideology—that is, a body of secular political dogmas) took form, in England and the Continent and to a lesser extent in America, it became clear that its disciples accepted certain postulates almost on faith. One of these was the idea of Progress—the notion that mankind, through its own efforts, is getting better and better, so that the Present is infinitely superior to any other age in history, and the Future will be better still, so long as private judgment and enlightened self-interest are allowed to prevail over tradition and authority. Another was an affection for Change on principle, and a detestation of Permanence—a craving for novelty. A third was the exaltation of Selfishness into a virtue—that is, a spiritual atomism, a world in which community should be discarded in favor of a thoroughgoing individualism. A fourth was the enthusiasm for Liberty, political and private opportunity to undo all things established and make the world anew, without much respect for two principles which Christian thinkers always had made coordinate with reasoned liberty, Justice and Order.

❖

In the states of Europe, the struggle between this liberalism and the Christian concept of society was undisguised. There the religious liberal was an anomaly, particularly after 1830. "Liberalism" meant detestation of the Church, usually hostility toward orthodox Christianity, and often a repudiation of religion in any form.

In England and America, because of peculiar circumstances, this inimicality was not so easily distinguished. Since the English Liberals took up the cause of the removal of religious disabilities against the defenders of the Anglican establishment, the bulk of Catholics and Nonconformists voted as Liberals, down to the times of Joseph Chamberlain and Stanley Baldwin, however little they might subscribe to the kernel of the liberal ideology. In the United States, though "liberalism" did not become a term of commendation until well within the present century, what are now looked upon as "liberal" causes were often supported by religious persons because they found it expedient, as in Britain, to make common cause with secularists whose immediate aims happened to coincide with theirs.

Brownson remarked in his day the impulse of American Catholics to side with radicals in politics because of a prejudice, acquired in Ireland or Europe, against established political institutions very unlike the constitutional structure of the United States. Besides, the "conservative" and "liberal" lines never were well defined in this country, and the popular confusion over the definition of either term persists down to the present time.

Now it appears to me that twentieth-century collectivism is in part a reaction against doctrinaire liberalism, and in part the natural consequence of that system of thought. The spiritual isolation and the decay of a sense of community which accompanied the triumph of liberalism cannot be endured long by any people. Love lacking, compulsion is employed to hold society together. And the materialism of the Marxist is only the logical culmination of the materialism of the doctrinaire liberal.

Once the insufficiency of private judgment to govern either society or character was revealed by the terrible events of this century, the body of liberal opinion began to break up, some going on to collectivism, others seeking to return to something like conservative values. The representative twentieth-century liberal, as Santayana observes, has given up the idea of liberation; the only tie which he would loosen is the marriage-bond. Having come full cycle, the liberal now, with ex-Mayor Clark of Philadelphia, is a devotee of the centralized state and the regulated society. He does not talk of Liberty or Justice or Order: he talks of Security. (I was surprised, recently, when Mr. William V. Shannon, writing in the *Commonweal*, maintained that American conservatives are fascinated by the delusion of stability. Surely stability, security, guaranteed welfare, and the like, are now the idols of the American liberal.)

❖

Until this century, nearly every American statesman desired to be thought a conservative: Calhoun did, and so did Lincoln. Mr. Colin Clark, in a recent number of *Encounter*, remarks the rather curious recent vogue of the word in this country. The American vaguely discontented with the shape of society, as Mr. Clark suggests, took for his model what he imagined English liberalism to be, although English liberalism already was far gone in decay: he imagined that it was some sort of the-middle-way policy, happily splitting the difference between individualism and collectivism.

Thus amorphous in its beginning, twentieth-century American liberalism has become almost impossible to describe, embracing a curious congeries of people all the way from rigid Manchesterians to the editors of the *Nation*. The dominant element among them, however, is now constituted by the devotees of the planned society, perceived at their frankest in R. G. Tugwell and Harry Hopkins: persons to whom regulation and uniformity are ends in themselves.

The word "liberal," in such circumstances, has lost any real meaning. For some "liberals," as Mr. Clark suggests, the chief value of the word is its employment as a convenient disguise: "liberal" has one meaning for the neophyte or outsider, and another for the initiate, in these circles. I found it amusing to observe the chagrin of some such persons when they read Orwell on Newspeak and Doublethink.

The liberal's distorted myth of private self-sufficiency in all things has been exploded; his complacent expectation of unchecked progress has been overwhelmed by social disorder and private discontent; his confidence in Rationality has been shattered beyond repair. To what, then, does he cling nowadays? To the feeble hope, ordinarily, of some sort of brummagem utopia of creature-comforts, characterized by equality of condition, uniformity of life and thought, pervasive state regulation, and the obliteration of traditional morality.

In a recent book by Mr. William H. McNeill, *Past and Future*, we see the best that the philosophers of American liberalism have to offer; and, as the *Times Literary Supplement* comments, "the alarming thing about his book is that the perfect world which he describes, and still more the means of achieving it, are far more terrifying and horrible" than the writings of our pessimistic realists. Mr. McNeill, as if determined to carry liberal neoterism to its logical absurdity, is in love with vertiginous speed, and exhorts us to run faster still, for running's sake. And where will this speed take us to? Why, to an omnipotent world state, a masterpiece of intricate regulation, which (like Marx's triumph of the proletariat) replaces change by changelessness, and imposes an eternal compulsory uniformity upon the whole human race, to which culmination Mr. McNeill looks forward cheerfully. Now I think that this is, indeed, the natural culmination of the Benthamite view of man and society; but I think that most people who call themselves liberals would find this society quite intolerable.

❖

In ordinary usage, the word "conservative" tends to imply a proclivity toward permanence, and "liberal" to imply a proclivity toward progression. But the twentieth-century liberal has come to care less and less about variety, individuality, moral improvement, and the other subjects which, in the eyes of John Stuart Mill, were the ends of liberalism: instead, he is willing to settle for an eternal and equalitarian stability.

The English Socialist has lowered his sights to the mark of middle-class comfort for the masses; the American liberal would be quite content with a universal suburbia. It is the genuine conservative, nowadays, who speaks out against an overweening complacency and a world that would be a life-in-death. It is the conservative who asserts the claims of Justice and Order and Liberty against the demand for a featureless Society.

Whatever the blessings of Security, the thinking conservative believes, it is possible to buy Security at too high a price. And the price we are now in danger of paying is very high indeed. It is the price of manhood.

Once real virtue, manhood, the courage and responsibility of free men, are extinguished in a society, presently security evaporates, too; but that is the lesser loss. The conservative maintains that there is something better than to know what it is to be guaranteed and protected and pensioned. The better state is to know what it is to be a man.

The liberal, old style or new style, always has tended to leave out of his calculations the tragic sense of life, without which men and women remain as children. Poverty is not in itself an evil; nor inequality; nor death. All these may be occasions for virtue. But a society which would deny men the right to struggle against evil for the sake of good, or which simply ceased to distinguish between good and evil, would constitute that domination of the Anti-Christ which now must seem to all reflective men a possibility so strong as to demonstrate the profound truth that takes the form of myth.

The gist of my reasoning is this: I think that whatever remains of nineteenth-century liberalism is rapidly sinking into an uninspired collectivism, which at best could bring to society only a dreary monotony. And I do not think that even this poor best could be realized; our fallen human nature would make short work even of a brummagem utopia. Although we might find it possible to extirpate heroism, with all the devices for suppression and indoctrination now at our command, we could scarcely succeed in extirpating villainy. Nineteenth-century liberal humanitarianism would come down at last to a domination of squalid oligarchs, all in the name of "democracy" and "progress" and "security."

❖

I am alarmed, therefore, at the dissolution of liberalism. This leaves a vacuum: and I do not want to see that vacuum filled by an intolerant radicalism of any description.

"Liberalism," though it remains for many people what Mr. Richard Weaver calls a god-term, really has ceased to signify anything, even among its more sincere partisans, than a vague good will. Good will divorced from right reason and free institutions can accomplish very little in this time of troubles. It is my hope that many people genuinely attached to justice and order and liberty, who in the past have called themselves liberals, now may see a new meaning in conservatism.

There are ages when custom and inertia lie insufferably heavy upon mankind; and such an age may come again; but this is not our age. Ours is a time when the moral and social heritage of many centuries of civilization is in imminent peril from the forces of vertiginous and indiscriminate change. The man who, in a different time, ought to be a reformer, now has the duty of being a conservator.

The liberal imagination has run out; the liberal myth, feeble in its beginnings, is now exhausted; and what is best in our society will have to be saved, if it is to be saved at all, by the advocates of some older and more stalwart system of thought.

It is not a new political party that I am recommending, or any neat program of positive legislation. The conservative task, if it is to be accomplished successfully, will be carried on within the minds of men. The bulk of both our national political parties is conservative, and this is all to the good. I do not mean that our parties ought to be unprincipled; quite the contrary; they need a good deal more principle than they manifest now. But the great labor of conserving our legacy of justice and order and liberty, of keeping mankind truly human, leaves much room for two conservative parties, differing about means, but substantially agreed upon the ends of life and society. We shall have fanaticism and radicalism enough to contend against in the rest of the world.

Nor do I think that this work of conservation can be accomplished by any particular class—certainly not by any idealization of "business rule." The late Robert Taft, with his accustomed forthrightness, said that the businessman is not calculated to be a statesman. The businessman, if he is as busy as his name implies, has little time to learn to be a philosopher or a legislator or a governor of men. Burke said this same thing a great while ago; it is no less true today.

Some men of business are able politicians, but this is in spite of their responsibilities in business, not because of them. We will do well to remember Dr. Johnson's adage that a man is seldom more innocently occupied than when he is engaged in making money; but innocence is not the same thing as statecraft. One of the principles of conservatism is the protection of private property and honest industry, and there is every reason just now why conservatives ought to emphasize this principle. Yet respect for the rights and duties of business does not mean that industrialists ought to write our laws and direct our state policies.

I hope that we Americans will conserve "free enterprise" and "economic stability" and all the best features of an economy governed by volition rather than compulsion. But we will conserve these things only if we set our sights higher and conserve something larger, a society of variety and tradition and veneration. The liberals cannot do that work for us. I do not know whether the conservatives can; but it is time they began to try.

["The Dissolution of Liberalism," Commonweal, *January 7, 1955, 374–78. Also found in* Beyond the Dreams of Avarice: Essays of a Social Critic *(Chicago: Henry Regnery Company, 1956), 32–42.]*

Ten Exemplary Conservatives

This essay appears in Kirk's The Politics of Prudence *(1993), a book which proposes to guide "the rising generation of the 1990s" in examining conservative principles, people, books, problems. In "Ten Exemplary Conservatives" Kirk sketches shapers of ideas who formed his opinions. The one thing that they share is affection for the Permanent Things and devotion to the conservative imagination. Kirk's list contains a Roman orator (Cicero), a Roman emperor (Marcus Aurelius), an English moralist and critic (Samuel Johnson), a Scottish romancer (Sir Walter Scott), a Virginia politician (John Randolph of Roanoke), a New England novelist and short-story writer (Nathaniel Hawthorne), a fighting, writing president (Theodore Roosevelt), a Polish sea-captain-novelist (Joseph Conrad), a recluse at the University of Chicago (Richard M. Weaver), and an English wanderer in antique lands (Freya Stark). Kirk hopes readers will gain from them teachings that inspired his own life and thought.*

In ways mysterious our political preferences are formed. "When did you decide to become a conservative?" people sometimes inquire of me. But I never did decide: I *found* myself a conservative, once I began to reflect upon such concerns. Others find themselves liberals or radicals, without quite being able to account for that inclination.

Occasionally, nevertheless, we contrive to recall a conversation, a book, a public meeting, a chance encounter, a rebuff, an opportunity, a moment of solitary reflection, or the example of some man or woman, which drew or pushed us in some degree toward a particular view of politics. I think, for example, of a Sunday afternoon in my father's company, resting on a slope high above the village millpond, I a little boy. We lay in the shade of great trees; and I recall reflecting on the peace and beauty of the scene, and the great age of the trees—and wishing that everything about us that day might never change. That is the fundamental conservative impulse: the longing for order and permanence, in the person and in the republic.

Or I think of walking with my grandfather, a sagacious and courageous man, along a railway cut through a glacial moraine, we talking of British history—for I had been reading Dickens's *A Child's History of England*. That communion with an old gentleman I admired infinitely, and our reflections that day upon the living past, were among the influences that have prevented me from becoming an evangel of Modernity.

Again, it may be the example of some eminent champion of the permanent things that moves us: some living man, perhaps, or some figure of antique grandeur, dust long ago. His actions shape our beliefs; and we find ourselves applying his convictions and emulating his policies, so far as possible, perhaps in a different age or land.

So I present to you brief sketches of ten people of a conservative cast of mind who did much to form my opinions over the years. I do not suggest that these ten are the grandest figures ever cast in the conservative mold, although the names of two or three of them would appear on almost any informed person's list of great defenders of an old order; I am merely including particular public figures or shapers of ideas who formed my conservative mind. Of course I was influenced by a hundred more; but the ones I am about to name worked upon my imagination fairly early—the first eight of them, at least. I refrain here from including any authors whom I discussed much in my earlier disquisition "Ten Conservative Books"—which deletion removes from consideration both Edmund Burke and T. S. Eliot, the men with whom my book *The Conservative Mind* begins and ends, respectively. Presumably everybody agrees that Burke is the greatest of conservative thinkers; but I omit him here because I have written and said so much about him already, over the past thirty-five years; and about Eliot, too, I have written a big book.

Thus I offer you this day ten *exemplary* conservatives, with much diversity of talents among them—the most recent among them separated in time by more than two thousand years from the first-born of their number. What they share is an affection for the permanent things, and the courage to affirm that truth was not born yesterday. They are the giants, upon whose shoulders stand such dwarfs as myself. Tall though they loom, I cannot allot many more than three hundred words to anyone of them. I hope merely to wake your memories of them, or to induce you to admire them for the first time. Here they are, in diminishing order of antiquity: first, Marcus Tullius Cicero.

In my high-school days, before the ghastly triumph of educational Instrumentalism, a large proportion of the pupils used to study ancient history for a year—and Latin for two years. Thus was I introduced to Cicero, a man of law and philosophy who set his face against a military revolution, and lost, and paid with his head. *Conservative* was not a term of politics during the first century before Christ, but presumably Cicero would not have objected to being so described, he being something of a philologist: the English word conservative is derived from the Latin *conservator*, signifying one who preserves from injury, violence, or infraction.

The orations and the life of the defender of the expiring Roman Republic were studied closely in every decent upper school in Britain and America, during the seventeenth and eighteenth centuries and well into the nineteenth. As a high-school senior, I read a novel about Cicero and Caesar, Phyllis Bentley's *Freedom, Farewell*; that led me to Plutarch's life of Cicero, and I recall sitting on my front porch by the railway station, most of one summer, reading Plutarch through, and being moved by Cicero especially.

Cicero died for the old Roman constitution; ever since then, men defending constitutional order have looked to Cicero as their exemplar. As I have said elsewhere, one heroic custom of the early Romans was to "devote" a man to the gods, that through his sacrifice the commonwealth might be for given for wrongdoing. To the *mores majorum*, and to the moral law, Cicero gave the last full measure of devotion. At times in his public life, Cicero had been timid or vacillating; yet at the end, the high old Roman virtue was his. That model of virtue endures in the conservative's consciousness. *Roma immortalis* is no vain boast, after all.

Thus my second conservative exemplar is Marcus Aurelius Antoninus, the Stoic emperor. I read him earnestly during my first years as a soldier, I often seated solitary on a sand-dune, the treeless desert stretching far away to grim mountains: appropriately enough, for Marcus Aurelius's book of meditations has been dear to soldiers over the centuries, among them John Smith at Jamestown and Gordon at Khartoum.

About Marcus Aurelius I corresponded with Albert Jay Nock, that strong individualist and essayist, during the last year of Nock's life. "The world has not once looked upon his like," Nock wrote of Marcus, in his essay "The Value of Useless Knowledge," "and his praise is for ever and ever. Yet hardly was the breath out of his body before the rotten social fabric of Rome disintegrated, and the empire crumbled to pieces."

Marcus Aurelius writes of the beauty of a ripe fig, trembling on the verge of deliquescence; I ventured to suggest to Nock that this passage in the *Meditations* may hint at a certain fascination with decadence; Nock denied it. However that may be, the Emperor acted in a decadent age, corruption all about him, so that, in his phrase, it was necessary for him to "live as upon a mountain," isolated from intimacies. Today's conservatives, too, see about them a bent world.

It was the heroic endeavor of Marcus Aurelius to conserve *Romanitas*, that grand system of law and order and culture. If he failed—even with his wife, even with his son—still he left an example of integrity that has endured, like his equestrian statue on the Capitoline, down to our time. In Nock's words, "The cancer of organized mendicancy, subvention, bureaucracy and centralization had so far weakened its host that at the death of Marcus Aurelius there was simply not enough producing-power to pay the bills." Eighty years of able Antonine rule "could not prevent the Roman populace from degenerating into the very scum of the earth, worthless, vicious, contemptible, sheer human sculch." We may make comparisons and draw analogies, near the end of the twentieth century. (Nock, by the way, wrote an admirable essay on conservatism, little noticed so far as I know: his model of a conservative is Lucius Cary, Lord Falkland, the mediator between Charles I and the Parliament.)

The lesson I learnt from Marcus Aurelius is the performance of duty. Take this passage from the *Meditations*—the Emperor being on a hard Danubian campaign when he set down these lines: "In the morning, when thou risest sore against thy will, summon up this thought: 'I am rising to do the work of a man. Why then this peevishness, if the way lies open to perform the tasks which I exist to perform, and for whose sake I was brought into the world? Or am I to say I was created for the purpose of lying in blankets and keeping myself warm?'" With that admonition I steel myself on January mornings at my ancestral village.

Everyone who contends against odds in defense of the permanent things is an heir of Marcus Aurelius.

We leap sixteen centuries to approach my third conservative, Samuel Johnson. That unforgettable moralist and critic sometimes is represented as a blustering bigot; actually the political Johnson was a reasonable, moderate, and generous champion of order, quick to sustain just authority, but suspicious of unchecked power. He was at once the friend and the adversary of Edmund Burke. His note on Whigs and Tories, written in 1781, suggests his reasonableness:

> A wise Tory and a wise Whig, I believe, will agree. Their principles are the same, though their modes of thinking are different. A high Tory makes government unintelligible; it is lost in the clouds. A violent Whig makes it impracticable; he is for allowing so much liberty to every man, that there is not enough power to govern any man. The prejudice of the Tory is for establishment; the prejudice of the Whig is for innovation. A Tory does not wish to give more real power to Government; but that Government should have more reverence. Then they differ as to the Church. The Tory is not for giving more legal power to the Clergy, but wishes they should have a considerable influence, founded on the opinion of mankind; the Whig is for limiting and watching them with a narrow jealousy.

At this point it is useful to recall that originally the word conservative implied a moderate attitude, an endeavor to find a middle way between extremes. Just that was the mission of Falkland and, sometimes, of Johnson.

Johnson I read at Behemoth University, called by some people Michigan State University. (It was a cow college when I enrolled there.) In morals, the sound sense of Dr. Johnson has been my mainstay; and *Rasselas* has taught me far more about human beings and humankind's vanities than has *Candide*.

To Scotland we turn for my fourth conservative, Sir Walter Scott. Through the Waverley Novels, the Wizard of the North disseminated Burke's conservative vision to a public that never would have read political tracts; but Scott's achievement is considerably more than this labor of popularizing political doctrines. For Scott wakes the imagination; he reminds us that we have ancestors and inherit a moral patrimony; he pictures for us the virtues of loyalty, fortitude, respect for women, duty toward those who will succeed us in time—and all this without seeming didactic. As D. C. Somervell puts it, Scott showed, "by concrete instances, most vividly depicted, the value and interest of a natural body of traditions."

My mother gave me five of Scott's romances for my eighth birthday, and I have been reading Scott ever since. Until fairly recent years, one saw cheap editions of Scott's novels on sale at British railway kiosks; but modern educational approaches are effacing that sort of literary taste. I do not mean to desert Sir Walter: (indeed, I shall re-read *The Antiquary* reasonably soon at my Michigan fastness). Popular influence of the novel departed when television was plumped into the living-room of nearly every household in the western world; I suppose that relatively few people will read Scott, although books about him continue to be published; but those who do read him may be won to his understanding of the great mysterious incorporation of the human race.

Let us cross the Atlantic now. A Virginian is my fifth exemplary conservative—not George Washington, or George Mason, or Madison, or Monroe, and certainly not Thomas Jefferson; but John Randolph of Roanoke, concerning whom I wrote my first book. Strange to say, Randolph, the enemy of change, was described at some length in my tenth-grade American history textbook; I wrote a school paper about him; by 1951, that effort had grown to a book published by the University of Chicago Press, *Randolph of Roanoke: A Study in Conservative Thought*—today published, in a fuller edition, by Liberty Fund.

Randolph's biting wit and extemporaneous eloquence, in the House or the Senate, still ring true against the centralizers, the meddlers in the affairs of distant nations, the demagogues, the men in office who "buy and sell corruption in the gross." Yet it was Randolph's intricate personality and burning emotion, as much as his political perceptions, that drew me to a study of him and of the history of the Southern states. Hugh Blair Grigsby describes Randolph at the Virginia Convention of 1829–30, when Randolph was not far from death's door:

> . . . It was easy to tell from the first sentence that fell from his lips when he was in fine tune and temper, and on such occasions the thrilling music of his speech fell upon the ears of that excited assembly like the voice of a bird singing in the pause of the storm. It is difficult to explain the influence which he exerted in that body. He inspired terror to a degree that even at this distance of time seems inexplicable. He was feared alike by East and West, by friend and foe. The arrows from his quiver, if not dipped in poison, were pointed and barbed, rarely missed the mark, and as seldom failed to make a rankling wound. He seemed to paralyze alike the mind and the body of his victim. What made his attack more vexatious, every sarcasm took effect amid the plaudits of his audience.

James Madison and James Monroe, near the end of their tether in 1829, listened closely and fearfully to the formidable Randolph, their heads bowed.

It was my study of this master of rhetoric, this hard hater of cant and sham, this American disciple of Burke, that led me deeper into an understanding of Edmund Burke's mind and heart. "Change is not reform!" Randolph cried to the Virginia Convention; that aphorism I cherish. Would that some chastening Randolph might stride into today's Senate or House! Henry Adams, whose ancestors Randolph denounced, called Randolph of Roanoke "a Saint Michael in politics."

From Southside Virginia we make haste to Salem, in Massachusetts, to encounter my sixth exemplary conservative, Nathaniel Hawthorne. My great-aunt Norma thoughtfully gave me her set of Hawthorne's works when I was about nine years old, and I have those volumes still, after reading them through a score of times.

It is significant of the modern temper that for the past three decades, the typical school anthology of American literature has found little space for Hawthorne, though a great deal for Walt Whitman—a disproportion that today, I note, begins to be remedied by some publishers. The anthologists and textbook publishers had sensed the conservatism of Hawthorne, and the flabby democratism of Whitman is obvious enough. Yet it has been Hawthorne, not Whitman, who has been taken very seriously at the higher levels of education and by learned literary critics.

Understanding the reality of sin, Hawthorne was contemptuous of radicals' designs for the perfection of man and society. It was Hawthorne, you may recall, who said that no man was ever more justly hanged than was John Brown of Osawatomie. Hawthorne's *Blithedale Romance* demolishes American utopians; his short tale "Earth's Holocaust" ridicules the radicals' fierce endeavor to destroy the civilized past. As did T. S. Eliot, I take Hawthorne for the most moving and enduring of American writers.

A fighting, writing President is my seventh exemplary conservative: Theodore Roosevelt. Once upon a time, when my grandfather took his small grandson to the movies, there happened to appear on the screen, briefly, the face of Roosevelt. My grandfather applauded loudly but solitarily, to my embarrassment. Had I then read *Hero Tales from American History*, written by Theodore Roosevelt and Henry Cabot Lodge, I too would have applauded. My grandfather gave me a copy of that book not long later, and I read it most eagerly. How I was stirred, at the age of twelve, by Roosevelt's sketches and vignettes of George Rogers Clark, King's Mountain, the storming of Stony Point, the battle of New Orleans, the death of Stonewall Jackson, the charge at Gettysburg, Farragut at Mobile Bay, the Alamo! When later I came to know Roosevelt's houses at Oyster Bay—where he ran the United States, summers, from a loft-office above a drug store at the principal corners of the village—and in Manhattan, it was as if I were visiting one of my teachers. Much else that Roosevelt wrote has not diminished in vigor. Much that Roosevelt did requires doing all over again.

To apprehend how conservative Roosevelt was, read the venomous chapter about him in that snarling book *The American Political Tradition and the Men Who Made It*, by Richard Hofstadter, a thoroughgoing Marxist if an unconfessed one.

Consider such a passage as this: "The frantic growth and rapid industrial expansion that filled America in his lifetime had heightened social tensions and left a legacy of bewilderment, anger, and fright, which had been suddenly precipitated by the depression of the nineties. His psychological function was to relieve these anxieties with a burst of hectic action and to discharge these fears by scolding authoritatively the demons that aroused them. Hardened and trained by a long fight with his own insecurity, he was the master therapist of the middle classes."

How shocking that a President should be concerned for the middle classes! When Hofstadter sneers with such neurotic malice, one may be quite sure that Theodore Roosevelt was a power for good.

For my eighth conservative, I select that Polish genius who wrote in English, Joseph Conrad. I discovered Conrad early in my high-school years; picked up a second-hand set of his works in Salt Lake City during my years as a sergeant; lost that set in our Great Fire of 1975; and now have replaced most of the burnt volumes. I commend to you especially, with an eye to the literature of politics, his novels *Under Western Eyes, The Secret Agent,* and *Nostromo*. Of those, the first shows us Russian revolutionary politics, sad and grisly; the second reveals to us the figure of the Terrorist, yesteryear and today; the third is the most penetrating study ever written of Latin-American politics and character, illustrating Bolivar's mournful observation that whoever tries to establish liberty in Latin America plows the salt sea. Do not neglect Conrad's short stories, notably "The Informer," which I reprint in *The Portable Conservative Reader*.

In Conrad a powerful critical intellect is joined to vast experience of the ways of East and West. The great novelist entertains no illusions about socialism, anarchism, feminism, nihilism, liberalism, or imperialism. Were Conrad, the foe of ideology, writing today—why, he might have difficulty finding a decent publisher, and his novels might be ignored by the mass-media reviewers; but happily for his influence, Conrad's reputation was impregnably established before the present Holy Liberal Inquisition in publishing and reviewing obtained its unsparing hegemony.

Ninth, I call your attention to Richard Weaver, whom I knew well. According to Ambrose of Milan, it has not pleased God that man should be saved through logic. Richard Weaver would have assented to this, knowing as he did the nature of the average sensual man and the limits of pure rationality. Yet with a high logical power, Weaver undertook an intellectual defense of culture and did what he might to rescue order, justice, and freedom from the perverters of language.

Weaver died before his time, in his room—its walls painted black—at a cheap hotel on the South Side of Chicago. He had lived austerely and with dignity, hoping one day to retire to Weaverville, North Carolina, his birthplace. He was a shy little bulldog of a man who detested much in the modern world—with reason. His slim strong book *Ideas Have Consequences*, published in 1948, was the first gun fired by American conservatives in their intellectual rebellion against the ritualistic liberalism that had prevailed since 1933, and which still aspires to dominion over this nation. In 1948 I was a bookseller; and recognizing promptly the virtue of *Ideas Have Consequences*, I organized a display of many copies, sold most of them, and invited Weaver to speak to our George Ade Society in Lansing—perhaps the first time Weaver had been asked to speak, outside the University of Chicago. (Although he was no very effective orator, in one year he was voted the most able instructor in the College of the University of Chicago.)

Among philosophers, Plato was Weaver's mentor; and among statesmen, Lincoln. (Although a declared Southerner, in politics Weaver was a conservative Republican.) Such views did not find him favor in the academy, but he persevered, gaining some ground with his second book *The Ethics of Rhetoric*, and the several volumes of his other essays, published posthumously, have brought a consciousness of enduring truth to many who never saw him or wrote to him. A high consistency and honesty won over, in some degree, even the more hostile of the reviewers of his books.

Some of his closer Chicago friends their number was not legion—might not see him during the course of an entire year. He never travelled; he endured stoically the ferocious Chicago winters, often wearing two overcoats, one over the other. Once a year he attended a church, and then a high Episcopalian service; the solemnity and mystery of the ritual, strongly though he was attracted by them, overwhelmed his soul: such a feast would last for months. The frugality woven into his character extended even to his very private religion.

No man was less romantic than Richard Weaver—yet none more inveterately attached to forlorn good causes. Vanity he knew not, and he despised the *hubris* of modern times. Although there exist no heirs of his body, the heirs of his mind may be many and stalwart.

Turn we at last to the gentler sex. Once upon a time I wrote a book entitled *The Intelligent Woman's Guide to Conservatism*; and it would be possible to compile *A Portable Conservative Women's Reader*, for during the past century there have flourished a good many eminent female conservatives.

As my tenth exemplary conservative, then, I designate Freya Stark, the author of several remarkable books of travel in the Levant and Iran. Miss Stark was no politician, but a conservative spirit runs strongly through all her books, particularly her moving volume of essays *Perseus in the Wind* and her important historical study *Rome on the Euphrates*. I began reading the books of Miss Stark (or Mrs. Stewart Perowne, as she became eventually) during my residence in Scotland, and have venerated her ever since. Her brief essay "Choice and Toleration" is included in *The Portable Conservative Reader*.

To apprehend how a civilization undoes itself, one cannot do better than to read attentively her *Rome on the Euphrates*, with its account of the destruction of the western world's middle classes by Roman taxation, centralization, bureaucracy, and foolish war. History does repeat itself, although always with variations. There must be noted one sentence by Freya Stark that every conservative ought to grave upon his lintel—should he possess a house with a lintel—or at least upon his memory: "Tolerance cannot afford to have anything to do with the fallacy that evil may convert itself to good."

What an *omnium gatherum* of people endowed with a conservative turn of thought and impulse! A Roman orator, a Roman emperor, a lexicographer, a Scottish romancer, a Virginia politician, a New England "boned pirate," a rough-riding President, a Polish sea-captain-novelist, a recluse at the University of Chicago, a wanderer in antique lands! Yet it was such who formed my own conservative mind; and their very diversity sufficiently demonstrates that conservatism is no ideology, but rather a complex of thought and sentiment, a deep attachment to the permanent things. Incidentally, I have taken the opportunity to pay tribute to some major figures not discussed at any length in my other books, to my shame: President Roosevelt, Dr. Weaver, and Miss Stark.

In the long run, the courses of nations are not determined by the candidates for office or the grandiose administrators whose names bulk large in the daily papers and echo in the television studios; whose names will be quite forgotten, most of them, a decade from now. Napoleon or Pitt, Stalin or Churchill, true, may leave real marks upon the world, for good or ill. Yet it is imagination that governs humankind: so the men and women who alter thought and sentiment are the true movers and shakers of the moral order and the civil social order.

The conservative imagination of the ten people I have presented to you was employed courageously to oppose that disorder which perpetually threatens to reduce the world to chaos. Profiting by their examples, we folk at the end of the twentieth century must rouse ourselves from the apathy of Lotos-land, taking counsel as to how we may defend the permanent things against the wrath of the enemies of order, so fierce and clamorous in our time; or how, at worst, to shore some fragments against our ruin.

["Ten Exemplary Conservatives," The Politics of Prudence *(Bryn Mawr, Pa.: Intercollegiate Studies Institute, 1993), 62–78.]*

Why I Am a Conservative

In this essay Kirk submits the articles of his conservative faith. We have here in fine a creedal statement of his beliefs, worth pondering for what it tells us about Kirk's lifelong defense of the conservative ethos. Even one who happens not to share Kirk's loyalties will be responsive to the inherent honesty of the testimony he presents, its succinctness of language, its reasonableness and good temper. Kirk is unyielding but not truculent in his positions. Quietly but firmly, he attempts to distinguish between the liberal and the conservative mind, between their attitudes and tendencies, between the aspirations of the liberal intent on having progress at any price and the hopes of the conservator to stave off "a society devoid of reverence, variety, and the higher imagination"—a society that promises a terrestrial paradise in defiance of the law of limits.

From the hour I began to reason, and possibly from the hour I began to feel, I have been a conservative. Worldly circumstances have little enough to do with social convictions. My boyhood, I may say, was spent in the railroad yards; at college, subsisting on peanut butter and crackers, I hugged my poverty about me like a cloak; and I have no expectation of eventual material wealth. If any young man is bent upon mundane advancement, I advise him to enlist in some "liberal" undertaking, for the conservative element which survives in our country does not have wealth, or influence, or even adequate means of expression.

Liberal prejudices—either old-style Manchesterian liberalism or new-style collectivistic liberalism—have dominated our climate of opinion for a great while; and the serious press, the private foundations, the universities, and even the surviving private patrons have been affected by this climate. The liberal, old style or new style, swears by the evangels of Progress; he thinks of society as a machine for aggrandizement, and of happiness as the gratification of appetites.

The conservative, on the contrary, thinks of society as what Burke called the great mysterious incorporation of the human race, held together by tradition and custom and immemorial usage, a living spirit; and he thinks that happiness comes from duty done, and from an understanding of the vanity of human wishes.

The American industrialist, by and large, has been a liberal, and so has the American labor organizer; they have differed about means, rather than ends. I do not mean that no industrialists, or no union leaders, are conservatives; some are truly conservative, but they are exceptional. The obsession with economics—a Benthamite and Marxist obsession—has oppressed nearly all discussion of Americans' wants for a good many years, and only now is beginning to give way to some serious talk of what we really want from life, and how we may keep life tolerable.

And it still is true that the writer, the scholar, and the aspiring public servant, if they are after the main chance, will do well to profess publicly a devotion to liberalism and progress and change for change's sake. Liberalism, old style or new style, remains the prevalent orthodoxy, with the usual rewards attached to conformity. One may safely cry up the virtues of big business, or may safely preach the gospel of the omnicompetent state. But neither attitude is conservative.

The American mind has certain archetypes. Of these, I think, two represent the old New England breed of men—leavening the nation—from whom I happen to be descended. One of these two types of New England intellect is that which I call the mind of Emerson. It is fond of alteration and tinkering, convinced of the inevitability of beneficent progress, unable to credit the reality of sin, inclined toward levelling, contemptuous of the past, and bent upon dissenting from all things established.

The other principal type of New England intellect is that which I call the mind of Hawthorne. It is suspicious of change, skeptical of Progress, convinced of the terrible power of sin, in favor of human nature (flawed though it is) in its present state rather than some radical revision of human character upon a Utopian design; it is reverent toward the past, mindful of the universe as a realm of mystery, and cognizant that proliferating variety is the mark of a healthful society, while uniformity is decadence.

From the beginning, I was in Hawthorne's camp. The modern "liberal" world, as I have come to understand it, is making its way straight toward what C. S. Lewis calls "the abolition of man"—toward a society devoid of reverence, variety, and the higher imagination; toward a society in which "everybody belongs to everybody else," in which there exists collectivism without community, equality without love.

The intelligent conservative does not set his face against reform. Prudent social change is the means for renewing society's vitality, much as the human body is perpetually renewing itself, and yet retains its identity. Without judicious change, we perish.

But change itself cannot be the end of existence: without permanence, we perish. Burke's standard of statesmanship was the union in one man of a disposition to preserve and an ability to reform. In some ages, the task of reformation looms gigantic; in other times, the task of conservation takes precedence.

Ours, I think, is an era afflicted by alteration at vertiginous speed, a time of material and moral innovation, in which no man can catch his breath, and reason is dethroned by appetite. What the twentieth century requires is not the goad, but the check-rein.

Precisely what does the American conservative hope to conserve?

First of all, he wants to keep humanity human: he is firmly determined not to allow men to be reduced to the sensual and egalitarian condition of Dr. Johnson's bull in a pasture, thinking, "Here is this cow, and here is this grass: what more could I ask?" There is grave reason to fear that the infatuation with material aggrandizement which marks our generation is leading us toward just that condition, in which we will be starved for imagination and hope and love.

Second, the conservative means to protect that heritage of civilization which the painful labor of numberless generations of men has bequeathed to us, and which now is menaced by fanaticism and the craze for novelty. The conservative knows that we are pygmies mounted upon the shoulders of giants, able to see further than our ancestors only because of their support, and liable to tumble into the abyss if, presumptuously, we sneer at the wisdom of our ancestors.

Third, the conservative seeks to protect the elaborate civil social edifice which, under Providence, has developed in America—our government of laws and not of men, our economy characterized by volition rather than compulsion, our institutions calculated to make a man his own master, our political system which prefers variety to centralized uniformity. A well-intentioned sentimental collectivism, the conservative believes, would deprive this nation of its vitality and its respect for individuality. Besides, power corrupting as it does, no Utopian collectivistic system long remains either well-intentioned or sentimental.

I am not disposed to exchange the manifest benefits of Christian civilization and American life for any New Morality or any New Order. We are plagued by many moral and social afflictions, and there is every reason for the true conservative to turn his hand to prudent reform. Yet, if worst comes to worst, I prefer the devil I know to the devil I don't.

For too many Americans, "liberalism" has become a god-term, a charismatic expression implying prosperity, security, freedom, novelty, progress, and the happy state of being in the swim. The time has come when we must inquire whether the actual policies of political liberalism lead to any such benefits.

It appears to me that our more advanced "liberals" have now quite given up any concern for freedom of the person, and are endeavouring to persuade us, instead, to submit to a regime of life in death, a colorless mediocrity and monotony in the world, an emptiness of heart, a penury of the imagination.

They no longer are interested in liberal education, or freedom of choice, or in asking themselves just what true human happiness amounts to. What, indeed, are our liberals liberal about? They do not aspire to make the human person truly free, under God; their aspiration is to make us into identical units in a monolithic society. To the representative modern liberal, the world is a very simple place, and man has only very simple—though consuming—material needs.

With Hawthorne, I think that we live in a universe of mystery. I think that men are better than beasts, and that life is something more than the gratifying of appetites. I think that variety and growth—not equality and uniformity—are the characteristics of a high culture.

Therefore I am a conservative. Quite possibly I am on the losing side; often I think so. Yet, out of a curious perversity, I had rather lose with Socrates, let us say, than win with Lenin.

["Why I Am a Conservative," Confessions of a Bohemian Tory: Episodes and Reflections of a Vagrant Career *(New York, Fleet, 1963), 304–8.]*

❖

II.

OUR SACRED PATRIMONY

The Law and the Prophets ❖ What Did Americans Inherit from the Ancients? ❖ The Light of the Middle Ages ❖ Civilization Without Religion? ❖ The Rarity of the God-Fearing Man ❖ The Necessity for a General Culture

Kirk's reverence for the wisdom of our ancestors imbues his view of the human world and of human destiny. All that we have and are, he stresses, we owe to the legacy of Western tradition and culture. Our civilization begins with the classical and biblical worlds, with what the ancient Greeks, Romans, and Hebrews bequeathed to us. Our spiritual and moral identity is Judaic and Christian in form and belief, shaped and ordered in a continuous historical process embracing the life of the community and the life of the soul. Kirk does not fail to acknowledge our indebtedness to the Middle Ages, singling out the religious essences of medieval ideas that influenced American society in its early stages. His conception of our sacred patrimony affirms the sacramental attributes of humankind and, above all, the eternal nature of man and woman.

In examining our cultural history and estimating the values of our heritage, Kirk assigns special significance to the religious concepts that helped define the origins and development of American civilization. It is imperative to understand the religious dimension of our heritage, and to renew its place in the modern era, if we are to resist nihilism and decadence. Kirk also pleads for the preservation of our Anglo-American heritage, especially in the context of English language and literature and the pattern of law and politics.

The failure to acknowledge what our sacred patrimony passes on to us in its totality conduces the worship of false gods and doctrines. Kirk is unyielding in his loyalty to the dual principle of continuity and conservatorship. Any softening of this principle inevitably ends in confusion and in the disappearance of the graces and virtues of a higher civilization. Our sacred patrimony ultimately enables us to discover a common unity in ourselves, in our institutions, and in our aspirations. We must guard with vigilance what has been handed down to us from age to age: this is at the center of Kirk's appreciation of our heritage.

The Law and the Prophets

The precepts of moral order, "the first need of all," come down to us from the ancient Hebrews through Moses, prophet and lawgiver. The Spirit spoke to Moses from outside human experience, revealing to him that all true law comes from God, and that law is the means for attaining order in the community and in the soul. Kirk stresses that Americans must have a firm conception of the foundational and covenantal place of the Hebrew law and the prophets: "Faith and hope may endure when cities are reduced to rubble: that, indeed, is a principal lesson from the experience of Israel under God." "The Law and the Prophets" shows a distinctly reverential grasp of history, philosophy, and theology. The religious legacy of Israel, Kirk iterates, teaches us that without faith human life ends in nothingness and without God we lose our souls.

From Mount Sinai to Massachusetts Bay

The tap-root of American order runs deep into a Levantine desert; it began to grow some thirteen centuries before the birth of Jesus of Nazareth. Through Moses, prophet and law-giver, the moral principles that move the civilization of Europe and America and much more of the world first obtained clear expression.

To a wandering people of obscure origin, the Hebrews, or Children of Israel, occurred then a tremendous "leap in being": that is, by an extraordinary perception, the Israelites came to understand the human condition as it had not been understood before. Even earlier than the time of Moses, the Israelites had experienced the moral workings of an unseen power, which had spoken to the consciousness of Noah and of Abraham. But through Moses, the Hebrews learned more distinctly that there watched over them an all-powerful intelligence or spirit which gave them their moral nature. In their sacred book called Exodus, later, the Jews who were the Israelites' descendants would set down the revelation which Moses received from Yahweh, or Jehovah, the unseen Lord of all.

"Revelation" means the unveiling of truths that men could not have obtained from simple experience in this world. It is a communication of knowledge from some source that transcends ordinary human perception. To the

Israelites, Moses made known that there exists but one God, Jehovah; that God had made a covenant or compact with His people; that He had decreed laws by which they should live. From that revelation have grown modern ethics and modern social institutions and much besides.

"Exodus" means departure: the Israelites were departing from Egypt into Palestine. Also they were departing from the old moral order of the cosmological empires—from that old order's capricious deities and arbitrary priest-kings—into a new moral order which would be called, later, the faith of Judaism. Later still, this moral order revealed at Sinai would become the foundation of the moral order called Christianity.

Some twenty-nine centuries after Moses heard the voice from the burning bush, a smaller band of wanderers would embark upon another exodus, farther in distance but swifter in time than the exodus of the Israelites. The people of this later exodus were the Puritans, sailing for the New World, and their ablest leader was John Winthrop. On the deck of the ship *Arbella*, halfway between England and Cape Cod, in the year 1630, Winthrop preached a lay sermon, to remind his fellow-voyagers how they had made a covenant with the God of Israel.

"We must delight in each other, make others' conditions our own, rejoice together, mourn together, labor and suffer together," Winthrop said: "always having before our eyes our commission and community in the work, our community as members of the same body. So shall we keep the unity of the spirit in the bond of peace, the Lord will be our God and delight to dwell among us, as His own people, and will command a blessing upon us in all our ways, so that we shall see much more of His wisdom, power, goodness, and truth than formerly we have been acquainted with.

"We shall find that the God of Israel is among us, when ten of us shall be able to resist a thousand of our enemies, when He shall make us a praise and glory, that men shall say of succeeding plantation, 'The Lord make it like that of New England.' For we must consider that we shall be as a city upon a hill, the eyes of all people are upon us. So that if we shall deal falsely with our God in this work we have undertaken, and so cause Him to withdraw His present help from us, we shall be made a story and a by-word throughout the world; we shall open the mouths of enemies to speak evil of the ways of God and all professors for God's sake; we shall shame the faces of many of God's worthy servants, and cause their prayers to be turned into curses upon us, till we be consumed out of the good land whither we are going."[1]

These words of Winthrop are in the spirit of what the Jews called the Torah, the Law. The moral commandments revealed to Moses upon Mount

Sinai were broken by the Israelites almost as soon as they were made known; the principles of order reaffirmed by Winthrop were violated by the settlers in New England not long after the landing in Massachusetts. Yet without knowledge of that moral order, the men of ancient Israel and Judah could not have lived in community. And so it is with the people of modern America, and of lands which inherit the moral understanding of Judaism or of Christianity.

Even the simplest human communities cannot endure without some form of laws, consciously held and enforced. Ants and bees may cooperate by instinct; men must have revelation and reason. What we call "biblical law" was not the first code of justice. Long before Moses and his brother Aaron led the Hebrew people out of Egypt, codes of law had been promulgated among the Babylonians, the Sumerians, the Akkadians, the Assyrians, and the Hittites. Yet it is the Law made known through Moses that has survived, and which still works upon the society in which we live.

The Israelites of the Exodus were a people without writing, nomads who left no archeological evidence behind them; they were far less civilized than certain other peoples of that age; indeed, having had no cities, they cannot properly be called civilized at all. We can know Moses and the people whom he led only through the Pentateuch, the first five books of what Christians call the Old Testament. The Moses of that sacred history was a "charismatic leader," a man of especial spiritual gifts, who perceived and expressed truths which until then had been glimpsed only dimly, if at all.

In the dawn of every religion, some such figure as Moses may be discerned: the "seer" who sees what others cannot see. The seer communicates such truth to his followers, teaching them how to order their lives and to live together in community. The other creeds of the ancient world are dust and ashes now, but the Decalogue of Moses and the understanding of man's existence under God which Moses communicated to the people remain a living power, the source of order.

All the aspects of any civilization arise out of a people's religion: its politics, its economics, its arts, its sciences, even its simple crafts are the by-products of religious insights and a religious cult. For until human beings are tied together by some common faith, and share certain moral principles, they prey upon one another. In the common worship of the cult, a community forms. At the heart of every culture is a body of ethics, of distinctions between good and evil; and in the beginning, at least, those distinctions are founded upon the authority of revealed religion. Not until a people have come to share religious belief are they able to work together satisfactorily, or even to make sense of the world in which they find themselves. Thus all order—

even the ideological order of modern totalist states, professing atheism—could not have come into existence, had it not grown out of general belief in truths that are perceived by the moral imagination.

This religious origin of private and public order has been described afresh in the twentieth century by such historians as Christopher Dawson, Eric Voegelin, and Arnold Toynbee. The first social organization, beyond mere family groups, is the cult that seeks to communicate with supernatural powers.

Animals survive by instinct; true human beings cannot. Possessing reason, even primitive men ask questions. They find themselves, as did the Israelites in the desert of Sinai, in a condition of danger, suffering, and ignorance. Led perhaps by some man of marvelous insights, they join together in seeking answers to their questions. So the cult, the religious association, comes into existence. Men try, through the cult, to acquire protection and knowledge from a power that is more than human. Without such communication, they cannot survive on the human level—and perhaps not even on the animal level.

This truth may be more readily understood in the troubled twentieth century than it was in the nineteenth. Under tribulation, men come to realize that they are feeble and imperfect, if they try to stand by themselves. They recognize their failings—what the Hebrews called their sinfulness.

"The nineteenth-century myth of inevitable and perpetual progress has been exploded by the impact of world wars, with their demonstration that autonomous man cannot solve the vast problems of racial and cultural conflict, economic welfare and political order," R. B. Y. Scott writes. "He is overwhelmed by his own machinery, and by social torrents set loose through his unwillingness to affirm his solidarity with his fellow men. The judgments of God are manifest in the world of today. The time has come to bring home to men that these are right judgments on human sin; that men bear these consequences inevitably, because they are morally responsible beings who have denied their own nature in denying their responsibility to their neighbors."[2]

It was so with the Israelites of the Exodus. Their problems of personal and social order, at bottom, were similar to the problems of order we confront today. How may human beings live with their own weaknesses and ruinous impulses? Can they turn to a source of goodness and wisdom that surpasses mere human talents? The revelation which came to Moses was in answer to perennial human longings. What is man doing in this hard world—man, with his vague aspirations and his power of reflection? How may a community live together in order and peace? Through Moses there came a response to these implicit questions, and that response endures in the twentieth century after Christ.

The Moses of the Pentateuch was a man acquainted with the civilization of Egypt at its higher levels, and so better prepared than the nomads whom he led in confronting these perplexities of private and public order. Yet the vision of order which he describes was more than the order which then existed in Egypt. That is why it has endured to our time.

When the fugitive Israelites struggled to survive in the ghastly desert of Sinai, between Egypt and Palestine, Moses ascended Mount Sinai—as desolate today as it was then, except that an ancient Christian monastery stands there now. Almost nowhere does physical nature seem more hostile to mankind than in Sinai, though the armies of Israel and Egypt have fought for that waste in recent years. Yet upon the Mount, a bush or tree burst into flame, and a voice said to Moses' consciousness, "I am that am." To Moses, a mortal human being, a timeless Power spoke. The Creator made Himself known to His creatures, telling them of His intention for them.

What Moses experienced and expressed was something more than what we call "intuition" and something more than even what we call "vision." Moses' perception was transcendent—that is, Moses perceived the nature of being through some means beyond the limits of human rationality and private experience. Moses was enabled to express truths about the human condition which could not have come out of his environment or even from the collective experience of the Israelites. This transcending of the five human senses and of memory, this communion with a source of wisdom more than human, is what we mean by the word "revelation."

So far as words could express his overwhelming experience of transcendence, Moses made known to the Israelites the existence of the Other, the divine Presence, the supreme being who had revealed Himself upon Mount Sinai: the existence of One whom they came to call Yahweh (incorrectly translated as "Jehovah" in English). Yahweh, Moses told the people, is the Lord of all creation; He is God, and no other gods exist. (Three centuries before the birth of Christ, the Jews would cease even to utter the word "Yahweh," lest they seem blasphemous, and would substitute other titles for the Lord.) Coming down from his solitary communion upon Mount Sinai with the eternal One, Moses gave Yahweh's commandments to the Children of Israel. He told them how to order their lives, and how to dwell together in community: that is, Moses communicated the principles of personal and social order. From outside human experience, the Spirit had spoken.

We cannot well understand order and disorder in America today, or elsewhere in the world, unless we know something of the beliefs and the experiences of the Hebrew people in a remote land and a remote time. In the lines of T. S. Eliot, "The communication of the dead is tongued with fire beyond the language of the living." Through Moses, long dead, meaning came into human existence. Our modern moral order, at least in what is called the West, runs back to the burning bush on Sinai.

American political institutions owe little, directly, to the example and the experience of the Israelites or the Jews. True, the Puritans of Massachusetts Bay endeavored to establish a "Bible state"; but in its extreme form that experiment endured only three years; even in its modified aspect it lasted merely for two generations. Nevertheless, the American moral order could not have come into existence at all, had it not been for the legacy left by Israel.

In the whole of John Adams's political writings, which draw heavily upon Greek and Roman political experience, there is no account of the states of Israel and Judah. It was not that Adams, a descendant of the Puritans, ignored the patrimony of the Hebrews: rather, he understood that the political experience of Israel and Judah was irrelevant to American circumstances. "I will insist that the Hebrews have done more to civilize men than any other nation," Adams wrote in 1809. "If I were an atheist, and believed in blind eternal fate, I should still believe that fate had ordained the Jews to be the most essential instrument for civilizing the nations. If I were an atheist of the other sect, who believe or pretend to believe that all is ordered by chance, I should believe that chance had ordered the Jews to preserve and propagate to all mankind the doctrine of a supreme, intelligent, wise, almighty sovereign of the universe, which I believe to be the great essential principle of all morality, and consequently of all civilization."[3]

As Adams understood, it is the prophets of Israel and Judah, not the kings, who teach us the meaning of order. Israel and Judah were petty states not very different in political structure from some other petty states of the ancient Levant; as states, they perished under the might of the vast empires that had menaced them from their beginnings. It is not Jerusalem the political capital that signifies much; it is Jerusalem—repeatedly ruined and depopulated, but always rising from the ashes—as Zion, the home of the name of God, that looms immense. To look at the spiritual experience of the Hebrews and the Jews in adequate perspective, however, it is well first to review briefly the political history of the kingdom that had Jerusalem for its capital.

Jerusalem: Disaster and Triumph

For nearly two centuries after Moses had led the Israelites to the threshold of the promised land of Canaan, the Hebrew tribes were engaged in occupying Palestine—sometimes by peaceful penetration, sometimes by conquest. At the height of their territorial power, Israel and Judah combined would occupy an area little bigger than modern Belgium. Joined in a loose confederation, the tribes were led by judges, or charismatic chieftains, whose duty it was to restore righteousness; these judges inherited the office of Moses.

About the year 1030 B.C., the Israelites chose a king, that they might withstand better the military power of their enemies. The kings of Israel and Judah would not claim to be divine, unlike the rulers of the Oriental empires in that age: at most, they declared that the Lord approved of them. Saul, the first king, fell to his ruin before his young rival David. Leading a band of mercenaries, David took the old Jebusite city of Jerusalem, and founded there both the religious sanctuary of the Israelites and their political capital. ("Zion" originally meant the hill on which David established Yahweh's shrine and built a palace.) The kingdom of a united Israel lasted only through the reigns of David and his son Solomon; after the year 926, this realm was split into a northern kingdom and a southern—into Israel (or Samaria) and Judah.

The kingdom of Israel, with its capital at Samaria, was five times the size of its southern rival, and included ten of the twelve Hebrew tribes. But after two centuries, it was crushed by the Assyrians, and the enslaved "Lost Ten Tribes" vanished forever into the heart of the Assyrian empire. Little Judah, nevertheless, survived until the year 587 (or, in a broken condition, a trifle longer), going down at last before the might of the Chaldeans of Babylon; the people of Judah, too, or most of them, were carried away into bondage.

In the year 538 B.C., a remnant of the Jews (as the descendants of the Israelites are called after their Babylonian captivity) were permitted to return to Jerusalem, where they rebuilt their Temple, or sanctuary of Jehovah, about 520. A people militarily weak and often impoverished, governed for centuries by high priests and later by kings or princes half Greek in their culture, the Jews of the Return were dominated successively by the Persians, the Greeks, the Hellenistic empires of Syria and Egypt, and the Romans. Under these foreign masters, some degree of autonomy was possessed by the Jews until the Romans crushed the revolt of the Jewish Zealots in the year AD 70. Then again the Jews were expelled from their sacred city and dispersed throughout the civilized world. Not until almost the middle of the twentieth century would there arise again in Palestine a state governed by people of Jewish stock.

This is a long grim history of civil war, foreign oppression, fire and slaughter. If the subjects of the monarchies of Israel and Judah, and of the later Jewish states, knew something more of freedom and justice than did the people of neighboring states, that was in part because their kings were too feeble, and too much harassed by enemies on their frontiers to rule with absolute authority.

What chiefly distinguished the Israelites and their successors the Jews from the political order of the despotisms by which they were surrounded, however, was the existence of a partial check upon the civil authority. For before the Babylonian Captivity, the great prophets restrained the kings' ambitions, and during the Hellenistic and Roman overlordships the people were protected by the Sanhedrin, or court of religious elders. Yet no one writes of the "political genius of the Jews" after the fashion in which historians praise the Greek and Roman contributions to worldly order.

The Israelites almost might be called a non-political people: they developed no political theories of a secular sort and no enduring practical political institutions on a national scale—though their local communities, clan and town, outlasted their monarchy and (until the Diaspora, or uprooting of the Jews) outlasted alien dominations. Their one clear political principle was a religious doctrine. Jehovah is King, they declared, and true laws are Jehovah's laws. Judges, kings, and high priests, the powers of this earth, are but surrogates of Jehovah at best, indulged by Him or sometimes made instruments of His wrath. "The human rulers of this people are chosen, accepted, or tolerated by God," as Roland de Vaux puts it, "but they remain subordinate to him and they are judged by the degree of their fidelity to the indissoluble covenant between Yahweh and his people. In their view of things the State, which in practice means the monarchy, is merely an accessory element; in actual fact Israel lived without it for the greater part of its history."[4]

This, then, is the high contribution of Israel to modern social order: the understanding that all true law comes from God, and that God is the source of order and justice. But of practical political establishments in Israel or Judah or the later Jewish principalities, nothing remains.

It is no wonder that the New England Puritans failed to establish a latter-day Bible state, on an Old Testament pattern, for that ideal state of justice and charity never really had existed in Israel and Judah; and the Jewish "theocracy" after the Babylonian exile could not be imitated successfully in seventeenth-century America, a land and an age profoundly different. The twentieth-century democracy of Israel, with its secular parties and western parliamentary structure, bears no resemblance to the Kingdom or to post-exile theocracy. Even had Israel and Judah not been overwhelmed by Nineveh and Babylon, the temporal order of those little kingdoms did not possess strength sufficient to endure long without thoroughgoing alteration.

Yet though scattered and persecuted, the Jewish people survived. When all the other civilizations and creeds of the ancient world have disappeared, Jewish faith and Jewish culture have persisted to our time, permeating the societies of many lands and reasserting their vigor. Similarly, the holy city of Jerusalem did not die, though Nineveh and Babylon and Memphis and Susa and Antioch, and other mighty imperial capitals of the ancient world, were destroyed utterly. The buildings of Jerusalem might be razed, the city's walls thrown down, its population put to the sword; still, under Byzantine and Arab and Crusader and Turk, the Jew would find his way back to the sanctuary of Zion, lamenting beside the Wailing Wall that was said to be a fragment of the ancient Temple, renewing community on those blood-soaked sacred hills.

From its foundation, the hill-town of Jerusalem was a fortress. Almost impossible to storm except from the north, and repeatedly strengthened by military works, this city would sustain sieges century after century—falling after desperate resistance against overwhelming odds, yet always restored after some interval. Only as a fortress did the place enjoy natural advantage: it did not lie upon the principal ancient trade routes, there was little water, the country round about was infertile; the city had no industry, and its commerce was such as a place of pilgrimage and minor political capital could attract.

For all that, this unlikely spot became the most holy ground for three great religions, so that the city on its plateau, nearly surrounded by deserts, magnetically drew back inhabitants after destruction, though mighty Babylon lay covered by the sands and the old capitals of Egypt gave way to Greek Alexandria. Jerusalem was denounced by the prophets for wickedness and hardness of heart, but the city was condemned so fiercely only because it was loved so passionately.

Where the Temple built by Solomon stood once, there rises today the Dome of the Rock, the Mosque of Omar, erected by the Moslems in 688 A.D. The Temple, with its most sacred chamber the Holy of Holies, was the reason for Jerusalem's symbolic power over all Jews; the palaces of King David and his successors were as nothing by the side of the Temple. Jerusalem, said the prophets and the priests, was the throne and dwelling of Jehovah: all the nations of the earth would come there to worship the one true God. And so it came to pass.

Out of Jerusalem, said the prophets, flows the river of life. This is the eternal city: salvation radiates from Jerusalem, for here God meets with man. Beyond the confines of time, Jerusalem will be the city of moral perfection and of joy. The material Jerusalem, down through the centuries, was squalid enough in one age or another. Yet the Jerusalem of prophecy—the symbolic Jerusalem, holy Zion—is the city of divine wisdom in which man is freed from sin.

So it was with the political order of the Israelites and the ancient Jews—imperfect at its best, weighed in the balance and found wanting. But the moral order of Israel, the sanctuary of the soul, has transcended time and circumstances. It lives in the modern world. The Bible is the record of the growth of that moral order.[5] Although America is no Bible state, without some knowledge of the Bible the fabric of American order cannot be understood tolerably well. Therefore the meaning of the Old Testament—which to many people in the twentieth century must seem a confused and confusing account of remote times and forgotten wars—is the subject of the next portion of this chapter.

The God of Justice

There is but one God; and He is just. That is the essence of the legacy of Israel. It may be platitudinous to say this, but the important thing about platitudes is that they are true—which is why they have become platitudes.

Through Moses, this fundamental understanding of the just God was given clear expression. But it was known before the voice spoke upon Sinai. In its most dramatic form, that truth is examined in the Book of Job.

As we know it in the Old Testament, the story of Job appears to have been set down during the Babylonian captivity of the Jews, about the time of Isaiah II. Yet its origin is immensely older—running back to an age more than two thousand years before the birth of Jesus. In the Book of Job one finds no mention of the Israelites. What are we to make of God's ways toward man? That question was asked many centuries before the Israelites came out of Egypt, and a voice from the whirlwind answered it.

God permits Satan to try the faith of a good man, Job, a kind of desert sheik. Deprived by Satan, the Evil One, of his children and his goods, Job sits like a leper upon a dunghill, afflicted by a loathsome disease. He is made what the Arabs call *sidi bu zibbula*—old father of the dunghill, outcast and despised. His wife tells him to curse God and die. Indeed he longs for death, but he will not renounce the Lord.

Job has been a just man: he has not lusted after virgins, acquired wealth wrongly, committed adultery, mistreated his slaves, refused charity to the poor, widowed, and orphaned, worshipped strange gods, rejoiced at enemies' misfortunes, thrust strangers into the street, or abused his land and his tenants. Yet God has decreed, or permitted, that Job should suffer beyond endurance. Why?

To Job amongst the ashes come his "comforters," friends who know only the letter of the law, with their smug and narrow interpretations of the ways of God. Job has offended against God, or else does not submit himself meekly to God's justice, they tell the sufferer. It is as if Job were upon trial. Can he not find a mediator with God, or even summon God to witness?

Then, to the confounding of the comforters, God does speak from a whirl of dust. Job has been more right than his comforters, God reveals; yet Job too has been wrong. The Lord of creation reminds Job that His ways are beyond human comprehension: Job has fallen into presumption by attempting to understand the will of God. To this revelation the tormented Job submits himself meekly. It is not for man to adjudge God, as if God and man were litigants. With this submission, Job's faith is made perfect. And in the end, there is restored to Job twice what he had before his loss.

Such faith in God's ultimate justice, a true perception coming down to the Children of Israel from the dawn of conscience, distinguished the Hebrews from the other peoples of the ancient world. The gods of Israel's neighbors were many, and they had little to do with justice. The "Baals" of Syria and Mesopotamia were local deities, propitiated sometimes by human sacrifice; they were arbitrary gods, in no kinship with human beings; no universal sovereignty was claimed for them. The gods of Assyria and Phoenicia and other nations were voracious and dreadful. The gods of Egypt were strange to the point of lunacy. The gods of the Greeks were mere personified forces of nature, whose passions and caprices no man would think of emulating. Greece excepted, those other nations called their rulers divine beings. But for Israel, the king was Jehovah's steward at most: the Israelites had their priests and their kings, but not priest-kings.

With their loathsome rites, their temple prostitutes, their indifference to justice, these alien religions were abhorrent to the Children of Israel. Unlike these false gods, Jehovah was not a mere force of nature, or the patron of a clan. His relation to Israel was *ethical*, from the time He spoke from the burning bush. He was the God of the Covenant: of an eternal pact between Him and His chosen people, a compact renewed by every worshipper at every formal sacrifice to Jehovah. Although man was made in God's image, man was forbidden to create any molten image of Jehovah, lest Israel come to worship idols rather than the reality of God. When, at the final ruin of the Jewish state, Roman soldiers burst into the Temple and tore away the veil of the innermost sanctuary, they were astonished to find no image there. Israel alone knew that no man might look upon the face of the Creator.

From the eighteenth century onward, humanitarian writers have protested that Yahweh, God of Israel, was merciless. But to so argue is to ignore the strange gods of those centuries. To those who lived by His laws, Jehovah was infinitely kind; in time, Israel learned through the prophets that God was not the lord of justice only, but also a deity loving His people and to be loved by them. Nothing of that sort could be said of the pagan gods: no worshipper of Astarte or Moloch or Ashur or even Zeus thought of his deity as the author of law for man, or fancied that a terrible and unpredictable divine force could be loved. Those ages considered, Jehovah was gentle, by the side of the false gods.

Only Jehovah had made with man a Covenant—a solemn bond between greater and lesser, revealed to men chosen by the Lord. To Noah, some knowledge of this Covenant was communicated; to Abraham, a further understanding; to Moses, a large revelation. The God who decreed the Covenant was a God who had made known the ways of justice among men. Potentially at least, the world that God had created was a world of order. That order had been broken by man's willful sinfulness, beginning with the disobedience of Adam and Eve in the Garden. "For the imagination of man's heart is evil from his youth," the Lord declares in the book of Genesis.[6]

"In Adam's fall we sinned all": that is the first line of the Puritans' *New England Primer*, the first book printed in North America. That doctrine was part of New England's legacy from Israel. What is called the "doctrine of original sin" passed from Judaism into Christianity, and became in time a fundamental principle with the Christian settlers in early America.

Man had fallen, the Israelites believed: that is, man had fallen away from what God intended man to be. The story of the Garden of Eden was a representation of that Fall. Although some understanding that man had sinned and fallen away from his better nature may be traced dimly in other religions of the ancient Near East, only in the faith of Israel had that conviction a dominating place. To Israel, "sin," in essence, was rebellion—insurrection against God by breaking the Covenant, or rebellion against moral and social order by failure to fulfill one's obligations. The people of Israel learned that violence and fraud are embedded in fallen human nature, and may be restrained only by obedience to divine authority. Their own fierce history confirmed this: the story of man's fall into sin was repeated in every generation. It was sin that set the men of Israel and Judah at one another's throats even in their hours of desperate common peril. Just after the Babylonians carried off the inhabitants of Jerusalem to captivity, the remnant of the people left in Judea fell to ruinous civil strife—one proof among many of the depravity afflicting even God's chosen people.

Yet in His mercy, Jehovah had given His people an opportunity to redeem themselves. If they would abide by the Covenant He had communicated to Moses, they might be saved from the destroying clutch of sin. The Law was not a punishment or an oppressive burden imposed upon the people: on the contrary, it was the precious gift of Jehovah, by which Israel might exist in justice. The Law of Jehovah was the means for living with one's self and living with one's neighbors; it was the means for regaining order in the soul and in the community.

Modern people, relatively secure, generally take it for granted that some sort of order is at work in the world. They assume, however vaguely, that certain principles of justice exist, and that life has purpose of some sort. But before the people of Israel experienced their "leap in being," by which they learned of the just God and His laws, no confidence prevailed anywhere that an abiding order governed the universe. Everything that happened might be chance, accident; the gods were ferocious or whimsical; those gods laid down no clear principles for the conduct of human life. At best, the pagan gods did as they pleased with human beings, regardless of justice. As Hesiod wrote of the chief of the Greek gods,

> *Zeus rules the world, and with resistless sway*
> *Takes back tomorrow what he grants today.*

True, the ancient civilizations desperately desired some principles of private and public order. One can make out an attempt to reach such principles in certain Greek myths; and the Egyptians, or some of them, endeavored to find ethical authority that would make life worth living. In the Egyptian "Coffin Text" entitled "Dispute over Suicide," written about the year 2,000 B.C., we find an awareness by the nameless author that all men are guilty of the disorder that afflicts society, and that only by participating in the divine essence of existence can a person—who is both man and soul—work to redeem the people from their degradation.[7] The quest for enduring order is a natural and necessary search among any people. But the first real success in that quest was achieved by Israel, and that surprising triumph has not been forgotten by mankind.

To the Israelites, the One God revealed Himself: that is, divine wisdom and power were made known to Israel by a deliberate act of God. Divine authority informed a people how they should live. The terror of existence without object or rule was dissipated by the revelation that man is not alone in the universe; that an Other exists; and that Other is the One God, who makes it possible for human beings to be something better than the beasts that perish. Through the revelation of order in the universe, men and women are given the possibility of becoming fully human—of finding pattern and purpose in existence, unlike dogs that live from day to day only.

So the Ten Commandments, the Decalogue, are not a set of harsh prohibitions imposed by an arbitrary tribal deity. Instead, they are liberating rules that enable a people to diminish the tyranny of sin; that teach a people how to live with one another and in relation with God, how to restrain violence and fraud, how to know justice and to raise themselves above the level of predatory animals.

Those Commandments are simple enough. They declare that there exists a Supreme Being; that all other "gods" are false; that material images delude; that God's name must not be used for evil purposes; that one day of the week should be devoted to contemplation of the divine; that parents must be honored; that murder and adultery and theft are evil; that in a process at law, one must not lie; that the inner desire for another's possessions is sinful. These principles are not the whole of morality, of course; but they are essential to morality. And they are as true for a complex modern civilization as they were for desert wanderers.

Through Moses, the Israelites received a body of lesser laws, still observed in large part by Orthodox Jews. Long later, after the remnant of the people of Judah had returned from their Babylonian exile, these rules and the revelations of the Hebrew prophets were written down in the Torah, the code of divine law, so that the Jews might govern their whole daily existence by religious principles. The Torah, and the rabbis who expounded it, would hold the Judaic faith and observance together while all the other creeds and religious communities of the ancient world dissolved. So it is that the Jews are known as the people of the Law; they possessed the Law before they possessed the Book, or the Bible.

The Law is not merely the decree of a monarch who may pretend to divine powers—that the Israelites learned. The Law is not merely a body of convenient customs and usages that men have developed for themselves. The Law is not the instrument of oppression by a class or a hierarchy. For the true Law is derived from the Covenant that God has made and reaffirmed with his people. The Law is revealed to save man from self-destruction; to redeem man from sin and its consequences; to keep man from becoming a Cain, his hand against every man's; to enable man to resemble the God in whose image he was created.

Throughout western civilization, and indeed in some degree through the later world, the Hebraic understanding of Covenant and Law would spread, in forms both religious and secular. The idea of an enduring Covenant, or compact, whether between God and people or merely between man and man, took various styles in various lands and ages; it passed into medieval society through Christian teaching, and became essential to the social order of Britain, from which society most settlers in North America came. This concept and reality of Covenant was not confined to those American colonics—notably the New England settlements and Pennsylvania—which were fundamentally religious in their motive. Like the people of Israel and Judah, the Americans broke solemn covenants repeatedly; but like Israel, America nevertheless knew that without a covenant, the people would be lost.

And from Israel, even more than from the Roman jurisconsults, America inherited an understanding of the sanctity of law. Certain root principles of justice exist, arising from the nature which God has conferred upon man; law is a means for realizing those principles, so far as we can. That assumption was in the minds of the men who wrote the Declaration of Independence and the Constitution of the United States. A conviction of man's sinfulness, and of the need for laws to restrain every man's will and appetite, influenced the legislators of the colonies and of the Republic. Thomas Jefferson, rationalist though he was, declared that in matters of political power, one must not trust in the alleged goodness of man, but "bind him down with the chains of the Constitution."

A principal difference between the American Revolution and the French Revolution was this: the American revolutionaries in general held a biblical view of man and his bent toward sin, while the French revolutionaries in general attempted to substitute for the biblical understanding an optimistic doctrine of human goodness advanced by the philosophes of the rationalistic Enlightenment. The American view led to the Constitution of 1787; the French view, to the Terror and to a new autocracy. The American Constitution is a practical secular covenant, drawn up by men who (with few exceptions) believed in a sacred Covenant, designed to restrain the human tendencies toward violence and fraud; the American Constitution is a fundamental law deliberately meant to place checks upon will and appetite. The French innovators would endure no such checks upon popular impulses; they ended under a far more arbitrary domination.

Israel's knowledge of the Law merely commenced with the experience under God imaginatively described in the books of Genesis and Exodus. This knowledge was broadened and deepened by a succession of prophets. The power of the prophets diminished with the fall of Jerusalem to the armies of Babylon, and ended in the first century of the Christian era. Without venturing rashly here into the labyrinths of biblical scholarship, it is possible to describe the prophets' enduring significance for modern men, and to suggest how deeply interwoven with the fabric of American order this prophetic teaching remains.

Righteousness and Wrath

The word "prophet" means a speaker—one who is called by God to speak to the people and to those in the seats of the mighty. Through the grace and favor of God, a prophet foretold the purpose of God; but he was not a magician, a soothsayer, or a man who predicted in detail the course of events. To put it another way, the Hebrew prophets were men endowed with moral imagination, convinced that Jehovah had commanded them to speak in His name, to tell the people of divine wrath and divine mercy.

"The Hebrew prophets kept the personality of God—kept it triumphantly, and abolished all other claimants to Godhead," T. R. Glover says. "God is personal, and God is one; God is righteous, and God is king—they are four great tenets on which to base any religion, and they were not lightly won. They were the outcome of experience, hard, bitter, and disillusioning—a gain acquired by the loss of all kinds of hopes and beliefs, national and personal, tested in every way that man or devil can invent for the testing of belief. . . . They made righteousness a thing no more of ritual and taboo but of attitude and conduct and spirit. They set religion free from ancient follies and reviving horrors."[8]

Moses was a prophet, and so was Samuel, the last of the judges of Israel. Here, however, we are concerned chiefly with the prophets of the eighth and seventh centuries before Christ, to whom was given courage to rebuke kings and to threaten a whole people with the anger of God. These were the solitary figures later recognized as true prophets, to whom Jehovah had revealed His will—though often they were without public honor in their own time. Amos, Hosea, the first Isaiah, Micah, Jeremiah, Habakkuk, and the second Isaiah have no counterparts in other religions. They were deeply involved in the wars and the domestic discontents of their age, but their message has transcended the events that compelled them to speak.

Israelites and Jews knew that many false prophets had gone forth into the land: court prophets attached to a royal household (though some of these might be true prophets, nevertheless); "sons of prophets," or wandering bands of enthusiasts; prophets who mistook their mere dreams for divine revelation; charlatans and demagogues who pretended to have gained the prophetic afflatus—that is, to have obtained supernatural communication of knowledge. But the false prophets were forgotten, and the true prophets endured.

Although the mouthpiece of God, each of the great prophets spoke in his own style. By their passion, their eloquence, their fearlessness, and their vindication through events, later generations weighed these prophets and found them truly the servants of Jehovah. In the earlier years of Israel, they were called seers—men who perceived what ordinary vision could not apprehend.

Out of their knowledge of the history and traditions and literature of Israel, these men spoke to their generation, reminding Israel of the Covenant and of Jehovah's wrath and purpose. But they spoke from something more than knowledge of the past. They had been inspired by God (often to their own alarm and astonishment) to announce His judgments. They transcended sensory perception and the realm of matter. They were media or conductors, so to speak, for the voice of the Other.

Their insights—or, rather, their communications from a power more than human—were not gained in dreams: God had addressed their minds directly. When they foretold tribulations, because of disobedience to Jehovah, those tribulations soon occurred. When they described the mercy of God, and the relations in which man should stand to his Creator, the resounding persuasiveness of their voices moved the minds and hearts of posterity, if not of those who met the prophets face to face.

The first prophet to set down in writing his revealed hard truths was Amos, who left his herds and his sycamore trees near the town of Tekoa at the command of Jehovah. Making his way to the high sanctuary of Bethel, in Samaria, about 765 B.C., this countryman—no more, apparently, than a shepherd or peasant—denounced king and people for having fallen away from the Covenant. To the high priest, Amos denied that he was a prophet—meaning that he was no professional foreteller of events, but instead a man overwhelmed by God. The luxury, the corruption, the injustice, the smugness of Israel he assailed, telling his hearers that the king would be put to the sword and the people carried into slavery; that the high priest of Bethel would die in exile, his children slain, and his wife made a harlot. What wonder that priests and people drove him out of Bethel? Yet those judgments came to pass.

What signifies most in Amos is his declaration that Jehovah is the God of all peoples, not of Israel only. The Covenant itself is the expression of a justice in the universe that existed long before Moses ascended Mount Sinai; the Israelites, true, are Jehovah's chosen people, in that God has chosen to instruct them directly, and not others; but for that very reason, God demands of Israel a righteousness greater than that of other nations. Amos tells of the anger of God with Tyre, Edom, Syria, Philistia, Amon, and Moab, states faithless and pitiless; but God's wrath with Israel is not less, for Israel has broken the Law. Ignoring the commandments of the Lord, Israel had trusted in sacrifices and rituals to appease Jehovah; so the Lord must chastise His people for sin and folly. There is but one God; and He is Lord of all nations, sparing none, forgetting none.

Like the earlier prophets, Amos delivers a commination for the abuse of power by kings. This conflict runs through the whole history of Israel and Judah. Occasionally a king would seek the counsel of a prophet and ask his blessing—ask, perhaps, for his intercession with the Lord; but commonly the prophets stood in unyielding opposition to royal policies. At the heart of this encounter, often, was this dilemma: the kings of Israel and Judah found it prudent to treat with the monarchs of neighboring states, to take other kings' daughters in marriage, to tolerate the cults of those alien nations within Israel, to form and break alliances with powers that knew not the Law. How might the little kingdoms of Israel and Judah survive without such unhallowed dealings? Trust in the Lord God, replied the prophets. But the kings knew the edge of Assyrian or Babylonian or Egyptian swords and spears. Down to the fall of Jerusalem, this struggle between king and prophet was not resolved.

"The ways of the Lord are right, and the just shall walk in them," the prophet Hosea, another countryman, declared to Samaria, in the late decades of the eighth century, "but the transgressors shall fall therein." Like Amos, but more than Amos, Hosea told of what must be, if Israel should continue to disobey the Law; and yet Hosea implied that this punishment might be revoked by God, should Israel return to obedience. (What the prophets "foretold," ordinarily, were probabilities, not immutable destinies.) For the Lord is compassionate: as a loving and dutiful husband forgives and redeems a licentious wife, so Jehovah seeks to save his people from the fruits of sin. Let the kingdom of Israel cease from harlotry; let Israel abjure alliances with Assyria or Egypt; and then the Lord will forgive and save.

As Samaria sank toward oblivion, in Judah there spoke Isaiah ben Amos, as high in station as Amos and Hosea had been lowly. The first prophet Isaiah told King Ahaz, in the name of the Lord, not to court the terrible Assyrians. Egypt and Assyria, the mortar and pestle of war, might devastate Judah, but a remnant of the chosen people would endure and return. And at the end of time, the world will be transformed; justice will triumph; Zion will be perfected; the people who have kept faith with Jehovah will be rewarded. Put no trust in worldly powers; let Judah stand still while imperial hosts are arming. Near the end of the eighth century, Isaiah described the divine order in history. By the mercy of the Lord, Judah should be saved from Sennacherib's sword, but the cunning and worldly-wise should be confounded: "Woe unto them that seek deep to hide their counsel from the Lord, and their words are in the dark, and they say, Who seeth us? and who knoweth us? . . . For the terrible one is brought to nought, and the scorner is consumed, and all that watch for iniquity are cut off."

In that same age, the prophet Micah exhorted the sinner to accept God's anger: the Lord, infinitely compassionate, will raise up those who have been chastened. Jerusalem will fall, but not forever. That catastrophe was not far distant. The prophet Habakkuk, called during the reign of King Jehoiakim, at the end of the seventh century and the beginning of the sixth, inquired why God had permitted the Chaldeans of Babylon to harass Judah and other nations so frightfully. And he found his answer: the Chaldeans had enforced the judgment of Jehovah upon the nations; the sinful were punished through the agency of the sinful. "The righteous shall live by his faith," the Lord told His prophet: wait on the Lord, rejoicing in Him. In the end, the righteous shall be redeemed.

Jeremiah, most tormented of the prophets, lived through the reigns of several kings, and he survived the devastation of Jerusalem that he had foretold. Standing in the court of the Temple, terrified at his dread call from God but fearless before the people, Jeremiah declared to the princes and the multitude that the Temple should be destroyed and the city lie desolate, unless Judah should repent and amend its ways. "This man is worthy to die, for he hath prophesied against this city, as ye have heard with your ears," the priests and the court prophets cried. But the princes saved Jeremiah, and his message was sent to King Jehoiakim—who burnt it.

Jeremiah declared that Judah must submit to Babylon, as a punishment decreed for sins; he would not pray for Jerusalem in her last extremity, for his master was not the king, but God. When the Babylonians took the city in the year 587, after a siege of more than a year and a half, they released the prophet from the dungeon into which King Zedekiah had thrust him. And then Nebuchadnezzar's soldiery sacked fallen Jerusalem; they burnt the Temple and the royal palace, threw down the city's walls, and carried off the people into bondage.

And yet Israel was not destroyed, Jeremiah prophesied; for Jehovah had made a new Covenant with his people. "After these days, saith Jehovah, I will put my law in their inward parts, and in their heart will I write it; and I will be their God, and they shall be my people. And they shall teach no more every man his neighbor, and every man his brother, saying, Know Jehovah: for they all shall know me, from the least of them unto the greatest of them, saith Jehovah: for I will forgive their iniquity, and their sin I will remember no more."

The old Covenant, that is, had worked upon the nation; the new Covenant would work upon the individual person, through conscience and private insight. Jehovah did not need His house upon Zion, nor did He need the kingdom of Judah, as He had not needed Samaria. He was the Lord of Hosts, and through the hearts and minds of those faithful to Him would He bring Israel to redemption; captives though they were, His people would spread the truth of Jehovah throughout the world. The Supreme Person would accomplish His will through a multitude of persons, not through a political state.

The last of the major prophets was the second Isaiah, living long after the first Isaiah (though his writings are Chapters 40 to 66 of the Book of Isaiah). He prophesied during the Babylonian Captivity, saying that mighty Babylon would fall before the power of Persia, and that the chosen people would be liberated by the conquering Cyrus. Upon the palace wall of Belshazzar, regent of Babylon, appeared the puzzling words *mene, mene, tekel, upharsin*;[9] Babylon did fall in a single night; as the second Isaiah (or the nameless prophet so designated) had foretold, the remnant of Judah returned to Jerusalem.

This was a healing prophecy. It is possible to know God, if one does not aspire to understand him utterly: "For my thoughts are not your thoughts, neither are your ways my ways, saith the Lord. For as the heavens are higher than the earth, so are my ways higher than your ways, and my thoughts than your thoughts." Israel had been the Lord's suffering servant, the representative of mankind; for the sins of all mankind had Israel been chastised. Now the remnant of Israel should be raised up, and the truth of the Lord should go forth to the Gentiles, Israel serving as a light to the nations. At the sins and the tribulations of Israel, the Lord had suffered like a woman in childbirth. Now He will comfort His people, for He loves them.

From first to last, the prophets often were detested by the kings, hated and menaced by the people; like Israel, they were suffering servants. They pointed the way to the salvation of man; man rejected them. Now God himself would intervene more directly in the world, the second Isaiah promised: God would send a new servant, with the divine spirit upon him, to establish justice in the earth.

What are we to make of these prophets, from Amos to the second Isaiah? If they were speaking only to the kings and the people of two petty Levantine states that fell to bits, the prophets would matter little enough in the history of mankind. If that were all, then the prophets failed, for even the restored Jerusalem of the Return went down to dust and ashes later. But in truth, the prophets were speaking to all men, in all times.

"The prophet was an individual who said No to his society, condemning its habits and assumptions, its complacency, waywardness, and syncretism," Abraham Heschel observes. "He was often compelled to proclaim the very opposite of what his heart expected. His fundamental objective was to reconcile man and God. Why do the two need reconciliation?" Why, because of man's overweening pride, man's resentment at God's intervention in history, man's abuse of freedom. Though Jews and Christians declare that no true prophets have been called for the past nineteen centuries, the old prophets endure.[10] "It is for us to decide whether freedom is self-assertion or response to a demand; whether the ultimate situation is conflict or concern."[11]

Through interpretation of Jehovah's ways with Israel, through their search for meaning in Israel's historical experience under God, the prophets descried order in the world. Early they perceived that man is made in the image of a Person who is invisible: the Lord of Creation, transcending matter and time. Out of His love, that Lord has prescribed ethical principles by which God's people may live in community, so that they will not be as the beasts that perish. The Children of Israel first knew God as the Lord of Israel; presently they came to know Him as the Lord of all nations; late, they knew Him for the Lord who works upon every human heart. He is the Lord of Justice, and the Lord of Mercy. Those who obey Him will be saved, redeemed from sin, suffer though they may in their time; at the end of days, theirs shall be the victory. The man who loves the Lord will obtain order in his soul, and the nation that is meek before the Lord will obtain order in the commonwealth. Without knowledge of the Lord, there can be only the outer darkness, where there is wailing and gnashing of teeth.

The Law and the Prophets gave clear ethical meaning to human existence; that is why the order of modern society is founded upon them. All the sins of man that Amos denounced are with mankind still: ghastly violence, corruption of justice, oppression of the weak, selfish indulgence, hypocrisy, ruinous complacency. Although thirty-three centuries have passed since Moses heard the voice of Jehovah, mankind in general has not succeeded satisfactorily in ordering either soul or commonwealth. Yet without the principles of order made known by the Law and the Prophets, modern man could not recognize standards for the person and the republic.

The common people of Israel understood only imperfectly the Law and the Prophets; the average man of the twentieth century understands them no better. Were it not for the legacy of Israel, nevertheless, the human condition would be unendurable for many. Like the ancient Egyptian of the "Dispute over Suicide," men would ask themselves whether it is not better to die by one's own hand than to live amidst corruption. Without the Law and the Prophets, order in existence could not endure.

Under God in Time and History

In the preceding account of Israel and of the sources of Jewish and Christian belief, the character of the Law and the teachings of the Prophets have been set down as they were understood by nearly all the early settlers in America, and by the vast majority of Americans at the time of the framing of the Constitution of the United States. Historically speaking, such are the Hebraic roots of American order, whether or not the reader of this book wholly accepts the Law and the Prophets. To undertake Jewish or Christian apologetics—that is, to undertake a theological defense of these beliefs on the basis of reason—is beyond our present purpose and beyond the limitations of space.

To many Americans in the twentieth century, the Old Testament may seem a puzzling and confused narration, in part incredible, in part irrelevant to the condition of modern man. No whale could have swallowed Jonah, any high-school student may object. The "historical Moses" may have been rather different from the Moses of Exodus, modern scholarship may suggest. During the past century, the decline of popular knowledge of the Bible, particularly of the Old Testament, has made it more difficult to relate the Hebraic experience to modern questions of order. For that matter, the Bible never was easy to understand.[12]

But what we need to bear in mind, if we wish to grasp the connection between the experience of order in biblical times and the experience of order in our own age, is that there exist two distinct forms of history: sacred history, and secular history. Sacred history consists of an account of mankind's experience with God; secular history consists of an account of mankind's experience in mundane affairs. The first form of history often can be expressed only through imagery—through parables, allegories, and the "high dream" of poetry. The second form of history, dealing with worldly events, tries to confine itself to such verifiable records and narrations as are available. Historians in either form must possess imagination, if their products are to have enduring significance.

Necessarily, sacred history describes through images, "as in a glass, darkly." For man's experiences of transcendence—man's sudden rare perceptions of a reality that cannot be measured accurately by his limited five senses—are unlike man's experiences of battles, diplomatic conferences, or elections. The poet sometimes obtains a glimpse of truth, which he then endeavors to test as best he can by his rational faculties: so it is with the scientist, too. And so it was with the prophets. In the seventeenth century, the great mathematician and philosopher Pascal had one intense experience of religious transcendence. What he had experienced in the depths of the soul, below the limits of ordinary consciousness, he could not put into words, though he was a master of prose. All he could say was "Fire, fire, fire!"

Therefore the Old Testament, a sacred history, ought not to be read as if it were simply an account of everyday events. Often it is symbolic and poetical, for many truths are most accurately expressed in symbol. The story of Jonah, for instance, really is a kind of parable: it teaches how a people, through their religious faith, may preserve their identity even though conquered and enslaved by some immense power—as if a man were to be swallowed by a sea monster. Just so the Jews, through faith in Jehovah, survived their Babylonian Captivity.

Similarly, it is not a conceivable "historical Moses"—unknown to us, because no documents or even artifacts or bones survive from that remote time and that obscure people—who really matters. The important Moses is the figure portrayed by the scribes—the man who experienced a "leap in being," who was granted moments of transcendence perhaps comparable to Pascal's, who through that experience was enabled to describe the Law for the Hebrews. One might as well search for "the historical Don Quixote de la Mancha." Even if somehow it could be shown that Cervantes had in mind a particular Spaniard of his acquaintance whom he used as model for his immortal character, it would not be the "historical" Quixote who would matter to the twentieth century: the significant Quixote is the Knight of the Sorrowful Countenance of Cervantes's novel. As Mark Twain said of Homer, the *Iliad* was written either by Homer or by another man with the same name. So it is with Moses and the Law.

Although a good deal of secular history is intermingled with the sacred history of the Bible, the Old Testament's purpose is not to present a chronicle of political and military events, but rather to describe in a variety of ways, and by various hands, how the Hebrews were made aware of the existence of Jehovah, and of Jehovah's laws, and of the Covenant that joins God and man. To criticize the Old Testament as if it were an attempt at chronological recording in the modern sense is to mistake its whole character.

By the truths about the human condition that were revealed from the lips of Moses and of the prophets, the Hebrews became aware of eternity. This is not easy for us to understand. For modern men generally think of what we call "time" much as the Greeks thought of time: that is, time seems "linear," extending in a kind of line from some point in remote antiquity to the present. But the Hebrews thought of time as "psychic"—that is, related to the soul, to spiritual experience. For God, all things are eternally present: God is not bound by human conventions of "time." What occurred to Moses and the prophets was a breakthrough in time, so to speak: for certain moments, or rather in certain abrupt experiences, time and the timeless coincided, and the Hebrews were given a glimpse of God's eternity. This is expressed by Thorleif Boman:

> For us space is like a great container that stores, arranges, and holds everything together; space is also the place where we live, breathe, and can expand freely. Time played a similar role for the Hebrews. Their consciousness is like a container in which their whole life from childhood on and the realities which they experienced or of which they had heard are stored. Because every person is and remains identical with himself, a consolidating unity adheres to each person's psychical content which could be expressed thus: all this is my world, my existence. A man who lives from the psychical impressions that the external world makes upon him has a world in his consciousness; he lives in time, but even while he actually lives in time, moments and intervals of time play a very subordinate role. It is the same I that once played as a child, went to school as a youth, and entered competitive life; body and appearance have changed, life's experiences have come, but the man himself, *i.e.* his consciousness, has remained the same self. Seen from the inside his personal experiences form a unity, a world; in that world he moves freely and with ease. Thus even while the Hebrew lives in time, time-distinctions play a very trifling role for him. Even in the divine consciousness all time-measurement disappears, because Yahweh remains identical with himself.[13]

For the Hebrew, then, in essence time is not simply a progression of events, marked by deaths and births. The true significance of time is its psychic relationship with eternity. One may say that what matters about time is the intensity of psychic consciousness in certain moments, not mere duration. For the Hebrew prophet, and for the Hebrew and the Jew who understood the prophet, then, to survive physically as an individual is not the aim of existence. The Hebrew's "time" is not merely the days and nights of individual life, but rather the existence of a people under God. God is outside of "time," even though time is His creation: for God, all events in the history of a people are simultaneously present. God is not bound by "past" or "future" or "present."

That being so, Hebrew thinkers are not much concerned with the question of personal immortality. The survival of the Hebrew *people*, chosen by God, is the burning concern of the prophets. The individual living in this moment is one of those people: he shares in the past of the people, and shares in their future. The order of the people, under the Covenant with God, transcends the momentary desires of any individual. If men are to be saved, they will be saved as persons among the people of God, not as isolated individuals.

With the revelation to Moses, made fuller by the prophets, God had broken into time. Thereafter the Hebrews, or those among them who understood the Law and the Prophets, held a view of history and the human condition very different from that of other peoples. "The God who became manifest through the Exodus deliverance obviously was not subject to any time but was rather a sovereign lord of time, or, to put it differently, a God transcending time," Gerhart Niemeyer writes. ". . . Furthermore, an eternal God manifested by a pinpointed intervention in time must be a God of purpose, will, and intelligence, rather than merely a god of cosmic potency. As manifested by His action in the past, He must be a God of judgment and redemption. . . . So now time became, in a way, an ocean inhibited by men, interrupted by the single island that was thrown up through God's past intervention." And God might intervene again.[14]

This brief digression about the Hebrew concept of time is closely related to the concept of order—and, through Jewish and Christian teaching, to the idea of order which still underlies America's personal and social order. If God is purposeful, consciously willing, intelligent, just, and redeeming—why, then man is foolish if he does not seek to know this Being: to understand the human condition, one tries to know God. If such is God's nature, then the "time" which matters is the time in which men commune with God and fulfill His purposes. Through God, man enters into eternity, redeemed from sin. If this is true, surely history takes on a new meaning: history becomes the life of a people in their search for God, or their flight from God. And accounts of the doings of captains and kings are important only so far as those events relate to God's purposes with mankind.

If one accepts the reality of a just and loving God, whose eternity is the escape from the shackles of time and the sufferings of this world, it must follow that a people should enter into the order which God has designed for them. If God has ordained an order for the soul or the person, and an order for the community, to flout that order is a destructive act of disobedience, by which a man would make himself a prisoner of time. It was this conviction which steeled the Hebrews and the Jews to live by the Law, despite all sufferings and all temptations.

Under fierce trials, often the Jews of the Diaspora must have asked themselves this question: what evidence exists that Moses and the prophets perceived clearly and spoke truly? They found pragmatic evidence, the evidence of the experience of their people: the fact that they had survived as a people, when other peoples had perished. In the passage of the centuries, they saw not only Jews, but Christians and Moslems, still living by the essence of Hebraic revelation; they saw even new secular philosophies and ideologies permeated by the Law, though the philosophers and ideologues might try to deny it. This might not be perfect evidence of the truth, but all evidence for things beyond the five senses is imperfect: survival and continuing relevance to the human condition are the best practical tests to determine whether a body of belief is right or wrong.

And, as Jeremiah had prophesied, Jehovah had put His law in their inward parts, and written it upon their hearts. In exile, their national community broken, they perceived the reality of God inwardly, through their worship. Personal knowledge of God's existence and justice and love, of God's eternity, entered into their lives—if as in a glass, darkly. But for that knowledge and that confidence, they would have perished altogether.

From the experience of the Jews in history, within the confines of time, it is possible to learn why men submit themselves to a personal order and a social order. To go to the heart of the matter, why do human beings conform to a prescribed personal order, when often their immediate pleasure and advantage would be served by disregarding that personal order? Why do they conform to a prescribed social order, when often they seem to have much to gain by breaking the laws?

The fundamental reason for such obedience is this: God has willed such an order, and that order is for man's great benefit. If a man defies that order, he becomes something less than human: he separates himself from the God who brought him into existence, and who offers him eternity. Disorder is rejection of divine wisdom and justice and love. So for the sake of sustaining that order, and of playing his part in it, a man who believes in the Law and the Prophets will sacrifice everything worldly. It is better that a man should die in time than that a people should perish for eternity.

It is the Hebraic order which has come down through the centuries to the American Republic—if altered by intervening circumstances and beliefs. God, the Lord of history, the timeless One, became known at Mount Sinai. His Law still is the source of order, even when the forms of that law have been secularized.

Other peoples have inherited other moral orders: such an order, for instance, as Gautama, the Buddha, communicated to India. Yet the rudiments of order seem everywhere similar. C. S. Lewis, in *The Abolition of Man*, collects parallel passages from a variety of religions and philosophies that illustrate the existence of a Natural Law universally recognized. He finds common acceptance, though variously expressed, of a law of general beneficence; a law of special beneficence; duties to parents, elders, ancestors; a law of justice; a law of magnanimity. Revelation in the Old Testament perhaps is not the only form that revelation has taken; but it is the form of revealed truth upon which American order depends.[15]

Revelation, in one form or another, everywhere has been the foundation of private and public order. It is not altogether surprising that the primitive Children of Israel, in an Arabian desert, should have experienced profound moral revelations; for such insights are not unknown among the moral leaders of peoples who remain primitive to the present day. In 1928, a small party led by a British explorer, L. M. Nesbitt, was trapped by a band of fierce Danakils in the Danakil Depression of Africa. They were saved from massacre by a kind of Danakil prophet, a very ancient man named Suni Maa, who lived by a moral order that the young men of his clan could not apprehend. Nesbitt asked this "living skeleton" if the lives of the explorers were in danger.

"In great danger indeed," replied Suni Maa, "especially with the younger men who are avaricious, and whose short life has not yet raised them above the soil to which they cling. They do not know that there are things, not of this world, but mysterious and superior, and worthy of being sought to the exclusion of everything else."[16]

Such perception of a truth beyond the senses, expressed in this century by a Danakil seer, was the revelation that Moses delivered to the Children of Israel. As the Hebrews learned, there exists a moral order which transcends time. In both its Christian and its Jewish forms, the order of Sinai still gives vitality to America.

The Old Testament and the New America

In colonial America, everyone with the rudiments of schooling knew one book thoroughly: the Bible. And the Old Testament mattered as much as the New, for the American colonies were founded in a time of renewed Hebrew scholarship, and the Calvinistic character of Christian faith in early America emphasized the legacy of Israel.

Marcionism—the heresy that Christians ought to cast aside Jewish doctrines—had no adherents in early America.[17] Only a handful of Jews settled in the colonies before the Revolution, and not a great many until the later decades of the nineteenth century; yet the patrimony of Israel was more powerful in America than in Europe.

The New England Puritans not only ordered their commonwealth by the Ten Commandments and the books of Leviticus and Deuteronomy, but constantly drew parallels, between themselves and the people of Israel and Judah. The Puritans thought of themselves as experiencing afresh, under God, the tribulations and the successes of the Hebrew people. "For answers to their problems," says Daniel Boorstin, "they drew as readily on Exodus, Kings, or Romans, as on the less narrative portions of the Bible. Their peculiar circumstances and their flair for the dramatic led them to see special significance in these narrative passages. The basic reality in their life was the analogy with the Children of Israel. They conceived that by going out into the Wilderness, they were reliving the story of Exodus and not merely obeying an explicit command to go into the wilderness. For them the Bible was less a body of legislation than a set of binding precedents."[18]

New England's intellectual leadership, which would give that region an influence over the United States disproportionate to New England's population, transmitted this understanding of the Hebrew patrimony far beyond the New England colonies. But also the teachings of John Calvin of Geneva, so strongly imprinted upon the Congregational churches of New England, worked as well (if less intensely) upon the other American colonies. The Presbyterians—Scottish, Scotch-Irish, and English—who came to the middle and southern colonies also were disciples of Calvin; even the Anglican settlers, until the middle of the seventeenth century, often emphasized the Calvinistic element in the doctrines of the Church of England.[19] The Baptists, too, were moved by Calvin.

John Calvin's Hebrew scholarship, and his expounding of the doctrine of sin and human depravity, impressed the Old Testament aspect of Christianity more strongly upon America than upon European states or other lands where Christians were in the majority. And of course the Lutherans, the Methodists, the Quakers, and other Christian bodies in the American colonies did not neglect the Old Testament, though they might tend to give it less weight than did the Calvinists.

"Because freedom from slavery and oppression were dominant themes in the Old Testament," Neal Riemer writes, the legacy of Israel and Judah nourished American liberty. "It warned—as in the story of the Tower of Babel—against Man's attempt to be God. It forced Man—as in the story of Adam and Eve—to recognize his mortality and fallibility and to appreciate that there can be no Utopia on earth. Again and again, it inveighed against the belief that Utopia can be captured and made concrete in idolatry. On the other hand, however, it left ample room for effort to make life better. This is the central meaning, as I read it, of God's Covenant with Noah and its reaffirmation with Abraham, with Moses, and with the later prophets."[20]

So the Old Testament helped to make social realists of the early Americans. As Edmund Burke would declare at the end of the colonial period, the religion of most of the Americans was "the dissidence of dissent, and the Protestantism of the Protestant religion"—suffused with the spirit of liberty. But it was not from the Law and the Prophets that the Americans dissented; the Calvinists' quarrel was not with the Children of Israel, but with the prerogatives of the Church of England. Generally the Calvinists believed more fervently in the authority of the Old Testament than Martin Luther had; the idea of the Covenant colored all their political convictions.

Clinton Rossiter expresses succinctly the cardinal point that American democratic society rests upon Puritan and other Calvinistic beliefs—and through those, in no small part upon the experience of Israel under God. "For all its faults and falterings, for all the distance it has yet to travel," Rossiter states, "American democracy has been and remains a highly moral adventure. Whatever doubts may exist about the sources of this democracy, there can be none about the chief source of the morality that gives it life and substance. . . . " From this Puritan inheritance, this transplanted Hebrew tradition, there come "the contract and all its corollaries; the higher law as something more than a 'brooding omnipresence in the sky'; the concept of the competent and responsible individual; certain key ingredients of economic individualism; the insistence on a citizenry educated to understand its rights and duties; and the middle-class virtues, that high plateau of moral stability on which, so Americans believe, successful democracy must always build."[21]

Of course Puritanism, and the other forms of Calvinism in America, were Christian in essence, not renewed Judaism merely. And the stern Calvinism of the early colonial years would be modified, presently, by the growth of a less Calvinistic Anglicanism, by the influence of Lutheranism, by the coming of millions of Catholic immigrants in the nineteenth century, and by the arrival of masses of immigrants of other confessions or persuasions. As generation succeeded generation, moreover, the New Englanders themselves would relax the strictness of the founders of Massachusetts Bay Colony.

That said, nevertheless American political theory and institutions, and the American moral order, cannot be well understood, or maintained, or renewed, without repairing to the Law and the Prophets. "In God we trust," the motto of the United States, is a reaffirmation of the Covenants made with Noah and Abraham and Moses and the Children of Israel, down to the last days of prophecy. The earthly Jerusalem never was an immense city: far more Jews live in New York City today than there were inhabitants of all Palestine at the height of Solomon's glory. But the eternal Jerusalem, the city of spirit, still has more to do with American order than has even Boston which the Puritans founded, or New York which the Dutch founded, or Washington which arose out of a political compromise between Jeffersonians and Hamiltonians. Faith and hope may endure when earthly cities are reduced to rubble: that, indeed, is a principal lesson from the experience of Israel under God.

["The Law and the Prophets," The Roots of American Order, *3rd ed. (Washington, DC: Regnery Gateway, 1991), 11–50.]*

❖

What Did Americans Inherit from the Ancients?

In this essay, Kirk examines the ways in which classical civilization influenced American thought and mores. He neither mythicizes nor romanticizes the ancient world, but sees things in proportion and in continuity. The Framers of the American constitution did not find in Greek political institutions a viable model of a good constitution, and even learned from their political flaws what ought to be avoided. The Roman Republic, with its system of checks and balances, was taken more seriously, however, and Rome's political and moral example served as a cautionary example to Americans of the early republic. What the Greeks and the Romans bequeathed to America was, above all, a body of great literature: "The poets, the philosophers, the rhetoricians, the historians, the biographers, the satirists, the dramatists of the ancient world move us still; their aphorisms are embedded in our schooling, their descriptions of the human condition tell us what is tragic and what pathetic."

It was British scholars and schoolmasters who imparted to the Americans of the thirteen colonies a knowledge of classical languages and literature, Greek and Roman history and politics and law. A translation of Plutarch's *Lives of the Noble Greeks and Romans* often stood on an American's bookshelf alongside the Bible; and the character of leading Americans was formed by both books. The influence of Greek and Roman literature upon the people of British North America is well described in Richard M. Gummere's book *The American Colonial Mind and the Classical Tradition*.[22] Second only to great English literature's influence upon yesteryear's Americans, classical philosophy and drama and rhetoric helped to shape American thought and mores.

Although those Americans who attended British universities, or the few American colleges established during the colonial era, acquired a good mastery of Ciceronian Latin often, and a tolerable acquaintance with ancient Greek, in general Americans read Plato and Aristotle, Plutarch and Livy, Sophocles and Seneca, in the great English translations published during the Tudor reigns, as the English commenced settling North America. Thus an English flavor permeated even the literary legacy Americans received from the ancient world.[23]

Just what is this classical patrimony that much influenced both the thought and the action of the people of the thirteen colonies, and that was cherished in the United States well into the twentieth century? To Europeans living west of the Elbe or south of the Danube, the remains of classical civilization are visible even today: intelligent observers are aware of a continuity extending over many generations. Englishmen can look upon Roman masonry at York, Chester, Colchester, and even today's London. For that matter, Roman ruins survive from the Atlantic shore of the Iberian peninsula all the way to the Euphrates, or from Scotland to Morocco. People who speak Romance tongues cannot be altogether unaware of the Roman past, nor can Greeks forget their distant cultural ancestors. But in North America, neither monuments of antiquity nor the roots of language can evoke memories of civilizations broken, yet somehow working through Americans in ghostly fashion. Nevertheless, Americans pay public homage to long-dead Greeks and Romans. Why is the public architecture of the District of Columbia still dominated by classical columns and domes? Why do Americans still pay some lip service to the disciplines of the humanities, the sources of which may be traced back to Greece six centuries before Christ?

It should be confessed that in some respects our debt to the ancients is not quite so great as certain historians and professors of politics would have us believe. The "lamp of experience" that Patrick Henry held high was not, in any positive and immediate fashion about 1775, the political experience of the Greeks and the Romans. That political and social experience "by which my feet are guided" (in Henry's famous phrase) was the British experience and the experience of British subjects in the colonies. Then as now, the great mass of men and women were guided by received custom and convention, not by Hebraic or Greek or Latin texts. Only the well-schooled, in any literate culture, are much influenced in their conduct by learned writings of yesteryear. Although Patrick Henry read much, he was not moved mightily by intellectual abstractions.[24]

In the Bicentennial years, a good deal was said about the Greek roots of Amerian democracy, the model of the Roman Republic for Americans, and that sort of thing. (Too little was said about the Hebraic and Hellenic patrimony of moral order.)

In truth America's political *institutions* owe next to nothing to the ancient world—although American modes of thinking about politics indeed were influenced, two centuries ago, by Greek and Roman philosophers long dead.

One learns much about constitutions from reading Plato and Aristotle and Polybius; constitutions monarchic, aristocratic, democratic; about oligarchies and timocracies; about tyrannies and kingships; about the polity, that blending of types of government. The educated Americans of the generation to which the Framers of the Constitution belonged studied the books of the Greeks and the Romans. But those books could not teach the Americans very much about constitutions that might be applied practically to the infant Republic of the United States.

For the people of the thirteen colonies had known almost from the first English settlements the institutions of representative government; while the ancient world had known nothing of that sort. Representative government, indeed, was what the War of Independence had been about. Only through some system of representation could a far-reading United States of America be conceivable. Even the most redoubtable Anti-Federalist did not fancy that the American Republic could consist of a league of infant city-states; a Congress there must be, and that Congress must be a *representative* assembly.

For Greek politics in ancient times were the politics of city-states for the most part, compact in territory, limited in population; and in the Greek democracies the entire body of male citizens was able to assemble in a forum for making public decisions of the gravest sort—sometimes foolish decisions with ghastly consequences. The United States, on the contrary, was a vast expanse of territory in which the few cities, in 1787, counted for little. And the Americans, unlike the Greeks, had the printing press to inform their democratic society. Many other differences existed.

Anyone who studies history seriously is liable to be disheartened by the repeated disastrous failures of human attempts to achieve a tolerable measure of order and justice and freedom, for any great length of time. Sir Ernest Barker, an eminent English professor of politics, commented on the views of that great historian of law Sir Henry Maine: "History has with Maine, what it tends to have with many of us, a way of numbing generous emotions. All things have happened already; nothing much came of them before; nothing much can be expected of them now."[25]

Maine, writing in the last quarter of the nineteenth century, knew from his studies in ancient law how the democratic republics of classical Greece had failed. A hundred years before Maine wrote, the authors of the *Federalist Papers*, and the other Framers of the American Constitution, had perceived that Americans could not find in the history of the Greek city-states any satisfactory model of a good constitution.

Study of Greek and Latin literature, and of the ancient world's history and politics, loomed much larger in American education during the latter half of the eighteenth century than it does in American education today. Most of the Framers at one time or another, in translation or in the original Greek or Latin, had read such ancient authors as Herodotus, Thucydides, Plato, Aristotle, Polybius, Cicero, Livy, and Plutarch—philosophers and historians who described the constitutions of the Greek and Roman civilizations. But from such study the American leaders of the War of Independence and the constitution-making era learned, by their own account, chiefly what political blunders of ancient times ought to be avoided by the Republic of the United States.

For the Greek city-states of the sixth and fifth and fourth centuries before Christ never succeeded in developing enduring constitutions that would give them order and justice and freedom. Civil war within those city-states was the rule, rather than the exception, class against class, family against family, faction against faction. And when half of those cities went to war against the other half, in the ruinous Peloponnesian struggle, during the last three decades of the fifth century—why, Greek civilization never wholly recovered from that disaster.

Leading Americans did study closely the old Greek constitutions. In his *Defense of the Constitutions of Government of the United States of America* (published in 1787, on the eve of America's Great Convention), John Adams examines critically twelve ancient democratic republics, three ancient aristocratic republics, and three ancient monarchial republics—and finds them all inferior to the political system of the new Republic of the United States. Alexander Hamilton, James Madison, and John Jay, the authors of the *Federalist Papers*, often referred to "the turbulent democracies of ancient Greece" (Madison's phrase) and to other ancient constitutions. In general, those three American statesmen found the political systems of Greece and Rome "as unfit for the imitation, as they are repugnant to the genius of America" (again, Madison's phrase). Old James Monroe, long after he had been president of the United States, wrote his little book *The People, the Sovereigns*, finding the ancient constitutions of Athens, Sparta, and Carthage woefully defective when contrasted with the Constitution of the United States, in which the sovereign people conferred power upon governors.[26] The American Framers and the early statesmen of the Republic, whether Federalists or Republicans, were no admirers of classical political structures.

Eighteenth-century Americans did respect Solon, the lawgiver of Athens in the sixth century before Christ. But Solon's good constitution for his native city had lasted merely some thirty years before a tyrant seized power in Athens. Nor did ancient political theory, as distinct from institutions, often obtain American approbation: John Adams wrote that he had learned from reading Plato two things only: "First, that Franklin's ideas of exempting husbandmen and mariners, &c., from the depredations of war, were borrowed from him; and second, that sneezing is a cure for the hiccough."[27]

Ancient Greek culture indeed did help to shape education in America, but Greek constitutions had next to no part in shaping the Constitution of the United States, nor the constitutions of the several states—except so far as Greek constitutional flaws suggested what Framers at Philadelphia and elsewhere ought not to adopt.

The Roman Republic was taken somewhat more seriously by leading Americans in the 1780s. The English word *constitution* is derived from the Latin *constitutio*, signifying a collection of laws or ordinances made by a Roman emperor. American boys at any decent school in the eighteenth century studied the orations and the life of Marcus Tullius Cicero, the defender of the Roman Republic in its declining years. The Roman term "Senate" was applied by the American Framers to the more select house of the legislative branch of their federal government—although the method for selecting senators in America would be very different from what it had been in Rome.

For the American constitutional delegates at Philadelphia, the most interesting feature of the Roman Republican constitution was its system of checks upon the power of men in high public authority, and its balancing of power among different public offices. The Americans had learned of these devices from the *History* by Polybius, a Greek statesman who had lived long in Rome—under compulsion. The two Roman consuls, or executives; the Roman Senate, made up of rich and powerful men who had served in several important offices before being made senators; the Roman assembly, or gathering of the common people—these three bodies exercised separate powers. And the Roman constitution (an "unwritten" one) included other provisions for preventing any one class from putting down other classes, and for preserving the republican form of government. Praised by Polybius as the best constitution of his age, this Roman constitutional system was bound up with a beneficial body of civil law, and with "the high old Roman virtue"—the traditional Roman morality, with its demand for the performance of duties and for determined courage.

The actual forms of checks and balances that the Americans incorporated into their Constitution in 1787 were derived from English precedent and from American colonial experience, rather than directly from the Roman model. Instances from the history of the Roman Republic, nevertheless, often were cited by the Framers and by other leading Americans of that time as reinforcement for the American concept and reality of political checks and balances. And the Americans' vision of a great and growing republic owed much to the annals of the Roman Republic.

In consequence of the long civil wars of Roman factions in the first century before Christ, the Republic fell, to be supplanted by the Roman empire. This Roman experience, and the decadence that oppressed Roman civilization as the centuries elapsed, were much in the minds of American leaders near the end of the eighteenth century. The grim consequences of political centralization under the Empire did something to discourage the notion of an American government that would be central rather than federal—much as the Greeks' disunity was remarked by some delegates as a warning against leaving the American Republic a mere confederation. Besides, Roman struggles of class against class reminded Americans that they must seek to reconcile different classes through their own constitutional structure.

Thus Rome's political and moral example was a cautionary lesson to Americans of the early Republic. Gibbon's grand history *The Decline and Fall of the Roman Empire* had been published between 1776 and 1783, the period of the American Revolution, and its details were vivid in the minds of the delegates at Philadelphia.

Yet it will not do to make too much of the influence of the Roman constitution upon the Constitution of the United States, two thousand years after Polybius wrote in praise of Roman character and institutions. The more immediate and practical examples of constitutional success were the British and the colonial American political structures; and the American Republic was joined with Britain and with her own colonial past by a continuity of culture that much exceeded the Americans' link with old Rome, so distant and so remote in time.

In ancient times and in modern, the central problem of political constitutions has been this: how to reconcile the claims of authority with the claims of freedom. In any tolerable society, there must exist a permanent authority that maintains order and enforces the laws. Also, in any tolerable society, individuals and voluntary groups ought to enjoy considerable freedom. If authority (whether a government or some other general authority) claims too much, despotism may come to pass. If too much is claimed for personal freedom, anarchy may result. The states of the ancient world never wholly succeeded, in their constitutions, in satisfactorily balancing authority and liberty.

It was the aspiration of the delegates at Philadelphia, in 1787, to reconcile the need for a strong federal government with the demand for much personal liberty and for guarantees of state and local powers. They could not find in the history of the ancient world any model that might achieve this purpose. In 1866, nine decades after the Great Convention at Philadelphia, Orestes Brownson—one of the more interesting of America's political thinkers—would write in his book *The American Republic* that America's mission under God was to realize the true idea of the political state or nation; to give flesh to that concept of the commonwealth "which secures at once the authority of the public and the freedom of the individual—the sovereignty of the people without social despotism, and individual freedom without anarchy. . . . The Greek and Roman republics asserted the state to the detriment of individual freedom; modern republics either do the same, or assert individual freedom to the detriment of the state. The American Republic has been instituted by Providence to realize the freedom of each with advantage to the other."[28]

Certainly such a high ambition, surpassing the political achievements of the ancient world, was the spirit of 1787 at Philadelphia.

If, then, the Greeks and the Romans bequeathed to America no political institutions—why, what is America's inheritance from the ancient world? Primarily, that patrimony is a body of great literature. The poets, the philosophers, the rhetoricians, the historians, the biographers, the satirists, the dramatists of the ancient world move us still; their aphorisms are embedded in our schooling, their descriptions of the human condition tell us what is tragic and what pathetic. Aye, the theologians of the late centuries of the Graeco-Roman culture move us, too; for Augustine of Hippo and Gregory the Great were men of the classical culture, and so were other Fathers of the Church, West and East.

Does not the preceding paragraph omit the patrimony of justice and law that has come down to our time from Greece, and more especially from Roman sources? No, I am not ignoring that great inheritance; I am merely pointing out that this is a literary, rather than an institutional, legacy, especially when one refers to the laws of the United States and of other countries basically English in their legal institutions. British and American jurisprudence was much influenced, formerly at least, by the writings of Plato, Aristotle, and Cicero; and British judges, reading Roman law surreptitiously despite repeated fulminations from the Crown, were not immune from the doctrines of Gaius, Ulpian, and the Corpus Juris. But obviously the juridical system of the United States is not copied directly from the Roman system of courts and procedures, any more than the Constitution of the United States is an embodiment of Greek political philosophy.

So it is through books of one sort or another that the ancient world moves us moderns. Once upon a time, well-educated men and women could read those books in the original Latin or Greek; but in the present century, and more particularly during the past seven decades, the proportion of people well acquainted with the classical languages has declined fearfully. In translation, however, the books of the greater writers of ancient times continue to work upon minds and consciences, if not so strongly as such writers did two centuries ago, when the Americans accepted "a more perfect Union."

Why is it that educational authorities, down to this writer's own youthful years, believed the teaching of the great literature of Greece and Rome highly important for the enlargement of wisdom and virtue, mind and character? Why was it that the British pattern of schooling, developed during the sixteenth and seventeenth and eighteenth centuries and continued little altered at the better schools down to recent decades, consisted in large part of careful study of Plato and Aristotle, the Greek dramatists and historians, Cicero, Vergil, Horace, Livy, Tacitus, Seneca, Plutarch? Why was it that well into the nineteenth century, even in wild Connaught, hedge schoolmasters like Yeats's Red Hanrahan went about with an inkpot hanging on a chain round the neck, a heavy copy of Vergil in a coat pocket, teaching Latin poetry to little barefoot Papist boys? Were the educational authorities of yesteryear absurdly mistaken about the importance of the ancient writers? Have today's educational authorities mercifully rescued the rising generation from servitude to the dead hand of the past, that the young may rejoice in the blessings of the new discipline of computer science?

On the contrary, the classical disciplines in schooling were immensely important, and for centuries successful. Their purpose was to bring about order in the soul and order in the commonwealth.

First, the poets and the philosophers of antiquity examined keenly the human condition. What are we mortals, and what are we to do in the short span of man's existence? Such ultimate questions were taken up boldly by both Greek and Roman writers of genius. People of the modern age were able to profit much from these discourses and disputations of some two thousand years ago, because the very remoteness in time of the ancient poets and philosophers emancipated modern readers from the tyranny of present-day passions and complexities. The Greeks and the Romans did not possess the Hebrews' treasures of the Book and the Law; but they possessed insights into human nature and even into physical nature—the theory of atoms, for instance—that people near the end of the twentieth century account for. Once this writer said to the Earl of Crawford, a considerable classical scholar, that the ancient Greeks knew everything important. "Yes," he replied, "and the question is, '*How* did they know it?'" Knowledge of ancient insight and speculation is the way to acquire a philosophical habit of mind.

Second, the literature of the ancient world was employed to form good character among the rising generation. Plutarch's heroes were exemplars for the men who framed the Constitution of the United States. In my own case, the *Meditations* of Marcus Aurelius have influenced me more strongly than has any other treatise, of any age, in any language. The high old Roman virtues were inculcated among the literate of many lands, century upon century: one might write an essay, I suppose, upon how the audacious character of the Polish nobility, say, down to very recent years, was formed in Roman molds, Latin being the language of the educated in Poland until well into the eighteenth century. Or one might trace the strong influence of Roman models upon the Spaniards—Iberia having been more Roman than Italy, in imperial times—and through the Spaniards, upon the upper classes of Latin America. Cicero's *Offices* became in medieval times a manual for the duties of the leaders of men; and although presumably no candidate for the presidency of these United States, in recent years, kept on his bedside table the *Offices*, nevertheless in subtle ways that book and the manuals of the Stoics still linger as exhortations to, or restraints upon, public men in this land—linger in ghostly fashion, transmuted through later writers or embedded in political customs. One may add that the very recent concern for restoring in American public schooling some measures to form good character has revived in certain quarters an interest in classical moral philosophy, as distinguished from religious instruction.

Third, the classical literature of jurisprudence and law obviously is a very important part of our patrimony from Greece and Rome. The theory of justice which prevailed in the West generally until the Russian Revolution, and which still prevails after a fashion in Western Europe and the Americas, has its roots in Aristotle's doctrine of "to each his own," and in Aristotle's observation that it is unjust to treat unequal things equally. The Ciceronian teaching of natural law, though much assailed and battered since the closing years of the eighteenth century, still has vitality—if sometimes in curiously distorted forms. And of course Justinian's *Corpus Juris* reconquered Europe, gradually, for *Romanitas*—long after Rome had fallen, and spreading its power even after the fall of Constantinople. And incorporated into canon law, Roman legal principles still function within the framework of the Catholic Church and are studied in this metamorphosed form today, in the law schools of Central and Southern Europe most notably.

One might go on to describe other great ways in which the civilization dominant in the Mediterranean world, more than two millennia gone, still works among us. But time runs on, runs on. I have emphasized strongly our classical literary patrimony, and have denied that we enjoy much inheritance from Greece and Rome in our political institutions. But I do not mean to argue that no Roman influence survives in social—as distinguished from political—institutions, even to this day.

In Italy, and to some degree in Spain, it still is possible to find functioning, especially in old-fashioned towns and villages, remnants of social usages that apparently have survived many centuries of devastation and radical social alteration—even of vast demographic changes. But when I refer to social institutions, I mean something larger and more widespread than remnants of ancient folkways.

Nay, I mean, rather, to give an eminent example, the institution of the family, still most close-knit in the south of Europe, but transplanted to northern Europe also, and across the Atlantic. The Roman state never forgot that the family was the footing of all civil social order; the state was solicitous for the family's well-being—if, at the end, unsuccessful in its protections. This function of safeguarding and upholding the family passed from the dying Roman state to the emerging universal church, gradually, but most notably during the reign of Gregory the Great. Thus the Church, in medieval times and in modern, labored skillfully to nurture family loves and family duties: the institutions of classical Rome transmuted into the institutions of Christian Rome. "Rome is the power that withholds," John Henry Newman wrote—the power, in ancient times and even in our own day, which restrains men and women from the indulgence of those appetites which, given their head, would shatter the human race. The strong family has been such an institution of restraint, life-giving restraint. No-fault divorce nowadays is only one of the socially destructive assaults upon the traditional family that, in the name of emancipation, would make us all into orphans. When that restraining power of Rome is broken, Newman declared, there will come the Anti-Christ. But such prophecies are not Delphic or Cumaean.[29]

However that may be, the institution of the family comes to us in part through Rome; yet through Roman principles absorbed into Britain, and reinforced by British social experience. This filtering is true of nearly all of America's classical patrimony: Americans know it through British eyes.

Fulbert of Chartres, in medieval times, declared that we moderns—that is, the people of his own age—are dwarfs standing upon the shoulders of giants: we see farther than do the giants, but merely because we are mounted upon their shoulders. Those giants are the wise men of classical and early Christian epochs. From them Americans have inherited the order of the soul and the order of the commonwealth. If we think to liberate ourselves from the past by leaping off those giants' shoulders—why, we tumble into the ditch of unreason. If we ignore the subtle wisdom of the classical past and the British past, we are left with a thin evanescent culture, a mere film upon the surface of the deep well of the past. Those who refuse to drink of that well may be drowned in it.

["What Did Americans Inherit from the Ancients?" America's British Culture *(New Brunswick, NJ, and London: Transaction Publishers, 1993), 95–106.]*

The Light of the Middle Ages

The Middle Ages mark the period from the fall of the Roman Empire in 476 to the fall of Constantinople to the Turks in 1453. It was an age, as T. S. Eliot has written, that sought to secure a "hold on permanent things, on permanent truths about man and God, and life and death." This excerpt from Kirk's The Roots of American Order *(1974) recalls "a neglected inheritance" in our intellectual history. For Kirk the great saint and the great knight were "the wonder of medieval Europe." Later the scholar and the gentleman would be their descendants. The chivalric ideal, in particular, bequeathed a spirit of honor and valor that was not lost on the men of colonial times. The writings of medieval English and Scottish scholars, Kirk also believes, "passed into the intellectual consciousness that was the seed-bed of American culture," and influenced the better-schooled American leaders in recognizing "the existence and perfection of the revealed God."*

The Sword of Faith

The time of the growth of common law and of parliaments was also the time of the Crusades. Two types of humanity were the wonder of medieval Europe: the great saint and the great knight. In later ages, their descendants would be the scholar and the gentleman. We have said something of saints already; now we look at one famous knight.

From the closing years of the eleventh century to the end of the thirteenth century, the feudal West engaged in that enormous adventure and tragedy called the Crusades. At the beginning of those two centuries of warfare in the East, the objects of the Christian kings and barons, or at least the objects of the popes, were to rescue the holy city of Jerusalem from the Moslems, and to aid the Eastern Empire of Constantinople against its Moslem foes. In the former object, the Crusaders succeeded—for eighty-eight years. In the latter object, they destroyed the Byzantine system instead of saving it, for the Latin Crusaders stormed Constantinople in 1204 and chose one of their own princes as emperor, and then carved the Byzantine territories into feudal fiefs.

By the year 1187, Jerusalem had fallen back into the hands of the Moslems, and the Latin Christians of *Outremer* (the overseas stronghold of Christendom) held little more than a strip of land along the Palestinian coast, with the fortress-town of Acre as their actual capital—though they still called their state the Kingdom of Jerusalem. By 1208, the European colonists of *Outremer* lacked even a king, though they had a girl-queen, Maria, seventeen years old. They besought the king of France to find them a husband for Maria: such a husband, such a king, as could withstand the outnumbering enemy and restore to them Jerusalem.

King Philip Augustus of France, who had been a Crusader himself, chose for their king a landless knight, sixty years old. This was such a knight-errant as wandered through the pages of medieval romances, who might have jousted with Gawain or Lancelot. Yet he was flesh and blood—very much flesh and blood, because gigantic in stature. John of Brienne, soon to be King of Jerusalem, came from Champagne, and had been reared for a priest, but liked the sword better. His brother, through marriage to a forsaken heiress to the overthrown Norman rulers of the South, vainly asserted a forlorn claim to the throne of Sicily. For forty years and more this John of Brienne had been a gallant squire of dames, a champion at tournaments, and a valiant commander in the French king's armies. This huge scarred veteran was married to the girl-queen of Jerusalem; and perhaps she loved him, which was infrequent in the noble marriages of medieval times. Ordinarily he was as gentle with women as he was heavy-handed with armed men; indeed, the only charge that could be brought against him as king and emperor was his excessive indulgence of wives and daughters. The king of France gave him forty thousand silver pounds because John had nothing of his own, and Pope Innocent gave him another forty thousand. In the stronghold of Acre, King John bided his time until he should have force enough to take the field against the sultans.

Maria of Jerusalem bore him a daughter, Yolande, and then died. The people of *Outremer* admired and obeyed him, for he was a man of political knowledge as well as a man of battle. By 1218, he was ready to lead the Fifth Crusade, and he meant to strike first at Egypt, the center of Moslem power. Pope Innocent III strained every nerve for this effort, and a hundred thousand armed men were gathered in Palestine for the undoing of Egypt and the recovery of Jerusalem: the king of Hungary, the duke of Austria, a fleet from the Frisian Islands, the king of Cyprus, and crusaders from many other lands joined King John, who already had the three military orders of monks and the levies of *Outremer*. They marched into Egypt.

John of Brienne beat the sultan's hosts and took the port of Damietta; the Sultan of Egypt offered the Crusaders Jerusalem and more besides if they would withdraw from his domains; that was enough to satisfy John. But the new pope, Honorius III, had dispatched to Egypt a Spanish cardinal, Pelagius, as papal legate. Although he had neither diplomatic skill nor military experience, Pelagius asserted command over John, and with that the opportunity was lost.

There came to Egypt at this time, too, the strangest and most holy man of that age, Saint Francis of Assisi. In his youth, Francis had fought in the war between Assisi and Perugia, and had been taken prisoner; now he was the fearless peacemaker. Following more boldly in Christ's steps than perhaps any man before or since the thirteenth century, Francis and his friars lived in extreme poverty and simplicity. He was the humblest and most successful of all the reformers who from time to time renewed the medieval Church. His love extended to all animate creation—even to "Brother Wolf."

What could the saintly enthusiast and the grand knight-errant have said to each other? We have no record of their talk. Yet John of Brienne, a cleric in his youth, was so won by the ascetic of Assisi that he became a Franciscan of sorts himself; long later, he would be buried in the gray gown of Francis's begging friars.

Saint Francis crossed over to the Saracen lines and charmed the Sultan of Egypt. He asked the Moslem monarch that he might be permitted to walk barefoot on hot coals to testify to his faith in Christ. The Sultan al-Kamil spared Francis that test, but he did discourse on religion with the gentle hero from Umbria. "The Moslem guards were suspicious at first," a twentieth-century historian of the Crusades writes, "but soon decided that anyone so simple, so gentle, and so dirty must be mad, and treated him with the respect due to a man who has been touched by God."[30] The mystic of Assisi could not persuade the two armies to the peace of God, nevertheless: once he was gone from the camp, they took again to the sword.

By Pelagius's meddling, John's campaign was undone. The Crusaders were defeated with tremendous loss, and John of Brienne withdrew to Acre. He had married again, this time an Armenian princess, Stephanie; but she tried to poison his baby daughter Yolande, so John beat his Armenian wife, and later she died of that thrashing, rumor said—for John was accustomed to striking hard.

Although the Fifth Crusade had failed, John still held his scrap of a kingdom, and must find aid in the West for his people; he must find, too, a strong husband for Yolande, she being eleven years old, he far into his seventies. In 1222, he sailed with Yolande to Italy, and sought out Pope Honorius at Rome.

The pope arranged that Yolande should marry the greatest sovereign in Christendom, Frederick II, Holy Roman Emperor—able, skeptical, licentious: then Frederick himself might go on crusade, and Jerusalem be delivered again. John hesitated; but the splendor of this match was too much for even the proudest knight-errant to resist.

While the marriage-treaty was being drawn up, John proceeded into France, seeking help for *Outremer*, and then into Spain. There he married another young bride, Berengaria, sister to the King of Castile. After grand ceremonies in Italy and *Outremer*, Yolande was married to Frederick at Brindisi, late in 1225. Frederick was masterful, learned, and the next thing to an atheist; also he was merciless and treacherous: the other side of the chivalric coin from John of Brienne.

No sooner had Frederick married Yolande—and debauched her cousin, a bridesmaid—than he deposed old John from the kingship of Jerusalem, assuming the throne himself on the strength of being now the husband of the young Queen Yolande. He deprived John even of fifty thousand marks that the dying King of France had given him for *Outremer*. Enraged, John of Brienne went to the pope at Rome; Yolande was dispatched to Frederick's harem in Sicily, where she died after bearing the emperor a son. Like Shakespeare's Lear, King John was desolate in his old age—or so it seemed.

Unlike Lear, however, John of Brienne was far from his dotage. Pope and emperor fell out; at last, in 1228, the excommunicated Frederick II sailed for Palestine on a crusade of sorts. Poor Yolande was dead and buried in Sicily now; John owed Frederick no love. With papal troops at his back, John marched into the absent emperor's Italian domains, taking towns and castles on behalf of the pope. John was nearly eighty years old in his hour of vengeance, and some thought he should be crowned king of England, that land then needing a king of might.

But then there came to John the offer of a more exotic throne. The Latin Empire of Constantinople, grandest of medieval cities, lacked a strong ruler. Who could defend that beleaguered realm better than John of Brienne? Berengaria had a little daughter by John, Maria, four years old: it was arranged that the baby Maria should be betrothed to Baldwin II, the boy-emperor of Constantinople, and that John himself should be emperor, as well as regent, until his death.

So to the palace on the Golden Horn John sailed, to become in title the successor of Constantine the Great. There he arrived in 1231, an emperor more than eighty-three years of age. For the time being, the terror of his name kept off the enemies to the north and the enemies to the east. John disbanded the armies and lived at ease with wife and daughter: his fire, it appeared, was extinguished at last.

So thought the Greek emperor of Nicaea and the formidable king of Bulgaria. In concert, they marched against Constantinople with a tremendous host and a large fleet, in 1235. At his immediate command, Emperor John had only a hundred and sixty knights, and a small force of sergeants and archers.

Constantinople was surrounded by the strongest fortifications in the world, but John of Brienne disdained them. Taking horse, he charged the enemy at the head of his chivalry; panic seized the Greeks and the Bulgars, and they broke; John's men gained much of their fleet. Then John sent messages to the vassal principalities of the Latin Empire, gathered the Westerners who held fiefs in what had been old Greece, and beat the Greeks and the Bulgars again in 1236.

That done, no one ventured to disturb him. At the age of ninety, full of glory but empty (as always) of pocket, John died peacefully in his imperial palace. By his command, he was buried in the habit of a Franciscan friar; at heart, this hero of the sword was brother to the mendicant of Assisi.

The age of chivalry was an age of wonders. Where did the actual begin and the imaginary end? No man knew. John of Brienne had done deeds marvellous as any knight's of romance. "Chivalry was the fine flower of honor growing from this soil," Henry Osborn Taylor comments, "embosomed in an abundant leafage of imagination. . . . For final exemplification of the actual and the ideally real in chivalry, the reader may look within himself, and observe the inextricable mingling of the imaginative and the real. He will recognize that what at one time seems part of his imagination, at another will prove itself the veriest reality of his life. Even such wavering verity of spirit was chivalry."[31]

The knights-errant of medieval times, most of them, were burly armored men who went about seeking causes to champion—widows' and orphans,' sometimes—but usually for a price. From their number could emerge such a one as John of Brienne, and in time from the ideals of chivalry emerged the idea of a gentleman. The civilization of Europe has been maintained by two powers, Edmund Burke would say in the eighteenth century: the Christian religion, and the spirit of a gentleman. By the time of Miguel de Cervantes, in the sixteenth century, the old knight-errant would have vanished, and his last emulator, Don Quixote de la Mancha, would appear absurd. Yet Don Quixote, venerating such heroes as John of Brienne and John's peers of the medieval romances, stands up a true gentleman, loftier far in spirit than those who mock him. "A lean and foolish knight forever rides in vain," in G. K. Chesterton's lines: but not altogether in vain. For the sense of honor and of duty, and the sword of faith, passed in some degree from the medieval world to later times.

In the English Renaissance, the courtier and the gentleman would take the knight-errant's place. They would be as quick to love and to hate as the old knight had been, but their graces would be more polished. Sir Walter Raleigh, having planted the first settlement in Virginia, would be flung into London Tower on a trumped-up charge of treason; there he would write his immense *History of the World*, and invent medicines. At last he would go to the block, King James wishing to please the Spanish ambassador by Raleigh's death; and as a gentleman he would die.

The poet Sir Philip Sidney, mortally wounded in the Low Countries, would give his cup of water to a dying common soldier: "Thy need is greater than mine." In this fashion, the chivalric ideal of the Middle Ages endured after the feudal institutions had been swept away.

America was no aristocratic land, but such examples were not lost on the men of colonial times and later days. Captain John Smith, commanding what force the early Virginian settlement could muster, was a kind of latter-day paladin, full of tales—half fanciful, perhaps, half genuine—of his wars against the Turks. America would have no nobles, but it would have gentlemen. And they would dare much. One of these, not fearing to take the sword, was George Washington; another would be a later Virginian, Robert E. Lee. It is well that war is so terrible, said General Lee, for otherwise we should grow to love it.

It has been said that a gentleman is a person who never calls himself one. Certainly few Americans lay claim to gentility nowadays. And yet the heavy-handed champion of medieval times bequeathed to later centuries a spirit of valor and honor and fortitude, and sometimes of generosity, that has not lost all its value. The communication of medieval saints echoes down to us, and so does the communication of medieval knights. As the poet-adventurer Roy Campbell said to me once, "If you are Don Quixote, all your windmills will be giants; but then, all your giants will be windmills." Francis of Assisi, born a person of quality, was fearless in one fashion, John of Brienne in another; faith sustained them both. Their light, blending, still illuminates our own century, which confronts its own windmills and its own giants.

Schoolmen and Universities

Knights have vanished almost, but scholars have multiplied. From medieval times, one inheritance comes down to us uninterrupted: the universities. The work of a university is the ordering and integrating of knowledge. That work began systematically in the twelfth century, and without it modern civilization would founder.

Although Americans in the formative years of this country were influenced indirectly by medieval thought, few of them understood how much they owed to that source. With few exceptions, they tended to think of the Middle Ages as barbarous. Yet in essence their own schooling, at every level, was developed out of medieval education.

The Schoolmen, the Christian philosophers of the medieval universities, transcended the barriers of nationality and language. For the language of the universities was Latin, not vernacular tongues; and both professors and students shifted without much impediment from country to country, teaching and studying with small regard for political loyalties. The very word "university" implies the universal, the general—something more than local and private; the universities' degrees were recognized as valid throughout Christendom.

And the Schoolmen were in search of universal truths. At the height of their intellectual power, in the thirteenth century, they developed an elaborate structure of philosophy, the purpose of which was to prove that reason is not contrary to Christian faith. The greatest of them, Thomas Aquinas, reconciled the writings of Aristotle with Christian doctrine. The Schoolmen of that age, the Realists, perceived the universe as ordered by divine wisdom and love. True reality, they declared, is found in "universals"—that is, in general laws of being, somewhat like Plato's "ideas."

In politics, as in metaphysics and ethics, the Schoolmen of the thirteenth century sought for "universals." The state should be guided by universal principles of justice. Saint Augustine, centuries earlier, had written that the state was a necessary evil, resulting from man's sinfulness. But Saint Thomas Aquinas saw the political state as natural and beneficial: even had mankind been innocent of sin, government would have been desirable, as a means for attaining the common good. In this, as in much else, Aquinas restored the authority of Aristotle.

Where the civil social order was concerned, the Schoolmen's principal problem was to describe the proper relation between Church and State: how to balance the "two swords," or two powers by whom this world is ruled, that

Saint Gelasius had defined when the Church was rising upon the ruins of the Roman imperial structure. How should pope and emperor share authority? At a time of crisis, should men be loyal to Church, rather than to State? Was the canon law of the Church independent of imperial or royal laws? These were immediately practical questions in medieval times, so that now and again they were tested by the witness of blood—as in the martyrdom of Thomas à Becket, archbishop of Canterbury, who by his death became the most popular of English saints.

One is tempted to discuss these questions in some detail here, for they have an enduring relevance to the problems of order. Yet scholastic debates were not much heeded by the Americans who established a new nation in the eighteenth century: the Reformation would form a towering barrier between the "Papist" philosophers of medieval times and the settlers in British North America. At best, the concepts of Aquinas and other Schoolmen of the thirteenth and fourteenth centuries would pass to some Americans only at second-hand, through the books of Richard Hooker and some other Anglican divines of the Reformation. The Schoolmen of the Continent were sealed away from Englishmen and therefore Americans, once the medieval Church dissolved in the sixteenth century.

Many of the more eminent medieval scholars, nevertheless, were Englishmen or Scots, and in some degree their writings passed into the intellectual consciousness that was the seed-bed of American culture. The earliest of these English thinkers was Saint Anselm, archbishop of Canterbury in Norman England: a native of Italy, but the intellectual and practical architect of the medieval Church in England. The better-schooled among the American leaders would know something of Anselm's powerful proofs of the existence and perfection of the revealed God.

There were other English and Scottish Schoolmen famous throughout Christendom: in the thirteenth century, the Franciscan Alexander of Hales; Robert Grosseteste, bishop of Lincoln; and Roger Bacon, whose ideas anticipated modern scientific method. In the first half of the fourteenth century, the subtle John Duns Scotus set himself against the system of Thomas Aquinas; and there rose up in England the formidable William of Ockham, the Nominalist.

That Englishman William of Ockham, indeed, undid the earlier Realism of the universities—and so, if unintentionally, helped to clear the way for Renaissance and Reformation. The mode of thought called "Nominalism" denied the existence of "universals": that is, the Nominalists held that only names are general, and only individuals exist. There is no universal "horse," for instance: "horse" is merely a word which we apply, for convenience, to certain creatures of a particular species that resemble one another. This nominalist concept would lead on to a personal and social individualism that opposed the medieval ideal of universality; practically, it would work to break down the "medieval synthesis" of authority in church and state, and would be a factor in the personal individualism of the Renaissance and the religious individualism of the Reformation.

A contemporary of William of Ockham, in the first half of the fourteenth century, was Marsilius of Padua, a Schoolman more radical than the English Nominalist. Marsilius, at the University of Paris, argued that the Church must be subordinated to the State: even though divine law is superior to human law, it is the State that must decide the interpretation of divine law. Thus Marsilius carried Aristotle's politics—the politics of the *polis*, the autonomous city-state—further than did Aquinas. In effect, the principles of Marsilius reduced papal authority and made conceivable the governing of churches by kings and princes—which would come to pass, in some countries, during the Reformation.

But for our purposes in this book, it will not do to go deeply into the debates of the Schoolmen, important though they were. For the majestic Schoolmen of the Continent—Albertus Magnus, Abelard, Hugh of St. Victor, even Aquinas—were little better than names even to the learned in eighteenth-century America. Only when Roman Catholic colleges and universities began to be founded in the United States, chiefly late in the nineteenth century, would the old Schoolmen's intellectual power be recognized in this country. Anglican and Presbyterian and Puritan divines, rather than the medieval philosophers, nurtured American faith and reason.

Despite that, the Schoolmen's medieval universities in Britain and northern Europe, converted into strongholds of Protestantism at the Reformation, have exercised a large influence upon American order, both in themselves and through the American colleges that in the beginning were modelled modestly upon them. The foundations which today are called Harvard, William and Mary, Yale, Princeton, and Columbia all were intended to carry into the colonies the English and Scottish patterns of higher learning. Even the state universities established early in the nineteenth century took "Oxbridge" or the Scottish universities for models, though later they would be much altered by emulation of German universities and by utilitarian aims.

The medieval university was an independent corporation of scholars, a body of schools of general studies, commonly with colleges of arts that prepared young men for the bachelor's or the master's degree, and also higher schools of theology, law, and medicine. The university arose out of the Church's monastic schools and cathedral schools, usually, in response to a thirst for higher learning.

In Britain and northern Europe, although not always in Italy or elsewhere in the South, these universities were dominated by the Church, and the students were clerks, or clerics, either in minor orders or about to take orders—some of those students very young indeed. At the University of Bologna, the students controlled everything—until the townsfolk of Bologna, objecting to the students' arrogant ways, contrived to end that. But the English and Scottish universities stood nominally under the direction of ecclesiastics, and were governed practically by their professors, who were priests, monks, and friars. Their first object was to pursue truth for the glory of God. Beyond that, they were meant to educate young men to become clergymen, to prepare some of those for prospective service with the State as well as with the Church, and to develop the other learned professions of law and medicine. In these universities, theology was queen of the sciences.

Thomas Aquinas, in the thirteenth century, held that there was no wall of separation between theology and philosophy: those studies differed merely in method. But William of Ockham, in the fourteenth century, divorced philosophy from theology, maintaining that he thereby freed Christian dogmas from the influence of pagan speculations. That divorce would lead to other speculations in the universities, however, and so toward the Reformation. Yet in their early centuries, Europe's universities were centers for the intellectual reinforcement of authority and tradition—even if professors quarreled passionately and students seemed lawless.

"They had no antique prototype," Henry Osborn Taylor writes of these medieval foundations: "nothing either in Athens or Rome ever resembled these corporations of masters and students, with their authoritative privileges, their fixed curriculum, and their grades of formally certified attainment. Even the Alexandria of the Ptolemies, with all the pedantry of its learned litterateurs and their minute study of the past, had nothing to offer like the scholastic obsequiousness of the medieval University, which sought to set upon one throne the antique philosophy and the Christian revelation, that it might with one and the same genuflection bow down before them both."[32]

The two English medieval universities, Oxford and Cambridge, had their origins near the end of the twelfth century and the beginning of the thirteenth, and so rank among the earliest of universities (as distinguished from monastic or cathedral schools). Both were unusual in that they did not grow out of old cathedral schools, but instead sprang up as guilds of teaching masters—though soon they would be endowed by great churchmen and by kings. The three medieval Scottish universities, on the other hand—St. Andrews, Glasgow, and Aberdeen—resembled most of the universities of northern Europe in being associated with cathedrals.

As a rather late specimen of the type and influence of medieval universities, we consider the oldest university of Scotland, St. Andrews. There are reasons for emphasizing here a Scottish university rather than Oxford or Cambridge. For one thing, by the eighteenth century Oxford and Cambridge would become aristocratic in character; but the Scottish universities would remain relatively democratic and popular foundations, and so their professors and students would more nearly resemble those of the early American colleges. Also the Scottish universities would be Calvinistic in their theology and pattern of church government, after the Reformation; while Oxford and Cambridge would be Anglican. And of the five early American colleges, Harvard, Yale, and the College of New Jersey (now Princeton) would be Calvinist.

Because the colonies were governed from London, sometimes Scottish contributions to young America are neglected by historians. But much of America's early energy, in politics, commerce, and on the frontier, was that of Scots—who would become more successful in America than any other ethnic group except the New England Puritans. James Wilson, signer of the Declaration of Independence, member of the Constitutional Convention, a principal author of the Constitution, and later an associate justice of the Supreme Court, was one of the more ardent advocates of popular sovereignty; he had been born and schooled at the Scottish university town of St. Andrews. Scottish Presbyterianism worked intricately upon American life and character.

So we turn for our representative university to a little center of learning on the North Sea, St. Andrews—a place that had drawn pilgrims in the Dark Ages because in its cathedral rested an arm-bone and some finger-bones of Saint Andrew the Apostle. The bishops and archbishops of St. Andrews were Scotland's primates, and often the Scots kings' chancellors, too. As Scottish patriotism flourished in the century after Robert Bruce's defeat of the English at Bannockburn, the first university of that austere land was founded in a spirit of national independence.

Schools there had been in St. Andrews almost at the dawn of Scottish history: they had been conducted first by the Culdees, a Celtic Christian sect of Irish origin. At the beginning of the fifteenth century, a number of little schools under private masters were prospering in the town. But the time had come when schooling must be regularized and the higher learning dignified.

A wise and strong bishop, Henry Wardlaw, was in St. Andrews; learned men among the clerics found him a patron competent to establish a university.

From its inception, this new university was intended to be a bulwark of orthodoxy. Lawrence of Lindores, Abbot of Scone and Inquisitor of Heretical Pravity for Scotland, appears to have been a master spirit in the undertaking, next to the bishop; and no man was more zealously orthodox. These ecclesiastics detected the first murmur of the storm that would be called the Reformation. They proceeded to buttress the wall of Faith with the prop of Reason.

It was a time troubled by heresy and schism. In the Great Schism of the medieval Church, Scotland adhered to the Avignon popes, while England supported the Roman claimants to the papacy. Thus the Scottish students who once would have walked south to Oxford and Cambridge now must risk falling into schism if they ventured over the Border. Ever since the Scottish wars of independence, Scottish clerks had crossed in increasing numbers to the Continent, especially to the Scots colleges at Paris and Orleans. But after 1408, France too forswore her allegiance to Benedict XIII, of the Avignon line of popes, and thus the whole of the Continent, except for Spain, was closed to Scots scholars. Besides, access to the English universities was impeded by the sore troubles of King Henry IV; while in France, civil war had hit the colleges at Paris and Orleans hard—it being perilous even to approach those cities.

Heresy was no less menacing than schism. The movement called Lollardry, bound up with the ideas of John Wycliffe (who had translated the Bible into English), seemed bent upon social revolution. The Lollards or Wycliffites declared that they would subject the Church to the authority of the Crown, confiscate and redistribute land, apply the laws of the Jews to England and Scotland, and sweep away the clergy together with their benefices. In 1407, John Resby, a Lollard preacher, had been burnt in Scotland, for he had denied that the pope was Christ's vicar, and had affirmed that bad character incapacitates priests from performing holy offices.

The late medieval Church in Scotland was tolerant of much, but these doctrines were perilous to its existence. The rising generation must be forewarned against these errors, before visionary reformers should seduce young men. With Lindores there joined other clergy, and they lectured in St. Andrews town upon theology, logic, the law of God, canon law, and civil law. In 1412, Bishop Wardlaw gave to these teachers a charter of incorporation, creating the University of St. Andrews.

But most medieval universities desired papal sanction. In 1413 there arrived from stern old Pope Benedict XIII, the last of the Avignon line, six papal bulls confirming the charter and authorizing faculties of theology, canon and civil law, arts, medicine, and other university subjects.

The new university had a chancellor, a grand personage intended to protect the foundation; and before the Reformation, the chancellor almost always was the bishop or archbishop of St. Andrews. From within the university was chosen a rector, who must be a graduate and a man in holy orders, and who exercised the university's wide civil and criminal jurisdiction, ordered its affairs, and prescribed its discipline: the first of these was Lawrence of Lindores, the Inquisitor. Scotland being thoroughly medieval still, no touch of the new humanism penetrated to the curriculum of St. Andrews. Lawrence of Lindores lectured on the *Sentences* of Peter Lombard, a textbook of the twelfth century; the scientific treatises of Aristotle, in their corrupt Latin version (for no teacher at St. Andrews knew Greek), provided the basis of philosophy; most of the masters were Nominalists.

Faculties at St. Andrews took the University of Paris for their model. *Bajans*, or entering students (most of whom were no more than fifteen years old, and many younger) were presumed to know grammar well enough; they were set to learning logic and rhetoric, and after those subjects, physics, metaphysics, and Aristotle's *Ethics*. A student might attain the baccalaureate after eighteen months, be capped as a licentiate after four years, and become a master almost immediately thereafter. Eight more years of study were required if one would become a doctor of theology. Lecturers and regents all were clerics, most of them holding priests' livings but devoting their time to the college.

In medieval times, nearly all university students were very poor. At St. Andrews, they subsisted on porridge (the oats being fetched from their families' farms) and some fish. Then, as now, students' motives were mixed: some felt a thirst for learning, most desired advancement in society. To become a learned clerk was a way to preferment in Church and State, and humble birth was no obstacle, if one should become a good and useful scholar. Professors and students at the medieval universities came to form an order, or "estate," distinct from other social classes.

St. Andrews University grew. The original College of St. John was eclipsed by the new College of St. Salvator, founded by Bishop Kennedy in 1450. The powerful bishop built handsomely, almost on the scale of Oxford or Cambridge. And he provided for a hierarchy of theologians and artists: a doctor for provost of his college, a licentiate and a bachelor of theology, four priests who would be masters of arts and theological students, and six poor clerks, students of the arts and choristers. These thirteen members of the corporation would officiate at the collegiate church of the Holy Savior; also they would lecture and study. Thirty more chaplaincies were endowed by 1475. By the beginning of the sixteenth century, sixty to eighty undergraduates were studying at St. Salvator's.

Joining worship with the advancement of learning, St. Salvator's became the model for all higher studies in Scotland. The sharp tower of St. Salvator still dominates the town of St. Andrews, and eighteen generations of scholars have passed through the archway at its foot.

One hundred years after the founding of the university, a third foundation arose: the College of Poor Clerks of the Church of St. Andrews. Its purpose was to educate novices of the Augustinian order, so that St. Andrews Priory might be served by men of learning. In its charter of 1512, establishing this College of Poor Clerks, the decay of the Church in Scotland is mentioned. That affliction could not be hid: for pilgrims no longer came to the shrine of St. Andrew. Rather uneasily, in the college charter this disappearance of pilgrims was attributed to the total triumph of Christian belief: God no longer needs to work miracles at saints' shrines, when all believe in Him.

But in truth, the Scottish Church was deep in disrepute by 1512, and the lack of pilgrims resulted from lack of belief in miraculous cures. From its beginnings, this new St. Leonard's College (as it came to be called) grew out of the decay of faith. It would not be long before this college, meant for a bastion of orthodoxy, would become a nest of Reformers. The phrase "to drink of St. Leonard's well" would signify contagion by Calvinism.

Patrick Hamilton, the first Scots Protestant martyr of the Reformation, was a St. Leonard's man; he was sent to the stake for heresy only sixteen years after the founding of the college. The greatest of Scottish humanists, George Buchanan, a stern Reformer, became principal of St. Leonard's and tutor to the young king. Before St. Leonard's well ran dry, every remnant of the old order that created St. Leonard's had been extirpated.

In 1537, just before the outbreak of the Reformation, Archbishop Beaton secured a papal bull for yet another college, which he built upon the site of the original St. John's. This "College of the Assumption of the Blessed Virgin Mary" remained rigorously scholastic, the Archbishop disregarding the entreaties of the principal, who would have commenced humane studies—Latin, Greek, and Hebrew. The last Catholic primate of Scotland, Archbishop Hamilton, completed the college. Then the Reformation swept over the place, submerging St. Mary's College along with everything else. The archbishop who completed the building was taken in arms when the Reformers stormed Dumbarton Castle, and they hanged him in his canonical dress upon Stirling rock. After the triumph of the Reformers, the college was directed to the training of ministers, and it remains to this day the university's divinity school.

"The stones cry out to us as we pass," Sir D'Arcy Thompson writes of St. Andrews, "and tell us the story of our land, the chronicle of popes and kings, the history of the Old Church and the New."[33] Beside the University of Paris, he remarks, St. Andrews was a small foundation. Yet Scottish learning would be written large in America.

The northern universities had been created to serve the Church; soon, however, they would serve Renaissance and Reformation—and revolution. In the paving-stones of St. Andrews market place, a stone cross is traced. Here stood the medieval market-cross, and here Paul Craw was burnt in 1433.

Craw, a physician from Bohemia, had been sent by the Hussites of central Europe to disturb the Church in Scotland. The Hussites were social revolutionaries, as well as forerunners of the Protestant Reformers. Bishop Wardlaw, the university's founder, ran Craw to earth in the very year when teaching commenced at St. Andrews University. Urged on by two Schoolmen, the bishop sent Craw to the stake, where he died amidst the flames with a brass ball thrust into his mouth, that he might not harangue the crowd. But more men like Craw would come, as the university grew, and not all of them could be silenced.

In Scotland, as in Germany and other lands, the Reformation would rise out of the universities; so would the Renaissance, in most countries. Thus the Middle Ages' grand intellectual achievement, the universities, became the Middle Ages' undoing. Dante, near the end of medieval times, thought of the universities as a distinct estate equal in influence to State and Church. He called upon the universities to share in the restoration of the medieval order; but shortly after his time, they would turn instead to new modes of thought, soon producing new modes of action.

The half-dozen little American colleges of colonial times would be bare and narrow places, if contrasted with the medieval universities on which they were humbly modelled. Yet *veritas*, Truth, Harvard's motto, was a courageous echo of the high aspiration of the English and Scottish universities. There was more truth to be learned from medieval civilization, in its many aspects, than Harvard or William and Mary College knew at first. Even in its collapse, the medieval order passed on to America its vision of synthesis and harmony.

It is misleading to think chiefly of the Crusades, or of the Hundred Years' War, when one sees the words "Middle Ages." In medieval times, disorder broke out frequently, over that span of a thousand years; nevertheless there endured generally a concept of order that was a high vision, and sometimes the practical achievement of that long age was orderly. The attempt to achieve balance between the claims of Church and the claims of State; the development of civic liberties, of representative assemblies, and, in England, of the common law; the strong feeling of community in church, guild, town, and family—all these were the marks of a healthy culture, however rough its vigor. Renaissance and Reformation would not altogether deprive America of this medieval inheritance.

["The Light of the Middle Ages," The Roots of American Order, *3rd ed. (Washingon, DC: Regnery Gateway, 1991), 200–219.]*

❖

Civilization Without Religion?

Kirk wrote the following essay for a symposium on "Christianity in Sight of the Third Millennium" published in Modern Age: A Quarterly Review *(Summer 1990). Ours is an advanced state of decadence, he says, a liberal society that surrenders to appetites and illusions. What especially ails modern civilization is the loss of religious vision out of which culture arises and flourishes. Refusing to give in to society's religious decline, Kirk urges us to resist the evils that shake the foundations of a moral social order. Renewal and restoration are words that loom large in his final writings, especially in his book* Redeeming the Time *(1996) and its earlier companion volume* The Politics of Prudence *(1993). With the Hebrew prophet of righteousness, Amos (Kirk's own middle name), he implores his contemporaries to "Hate evil, love good; establish justice in the gate."*

Sobering voices tell us nowadays that the civilization in which we participate is not long for this world. Many countries have fallen under the domination of squalid oligarchs; other lands are reduced to anarchy. "Cultural revolution," rejecting our patrimony of learning and manners, has done nearly as much mischief in the West as in the East, if less violently. Religious belief is attenuated at best, for many—or else converted, after being secularized, into an instrument for social transformation. Books give way to television and videos; universities, intellectually democratized, are sunk to the condition of centers for job certification. An increasing proportion of the population, in America especially, is dehumanized by addiction to narcotics and insane sexuality.

These afflictions are only some of the symptoms of social and personal disintegration. One has but to look at our half-ruined American cities, with their ghastly rates of murder and rape, to perceive that we moderns lack the moral imagination and the right reason required to maintain tolerable community. Writers in learned quarterlies or in daily syndicated columns use the terms "post-Christian era" or "post-modern epoch" to imply that we are breaking altogether with our cultural past, and are entering upon some new age of a bewildering character.

Some people, the militant secular humanists in particular, seem pleased by this prospect; but yesteryear's meliorism is greatly weakened in most quarters. Even Marxist ideologues virtually have ceased to predict the approach of a Golden Age. To most observers, T. S. Eliot among them, it has seemed far more probable that we are stumbling into a new Dark Age, inhumane, merciless, a totalist political domination in which the life of spirit and the inquiring intellect will be denounced, harassed, and propagandized against: Orwell's *Nineteen Eighty-Four*, rather than Huxley's *Brave New World* of cloying sensuality. Or perhaps Tolkien's blasted and servile land of Mordor may serve as symbol of the human condition in the twenty-first century (which, however, may not be called the twenty-first century, the tag *Anno Domini* having been abolished as joined to one of the superstitions of the childhood of the race).

Some years ago I was sitting in the parlor of an ancient house in the close of York Minster. My host, Basil Smith, the Minster's Treasurer then, a man of learning and of faith, said to me that we linger at the end of an era; soon the culture we have known will be swept into the dustbin of history. About us, as we talked in that medieval mansion, loomed Canon Smith's tall bookcases lined with handsome volumes; his doxological clock chimed the half-hour musically; flames flared up in his fireplace. Was all this setting of culture, and much more besides, to vanish away as if the Evil Spirit had condemned it? Basil Smith is buried now, and so is much of the society he ornamented and tried to redeem. At the time I thought him too gloomy, but already a great deal that he foresaw has come to pass.

The final paragraph of Malcolm Muggeridge's essay "The Great Liberal Death Wish" must suffice as a summing-up of the human predicament at the end of the twentieth century.

"As the astronauts soar into the vast eternities of space," Muggeridge writes, "on earth the garbage piles higher; as the groves of academe extend their domain, their alumni's arms reach lower; as the phallic cult spreads, so does impotence. In great wealth, great poverty; in health, sickness; in numbers, deception. Gorging, left hungry; sedated, left restless; telling all, hiding all; in flesh united, forever separate. So we press on through the valley of abundance that leads to the wasteland of satiety, passing through the gardens of fantasy; seeking happiness ever more ardently, and finding despair ever more surely."

Just so. Such recent American ethical writers as Stanley Hauerwas and Alasdair MacIntyre concur in Muggeridge's verdict on the society of our time, concluding that nothing can be done, except for a remnant to gather in little "communities of character" while society slides toward its ruin. Over the past half-century, many other voices of reflective men and women have been heard to the same effect. Yet let us explore the question of whether a reinvigoration of our culture is conceivable.

Is the course of nations inevitable? Is there some fixed destiny for great states? In 1796, a dread year for Britain, old Edmund Burke declared that we cannot foresee the future; often the historical determinists are undone by the coming of events that nobody has predicted. At the very moment when some states "seemed plunged in unfathomable abysses of disgrace and disaster," Burke wrote in his *First Letter on a Regicide Peace*,

> they have suddenly emerged. They have begun a new course, and opened a new reckoning; and even in the depths of their calamity, and on the very ruins of their country, have laid the foundations of a towering and durable greatness. All this has happened without any apparent previous change in the general circumstances which had brought on their distress. The death of a man at a critical juncture, his disgust, his retreat, his disgrace, have brought innumerable calamities on a whole nation. A common soldier, a child, a girl at the door of an inn, have changed the face of fortune, and almost of Nature.

The "common soldier" to whom Burke refers is Arnold of Winkelried, who flung himself upon the Austrian spears to save his country; the child is the young Hannibal, told by his father to wage ruthless war upon Rome; the girl at the door of an inn is Joan of Arc. We do not know why such abrupt reversals or advances occur, Burke remarks; perhaps they are indeed the work of Providence.

"Nothing is, but thinking makes it so," the old adage runs. If most folk come to believe that our culture must collapse—why, then collapse it will.

Yet Burke, after all, was right in that dreadful year of 1796. For despite the overwhelming power of the French revolutionary movement in that year, in the long run Britain defeated her adversaries, and after the year 1812 Britain emerged from her years of adversity to the height of her power. Is it conceivable that American civilization, and in general what we call "Western civilization," may recover from the Time of Troubles that commenced in 1914 (so Arnold Toynbee instructs us) and in the twenty-first century enter upon an Augustan age of peace and restored order?

To understand these words "civilization" and "culture," the best book to read is T. S. Eliot's slim volume *Notes Towards the Definition of Culture*.

Once upon a time I commended that book to President Nixon, in a private discussion of modern disorders, as the one book which he ought to read for guidance in his high office. Man is the only creature possessing culture, as distinguished from instinct; and if culture is effaced, so is the distinction between man and the brutes that perish. "Art is man's nature," in Edmund Burke's phrase; and if the human arts, or culture, cease to be, then human nature ceases to be.

From what source did humankind's many cultures arise? Why, from cults. A cult is a joining together for worship—that is, the attempt of people to commune with a transcendent power. It is from association in the cult, the body of worshippers, that human community grows. This basic truth has been expounded in recent decades by such eminent historians as Christopher Dawson, Eric Voegelin, and Arnold Toynbee.

Once people are joined in a cult, cooperation in many other things becomes possible. Common defense, irrigation, systematic agriculture, architecture, the visual arts, music, the more intricate crafts, economic production and distribution, courts and government—all these aspects of a culture arise gradually from the cult, the religious tie.

Out of little knots of worshippers, in Egypt, the Fertile Crescent, India, or China, there grew up simple cultures; for those joined by religion can dwell together and work together in relative peace. Presently such simple cultures may develop into intricate cultures, and those intricate cultures into great civilizations. American civilization of our era is rooted, strange though the fact may seem to us, in tiny knots of worshippers in Palestine, Greece, and Italy, thousands of years ago. The enormous material achievements of our civilization have resulted, if remotely, from the spiritual insights of prophets and seers.

But suppose that the cult withers, with the elapse of centuries. What then of the culture that is rooted in the cult? What then of the civilization which is the culture's grand manifestation? For an answer to such uneasy questions, we can turn to a twentieth-century parable. Here I think of G. K. Chesterton's observation that all life being an allegory, we can understand it only in parable.

The author of my parable, however, is not Chesterton, but a quite different writer, the late Robert Graves, whom I once visited in Mallorca. I have in mind Graves's romance *Seven Days in New Crete*—published in America under the title *Watch the North Wind Rise*.

In that highly readable romance of a possible future, we are told that by the close of the "Late Christian epoch" the world will have fallen altogether, after a catastrophic war and devastation, under a collectivistic domination, a variant of Communism. Religion, the moral imagination, and nearly everything that makes life worth living have been virtually extirpated by ideology and nuclear war. A system of thought and government called Logicalism, "pantisocratic economics divorced from any religious or national theory," rules the world—for a brief time.

In Graves's words:

> Logicalism, hinged on international science, ushered in a gloomy and anti-poetic age. It lasted only a generation or two and ended with a grand defeatism, a sense of perfect futility, that slowly crept over the directors and managers of the regime. The common man had triumphed over his spiritual betters at last, but what was to follow? To what could he look forward with either hope or fear? By the abolition of sovereign states and the disarming of even the police forces, war had become impossible. No one who cherished any religious beliefs whatever, or was interested in sport, poetry, or the arts, was allowed to hold a position of public responsibility. "Ice-cold logic" was the most valued civic quality, and those who could not pretend to it were held of no account. Science continued laboriously to expand its over-large corpus of information, and the subjects of research grew more and more beautifully remote and abstract; yet the scientific obsession, so strong at the beginning of the third millennium A.D., was on the wane. Logicalist officials who were neither defeatist nor secretly religious and who kept their noses to the grindstone from a sense of duty, fell prey to colobromania, a mental disturbance. . . .

Rates of abortion and infanticide, of suicide, and other indices of social boredom rise with terrifying speed under this Logicalist regime. Gangs of young people go about robbing, beating, and murdering, for the sake of excitement. It appears that the human race will become extinct if such tendencies continue; for men and women find life not worth living under such a domination. The deeper longings of humanity have been outraged, so that the soul and the state stagger on the verge of final darkness. But in this crisis an Israeli Sophocrat writes a book called *A Critique of Utopias*, in which he examines seventy Utopian writings, from Plato to Aldous Huxley. "We must retrace our steps," he concludes, "or perish." Only by the resurrection of religious faith, the Sophocrats discover, can mankind be kept from total destruction; and that religion, as Graves describes it in his romance, springs from the primitive soil of myth and symbol.

Graves really is writing about our own age, not of some remote future: of life in today's United States and in the former Soviet Union. He is saying that culture arises from the cult; and that when belief in the cult has been wretchedly enfeebled, the culture will decay swiftly. The material order rests upon the spiritual order.

So it has come to pass, . . . in the closing years of the twentieth century. With the weakening of the moral order, "Things fall apart; / . . . Mere anarchy is loosed upon the world. . . ." The Hellenic and the Roman cultures went down to dusty death after this fashion. What may be done to achieve reinvigoration?

Some well-meaning folk talk of a "civil religion," a kind of cult of patriotism, founded upon a myth of national virtue and upon veneration of certain historic documents, together with a utilitarian morality. But such experiments of a secular character never have functioned satisfactorily; and it scarcely is necessary for me to point out the perils of such an artificial creed, bound up with nationalism: the example of the ideology of the National Socialist Party in Germany, half a century ago, may suffice. Worship of the state, or of the national commonwealth, is no healthy substitute for communion with transcendent love and wisdom.

Nor can attempts at persuading people that religion is "useful" meet with much genuine success. No man sincerely goes down his knees to the divine because he has been told that such rituals lead to the beneficial consequences of tolerably honest behavior in commerce. People will conform their actions to the precepts of religion only when they earnestly believe the doctrines of that religion to be true.

Still less can it suffice to assert that the Bible is an infallible authority on everything, literally interpreted, in defiance of the natural sciences and of other learned disciplines; to claim to have received private revelations from Jehovah; or to embrace some self-proclaimed mystic from the gorgeous East, whose teachings are patently absurd.

In short, the culture can be renewed only if the cult is renewed; and faith in divine power cannot be summoned up merely when that is found expedient. Faith no longer works wonders among us: one has but to glance at the typical church built nowadays, ugly and shoddy, to discern how architecture no longer is nurtured by the religious imagination. It is so in nearly all the works of twentieth-century civilization: the modern mind has been secularized so thoroughly that "culture" is assumed by most people to have no connection with the love of God.

How are we to account for this widespread decay of the religious impulse? It appears that the principal cause of the loss of the idea of the holy is the attitude called "scientism"—that is, the popular notion that the revelations of natural science, over the past century and a half or two centuries, somehow have proved that men and women are naked apes merely; that the ends of existence are production and consumption merely; that happiness is the gratification of sensual impulses; and that concepts of the resurrection of the flesh and the life everlasting are mere exploded superstitions. Upon these scientistic assumptions, public schooling in America is founded nowadays, implicitly.

This view of the human condition has been called—by C. S. Lewis, in particular—reductionism: it reduces human beings almost to mindlessness; it denies the existence of the soul. Reductionism has become almost an ideology. It is scientistic, but not scientific: for it is a far cry from the understanding of matter and energy that one finds in the addresses of Nobel prize winners in physics, say. Popular notions of "what science says" are archaic, reflecting the assertions of the scientists of the middle of the nineteenth century; such views are a world away from the writings of Stanley Jaki, the cosmologist and historian of science, who was awarded the Templeton Prize for progress in religion.

As Arthur Koestler remarks in his little book *The Roots of Coincidence*, yesterday's scientific doctrines of materialism and mechanism ought to be buried now with a requiem of electronic music. Once more, in biology as in physics, the scientific disciplines enter upon the realm of mystery.

Yet the great public always suffers from the affliction called cultural lag. If most people continue to fancy that scientific theory of a century ago is the verdict of serious scientists today, will not the religious understanding of life continue to wither, and civilization continue to crumble?

Perhaps; but the future is unknowable. Conceivably we may be given a Sign. Yet such an event, if it is to occur at all, is in the hand of God. Meanwhile, some reflective people declare that our culture must be reanimated, by a great effort of will.

More than forty years ago, that remarkable historian Christopher Dawson, in his book *Religion and Culture*, expressed this hard truth strongly. "The events of the last few years," Dawson wrote, "portend either the end of human history or a turning point in it. They have warned us in letters of fire that our civilization has been tried in the balance and found wanting—that there is an absolute limit to the progress that can be achieved by the perfectionment of scientific techniques detached from spiritual aims and moral values. . . . The recovery of moral control and the return to spiritual order have become the indispensable conditions of human survival. But they can be achieved only by a profound change in the spirit of modern civilization. This does not mean a new religion or a new culture but a movement of spiritual reintegration which would restore that vital relation between religion and culture which has existed at every age and on every level of human development."

Amen to that. The alternative to such a successful endeavor, a conservative endeavor, to reinvigorate our culture would be a series of catastrophic events, the sort predicted by Pitirim Sorokin and other sociologists, which eventually might efface our present sensate culture and bring about a new ideational culture, the character of which we cannot even imagine. Such an ideational culture doubtless would have its religion: but it might be the worship of what has been called the Savage God.

Such ruin has occurred repeatedly in history. When the classical religion ceased to move hearts and minds, two millennia ago, thus the Graeco-Roman civilization went down to Avernus. As my little daughter Cecilia put it unprompted, some years ago looking at a picture book of Roman history, "And then, at the end of a long summer's day, there came Death, Mud, Crud."

Great civilizations have ended in slime. Outside the ancient city of York, where York Minster stands upon the site of the Roman praetorium, there lies a racecourse known as the Knavesmire. Here in medieval time were buried the knaves—the felons and paupers. When, a few years ago, the racecourse was being enlarged, the diggers came upon a Roman graveyard beneath, or in part abutting upon, the medieval burial ground. This appeared to have been a cemetery of the poor of Romano-British times. Few valuable artifacts were uncovered, but the bones were of interest. Many of the people there interred, in the closing years of Roman power in Britain, had been severely deformed, apparently suffering from rickets and other afflictions—deformed spines and limbs and skulls. Presumably they had suffered lifelong, and died, from extreme malnutrition. At the end, decadence comes down to that, for nearly everybody.

It was at York that the dying Septimius Severus, after his last campaign (against the Scots), was asked by his brutal sons, Geta and Caracalla, "Father, when you are gone, how shall we govern the empire?" The hard old emperor had his laconic reply ready: "Pay the soldiers. The rest do not matter." There would come a time when the soldiers could not be paid, and then civilization would fall to pieces. The last Roman army in Italy—it is said to have been composed entirely of cavalry—fought in league with the barbarian general Odoacer against Theodoric, King of the Ostrogoths, in the year 491; on Odoacer's defeat, the Roman soldiers drifted home, nevermore to take arms: the end of an old song. Only the earlier stages of social decadence seem liberating to some people; the last act, as Cecilia Kirk perceived, consists of Death, Mud, Crud.

In short, it appears to me that our culture labors in an advanced state of decadence; that what many people mistake for the triumph of our civilization actually consists of powers that are disintegrating our culture; that the vaunted "democratic freedom" of liberal society in reality is servitude to appetites and illusions which attack religious belief; which destroy community through excessive centralization and urbanization; which efface life-giving tradition and custom.

History has many cunning passages, contrived corridors
And issues, deceives with whispering ambitions,
Guides us by vanities.

So Gerontion instructs us, in T. S. Eliot's famous grim poem. By those and some succeeding lines, Eliot means that human experience lived without the Logos, the Word; lived merely by the asserted knowledge of empirical science—why, history in that sense is a treacherous gypsy witch. Civilizations that reject or abandon the religious imagination must end, as did Gerontion, in fractured atoms.

In conclusion, it is my argument that the elaborate civilization we have known stands in peril; that it may expire of lethargy, or be destroyed by violence, or perish, from a combination of both evils. We who think that life remains worth living ought to address ourselves to means by which a restoration of our culture may be achieved. A prime necessity for us is to restore an apprehension of religious insights in our clumsy apparatus of public instruction, which—bullied by militant secular humanists and presumptuous federal courts—has been left with only ruinous answers to the ultimate questions.

What ails modern civilization? Fundamentally, our society's affliction is the decay of religious belief. If a culture is to survive and flourish, it must not be severed from the religious vision out of which it arose. The high necessity of reflective men and women, then, is to labor for the restoration of religious teachings as a credible body of doctrine.

"Redeem the time; redeem the dream," T. S. Eliot wrote. It remains possible, given right reason and moral imagination, to confront boldly the age's disorders. The restoration of true learning, humane and scientific; the reform of many public policies; the renewal of our awareness of a transcendent order, and of the presence of an Other; the brightening of the corners where we find ourselves—such approaches are open to those among the rising generation who look for a purpose in life. It is just conceivable that we may be given a Sign . . . , yet Sign or no Sign, a Remnant must strive against the follies of the time.

["Civilization Without Religion?" Redeeming the Time, *edited by Jeffrey O. Nelson (Wilmington, DE: Intercollegiate Studies Institute, 1996), 3–15.]*

❖

The Rarity of the God-Fearing Man

"Without a knowledge of fear, we cannot know order in personality or society." "To fear to commit evil, and to hate what is abominable, is the mark of manliness." "What raises up heroes and martyrs is the fear of God." The aphoristic forcefulness of these statements distinguishes this essay. Fashionable opinions, enlightened education, the media elites, liberation theology, political radicalism emerge as allies bent on extinguishing what Rudolf Otto calls "the idea of the holy" in the moral and religious order of life and faith. Post-Christian man has been persuaded by the followers of neoterism and meliorism to renounce the fear of the Lord. We purchase freedom from fear, Kirk says, at the cost of our spiritual impoverishment. The God of our fathers is thus diminished in majesty and power, reshaped into vulgar images of devotion, subservient to the doctrine of progress and to profane attitudes contemptuous of our biblical patrimony.

A Michigan farmer, some years ago, climbed to the roof of his silo, and there he painted, in great red letters that the Deity could see, "The fear of the Lord is the beginning of wisdom." These words are on that roof yet. When in his cups, which was often enough, that farmer thrashed his daughter to fill her with a holy terror.

In his way, I suppose, the drunken brute did fear God. Surviving the thrashings, his daughter grew to be a woman; and though she did not much fancy her father's company, she lived as decent a life as most. Her upbringing, bad though it was, may have been better than the formative years of the average American child nowadays, "permissively" reared. To the permitted brat with the permissive parents, few appetites are denied, and he grows up ignorant of the norms of human existence. Never learning in childhood that certain things exist which we ought to fear, he slides into physical maturity, bored, flabby in character, and moved by irrational impulses toward violence and defiance, the consequence of a profound disorder in personality.

Without a knowledge of fear, we cannot know order in personality or society. Fear forms an ineluctable part of the human condition. Fear lacking, hope and aspiration fail. To demand for mankind "freedom from fear," as politically attainable, was a silly piece of demagogic sophistry. If, *per impossibile*, fear were wiped altogether out of our lives, we would be desperately bored, yearning for old or new terrors; vegetating, we would cease to be human beings. A child's fearful joy in stories of goblins, witches, and ghosts is a natural yearning after the challenge of the dreadful: raw head and bloody bones, in one form or another, the imagination demands. From the great instinct to survive, to struggle, to triumph, comes the urge to contend with fear.

And there are things which rightfully we ought to fear, if we are to enjoy any dignity as men. When, in an age of smugness and softness, fear has been pushed temporarily into the dark corners of personality and society, then soon the gods of the copybook headings with fire and sword return. To fear to commit evil, and to hate what is abominable, is the mark of manliness. "They will never love where they ought to love," Burke says, "who do not hate where they ought to hate." It may be added that they will never dare when they ought to dare, who do not fear when they ought to fear.

Time was when there lay too heavy upon man that fear of the Lord which is the beginning of wisdom. Soul-searching can sink into morbidity, and truly conscience can make cowards of us all. Scotland in the seventeenth century, for instance, tormented itself into a kind of spiritual hypochondria by an incessant melancholy fawning upon the Lord's favor. But no such age is ours.

Forgetting that there exists such a state as salutary dread, modern man has become spiritually foolhardy. His bravado, I suspect, will stand the test no better than ancient Pistol's. He who admits no fear of God is really a post-Christian man; for at the heart of Judaism and Christianity lies a holy dread. And a good many people, outwardly and perhaps inwardly religious—

for *religio* implies the cult, the common worship, the binding together, rather than the relationship between the Almighty and lonely man—today deny the reality of reverential fear, and thus are post-Christian without confessing it.

Christianity always was a scandal; and I rather think I began to fear God because I discovered that terror to be so unconventional, impractical, and off-color in our era. (Men are moved in divers ways, and belief actually will follow action.) Before I began to think much on the spiritual diseases of our century, I revolted against the disgusting smugness of modern America—particularly the complacency of professors and clergymen, the flabby clerisy of a sensate time. Once I found myself in a circle of scholars who were discussing solemnly the conditions necessary for arriving at scientific truth. Chiefly from a perverse impulse to shock this Academy of Lagado, perhaps, I muttered, "We have to begin with the dogma that the fear of God is the beginning of wisdom."

I succeeded in scandalizing. Some gentlemen and scholars took this for indecent levity; others, unable to convince themselves that anyone could mean this literally, groped for the presumptive allegorical or symbolical meaning behind my words. But two or three churchgoers in the gathering were not displeased. These were given to passing the collection plate and to looking upon the church as a means to social reform; incense, vestments, and the liturgy have their aesthetic charms, even among doctors of philosophy. Faintly pleased, yes, these latter professors, to hear the echo of fife and drum ecclesiastic; but also embarrassed at such radicalism. "Oh no," they murmured, "not the *fear* of God. You mean the *love* of God, don't you?"

For them the word of Scripture was no warrant, their Anglo-Catholicism notwithstanding. With Henry Ward Beecher, they were eager to declare that God is Love—though hardly a love which passes all understanding. Theirs was a thoroughly permissive God the Father, properly instructed by Freud. Looking upon their mild and diffident faces, I wondered how much trust I might put in such love as they knew. Their meekness was not that of Moses. Meek before Jehovah, Moses had no fear of Pharoah; but these doctors of the schools, much at ease in Zion, were timid in the presence of a traffic policeman. Although convinced that God is too indulgent to punish much of anything, they were given to trembling before Caesar. Christian love is the willingness to sacrifice oneself; yet I would not have counted upon these gentlemen to adventure anything of consequence for my sake, nor even for those with greater claims upon them. I doubted whether the Lord would adventure much on their behalf: the vessels for dishonor are not necessarily the sots of

Skid Row. If, for instance, there should come a moment in which these particular churchgoers should be confronted with the squalid oligarchs of our time, the gauleiters and the commissars—why, I would look for precious little sacrifice from them. Theirs was a light love. Gauleiters and commissars? Why, their fellowship and charity were not proof against a dean or a divisional head.

"Me supreme Wisdom and primal Love sustain": this is the legend above the gate of the Inferno. The great grim Love which makes Hell a part of the nature of things, my colleagues could not apprehend. And, lacking knowledge of that Love, at once compassionate and retributive, their sort may bring us presently to a terrestrial hell, which is the absence of God from the affairs of men—with certain unattractive personal and social consequences.

In ceasing to fear God, their sort would find themselves, soon or late, naked before earthly frights; in mistaking God for a Sunday-afternoon dad reading the comics, or for a progressive kindergarten teacher, they would dawdle down the path to the bushes at the bottom of the garden—and find behind the prickly pear the King of Terrors. The guillotine made a Christian of the mocking La Harpe; the humanitarian professor made a God-fearing man of me.

Religiosity, or at least a festive and indolent and church-plate-passing Sabbatarianism, is sufficiently established in our America. But the God-fearing man is sufficiently rare among us, and not noticeably welcome in pulpit or pew. I have known of ministers given the sack by their congregations for fretting overmuch about the wrath of the Lord; indeed, there is ample precedent for this, Jonathan Edwards, our only theologian of mark, having been pushed into the backwoods for precisely such excess of zeal. Not many among us subscribe to James Fitzjames Stephen's concept of God, though it is orthodox enough:

> I think of [this Being] as conscious and having will, as infinitely powerful, and as one who, whatever lie may be in his own nature, has so arranged the world or worlds in which I live as to let me know that virtue is the law which he has prescribed to me and to others. If still further asked, Can you love such a Being? I should answer, Love is not the word which I should choose, but awe. The law under which we live is stern, and, as far as we can judge, inflexible, but it is noble and excites a feeling of awful respect for its Author and for the constitution established in the world which it governs, and a sincere wish to act up to and carry it out as far as possible. If we believe in God at all, this, I think, is the rational and manly way of thinking of him.[34]

With Stephen's description of God as judge, it is not unprofitable to contrast the vision of the Lord vouchsafed to a certain immensely rich and well-known living American, eminently successful in business and politics. This gentleman freely confesses that he is not wholly a self-made man: God loves him and has helped him on his way. "God always has his arm around my shoulder." As a species of junior partner, God has been properly permissive and submissive. Our successful American does not fear God. Why in Heaven's name should he? God knows his place.

Every age portrays God in the image of its poetry and its politics. In one century, God is an absolute monarch, exacting his due; in another century, still an absolute sovereign, but a benevolent despot; again, perhaps a grand gentleman among aristocrats; at a different time, a democratic president, with an eye to the ballot box. It has been said that to many of our generation, God is a Republican and works in a bank; but this image is giving way, I think, to God as Chum—at worst, God as a playground supervisor. So much for the images. But in reality God does not alter.

Because the graven image deludes, it is forbidden. Yet a mental image of some sort men demand, in any time. C. S. Lewis tells of a small girl who, on inquiring of her parents what God looked like, was carefully informed that God is a Perfect Substance. To the girl, a Perfect Substance meant tapioca pudding; and since she detested tapioca pudding, she grew up with a marked prejudice against God. God the patriarch, with the flowing white beard, is perhaps as true an image as little girls or big ones are likely to hit upon. The deceptive image, formed by our petty preferences in taste or politics, may do remarkable mischief. And God the Chum, never to be dreaded because He is indiscriminately affectionate—even promiscuous—may be a more treacherous idol, and more potent for the destruction of personality and of the civil social order, than the vision of God that had Agag hewed in pieces.

If in Scripture one thing is beyond dispute, it is the injunction to fear God. But in this enlightened era it is almost blasphemous to whisper this awkward doctrine in the sensitive ears of churchgoing folk. A vulgarized Pelagianism proscribes the description of sinners in the hands of an angry God; and, correspondingly, the idea of a retributive Providence is out of fashion. So far as Providence really is credited at all by most professed Christians . . . , that Providence is regularly beneficent, dispensing fur coats and Jaguars. Hints to the contrary are more often encountered in the writings of philosophical historians than in sermons. It must come as a shock to many positivistic professors of history to read professor Herbert Butterfield's account of the workings of Providence; for Butterfield's is the archaic, orthodox, calm, and ultimately hopeful view that Providence is the operation of laws made for man, immutable and at least as often destructive as rewarding. "If atomic research should by some accident splinter and destroy this whole globe tomorrow," Mr. Butterfield writes in his *Christianity in History*,

> I imagine that it will hurt us no more than that "death on the road" under the menace of which we pass every day of our lives. It will only put an end to a globe which we always knew was doomed to a bad end in any case. I am not sure that it would not be typical of human history if—assuming that the world was bound some day to cease to be a possible habitation for living creatures—men should by their own contrivance hasten that end and anticipate the operation of nature or of time—because it is so much in the character of Divine judgment in history that men are made to execute it upon themselves.[35]

Yes, this has become unpopular doctrine. Despite the catastrophes of our century, despite the evidence of the newspapers that the fountains of the great deep are broken up, the meliorism of the Enlightenment—now what the sociologists call a cultural lag, but none the less pervasive for that—still dominates all classes of modern society. In some quarters, it has assumed the ideological form of apocalyptic Marxism; in others, the garments of a "progressive people's capitalism," with its "revolution of rising expectations"; or it may be blended with the "Freudian ethic," managing somehow to reconcile with the womb-gloom of Freud a cheerful confidence that all will be well if only we soothe and adjust and recognize or liberate repressed desires—and pay the psychiatrist. This obsolete but persistent meliorism inspires the rosy dreams of a universal political system, to be attained almost instanter by the United Nations Organization or some other instrument, despite the clearly centrifugal motion of twentieth-century nationalism.

Probably the most influential popularizer of these notions was John Stuart Mill, with his conviction that if only want, disease, and war should be abolished—through economic progress and positive law—the human condition would be hunky-dory. Mill, rather than St. Augustine, is the authority for post-Christian man; and Stephen's concept of God was inconceivable to Mill. How can we fear what rationalism cannot demonstrate?

"Do you feel happy inside?" asks the modern young minister in Marquand's *Women and Thomas Harrow* (1958). That clergyman himself is trapped into confessing that he often does not feel happy inside; but it never would do to let slip such heresies from the pulpit. What renewed consciousness of the need for fearing the Lord as has been expressed in our century, often has come from quarters notoriously unclerical. We find, for instance, a striking passage in Bernard Shaw's preface to *Back to Methuselah* (1922): "Goodnatured unambitious men," Shaw observes, "are cowards when they have no religion." Before the spectacle of half of Europe being kicked to death by the other half, they stare in helpless horror, or are persuaded by the newspapers that this is a sound commercial investment and an act of divine justice:

> They are dominated and exploited not only by greedy and often half-witted and half-alive weaklings who will do anything for cigars, champagne, motor cars, and the more childish and selfish uses of money, but by able and sound administrators who can do nothing else with them than dominate and exploit them. Government and exploitation become synonymous under such circumstances; and the world is finally ruled by the childish, the brigands, and the blackguards.

Such is the post-Christian man, contemptuous of God but fearful of everything else, for whom Shaw would have invented a new sort of faith. Politically, the man who does not fear God is prey to the squalid oligarchs; and this is no paradox. What raises up heroes and martyrs is the fear of God. Beside the terror of God's judgment, the atrocities of the totalist tyrant are pinpricks. A God-intoxicated man, knowing that divine love and divine wrath are but different aspects of a unity, is sustained against the worst this world can do to him; while the good-natured unambitious man, lacking religion, fearing no ultimate judgment, denying that he is made for eternity, has in him no iron to maintain order and justice and freedom.

Mere enlightened self-interest will submit to any strong evil. In one aspect or another, fear insists upon forcing itself into our lives. If the fear of God is obscured, then obsessive fear of suffering, poverty, and sickness will come to the front; or if a well-cushioned state keeps most of these worries at bay, then the tormenting neuroses of modern man, under the labels of "insecurity" and "anxiety" and "constitutional inferiority," will be the dominant mode of fear. And these latter forms of fear are the more dismaying, for there are disciplines by which one may diminish one's fear of God. But to remedy the causes of fear from the troubles of our time is beyond the power of the ordinary individual; and to put the neuroses to sleep, supposing any belief in a transcendent order to be absent, there is only the chilly comfort of the analyst's couch or the tranquillizing drug.

By the fashionable philodoxies of our modern era, by our dominant system of education, by the tone of the serious and the popular press, by the assumptions of the politicians, by most of the sermons to the churchgoers, post-Christian man has been persuaded to do what man always has longed to do—that is, to forget the fear of the Lord. And with that fear have also departed his wisdom and his courage. Only a ferocious drunken farmer is unenlightened enough to affirm a primary tenet of religion in great red letters, and he does not know its meaning. Freedom from fear, if I read St. John aright, is one of the planks in the platform of the Antichrist. But that freedom is delusory and evanescent, and is purchased only at the cost of spiritual and political enslavement. It ends at Armageddon. So in our time, as Yeats saw,

> *Things fall apart; the centre cannot hold;*
> *Mere anarchy is loosed upon the world,*
> *The blood-dimmed tide is loosed, and everywhere*
> *The ceremony of innocence is drowned;*
> *The best lack all conviction, while the worst*
> *Are full of passionate intensity.*

Lacking conviction that the fear of the Lord is the beginning of wisdom, the captains and the kings yield to the fierce ideologues, the merciless adventurers, the charlatans and the metaphysically mad. And then, truly, when the stern and righteous God of fear and love has been denied, the Savage God lays down his new commandments.

Sincere God-fearing men, I believe, are now a scattered remnant. Yet as it was with Isaiah, so it may yet be with us, that disaster brings consciousness of that stubborn remnant and brings, too, a renewed knowledge of the source of wisdom. Truth and hardihood may find a lodging in some modern hearts when the new schoolmen and the parsons, or some of them, are brought to confess that it is a terrible thing to be delivered into the hands of the living God.

In a Michigan college town stands an immense quasi-Gothic church building, and the sign upon the porch informs the world that this is "The People's Church, Nondenominational and Nonsectarian." Sometimes, passing by, a friend of mine murmurs, "The People's Church—formerly God's." In The People's Church, the sermons have to do with the frightful evils of beer and cigarettes; all too probably, such townsfolk as are not present on the Sabbath have sunk themselves in these sins; and the congregation is congratulated by their pastor on their godliness in occupying the pews. A heavy complacency glows faintly in the eyes of these good people.

From The People's Church, the fear of God, with its allied wisdom, has been swept away. So have I. Who could fear a teetotaling, nonsmoking, nondenominational, nonsectarian God? Not the professors and the shopkeepers and the landladies of this happy college town. If by any amazing chance they ever should find themselves in God's hands—which is beyond reason, since they know that the real purpose of the church is merely to serve as a moral police—the members of this virtuous congregation, surely, would simply be patted and soothed like spaniels.

From this post-Christian church the fear of God, together with the odor of sanctity, has been cleansed quite away. In the cleansing, the college has assisted. Within the doors there remains, spiritually considered, only a vacuum—which nature abhors. Presently something will fill that vacuum; and it may be a rough beast, its hour come round at last, with the stench of death in its fur.

["The Rarity of the God-Fearing Man," The Intemperate Professor and Other Cultural Splenetics *(Baton Rouge, LA: Louisiana State University Press, 1965), 73–81.]*

❖

The Necessity for a General Culture

"The Necessity for a General Culture" is the first chapter in America's British Culture *(1993), in which book Kirk surveys "the dominant British culture of North America." In the past half century, he finds, the fundamental constituents of British culture in America have come under attack by those who would divorce democratic culture from the values of higher culture. Whatever the ethnic and racial origins of Americans happen to be, the bastions of their culture are British in principle, of which the English language and literature are an enduring legacy. Rule of law, American common law, and positive law derive from English law, even as forms of representative government derive from English institutions. In an age when, as José Ortega y Gasset wrote in* The Revolt of the Masses *(1930), "The mass crushes beneath it everything that is different, everything that is excellent, individual, qualified and select," an active defense of a viable culture is required.*

What Does "Culture" Mean?

This slim book is a summary account of the culture that the people of the United States have inherited from Britain. Sometimes this is called the Anglo-Saxon culture—although it is not simply English, for much in British culture has had its origins in Scotland, Ireland, and Wales. So dominant has British culture been in America, north of the Rio Grande, from the seventeenth century to the present, that if somehow the British elements could be eliminated from all the cultural patterns of the United States—why, Americans would be left with no coherent culture in public or in private life.

When we employ this word *culture*, what do we signify by it? Does "culture" mean refinement and learning, urbanity and good taste? Or does this "culture" mean the folkways of a people? Nowadays the word may be employed in either of the above significations; nor are these different meanings necessarily opposed one to the other.

Our English word *culture* is derived from the Latin word *cultus*, which to the Romans signified both tilling the soil and worshipping the divine. In the beginning, culture arises from the cult: that is, people are joined together in worship, and out of their religious association grows the organized human community. Common cultivation of crops, common defense, common laws, cooperation in much else—these are the rudiments of a people's culture. If that culture succeeds, it may grow into a civilization.

During the past half-century, such eminent historians as Christopher Dawson, Eric Voegelin, and Arnold Toynbee have described the close connections between religion and culture. As Dawson put it in his Gifford Lectures of 1947,

> A social culture is an organized way of life which is based on a common tradition and conditioned by a common environment. . . . It is clear that a common way of life involves a common view of life, common standards of behavior and common standards of value, and consequently a culture is a spiritual community which owes its unity to common beliefs and common ways of thought far more than to any unanimity of physical type. . . . Therefore from the beginning the social way of life which is culture has been deliberately ordered and directed in accordance with the higher laws of life which are religion.[36]

Dawson gives us here a quasi-anthropological definition of culture. At the beginning of the twentieth century, historians and men of letters would have raised their eyebrows at this sociological approach. The principal dictionaries of nine decades ago offered diverse definitions of the word—the agricultural meaning, the biological one, the bacteriological one, and others; but the common apprehension of *culture* ran much like this: "The result of mental cultivation, or the state of being cultivated; refinement or enlightenment; learning and taste; in a broad sense, civilization, as, a man of *culture*."

This latter employment of the word, connoting personal achievement of high standards in manners, taste, and knowledge, conjuring up the image of the virtuoso, is not archaic today. But the prevailing anthropological understanding of the word signifies the many elements which a people develop in common. We may take as a working anthropological definition that offered by H. J. Rose, in a footnote to his *Handbook of Latin Literature* (1936).

"By 'culture' is meant simply a mode of communal life characteristically human, *i.e.*, beyond the capacity of any beast," Rose writes. "Refinement and civilization are not implied, although not excluded. Thus we may speak alike of the 'culture' of the Australian blacks and of the modern French, distinguishing them as lower and higher respectively."[37]

To apprehend the relationships between "culture" as the word is employed by anthropologists and "culture" as that word is understood by the champions of high achievements in mind and art, we may turn to the chief poet of this century, T. S. Eliot. Since fairly early in the nineteenth century, reflective men and women have tended to regard this latter sort of culture as something to be sought after. Just what is it that the champions of culture seek? Why, "improvement of the human mind and spirit."[38]

Eliot suggests that this high culture consists of a mingling of manners, aesthetic attainment, and intellectual attainment. He argues too that we should regard culture in three senses, that is, whether we have in mind the development of an individual, or the development of a group or class, or the development of a whole society.

As Eliot explains, the different types of culture are interdependent. The question is not really one of conflict between "democratic" and "aristocratic" modes of culture. A nation's culture may be diverse, seemingly; yet the personal culture cannot long survive if cut off from the culture of a group or class. Nor may the high culture of a class endure if the popular culture is debased, or if the popular culture is at odds with personal and class cultures.

"Cultural disintegration is present when two or more strata so separate that these become in effect distinct cultures, and also when culture at the upper group level breaks into fragments each of which represents one cultural activity alone," Eliot writes. "If I am not mistaken, some disintegration of the classes in which culture is, or should be, most highly developed, has already taken place in western society—as well as some cultural separation between one level of society and another. Religious thought and practice, philosophy and art, all tend to become isolated areas cultivated by groups in no communication with each other."[39]

With increased speed, that lamentable process of disintegration and separation has continued since Eliot wrote those sentences . . . decades ago; it is especially conspicuous in American higher education. If the decay goes far enough, in the long run a society's culture sinks to a low level; or the society may fall apart altogether. We Americans live . . . in an era when the general outlines and institutions of our inherited culture still are recognizable; yet it does not follow that our children or our grandchildren . . . will retain a great part of that old culture.

To resume T. S. Eliot's argument, any healthy culture is represented at its higher levels by a class or body of persons of remarkable intelligence and taste, leaders in mind and conscience. Often such persons inherit their positions as guardians of culture; to borrow a phrase from Edmund Burke, these are the men and women who have been reared in "the unbought grace of life."

Either within such a cultured class, or sometimes temporarily outside it, there should be found individuals of cultural attainments whose private talents may contribute much to the improvement of the human mind and spirit. Yet such persons cannot be expected to sustain culture on their own shoulders somehow, Atlas-like, if they lack the support of a class or group, or if the tendency of the great mass of people is in an opposite direction. As Eliot puts it, "People are always ready to consider themselves persons of culture, on the strengths of one proficiency, when they are not only lacking in others, but blind to those they lack."[40]

Beyond the men and women of personal culture, beyond the high culture of class or group, lies the democratic culture of the folk—if we are to speak, like anthropologists, of cultural folkways. The popular culture ordinarily has had its origins, perhaps long ago, in the concepts and customs of a cultural aristocracy, much as the Children of Israel received their culture from Moses and Aaron. And yet once cultural beliefs, traits, conventions, and institutions have taken hold among a people, the most ardent and able adherents and defenders of an inherited culture may be obscure men and women, members of the democratic culture, who maintain the good old cause.

But if the mass culture, the democratic culture, becomes much alienated from the culture of the educated classes—why, presently the mass culture falls into decadence. That has been happening swiftly in recent decades, in America and elsewhere. Thomas Molnar, in his recent book *Twin Powers*, describes the consequences:

> *Culture* has come to mean, of course, anything that happens to catch the fancy of a group: rock concerts, supposedly for the famished of the third world; the drug culture and other subcultures; sects and cults; sexual excess and aberration; blasphemy on stage and screen; frightening and obscene shapes; the plastic wrapping of the Pont-Neuf or the California coast; to smashing of the family and other institutions; the display of the queer, abject, the sick. These instant products, meant to provide instant satisfaction to a society itself unmoored from foundation and tradition, accordingly deny the work of mediation and maturation and favor the incoherent, the shapeless and the repulsive.[41]

Dr. Molnar adds that if this sort of culture "spreads out in movie-house, museum, festival, press, and university, the reason may be that it embodies society's ideal." Here Molnar is writing of what commonly is called the counterculture—an anticulture which may extend to the very people who are supposed to set high cultural standards. This revolt against inherited culture often hardens into a detestation of those classes and groups, and their standards, which once upon a time shaped the thought and the taste of the whole society. Eliot touches upon this ideological hostility toward any sort of superior culture.

"It is commonly assumed," Eliot puts it, "that there is culture, but that it is the property of a small section of society; and from this assumption it is usual to proceed to one of two conclusions: either that culture can only be the concern of a small minority, and that therefore there is no place for it in the society of the future: or that in the society of the future the culture which has been the possession of the few must be put at the disposal of everybody."[42]

The preferences, mores, and customs that make up the democratic culture used to find their sanction in the judgment of individuals of remarkable talents, or in the manners and attitudes of a class or group of arbiters of culture. For instance, if Chaucer still is taught in some degree in America's public schools, that is not because the Common Teacher or the Common Pupil instinctively recognizes Chaucer's merits; rather, it is because, a good while ago, the people who make up school curricula and publish school textbooks decided that Chaucer ought to be studied, being a great author of historical importance; and so Chaucer has lingered on, as of "cultural value," despite large changes in the schools. If directors of curricula and publishers of textbooks should decide tomorrow to delete Geoffrey Chaucer, the democratic culture of the Representative Parent would not restore poor Chaucer; indeed, the Representative Parent might sigh with relief at the expulsion of the funny old fellow who couldn't write real English.

The culture of the crowd, then, is dependent in the long run upon the culture of the man of genius and the culture of the educated classes. It is equally true that the cultured individual and the cultured class cannot prevail—indeed, cannot survive—if a great wall of separation should be erected between them and the mass of people. What happens to a talented musicologist, say, when ninety-five percent of the rising generation have been subjected in their formative years to acid rock, and have paid no attention whatsoever to the music of elevation and order? What happens to the class of professors of literature, say, when the accustomed reading of most of their male students has been *Playboy* and *Penthouse*?

A received culture may be betrayed by the talented individual or the culturally schooled class of men and women, quite as fatally as by the crowd. A musicologist who casts aside the great composers of the eighteenth and nineteenth centuries out of his enthusiasm for electronic dissonance; a professor of humane letters who lectures obsessively on the perverse in literature—such persons are false to their duty of upholding certain norms of culture. And any hungry sheep of the democratic culture who happen to look up at these mentors—why, if they are fed, it is upon the inedible or the putrescent.

It will not suffice for us who enjoy the old received culture to seek refuge in the embrace of Common, or Popular, Culture. For the Common Culture commonly decides to do tomorrow what the Uncommon Culture does today; or, worse, the Common Culture, bewildered, converts itself into the Common Counterculture. The defense of inherited culture must be conducted here and now, with what weapons may be snatched from the walls—here on this darkling plain at the end of the twentieth century. With Eliot, we conduct

> *. . . a raid on the inarticulate*
> *With shabby equipment always deteriorating. . . .*

A nation's traditional culture can endure only if the several elements that compose it admit an underlying unity or fidelity to a common cause. The high culture and the common culture, of necessity, are interdependent; so are the national culture and the regional culture. What American culture urgently requires just now is solidarity: that is, a common front against the operations of Chaos and old Night.

The Enemies of Inherited Culture

"Down with Euroculture!" During the past several years, strident voices have been crying that commination in many states of the Union. The adversaries of the dominant culture in the United States demand that in American schooling, and in American life generally, Eurocentric assumptions must be supplanted by a "multiculture" emphasizing the cultural achievements of "African Americans, Asian Americans, Puerto Ricans/Latinos, and Native Americans." (This list of "minorities" is found in an official report of a task force appointed by the educational commissioner of the State of New York.) The culture of women also is incorporated in some demands for a cultural revolution in America—despite the fact that America's dominant higher culture already, in considerable part, is sustained by intelligent and conscientious women.

Of course it is true that into the culture, the British culture, of North America have entered large elements, in the nineteenth and twentieth centuries, of other major cultures, chiefly from Europe—but also, and increasingly, from China, Japan, the Levant, Mexico, Puerto Rico, and (quite recently) Korea and Indochina. But these and other cultures from abroad have been peacefully incorporated into the dominant British culture of North America. Even Mexican culture, which soon may be the biggest minority ethnic bloc in the United States, commonly is woven into the fabric of American society—after the passage of a single generation.

Now American society is imperfect, as is everything else here below. Yet the transplanted culture of Britain in America has been one of humankind's more successful achievements. The United States today is flooded with immigrants, lawful or unlawful, eager to enjoy the security, prosperity, freedom, and cultural opportunities of America. America's successes, substantially, have been made possible by the vigor of the British culture that most Americans now take for granted. Who, then, are the people desiring to pull down this dominant culture and set up in its place some amorphous "multiculture"?

One does not find the Vietnamese, or other Asiatics who have taken refuge in America, complaining about "cultural oppression." Most of them swiftly and intelligently adapt themselves to American culture. Most Spanish-surname Americans do not deny the merits of European civilization. Of "Native Americans," only a handful pretend to desire some sort of return to their ancestors' folkways of the eighteenth century. One hears no cultural howls of rage from Eskimo or Aleut.

In truth, the adversaries of America's dominant culture may be classified in three categories: certain militant blacks; white radicals, mostly "civil rights" zealots of yesteryear; and a mob of bored, indolent students to whom any culture but pop culture is anathema. Near the close of the twentieth century, the hardest haters of inherited high culture are to be found within the Academy—embittered ideologues, their character warped in the turbulent sixties, whose ambition it is to pull down whatever has long been regarded as true and noble. On nearly every campus, some of the purported guardians of culture have become the destroyers of culture. Ratlike, they gnaw at the foundations of society—quite as Karl Marx admonished intellectuals to do. At bottom, this "Down with Euroculture!" is the symptom of an intellectual disease that has been festering for a quarter of a century and longer.

The malign silliness of the academic radicals' shrieks is sufficiently suggested by their complaint that most books prescribed for college reading were written by "dead white males"—as if one might alter retroactively the pigmentation and the gender of William Shakespeare or Isaac Newton. This is like endeavoring to repeal the law of gravity, or to annul all human history. (Newton is mentioned here because the denouncers of "Euroculture" declare that the scientific departments, too, must be purged of racism, sexism, and the dread sin of Eurocentrism.)

Much in American education requires improvement. Indeed oppression exists in the typical curriculum; but it is the tyranny of Giant Dullness, not the despotism of White Capitalistic Exploitation. So Multiculturalists' denunciation of existing educational programs sometimes hits the mark. Yet what would the multiculturalist champions of the intellectual rights of blacks, Latinos, and American Indians bestow upon high school and college by way of substitutions? Apparently an omnium-gatherum, in American history, of incidents of oppression of minorities or of "minority" heroism, mingled with ideological denunciations of the American Republic. They would erect historical falsehoods in the interest of equality of condition; they would establish on the American campus a proletarian dictatorship of the mind. In the teaching of literature, they would efface the "Euroculture" of Plato and Aristotle, Dante and Cervantes and Shakespeare, supplanting these old fuddy-duddies with minor writers of approved "minority" affiliations, and feminist ideologues of the present century. As for English literature, or American literature in the British tradition, the radicals would chuck it all down the memory-hole—except for such "workers in the dawn" writing as might seem sufficiently denunciatory of capitalism and white supremacy.

The culture of America is but two centuries old—or little more than three centuries and a half, if we turn back to the earliest English settlements on the Atlantic shore. The culture of Britain is some sixteen centuries old, if we begin with the triumph of the Angles and the Saxons. If Americans lose that British patrimony, they must become barbarians, and on their darkling plains ignorant armies of ideologues may clash by night.

The Case for a Defense of the English-Speaking Cultures

The majority of American citizens nowadays are not descended from English-speaking ancestors. They are outnumbered by people descended from German-speaking stock: Germans, Austrians, and German-speakers of central Europe. And the proportion of America's population with Italian, Polish, and other European language-roots bulks large. Spanish was spoken, and often still is spoken, by the parents or the grandparents of the ethnic group most rapidly increasing in the United States—that is, Latin-Americans. Asiatic and African immigrants, fugitives most of them from the twentieth-century Time of Troubles, must acquire some proficiency in the English language, a tongue altogether unrelated to their ancestral languages.

Nevertheless, whatever the racial or ethnic or national origins of Americans, the principal features of the culture within which they have their being are British in origin. It is not possible to participate effectively in American society without acquiring that English-speaking culture. For, as Thomas Sowell (some of whose ancestors were African) remarked recently, "Cultural features do not exist merely as badges of 'identity' to which we have some emotional attachment. They exist to meet the necessities and forward the purposes of human life."[43]

In June 1991, the Social Studies Syllabus Review Committee of the state of New York issued a report embracing the notion of "multicultural education" in public schools and rejecting "previous ideals of assimilation to an Anglo-American model." This Syllabus Review Committee, under the authority of the New York State Board of Regents, approved a new "Curriculum of Inclusion" drafted by Leonard Jeffries, a radical black professor who called the existing syllabus "White Nationalism" and ethnocentric.

Professor Arthur Schlesinger, Jr., had been a member of that Syllabus Review Committee; he dissented strongly from the "multicultural" report that the Committee endorsed. His remarks on the report carry weight:

> The underlying philosophy of the report, as I read it, is that ethnicity is the defining experience for most Americans, that ethnic ties are permanent and indelible, that the division into ethnic groups establishes the basic structure of American society and that a main objective of public education should be the protection, strengthening, celebration, and perpetuation of ethnic origins and identities. Implicit in the report is the classification of all Americans according to ethnic and racial criteria.[44]

Similar endeavors to repudiate the long-established common culture of America, rooted in many centuries of thought and experience on either side of the Atlantic, have been militant in states other than New York. Were the zealots of multiculturalism to succeed, Americans of differing ethnic origins would scarcely be able to converse together, let alone work together.

Assailants of "the Anglo-American model" for culture often seem to assume that sweeping aside America's established culture would be merely a matter of public policy, with no consequences except a different teaching in classrooms. Thomas Sowell refutes that assumption:

> Cultures exist to serve the vital practical requirements of human life—to structure a society so as to perpetuate the species, to pass on the hard-earned knowledge and experience of generations past and centuries past to the young and inexperienced, in order to spare the next generation the costly and dangerous process of learning everything all over again from scratch through trial and error—including fatal errors.

> Cultures exist so that people can know how to get food and put a roof over their heads, how to cure the sick, how to cope with the death of loved ones and how to get along with the living. Cultures are not bumper stickers. They are living, changing ways of doing all the things that have to be done in life.[45]

Professor Schlesinger points out that America's language and political purposes and institutions are derived from Britain: "To pretend otherwise is to falsify history. To teach otherwise is to mislead our students." But he adds that "the British legacy has been modified, enriched, and reconstituted by the absorption of non-Anglo cultures and traditions as well as by the distinctive experiences of American life." Very true that is. Yet the British culture is central in certain ways; the other cultures often are peripheral.

Schlesinger concludes by asking his colleagues "to consider what kind of nation we will have if we press further down the road to cultural separatism and ethnic fragmentation, if we institutionalize the classification of our citizens by ethnic and racial criteria and if we abandon our historic commitment to an American identity. What will hold our people together then?"[46] Amen to that! . . .

In four major fashions—folkways, if you will—the British mind and British experience, for more than a dozen generations, have shaped the American culture.

The first of these three ways is the English language and the wealth of great literature in that language. Bestriding the world, that English language should be of even greater advantage to Americans today than it has been in the past.

The second of these ways is the rule of law, American common law and positive law being derived chiefly from English law. This body of laws gives fuller protection to the individual person than does the legal system of any other country.

The third of these ways is representative government, patterned upon British institutions that began to develop in medieval times, and patterned especially upon "the mother of parliaments," at Westminster.

The fourth of these ways is a body of mores, or moral habits and beliefs and conventions and customs, joined to certain intellectual disciplines. These compose an ethical heritage. According to Tocqueville, Americans' mores have been the cause of the success of the American Republic.

In yet other ways, the United States benefits from a British patrimony: the American economy, for instance, developed out of British experience and precedent; and American patterns of community and of family life are British in considerable part. But time being limited, we confine ourselves here to British beliefs and social institutions of which the influence upon Americans has not much diminished with the elapse of four centuries. They will be rejected by those interesting persons who demand that Swahili, rather than English, be taught in urban schools; but most Americans, today as well as yesteryear, take for granted the patterns of Anglo-American culture that I describe.

A culture is perennially in need of renewal. . . . A culture does not survive and prosper merely by being taken for granted; active defense always is required, and imaginative growth, too. Let us brighten the cultural corner where we find ourselves. For, as T. S. Eliot remarked more than four decades ago, "Culture may even be described simply as that which makes life worth living."[47]

["The Necessity for a General Culture," America's British Culture *(New Brunswick, NJ: Transaction Publishers, 1993), 1–12.]*

❖

III.

PRINCIPLES OF ORDER

Edmund Burke: A Revolution of Theoretic Dogma ❖ The Prescience of Tocqueville ❖ T. S. Eliot's Permanent Things ❖ Eric Voegelin's Normative Labor

The renowned French religious philosopher Simone Weil stipulates that the first need of all things, human and spiritual, is order. Order signifies stability, control, responsibility, restraint, moderation, harmony. Order is especially prominent among the first principles that Kirk sees as central to the health of the community and of the human soul. When the living principle of order is weakened, and its constituent qualities dismantled, then disorder—whether as confusion, or agitation, or deterioration—spreads like a plague. This process of disorder concludes in extremisms like anarchy and tyranny, which visionaries like Edmund Burke and Alexis de Tocqueville warned against. In his exposition of the need for order, Kirk is a twentieth-century successor to these earlier political thinkers.

For Kirk the disciplines of order produce civilization, which is often at the mercy not only of the destructive impulse but also of liberal and radical doctrinaires who chase after illusory schemes of reconstruction. He sees principles of order as being singularly necessary to the recovery of the "permanent things" that T. S. Eliot associated with the affirmation of transcendent reality, wisdom, truth. Order plays an active, life-giving part in what Eliot calls the "supreme struggle" in the "divine darkness" "to force the moment to its crisis." Kirk believes that for the conservative there exists an enduring moral order, which in the twentieth century has eroded, with all the dire consequences for both the individual and society.

Closely connected with the principle of order, Kirk asserts, is the principle of prudence, one of the four "classical virtues" advocated by philosophers from Plato to Eric Voegelin. Prudence is the ability to discern the maximal course of action from the standpoint of conduct, foresight, discretion. Order emerges from prudence, from prudent thought, judgments, decisions. Burke captures the full normative and salutary value of prudence and order in these words: "Indeed, all that wise men ever aim at is to keep things from coming to the worse. Those who expect perfect reformations, either deceive or are deceived miserably."

❖

EDMUND BURKE:

A REVOLUTION OF THEORETIC DOGMA

Edmund Burke (1729–97) holds a preeminent place in the work and thought of Russell Kirk. Visionary statesman and political philosopher, Burke "speaks up for honor and the unbought grace of life." Kirk's book entitled Edmund Burke: A Genius Reconsidered, *first published in 1967, was reissued, with revisions, in 1997. A model of excellence in exposition and commentation, it exhibits Kirk's powers of analysis and judgment. "A Revolution of Theoretic Dogma," a major chapter, calls attention to the "inspired wisdom" of an "enduring Burke." In examining Burke's* Reflections on the Revolution in France *(1790), Kirk focuses on the "metaphysical madness" of radicals whose schemes culminate in tyranny. Burke sought to present a system of truths obtained from the wisdom of the ages, in short, principles which save civilized society and prescriptive institutions from what Burke terms the "antagonist world" of "madness, discord, vice, confusion, and unavailing sorrow." Kirk sees Burke as a hero combating "armed doctrines" and defending the spirit of religion and the spirit of the gentleman.*

Burke's greatest hour came to him late. When the Paris mob stormed the Bastille, slaughtered its garrison of pensioners, and scattered its stones abroad, Edmund Burke was sixty years old: a party leader who had been out of office most of his career, an orator celebrated for his espousal of the cause of the unfortunate—but also, in 1789, a man whose reputation had declined. His immoderate zeal in the "Regency crisis" at the time of George III's first fit of madness had damaged his fair fame;[1] and then the King had recovered, to make Burke a laughingstock. He was unpopular with many, too, because of his prosecution of Hastings and his solicitude for Irish Catholics.

Already he thought of retirement from Parliament. Within his party, the suppler Fox had surpassed him in power—and, many said, in eloquence; after Rockingham's death, Burke's influence among the grand Whigs had diminished. Even to himself, he seemed to contend against the stars in their courses: Hastings, he knew, would go free; the Tories were well entrenched in office; his own affairs proceeded badly. He struggled for Catholic emancipation; should he not soon ask for the Chiltern Hundreds, seeking his own emancipation from "crooked politicks"?

Then, of a sudden, Sansculottism asked, "What think ye of me?" Burke's prompt reply was his most enduring gift to the rising generation and to those yet unborn.

"Burke gave the most striking proofs of his character and genius in the evil days in which his life ended—not when he was a leader in the Commons, but when he was a stricken old man at Beaconsfield." So wrote Woodrow Wilson. "What a man was you may often discover in the records of his days of bitterness and pain better than in what is told of his seasons of cheer and hope; for if the noble qualities triumph then and show themselves still sound and sweet, if his courage sink not, if he show himself still capable of self-forgetfulness, if he still stir with a passion for the service of causes and polities which are beyond himself, his stricken age is even greater than his full-pulsed years of manhood. This is the test which Burke endures—the test of fire."[2]

Edmund Burke never had feared to attack the powerful, or to defend the weak, or to oppose to established interests the high power of his imagination. His chief constructive measure had been the Economical Reform, which mightily amended the structure and operation of the Civil List, in despite of everything that placeholders and royal influence could do to prevent him. He had been the most outspoken champion of oppressed Catholics—and, often, of Dissenters. He had insisted, when first he rose to eminence in the House of Commons, that Americans possessed both the rights of Englishmen and the prescriptive usages which they had acquired in the course of their colonial experience. He had steadfastly opposed all policies calculated to reduce private liberties, to centralize authority in the Crown, or to diminish the prerogatives of Parliament. His generous sympathies for the chartered rights of civilized men extended far beyond England and Ireland, to Quebec and Madras. Even his own party—let alone the Crown—never had rewarded him properly for his courage, his brilliance, his scholarship, and his energy. It seemed, therefore, to many of the leaders of liberal opinion in revolutionary France (which country Burke had visited thrice, returning to London dismayed at the rise of atheism among the French) that Burke, more than any other English political leader, was admirably calculated to head in Britain a radical movement of reform on French principles.

But the French radicals reckoned without their man. At one time or another, Mirabeau, Thomas Paine, "Anacharsis" Cloots, and a young gentleman named DePont had visited Burke at Beaconsfield, and had enjoyed his kindnesses; the latter three wrote to him, in 1789, in the expectation that he would approve their sweeping alteration of French institutions.[3] They had mistaken Burke's whole nature. He was not a man of the Enlightenment, but a Christian, much read in Aristotle, Cicero, the Fathers of the Church, the Schoolmen (including Aquinas) and the great English divines. The presumption of the Age of Reason roused Burke's indignation and contempt. Endowed with a prophet's vision, he marvellously foresaw the whole course of events which would follow upon the French attempt to reconstruct society after an abstract pattern. The Revolution, after careering fiercely through a series of stages of hysterical violence, would end in a despotism; but by that time, it would have brought down in ruins most of what was fine and noble in traditional society. Burke resolved that Britain should not share in France's folly, and that the whole of the civilized world must be awakened to the menace of these abstractions of impractical speculators, which would expose mankind to the cruelty of the brute that lurks beneath our fallen human nature, instead of conjuring up the Noble Savage of romantic fiction.

As Lord Percy of Newcastle writes, Burke was the chief formulator of the modern Christian understanding of true civil freedom: yet he has been "until quite recently, almost persistently misunderstood. His party pamphlets have been taken as sound history, while his anti-revolutionary philosophy has been dismissed as a crotchet of old age and declining powers. This is almost the exact reverse of the truth. Burke was a Whig partisan, no more reliable as a witness to contemporary fact than any other party politician. But, as other such politicians have not seldom been shocked into statesmanship by war, he was shocked into philosophy by, first, the American and, then, the French Revolution."[4]

Much read in history and much practiced in the conduct of political affairs, Burke knew that men are not naturally good, but are beings of mingled good and evil, kept in obedience to a moral law chiefly by the force of custom and habit, which the revolutionaries would discard as so much antiquated rubbish. He knew that all the advantages of society are the product of intricate human experience over many centuries, not to be amended overnight by some coffee-house philosopher. He knew religion to be man's greatest good, and established order to be the fundamental of civilization, and hereditary possessions to be the prop of liberty and justice, and the mass of beliefs we often call "prejudices" to be the moral sense of humanity. He set his face against the revolutionaries like a man who finds himself suddenly beset by robbers.

Burke had defended the claims of some of the American colonists because they were the "chartered rights of Englishmen" overseas, developed by an historical process. He attacked the fallacy of the "Rights of Man," expounded by the French theorists, because he recognized in this abstract notion of rights an insensate desire to be emancipated from all duties. Unlike the "Glorious Revolution" of 1688, the French Revolution was intended to uproot the delicate growth that is human society; if not impeded, this revolutionary passion would end by subjecting all men first to anarchy and then to a ruthless master. In the pursuit of pretended abstract rights, men would have lost all real prescriptive rights.

Burke's reaction was then, and later, astounding to the votaries of the cult of Progress. In the middle of the nineteenth century, the historian Buckle argued that Burke must have gone mad in 1789. But men of the twentieth century have had much experience of revolutions undertaken on unexamined *a priori* assumptions; so few echo Buckle's theory today. The madness was rather that of the *philosophes* and people of fashion to whom Cazotte uttered his bloody prophecies: theirs was what Edmund Burke called "metaphysical madness," a rationalistic lunacy, founded upon a fantastic misunderstanding of human nature.[5] In Woodrow Wilson's phrase, "Burke was right, and was himself, when he sought to keep the French infection out of England."[6]

In Parliament, Burke's majestic denunciations of the Revolution at first had little effect. His own close friend and fellow leader of the Whigs, Charles James Fox, looked upon the French upheaval as a splendid triumph of progress and liberty; while William Pitt, though more cautious, thought the collapse of the French monarchy's authority more an opportunity for English advantage in the old rivalry than a menace to established English society. Perceiving that he must appeal beyond St. Stephen's Chapel to the sound sense of the British public, Burke set to work writing a tremendous pamphlet, which became the most brilliant work of English political philosophy, and which for eloquence combined with wisdom has no equal in any language's literature of politics: *Reflections on the Revolution in France*, published on November 1, 1790. This began as a letter to a young French friend, Charles DePont, who had visited Burke at Gregories in 1785 and had commenced a correspondence with him in the first stages of the Revolution, asking for Burke's opinion whether the French would succeed (knowing how to distinguish between liberty and license) in creating a better order.

DePont doubtless expected a favorable reply. But Burke, suspicious of certain tendencies of the Revolution from the first, within a few months perceived that the revolutionaries actually were subverting true "social freedom," which is maintained by wise laws and well constructed institutions; they were seeking what never can be found, perfect liberty—which must mean that the bonds of social community are dissolved, and men are left little human atoms, at war with one another. By November, 1789, Burke was thoroughly alarmed—especially by a sermon of the radical Unitarian minister Dr. Richard Price, a friend of Lord Shelburne. Price had talked of "cashiering kings." Thus the purported letter to DePont actually commenced as a denunciation of Price's errors, and then developed into a defense of tradition, prescription, and the established order of civilized society against the radical innovators.

This book can no more be analyzed competently here than one could condense the writings of Plato, say, into a few paragraphs: the *Reflections* must be read by anyone who wishes to understand the great controversies of modern politics.[7] In this chapter, it is possible only to suggest Burke's principal arguments and overwhelming eloquence.

The immediate effect of the *Reflections* was titanic. Burke's popularity had been at its lowest ebb, especially after the "Regency crisis" concerned with the state of the Crown during the temporary madness of George III; Fox, Burke, and other Portland Whigs had harmed themselves by their espousing of the Prince of Wales's claim to a regency by right. What Burke never expected, his tract abruptly raised him high in the opinion of the strong majority of the literate public. The King himself (his wits recovered) said that the *Reflections* was "a good book, a very good book; and every gentleman ought to read it." Nearly every gentleman did.

Most of the Tories, some of the Portland Whigs, and a great many people who ordinarily took little active part in English politics, began to perceive the dread danger of revolution, and shifted toward that course of action which, in the long run, would crush Napoleon. Fox's Whigs, on the contrary, cried down Burke as an apostate, and in time the Duke of Bedford was rash enough to accuse Burke of self-seeking—which, after Burke's retirement from the House of Commons, provoked Burke's crushing reply, *A Letter to a Noble Lord*. A flood of pamphlets in answer to Burke's book appeared; in English, the two most influential retorts were those of James Mackintosh and Thomas Paine.[8]

As the Revolution progressed, Mackintosh confessed that Burke was altogether right, becoming one of Burke's ablest disciples; and though Paine never disavowed his own radicalism, his narrow escape from the guillotine in Paris was some refutation of his early high hopes for liberty, equality, and fraternity.

Burke, said Paine, pitied the plumage but forgot the dying bird:

> When we see a man dramatically lamenting in a publication intended to be believed that "*The Age of chivalry is gone!* that *The glory of Europe is extinguished for ever!* that *The unbought grace of life* (if anyone knows what it is), *the cheap defense of nations, the nurse of manly sentiment and heroic enterprise is gone!"* and all this because the Quixot age of chivalry nonsense is gone, what opinion can we form of his judgment, or what regard can we pay to his facts? In the rhapsody of his imagination he has discovered a world of wind mills, and his sorrows are that there are no Quixots to attack them. But if the age of aristocracy, like that of chivalry, should fall (and they had originally some connection), Mr. Burke, the trumpeter of the order, may continue his parody to the end, and finish with exclaiming: "*Othello's occupation's gone*!"

This passage is from *The Rights* of *Man*. In the minds of liberals as well as the minds of conservatives, however, from Woodrow Wilson to Harold Laski, from Samuel Taylor Coleridge to Paul Elmer More, Burke vanquished Paine in this debate; and certainly he won the immense majority of his countrymen, so that Britain turned all her energies toward the defeat of revolutionary violence. The leadership which is inspired by honor, that love of things established which grows out of a veneration of the wisdom of our ancestors, that sagacity which reconciles necessary change with the best in the old order—these things Burke knew to be superior to the pretended Rights of Man that Paine extolled; and British and American society have been incalculably influenced by Burke ever since the *Reflections* was published.[9]

On first examination, the *Reflections* may seem to be a loose-knit book; but really it is nothing of the sort. Burke "winds into his subject like a serpent," lending history with principle, splendid imagery with profound practical aphorisms. All his life, he detested "abstractions"—that is, speculative notions with no secure foundation in history or in knowledge of the world. What Burke is doing in this book, then, is to set forth a system of "principles"—by which he meant general truths obtained from the wisdom of our ancestors, practical experience, and a knowledge of the human heart. He never indulges in "pure" philosophy because he will not admit that the statesman has any right to look at man in the abstract, rather than at particular men in particular circumstances.

The first portion of the book is a comparison of the political convictions of Englishmen with those of the French revolutionaries. Burke demolishes Dr. Price, and proceeds to show that the Glorious Revolution of 1688 was not a radical break with English traditions, but rather a preservation of prescriptive institutions. Then he passes on to expose the sophistries and fallacies of the French reformers, and to analyze the rights of men, true and false.

Burke defends the church against the zealots of Reason, and the old constitution of France against the fanatic advocates of turning society inside out. He speaks up for honor and the unbought grace of life. Then, in the latter portion of his tract, he assails the National Assembly, which by presumption has been delivered up to folly and crime, and which will end by ruining justice and terminating its own existence.

Written at white heat, the *Reflections* burns with all the wrath and anguish of a prophet who saw the traditions of Christendom and the fabric of civil society dissolving before his eyes. Yet his words are suffused with a keenness of observation, the mark of a practical statesman. This book is polemic at its most magnificent, and one of the most influential political treatises in the history of the world.

Few books have had so immediate and so enduring an influence, indeed—as Walter Scott observed. "About 1792, when I was entering life, the admiration of the god-like system of the French Revolution was so rife, that only a few old-fashioned Jacobites and the like ventured to hint a preference for the land they lived in," Scott wrote, in 1831, "or pretended to doubt that the new principles must be infused into our worn-out constitution. Burke appeared, and all the gibberish about the superior legislation of the French dissolved like an enchanted castle when the destined knight blows his horn before it."[10]

Although more copies of Paine's reply were sold than of the *Reflections*, Burke captured, soon or late, the minds of the English and Scottish writers of the rising generation, so that his indirect influence was incalculable. Walter Scott's romances are shot through and through with Burke's convictions; while Wordsworth, Coleridge, Southey, and other poets became Burke's disciples.

Nowadays, political debate is sufficiently dreary-blighted by cant, slogan, and arid commonplace. Even though the fountains of the great deep are broken up, the political rhetoric of the twentieth century is enfeebled, and—at least in America and Britain—scarcely equal in style to the daily newspaper.

It was not so in Burke's day. In the latter half of the eighteenth century, the rhetoric of politics possessed true power and subtlety. As in the age of

Cicero, political speaking and writing then formed the most extensive province of the realm of humane letters. The very demagogue, such as Wilkes, was splendid as orator and pamphleteer; today he has lost his tongue.

And Burke endures, though the other political polemicists of that time are nearly forgotten. Paine has a following still: with interesting archaism, the village atheist continues to pass out paper-backed copies of *The Age of Reason*. Radicalism having passed Paine by long ago, the twentieth century does not turn to him for political wisdom—merely for brilliant examples of what James Boulton accurately calls "the vulgar style" of political rhetoric.[11] The enormous immediate popularity of Paine's rejoinder, Boulton suggests, was produced by the simplicity of Paine's argument and by a rhetorical method calculated to make Paine appear a plain man of the people, full of homely allusions. Yet this very simplicity now makes Paine's pamphlets shallow. As Boulton puts it, "However astute Paine's motives in 1791, the *Rights of Man* does not give the reader the same degree of permanent pleasure that he experiences from reading the *Reflections;* Paine cannot command that complex subtlety of style and sensitivity to the resources of language displayed by Burke."[12]

Unlike Paine, Burke did not hope to reach directly the mass of Englishmen. At best, he wrote for what he called the real nation—that is, some four hundred thousand citizens, qualified by education, profession, or substance to take some part in public affairs. And he expected to be read by only a fraction of this select body: he appealed to a cultural aristocracy, as did Samuel Johnson.

As a contemporary wrote, Burke reasoned in metaphor. Evoking images, Burke sought to persuade by his appeal to the moral imagination—not by setting his own abstractions against the abstractions of the *philosophes*. As Boulton observes, the most significant and persuasive portion of the *Reflections* is the apostrophe to Marie Antoinette—not the "philosophical center" of that book, Burke's refutation of the revolutionary concept of the social contract. Abhorring the "abstract metaphysician," the merciless rationalist, Burke was not attempting a systematic treatise on political theory, after the fashion of William Godwin. Enduring political wisdom, both practical and theoretical, runs through Burke's speeches and tracts; but Burke's method is a world away from that of the Encyclopedists.

For all that, Burke outmatched the French doctrinaires at their own appeal to reason. His central argument on the nature of the rights of men is sufficient illustration. The French revolutionaries talked incessantly of abstract and misty "rights of man," universal and imprescriptible. Burke retorted that practical civil liberty is quite different from these amorphous concepts:

Far am I from denying in theory, full as far is my heart from withholding in practice (if I were of power to give or to withhold) the real rights of men. In denying those false claims of right, I do not mean to injure those which are real, and are such as their pretended rights would totally destroy. If civil society be made for the advantage of man, all the advantages for which it is made become his right. It is an institution of beneficence, and law itself is only beneficence acting by a rule. Men have a right to live by that rule; they have a right to do justice as between their fellows, whether their fellows are in politick function or in ordinary occupation. They have a right to the fruits of their industry; and to the means of making their industry fruitful. They have a right to the acquisitions of their parents; to the nourishment and improvement of their offspring; to instruction in life, and to consolation in death. Whatever each man can separately do, without trespassing upon others, he has a right to do for himself, and he has a right to a fair portion of all which society, with all its combinations of skill and force, can do in his favour. In this partnership all men have equal rights; but not to equal things. He that has but five shillings in the partnership, has as good a right to it, as he that has five hundred pounds has to his larger proportion. But he has not a right to an equal dividend in the product of the joint stock; and as to the share of power, authority, and direction which each individual ought to have in the management of the state, that I deny to be amongst the direct original rights of man in civil society; for I have in my contemplation the civil social man, and no other. It is a thing to be settled by convention.

If civil society be the offspring of convention, that convention must be its law. That convention must limit and modify all the descriptions of constitution which are formed under it. Every sort of legislative, judicial, or executory power, are its creatures. . . .

Government is not made in virtue of natural rights, which may and do exist in total independence of it; and exist in much greater clearness, and in a much greater degree of abstract perfection: but their abstract perfection is their practical defect. By having a right to every thing they want every thing. Government is a contrivance of human wisdom to provide for human wants. Men have a right that these wants should be provided for by this wisdom. Among these wants is to be reckoned the want, out of civil society, of a sufficient restraint upon their passions. Society requires not only that the passions of individuals should be subjected, but that even in the mass and body as well as in the individuals, the inclinations of men should frequently be thwarted, their will controlled, and their passions brought into subjection. This can only be done by a *power out of themselves*; and not, in

> the exercise of its function, subject to that will and to those passions which it is its office to bridle and subdue. In this sense the restraints on men, as well as their liberties, are to be reckoned among their rights.

Only in a state governed by constitution, convention, and prescription can the rights—or the aspirations—of men be realized. Rousseau's disciples destroy the framework which makes possible the chartered rights of men, and so reduce men to anarchy or slavery—including servitude to their own passions, for "men of intemperate mind never can be free; their passions forge their fetters."[13]

Wavering Whig peers learned from Burke that they must set their faces against the Revolution, or see all order uprooted and all property in peril of confiscation; the Anglican clergy—two-thirds of whom, by Burke's estimate, had smiled hesitantly upon events in France—were taught that religion and manners could not survive Jacobinism. Peers and parsons had read Virgil and Cicero, and often a good deal besides; and upon them Burke's metaphors and imagery worked powerfully, as did his practical reasoning. When they moved, so did the nation, despite all that Paine and Mackintosh and Wollstonecraft and the other counter-pamphleteers could say.

The twentieth-century leader of party cannot address himself to so coherent an aristocracy of culture as did Burke. The contemporary politician thinks that he must move the masses; yet he does not successfully employ a vigorous vulgar rhetoric like that of Paine. Even the political tracts of our time aspire, at most, to the "sober, honest, plain-speaking but temperate" method of Mackintosh (in James Boulton's phrases), calculated to influence the middle classes. The clichés of daily journalism, unrelieved by wit, are the sum and substance of most political oratory in this hour—even among those politicians with some reputation for learning.

Early in the nineteenth century, according to Burke's most ardent American disciple, John Randolph of Roanoke, one could quote to Congressmen only Shakespeare and the Bible, if one desired the signs of recognition. That was nearly a century and a half ago: Shakespeare and the Authorized Version might not always be evocative in Senate and House today, nor in the House of Commons.

Burke's *Reflections* did pass beyond the comparatively small audience which he had expected; but to reach a wide public, even at the end of the eighteenth century, it was necessary to abridge the book, with judicious deletions. Boulton draws attention, for instance, to the popular misunderstanding of Burke's phrase "the swinish multitude," referring to the fate of learning when a revolution should sweep away the natural guardians of culture, and which "was used by Burke to denote the unthinking, uncultivated masses, the irresponsible elements in society whose lack of involvement in sustaining the cultural heritage would lead them to destroy it." This passage, widely misinterpreted or misunderstood, and fiercely attacked, was omitted by Burke's abridger, "S. J.," in 1793, for "it would prove either repugnant or unintelligible to poorer readers."[14]

In the age of one-man, one-vote, any such striking phrase, however true, is the more liable to partisan attack and popular resentment or bewilderment. Thus the political orator or pamphleteer in the twentieth century tends to confine himself to platitudes which few will challenge, and to avoid words tending toward that "obscurity" with which Paine charged Burke. By such blandness, most of the time, elections are won; but the language of politics suffers—and often the public welfare suffers, too, since an impoverished and timid vocabulary means impoverished and timid political action.

But Burke's vocabulary of politics resulted in action far from impoverished or timid; even today, Burke's words are rallying cries. Today the pertinence of the *Reflections* is greater for both conservatives and liberals (Burke himself was both) than it was half a century ago. The revolutions of our times having dissipated the shallow optimism of the early years of the nineteenth century, we now perceive in the Russian Revolution and the rise of Communism elsewhere the counterpart, still more terrible, of the French Revolution and its expansion; we behold in the grinding tyranny of the Soviets and of Communist China the full realization of Burke's prophecies. Having broken with the old sanctions to integrity, Burke wrote, revolutionaries must come down to terror and force, the only influences which suffice to govern a society that has forgotten prudence and charity.

The spirit of religion and the spirit of a gentleman, Burke declared, gave to Europe everything generous and admirable in modern culture. A speculative system which detests piety, manners, the traditional morality, and all ancient usages speedily must repudiate even the pretended affection for equality which gives that innovating system its initial appeal to the masses.

> All the decent drapery of life is to be rudely torn off. All the superadded ideas, furnished from the wardrobe of a moral imagination, which the heart owns and the understanding ratifies, as necessary to cover the defects of our naked, shivering nature, and to raise it to dignity in our own estimation, are to be exploded, as a ridiculous, absurd, and antiquated fashion.

> On this scheme of things, a king is but a man, a queen is but a woman, a woman is but an animal—and an animal not of the highest order. . . . On the scheme of this barbarous philosophy, which is the offspring of cold hearts and muddy understandings, and which is as void of solid wisdom as it is destitute of all taste and elegance, laws are to be supported only by their own terrors, and by the concern which each individual may find in them from his own private speculations, or can spare to them from his own private interests. In the groves of their academy, at the end of every vista, you see nothing but the gallows.

Nineteenth-century meliorists took for mere distempered fancy the preceding paragraph, once the French Revolution was over; but in truth, Burke was describing the necessary character of all ideologies, or armed doctrines. To our sorrow, we dwell (except for those of us who are temporarily secure upon virtual islands of refuge in the modern flood) in the twentieth-century "antagonist world" of madness, confusion, despair, and unavailing sorrow that Burke contrasted with the just civil social order, founded on conscientious leadership and prescriptive institutions.

A year after the *Reflections* was published, the ascendancy of that book was not yet complete among Burke's old friends of the Rockingham-Fitzwilliam connection, though by 1793 the power of Burke's mind, combining with the reaction against the Terror in Paris, would turn the bulk of thinking Englishmen toward plans for striking a counter-blow at Jacobinism. Even Earl Fitzwilliam, cast (with some flaws) in Rockingham's mold, still hoped, late in 1791, that a clash with Continental radicalism might be averted; he hesitated to enlist in a crusade against the revolutionary regime. (Like Rockingham before him, Fitzwilliam had been extending large financial assistance to Burke; when Fitzwilliam seemed to dissent in part from Burke's convictions on this point, the hard-pressed statesman, declining in health and deprived of many friends, nevertheless resolutely told the Earl that he would accept no more such help from him—and offered to give up his parliamentary seat at Malton.)

By 1793, however, the pamphlets of Paine and Priestley, the sermons of Dr. Price, the intrigues of the Constitutional Society and the Revolutionary Society, even the eloquence of Fox, all were scattered like chaff in the blast of Burke's whirlwind wrath. "I am come to a time of life," he wrote to Lord Fitzwilliam, "in which it is not permitted that we should trifle with our existence. I am fallen into a state of the world, that will not suffer me to play at little sports, or to enfeeble the part I am bound to take, by smaller collateral considerations. I cannot proceed, as if things went on in the beaten circle of events, such as I have known them for half a century."[15]

To save men from silly little catechisms of rights without duties; to save them from ungovernable passions aroused by filling men with aspirations that cannot be gratified in nature; to save men from sham and cant—that was Burke's endeavor in his assault upon the *philosophes* and the Jacobins. In truth, it was Burke, not Napoleon, who laid the fell spirit of innovation which was bestriding the world. Abstract doctrine and theoretic dogma had made the Revolution; Burke evoked the wisdom of the species to restrain the hard heart of the "pure metaphysician." Human nature is a constant, and the metaphysicians of the Enlightenment could not make man and society anew: they could only ruin the constructions of thousands of years of painful human endeavor.

"We," he wrote of the English, "are not the converts of Rousseau; we are not the disciples of Voltaire; Helvétius has made no progress amongst us. . . . We know that *we* have made no discoveries, and we think that no discoveries are to be made, in morality; nor many in the great principles of government, nor in the idea of liberty, which were understood long before we were born, altogether as well as they will be after the grave has heaped its mould upon our presumption, and the silent tomb shall have imposed its law upon our pert loquacity."

As Louis Bredvold comments upon this passage,

> Politics then, according to Burke, ought to be adjusted, not to bare human reason, but to human nature, of which reason is but a part, and, he adds, by no means the greatest part. Burke could not have conceived of a nation or a people or a community as anything like a collection of machines in a factory, all beautifully adjusted and synchronized by a system of belts and transmissions, regulated by human engineering; neither would he believe that human felicity could be found in any anarchic state of society. To form a good and humane society, Burke thought, many things are necessary, in addition to good laws; he emphasized the importance of religion, traditions of living, a rich heritage of customs, a complex pattern of relationships of all kinds, such as would not only develop the personality of the individual—to use the popular phrase of our day—but which would also teach him the truth about his own nature by their discipline of him.[16]

At bottom, the difference of Burke from the revolutionaries—like all large differences of opinion—was theological. Burke's was the Christian understanding of human nature, which the men of the Enlightenment violently rejected. We must leave much to Providence; to presume to perfect man and society by a neat "rational" scheme is a monstrous act of *hubris*. With his friend Johnson, Burke abided by Christian resignation—and Christian hope.

To the revolutionaries, Christianity was superstition—and an enemy. The dogmas and doctrines of Christianity must go by the board. But in short order, theological dogmas were supplanted by secular dogmas. Christian charity was supplanted by "fraternity"—which, in effect, led to the attitude "Be my brother, or I must kill you." The Christian symbols of transcendence were adapted to the new order, but in a degraded form: for perfection through grace in death, the French theorists substituted the promise of perfection in this world, with every appetite satisfied. And when perfection was not promptly attained, wicked obscurants and reactionaries must be hunted down, for Progress surely would triumph, were it not for ignorant or malicious human obstruction.

Thus arose the "armed doctrine," an inverted religion, employing central political power and strength of arms to enforce conformity to its "rational" creed. Through destruction of ancient institutions and beliefs, the way must be cleared to Utopia. Since Burke's day, the label "ideology" has been affixed to what he called "the armed doctrine"—political fanaticism, promising general redemption and idyllic general happiness to be achieved through radical social alteration.

But Utopia never will be found here below, Burke knew; politics is the art of the possible, not of perfectibility. We never will be as gods. Improvement is the work of slow exploration and persuasion, never unfixing old interests at once. Mere sweeping innovation is not reform. Once immemorial moral habits are broken by the rash Utopian, once the old checks upon will and appetite are discarded, the inescapable sinfulness of human nature asserts itself: and those who aspired to usurp the throne of God find that they have contrived a terrestrial Hell.

For seven years, Burke contended against the Jacobin heresy. Danton demanded to behold "the bronze seething and foaming and purifying itself in the cauldron"—that is, society in white-hot ferment, every impurity burnt out. But Danton was consumed in his own revolutionary cauldron. Burke knew that the just society is nothing like a cauldron; on the contrary, society is a spiritual corporation, formed by a covenant with the Author of our being:

> Each contract of each particular state is but a clause in the great primeval contract of eternal society, linking the lower with the higher natures, connecting the visible and invisible world, according to a fixed compact which holds all physical and all moral natures each in their appointed place. This

> law is not subject to the will of those, who, by an obligation above them, and infinitely superior, are bound to submit their will to that law. The municipal corporations of that universal kingdom are not morally at liberty at their pleasure, and on their speculations of a contingent improvement, wholly to separate and tear asunder the bonds of their subordinate community, and dissolve it into an unsocial, uncivil, unconnected chaos of elementary principles.

In 1790, it appeared that the ancient states of Europe were dissolving into the dust and powder of an atomic age; generation would not link with generation, men would be as the flies of a summer, and whole classes would be proscribed and hunted down like beasts. "What shadows we are, and what shadows we pursue!" Burke had said, ten years before, on declining the poll at Bristol. What one man might do to resist this disintegration, Burke would undertake.

In 1805, William Wordsworth, abjuring the radicalism of his youth, asked the dead Burke's pardon for his early errors. The lines of *The Prelude* describe Burke in 1791:

> *I see him,—old, but vigorous in age,—*
> *Stand like an oak whose stag-horn branches start*
> *Out of its leafy brow, the more to awe*
> *The younger brethren of the grove, . . .*
> *While he forewarns, denounces, launches forth*
> *Against all systems built on abstract rights,*
> *Keen ridicule; the majesty proclaims*
> *Of Institutes and Laws, hallowed by time;*
> *Declares the vital power of social ties*
> *Endeared by Custom; and with high disdain,*
> *Exploding upstart Theory, insists*
> *Upon the allegiance to which men are born. . . .*

To Coleridge, also, once he had renounced his Gallic enthusiasm, Burke's moral imagination became the source of poetic truth. As Coleridge wrote in his ode on France, in 1798:

> *The Sensual and the Dark rebel in vain,*
> *Slaves by their own compulsion!*

This is the spirit, and almost the phrase, of Edmund Burke, whom the rising generation heard, and not in vain.[17]

["A Revolution of Theoretic Dogma," Edmund Burke: A Genius Reconsidered *(New Rochelle, NY: Arlington House, 1967), 145–70. Rev. and updated ed. (Wilmington, DE: Intercollegiate Studies Institute, 1997).]*

❖

The Prescience of Tocqueville

Like those of Edmund Burke, the writings of Alexis de Tocqueville (1805–59), the French historian and political thinker, Kirk was to count of high importance, "for every sentence has significance, every observation sagacity." Tocqueville, he continues, "was the best friend democracy ever has had, and democracy's most candid and judicious critic." We can learn much from him in stemming the tide of dissolution and resisting the "sacrifice of democracy's virtues upon the altar of democracy's lusts." What menaces democracy most, according to Tocqueville, is "a tyranny of mediocrity" in the form of "a standardization of mind and spirit and condition enforced by the central government." Tocqueville's magisterial work, Democracy in America *(1835, 1840), Kirk emphasizes, both analyzes and warns against those tendencies and practices of the super-state that dilute the structure of life and the spiritual condition of man. Tocqueville's critique thus helps to identify the "insidious vices" that reside in social democracy and culminate in "democratic despotism."*

> It is believed by some that modern society will be always changing its aspect; for myself, I fear that it will ultimately be too invariably fixed in the same institutions, the same prejudices, the same manners, so that mankind will be stopped and circumscribed; that the mind will swing backwards and forwards forever without begetting fresh ideas; that man will waste his strength in bootless and solitary trifling, and, though in continual motion, that humanity will cease to advance.
>
> —Tocqueville, *Democracy in America*

In Tocqueville that facility of the French for generalization, which turned the world upside down, reached its apex. He employed methods of this style of the philosophes and the Encyclopedists to alleviate, more than half a century later, the consequences of their books. In some respects, the pupil, Tocqueville, excels his philosophical master, Burke: certainly his *Democracy in America* contains an impartial examination of the new order which Burke never had time or patience to undertake, even had it taken distinct form before

Burke's death. Tocqueville is a writer who should be read not in abridgement, but wholly; for every sentence has significance, every observation sagacity. The two big volumes of *Democracy in America* are a mine of aphorisms, his *Old Regime* is the germ of a hundred books, his *Recollections* have a terse brilliance of narrative that few memoirs possess. Some people besides professors still read Tocqueville. They ought to, because he was the best friend democracy ever has had, and democracy's most candid and judicious critic. A century has elapsed since the triumph of Louis Napoleon cut short Tocqueville's public career, but his like as a political philosopher and a sociologist has not been seen since.

Although he was judge and legislator and foreign minister, and enjoyed a great literary reputation, Tocqueville felt himself to be nearly a failure. In Macaulay's essay on Machiavelli is a passage which struck the fancy of that omnivorous reader John Randolph of Roanoke, though he did not know the author's name when he came upon the article in the *Edinburgh Review.* Randolph applied this description to his own situation; and certainly Tocqueville's sentiments were similar. "It is difficult to conceive of any situation more painful than that of a great man condemned to watch the lingering agony of an exhausted country, to tend it during the alternate fits of stupefaction and raving which precede its dissolution, and to see the symptoms of vitality disappear one by one, till nothing is left but coldness, darkness, and corruption." The spirit of a gentleman and the high talents of remarkable individuals, Tocqueville thought, were sliding into an engulfing mediocrity, and the society of his day was confronted with the prospect of life-in-death. The futility of crying against the monstrous deaf and blind tendency of the times made Tocqueville painfully conscious of his impotent insignificance. But he was no mere railer against circumstance; he never lost hope of ameliorating those problems which resulted from the levelling inclination of society; and his influence upon posterity has been more considerable than he expected.

Democratic despotism: in this phrase, which the hesitating Tocqueville adopted only for lack of a better, he described the conundrum of modern society. The analysis of democratic despotism is his supreme achievement as political theorist, sociologist, liberal, and conservative. "I am not opposed to democracies," he wrote to M. de Freslon, in 1857. "They may be great, they may be in accordance with the will of God, if they be free. What saddens me is, not that our society is democratic, but that the vices which we have inherited and acquired make it so difficult for us to obtain or to keep well-regulated liberty. And I know nothing so miserable as a democracy without liberty."[18] Harold Laski remarks that Tocqueville, essentially an aristocrat, was "unable to accept without pain the collectivist discipline" toward which centralized democratic politics remorsely tend. Legislative power, once it is wholly in the hands of the mass of men, is applied to purposes of economic and cultural levelling.[19] Quite so; the collectivist discipline was more repugnant to Tocqueville—or to any liberal or conservative, of whatever origins—than the worst stupidities of the old régime. Like Aristotle (and some reputable writers have declared that Tocqueville was the greatest political thinker since Aristotle, although Tocqueville himself found little in Aristotle's *Politics* which he thought applicable to modern problems), Tocqueville was always searching for ends. A political system which forgets ends and worships averages, a "collectivist discipline," for Tocqueville was bondage worse than slavery of the old sort. Society ought to be designed to encourage the highest moral and intellectual qualities in man; the worst threat of the new democratic system is that mediocrity not only will be encouraged, but may be enforced. Tocqueville dreads the reduction of human society to an insect-like arrangement, the real gravitation toward which state was described recently by Professor C. E. M. Joad.[20] Variety, individuality, progress: these Tocqueville struggles to conserve.

> Whenever social conditions are equal, public opinion presses with enormous weight upon the mind of each individual; it surrounds, directs, and oppresses him; and this arises from the very constitution of society much more than from its political laws. As men grow more alike, each man feels himself weaker in regard to all the rest; as he discerns nothing by which he is considerably raised above them or distinguished from them, he mistrusts himself as soon as they assail him. Not only does he mistrust his strength, but he even doubts of his right, and he is very near acknowledging that he is in the wrong, when the great number of his countrymen assert that he is so. The majority do not need to force him; they convince him. In whatever way the powers of a democratic community may be organized and balanced, then, it will always be extremely difficult to believe what the bulk of the people reject or to profess what they condemn.[21]

Such generalizations, though bold as those of the *philosophes*, were far better grounded than the speculations on *a priori* assumptions in which French thinkers of the preceding century had delighted. By his extensive acquaintance with England, by his political career, by his investigations into American life, and by his unassuming erudition, Tocqueville was prepared to pronounce with authority concerning human and social nature. He wrote with extreme care, anxious to be moderate, zealous to be just. "Of all writers, he is the most widely acceptable, and the hardest to find fault with. He is always wise, always right, and as just as Aristides." This is the judgment of Lord Acton.[22] Tocqueville was determined to escape self-delusion, at whatever expense to peace of mind. Believing with Burke that Providence paves the way for enormous changes in the world, and that to oppose such changes when their tendency is manifest amounts to impiety, he was willing to surrender much to the new democracy—even, to a considerable extent, elevation of mind. "In the democratic society of which you are so proud," said that courageous genius Royer-Collard to Tocqueville, "there will not be ten persons who will thoroughly enter into the spirit of your book."[23] But Tocqueville was not willing to let democracy become a cannibal; he would resist, so far as he could, the sacrifice of democracy's virtues upon the altar of democracy's lusts.

The insidious vice of democracy, Tocqueville discerned, is that democracy preys upon itself, and presently exists only corrupt and hideous—still, perhaps, preserving its essential characteristic of equality, but devoid of all those aspirations toward liberty and progress which had inspired its earlier triumph. Most critics of democracy had declared that political equalitarianism must end in anarchy—or, barring that, tyranny. Tocqueville was not in bondage to the past, although he had a strong respect for historical knowledge: the future need not always be like what went before, he wrote, and neither of these hoary alternatives is the probable consummation of modern equalitarianism. What menaces democratic society in this age is not a simple collapse of order, nor yet usurpation by a single powerful man, but a tyranny of mediocrity, a standardization of mind and spirit and condition enforced by the central government, precisely what Laski calls "the collectivist discipline." Tocqueville foresaw the coming of the "social welfare state," which agrees to provide all for its subjects, and in turn exacts rigid conformity. The name democracy remains; but government is exerted from the top downward, as in the Old Régime, not from the bottom upward, the democratic ideal. It is a planners' society, dominated by a bureaucratic *élite*; the old liberties and privileges and individuality which aristocracy cherishes have been eradicated to make way for a monotonous equality which the managers of society share.

> I seek to trace the novel features under which despotism may appear in the world. The first thing that strikes the observation is an innumerable multitude of men, all equal and all alike incessantly endeavouring to procure the petty and paltry pleasures with which they glut their lives. Each of them, living apart, is as a stranger to the fate of all the rest; his children and his private friends constitute for him the whole of mankind. As for the rest of his fellow citizens, he is close to them, but he does not see them; he touches

> them, but he does not feel them; he exists only in himself and for himself alone; and if his kindred still remain to him, he may be said at any rate to have lost his country.

This is the "American-standard-of-living" ideal of social existence, devastatingly outlined and condemned in a paragraph; and American society, like democratic societies throughout the world in countries which have undergone similar economic development, has arrived very nearly at a condition which fulfils this melancholy prophecy, four generations after Tocqueville wrote.[24]

But in the long run this society, though deprived of true community of spirit, cannot continue to be democratic or libertarian: its appetite for economic security and physical contentment exacts the sacrifice of liberty and true culture. A Colossus bestrides this world:

> Above this race of men stands an immense and tutelary power, which takes upon itself alone to secure their gratifications and to watch over their fate. That power is absolute, minute, regular, provident, and mild. It would be like the authority of a parent if, like that authority, its object was to prepare men for manhood; but it seeks, on the contrary, to keep them in perpetual childhood; it is well content that the people should rejoice, provided that they think of nothing but rejoicing. For their happiness such a government willingly labors, but it chooses to be the sole agent and the only arbiter of their necessities, facilitates their pleasures, manages their principal concerns, directs their industry, regulates the descent of property, and subdivides their inheritances; what remains, but to spare them all the care of thinking and all the trouble of living?
>
> Thus it every day renders the exercise of the free agency of man less useful and less frequent; it circumscribes the will within a narrower range and gradually robs a man of all the uses of himself. The principle of equality has prepared men for these things; it has predisposed them to endure them and often to look on them as benefits.[25]

Here a kind of humanitarian Egyptian or Peruvian society is described—just the sort of state which British and American collectivistic reformers project today. Most advocates of planned economy, indeed, are scarcely able to understand Tocqueville's distaste for an existence like this. The omnicompetent, paternalistic state, guiding all the affairs of mankind, satisfying all individuals' wants, is the ideal of twentieth-century social planners. This arrangement is intended to gratify the material demands of humanity, and twentieth-century social aspiration, saturated with the ideas of Bentham and Marx, scarcely conceives of wants that are not material. That men are kept in perpetual childhood—that, in spirit, they never become full human beings—seems no great loss to a generation of thinkers accustomed to compulsory schooling, compulsory insurance, compulsory military service, and even compulsory voting. A world of uniform compulsion is death to variety and the life of the mind; knowing this, Tocqueville felt that the materialism which democracy encourages may so far obsess the public consciousness as to stifle, in all but a few independent souls, the notions of freedom and variety.

"A native of the United States clings to this world's goods as if he were certain never to die; and he is so hasty in grasping at all within his reach that one would suppose he was constantly afraid of not living long enough to enjoy them. He clutches everything, he holds nothing fast, but soon loosens his grasp to pursue fresh gratifications."[26] This passion of avarice is not a vice peculiar to America, Tocqueville explains: it is a product of democratic times generally. An aristocrat, and the society to which he furnishes the tone, may hold riches in contempt—valour, honour, and pride of family being stronger impulses; but where commercialism fascinates even the most influential class among a people, presently that interest excludes almost all others. The middle classes, by their example, convince the mass of men that aggrandizement is the object of existence. And once the masses embrace this conviction, they do not rest until the state is reorganized to furnish them with material gratifications. Already, in America, this materialism tends toward standardization of character: "This gives to all their passions a sort of family likeness and soon renders the survey of them monotonous."[27] As older nations surrender to the democratic impulse, they succumb to materialism proportionately.

Materialism, as a governing force in society, is open to two overpowering objections: first, it enervates the higher faculties of man; second, it undoes itself. Materialism may be a negative vice, rather than a positive: "The reproach I address to the principle of equality is not that it leads men away in the pursuit of forbidden enjoyments, but that it absorbs men wholly in quest of those which are allowed. By these means a kind of virtuous materialism may ultimately be established in the world, which would not corrupt, but enervate, the soul and noiselessly unbend its springs of action.[28] (How much more penetrating is this than Macaulay's naive delight in new villas and "beautiful and costly machinery"!) Presently such absorption in the finite quite eclipses any realization of the infinite; and man, oblivious to the existence of spiritual powers or of God himself, ceases to be truly human. "Democracy encourages a taste for physical gratification; this taste, if it becomes excessive, soon disposes men to believe that all is matter only; and materialism, in its turn, hurries them on with mad impatience to these same delights; such is the fatal circle within which democratic nations are driven round. It were well that they should see the danger and turn back."[29]

After some passage of time, this preoccupation with getting and spending undermines the social structure which makes material accumulation possible. "If men were ever to content themselves with material objects, it is probable that they would lose by degrees the art of producing them; and they would enjoy them in the end, like the brutes, without discernment and without improvement."[30] For whatever enlarges the soul, renders the soul more fit, for practical undertakings; and whatever contracts the soul, enervates practical abilities in the process. Moral decay first hampers and then strangles honest government, regular commerce, and even the ability to take genuine pleasure in the goods of this world. Compulsion is applied from above as self-discipline relaxes below, and the last liberties expire under the weight of a unitary state. Once a society has slipped so far, almost no barrier remains to withstand absolutism. "Since religion has lost its empire over the souls of men, the most prominent boundary that divided good from evil is overthrown; kings and nations are guided by chance and none can say where are the natural limits of despotism and the bounds of license."[31] The state assumes the right to invade every detail of private life; this usurpation is endorsed by the dislike which undiscriminating democracies manifest toward individual differences; and at length the commercial and industrial impulse which commenced this chain of causation is broken by the importunate interference and insufferable burden of the super-state.

Is this triumph of democratic despotism inevitable? The extension of democratic institutions throughout the civilized world certainly is inevitable, Tocqueville answers, and seems so much a work of Providence that we ought to accept it as a process divinely ordained. But the perversion of democratic society into a sea of anonymous beings, social droplets, deprived of true family, true freedom, and true purpose, although terribly possible, is not yet inevitable. Against this, intelligent men should struggle like fanatics; for the Benthamite dream of social organization, in which the lonely, friendless, selfish, and hopeless individual confronts the leviathan state, in which all ancient affections and groupings have been eradicated and materialism has been substituted for traditional satisfactions—this may be averted by the force of ideas, or so we must hope. Eternal vigilance and incessant criticism will be required, however, if the tendency of democratic peoples toward a life-in-death monotony, a Byzantine dreariness, is in any degree to be arrested. The forces which impel mankind toward democratic despotism are of tremendous power. Tocqueville analyses them at length, chiefly in the fourth book of the second volume of *Democracy in America*. Chief among these causes, in addition to the materialism already remarked, are the democratic proclivities to simplicity of concept and structure, to centralization, and to standardization.

First, democratic peoples have a deep-founded dislike for hierarchy, intermediate orders, privileges, and special associations of all descriptions. Complexity and diversity are annoyingly difficult for common minds to appreciate, and this vexation is erected into detestation on principle. Even supernatural beings, intermediate between God and man, tend to fade from the religion of democratic societies: the average man prefers the simple relationship of individual confronting Divinity directly. If democracies do not tolerate angels or devils, they will hardly endure vestiges of aristocracy, limited franchises, privileged persons, and those other institutions which interpose barriers between the government and the private concerns of citizens. Thus the trend of democratic simplification is to efface the very safeguards which make libertarian democracy possible. Tocqueville repeatedly describes the function of an aristocracy in protecting freedom. "Nothing in the world is so conservative in its views as an aristocracy. The mass of the people may be led astray by ignorance or passion; the mind of a king may be biased and made to vacillate in his designs; and, besides, a king is not immortal. But an aristocratic body is too numerous to be led astray by intrigue, and yet not numerous enough to yield readily to the intoxication of unreflecting passion. An aristocracy is a firm and enlightened body that never dies."[32] But this instrument for checking arbitrary power and ensuring the continuity of civilization invariably is extirpated by a triumphant democracy.

Second, the readiness of democratic states to concentrate in the central government all real power soon withers true democracy at the root; for democracy is a product of local institutions and self-reliance. More perspicacious than the Federalists and many of the Tories, Tocqueville perceived, like Randolph and Calhoun, that liberty is intimately connected with particularism. Consolidation is the instrument of innovation and despotism. The Old Régime in France erred in considering consolidation a conservative device: on the contrary, consolidation made possible the overthrow of a multitude of ancient interests by one single wave of revolutionary violence. The consolidated machine of government which the Bourbons had established was promptly converted to Jacobinical purposes.

> Not only is a democratic people led by its own taste to centralize its government, but the passions of all the men by whom it is governed constantly urge it in the same direction. It may easily be foreseen that almost all the able and ambitious members of a democratic community will labor unceasingly to extend the powers of government, because they all hope at some time or other to wield those powers themselves. It would be a waste of time to attempt to prove to them that extreme centralization may be injurious to the state, since they are centralizing it for their own benefit. Among the public men of democracies, there are hardly any but men of great disinterestedness or extreme mediocrity who seek to oppose the centralization of government; the former are scarce, the latter powerless.[33]

The situation of the states of the American union today—resentful yet mendicant-like before increasing influence by the federal government, fearful of consolidation but cursed with an insatiable appetite for federal grants-in-aid—is sufficient illustration of Tocqueville's observation. Only one thing is safe from revolution, said Tocqueville: centralization. Only one thing could not be set up in France—a free government; and only one thing could not be destroyed—the centralizing principle. Even with men aware of its dangerous nature, "The pleasure it procures them of interfering with everyone and holding everything in their hands atones to them for its dangers."[34] Centralization promises special favours to all sorts of interests, and its possibilities tempt simple democrats almost irresistibly. Yet centralization is wholly inimical to democracy, transferring power to the operator of the machine of government. "I am of the opinion that, in the democratic ages which are opening upon us, individual independence and local liberties will ever be the products of art; that centralization will be the natural government."[35]

Third, democratic nations are enamoured of uniformity, standardization; they hate the eccentric, the grand, the mysterious. They demand that legislation be comprehensive and inflexible. "As every man sees that he differs but little from those about him, he cannot understand why a rule that is applicable to one man should not be equally applicable to all others. Hence the slightest privileges are repugnant to his reason; the faintest dissimilarities in the political institutions of the same people offends him, and uniformity of legislation appears to him to be the first condition of good government."[36]

When classes vanish, presently even the taste to be different, to be a distinct individual, wanes; men grow ashamed of personality. In the ages of aristocracy men sought to create imaginary differences even where no actual distinctions existed; in democratic times everything slides toward the blur of mediocrity. "Men are much alike, and they are annoyed, as it were, by any deviation from that likeness; far from seeking to preserve their own distinguishing singularities, they endeavor to shake them off in order to identify themselves with the general mass of people, which is the sole representative of right and of might in their eyes."[37] Leadership dwindles in consequence, the enlivening energy of contrast evaporates from a people, and men become almost featureless, mere ciphers, identical and interchangeable in the social system. Intelligence shrinks proportionately. As candidates for any sort of advancement appear more and more alike, democracies tend to select men for preferment not by recognition of their peculiar talents, but by wearisome regulations and routines. "From hatred of privilege and from the embarrassment of choosing, all men are at last forced, whatever may be their standard, to pass the same ordeal; all are indiscriminately subjected to a multitude of petty preliminary exercises, in which their youth is wasted and their imagination quenched, so that they despair of ever fully attaining what is held out to them; and when at length they are in a condition to perform any extraordinary acts, the taste for such things has forsaken them."[38] Anyone familiar with the methods of modern educationists and administrators—in the graduate schools of American universities, for instance—knows what Tocqueville means. When ambition is stifled deliberately after this fashion, the tone of collective life must suffer.

Altogether, this analysis of democratic follies is a dismaying picture of society's stumbling progress toward a condition of servitude called democracy but in actuality a new absolutism. Its outlines have become clearer in the twentieth century. Tocqueville's most succinct description of this yawning peril occurs near the beginning of his *Democracy*:

> I perceive that we have destroyed those individual powers which were able, single-handed, to cope with tyranny; but it is the government alone that has inherited all the privileges of which families, guilds, and individuals have been deprived; to the power of a small number of persons, which if it was sometimes oppressive was often conservative, has succeeded the weakness of the whole community.
>
> The distribution of property has lessened the distance which separated the rich from the poor; but it would seem that, the nearer they draw to each other, the greater is their mutual hatred and the more vehement the envy and the dread with which they resist each other's claims to power; the idea of right does not exist for either party, and force affords to both the only security for the present and the only guarantee for the future.[39]

What should be done? Marx, in these very years, was full of visions of a world purged utterly of the old order, problems solved in a proletarian upheaval, society reconstituted from base to pinnacle—or rather, all society above the base lopped away. The calm, intricate, and analytical mind of Tocqueville, aware that no knot really is untied after the method Alexander used with Gordius's, turned instead to the weary necessity of reconciling old values with new faiths—the conservative function, so much derided, so difficult to execute, so indispensable to the survival of civilization.

"I have always thought that in revolutions, especially democratic revolutions, madmen, not those so called by courtesy, but genuine madmen, have played a very considerable political part. One thing at least is certain, and that is that a condition of semi-madness is not unbecoming at such times, and often even leads to success."[40] This is Tocqueville writing of the frightful days of 1848—when, like ghosts of '93, such raving figures as Blanqui and Barbès invaded the Tribune of the Chamber of Deputies and cried out for a new Terror. Tocqueville was present at the wild street-fighting of this first strong socialist snatch at power; he saw the balloon of Marxism pricked, for the time being; and soon he was foreign minister under Louis Napoleon, until the *coup d'état* ended the public life of the critic of democracy, who would no more bow to a plebiscitary dictator than to the Parisian mob. That Tocqueville could witness these swings of the revolutionary pendulum and still hope for the future of society is testimony to his remarkable strength of mind.

Tocqueville knew that men and societies possess free will. Holding Hegel and all his school in contempt, he scoffed at deterministic theories of history, with their chain of fatality, and described the factors of chance and unknown causation in historical movements—"chance, or rather that tangle of secondary causes which we call chance." His faith in Providence, genuine and pervasive as Burke's, denied these pretentious theories of fixed fate and national destinies. "If this doctrine of necessity, which is so attractive to those who read history in democratic ages, passes from authors to their readers till it infects the whole mass of the community and gets possession of the public mind, it will soon paralyze the activity of modern society and reduce Christians to the level of the Turks."[41] Great and mysterious movements indeed were at work in the world of the nineteenth century; but opinion and political institutions could modify and mould the shape of these tendencies. Granted patience and good conduct, even the Old Régime could have been preserved and reformed without indiscriminate destruction: "The revolution broke out not when evils were at their worst, but when reform was beginning," he wrote to Freslon. "Half-way down the staircase we threw ourselves out of the window, in order to get sooner to the bottom. Such, in fact, is the common course of events."[42] The common course, yes; but not the inevitable course; and a determined stand still may avert the coming of democratic despotism.

Tocqueville's liberal conservatism is no forlorn cause yet. To inevitable democracy he rendered the invaluable service of strict criticism and delineated reform. Mr. A. J. P. Taylor, in his recent book *From Napoleon to Stalin*, thinks that Tocqueville failed in his course of action and his analysis of events during 1848: "The greatest invention of 1848," Taylor writes, "which Tocqueville disowned, was Social Democracy; this was the only way in which civilization could be saved. . . . Above all, he who loves liberty must have faith in the people."[43]

This is as if Morelly or Mably were disinterred to criticize Alexis de Tocqueville. For Tocqueville knew all too well the nature of "Social Democracy," a euphemism coined to describe the centralized equalitarian state, governed (with, perhaps, occasional plebiscites) by the central new *élite*, which does not so much choke freedom as simply ignores it. And, being Burke's pupil, Tocqueville never could submit to the delusion that "the people" exist as an abstraction to be trusted or feared or hated or revered in place of Jehovah.

None understood better than Burke and Tocqueville the idea of nationality and the eternal union of all generations of mankind; but the People, or masses, do not live a mystic, beneficent existence somehow independent of parties, passions, and the ordinary failings of humanity. The people do not think or act uninfluenced by ideas and leaders. Without ideas and leaders, indeed, a people cannot truly be said to exist: in the absence of such a leaven, the people subsist only as an inchoate mass of loosely cohering units, a tapioca-pudding state, which condition many utilitarian social planners contemplate with equanimity. The people, under the influence of high principle, sometimes may be capable of great courage and sacrifice; they may also, under the dominion of other principles, shout for Hitler or Stalin or any man who wishes to burn a witch. Lacking the influence of those virtuous customs and establishments that Tocqueville described, the people become Hamilton's "great beast"; and to trust them in the abstract is an act of faith more recklessly credulous than medieval men's trust in relics. Precisely this blind stumbling in the wake of the multitude is the error which *Democracy in America* was written to remedy.

["The Prescience of Tocqueville," University of Toronto Quarterly, *Vol. 22 (July 1953), 342–53. This selection also appears in Chapter VI, Section 4, "Tocqueville on Democratic Despotism,"* The Conservative Mind: From Burke to Eliot, *7th rev. ed. (Washington, DC: Regnery Publishing, Inc., 1986, c1953), 204–24.]*

T. S. Eliot's Permanent Things

Kirk was unyielding in his belief that "[w]e cling to the permanent things, the norms of our being, because all other grounds are quicksand." "The permanent things," words that come from T. S. Eliot, is a phrase that recurs in Kirk's works. To Kirk "the permanent things" signify "the creations of an intention and a wisdom more than natural, more than private, more than human," in other words, a transcendent reality of higher certitudes and acceptations that in turn metamorphose into universal paradigms of truth. "The permanent things" are not only the bedrock of normative principles of order, but also the intrinsic recognition of the authority of the Bible, of Antiquity and Tradition, of Revelation. The "enemies of the permanent things" are those who spurn the natural or "informal" inferences we draw from religious doctrine, or the "illative sense," a term Kirk frequently quoted from John Henry Newman's The Grammar of Assent *(1870).*

In every age, the dominant man of letters has been a champion of normality, with only here and there a national or a temporary exception. Frequently he has swum against the strong intellectual and social currents of his time. So it was even with Homer, before classical history began: the *Iliad* is a noble appeal to divine justice and order, against the violence of a brutal epoch and the confused passions of its masters. Homer's strong and subtle portrait of Achilles in his wrath, delivered up to *ate* (folly and guilt), is an epitome of the impious errors of a people and an age.

In the twentieth century, T. S. Eliot became the principal poet and critic in this ethical continuity. Like Samuel Johnson in the eighteenth century, Eliot held in contempt the climate of "progressive" opinion in which he found himself. He was as much amused as vexed at those intellectuals who mistook Eliot's analysis of the modern temper for assent to the modern temper, with its weariness and futility. At length the reviewers perceived what way Eliot was rowing—and grew indignant. As Eliot remarks in "Thoughts after Lambeth" (1931):

> When . . . I brought out a small book of essays, several years ago, called *For Lancelot Andrewes*, the anonymous reviewer in the *Times Literary Supplement* made it the occasion for what I can only describe as a flattering obituary

> notice. In words of great seriousness and manifest sincerity, he pointed out that I had suddenly arrested my progress—whither he had supposed me to be moving I do not know—and that to his distress I was unmistakably making off in the wrong direction. Somehow I had failed, and had admitted my failure; if not a lost leader, at least a lost sheep; what is more, I was a kind of traitor; and those who were to find their way to the promised land beyond the waste, might drop a tear at my absence from the roll-call of the new saints.[44]

In fact, from the beginning it had been Eliot's purpose to attack this new inverted orthodoxy of "progressivism." He meant to defend "lost" causes, because he knew that no cause worth upholding ever is lost altogether. He had sworn fealty to what he called "the permanent things," and he understood that these permanent things were the creations of an intention and a wisdom more than natural, more than private, more than human.

Any attentive reader may discern without difficulty this dedication in *The Waste Land* (1922) and *The Cocktail Party* (1949). It is no less strong in Eliot's later writings. I attended the first performance, at the Edinburgh Festival, of Eliot's comedy *The Confidential Clerk* (1953), and soon after published a criticism of that play. When next we met, Eliot told me that I had understood him better than had anyone else who had ventured to write about *The Confidential Clerk* before that comedy was printed; and, indeed, when the British and American editions of the play appeared, I was surprised to find that some of my own remarks had been chosen to appear on the jackets of both editions, in pride of place. This approbation from a gentleman who almost invariably refrained, on principle, from comment upon interpretations of his writings may be sufficient excuse for examining here *The Confidential Clerk* as a less-known model of Eliot's normative undertaking, which ran through almost everything he wrote.

The sinister suggestions latent in the title of this play are not realized: for Eliot's clerk is simply a man of business, and all the characters are people ordinary enough, with the partial exception of Colby, the new clerk. Their ordinariness, indeed, is the cause of their unhappiness, and provides the play with its principal theme: the prison of Self.

Sir Claude Mulhammer the financier, and his flighty wife Lady Elizabeth, and his protégés Lucasta Angel and Colby, and B. Kaghan the rising young broker, do not understand one another, or themselves, or even from whence they came. The younger people know that they were born out of wedlock, but apprehend little else about their world. Sir Claude, in the first act, declares that his principle of action is always to assume that he understands nothing about any man he meets; yet to assume that the other man understands *him* thoroughly. Yet even this premise betrays Mulhammer in the end, until he cries, with his eyes shut, "Is Colby coming back?"—knowing now that even the presumed existence of his own son had been an illusion for twenty-five years.

These people, the wrack of broken families, specimens of a generation without certitudes and deprived of continuity with the past, are involved in the very oldest of dramatic plots—mistaken identity, the missing son, and the classical comedy of errors. Eliot revives these devices ingeniously, doubtless with some pleasure in his anachronisms; and, perhaps consciously, he writes whole speeches that could have been Shaw's, and others that could have been the work of Wilde, and others Ibsen's. Lady Elizabeth with her "mind study," her Swiss clinics, and her intuitions, would have done credit to Wilde; the bond between Lucasta and Colby, broken by Colby's discovery that they may be brother and sister, has a Shavian touch; while through all three acts, somberly, the ghost of *The Wild Duck* (1884) whispers that the truth we ween about ourselves may be our undoing. When all is over, Colby and Lucasta and Kaghan, at least, do know who they are, and in some degree realize their end in life, but they accept the discovery of their true nature with resignation, not with relief. Upon them all, though most heavily upon Mulhammer, descends a consciousness of the vanity of human wishes.

Everyone in the play (except, possibly, for old Eggerson, the retiring clerk, with his wife and garden and simple virtues) is haunted by a terrifying loneliness and a regret for talents frustrated. Even accomplishment in the arts (Mulhammer would have liked to be a praiseworthy potter, and Colby a talented organist and composer) is baffled by the spirit of our age, Eliot seems to suggest. These people are what Burke called the flies of a summer, unable to link with dead generations or those yet unborn, lacking memories or high hope. They seek for continuity, status, faith; and, beyond all these (though only Colby, probably, knows this) they seek for some assurance that their lives *matter*, and that the barriers which separate every man from his fellows are transcended by a Reality more than fleshly.

In structure, *The Confidential Clerk* is close to *The Importance of Being Earnest* (1895), even to the revelations in the final act by the old nurse (or rather, here, Mrs. Guzzard, the foster-mother); and it is possible to laugh at certain lines and certain characters. Yet the man who sees *The Confidential Clerk* laughs only after the fashion of Democritus, at the pathos of all evanescent things; for in its essence this play is sad, profoundly sad, as sad as *The Waste Land*. In the second part, especially, occur lines of high tenderness and pathos, as when Lucasta comes to believe that she understands Colby and herself, and is on the brink of self-realization—and then this is overwhelmed, the next instant, by disillusion, or rather by illusion of a different sort. Throughout the play, Eliot treats his people with mercy and sympathy; they become lovable, indeed, all of them. From Sir Claude to Mrs. Guzzard, they are men and women of kindly natures, honest inclinations, and generous hearts. But, being human and modern, they are heir to all the imperfections of the spirit and the flesh; thus they cannot escape the rootlessness of their time, nor the sense of talents run to waste, nor the prison of Self. They do not know themselves, nor the nature of being.

Lucasta thinks that Colby is different from the rest of them, for he can withdraw from their midst into his garden of the imagination, a sanctuary from the desolated material world. But Colby himself knows better: his garden of mind is as lonely as the real world without. If Colby were endowed with conviction of an abiding reality that surpassed the Waste Land—why, then indeed he never would be solitary in his domain of fancy, for "God would walk in my garden." Wanting this faith, however, the man is left melancholy and unnerved, deprived of love, and scarcely caring to know the identity of his parents. We see him, near the end of the third act, groping toward a churchly vocation; yet only Eggerson, the practical old clerk, has come close to understanding Colby. Lucasta, turning back to Kaghan for some sense of affection and belonging, thinks that Colby needs no human company, being secure in the citadel of self-knowledge. She does not understand how like a citadel is to a prison.

Although successful enough as a dramatic production, *The Confidential Clerk* will be remembered more for its occasional lines of twilight beauty and its penetration into the recesses of Self than as a neat and close-knit comedy. Few consider it one of Eliot's principal works. Yet I am not sure of this judgment; for this is a play which touches most movingly upon the sources of longing and the need for enduring love, and so bears the mark of a man of genius.

Now the permanent things for which Eliot stands, in this comedy and in all his writing, are not difficult to make out. First, he is governed by what Unamuno called "the tragic sense of life," the Christian knowledge that men never will be as gods; that we all are imperfectible creatures, necessarily discontented even in our sensate triumphs. Were it not for the hope that man is made for eternity, we should be the most miserable of creatures; but that hope is compensation for all our mishaps here below, and it sets the Christian world high above the gloomy classical world.

Second, Eliot abides by the wisdom of our ancestors: the Christian and Judaic and classical patrimony, incorporated in tradition. As Eliot expressed this in his essay "Tradition and the Individual Talent" (1917), "Some one said: 'The dead writers are remote from us because we *know* so much more than they did.' Precisely, and they are that which we know."[45] Here are Fulbert's giants again. As Virgil, in his Fourth Eclogue, seems to have prophesied the coming of Christ, so the writer of vision may foresee and describe what he does not wholly understand himself. In this vein, Eliot wrote in "Virgil and the Christian World" (1951):

> A poet may believe that he is expressing only his private experience; his lines may be for him only a means of talking about himself without giving himself away; yet for his readers what he has written may come to be the expression both of their own secret feelings and of the exultation or despair of a generation. He need not know what his poetry will come to mean to others; and a prophet need not understand the meaning of his private utterance.[46]

Because the poet lives in a tradition, he may become a prophet; the great mysterious incorporation of the human race speaks through him, so that he says more than he comprehends. Tradition is not mere purblind stumbling in the track of yesterday's common men; and Eliot makes this point clear in "Tradition and the Individual Talent":

> Yet if the only form of tradition, of handing down, consisted in following the ways of the immediate generation before us in a blind or timid adherence to its ways, "tradition" should positively be discouraged. We have seen many such simple currents soon lost in the sand; and novelty is better than repetition. Tradition is a matter of much wider significance. It cannot be inherited, and if you want it you must obtain it by great labour. It involves, in the first place, the historical sense, which we may call nearly indispensable to any one who would continue to be a poet beyond his twenty-fifth year; and the historical sense involves a perception, not only of the pastness of the past, but of its presence; the historical sense compels a man to write not merely with his own generation in his bones, but with a feeling that the whole of the literature of Europe from Homer and within it the whole of the literature of his country has a simultaneous existence and composes a simultaneous order. This historical sense, which is a sense of the timeless as well as of the temporal and of the timeless and of the temporal together, is what makes a writer traditional. And it is at the same time what makes a writer most acutely conscious of his place in time, of his own contemporaneity.[47]

Third, Eliot seeks to recover the idea of a Christian society, in which order and justice and freedom obtain their fullest possible expression in a world irremediably flawed. As he wrote in 1939:

> So long . . . as we consider finance, industry, trade, agriculture merely as competing interests to be reconciled from time to time as best they may, so long as we consider "education" as a good in itself of which everyone has a right to the utmost, without any ideal of the good life for society or for the individual, we shall move from one uneasy compromise to another. To the quick and simple organization of society for ends which, being only material and worldly, must be as ephemeral as worldly success, there is only one alternative. As political philosophy derives its sanction from ethics, and ethics from the truth of religion, it is only by returning to the eternal source of truth that we can hope for any social organization which will not, to its ultimate destruction, ignore some essential aspect of reality. The term "democracy," as I have said again and again, does not contain enough positive content to stand alone against the forces that you dislike—it can easily be transformed by them. If you will not have God (and He is a jealous God) you should pay your respects to Hitler or Stalin.[48]

Only a civil social order, that is, which retains some understanding of consecration, ordination, and reverence can withstand fanatic ideologues and squalid oligarchs. It is not a theocracy that Eliot desires, but a commonwealth in which the leaders and the people alike acknowledge their mystical brotherhood in Christ, with the social consequences which arise from that community of spirit.

These standards—the tragic view of life, the adherence to real tradition, the Christian community expressed in the political order—are Eliot's fundamentals. We cannot retain or regain normative principles, he reasons, without an authoritative source of knowledge. And that fountain of authority, for Eliot, is the revelation—from prophets and from poets—which we possess already. As I mentioned earlier, David Hume maintains that we are governed by "impressions," or innate ideas, the source of which is unknowable. Basil Willey, in *The Eighteenth Century Background* (1940), paraphrases Hume's argument: "Religion is irrational, theism is permissible only in utter attenuation: oh for a revelation! but not, if you please, the one we are supposed to have had already."

Such skepticism is a far cry from Eliot's premises. "Impressions," Eliot says, are perilous guides, in private affairs as in public; nor will Irving Babbitt's "inner check" upon appetite suffice. John Middleton Murry had declared that an impressionistic "inner voice"—of what?—is quite enough, and preferable far to obeying tradition. Eliot replied in his essay "The Function of Criticism" (1923):

> Those of us who find ourselves supporting what Mr. Murry calls Classicism believe that men cannot get on without giving allegiance to something outside themselves. . . . "The English writer, the English statesman, inherit no rules from their forebears; they inherit only this: a sense that in the last resort they must depend upon the inner voice." This statement does, I admit, appear to cover certain cases; it throws a flood of light upon Mr. Lloyd George. But why "in the last resort"? Do they, then, avoid the dictates of the inner voice up to the last extremity? My belief is that those who possess this inner voice are ready enough to hearken to it, and will hear no other. The inner voice, in fact, sounds remarkably like an old principle which has been formulated by an elder critic in the now familiar phrase of "doing as one likes." The possessors of the inner voice ride ten in a compartment to a football match at Swansea, listening to the inner voice, which breathes the eternal message of vanity, fear, and lust.[49]

So Eliot submits himself to Authority, as described by Cardinal Newman: "Conscience is an authority; the Bible is an authority; such is the Church; such is Antiquity; such are the words of the wise, such are hereditary memories, such are legal saws and state maxims; such are proverbs; such are sentiments, presages, and prepossessions." The inner voice speaks often of desires, but seldom of norms; and only from authority may we learn normality.

Accordingly, genuine education is the conveying of normative wisdom, through study of authorities. The liberals, says Eliot, have gone astray in education by their assumption that we learn chiefly through personal experience. Having declared this (in "Religion and Literature," 1934), Eliot struck out at the liberals' fallacies:

> At this point I anticipate a rejoinder from the liberal-minded, from all those who are convinced that if everybody says what he thinks, and does what he likes, things will somehow, by some automatic compensation and adjustment, come right in the end. "Let everything be tried," they say, "and if it is a mistake, then we shall learn by experience." This argument might have some value, if we were always the same generation upon earth; or if, as we know to be not the case, people ever learned much from the experience of their elders. The liberals are convinced that only by what is called unrestrained individualism, will truth ever emerge. Ideas, views of life, they

> think, issue distinct from independent heads, and in consequence of their knocking violently against each other, the fittest survives, and truth rises triumphant. Anyone who dissents from this view must be either a mediaevalist, wishful only to set back the clock, or else a fascist, and probably both."[50]

But wisdom is not got through shouting-matches within one generation. Culture is the creation of a talented little minority, over centuries; what we call "mass culture" either is the emulation by the crowd of the culture conferred—even imposed—by Fulbert's giants, or else it is a popular degradation and caricature of a dying genuine culture. In *Notes Towards the Definition of Culture* (1948), Eliot describes the destruction of civilization by educationists' "mass culture":

> And yet the culture of Europe has deteriorated visibly within the memory of many of us who are by no means the oldest among us. And we know, that whether education can foster and improve culture or not, it can surely adulterate and degrade it. For there is no doubt that in our headlong rush to educate everybody, we are lowering our standards, and more and more abandoning the study of those subjects by which the essentials of our culture—of that part of it which is transmissible by education—are transmitted; destroying our ancient edifices to make ready the ground upon which the barbarian nomads of the future will encamp in their mechanized caravans.[51]

The Church is the great repository of authoritative wisdom; so real education necessarily is religious; "secularized" instruction undoes itself. "As only the Catholic and the communist know," Eliot wrote in 1933, "*all* education must be ultimately religious education. I do not mean that education should be confined to postulants for the priesthood or for the higher ranks of Soviet bureaucracy; I mean that the hierarchy of education should be a religious hierarchy."

The rationalist liberal will protest promptly that we must no longer be suckled in a creed outworn. Yet Eliot replies in "The *Pensées* of Pascal" (1933) that Christianity is not merely a credible body of belief, but the only source of certitude:

> The Christian thinker—and I mean the man who is trying consciously and conscientiously to explain to himself the sequence which culminates in faith, rather than the public apologist—proceeds by rejection and elimination.

> He finds the world to be so and so; he finds its character inexplicable by any non-religious theory; among religions he finds Christianity, and Catholic Christianity, to account most satisfactorily for the world, and especially for the world within; and thus, by what Newman calls "powerful and concurrent" reasons, he finds himself inexorably committed to the dogma of the Incarnation. To the unbeliever, this method seems disingenuous and perverse: for the unbeliever is, as a rule, not so greatly troubled to explain the world to himself, nor so greatly distressed by its disorder; nor is he generally concerned (in modern terms) to "preserve values." He does not consider that if certain emotional states, certain development of character, and what in the highest sense can be called "saintliness" are inherently and by inspection known to be good, then the satisfactory explanation of the world must be an explanation which will admit the "reality" of those values.[52]

If men reject authority and reject all the inferences which we draw from religious doctrine, then they are left with no better ethics than the moral system of Thomas Hobbes. As Eliot writes in his essay on John Bramhall (1927), the modern notion that value resides "entirely in the degree of organization of natural impulses" is close akin to Hobbes's assumptions. Eliot proceeds to quote a passage from I. A. Richards's *Principles of Literary Criticism* (1924), by way of illustrating the narrow naturalism of the liberal who will not accept authority, tradition, and the illative sense:

> Anything is valuable which will satisfy an appetency without involving the frustration of some equal or more important appetency; in other words, the only reason which can be given for not satisfying a desire is that more important desires will thereby be thwarted. Thus morals become purely prudential, and ethical codes merely the expression of the most general schemes of expediency to which an individual or a race has attained.[53]

These "values" of I. A. Richards or Bertrand Russell, it appears, are no better than the satisfaction of appetites upon a Benthamite moral calculus. For ethical codes which are simply "general schemes of expediency," Eliot had no respect. What revelation, tradition, and normative insight dictate often is highly inexpedient for a particular person at a particular time, or indeed for certain communities; yet those commands must be obeyed. In the intricate and unending calculation of appetite-preferences, every man must be bewildered all his life, and so must any society that tries to govern itself expediently by a perpetual measuring of relative frustrations. We cling to the permanent things, the norms of our being, because all other grounds are quicksand.

Only by the recovery of normative truths, Eliot argued decade after decade, can we save ourselves from the forces of disintegration. Perhaps he put this best in "Thoughts after Lambeth":

> I do not mean that our times are particularly corrupt; all times are corrupt. I mean that Christianity, in spite of certain local appearances, is not, and cannot be within measurable time, "official." The World is trying the experiment of attempting to form a civilized but non-Christian mentality. The experiment will fail; but we must be very patient in awaiting its collapse; meanwhile redeeming the time: so that the Faith may be preserved alive through the dark ages before us; to renew and rebuild civilization, and save the World from suicide.[54]

To those chilled by the foggy climate of opinion in which we dwell now, it should be some comfort and encouragement that the greatest man of letters of this century, with his penetrating critical intellect (which did not spare certain insufficiencies in important Christian writers), set his face unflinchingly against the enemies of the permanent things. In the long run, it is the man of vision who prevails, not the eager little knot of intellectuals hot after novelties. We speak, long later, of an "Age of Milton," an "Age of Dryden," an "Age of Johnson"—not an age of this or that neoterist. The little dogs and all, Tray, Blanch, and Sweet-heart, will bark at Eliot; he is feared and disliked by those "intellectualists" disparaged by Francis Bacon (after Heraclitus) as cloudy speculators "which are, notwithstanding, commonly taken for the most sublime and divine philosophers." The modern ideologue is such an intellectualist, and the modern ideologue detests Eliot—precisely because Eliot is so persuasive and so difficult to refute. Yet in the fullness of time, if indeed not tomorrow, the greater part of the twentieth century will be known, in letters, as the Age of Eliot. . . .

["T. S. Eliot's Permanent Things," Enemies of the Permanent Things*:* Observations of Abnormity in Literature and Politics*, Rev. ed. (La Salle, IL: Sherwood Sugden & Company, 1969), 51–62.]*

❖

Eric Voegelin's Normative Labor

Among the keen-sighted few who perceived the magnitude of a modern "disordered world of metaphysical madness," Kirk said, was Eric Voegelin (1901–85), a German political philosopher who immigrated to the United States in 1936 to escape Nazism. Author of the multivolume Order and History *(1956–87), Voegelin maintained that politics arises out of the acceptance of transcendent religious principles. When these principles are compromised political order falters. From the very beginning, Kirk championed Voegelin's ideas, seeing in them a source of principles of order liberated from ideology. In any striving for political normality, Voegelin insisted, the first of the moral virtues is prudence, a virtue Kirk much valued. His espousal of Voegelin's achievement refutes "enlightened historians" who purvey "illusory opinions and vain wishes." If we are to reclaim our patrimony, Kirk avows, we must heed a philosopher—a* spoudaios *in Aristotle's sense of a serious man of thought—of moral excellence and wisdom like Eric Voegelin.*

Understanding Politics through History

In healthy reaction to the enemies of the permanent things in politics, a considerable body of serious political and historical scholarship has appeared in recent years. Some of these writers have been mentioned in earlier chapters. Perhaps the most systematic of them is Dr. Eric Voegelin, whose historical studies are intended to point the way toward a recovery of political normality.

"The true dividing line in the contemporary crisis," Voegelin wrote fifteen years ago, "does not run between liberals and totalitarians, but between the religious and philosophical transcendentalists on the one side, and the liberal and totalitarian immanentist sectarians on the other." This theme runs through his influential little book *The New Science of Politics* (1952), and through his massive work *Order and History* (1956–87) (in four volumes, one of which, at this writing, remains to be published).[55] The delusion that human rationality may convert the world into an earthly paradise is, in Voegelin's view, the principal source of our modern political catastrophes. For politics, like science, like art, arises out of belief in a transcendent religion; and when that faith decays, politics degenerates.

Professor Voegelin's personal experience of social disorder is considerable, extending from persecution by the Nazis to being knocked on the head by a gang of young criminals not far from the University of Notre Dame, in Indiana. Witty, good-natured, master of classical and Christian learning, Voegelin is thoroughly familiar with English and American political philosophy. Describing himself as a "pre-Reformation Christian," he draws upon both Protestant and Catholic theologians. He sees in the United States and Britain the two nations least seriously infected by ideology and Gnosticism, and in them a hope for the regeneration of our civilization.

"On my religious 'position,'" Voegelin writes of ideologues' attacks, "I have been classified as a Protestant, a Catholic, as anti-semitic and as a typical Jew; politically, as a Liberal, a Fascist, a National Socialist, and a Conservative; and on my theoretical position, as a Platonist, a Neo-Augustinian, a Thomist, a disciple of Hegel, an existentialist, a historical relativist, and an empirical sceptic; in recent years the suspicion has frequently been voiced that I am a Christian. All these classifications have been made by university professors and people with academic degrees. They give ample food for thought regarding the state of our universities."[56]

Such labels wake passions, when dispassionate discourse is required. And Voegelin endeavors to restore among us an understanding of general principles, emancipated from ideology.

Gnosticism, the heresy which substitutes a dream of a perfect mundane society for the City of God, lies at the root of the clamorous ideologies which compete for the support of the modern crowd. To ideology, Voegelin opposes science, or understanding of man and society founded upon observation throughout history. In disavowing ideology, Voegelin espouses political principle. Like Burke, he draws a distinction between "abstraction" (or an *a priori* assumption unsupported by history or common experience or what we call revelation) and "principle," or a justified deduction from what we have learnt, over the ages, about men and their commonwealths. With Burke, and with Richard Hooker, he makes the virtue of prudence the means of political wisdom:

> In classic and Christian ethics the first of the moral virtues is *sophia* or *prudentia*, because without adequate understanding of the structure of society, including the *conditio humana*, moral action with rational co-ordination of means and ends is hardly possible. In the Gnostic dream world, on the other hand, non-recognition of reality is the first principle.

Recognition of a transcendent order in the universe does not make the statesman into a dreamer, but into a realist. Knowing his theology and his history, he takes it for granted that man is not a perfect nor a perfectible being, and that the prudent statist will endeavor to make life in the civil social order tolerable, not perfect. It is utopianism, the Gnostic delusion, which leads (in Voegelin's words) "with increasing theoretical illiteracy to the form of various social idealisms, such as the abolition of war, of unequal distribution of property, of fear and want. And, finally, immanentization may extend to the complete Christian symbol. The result will then be the active mysticism of a state of perfection, to be achieved through a revolutionary transfiguration of the nature of man, as, for instance, in Marxism."

By definition, human nature is a constant; knowing this, the statesman is aware that human longing never can be satisfied upon this earth. For him, politics indeed is the art of the possible, and he remains content with patching and improving society here and there; he feels he has done well if he has preserved a tolerable measure of justice and order and freedom.

In modern political action, Gnosticism has two manifestations, its left wing and its right: communism and liberalism. "If liberalism is understood as the immanent salvation of man and society, communism certainly is its most radical expression; it is an evolution that was already anticipated by John Stuart Mill's faith in the ultimate advent of communism for mankind."

In the year of the Communist Manifesto, Orestes Brownson declared that communism was a heresy from Christianity; and this view is Voegelin's, as it is that of Father Martin D'Arcy and other philosophers of our time. But liberalism is only a more moderate form of the same heresy, the notion that Progress consists in material aggrandizement. A culture which abandons knowledge of God in the expectation of creature-comforts already is far gone in decadence:

> A civilization can, indeed, advance and decline at the same time—but not forever. There is a limit toward which the ambiguous process moves; the limit is reached when an activist sect which represents the Gnostic truth organizes the civilization into an empire under its rule. Totalitarianism, defined as the existential rule of Gnostic activists, is the end form of progressive civilization.

Now this is repudiation of liberalism root and branch, whether old-style individualistic liberalism or new-style collectivistic liberalism. The premises upon which liberalism is established must lead, according to Voegelin, to a total state, soon or late; for the Gnostic passion to alter society and human nature endures no opposition; and when it can, it destroys all the institutions which impede its consolidatory advance. If the only purpose of life is material success, why should reactionaries be permitted to delay the advent of utopia? Voegelin cites Harold Laski, in *Faith, Reason, and Civilization* (1944), to illustrate his point; as Laski put it, "It is, indeed, true in a sense to argue that the Russian principle cuts deeper than the Christian, since it seeks salvation for the masses by fulfillment in this life, and, thereby, orders anew the actual world we know."

The hour is very late, Voegelin writes; our society is terribly corrupt; and "it will require all our efforts to kindle this glimmer into a flame by repressing Gnostic corruption and restoring the forces of civilization. At present the fate is in the balance."

Voegelin's primary concern is order—which is also the first concern of jurisprudence. Now "order" means the principle and the process by which the peace and harmony of society are maintained. It is the arrangement of rights and duties in a state to ensure that people may find just leaders, may be loyal citizens, and may obtain public tranquillity. "Order" implies the obedience of a nation to the laws of God, and the obedience of individuals to just authority. Without order, justice rarely can be enforced, and freedom cannot be maintained.

Yet since the French Revolution, "order" has been an unpopular word. Order implies leadership, discipline, self-restraint, duty; and the doctrinaire ideological pamphleteers, from Tom Paine onward, have been hostile to these concepts. Emancipation from all restraints, inner or outer, has been the desire of the more extreme liberals of modern times. That this anarchic emancipation ends only in tyranny is a fact which the ritualistic liberal still refuses to recognize. The terrible events of our time of troubles have suggested to many people that we no longer can expect to obtain a free and just society merely by echoing vague slogans about "democracy," "progress," and "equality." For a high civilization to subsist, and for men to live in peace with one another, some coherent principle of order must prevail. "Without order," Richard Hooker wrote, "there is no living in public society, because the want thereof is the mother of confusion."

Such arguments, advanced or implied by Voegelin in *The New Science of Politics*, are disagreeable in the extreme to rationalistic liberals—let alone political totalists—who maintain that men have no souls, and that there exists no source from which transcendent knowledge can come; and who, besides, simply do not understand the language of poetic and religious symbol, being altogether prosy. With their master Bentham, these scholars and gentlemen tend to equate poetry with pushpin; while as for religious insight, they take it for granted that all such rubbish was discarded long ago—or should have been.

Resentments of this character against Voegelin's approach were conspicuous in various reviews of *The New Science of Politics*; one professor at a middlewestern university, who previously had confined himself to the behavioral and institutional disciplines, burst in print into a denunciation of Voegelin's theories, which (he insisted) were merely an exhortation to "repression." (Voegelin, in a passage quoted earlier, feels that evil ought to be repressed; his reviewer apparently would not discriminate against evil.) They could not understand what Voegelin was writing about, these critics implied, and so he must be up to dark mischief. Once the first three volumes of *Order and History* had been published, Professor Moses Hadas, a classicist, indulged in an assault upon Voegelin's motives fortunately rare in the pages of learned journals. Voegelin simply can't believe in all this talk about transcendence and the divine sanctions for order, Hadas assumed; so Voegelin must be simply a political Christian, at best, disguising his ugly Fascism (though he was removed from his Austrian professorship by the National Socialists) under the tattered cloak of old-fangled piety:

"Reduced to simple terms," Hadas wrote, "Professor Voegelin's 'order' rests upon a hoax, which is justified by attributing divine afflatus to the elite which usurps the power to work it. . . . Professor Voegelin is by no means alone in his doctrine—such eminent teachers as Karl Jaspers have spoken of 'elitarian activism'—and no one can impugn the sincerity of his convictions or his right to voice them. What is disturbing is that his pietistic coloring makes it difficult for an unwary reader to apprehend what these convictions amount to. One wonders whether the 'institution that wishes to remain unnamed' which Professor Voegelin thanks for material aid in each of his Prefaces was aware of the nature of his work, and one remembers a remark attributed to a notable patron of the institution which Professor Voegelin serves: 'Sure, we'll have fascism in this country, but of course we'll call it something else.' Leap in being?"[57]

The preceding academic vituperation probably did greater harm to the reputation of its author than to that of Voegelin. Nearly anyone who reads *Order and History* must perceive that Hadas's review of the three volumes was studded with gross misrepresentations and groundless imputations. The "unnamed institution" to which Hadas referred ominously was a well-known American charitable foundation. And the sinister "institution which Professor Voegelin serves" is merely Hadas's slurring reference (incorrect at the time he wrote, incidentally) to Louisiana State University, where Voegelin formerly taught (*not* in Huey Long's time, though it is Long to whom the remarks about American Fascism are attributed). Guilt by association?

Yet such quasi-scholarly abuse does serve one purpose: to illustrate how the problem of order is quite as perplexing in our time as it was in the age of Socrates and Plato. Hadas sounds very like certain antagonists of Socrates—who, unable to defeat him in reasoned argument, turned then to vituperation and menaces. Apropos of one of these, Callicles in the *Gorgias*, Voegelin himself writes: "The social conventions, which Callicles despises, are wearing thin; and the advocate of nature is brought to realize that he is a murderer face to face with his victim. The situation is fascinating for those among us who find ourselves in the Platonic position and who recognize in the men with whom we associate today the intellectual pimps for power who will connive in our murder tomorrow."

It is ideological ferocity of Hadas's sort which Voegelin's books are written to resist. Humanitarian ideologues, good though their intentions may be, can bring about a dreadful decay of order. For the order of society is merely the order of souls writ large; there cannot be a good society without individual goodness of heart; and that goodness of heart is possible only when human beings perceive, with Socrates, that man is not the measure: God is the measure.

"In our time," as Voegelin puts it, "we can observe the same phenomenon in that people are shocked by the horrors of war and by Nazi atrocities but are unable to see that these horrors are no more than a translation, to the physical level, of the spiritual and intellectual horrors which characterize progressive civilization in its most 'peaceful' phase; that the physical horrors are no more than the execution of the judgment (*krisis*) passed upon the historical polity."

Historical study of this sort—works like those of Christopher Dawson (1889–1970) and Herbert Butterfield (1890–1979) and J. L. Talmon (1916–80)—will affect our social order within this century, I believe. At one time, poets had a strong influence upon men of law and statecraft. At present, the sociologists have their hour of ascendancy. Yet the time is not far distant when the philosophical historians will begin to alter the minds of judges and presidents. A few years ago, we were informed by enthusiastic reviewers that for many years to come, all sensible magistrates and politicians must be deeply affected by the researches of Dr. Alfred Kinsey. I think not. We begin to seek again the norm for man, not the norm for wasp or snake.

Behind the Veil of History

"History is the revelation of the way of God with man," Voegelin declares in the first volume of *Order and History*, which is entitled *Israel and Revelation* (1956). With this sentence, he becomes perhaps the most influential historian of our century, and certainly the most provocative. His first principles go against the grain of the chief schools of historical thought since the seventeenth century.

Nothing ever has happened in history, according to one school of liberal historians of the nineteenth and twentieth centuries: that is, events simply have glided one into another without discernible purpose or significance; everything has been "evolutionary development" or mere flux. All the endeavors of famous men, and all the aspirations of great nations, have had as little influence upon the stream—or web—of history as the buzzing of the flies of a summer. As for intervention in history, or creation in history, by influences more than human—why, such notions belong to the childhood of the race. For those historians, Providence does not exist; and though the Greeks (who took a view of history somewhat similar in that they found history inscrutable) at least acknowledged the existence of Fate and Fortune, the latter-day theorists of historical flux are unwilling to admit even those vague and impersonal powers to influence upon human existence. This school of writers has taken more literally than did Hegel himself the Hegelian observation that "What experience and history teach is this—that people and governments never have learned anything from history, or acted on principles deduced from it."

Another school of historians—the positivists, attached to what Voegelin calls Gnostic assumptions—strong in influence ever since the Enlightenment, has taken a very different tack: for these scholars, history has been the record of progress toward some grand terrestrial culmination and perfection—a progress sometimes impeded, but sure of ultimate triumph. Condorcet, Comte, and Marx, whatever their differences of opinion, all represent this school; and it has milder devotees. Governed by the idea of Progress, this concept—"progressivism" or "futurism" applied to historical study—dominated the writing of popular histories for a good many years, until the fearful events of our own century disconcerted the leaders of the movement.

A third school, reviving an ancient theory in modern times, has advanced the concept of historical cycles: stages of growth, maturity, and decadence, predictable and perhaps inevitable, recurring with fair regularity throughout the ages. Such was the cast of mind of Henry and Brooks Adams;

Spengler's *Decline of the West* (1918–22) gave this theory a popular success almost scandalous; and Toynbee's *Study of History* (1934–61) depends upon this interpretation, though now and again tinged with meliorism.

These three schools have dominated so thoroughly the discussion of historical problems for the past century that many people seem unaware that a fourth interpretation of history exists. That fourth interpretation, nevertheless, is a venerable theory, long known to the higher civilizations, though most thoroughly developed in Christian civilization. I mean the belief that history is the record of human existence under God, meaningful only so far as it reflects and explains and illustrates the order in the soul and in society which emanates from divine purpose. The aim of history, in the eyes of this school, is not antiquarian, nor yet programmatic: that purpose is to reveal to existing men and societies the true nature of being. Without this history, indeed, no society long endures. "The order of history," so Voegelin's first sentence in *Israel and Revelation* runs, "emerges from the history of order."

In the view of this last school of historians, history is not law, in the sense of fixed fate, foreknowledge absolute; nor does it have "meaning" in the sense of providing a Grand Design for immanent improvement. A study of history reveals the general principles to which men and societies, in all ages, are subject; but it cannot confer upon the scholar a prophetic afflatus; it cannot describe the wave of the future. "For the ray of light that penetrates from an historical present into the past," Voegelin writes, "does not produce a 'meaning of history' that could be stored away as a piece of information once for all, nor does it gather in a 'legacy' or 'heritage' on which the present could sit contentedly. It rather reveals a mankind striving for its order of existence within the world while attuning itself with the truth of being beyond the world, and gaining in the process not a substantially better order within the world but an increased understanding of the gulf that lies beyond immanent existence and the transcendent truth of being. Canaan is as far away today as it has always been in the past." We tremble "before the abysmal mystery of history as the instrument of divine revelation for ultimate purposes that are unknown equally to the men of all ages."

"Immanent" and "transcendent" are words that a reader must apprehend before he essays to fight his way into the learning of *Israel and Revelation*. The historian who espouses the cause of immanentization believes that the origin and end of everything in history, including mankind's religions, is to be found within the world of sensation, the world apprehended by the average sensual man. The historian who takes the transcendental view believes that the origin and end of everything in history must be sought, often symbolically, in realities more than human and more than terrestrial. We might call the school to which Voegelin belongs the "transcendentalist school," were there not danger of confounding the opinions of Voegelin and Emerson.

The historians of this latter school are at odds with Hegel's concept of remorseless destiny operating in history, with Marx's idea of the resolution of thesis and antithesis in a classless society, and with Toynbee's endeavor to predict the coming of a new religion and a new society formed out of a world-wide synthesis. With Gabriel Marcel, the historian of this school—let us call it, for immediate purposes, the Christian school of historical scholarship—sets his face against "this crowned ghost, the meaning of history."

For the ends of man and society are not to be found in history: those ends are transcendent, attaining fruition only beyond the limits of the time and the space which we know in this little world of ours. History has many meanings, but they are particular meanings for the regulation of private conduct and public polity, not a Gnostic plan for immanent regeneration before which we must abase ourselves. Who are the historians of this Christian school? To name three almost at random, St. Augustine, Bossuet, Edmund Burke. Voegelin is our present principal representative of this body of conviction, which he presents with system.

The term "Christian school" of historical scholarship is not entirely adequate, perhaps, for this theory of history is rooted in Judaic and Greek and Roman thought and experience, as well as in Christian doctrine and knowledge, and there exist parallels in other religions. But the fullest expression of this understanding of history is found among Christian thinkers. Voegelin stands for religious insight as opposed to "political religion," ideology, which, he writes, is "rebellion against God and man." Voegelin is no vulgarizer, but a scholar of such breadth and depth as the educational tendency of our age has made rare among us. His work requires interpreters, if it is to exert influence. Voegelin makes no concessions to theoretical illiteracy in our age: he takes for granted in his readers a familiarity with metaphysical terms, historical events, Biblical texts, and modes of reasoning which a pragmatic schooling neglects. Nor can he do otherwise: though he spreads his learning over several volumes, the field is so wide that he must sacrifice illustration and simplification, much of the time, to compactness and precision.

But *Order and History* cannot be ignored by anyone seriously concerned with our time of troubles. It should be read, as Voegelin recommends, "not as an attempt to explore curiosities of a dead past, but as an inquiry into the structure of the order in which we live presently."

To employ a loose and risky analogy, history is a veil upon the face of a gigantic significance. The Christian historian, though denying the existence of any simple pattern of progress or cycles, running through history, nevertheless detects beneath the surface of events an intelligible structure. This, in Voegelin's words, "is not a project for human or social action, but a reality to be discerned retrospectively in a flow of events that extends, through the present of the observer, indefinitely into the future. Philosophers of history have spoken of this reality as providence, when they still lived within the orbit of Christianity, or as *List der Vernunft*, when they were affected by the trauma of enlightenment. In either case they referred to a reality beyond the plans of concrete human beings—a reality of which the origin and end is unknown and which for that reason cannot be brought within the grasp of finite action."

So history is a reality, but a veiled reality, of which our knowledge always is imperfect and upon which our mundane designs can operate only slightly. History is our tool only in the sense that we employ our knowledge of history to bring ourselves to an understanding and realization, so far as we may, of the principles of private and public order. When the first school of historians I described above—the "nothing-ever-happened" school—lifts the veil upon the face of the significance behind history, that school, like Titus's soldiery in the Temple, finds the sanctuary empty—or, at best, inhabited only by Chaos and old Night. When the second school of historians—the positivistic school—lifts that veil, there looms up the voluptuous form of the Earthly Paradise. When the third school—the cyclical school—lifts that same veil, there stands revealed a species of clockwork, Ixion's wheel, with humanity bound upon it. But when the fourth school of historians, the Christian or transcendental school, lifts the veil of history, there emerges a pattern of order, a body of enduring truth, the filtered wisdom of the species, the considered opinions and experiences of the many wise men who have preceded us in time: the normative consciousness. And this complex record is rendered intelligible by a strong and subtle thread running through it, the continuity of Providence. The significance behind the veil is not simply the corpus of worldly wisdom, but—still more important—the contract of eternal society which joins our mundane order to an abiding, transcendent order.

This is the understanding of history possessed also—with varying interpretations—by Reinhold Niebuhr, Leo Strauss, and other philosophical historians I have named already. This is a revived theory of history, transcending doctrinal barriers, which gives first consideration to religious knowledge and traditional belief and classical theories as means to the proper apprehension of history. Professor Butterfield, for instance, in his book *Man on His Past* affirms a faith in Providence which would have been astounding and shocking—but was not Christianity always a scandal?—to the rationalist and positivist historians of the nineteenth century, and which will wake indignation in many quarters today. Butterfield writes, "And here is a Providence which does not merely act (as Ranke's Providence seemed to act) at marginal points or by remote control, but which touches all the details and the intimacies of life. . . . And we, too, need not be the slaves of our analytical methods—we may still praise God, and not merely do honor to scientific laws, at the coming of spring; and we may thank Providence rather than chance for those 'conjectures' which seem to matter so much both in life and in history."

Yes, the climate of opinion among historians is clearing; and the work which may do more to effect a general revision of learned opinion than any other historical production of this century is Voegelin's. *Israel and Revelation* treats of the order, spiritual and social, that arose among the people of Israel, in contrast with the cosmological order of the ancient empires; and it traces and analyzes the struggle between Israel as a faith and the kingdom of Judah. This is a work of original insight, sustained by a startling knowledge of the literary sources.

A young lion of political science, Mr. John Roche [1923–94]—an official intellectual apologist for the Johnson administration—once addressed a convention of his colleagues, and made it one of his claims to fame that he had not read *The New Science of Politics*, and did not intend to, because it seemed to be all about "someone called Saint Joachim of Flora," and therefore irrelevant to political science; he would be even more dismayed by *Israel and Revelation*. Voegelin has his work cut out for him when he attempts to reason with minds of this cast; yet he may prevail.

Israel and Revelation, though concise and even witty, is no book for the historical dilettante. It pleases neither the social gospeller nor the Bibliolater. To criticize it properly would require a book as long as the volume itself. But possibly a very brief summary may suggest its importance. Human nature is a constant; and the same problems of order—order in the realm of spirit and order in society—arise in every civilization, from the anonymous "Dialogue on Suicide" of an Egyptian who died two thousand years before Christ, dismayed at the disorder of his age, to our own present discontents.

> Every society is burdened with the task, under concrete conditions, of creating an order that will endow the fact of its existence with meanings in terms of ends divine and human. And the attempts to find the symbolic forms that will adequately express the meaning, while imperfect, do not

> form a senseless series of failures. For the great societies, beginning with the civilizations of the Ancient Near East, have created a sequence of orders, intelligibly connected with one another as advances toward, or recessions from, an adequate symbolization of truth concerning the order of being of which the order of society is a part.

The Kingdom of Judah became dust and ashes, but the revelation of divine and human nature which Israel received lies at the foundation of our whole present order.

Israelite history, Voegelin argues, cannot be received as a literal account of the events which occurred to the Israelite people. It is, rather, a symbolic history; and the deep truths of revelation commonly are expressed in symbol, not literally. In the symbol of the voice from out the Burning Bush, there was expressed a reality the cosmological empires had not known—and which Spengler and Toynbee, toiling in "the intellectual climate in which 'religious founders' were busy with founding 'religions,' when in fact they were concerned with the ordering of human souls," still had not learnt many centuries after. What took place on Sinai was a leap in being, a revelation quite new in human experience; and any close examination of the literary sources will reveal that here commenced the historical form of existence in the present under God, with history as the symbolism of that form. Moses (as distinguished from the mythical Moses of the Deuteronomic Code) was not the "founder of a religion," but the intermediary between man and the God previously unknown, who declared, "I am who I am." The Israelites, the Chosen People, the collective Son of God, did not desire to be chosen; it is improbable that they understood the revelation when it came from the lips of Moses; indeed, throughout the history of Israel and Judah, the spiritual and temporal order was perplexed by confusion; and when the Temple fell, that misunderstanding was as baleful as ever. Here lay the difficulty: "In Israel the spirit of God, the *ruach* of Yahweh, is present with the community and with individuals in their capacity as representatives of the community, but it is not present as the ordering force in the soul of every man, as the Nous of the philosophers or the Logos of Christ is present in every member of the Mystical Body, creating by its presence the *homonoia*, the likemindedness of the community."

The soul, to the Israelites, had no destiny beyond death; therefore the hope of Israel was fixed upon a mundane realization of Yahweh's promises to Israel. Only the Remnant who followed the Prophets preferred the Spirit to the Letter, and were willing to sacrifice existential triumph to the keeping of the Covenant. But the Prophets, in their contest with the Kings, were hopelessly impractical, leaving no place to worldly wisdom; they were "torn by the conflict between spiritual universalism and patriotic parochialism that had been inherent from the beginning in the conception of a Chosen People." Judah was doomed to dissolution, whatever her kings might do by way of compromise with the Baals and Ashtaroths. Yet "from the struggle for the bare survival of order in the soul of man emerged the Jewish community victoriously, both in its own right and as the matrix of Christianity."

Emancipated from "ideological mortgages upon science," Voegelin proceeds to trace the alteration of the prophetic understanding from Isaiah to Jeremiah. Isaiah, denouncing the king's unfaithfulness to the moral ideal of Israel, refused to come to terms at all with existential circumstances; he expected faith alone to reconstitute the order of human personality and of society. This is what Voegelin calls "metastasis," the will "to transform reality into something which by essence it is not . . . the rebellion against the nature of things as ordained by God." In a much later age, this impulse expressed itself as Gnosis. "Isaiah, we may say, has tried the impossible: to make the leap in being a leap out of existence into a divinely transfigured world beyond the laws of mundane existence." But Isaiah stopped short of an attempt to realize the Terrestrial Paradise by human endeavors. "If the prophets, in their despair over Israel, indulged in metastatic dreams, in which the tension of historical order was abolished by a divine act of grace, at least they did not indulge in tetastatic nightmares, in which the *opus* was performed by human acts of revolution." Yet Jeremiah, going to his trial, passed beyond metastasis. "The great motive that had animated the prophetic criticism of conduct and commendation of the virtues had at last been traced to its source in the concern with the order of personal existence under God. In Jeremiah the human personality had broken the compactness of collective existence and recognized itself as the authoritative source of order in society."

Jeremiah "had at least a glimpse of the terrible truth: that the existence of a concrete society in a definite form will not resolve the problem of order in history, that no Chosen People in any form will be the ultimate omphalos of the true order of mankind. . . . With Isaiah's and Jeremiah's movement away from the concrete Israel begins the anguish of the third procreative act of divine order in history: the Exodus of Israel from itself." The Deutero-Isaiah, with his song of the Suffering Servant, completes this Exodus from the cosmic-divine order of empire. God becomes known successively as Creator, as Lord and Judge of history, and as Redeemer. "The Servant who suffers many a death to live, who is humiliated to be exalted, who bears the guilt of the many to see them saved as his offspring, is the King above the kings, the representative of divine above imperial order. And the history of Israel as the people under God is consummated in the vision of the unknown genius, for as the representative sufferer Israel has gone beyond itself and become the light of salvation to mankind." The Zadokite fragment and the Dead Sea scrolls prove that the symbol of the Suffering Servant was not forgotten, during the five hundred years that followed. In Israel, the prophets had shared the suffering of God; now, in Jerusalem, the greatest event in history was to be consummated: God was to share the suffering of man.

Yes, Voegelin's work of scholarship will stick in the craws of the schools of historical theory still dominant; they may receive *Israel and Revelation* much as Jehoiakim received the scroll of Jeremiah, sent by Baruch: "It was in the wintry season, and a fire was burning before him in a brazier as an attendant read the scroll to him. Whenever three or four columns had been read, the King, who had listened in stony silence, would cut them off with his knife—and then Jehoiakim, the King of Judah, dropped the words of Yahweh, the King of Israel, on the brazier until the whole scroll was consumed by fire."

This volume and its companions, the work of a man of intellectual power, boldly deny the assumptions of the hegemony of intellectuals. With Isaiah, its author seems to say,

> Thy wisdom and thy knowledge,
> It hath perverted thee;
> And thou hast said in thine heart,
> I am, and none else beside me.

This dreary loneliness of the modern ego, this denial of the divine guidance which is the source of all order in personality and in society, becomes the parent of fanatic ideology. From that isolation of spirit, Voegelin's labor of historical and theoretical reconstruction is intended to redeem us.

Philosophers and Philodoxers

A philosopher aspires to teach wisdom; a philodoxer is a purveyor of *doxa*, illusory opinions and vain wishes. Out of the *doxa* comes disorder, in the soul and in the body politic. But *eunomia*, righteousness, the disciplined harmony of a man's soul, Solon said, makes "all things proper and sensible in the affairs of men." Eric Voegelin is a philosopher, as well as an historian and a professor of the *nomos*—that is, of institutions and traditions.

His knowledge of early civilizations and Old Testament scholarship, manifested in the first volume of *Order and History*, is equalled by his understanding of the Greek poets and philosophers whose thought is the subject of the two succeeding volumes, *The World of the Polis* (1957) and *Plato and Aristotle* (1957). Yet the serious reader of these two volumes might do well to turn, before opening them, to the one twentieth-century critic whose ends and convictions seem closest to Voegelin's own: Paul Elmer More. For More was a more lucid writer, though Voegelin is the more thoroughgoing. In the concluding chapter of More's *Platonism*, indeed, occurs a summary of Voegelin's own intention clearer than any passage in the two volumes of *Order and History* concerned with the Greeks.

"It is a fact, sad and indisputable," More wrote,

> that no one is more likely to call himself, or to be called by his admirers, a Platonist than the reformer with a futile scheme for the regeneration of the world, or the dreamer who has spurned the realities of human nature for some illusion of easy perfection, or the romantic visionary who has set the spontaneity of fancy above the rational imagination, the "fair soul" who has withdrawn from the conflict of life into the indulgence of a morbid introspection, or the votary of faith as a law abrogating the sterner law of works and retribution. Half the enthusiasts and inspired maniacs of society have shielded themselves under the aegis of the great Athenian. . . . If these are the only products of Platonism, then it is a pity the works of Plato were not lost altogether, with the books of so many other ancient philosophers, and we who busy ourselves with interpreting the Dialogues are merely adding to the sum of the world's folly. But it is not so. It is with Platonism as with Christianity and every other strong excitement of the human heart. Liberty is the noblest and, at the same time the most perilous possession that can be given to mankind; and, unless we are prepared to silence the higher call of religion and philosophy altogether for the safer demands of a purely practical wisdom, we must expect, while we try to expose, the vagaries of minds made drunk with excess of enthusiasm. . . . "Believe not every spirit, but try the spirits whether they are of God, because many false prophets are gone out into the world."

In this endeavor justly to distinguish between the lovers of wisdom and the devotees of illusion (and, as More says, perhaps the best definition of a true Platonist is "a lover of distinctions"), we are handicapped by our imperfect terms, tools that snap in the hand; for nowadays, in our language, the wise man is caught with the label of the persons whom Plato opposed, the Sophists; while for "philodoxer," the man whose desires override his righteousness, the perverter of the intellect, the ideologue, we have no precise equivalent in English. ("Sophist" expresses only in part the concept of the preacher of the *doxa.*) A principal portion of Voegelin's labor is to restore a sound vocabulary to philosophy and politics. Nowhere, surely, is this restoration more important than in the discussion of Plato, the central figure in these two volumes. The Serbonian bog of controversy over *The Republic*, for instance, is watered by writers and teachers who do not understand their own words; who, as Voegelin observes, repeat in our century the errors of the muddled, well-meaning Old School Tie and of the arrogant "amoral" controversalists: "The way from the well-intentioned, but philosophically no longer sensitive generation, which translated the 'good polis' as an 'ideal state,' to the generation which attacks Plato as an 'ideologue,' is the way from Cephalus to Thrasymachus."

Every serious discussion of order runs back, eventually, to Moses and Plato. Voegelin's discussion of Plato is as interesting as his examination of Moses; and the controversy which it has begun to arouse may serve here to illustrate how the problem of order has become central in men's minds once more.

Plato's theories of justice and order have been variously criticized in different ages, the critics of any period tending to see in *The Republic* and *The Laws* the reflection of opinion and event in their own time, and to commend or denounce Plato as he seemed to sympathize with, or to oppose, their own climate of opinion. At the end of the last century and the beginning of this, Plato generally was approved of as an "idealist," who commendably desired to shape this world nearer to our hearts' desire: for this interpretation suited the humanitarian and melioristic inclinations of the dominant critical school among professors of philosophy and politics.

With the coming of the ideological struggles since 1917, however, the scholarly partisans of this or that particular twentieth-century brand of politics began to convert Plato into an ideologue; and most of them denounced him as a totalist, though some Socialists ventured to welcome Plato as a forward-looking advocate of social planning. A number of writers condemned Plato as a Communist; others, as a Fascist; *The Republic* and *The Laws* were assumed to be merely embryo versions of our own ideological tracts, and so were fitted into convenient pigeon-holes to Right and Left.

The most influential criticism of this sort has been that of Karl Popper, in his book *The Open Society and its Enemies* (1950). Professor Popper, an old-school doctrinaire liberal, rationalistic and utilitarian, bitterly opposed to "myth" (in which he includes religion), warns all true democrats and liberals that Plato was a totalitarian, a Fascist, and a racist, an inveterate enemy of freedom. Popper makes no secret of his own hostility toward any long-established principle of order; for to him, equality, competition, and emancipation from tradition seem sufficient guarantees of "the open society." What Popper never intended, his condemnation of Plato aroused a good deal of serious interest in Plato's doctrines, and attracted a number of replies.

Intemperance of Popper's sort, however, was not the only approach to Plato provoked by the troubles of this age. A temperate and learned classical scholar, David Grene, re-examined the political ideas of Thucydides and Plato as reflections upon an age of disorder remarkably similar to our own time. Mr. Grene understands clearly what Popper does not understand at all—the motive of Plato in writing *The Republic*: that is, to offer a decadent society, which had lost faith in its religion, its traditions, and its customs, a means to make possible once more the life of the soul and the life of civilization. Yet Grene, in his book *Man in His Pride*, sees two Platos, young and old, the Plato of *The Republic* and the Plato of *The Laws*, at loggerheads one with the other.

"In the *Timaeus* and *Laws* trilogy," Grene writes, "the ideal state has become historical; somewhere in the past it can be thought of as having been, and its past actions can be imagined and fitted into a scheme which will lead all the way to the 'best' state of the future. But for the earlier Plato, the Plato of the *Republic*, there could be no assertion, lightly made, that his model city had been achieved, or even that it would be, exactly as outlined, the 'best' state for the future. The possibility of its actual existence meant far too much to him."

In short, Grene believes that Plato meant his Republic to take on actuality in this world, and looks sympathetically upon Plato's design—while Popper recoils in horror from the same prospect. "In the *Laws*," Grene continues, "the importance of the actual historical past is gone; history can become myth rich in meaning, and myth, history; and both can point to the future, which has no hopes of fulfillment and no agonies of frustration."

Now Voegelin, in his detailed analysis of Plato in the third volume of *Order and History*—possibly the most important section of his whole series—takes a position quite different from that of either Popper or Grene. Voegelin reasons, convincingly, that Plato's intention and accomplishment is to teach obedience to the incarnate Truth; not to preach some dismal set of totalist dogmas, nor yet to bring into being an "ideal" state in his own time, but rather to reveal those principles of order in the soul and order in the commonwealth which make us truly human and which keep the knife from our throats.

"The philosopher who is in possession of the Truth should consistently go the way of Plato in the *Republic*; he should issue the call for repentance and submission to the theocratic rule of the incarnate Truth." *The Republic* is an analogy or allegory of order, not a model constitution, though it will suggest reforms in the existential state; and there exists no opposition between *Republic* and *Laws*, but only a continuous development of the complex theme. Men cannot well remain pure in a corrupt society, Plato says repeatedly; nor can corrupt men maintain a high and just order. Therefore the problem of ordered soul and ordered state cannot be split into halves. Plato is seeking transcendent reality; his work is a leap in being, a glimpse of an eternal order, divinely ordained, which we must try to imitate in our souls and our institutions. "When the philosopher explores the spiritual order of the soul," Voegelin says, "he explores a realm of experiences which he can appropriately describe only in the language of symbols expressing the movement of the soul toward transcendental reality and the flooding of the soul by transcendence. At the border of transcendence the language of philosophical anthropology must become the language of religious symbolization."

Voegelin tells us, that is, with Plato, that order in society is possible only if there is true order in individual souls; and that there cannot be order in souls unless those souls, in some degree, know the author of their being and His intention for them. Plato writes in symbol, for there is no other way in which transcendent knowledge can be expressed; and, at its highest level, the truth about man and his state must be religious truth, and in some degree mystery.

From the age of Moses onward, there have been men—prophets or philosophers—who sought for the transcendent meaning in history: who groped for knowledge of the soul, and glimpsed in the record of history a divine meaning, a revelation of the way of God with man, and of the reality of the soul. Yet in Israel and in Athens, as today, there were men who, succumbing to *doxa*, endeavored to make immanent the transcendent symbols of order: to take by storm the Kingdom of Heaven, but to annex that Kingdom to an earthly realm, rather than to enter into eternity. Such were those Jews who hoped vainly that Judah would prevail in this world over her great enemies, and those Greek philodoxers who made power and success the objects of life, and those medieval Gnostics who looked for salvation and perfection in time and space, and those enthusiasts for the Enlightenment who expected the French Revolution to usher in the unending regime of universal happiness. Such are the "progressivists" and utopians of our own century, whether "liberal" or "totalitarian" in their factional affiliations. This is *doxa*: for human nature is not perfectible by human means, nor is society. And men intoxicated with *doxa*, even famous philodoxers, break up the order in personality when they blind men to the nature of the soul; and they upset the balance in any good society when they conjure up visions of desire satisfied which really are impossible of attainment.

So long as man is a mere part of nature, bound to this life and earth, impotent beneath mighty cosmological empires, he cannot tell or understand significant history: existence remains mere existence, a dog's life, full of sound and fury, perhaps, but empty of meaning as the idiot's tale; a simple bloody jumble of coronations and conquests. A leap in being is necessary for the ascent from cosmological myth to transcendent perception of the soul; and so there cannot be true history without this leap in being. Such a leap is not a mere "stage in cultural progress," though of course, once accomplished, that leap produces enduring cultural changes. The nature of the leap varies from one people to another; and it is not a single leap which is required, but a series of leaps.

In Israel, the problems of order—that is, of human existence under God—were the concern of the prophets; and through the prophets came the leap in being. In Hellas, the problems of order—that is, of an enduring justice and its sanctions—were the concern of the poets and the philosophers; and through the poets and the philosophers came the leap in being. Revelation and reason both are ways to order, and by either can a transcending leap be achieved. But that leap is not the work of narrow logic; instead, it is accomplished by the higher imagination, by the perceptions of genius, by an intuition which transcends ordinary experience—by a means, in fine, which we cannot adequately describe with those tools called words. Neither the leap of Israel nor the leap of Hellas brought full knowledge of the transcendent order; it required the fusing of Jewish and Greek genius in Christianity for a leap still higher.

Among the Greeks, the leap in being was principally the achievement of Plato; yet Plato's insight was attained only after the existential order of the polis was far sunk in decadence. Man's dreadful experience of the decay of his society, from the dawn of things, has been an impelling motive to the search for an order that is not transitory. From terror, man learns that the existential order is not real order—that mere fleshly existence is not the end of all. He awakens, Voegelin says, "to the untruth of existence." With St. Paul, man's existence before the leap in being is only "opaque existence." In Paul's words, "I once was alive without the law." The law is the *nomos*, which after the leap in being means not merely traditions and institutions, but norms, laws, that transcend things existential. Man awakens to his own nature, to his soul. Then he may "transform the succession of societies preceding in time into a past of mankind."This does not end the struggle for the knowledge of order; it only makes the search for order intelligible. Mankind becomes conscious "of the open horizon of its future."

The leaps of Israel and Hellas, roughly parallel in time and quite independent of each other, were achieved only after much travail, and the mass of men never really understood the nature of these discoveries; indeed, many of the learned and the clever sought to demolish the consciousness of the soul already acquired: such were the philodoxers. The power of the *doxa* is enormous. From early times in the Hellenic age, nevertheless, the Greek genius groped and toiled toward order: toward an apprehension of divine purpose and divine justice, toward a moral order among men. The principal expressions of this search are the writings of Homer, Hesiod, Xenophanes, Parmenides, Heraclitus, Aeschylus, Sophocles, Herodotus, the Old Oligarch, Thucydides, Plato, and Aristotle.

In Homer, the soul still is opaque; and so there can be no transcendence of the existential order. Achilles had rather be the meanest thrall in Boeotia than king among the shades. But Homer is struggling toward principles of order. In the disintegrated world of the ruined Mycenaean civilization, where Whirl seems master of all, where every moral tradition is broken, Homer—the blind one who sees—

> astutely observed that the disorder of a society was a disorder in the soul of its component members, and especially in the soul of the ruling class. . . . Without having a term for it, he envisaged man as having a psyche with an internal organization through a center of passions and a second center of ordering and judging knowledge. . . . And he strove valiantly for the insight that ordering action is action in conformity with transcendent divine order, while disruptive action is a fall from the divine order into the specifically human disorder. . . . But the historical process in which a society declines, as well as the infinitude of acts which in the aggregate of centuries spell destruction, had a pattern of their own that could not be described in terms of individual misdeeds. Homer had to face the problem that the day-to-day causality of human action will explain the detail of the historical process but not its configuration. His answer to this mystery of the rise and fall of civilizations was the extraordinary Olympian assembly at which Zeus and Hera agreed on their program for the destruction of Mycenaean civilization, including both Trojans and Achaeans.

Hesiod, too, tried to describe the divine justice, beneficent or retributory, which orders the universe. By mighty struggles, Zeus brought out of

Chaos a precarious order. "Zeus rules the world, and with tremendous sway takes back tomorrow what he grants today." The vengeance of Zeus visits the unjust upon earth. Though still encompassed by cosmological myth, Hesiod searches for an answer to the ills to which flesh is heir—an answer that must be more than the grip of Force and Power upon Prometheus. But Hesiod can discern no relief beyond the confines of the existential order; he is driven back upon the dream of an immanent salvation, as expressed in the fable of Pandora.

> The Hesiodian dream of no work, no hunger, no sickness, no old age and death, no women, lists the negatives of the experiences which are the principal sources of anxiety in human life. The paradise in this sense, as the dream of freedom from the burden and anxiety of existence, is a constant dimension of the soul that will express itself not only in the imagery of immortal existence in the beyond but generally pervades the imaginative occupation with a desirable state of mundane existence. One does not have to insist on coarse expressions that will first come to mind, such as the "freedom from want and fear" of the Atlantic Charter. More subtly, the dream is the dynamic component in the attempts to create an earthly paradise by reducing the hours of labor (no work), by getting a living wage (no hunger), and medical care (no sickness) for everybody, and by increasing the length of human life (no death). And even the problem that man is created both man and woman, while it can not be resolved, can be psychologically diminished to the famous "satisfaction of biological urges."

It will be observed from the preceding passage that Voegelin is no mere antiquarian in ideas. Human nature, and its difficulties, are constants; and the *doxa* of immanence springs eternal among men. Though ancient, it is nevertheless an error. A strong vein of passionate awareness runs through *Order and History*: a knowledge that the disorder of the smashed Mycenaean culture, and the disorder of the disintegrating polis of the fifth century, are one with the disorder of the twentieth century. And amid such disorder, there rises the figure of the philodoxer, "realistic," sardonic, driven by *pleonexia*, discarding *peitho* (righteous persuasion) in favor of trickery or intimidation; impelled by his passions and low interests, his illusions, even at the moment he claims to speak as practical logician and champion of common sense. These are men of today—who, like their predecessors in history, would obtain in the confusion of a bent world the realization of their dream-lusts. Take this passage from *Plato and Aristotle*:

> The condition of Socrates touches upon a problem, familiar to all of us who have had experiences with rightist or leftist intellectuals. Discussion is indeed impossible with a man who is intellectually dishonest, who misuses the rules of the game, who by irrelevant profuseness seeks to avoid being nailed down on a point, and who gains the semblance of victory by exhausting the time which sets an inevitable limit to a discussion.

Truly, it is history which teaches us the principles of order. It is the decay of men's apprehension of transcendent order that brings on *hubris* and *nemesis:* that is, the collapse of existential order. The philodoxers are the precursors of the atrocity-men.

Those truths of reason and revelation which men painfully have obtained over many centuries, the philodoxer endeavors to demolish in a generation. Voegelin traces with care the ascent of Greek thought toward the leap in being which came with Plato: a long story, full of interest, full of tribulation. Xenophanes, breaking with the myth, declared that "One God is greatest among gods and men, not like mortals in body or thought." Heraclitus set against "much-knowing" (*polys*) his "deep-knowing" (*bathys*); and if he did not attain to the height of transcendence, still he penetrated to the luminous depths of the soul: the mystic-philosophers had taken a leap in being, for they knew what Homer and Hesiod had not known, the soul as a source of knowledge. Solon taught the Athenians *eunomia*, righteousness, ordained by *Dike*, Justice. *Doxa*, Solon discovered, is the source of disorder; the passion of life, the *doxa*, must be disciplined for the sake of order, *eunomia*. "He passionately loves the magnificence and exuberance of life; but he experiences it as a gift of the gods, not as an aim to be realized by crooked means against the divine order."

From Heraclitus onward, the Greek philosophers—though not the philodoxers—apprehended the life of the soul. The men of Homer's time had known only the *psyche*, the life-force that departs with death, never to live after but in dreams. To Homer, a dead man was but a *soma*, a corpse. But the mystic-philosophers penetrated beyond the bounds of flesh. Their search for truth was continued in the tragedy: "The newly discovered humanity of the soul expands into the realm of action." Aristotle, living in the decadence of tragedy, thought of the tragic art only as *katharsis*, purging of emotions, a kind of group-therapy. But for Aeschylus and Sophocles, Voegelin writes, tragedy was the opening of the soul to the conflicting demands of *Dike*: not, it is true, a leap to the revelation of God, but a descent to the depths of the soul where *Dike* may be found. The tragic hero cannot merely weigh utilitarian consequences, or seek practical advice from gods and men: he must search his soul. Only an audience capable at least of appreciating heroic action, if not of participating in it, could understand and support the tragic drama—and by Aristotle's time, that audience was gone. But in the grand hour of Athens, Aeschylus and Sophocles spoke to men who still understood:

> The heroic soul-searching and suffering of consequences must be experienced as the cult of Dike, and the fate of the hero must arouse the shudder of his own fate in the soul of the spectator—even if he himself should succumb to his weakness in a similar situation. The binding of the soul to its own fate through representative suffering, rather than the Aristotelian catharsis through pity and fear, is the function of tragedy.

At the moment when the tragic drama towered over Athens, nevertheless, the Sophists already were at their work: and among them, in politics at least, the greatest was Protagoras. Man is the measure of all things, Protagoras taught. He was by no means wholly a philodoxer, for Protagoras declared that reverence and justice must live in the soul of every man, or else the polis would perish; for Protagoras a man with a diseased soul brought disease to the polis, and ought to be put to death if, after five years of reformatory education, he should turn out incorrigible. Yet the general ethical tendency of the Sophists is sufficiently suggested in our word "sophistry"; and out of the struggles of Socrates and Plato against sophistry came the definitions of the Platonic virtues: justice, wisdom, fortitude, and temperance.

Against Protagoras, Socrates and Plato affirmed that God is the measure of all things. Here was the supreme Greek leap in being. Gorgias, another powerful Sophist, assailed Parmenides' concept of Being; and Gorgias' *On Being* is "one of the earliest, if not the very first, instance of the perennial type of enlightened philosophizing. Its arguments could be directed against all the symbols of transcendence." For Voegelin, "enlightenment, with its eighteenth-century rationalistic associations, is no term of commendation." Of the time of the Sophists, he writes, "We may say that the age indeed has a streak of enlightenment in so far as its representative thinkers show the same kind of insensitiveness toward experiences of transcendence that was characteristic of the Enlightenment of the eighteenth century A.D., and in so far as this sensitiveness has the same result of destroying philosophy—for philosophy by definition has its center in the experiences of transcendence."

Gomperz, in his *Greek Thinkers* (1901–12) made Socrates the leader of rationalistic Enlightenment. As Paul Elmer More says, this description is totally inadequate. Voegelin puts an end, probably forever, to the attempt of positivists and rationalists to claim Socrates for their own. "Whatever the formulations of the 'historic' Socrates may have been, the 'essence' of his identification of virtue with knowledge, as a principle in opposition to the Sophists, makes sense only if the distortions of time were meant to be corrected by the love of the measure that is out of time." Socrates and Plato set to work restoring and elaborating the problems of order. *Physis*, nature, was not their light, but *nomos*, divine law.

David Grene calls Plato "the man in the duststorm."[58] He alludes to a passage in *The Republic*. Socrates is speaking of the philosopher in a decadent and violent age:

> He is like one who, in the storm of dust and sleet which the driving wind hurries along, retires under the shelter of a wall; and seeing the rest of mankind full of wickedness, he is content, if only he can live his own life and be pure from evil or unrighteousness, and depart in peace and good-will, with bright hopes.

Yet Plato, like Socrates, did not sit perpetually in the shelter of a wall. His expeditions to Syracuse were only the most conspicuous examples of his endeavor to regenerate Greek civilization by a reform at once internal and external. Socrates died for the sake of speaking the truth; Plato came near to dying like his teacher. As the glory of Greece had gone down to ruin in the quarries of Syracuse, Plato aspired sternly to raise up that glory again, even with Syracuse as its center. In that existential effort, he failed; but in his transcendent effort—his erection of the symbols of transcendence, with God as the measure—he triumphed; and all his detractors, ancient or modern, have not wholly undone his work. His leap in being occurred in a society much corrupted; his science of order was preached amidst existential disorder. The recovery of order in the soul cannot be separated from the restoration of order in the body politic, Plato knew, for even the philosopher may be seduced by the degeneracy of his age; and the average sensual man finds it next to impossible to maintain the order of his soul if he dwells in a corrupt community.

"Society can destroy a man's soul," Voegelin observes, "because the disorder of society is a disease in the psyche of its members. The troubles which the philosopher experiences in his own soul are the troubles in the psyche of the surrounding society which press on him. And the diagnosis of health and disease in the soul is, therefore, at the same time a diagnosis of order and disorder in society. On the level of conceptual symbols, Plato expressed his insight through the principle that society is man written in larger letters."

Plato was not an "idealist" in the sense that he entertained any notion of forcing upon a reluctant world some social trauma of his fancy. His *Republic* is a paradigm of the individual soul in harmony, not a scheme to be given actuality in positive law; Socrates says that the Republic, so far as it can be adapted to the world we know, can—nay, must—be modified. The *Republic* is a *zetema*, an inquiry, into the real nature of spiritual and social harmony. In Voegelin's phrases, "It should be clear that the inquiry is concerned with the reality of order in soul and society, not with 'ideals.'"

Plato was an inveterate foe to *doxa*—that is, to illusory social opinions, which attempt to force reality into a pattern that has no sanction in the nature of things. We moderns live in a political Babel, distorting Plato along with much else, Voegelin tells us:

> Within a few generations the Plato of the "ideal state" has been transformed into a "political ideologue." This astounding transformation will be intelligible if we see it in the light of Plato's own analysis of social corruption. The generation which attributed to Plato the creation of an "ideal state" had no evil intentions. Ideals were quite respectable at the time, and to ascribe them to Plato was praise. But even at that time the evil was lurking, for in common parlance an idealist was an impractical person who indulged his subjective valuations in opposition to reality; and the connotation of subjectivity in "ideal" undermined the objectivity of Plato's inquiry into the nature of reality.

Thus the passionate and confused modern critic Karl Popper—as the silliest example—ascribes to Plato precisely the *doxa* entertained by Plato's sophistical adversaries. Perhaps this is not surprising: after all, the Athenian jury did just this in the trial of Socrates. But the Athenian jurors did not set up as professors of logic.

Voegelin's close analysis of all the important Platonic dialogues, in scholarship the most valuable portion of these two volumes, cannot be examined here. It must suffice to quote from his concluding remarks, which serve to summarize both the purpose of his own study and the achievement of Plato: "Truth is not a body of propositions about a world-immanent object; it is the world-transcendent *summum bonum*, experienced as an orienting force in the soul, about which we can speak only in analogical symbols."

This was the endeavor and the method of Plato. It was the error—and perhaps even the malice—of Aristotle to treat Plato's Ideas, in part, as if they were world-immanent data. But in a time that requires most urgently the restoration of the theory and the vocabulary of order, we cannot afford to misunderstand and misinterpret Plato's end and method for the sake of a scholastic wrangle.

Aristotle's partial immanentizing of Platonic Ideas resulted in an "intellectual thinning-out. . . . The mystical *via negativa* by which the soul ascends to the vision of the Idea in the *Symposium* is thinned out to rise toward the dianoetic virtues and the *bios theoretikos*." When symbols are treated as if they were objects of sensory experience, order is in imminent danger. "When the Christian idea of supernatural perfection through grace in death was immanentized to become the idea of perfection of mankind in history through individual and collective mass action, the foundation was laid for the mass creeds of modern Gnosis."

The leap in being of the Hellenic philosophers was a great stride toward the apprehension of order; but, in this, unlike the Mosaic and prophetic leap in being, it did not disengage the order of history from cosmological myth. Both Israel and Hellas were to wait some centuries for the next leap in human consciousness of the soul and the order the soul dictates. They were to wait for the truth of perfection through grace in death, which idea Socrates foreshadowed, but did not fully express.

The philodoxers are with us still, and their name is legion; while our philosophers are few. Even among our professors of philosophy, there are not many who can understand Eric Voegelin, and fewer who will sympathize: for most of them, too, are philodoxers. We dwell in the disordered world of metaphysical madness that the fourth and fifth centuries knew; and for us, as for the Greeks, spiritual disorder brings on political anarchy. Yet *Order and History* will restore to some modern minds an understanding of transcendence. And some few may speak out, as did Socrates and Plato, in the teeth of the dust-storm.

["Eric Voegelin's Normative Labor," Enemies of the Permanent Things: Observations of Abnormity in Literature and Politics, *Rev. ed. (La Salle, IL: Sherwood Sugden & Company, 1969), 253–81.]*

IV.

THE MORAL IMAGINATION

The Moral Imagination ❖ Normative Art and Modern Vices ❖ A Cautionary Note on the Ghostly Tale ❖ Who Knows George Gissing? ❖ Wyndham Lewis's First Principles ❖ T. S. Eliot's *The Waste Land*

Russell Kirk views the "moral imagination" as the gift of Plato, Virgil, Dante; and he joins Edmund Burke, who is the father of the term, in ascribing to the moral imagination the power of perception, one that possesses universal value and testifies to the dignity of human nature. Modern political and educational leaders, as well as writers of fiction, Kirk charges, lack moral imagination when they degrade its standards, principles, centralities, norms. The moral imagination, for Kirk, saves us from what Irving Babbitt cited as a dangerous modern phenomenon: "anarchy of the imagination," and all the literary violence, perversity, decadence, and depravity that it unleashes, as well as the narcotic illusions it cheaply manufactures.

The creative imagination that is at once reverent and prescriptive nourishes the purpose of humane letters and thus fulfills its ethical obligations to the principles of order. Great art, we are reminded by Kirk, is at its maximum moral, allegiant both to the humanistic law of measure and to the religious virtues—awe, reverence, and humility. It is hardly enough to say, with Napoleon, that "imagination governs mankind," since, as Kirk specifies, there are always erroneous forms and cults of the imagination that lack a controlling power. In this respect, Kirk is wary of the perils of imagination, or what is morbidly emotional, temperamental, impressionistic, romantic.

The rejection of moral criteria has adverse effects on the normative function of letters and inevitably on the normative consciousness. This rejection, Kirk stresses, produces a vacuum as normative knowledge and understanding are usurped by moral indolence, when, as Plato observes, "evil and foulness and the opposite of good" emerge. The pursuit of virtue is confluent with the common pursuit of standards of discrimination that resist the aims and designs of the "enemies of the permanent things." For Kirk, then, the moral imagination is one of high seriousness, supremely sapient and contemplative, an enduring source of inspiration that elevates us to first principles as it guides us upwards towards virtue and wisdom and redemption.

In a culture that now enshrines what is called postmodernism, which is a disintegrated species of modernism that assails order and history, the moral imagination, Kirk also reminds us, is a crucial necessity.

❖

THE MORAL IMAGINATION

Any estimate of Kirk's achievement must include reference to his ethical view of the purpose of literature, epitomized in Edmund Burke's phrase "moral imagination," which appears in his Reflections on the Revolution in France *(1790), and which is found in this passage describing the destruction of civilizing manners by the revolutionaries: "All the decent drapery of life is to be rudely torn off. All the superadded ideas, furnished from the wardrobe of a* moral imagination, *which the heart owns, and the understanding ratifies, as necessary to cover the defects of our naked shivering nature, and to raise it to dignity in our own estimation, are to be exploded as a ridiculous, absurd, and antiquated fashion." The "moral imagination" is, for Kirk, infinitely superior to what Irving Babbitt calls the "idyllic imagination" and to what T. S. Eliot calls the "diabolic imagination." Kirk thus enunciates this clear and simple principle: "Great books do influence societies for the better, and bad books do drag down the general level of personal and social conduct."*

In the franchise bookshops of the year of our Lord one thousand nine hundred eighty-one, the shelves are crowded with the prickly pears and the Dead Sea fruit of literary decadence. Yet no civilization rests forever content with literary boredom and literary violence. Once again, a conscience may speak to a conscience in the pages of books, and the parched rising generation may grope their way toward the springs of moral imagination. The first annual lecture at this new Center for the Study of Christian Values in Literature is an endeavor to describe that high power of perception and description which has been called "the moral imagination," and to relate that imagination to what Chateaubriand called "the genius of Christianity." What once has been, may be again.

What is this "moral imagination"? The phrase is Edmund Burke's, and it occurs in his *Reflections on the Revolution in France*. Burke describes the destruction of civilizing manners by the revolutionaries:

> All the decent drapery of life is to be rudely torn off. All the superadded ideas, furnished from the wardrobe of a moral imagination, which the heart owns, and the understanding ratifies, as necessary to cover the defects of our naked shivering nature, and to raise it to dignity in our own estimation, are to be exploded as a ridiculous, absurd, and antiquated fashion.
>
> On this scheme of things, a king is but a man; a queen is but a woman; a woman is but an animal; and an animal not of the highest order. All homage paid to the sex in general as such, and without distinct views, is to be regarded as romance and folly. . . . On the scheme of this barbarous philosophy, which is the offspring of cold hearts and muddy understandings, and which is as void of solid wisdom as it is destitute of all taste and elegance, laws are to be supported only by their own terrors, and by the concern which each individual may find in them from his own private speculations, or can spate to them from his own private interests. In the groves of *their* academy, at the end of every vista, you see nothing but the gallows . . .
>
> Nothing is more certain than that our manners, our civilization, and all the good things which are connected with manners, and with civilization, have, in this European world of ours, depended for ages upon two principles; I mean the spirit of a gentleman, and the spirit of religion.

By this "moral imagination," Burke signifies that power of ethical perception which strides beyond the barriers of private experience and momentary events—"especially," as the dictionary has it, "the higher form of this power exercised in poetry and art." The moral imagination aspires to the apprehending of right order in the soul and right order in the commonwealth. This moral imagination was the gift and the obsession of Plato and Vergil and Dante. Drawn from centuries of human consciousness, these concepts of the moral imagination—so powerfully if briefly put by Burke—are expressed afresh from age to age. So it is that the men of humane letters in our century whose work seems most likely to endure have not been neoterists, but rather bearers of an old standard, tossed by our modern winds of doctrine: the names of Eliot, Frost, Faulkner, Waugh, and Yeats may suffice to suggest the variety of this moral imagination in the twentieth century.

It is the moral imagination which informs us concerning the dignity of human nature, which instructs us that we are more than naked apes. As Burke suggested in 1790, letters and learning are hollow if deprived of the moral imagination. And, as Burke suggested, the spirit of religion long sustained this moral imagination, along with a whole system of manners. Such imagination lacking, to quote another passage from Burke, we are cast forth "from this world of reason, and order, and peace, and virtue, and fruitful penitence, into the antagonist world of madness, discord, vice, confusion, and unavailing sorrow."

Burke implies that there exist other forms of imagination than the moral imagination. He was well aware of the power of imagination of Jean Jacques Rousseau, "the insane Socrates of the National Assembly." With Irving Babbitt, we may call the mode of imagination represented by Rousseau "the idyllic imagination"—that is, the imagination which rejects old dogmas and old manners and rejoices in the notion of emancipation from duty and convention. We saw this "idyllic imagination" infatuate a great many young people in America during the sixties and seventies—even though most of those devotees never read Rousseau. The idyllic imagination ordinarily terminates in disillusion and boredom.

When that occurs, too often a third form of imagination obtains ascendancy. In his lectures entitled *After Strange Gods* (1934), T. S. Eliot touches upon the diabolic imagination: that kind of imagination which delights in the perverse and subhuman. The name of Sade comes to mind at once; but Eliot finds "the fruitful operations of the Evil Spirit" in the writings of Thomas Hardy and D. H. Lawrence, as well. Anyone interested in the moral imagination and in the anti-moral imagination should read carefully *After Strange Gods*. "The number of people in possession of any criteria for discriminating between good and evil is very small," Eliot concludes; "the number of the half-alive hungry for any form of spiritual experience, or for what offers itself as spiritual experience, high or low, good or bad, is considerable. My own generation has not served them very well. Never has the printing press been so busy, and never have such varieties of buncombe and false doctrine come from it. *Woe unto the foolish prophets, that follow their own spirit, and have seen nothing!*"

This "diabolic imagination" dominates most popular fiction today; and on television and in the theaters, too, the diabolic imagination struts and postures. The other night I lodged at a fashionable new hotel; my single room cost about eighty dollars. One could tune the room's television set to certain movies, for an extra five dollars. After ten o'clock, all the films offered were nastily pornographic. But even the "early" films, before ten, without exception were products of the diabolic imagination, in that they pandered to the lust for violence, destruction, cruelty, and sensational disorder. Apparently it never occurred to the managers of this fashionable hotel that any of their affluent patrons, of whatever age and whichever sex, might desire decent films. Since Eliot spoke at the University of Virginia in 1933, we have come a great way farther down the road to Avernus. And as literature sinks into the perverse, so modern civilization falls to its ruin: "The blood-dimmed tide is loosed, and everywhere / The ceremony of innocence is drowned."

So, having remarked the existence of the moral imagination, the idyllic imagination, and the diabolic imagination, I venture to remind you of the true purpose of humane letters. As C. E. M. Joad points out in his book *Decadence: A Philosophical Inquiry* (1948), what we call "decadence" amounts to the loss of an end, an object. When literature has lost sight of its real object or purpose, literature is decadent.

What then is the end, object, or purpose of humane letters? Why, the expression of the moral imagination; or, to put this truth in a more familiar phrase, the end of great books is ethical—to teach us what it means to be genuinely human.

Every major form of literary art has taken for its deeper themes the norms of human nature. What Eliot calls "the permanent things"—the norms, the standards—have been the concern of the poet ever since the time of Job, or ever since Homer: "the blind man who sees," sang of the ways of the gods with men. Until very recent years, men took it for granted that literature exists to form the normative consciousness—that is, to teach human beings their true nature, their dignity, and their place in the scheme of things. Such was the endeavor of Sophocles and Aristophanes, of Thucydides and Tacitus, of Plato and Cicero, of Hesiod and Vergil, of Dante and Shakespeare, of Dryden and Pope.

The very phrase "humane letters" implies that great literature is meant to teach us what it is to be fully human. As Irving Babbitt observes in his slim book *Literature and the American College* (1908), humanism (derived from the Latin *humanitas*) is an ethical discipline, intended to develop the truly human person, the qualities of manliness, through the study of great books. The literature of nihilism, of pornography and of sensationalism, as Albert Salomon suggests in *The Tyranny of Progress* (1955), is a recent development, arising in the eighteenth century—though reaching its height in our time—with the decay of the religious view of life and with the decline of what has been called "The Great Tradition" in philosophy.

This normative purpose of letters is especially powerful in English literature, which never succumbed to the egoism that came to dominate French letters at the end of the eighteenth century. The names of Milton, Bunyan, and Johnson—or, in America, of Emerson, Hawthorne, and Melville—may be sufficient illustrations of the point. The great popular novelists of the nineteenth century—Scott, Dickens, Thackeray, Trollope—all assumed that the writer is under a moral obligation to normality—that is, explicitly or implicitly, to certain enduring standards of private and public conduct.

Now I do not mean that the great writer incessantly utters homilies. With Ben Jonson, he may "scourge the naked follies of the time," but he does not often murmur, "Be good, sweet maid, and let who will be clever." Rather, the man of letters teaches the norms of our existence through allegory, analogy, and holding up the mirror to nature. The writer may, like William Faulkner, write much more of what is evil than of what is good; and yet, exhibiting the depravity of human nature, he establishes in his reader's mind the awareness that there exist enduring standards from which we fall away; and that fallen human nature is an ugly sight.

Or the writer may deal, as did J. P. Marquand, chiefly with the triviality and emptiness of a society that has forgotten standards. Often, in his appeal of a conscience to a conscience, he may row with muffled oars; sometimes he may be aware only dimly of his normative function. The better the artist, one almost may say, the more subtle the preacher. Imaginative persuasion, not blunt exhortation, commonly is the method of the literary champion of norms.

It is worth remarking that the most influential poet of our age, Eliot, endeavored to restore to modern poetry, drama, and criticism their traditional normative functions. In this he saw himself as the heir of Vergil and Dante. The poet ought not to force his ego upon the public; rather, the poet's mission is to transcend the personal and the particular. As Eliot wrote in "Tradition and the Individual Talent," the very first essay found in *Selected Essays, 1917–1932* (1932):

> It is not in his personal emotions, the emotions provoked by particular events in his life, that the poet is in any way remarkable or interesting. His particular emotions may be simple, or crude, or flat. The emotion in his poetry will be a very complex thing, but not with the complexity of the emotions of people who have very complex or unusual emotions in life. One error, in fact, of eccentricity in poetry is to seek for new human emotions to express; and in this search for novelty in the wrong place it discovers the

> perverse. The business of the poet is not to find new emotions, but to use the ordinary ones and, in working them up into poetry, to express feelings which are not in actual emotions at all.

So pure poetry, and the other forms of great literature, search the human heart to find in it the laws of moral existence, distinguishing man from beast. Or so it was until almost the end of the eighteenth century. Since then, the egoism of one school of the Romantics has obscured the primary purpose of humane letters. And many of the Realists have written of man as if he were brutal only—or brutalized by institutions, at best. (So arose Ambrose Bierce's definition in *The Devil's Dictionary* (1906): "Realism, *n.* An accurate representation of human nature, as seen by toads.") In our time, and particularly in America, we have seen the rise to popularity of a school of writers more nihilistic than ever were the Russian nihilists: the literature of disgust and denunciation, sufficiently described in Edmund Fuller's *Man in Modern Fiction* (1958). To members of this school, the writer is no defender or expositor of standards, for there are no values to explain or defend; a writer merely registers, unreservedly, his disgust with humanity and himself. (This is a world away from Dean Swift—who, despite his loathing of most human beings, detested them only because they fell short of what they were meant to be.)

Yet the names of our twentieth-century nihilistic authors will be forgotten in less than a generation, I suspect, while there will endure from our age the works of a few men of letters whose appeal is to the enduring things, and therefore to posterity. I think, for instance of Gironella's novel *The Cypresses Believe in God* (1951). The gentle novice who trims the hair and washes the bodies of the poorest of the poor in old Gerona, though he dies by Communist bullets, will live a great span in the realm of letters; while the scantily-disguised personalities of our nihilistic authors, swaggering nastily as characters in best sellers, will be extinguished the moment when the public's fancy veers to some newer sensation. For as the normative consciousness breathes life into the soul and the social order, so the normative understanding gives an author lasting fame.

Malcolm Cowley, writing a few years ago in *Horizon* of the recent crop of first- novelists, observed that the several writers he discussed scarcely had heard of the Seven Cardinal Virtues or of the Seven Deadly Sins. Crimes and sins are only mischances to these young novelists; real love and real hatred are absent from their books. To this rising generation of writers, the world seems purposeless, and human actions meaningless. They seek to express nothing but a vagrant ego. (Jacques Barzun, in *The House of Intellect* [1959], has some shrewd things to say about the unjustified pride of the decade's array of aspiring writers.) And Mr. Cowley suggests that these young men and women, introduced to no norms in childhood and youth except the vague attitude that one is entitled to do as one likes, so long as it doesn't injure someone else, are devoid of spiritual and intellectual discipline—empty, indeed, of real desire for anything.

This sort of aimless and unhappy writer is the product of a time in which the normative function of letters has been greatly neglected. Ignorant of his own mission, such a writer tends to think of his occupation as a mere skill, possibly lucrative, sometimes satisfying to one's vanity, but dedicated to no end. Even the "proletarian" writing of the twenties and thirties acknowledged some end; but that has died of disillusion and inanition. If writers are in this plight, in consequence of the prevailing "permissive" climate of opinion, what of their readers? Comparatively few book-readers nowadays, I suspect, seek normative knowledge. They are after amusement, sometimes of a vicariously gross character, or else pursue a vague "awareness" of current affairs and intellectual currents, suitable for cocktail-party conversation.

The young novelists described by Mr. Cowley are of the number of Eliot's "Hollow Men." Nature abhors a vacuum; into minds that are vacant of norms must come some new force; and often that new force has a diabolical character.

A perceptive critic, Mr. Albert Fowler, writing in *Modern Age*, asks the question, "Can Literature Corrupt?"—and answers in the affirmative.[1] So literature can; and also it is possible to be corrupted by an ignorance of humane letters, much of our normative knowledge necessarily being derived from our reading. The person who reads bad books instead of good may be subtly corrupted; the person who reads nothing at all may be forever adrift in life unless he lives in a community still powerfully influenced by what Gustave Thibon calls "moral habits" and by oral tradition. And absolute abstinence from printed matter has become rare. If a small boy does not read Robert Louis Stevenson's *Treasure Island* (1883), the odds are that he will read *Mad Ghoul Comics*.

So I think it is worthwhile to suggest the outlines of the literary discipline which induces some understanding of enduring values. For centuries, such a program of reading—though never called a program—existed in Western nations. It powerfully influenced the minds and actions of the leaders of the infant American Republic, for instance. If one pokes into what books were read by the leaders of the Revolution, the framers of the Constitution and the principal men of America before 1800, one finds that nearly all of them were acquainted with a few important books: the King James version of the Bible, Plutarch's *Lives*, Shakespeare, something of Cicero, something of Vergil. This was a body of literature highly normative. The founders of the Republic thought of their new commonwealth as a blending of the Roman Republic with prescriptive English institutions; and they took for their models in leadership the prophets and kings and apostles of the Bible, and the noble Greeks and Romans of Plutarch. Cato's stubborn virtue, Demosthene's eloquent vaticinations, Cleomenes' rash reforming impulse—these were in their minds' eyes; and they tempered their conduct accordingly. "But nowadays," as Chateaubriand wrote more than a century ago, "statesmen understand only the stock market—and that badly."

Of course it was not by books alone that the normative understanding of the framers of the Constitution, for instance, was formed. Their apprehension of norms was acquired also in family, church, and school, and in the business of ordinary life. But that portion of their normative understanding which was got from books did loom large. For we cannot attain very well to enduring standards if we rely simply on actual personal experience as a normative mentor. Sheer experience, as Franklin suggested, is the teacher of born fools. Our lives are too brief and confused for most men to develop any normative pattern from their private experience; and as Newman wrote, "Life is for action." Therefore we turn to the bank and capital of the ages, the normative knowledge found in revelation, authority, and historical experience, if we seek guidance in morals, taste, and politics. Ever since the invention of printing, this normative understanding has been expressed, increasingly in books, so that nowadays most people form their opinions, in considerable part, from the printed page. This may be regrettable sometimes; it may be what D. H. Lawrence called "chewing the newspapers"; but it is a fact. Deny a fact, and that fact will be your master.

Another fact is that for some thirty years we have been failing, here in America, to develop a normative consciousness in young people through a careful program of reading great literature. We have talked about "education for life" and "training for life adjustment"; but many of us seem to have forgotten that literary disciplines are a principal means for learning to adjust to the necessities of life. Moreover, unless the life to which we are urged to adjust ourselves is governed by norms, it may be a very bad life for everyone.

One of the faults of the typical "life adjustment" or "permissive" curriculum in the schools—paralleled, commonly, by similarly indulgent attitudes in the family—has been the substitution of "real life situations" reading for the study of truly imaginative literature. This tendency has been especially noticeable in the lower grades of school, but it extends upward in some degree through high school. The "Dick and Jane" and "run, Spot, run" school of letters does not stir the imagination; and it imparts small apprehension of norms. Apologists for this aspect of life-adjustment schooling believe that they are inculcating respect for values by prescribing simple readings that commend tolerant, kindly, co-operative behavior. Yet this is no effective way to impart a knowledge of norms: direct moral didacticism, whether of the Victorian or the twentieth century variety, usually awakens resistance in the recipient, particularly if he has some natural intellectual power.

The fulsome praise of goodness can alienate; it can whet the appetite for the cookie-jar on the top shelf. In Saki's "The Story-Teller," a mischievous bachelor tells three children on a train the tale of a wondrously good little girl, awarded medals for her propriety. But she met a wolf in the park; and though she ran, the jangling of her medals led the wolf straight to her, so that she was devoured utterly. Though the children were delighted with this unconventional narrative, their aunt protests, "A most improper story to tell to young children!" "Unhappy woman!" the departing bachelor murmurs. "For the next six months or so those children will assail her in public with demands for an improper story!"

Well, Greek and Norse myths, for instance, sometimes are not very proper; yet, stirring the imagination, they do more to bring about an early apprehension of norms than do any number of the dull and interminable doings of Dick and Jane. The story of Pandora, or of Thor's adventure with the old woman and her cat, gives any child an insight into the conditions of existence—dimly grasped at the moment, perhaps, but gaining in power as the years pass—that no utilitarian "real-life situation" fiction can match. Because they are eternally valid, Hesiod and the saga-singers are modern. And versions of Hawthorne or of Andrew Lang are far better prose than the quasi-basic English thrust upon young people in many recent textbooks.

If we starve young people for imagination, adventure, and some sort of heroism—to turn now to a later level of learning—they are not likely to embrace Good Approved Real-Life Tales for Good Approved Real-Life Boys and Girls; on the contrary, they may resort to the dregs of letters, rather than be bored altogether. If they are not introduced to Stevenson and Conrad, say—and that fairly early—they will find the nearest and newest Grub Street pornographers. And the consequences will be felt not merely in their failure of taste, but in their misapprehension of human nature, lifelong; and eventually, in the whole tone of a nation. "On this scheme of things . . . a woman is but an animal; and an animal not of the highest order." The Naked Ape theory of human nature, the "reductionist" notion of man as a breathing automaton, is reinforced by ignorance of literature's moral imagination.

In one of his *Causeries*, Sainte-Beuve tells of a playwright standing at a friend's window to watch a frantic Parisian mob pouring through the street: "See my pageant passing!" the author complacently murmurs. Art is man's nature; and it is true enough, as Oscar Wilde said whimsically, that nature imitates art. Our private and public actions, in mature years, have been determined by the opinions and tastes we acquired in youth. Great books do influence societies for the better; and bad books do drag down the general level of personal and social conduct. Having seen the pageant, the mob proceeds to behave as a playwright thinks it should. I suppose that a public which goes often enough to the plays of Tennessee Williams may begin to behave as Mr. Williams thinks Americans behave already. We become what others, in a voice of authority, tell us we are or ought to be.

So I think that in the teaching of literature, some of the theories of the life-adjustment education and permissive schools have done considerable mischief. Nowadays the advocates of life-adjustment education are giving ground, sullenly, before their critics. The intellectual ancestor of their doctrines is Rousseau. Though I am no warm admirer of the ideas of Rousseau, I like still less the doctrines of Gradgrind, in *Hard Times* (1845); so I hope that life-adjustment methods of teaching literature will not be supplanted by something yet worse conceived. After all, *real* adjustment to the conditions of human existence is adjustment to norms. Even an ineffectual endeavor to teach norms is better than to ignore or deny all standards. A mistaken zeal for utilitarian, vocational training in place of normative instruction; an emphasis upon the physical and biological sciences that would push literature into a dusty corner of the curriculum; an attempt to secure spoken competency in foreign languages at the expense of the great works of our language—these might be changes in education as hostile to the imparting of norms through literature as anything which the life-adjustment and permissive people have done.

So I venture to suggest here, in scanty outline, how it is possible to form a normative consciousness through the study of humane letters. What I have to say ought to be commonplace; but these ideas seem to have been forgotten in many quarters. This normative endeavor ought to be the joint work of family and school. As the art of reading often is better taught by parents than it can be taught in a large class in school, so a knowledge of good books comes at least as frequently from the home as from the school. My own taste for books grew from both sources: my grandfather's and my mother's bookshelves, and from a very good little grade-school library. And if a school is failing to impart a taste for good books, this often can be remedied by interested attention in the family.

Tentatively, I distinguished four levels of literature by which a normative consciousness is developed. The upper levels do not supplant the earlier, but rather supplement and blend with them; and the process of becoming familiar with these four levels or bodies of normative knowledge extends from the age of three or four to the studies of college and university. We may call these levels fantasy; narrative history and biography; reflective prose and poetic fiction; and philosophy and theology.

1. *Fantasy*. The fantastic and the fey, far from being unhealthy for small children, are precisely what a healthy child needs; under such stimulus a child's moral imagination quickens. Out of the early tales of wonder come a sense of awe and the beginning of philosphy. All things begin and end in mystery. For that matter, a normative consciousness may be aroused by themes less striking than the Arthurian legends or the Norse tales. The second book I had read to me was *Little Black Sambo* (1899). Learning it by heart then, I can recite it still. (One symptom of the growing silliness of our time was the demand a few years ago, that *Little Black Sambo* be banned as "racist.") Though I risk falling into pathos, I cannot resist remarking that even *Little Black Sambo* touches upon norms. What child fails to reflect upon the *hubris* of the tigers, of the prudence of Sambo?

If children are to begin to understand themselves, and other people, and the laws that govern our nature, they ought to be encouraged to read Lang's collection of fairy tales, and the Brothers Grimm (even at their grimmest), and Andersen, and the Arabian Nights, and all the rest; and presently the better romancers for young people, like Blackmore and Howard Pyle. Even the Bible, in the beginning, is fantasy for the young. The allegory of Jonah and the whale is accepted, initially, as a tale of the marvelous, and so sticks in the memory. Only in later years does one recognize the story as the symbol of the Jews' exile in Babylon, and of how faith may preserve men and nations through the most terrible of trials.

2. *Narrative History and Biography*. My grandfather and I, during the long walks that we used to take when I was six or seven years old, would talk of the character of Richard II, and of Puritan domestic life, and of the ferocity of Assyrians. The intellectual partnership of an imaginative man of sixty and an inquisitive boy of seven is an edifying thing. My preparation for these conversations came from books in my grandfather's library: Dickens's *A Child's History of England* (1910), Hawthorne's *Grandfather's Chair* (1840), Ridpath's four-volume illustrated *History of the World* (1897). Later my grandfather gave me

H. G. Wells's *Outline of History* (1920). In the fullness of time, I came to disagree with Dickens's and Wells's interpretations of history; but that was all to the good, for it stimulated my critical faculties and led me to the proper study of mankind—and to the great historians, Herodotus, Thucydides, Xenophon, Polybius, Tacitus, and all the rest; to the great biographies, also, like Plutarch's *Lives* and Boswell's *Johnson* (1791), and Lockhart's *Scott*. Reading of great lives does something to make decent lives.

3. *Reflective Prose and Poetic Fiction*. When I was seven, my mother gave me a set of James Fenimore Cooper's novels; and about the same time I inherited from a great-uncle my set of Hawthorne. That launched me upon novel-reading, so that by the time I was ten I had read all of Hugo, Dickens, and Twain. Fiction is truer than fact: I mean that in great fiction we obtain the distilled wisdom of men of genius, understandings of human nature which we could attain—if at all—unaided by books, only at the end of life, after numberless painful experiences. I began to read Sir Walter Scott when I was twelve or thirteen; and I think I learnt from the Waverley novels, and from Shakespeare, more of the varieties of character than ever I have got since from the manuals of psychology.

Such miscellaneous browsing in the realm of fiction rarely does mischief. When I was eleven or twelve, I was much influenced by Twain's *Mysterious Stranger* (1916), an atheist tract disguised as a romance of medieval Austria. It did not turn me into a juvenile atheist; but it set me to inquiring after first causes—and in time, paradoxically, it led me to Dante, my mainstay ever since. In certain ways, the great novel and the great poem can teach more of norms than can philosophy and theology.

4. *Philosophy and Theology*. For the crown of normative literary studies, we turn, about the age of nineteen or twenty, to abstraction and generalization, chastened by logic. It simply is not true that

One impulse from a vernal wood
May teach you more of man,
Of moral evil and of good,
Than all the sages can.

It is not from vegetal nature that one acquires some knowledge of human passions and longings. There exist, rather in Emerson's phrase, law for man and law for thing. The law for man we learn from Plato, Aristotle, Seneca, Marcus Aurelius; from the Hebrew prophets, St. Paul, St. Augustine, and so many other Christian writers. Our petty private rationality is founded upon the wisdom of the men of dead ages; and if we endeavor to guide ourselves solely by our limited private insights, we tumble down into the ditch of unreason.

"Scientific" truth, or what is popularly taken to be scientific truth, alters from year to year—with accelerating speed in our day. But poetic and moral truth changes little with the elapse of the centuries. To the unalterable in human existence, humane letters are a great guide.

What I have been trying to describe in the preceding summary analysis is that body of literature which helps to form the normative consciousness of the rising generation: that is, to enliven the moral imagination. Here I have been historian and diagnostician; I have not endeavored to offer you facile remedies for our present bent condition.

If a public will not have the moral imagination, I have been saying, then it will fall first to the idyllic imagination; and presently into the diabolic imagination—this last becoming a state of narcosis, figuratively and literally. For we are created moral beings; and when we deny our nature, in letters as in action, the gods of the copybook headings with fire and slaughter return. I attest the moral vision of men like Aleksandr Solzhenitsyn; some have begun to make a stand, in the republic of letters, against the diabolic imagination and the diabolic regime. A human body that cannot react is a corpse; and a body of letters that cannot react against narcotic illusions might better be buried. The theological virtues may find hardy champions in these closing years of the twentieth century: men and women who remember that in the beginning was the Word.

["The Moral Imagination," Literature and Belief, *Vol. 1 (1981), 37–49. Also published in* Reclaiming a Patrimony *(Washington, DC: The Heritage Foundation, 1982), 45–58.]*

❖

Normative Art and Modern Vices

"To be a conservative is to be a conservator—a guardian of old truths and old rights." These words, found in the opening chapter of Enemies of the Permanent Things *(1969), identify Kirk's mission as a man of letters. He accepts as a major task the need to recover ethical standards subverted by "the malady of growing decay" in literature and politics. To surmount this affliction we have to understand the meaning of "norm" as an enduring standard that separates virtue from vice. The spread of decadence in modern society, Kirk believes, is tied to the disappearance of norms and conventions, and to the inclination toward the aberrant and the monstrous. Spontaneity, originality, and eccentricity, for instance, when cut off from norms, contribute to the moral malaise that so much of modern literature reflects. As the moral virtues crumble a pattern of abnormity accelerates in virulent forms of the degradation of literature.*

The malady of normative decay gnaws at order in the person and at order in the republic. Until we recognize the nature of this affliction, we must sink ever deeper into the disorder of the soul and the disorder of the state. A recovery of norms can be commenced only when we moderns come to understand in what manner we have fallen away from old truths.

Good literature and bad literature exert powerful influences upon private character and upon the polity of the commonwealth. Sound political theory and practice make it possible to maintain and improve private virtue; debased politics must debase human character. If ethical understanding, then, is ignored in modern letters and politics, we are left at the mercy of consuming private appetite and oppressive political power. We end in Darkness. . . .

My endeavor is to help to refurbish what Edmund Burke called "the wardrobe of a moral imagination." When the moral imagination is enriched, a people find themselves capable of great things; when it is impoverished, they cannot act effectively even for their own survival, no matter how immense their material resources. I am suggesting in these pages no panacea, then, but am attempting to point the way to first principles. Most of these principles are very old ones, obscured by neglect.

"Art is man's nature," said Burke, playing upon Aristotle's remark that art is the imitation of nature. We are not wholly subject to Fate and Fortune:

for the art of the man of letters, and the art of the statist, determine in large part whether we become normal human beings, or are perverted into abnormal creatures. In erring Reason's spite, as Samuel Johnson knew, the will is free. All argument may be against it, but all necessity is for it. Personal and social decadence are not the work of ineluctable forces, but are the consequences of defying normative truth: a failure of right reason, if you will, resulting in abnormality. When we distort the arts of literature and statecraft, we warp our nature before long.

An abnormity, in its Latin root, means a monstrosity, defying the norm, the nature of things. (These words "abnormality" and "abnormity" are interchangeable.) An abnormal generation is a generation of monsters, enslaved by will and appetite. To recover an apprehension of normality, then, is to acquire an understanding of one's real nature. The alternative to such recovery is not a piquant pose of "nonconformity," but monstrosity in the soul and in society. If normative art expires, the people perish. . . .

Standardization without Standards

On few subjects has more nonsense been uttered, in our own time, than the meaning of the concept "norm." The confused discussion, these past few years, of convention, conformity, and intellectuality is bound up necessarily with the understanding—or misunderstanding—of this word "norm." I propose here to bring some order into this discussion, and to relate my considerations to the moral imagination.

A norm means an enduring standard. It is a law of nature, which we ignore at our peril. It is a rule of human conduct and a measure of public virtue. The norm does not signify the average, the median, the mean, the mediocre. The norm is not the conduct of the average sensual man. A norm is not simply a measure of average performance within a group. There is law for man, and law for thing; the late Alfred Kinsey notwithstanding, the norm for the wasp and the snake is not the norm for man. A norm exists: though men may ignore or forget a norm, still that norm does not cease to be, nor does it cease to influence men. A man apprehends a norm, or fails to apprehend it; but he does not create or destroy important norms.

We have learnt something, in this century, about the ineluctable character of norms; we have learnt from the disasters of an era in which norms were forgotten or defied—in which ideology did duty for moral standards and principles of justice. We have discovered that were there no norms for man, it would be necessary for us to invent some.

But I do not propose to invent norms. The sanction for obedience to norms must come from a source higher than private speculation: men do not submit long to their own creations. Standards erected out of expediency will be hurled down, soon enough, also out of expediency. Either norms have a reality independent of immediate social utility, or they are mere fictions. If men assume that norms are no better than the pompous fabrications of their ancestors, got up to serve the interests of a faction or an age, then every rising generation will challenge the principles of personal and social order, and will learn wisdom only through agony. For half a century, we have been experiencing the consequences of moral and social neoterism: so, like the generation of Socrates and Thucydides in the fifth century, we begin to perceive that somehow we have acted on false assumptions. No, norms cannot be invented. All that we can do is to reawaken our consciousness to the existence of norms; to confess that there are enduring standards superior to our petty private stock of rationality.

An inhumane view of life speedily leads to an inhumane social order. Men in society must subscribe to some body of principles; and when they have lost sight of norms, they attach themselves in panic to some fanatic set of secular dogmas. For a generation and more, many men have tried to make an ideology serve a normative end; and they have failed.

Indulge me in one anecdote of my undergraduate days. An old friend of mine—agent of a textbook publisher—whom we may call Mr. Stewart, for years went about quizzing people as to their first principles, after the fashion of Socrates. He was interested especially in whether they made any distinction between virtue and vice; or, at least, whether they acknowledged any means for measuring vice and virtue. One day he was in colloquy with a learned professor of languages, whom we may call Dr. Nemo. Mr. Stewart experienced some difficulty in persuading Dr. Nemo to affirm any first principle. Everything, Dr. Nemo implied, is subjective and relative and tentative and—well, ambivalent. Indeed, Dr. Nemo would not affirm positively, on being pressed, that two and two are four.

"Which was the better person, do you think," Mr. Stewart inquired presently, "Jesus or Nero?"

But Dr. Nemo declined to sit in judgment on this vexed question, lest he be judged. We don't have all the facts, he said; and there is Nero's childhood to consider; and the two held different social stations; and, after all, one of these persons held one set of value-preferences, and the other subscribed to a different set. Who could say which was the worthier?

It became clear that Dr. Nemo felt a marked aversion to acknowledging any norm. Dr. Nemo affirmed one thing only: that he was a liberal. Liberals, he explained, know that there exist two sides to every question, and that we ought to sheer away from prejudices, and that we have no right to come to any conclusion until all the facts are available and scientific tests are applied. Morals, besides, are the product of cultural circumstances.

"Who is the better man," Mr. Stewart persisted—this was shortly before the Second World War—"Hitler or Stalin?"

"Let's not reduce matters to absurdity," said Dr. Nemo. "Stalin's the better man, of course."

So, after all, Dr. Nemo did recognize the existence of some norms. Stalin, he then believed, was a Man of Good Will—however much he might suffer from peccadilloes of taste and temper—a champion of Progress and Equality. Conceivably Dr. Nemo's opinion is modified today. Just here, however, I am not concerned with the relative degrees of iniquity of Hitler and Stalin. My point is that Dr. Nemo and persons like him—persons influenced by what the late Gordon Chalmers called "disintegrated liberalism"—recognize certain norms even at the moment they deny the existence of permanent standards. But their norms have the sanction only of ideological commitment; and that is a perilous sanction, often leading to erroneous judgments of men like Stalin.

Dr. Nemo held rather a friendly opinion of Stalin because he thought Stalin shared his own vague humanitarian value-preferences. Progress and Equality are charismatic terms, god-terms, for Dr. Nemo and his friends. These abstract concepts of his are derived, however remotely, from certain traditional norms. Had Dr. Nemo really discarded norms altogether, he would not have been able to believe even in Progress and Equality. Although he feared that Mr. Stewart might entrap him in some illiberal set of doctrines by obtaining his judgment concerning Jesus and Nero, he could not resist sitting in judgment when his ideological affections were in question.

With a man who maintains that he can discover no real standards for moral judgment of any sort, it is impossible to argue. Even Samuel Johnson, when told of a gentleman who maintained that virtue and vice are indistinguishable, contented himself with observing, "Why, sir, when he leaves our houses let us count our spoons." The most formidable of skeptics, David Hume, in his *Enquiry Concerning the Principles of Morals* (1751), put this difficulty with his usual acuteness:

"Disputes with men, pertinaciously obstinate in their principles, are, of all others, the most irksome; except, perhaps, those with persons, entirely disingenuous, who really do not believe the opinions they defend, but engage in the controversy, from affectation, from a spirit of opposition, or from a desire of showing wit and ingenuity, superior to the rest of mankind." It is best to shun their company. "Those who have denied the reality of moral distinctions," Hume continues, "may be ranked among the disingenuous disputants; nor is it conceivable, that any human creature could ever seriously believe, that all characters and actions were alike entitled to the affection and regard of everyone. . . . Let a man's insensibility be ever so great, he must often be touched with the images of Right and Wrong; and let his prejudices be ever so obstinate, he must observe, that others are susceptible of like impressions. The only way, therefore, of converting an antagonist of this kind, is to leave him to himself."

So I do not propose to undertake just now a task from which even the philosopher of Ninewells shrank; I do not intend to try to refute the nihilist by the methods of pure reason. I do not mean to survey the whole hoary controversy which has recurred perennially, over twenty-six centuries, concerning the existence or character of norms. To awaken an apprehension of norms was the high endeavor of Socrates and Plato; it was the constant theme of the Christian divines; it weighed on the minds of the rationalists of the eighteenth century and the positivists of the nineteenth. Nor shall I attempt a systematic refutation of the positions held by the instrumentalists and the logical positivists of our century: that work already has been commenced by a variety of writers.

But I do propose to assist in the rescue of normative consciousness from the clutch of ideology. For it ought to be the moral imagination which creates political doctrines, and not political doctrines which seduce the moral imagination. Our first task here is the restoration of a proper vocabulary.

A norm, I have said, is an enduring standard for private and public conduct. It is a canon of human nature. Real progress consists in the movement of mankind toward the understanding of norms, and toward conformity to norms. Real decadence consists in the movement of mankind away from the understanding of norms, and away from obedience to norms. The decay of the Greek civilization in the fifth and fourth centuries before Christ; the decline of the Roman order in the four centuries after Christ; the collapse of the medieval world in the fourteenth century; the decline of culture and the eruption of dark powers in our own twentieth century—these were times in which norms were forgotten or defied. The disintegration of moral understanding was at once cause and consequence of confusion in the social order.

One cannot draw up a catalogue of norms as if it were an inventory of goods. Normality inheres in some sensible object, and norms depend one upon another, like the stones of a cathedral. But it is possible to say that there is a norm of charity; a norm of justice; a norm of freedom; a norm of duty; a norm of fortitude. Most of us perceive these norms clearly only when they are part and parcel of the life of a human being. Aristotle made norms recognizable by describing his "magnanimous man," the upright person and citizen. For the Christian, the norm is made flesh in the person of Christ. Normality is not what the average sensual man ordinarily possesses: it is what he ought to try to possess.

When I write of a "norm," I do not mean a "value" merely. A value is the quality of worth. Many things are worthwhile that are not normative. When most writers nowadays employ the word "value" as a term of philosophy, moreover, they mean "subjective value"—that is, the quality of being worthwhile, of giving pleasure or satisfaction to individuals, without judgment upon the intrinsic, absolute, essential merit of the sensation or action in question; without reference to its objective deserts. In the subjective sense, going to church is a value for some persons, and taking one's ease in a brothel is a value for others. A norm has value, but has more than value. A norm endures in its own right, whether or not it gives pleasure to particular individuals. A norm is the standard against which any alleged value must be measured objectively.

So much, just now, for definition. I am embarked upon a labor thoroughly conservative and thoroughly unpopular. The unabashed defender of traditional norms, and the unregenerate champion of prescriptive institutions—though they may have gained some ground in recent years—remain members of a Remnant. To be conservative is to be a conservator—a guardian of old truths and old rights. This rarely has been a popular office—not with the leaders of the crowd.

Yet for the restoration of normality, the understanding of the problem must extend beyond any narrow circle of intellectuals. The little knots of Stoics, isolated from the Roman masses, could retard the decay of their sprawling society; but they could not renew the vitality of their social order: and it was only in the hour of that order's destruction that inner order in soul and personality was restored by Christian faith—or by that religion which has existed since the beginning of the world, but which now takes the name of Christianity.

At least the urgency of this need for the recovery of a normative consciousness is conceded grudgingly by some who never thought of themselves as guardians—for instance, by many contributors to the pages of those journals long devoted to the cause of a pragmatic or a positivistic secularism. But it may suffice to quote here from a man of skeptical and sardonic genius, George Bernard Shaw. In *Back to Methuselah* (1921), Shaw recognized that if religion is lacking, human society becomes intolerable; for if no norms are observed, men behave like the beasts from which they are ascended.

"Goodnatured unambitious men," Shaw wrote,

> are cowards when they have no religion. They are dominated and exploited not only by greedy and often halfwitted and half-alive weaklings who will do anything for cigars, champagne, motor cars, and the more childish and selfish uses of money, but by able and sound administrators who can do nothing else with them than dominate and exploit them. Government and exploitation become synonymous under such circumstances; and the world is finally ruled by the childish, the brigands, and the blackguards. Those who refuse to stand in with them are persecuted and occasionally executed when they give any trouble to the exploiters. They fall into poverty when they lack lucrative specific talents. At the present moment one half of Europe, having knocked the other half down, is trying to kick it to death, and may succeed: a procedure which is, logically, sound Neo-Darwinism. And the goodnatured majority are looking on in helpless horror, or allowing themselves to be persuaded by the newspapers of their exploiters that the kicking is not only a sound commercial investment, but an act of divine justice of which they are the ardent instruments.

One may acknowledge the acuteness of this insight without subscribing to the curious religion, or quasi-religion, which Shaw preaches—half soberly, half whimsically—in *Back to Methuselah*. And it ought to be said also for Shaw that he never succumbed to the illusion that ideology may substitute satisfactorily for religious conviction. Unlike certain American professors of education and sociology, Shaw never indulged the fond hope that Democracy—a condition or a means, but no end—could become the religion of the future. Nor, despite his flirtations with Fascism and Communism, did Shaw expect the totalist ideologies to realize this necessity. Man cannot be satisfied by worship of himself in the mass.

So it is not conservators only who are beginning to perceive that traditional norms have at least a pragmatic sanction. Still, the discussion of this sombre conundrum remains perplexed by many obsolete feuds and inconsistent arguments. Some of the people most thoroughly aware of the dangers of ideology and the terrors of life without principle nevertheless continue to denounce convention, custom, and all conformity as the enemies of private and social freedom. I think, for instance, of David Riesman. . . .

After describing the sad state of the "other-directed man"—a being who has no guide but the fads and foibles of his neighbors, who also are other-directed men, unable to guide him—Mr. Riesman still appoints himself the champion of an "individualism" received like Holy Writ from John Stuart Mill. It is an individualism without norms, a passion for being different merely for the sake of differing, an undiscriminating defiance of authority, convention, and conformity for the sake of being "autonomous."[2] The only end of existence to be discerned in Riesman's argument is Diversion: an uneasy search for new pleasures.

Riesman is a latter-day liberal, well aware of the traps in ideology (except when he falls back into a petition-signing mood, after having warned other liberals against signing manifestoes in the gross). His views of convention and conformity, however, are shared (with minor exceptions) by a writer professedly conservative, Peter Viereck. In his *Unadjusted Man* (1956), Mr. Viereck holds that to be unadjusted is a good in itself; the unadjusted man is "the stubborn grit in the machine," delaying the standardizing tendency of our age. Although a hard hater of Romanticism and a defender of Classicism, Viereck himself falls into the deep pit of sentimental Romanticism when he commends spontaneity, originality, and eccentricity as positive merits. Now spontaneity, originality, and eccentricity all have their proper part in life and letters; but when they are cut adrift altogether from norms—when they acknowledge no general principles—spontaneity becomes mere effervescence, originality becomes offensive egoism, and eccentricity becomes deliberate bad taste. I do not say that Viereck is unable to reconcile his opinions with a recognition of norms; I point out merely that he never makes the effort, nor does he seem to be aware of this gaping hole in his argument.

Yet Riesman and Viereck at least recognize that defiance of convention and militant nonconformity require some sort of apology. Others among us deny outright—or remain ignorant of the fact—that an intelligent case may be made for a convention in the service of normality and a conformity to enduring principles. These latter cry up a new convention of unconventionality and a new conformity of nonconformity, as if the civil social order had been created only so that we might have the fun of knocking it down again.

To deny for the sake of denial is to live with a sour taste in one's mouth. The sort of person whom Sidney Hook calls the "ritualistic liberal" is intolerant in the cause of toleration, conformist in the championship of nonconformity.

These excesses of the ritualistic liberal, nevertheless, sometimes produce a reaction among well-intentioned men which has its own blindness. "Let's be pragmatic, and forget about abstract theory." Because the ritualistic liberal, captive to ideology, has cried "wolf, wolf!" so shrilly and often so pointlessly, some among us suggest that all this fretting about the state of society is no better than a pathological condition of the critic: that somehow sweet reason and moderation and social legislation will carry us through our time of troubles without any need for discussion of general principles and aims. The complaints of the critic of society, whether he is conservative or liberal, are dismissed "pragmatically" as mere Anxiety.

"Anxiety" means distress of mind produced by prolonged apprehension of impending disaster. In our century, the dominant schools of psychology have arrogated the word as a term of pathology; and when many psychologists employ it, they imply that anxiety is apprehension without real cause: that is, a dread purely subjective, conjured up by the sufferer's mental sickness.

But in truth, anxiety is produced by disorder: disorder in private existence, and disorder in social existence. If the disorder which afflicts the anxious man is purely illusory, the product of his sick fancy, then anxiety falls within the borders of pathology; but if the disorder, internal and external, which the anxious man experiences is the product of a real moral and social confusion in his time, then the cure for anxiety lies not in psychiatric and physiological treatment, but in a stem endeavor to lessen this real disorder—an endeavor best lightened occasionally by letting cheerfulness break in.

A condition of anxiety brought on by a demonstrably real decay of order can be alleviated only by a restoration of order—or, at least, by satisfying work toward such a restoration, both in the order of the soul and in the order of politics. Anxiety results from the collapse of normative belief, the dissolution of standards of private conduct and public justice. Before anxiety may be dissipated, norms must be recognized and obeyed. It is not necessary for the dispelling of anxiety that the norms be wholly triumphant in society at large: no society ever has been wholly submissive to normative precepts. But it is essential that the sufferer from anxiety become aware of the reality of norms, and that he do something to signify his recognition of those standards, at least in his inner life, before he can be relieved from his affliction in any degree. Anxiety battens on fecklessness, impotence, frustration; it shrinks when conformity to norms restores purpose to a man's existence.

Dante knew all the woes to which humanity is heir. Yet Dante was not an Anxious Man, though he lived in a time of violent disorder. He knew that the principles of order abide, and that justice is more than human, and that art is the servant of enduring standards. His vision of eternal happiness and eternal torment was not a vision of disharmony; it was governed by norms; and in the certitude of those standards, all his mundane sorrows found their remedy. He faced Terror unflinchingly, and his achievement was not simply artistic mastery, nor yet remedy of the immediate distresses of his century, but rather the burning renewal of certain ancient moral insights, which he bequeathed as a legacy beyond price to the troubled souls who were to succeed him in time. It is thus that the consummate artist fights his battle against obsessive Anxiety.

Finally, so far as anxiety is bound up with the stress and tension essential to human nature, anxiety never can be abolished; and if it could, great literature would be written no longer. For a body that has ceased to react is a corpse, and an artist who has ceased to dread disorder is a vegetable. Anxiety in the artist and the statesman and the moralist is one of the products of that "fortunate fall," that contradiction which lies at the heart of human life—a contradiction which even the melioristic liberal mind, long dominant among us, now is beginning to make out. "This inner contradiction," as Arnold Toynbee writes in *An Historian's Approach to Religion* (1956), "means that ordinary life is a tension for which another name is Suffering." We are not constituted for perfect happiness; we are meant to struggle; we are Suffering Servants. The world always is full of genuine reasons for serious anxiety among thinking men. Our hope, and the mission of the man of letters, the statist, and the ethical philosopher, is not to sweep away that anxiety—for such an aspiration would be Gnostic illusion—but to keep anxiety from usurping the whole of life. Only when man perceives the norms that regulate inner and outer order is he armed to contend against anxiety as an obsession.

So the moral and cultural conservative, the guardian of normality, declines to embrace dime-store pragmatism: in rejecting ideology, he does not deny the reality of much anxiety about the state of the person and the state of the republic. He neither denounces convention and conformity indiscriminately, nor defends every popular fashion of the evanescent hour. What he respects is a sound conformity to abiding principles and a healthy convention which keeps the knife from our throats. Conformity to enduring moral truths is not servile. Obedience to the conventions of the just civil social order is not stupid.

In our time, when the fountains of the great deep are broken up, conformity and convention of the higher sort deserve the support of every man who values civilization. Coleridge says that there are two great elements in any society, its Permanence and its Progression. The Permanence of a state, roughly speaking, is its conservative interest; its Progression, what nowadays we call its liberal interest. There are ages in which intelligent people would do well to ally themselves with the Progression of their nation, to contend against stagnation; for a society without the means of renewal is not long for this world.

But our time is not such an age. We do not live in an ancient Egyptian or Peruvian culture, where the dead hand of the past seems to lie mercilessly upon a whole people, and where the only change is corruption. Our modern peril, rather, is that of vertiginous speed: the traditions of civility may be swallowed up by will and appetite; with us, the expectation of change is greater than the expectation of continuity, and generation scarcely links with generation. In the twentieth century, it is our Permanence, not our Progression, which needs the adherence of thinking men and women.

The twentieth-century ideologue—who, as Hawthorne said of the Abolitionist, brandishes his one idea like an iron flail—detests the champions of norms and conventions. To the Gnostic visionary, to the secularist worshipper of Progress and Uniformity, respect for norms and conventions is the mark of the beast. He hopes to sweep away every obstacle to the attainment of his standardized, regulated, mechanized, unified world, purged of faith, variety, and ancient longings. Permanence he cannot abide. He hungers after a state like a tapioca pudding, composed of so many identical globules of other-directed men.

Yet the troubles of our time have worried this zealot for heaven upon earth; he experiences secret misgivings nowadays; and the more he suffers from inner doubts of the perfectibility of man and society, the harder does he flail against the defenders of norm and convention, endeavoring in the heat of his assault to forget the disquieting voice—in Santayana's phrase—of a forlorn and dispossessed orthodoxy that prophesies disaster for men who would be as gods.

Lacking an apprehension of norms, there is no living in society or out of it. Lacking sound conventions, the civil social order dissolves. And lacking variety of life and diversity of institutions, normality succumbs to the tyranny of standardization without standards.

The Shoulders of Giants

"We are dwarfs mounted upon the shoulders of giants," Fulbert of Chartres told his scholars in the eleventh century. The great Schoolman meant that we modern folk—and the people of the eleventh century thought themselves quite as modern as we do—incline toward the opinion that wisdom was born with our generation. In a number of respects, whether in the twelfth century or the twentieth, the living generation knows more than did its grandparents' or great-grandparents' generation. The folk of Fulbert's generation knew more about the principles of architecture, for instance, than the folk of the tenth century had known. We people of the twentieth century, in our turn, know more about physics or chemistry, for example, than did the finest scholars at Chartres.

But for all that, Fulbert argued, we are no better than dwarfs mounted upon the shoulders of giants. We see so far only because of the tremendous stature of those giants, our ancestors, upon whose shoulders we stand. Gothic architecture in the eleventh century could not have existed without its foundations in the ninth and tenth centuries—or, for that matter, in the architecture of ancient Syria. Atomic physics in our sense could not have come into being without the speculative spirit of the seventeenth century—or, for that matter, without the intuitions of the pre-Socratic Greeks. Our civilization is an immense continuity and essence. Fulbert, Bishop of Chartres, was right: if we ignore or disdain those ancestral giants who uphold us in our modern vainglory, we tumble down into the ditch of unreason.

So if it is true that even our scientific knowledge, in considerable part, is a legacy from our forbears, it is still more certain that our moral, our social, and our artistic knowledge is an inheritance from men long dead. G. K. Chesterton coined the phrase "the democracy of the dead." In deciding any important moral or political question, Chesterton writes, we have the obligation to consult the considered opinions of the wise men who have preceded us in time. We owe these dead an immense debt, and their ballots deserve to be counted. Thus we have no right simply to decide any question by what the momentary advantage may be to us privately: we have the duty of respecting the wisdom of our ancestors; and also we have the duty of respecting the rights of posterity, the generations that are to come after us. This complex of duties is what the old Romans called piety: reverence for our nation, our family in the larger sense, our ancestors, in a spirit of religious veneration. A French philosopher of our time, Gabriel Marcel, writes that the only healthy society is the society which respects tradition. We ought to live, Marcel says, in an atmosphere of "diffused gratitude"—of sympathy for the hopes and achievements of our ancestors, from whom we derive our life and our culture, and which we are morally obliged to pass on undiminished, if not enhanced, to our descendants. We are grateful to the giants upon whose shoulders we stand. This feeling or atmosphere of diffused veneration is weakened in our modern age, for many people live only for themselves, ignoring the debt they owe to the past and the responsibility they owe to the future. They are ungrateful; and ingratitude brings on its own punishment.

Normative knowledge, then, is no burden, but instead a rich patrimony. Those who refuse it must be taught by personal experience—a hard master, as Benjamin Franklin says, though fools will have no other. Edmund Burke gave this concept of willing obligation to the dead, the living, and those yet unborn its most moving expression. We all are subject, he wrote, to "the contract of eternal society." This immortal contract is made between God and mankind, and between the generations that have perished from the earth, and the generation that is living now, and the generations that are yet to come. It is a covenant binding upon us all. No man has a right to abridge that contract at will; and if we do break it, we suffer personally and all society suffers; and we are cast out of this civil social order (built by the giants) into an "antagonist world" of total disorder—or, as the New Testament has it, into the outer darkness, where there shall be wailing and gnashing of teeth.

We moderns, Burke continued, tend to be puffed up with a little petty private rationality, thinking ourselves wiser than the prophets and the law-givers, and are disposed to trade upon the trifling bank and capital of our private intelligence. That way lies ruin. But though the individual is foolish, the species is wise; and, given time, the species judges rightly. The moral precepts and the social conventions which we obey represent the considered judgments and filtered experience of many generations of prudent and dutiful human beings—the most sagacious of our species. It is folly to ignore this inherited wisdom in favor of our own arrogant little notions of right and wrong, of profit and loss, of justice and injustice. Burke, though the most prophetic man of his age, never thought himself taller than the giants from whom came his strength.

This is no less true in the twentieth century, and in America. Our normative inheritance in the United States is of European and Asiatic origin: normality does not recognize frontiers.

In *The Revolt of the Masses* (1930), Ortega declared that American civilization could not long endure, were it severed from European culture. Ortega was right: American culture, and the American civil social order, share with modern European civilization a common patrimony. The principal elements in that inheritance are Christian faith (with its Judaic roots); the Roman and medieval heritage of ordered liberty; and the continuity of great "Western" literature. It is a legacy of belief, not of blood.

So far as race and nationality are concerned, the continuity between Europe and America is confused and imperfect. Take, for instance, my own little village of Mecosta, in the pine barrens of central Michigan, where my great-grandfather and his uncle settled nearly a century ago. The original population of the region was composed of Pottawattomies and Chippewas. Among the first civilized folk to establish themselves here were Negroes (escaped or emancipated slaves, most of whom had fled the Southern states across the Ohio and north to Canada, and then had entered Michigan from Canada, after the Emancipation Proclamation). The descendants of those colored people are in Mecosta and round about still, mixed in blood with white and Indian, but forming a distinct community, centered about their own church.

To this same region of Mecosta, in the days of Michigan lumbering, came New Englanders and New Yorkers of old Puritan stock, among them my great-grandfather. There had arrived a little earlier numbers of German peasants, whose church of St. Michael remains their bond of union. These Catholics were joined, presently, by Irish settlers. In recent years, Mecosta has gained some additional population, chiefly Polish and Ukrainian, filtering from the industrial cities into the countryside. All in all, my little Mecosta is a microcosm of America, curiously diverse in ancestry and cultural origins. What link is there between a village and a nation like this, and the ancient communities of Europe?

Why, what joins the cultures on either side of the Atlantic is a complex of religious and moral and social convictions, given expression in literature, that Europe and America have received from common spiritual and intellectual ancestors. If this inheritance should be much diminished, all the elaborate fabric of our material civilization could not long survive, either side of the ocean, the collapse of this subtle inner order and this intricate institutional order.

The first article in this common patrimony, I have said, is the Christian faith, including its origins in Judah and Israel. All the important aspects of any civilization arise from its religion—even the economic system of that civilization. As Irving Babbitt wrote a generation ago, economics moves upward into politics, politics into ethics, ethics into theology. This is no less true in the United States of America than it was in ancient Egypt or than it is in modern India. And the United States is a Christian nation, notwithstanding the opinion expressed by Thomas Jefferson in his message to the Bey of Tunis. The great majority of Americans voluntarily subscribe to the faith we call Christianity. In the things which most nearly concern the private life and the public good, they draw their moral and intellectual sustenance from the Old World. (It may be true, as some critics argue, that much of the high rate of church-attendance in this country reflects not so much religious conviction as mere religiosity; but that always has been true of church-attendance everywhere.) The prophets of Israel, the words of Christ and His disciples, the writings of the fathers of the Church, the treatises of the Schoolmen, the discourses of the great divines of Reformation and Counter-Reformation—these are the springs of American metaphysics and American morality, as they are of European metaphysics and morality. They underlie the beliefs even of those Americans and Europeans who deny the validity of Christianity. And with Christian doctrine there are blended certain elaborate elements of classical philosophy.

In its immediate influence upon culture, perhaps the most important aspect of Christianity is its account of the human personality: its doctrine of the immortal soul, the unique character of every soul, the concept of human dignity, the nature of rights and duties, the obligation to practice charity, the insistence upon personal responsibility. European and American civilization has been erected upon the foundation of the dignity of man—upon the assumption that man is made for eternity, and that he possesses dignity because he has some share in an order that is more than temporal and more than human.

Christianity always has been an immense moving force among Americans. The student who endeavors to ignore the power of Christianity in European and American culture is as foolish as would be any physician who should endeavor to ignore a patient's personality. Christianity is the core of our civilization—its vitality, indeed. Even the virulent totalist ideologies of our century are influenced by Christianity, inspired by a misunderstanding of Christian doctrines, or by a reaction against Christian principles; hate it though they may, the ideologues cannot break altogether with the Christian religion.

The second article in our common patrimony is our theory and practice of ordered liberty: our system of law and politics. This is derived from Roman and from medieval sources—and in part, more remotely, from Greek philosophy and historic experience. To the classical and medieval ideas of justice, and to the classical and medieval social experience, there has been added a modern body of theory and practice—although too often we modern folk, including the scholars among us, exaggerate the importance of "liberal" contributions in the eighteenth and nineteenth centuries, some of which latter contributions have not stoutly withstood the severe tests of our twentieth-century time of troubles.

The doctrines of natural law; the concept of a polity, a just and balanced commonwealth; the principle of a government of laws, not of men; the understanding that justice means "to each his own"; the idea of a healthful tension between the claims of order and the claims of freedom—these passed directly from Europe into American theory and institution. More than any other single figure, Cicero influenced the theory of both European and American politics—and through that theory, our political institutions.

To this general heritage, the English added their common law and their prudent, prescriptive politics; and the English patrimony was directly incorporated in the American social order. The founders of the American Republic, especially the lawyers and politicians among them, took for granted this English pattern of politics, modifying it only slightly to conform to colonial usage and to suit the new nation—and even then modifying it not in favor of some newfangled abstract scheme, but rather on the model of the Roman Republic.

The principle of elaborate restraints upon political power, for instance, is conspicuous in the political theory and practice of Britain and in that of the United States. It has been so since the beginning of American society. John Cotton declared in Massachusetts in the third decade of the seventeenth century:

> Let all the world learn to give mortal men no greater power than they are content they shall use—for use it they will. . . . This is one of the strains of nature: it affects boundless liberty, and to run to the utmost extent. Whatever power he hath received, he hath a corrupt nature that will improve it in one thing or other; if he have liberty, he will think why may he not use it. . . . There is a strain in a man's heart that sometime or other runs out to excess, unless the Lord restrain it; but it is not good to venture it.

Yet the third article in this common patrimony is more enduring, perhaps, than even political usage. Great works of literature join us in an intellectual community. And the ethical cast of enduring humane letters, working upon the imagination, is as normative as is religious doctrine or political principle. Humane literature teaches us what it is to be a man. Homer and Hesiod; Herodotus and Thucydides; Sophocles and Plato; Vergil and Horace; Livy and Tacitus; Cicero and Seneca; Epictetus and Marcus Aurelius; Dante, Petrarch, Erasmus, Shakespeare, Cervantes, Goethe, and all the rest—these have formed the mind and character of Americans as well as of Europeans. The best of American literature is part and parcel of the normative continuity of literature, extending back beyond the dawn of history.

In all essential respects, then, Europe and America enjoy a common faith, a common system of law and politics, and a common body of great literature. They make one civilization still. These normative and cultural bonds have outlasted dynasties, empire, and even philosophies; though injured now and again by war or social dissolution, they rise with renewed vigor or after every period of violence or decadence. Whether this heritage is to survive the twentieth century must depend, in no small part, upon the reinvigoration of a popular normative consciousness. . . .

The soul of a civilization may be lost at the very moment of that culture's material triumph. In our time, we run no risk of experiencing too little change; whether we like it or not, we ride the whirlwind of innovation. To give direction to this change, and to insure that generation may link with generation, some of us must undertake the rescue of the moral imagination.

The undisciplined modern mind, thinking it pursues facts, often follows a corpse-candle to the brink of the abyss—and, sometimes, over that brink. "The Devil played at chess with me," wrote Sir Thomas Browne, "and yielding a Pawn, thought to gain a Queen of me, taking advantage of my honest endeavours; and whilst I laboured to raise the structure of my Reason, he strived to undermine the edifice of my Faith." If a man relies wholly upon his private rational powers, he will lose his faith—and perhaps the world as well, risking his nature at the Devil's chess-game. But if a man fortifies himself with the normative disciplines, he draws upon the imagination and the lessons of the ages, and so is fit to confront even a diabolical adversary.

The Doors of Normative Perception

"How were the giants so wise?" Sincerely or mordantly, this question will be asked. To phrase it another way, what are the sources of the enduring norms? Why should we take them on authority?

The answer . . . is not simple. . . . But for the moment, we may indicate three doors of normative perception: revelation, custom or common sense, and the insights of the seer.

For the man of religious convictions—Christian, or Jew, or Moslem—the primary source of knowledge about faith and morals is divine revelation. Yet this will not suffice for the unbeliever or the skeptic; neither will revelation tell us much about political prudence, nor about the standards of art. I am one who embraces the transcendent truth of revelation. . . . I argue chiefly on the foundation of the other two means of normative perception—both because the discussion of revelation's validity would be too intricate and lengthy for these pages, and because I address myself to doubters, as well as to the converted.

Direct revelation, moreover, has been extremely rare: on most occasions, divine wisdom was expressed through the mouths of very human prophets—who may be categorized, if you wish, under the later classification of "seer." The most important of all direct revelations was simply the sentence that Moses heard from the burning bush: "I am the God of thy father, the God of Abraham, the God of Isaac, and the God of Jacob." (The first phrase, I am told, is more accurately rendered, "I am that am.") And those words were heard not by the Israelite people collectively, but by Moses in solitude; revelation requires its agents, and the man who has penetrated beyond the veil of sense may be able to say only, with Pascal, "Fire, fire, fire!"—the rest being inexpressible in language, and almost unthinkable in thought.

To maintain that all normative truth may be found in the Bible, or in any other sacred book, is to fall into the error of what Coleridge called "bibliolatry." Though the Decalogue is the word of God, it is not the sole source of the commandments for mankind. The universality of such moral laws is summed up succinctly by C. S. Lewis, in his *Abolition of Man* (1947); Lewis calls these universal commandments, perceived and expressed variously in every culture, "the Tao." "Honor thy father and thy mother, that thy days may be long in the land," for example, is an injunction of which every people have been made aware. Although in our Father's house are many mansions, they are not all on the same floor, true enough; yet Jewish and Christian dogmas, if the clearest and highest expression of moral normality, nevertheless do not enjoy an exclusive claim to such revelation.

"Orthodoxy is my doxy; heterodoxy is another man's doxy." I subscribe to Samuel Johnson's profession. When the art of worldly wisdom is in question, for all that, the modern opponent of abnormality, if he means to persuade the heterodox, repairs to the arguments of Johnson's "Tory by accident," David Hume. In morals and taste, says Hume, we govern ourselves by custom—that is, by the habits of the human race. The standards of morality are shown to us by study of the story of mankind, and the arbiters of those standards are men of strong sense and delicate sentiment, whose impressions force themselves upon the wills of their fellow-men.

This is another way of saying what I suggested a few paragraphs ago: that for the most part our norms are derived from the experience of the species, the ancient usages of humanity; and from the perceptions of genius, of those rare men who have seen profoundly into the human condition—and whose wisdom soon is accepted by the mass of men, down the generations. I turn first to custom, or what we call common sense.

The good citizen, Vergil remarks, is a law-abiding traditionalist: that is, a man governing himself by custom, deferring to the habits formed among a people through their painful process of trial and error, their encounters with gods and men over a great many years. Custom is the expression of a people's collective experience, some of it accumulated before that people had a history. "Custom, then, is the great guide of human life," says Hume. "It is that principle alone which renders our experience useful to us, and makes us expect, for the future, a similar train of events with those which have appeared in the past. Without the influence of custom, we should be entirely ignorant of every matter of fact beyond what is immediately present to the memory and senses."

Custom is closely allied with common sense, "those convictions which we receive from nature, which all men possess in common, and by which they test the truth of knowledge and the morality of actions; the practical sense of the greater part of mankind, especially as unaffected by logical subtleties or imagination," as the old *Century Dictionary* (1889–1914) puts it. Common sense is "consensus," or general agreement on first principles—a word somewhat tarnished by politicians in recent years. In the vast majority of our normative decisions, we defer to the consensus of mankind—that is, we feel ourselves bound to think and behave as decent men always have thought and behaved. Conformity to custom—call it prejudice, if you will—makes a man's virtue his habit, as Burke expressed this idea. Without the power of custom to control and instruct us, we should be involved perpetually in "agonizing reappraisals," endeavoring to decide every question upon its particular merits and advantages of the moment; we would be unnerved incessantly by doubt and vacillation.

Common sense and custom, then, are the practical expressions of what mankind has learnt in the school of hard knocks. There exists a legitimate presumption in favor of venerable usages; for your or my private experience is brief and confused, but the experience of the race takes into account the consequences suffered or the rewards obtained by multitudes of human beings in circumstances similar to yours and mine. Custom and common sense constitute an immemorial empiricism, with roots so antique and obscure that we can only conjecture the origins of any general habit. One thing we do know: it is dangerous to break with ways that have been intertwined so intricately in human longings and satisfactions. Those who toss the cake of custom into the rubbish-bin may find themselves supperless. And if common sense is discarded—why, it is supplanted not by a universal intellectualism, but by common nonsense.

Yet how did folk-wisdom come into being? It cannot be that a crowd of dullards, merely by the accumulation of numbers and the passage of time, somehow produce a collective sagacity. Penetrating insights guided the Greeks before Homer. "The old Greeks knew everything," a talented friend said to me once. "But how did they know it?"

The answer may be that at the beginnings of anything resembling a true civil social order, individual men possessed of genius—obscure men whose very names have perished—were the discoverers of the truths which we now call custom and common sense. Hume's men of strong sense and delicate sentiment, or their primitive forerunners, presumably existed when man was becoming true man; and their insights were impressed upon their primitive fellows. It is believed that those old-fangled and picturesque garments we now call "folk costumes" once were the dress of a local aristocracy; the peasants adopted these fashions, but have retained them long after the aristocracy has gone on to newer modes—or perhaps has gone on to extinction. So it may be with the practices and beliefs which we call custom and common sense: originally these may have been the intuitions or the empirical conclusions of gifted individuals, who were emulated by the common man; but as the elapse of centuries has hidden the original authorship of folkways and popular convictions, so mankind has come to assume that the multitude itself always apprehended these truths, much as the ant-hill and the hive seem to be governed by a collective consciousness without the direction of commanding intellects.

Such reflections—perhaps impossible to demonstrate or to disprove—lead us to the third principal door to normative understanding: the astounding perceptions of the seer—"the blind man who sees," like Homer. A few men mysteriously endowed with a power of vision denied to the overwhelming majority of us have been the Hammurabis of our moral and political and literary codes. We know their names, although sometimes we know little but their names and some appended scanty legends. (As Mark Twain put it, the *Iliad* and the *Odyssey* were written either by Homer or by another man with the same name.) We accept such men of genius as authorities because we recognize, however imperfectly, that they see farther than you or I see.

A typical undergraduate may inquire at this point, "Who made these seers normative authorities?" Why, no one appointed them: their strength of mind and eloquence of expression conquered the mass of men. Their authority in part is vindicated by the immense influence which their words have exerted ever since those words were uttered; and in part by the fact that intelligent men in every age, upon reflection, have assented to the truths exerted by these prophets and poets and philosophers. You and I see as in a glass, darkly—the riddle of a mirror; but those few men of vision saw something of the real nature of things. It is as if they had the eyes of eagles, and we the eyes of moles. (A mole, it is true, knows the eagle only by his talons, when unhappily that mole has ventured above ground.) Presumably the mole cannot even dream of that power of vision which the eagle takes as his birthright.

Moses and Solon were such seers for the Jews and for the Athenians. Through the moral perception of these law-givers, these half-symbolic figures who burst the bounds of pragmatic reasoning, their peoples experienced what Eric Voegelin calls "a leap in being," a new and stronger apprehension of truth. What before had been mere cloudy surmises became norms: the law for man.

Such seers were the unknown author of the Book of Job, and the prophet called Isaiah; such were Heraclitus and Democritus, and such Sophocles and Plato. Such, in the Orient, were Confucius and Lao-tse, and Gautama. Such was Vergil for the Romans—and, in some sense, Livy. In the Christian continuity, such seers were St. Paul, St. Augustine, St. Thomas Aquinas, Dante, and Pascal. Yet other seers will appear in our midst, no doubt, unless we make it impossible for them to exist, or unless we close our eyes and ears to the very possibility of the transcendent.

These are the giants, upon whose shoulders we stand. No one knows better than a great scientist the extent of our debt to men of vision who have preceded us in time. "If I have seen farther, it is by standing on the shoulders of giants," said Sir Isaac Newton, echoing Fulbert of Chartres. To overthrow a giant, it is necessary either to be a giant one's self, or else a David favored of the Lord; and few of us are either. Therefore we yield to the seers—the prophets and poets and philosophers of the Great Tradition—as authorities, because without their guidance we would wander hungry in a dark wood. The life of pygmies in the modern world would be poor, nasty, brutish, and short.

We are governed by the normative insights of the giants because we are incapable of inventing better rules for ourselves. A college sophomore once informed me that he was ready to work out a complete moral system without reference to the opinions of our ancestors. I inquired whether he thought himself capable of constructing, unaided, an automobile. He confessed that he did not so think. I then suggested that a contraption merely mechanical, like an automobile, is simple when compared with an instrument for controlling the passions of men. Indeed, this student's system of morality would be patched together, at best, from fragments of Christian doctrine and classical philosophy: he might regard our moral order as a junkyard, yet only there would he find his parts.

Karl Marx had some of the qualities of a seer, and he postulated a new normative order. His moral system, nevertheless, was a caricature of Christian doctrine, combined with ideas from Bentham and Hegel (both of whom

Marx reviled); and, once tested, Marxism turned out to be hideous, and quite contrary to its inventor's expectations. Many false prophets have gone forth into the world; but by their works may they be known.

By definition, human nature is constant. Because of that constancy, men of vision are able to describe the norms, the rules, for mankind. From revelation, from custom and common sense, and from the intuitive powers of men possessed by genius, we know that there exist law for man and law for thing. Normality is the goal of human striving; abnormity is the descent toward a condition less than human, surrender to vice. . . .

["Normative Art and Modern Vices," Enemies of the Permanent Things: Observations of Abnormity in Literature and Art, *Rev. ed. (La Salle, IL: Sherwood Sugden & Company, 1984), 15–39.]*

❖

A Cautionary Note on the Ghostly Tale

"A Cautionary Note on the Ghostly Tale" is the preface to Watchers at the Strait Gate *(1984), one of Kirk's several books of ghost stories, which he calls "experiments in the moral imagination." In them he seeks to bring about a spiritual awakening in the face of a profane secularism. A ghost story, he says, can induce awareness of the character of evil, offer glimpses of transcendent reality, and overcome "the heavy hand of 'scientific' materialism and mechanism, which regime in effect denie[s] the existence of souls." By combining elements of parable and fable, a writer of the fantastic expands our understanding of human nature and helps us perceive supernal truths. Kirk's personal and critical testimony introduces us to a spinner of uncanny tales as he broods over his craft. His testimony also helps us to appreciate the infinite mystery of the ways of the creative process.*

Elaborated from certain encounters of mine with life and death, these stories were not written for children. Some of my perceptions, impressions, or experiences occurred three or four decades ago—which dusty fact accounts for the very modest prices and wages incidentally mentioned in a number of my yarns. Worse, a few of my stage-settings and backgrounds—

from Los Angeles to Stari Bar, from Pittenweem to Marrakesh—have been knocked about, since I wrote, by urban renewers and other misguided evangels of progress.

Such nostalgic archaism (though unintended when I wrote these stories) has its literary advantages. As M. R. James remarked while praising Sheridan Le Fanu, "The ghost story is in itself a slightly old-fashioned form; it needs some deliberateness in the telling; we listen to it the more readily if the narrator poses as elderly, or throws back his experience to 'some thirty years ago.'"

Alarming though (I hope) readers may find these tales, I did not write them to impose meaningless terror upon the innocent. The political ferocity of our age is sufficiently dismaying: men of letters need not conjure up horrors worse than those suffered during the past decade by Cambodians and Ugandans, Afghans and Ethiopians.

What I have attempted, rather, are experiments in the moral imagination. Readers will encounter elements of parable and fable. Gerald Heard said to me once that the good ghost story must have for its kernel some clear premise about the character of human existence—some theological premise, if you will. Literary naturalism is not the only path to apprehension of reality. All important literature has some ethical end; and the tale of the preternatural—as written by George Macdonald, C. S. Lewis, Charles Williams, and other masters—can be an instrument for the recovery of moral order.

The better uncanny stories are underlain by a healthy concept of the character of evil. Defying nature, the necromancer conjures up what ought not to rise again this side of Judgment Day. But these dark powers do not rule the universe: by bell, book, and candle, symbolically at least, we can push them down under.

Because the limbo of the occult has no defined boundaries, remaining *terra incognita* interiorly, the imaginative writer's fancy can wander there unburdened by the impedimenta of twentieth century naturalism. For symbol and allegory, the shadow-world is a better realm than the mechanized empire of science-fiction. The story of the supernatural or the mystical can disclose aspects of human conduct and human longing to which the positivistic psychologist has blinded himself. The more talented fabulists of the occult and the crepuscular—among these, Mircea Eliade and Robert Aickman, in their different fashions—piece together into a pattern those hints and glimpses offered fragmentarily by mystical vision, second sight, hauntings, dreams, wondrous coincidences.

As a literary form, then, the uncanny tale can be a means for expressing truths enchantingly. But I do not ask the artist of the fantastic to turn didactic moralist; and I trust that he will not fall into the error that the shapes and voices half-glimpsed and half-heard are symbols *merely*. For the sake of his art, the teller of ghostly narrations ought never to enjoy freedom from fear. As Samuel Johnson lived in dread of real torment beyond the grave—not mere "mental anguish"—so the "invisible prince," Le Fanu, archetype of the literary men of this genre, is believed to have died literally of fright. He knew that his creations were not his inventions merely, but glimpses of the abyss.

In an era of the decay of religious belief, can fiction of the supernatural or preternatural, with its roots in myth and transcendent perception, succeed in being anything better than playful or absurd? The lingering domination of yesteryear's materialistic and mechanistic theories in natural science persuades most people that if they have encountered inexplicable phenomena—why, they must have been mistaken. How is it possible to perceive a *revenant* if there cannot possibly be *revenants* to perceive?

Take George Orwell. In 1931 he wrote to a friend "about a ghost I saw in Walberswick cemetery." He described his encounter in considerable detail, including a plan of church and graveyard. But he concluded, "Presumably an hallucination." Ghosts did not square with Orwell's rather belligerent denial of the possibility of the life eternal. Yet he would have liked to believe. And what is an hallucination? On reading Orwell's letter, I was reminded of an acquaintance of mine who accounted for several astounding simultaneous occurrences in a house as "entropy." What is entropy? I inquired. "Oh, things like that." A scientific term sufficed him.

Most people nowadays continue to share Orwell's uneasy rejection of "psychic" phenomena. An English *aficionada* of the ghostly tale instructs us at considerable length that the ghost story has died: Sigmund Freud slew the poor thing. Wisdom began and ended with Freud.

But did it? C. G. Jung's theories about psychic phenomena differed radically from Freud's. Startling personal experience converted Jung from his previous belief that such phenomena were subjective "unconscious projections" to his later conviction that "an exclusively psychological approach" cannot suffice for study of psychic phenomena of the ghostly variety. And no wonder! For while Jung was staying in an English country house, there abruptly appeared on his pillow "the head of an old woman whose right eye, wide open, was staring at me. The left half of her face, including the eye, was missing. I leapt out of bed and lit a candle"—at which point the head vanished.

Although a vulgarized Freudianism remains popular today, as an intellectual force Freudianism is nearly spent. The philosophical and ideological currents of a period necessarily affecting its imaginative literature, the supernatural in fiction has seemed ridiculous to most, nearly all this century. Yet as the rising generation regains the awareness that "nature" is something more than mere fleshly sensation, and that something may lie above human nature, and something below it—why, the divine and the diabolical rise up again in serious literature. In this renewal of imagination, fiction of the preternatural and the occult may have a part. *Tenebrae* are woven into human nature, despite all that meliorists declare.

"We have heard a whole chorus of Nobel Laureates in physics informing us that matter is dead, causality is dead, determinism is dead," Arthur Koestler wrote in 1972. "If that is so, let us give them a decent burial, with a requiem of electronic music. It is time for us to draw the lessons from twentieth-century post-mechanistic science, and to get out of the straitjacket which nineteenth-century materialism imposed on our philosophical outlook."

Amen to that. Our literary assumptions and modes, like our philosophical outlook, were oppressed by the heavy hand of "scientific" materialism and mechanism, which regime in effect denied the existence of souls. It becomes possible to admit once more the reality of a realm of spirit. It does not follow necessarily that we will acquire a great deal more knowledge about shadowland. "The limitations of our biological equipment may condemn us to the role of Peeping Toms at the keyhole of eternity," Koestler concludes his slim book *The Roots of Coincidence* (1972). "But at least let us take the stuffing out of the keyhole, which blocks even our limited view."

A reason why I write stories like those in this present collection—aside from the fun of the process, which scandalizes—is that I aspire to help extract the stuffing from the keyhole. The tales in this volume have retributive ghosts, malign magicians, blind angels, beneficent phantoms, conjuring witches, demonic possession, creatures of the twilight, divided selves. I present them to you unabashed. They may impart some arcane truths about good and evil: as Chesterton put it, all life is an allegory, and we can understand it only in parable.

But let me say also that my bogles are not to be taken lightly. I could offer you True Relations—my own experiences, or those of friends—quite as startling as my fictional narratives, though more fragmentary and inconclusive. I do tell such "true ghost stories" aloud to audiences; but the True Relation, a sudden puzzling phenomenon, does not make by itself a polished piece of humane letters; it must be embroidered and enlarged by literary art, to be worth printing.

No one ever has satisfactorily supported by evidence a general theory accounting for ghostly apparitions and similar phenomena. Yet a mass of testimony from all countries and all ages exists to inform us that strange happenings beyond the ordinary course of life and matter have occurred at irregular intervals and in widely varied circumstances.

Possibly we never will understand the character of such phenomena better than we do already. Suppose, suggests C. E. M. Joad, that we appoint a sober committee of three to sit in the haunted room at midnight and take notes on the appearance of the reputed ghost. But suppose also that one of the conditions essential for the occurrence of this particular phenomenon is that there not be present a sober committee of three: well, then, the very scientific method has precluded the possibility of reaching a scientific determination. Our human faculties may not suffice to extract the stuffing from the keyhole. If so, our mere inadequacy does not prove that nothing lies beyond the keyhole. From behind that locked door still may come thumps and moans, which some of us hear better than others do. It is well to be skeptical in such concerns—skeptical of the "light at the end of the tunnel" enthusiasts, but equally skeptical of the old-fogy doctrinaire mechanists.

Enough: I do not intend to let this preface to grimly amusing tales become a didactic treatise on a shrouded huge subject. I am merely a humble follower in the steps of Defoe, Scott, Coleridge, Stevenson, Kipling, the Sitwells; of Hawthorne, Poe, Henry James, Edith Wharton—and many other writers of high talent who did not blush to fancy that something may lurk on the other side of the keyhole. If I bring discredit upon their genre, I will deserve to be hounded to my doom by James Thurber's monster the Todal (who, in *The Thirteen Clocks* [1950], smells like long-unopened rooms, and gleeps), "an agent of the Devil, sent to punish evil doers for having done less evil than they should."

Nearly all these tales were published in periodicals or anthologies, over the years: *Fantasy and Science Fiction, London Mystery Magazine, The Critic, World Review, Frights, Dark Forces, Whispers, New Terrors*. They were written in haunted St. Andrews, in the Isle of Eigg, at Kellie Castle, at Balcarres House, at Durie House (which has the most persistent of all country-house spectres), and at my ancestral spooky house at Mecosta, Michigan—this last house totally destroyed by fire on Ash Wednesday, 1975; also nocturnally in my silent library (once a factory) at Mecosta.

These lines are written at the hour of three, the witching hour, when most men's energies are at ebb, "in the silent croaking night," a cricket for company. "The small creatures chirp thinly through the dust, through the night." Pray for us scribbling sinners now and at the hour of our death.

["A Cautionary Note on the Ghostly Tale," Watchers at the Strait Gate*:* Mystical Tales *(Sauk City, WI: Arkham House, 1984), ix–xiv.]*

❖

Who Knows George Gissing?

While yet in his twenties Kirk came across in an Atlanta bookshop George Gissing's The Unclassed *(1884). From that time on he championed the English novelist who lived in the years 1857–1903. Gissing's* New Grub Street *(1891), a "protest against the modern temper," was one of Kirk's favorite novels. His enthusiasm is contagious, as he cites Gissing's prolixity and unevenness, but at the same time insists on his genius. Gissing's was, Kirk admits, an unadulterated realism, "but the realism of a man with taste and discrimination" who put "living beings into our imagination" through "the power of the word and the appeal to universal experience." In pleading for a just critical valuation of Gissing, Kirk was to follow in the steps of two great twentieth-century English moralists: Q. D. Leavis, who considered* New Grub Street *"an ancestor of the novel of our time"; and George Orwell, who contended that Gissing spoke "for the exceptional man, the sensitive man, isolated among barbarians."*

About Wakefield, in West Riding, lies what we might call the Gissing country. Ride the circuit of this interminable chain of mill towns—Leeds, Bradford, Halifax, Dewsbury, Wakefield—with their halo of smutty mist, their dismal walls of soiled stone or half-brick, their desolation of slack-jawed streets, and one may reflect that they seem ingeniously designed for the torment of any man who cares for beauty and tradition. Wakefield, which of them all appears most nearly heartless, has a fine parish church (now a cathedral) built six hundred years before George Gissing came into the world; and it has a decent public library, established some years after he died; otherwise, it is one of Cobbett's hell-holes. On a principal street, opposite "Betty's Snack Bar," *à la* U. S. A., is rather an old brick house of three stories, one of the few buildings in the city that can claim even Georgian venerability. The ground floor is a chemist's shop, a unit in the great chain of Boots, Ltd. In 1857, there was a chemist's shop in the same place—the establishment of a scholarly pharmacist named Gissing. In that year, a brass plate at the door records, was born in the room above the shop George Gissing, "novelist and man of letters." The automobiles honk past the house in the ugly road.

I

Fifty years ago, early in 1900, George Gissing was beginning to die at the age of forty-three; he had left England for the Continent, to spend in France nearly the whole of what remained to him of life. With him was his Gabrielle, whom he could not make his wife, for the fate that spoiled all his loves followed him to the end. When hardly more than a boy, he had half relished the idea of a life like one of Murger's Bohemians; very nearly such a life, or its English counterpart, had been his; and it had been a long curse of poverty and solitude. Few people ever had read his books; now, he feared, these few were commencing to forget him; and it was to supply the means of existence in the shadow of the Pyrenees that he finished the book which was to bring him, dead, the reputation he had coveted in his London garrets and cellars: *The Private Papers of Henry Ryecroft* (1903). Of this, the novelist wrote that it was "the thing most likely to last when all my other futile work has followed my futile life." The twentieth century was arrived—1900, of which he had said to his brother two decades before: "That year ought to be fertile in great things." Gissing had altered; and when the year was come indeed, he now told a friend, "The barbarization of the world goes merrily on. No doubt there will be continuous warfare for many a long year. It sickens me to read the newspapers; I turn as much as possible to the old poets." First he had wanted to be the reformer of society, and later to be the servant of art; and he ended as the connoisseur of misery.

Dead half a century, nearly! To the reader of *Ryecroft* or *The New Grub Street,* this is a curious thought, for in Gissing's pages lives the sense of an evening's conversation, an exchange of opinions with a contemporary, the voice of a conscience speaking to a conscience. Older authors there are from whose books comes the same illusion—Plutarch, for one; but they are not many. And, then, Gissing died young; comrades of his like H. G. Wells were with us only yesterday. Having read something of Gissing's, one feels that he would really have liked to know the man. Perhaps the glow of intellectual fellowship that seems to emanate from Gissing is a reflection of a chief pleasure of Gissing's own, good talk of people and books with men who understood. Certainly he got little pleasure from the sources of satisfaction which generally rank high—fine houses, good food, loving women—dearly though he coveted these, too. One glimpses a genuine manliness in Gissing, a manliness transcending the flaws of character he recognized in himself, a manliness of which many a literary figure of the past seventy years could have used a share.

Yet quite dead, and buried at St. Jean-de-Luz, and fitly so, this man with whom one would have liked to talk. There is about Gissing's career the fitness which is stamped upon the classical models he reverenced. It was fit that he should labor for a pittance, and fit that he should die abroad, brooding and exhausted, at a time when most men are only beginning to master life. It seems as fit in Gissing as it does in all his better stories, for he was a species of incarnation of protest against the modern temper. Remorselessly true, in his novels, to the candid observation of human nature, this Gissing: the naïve enthusiast is baffled, the rebel wearied or corrupted, the weakling broken. Just so was he uncompromisingly true to his own character. Having commenced as a Quixote, he clung stubbornly, even when the mists of youth had drifted away from his eyes, to an ideal of life and work that he would not abandon. Can we imagine a successful Gissing, writing to please Mr. Mudie's subscribers, holding the admiration of Amy Reardon, aping his own Jasper Milvain? Can we even imagine him tranquil as Ryecroft? He lived and died as it befitted a man of his ideals to endure and perish, and that without a drop of the heavy dose of *poseur* which infected so many writers of his generation—Moore, Wilde, Rimbaud. Thus the story of Gissing is better than any of his novels, all of which were patches ripped from the Nessus's shirt of his existence.

A moving story, Gissing's life, but a story not many know except for rags and tatters of scandal and sentimental commiseration. The public for which Gissing wrote, and the admirers of his talent since his death, always were few. Once, visiting a family of teachers in Bradford, close to the scenes of Gissing's boyhood, I mentioned that I was going to Wakefield to photograph Gissing's house. Who was Gissing? my hosts wanted to know; and, on being told, what sort of thing did he write? These were people of some schooling, of as much schooling as Gissing himself had; but I was not surprised. On the other hand, one afternoon in a prosperous bookshop in San Francisco I came upon old copies of two novels of Gissing's which, like most of his, are hard to find; and presenting these at the cashier's counter, I found myself envied by the clerk, who would have taken them for himself had he known they were in the shop. The scattered confraternity of those who really know Gissing is conspicuous not for size, but for sincerity and persistence of esteem. The man had something in him, thus to find his way obscurely into odd comers of society and stick there.

At intervals a flurry of renewed attention to Gissing's books and character breaks into print. One such commotion followed close upon his death; another, after the publication in 1912 of those two curious, condescending books *The Private Life of Henry Maitland* and *George Gissing, a Critical Study*; a third, at the time of the re-publication of both those volumes, 1923. In this year, even his best-known books, except for *Ryecroft*, are out of print in America and Britain; but presently they will return to booksellers' shelves, for a regular though subtle demand induces new editions.

What manner of man remembers Gissing? Frank Swinnerton, whose chief, but convincing, tribute to Gissing is imitation, would have us think that "ill-educated egoists," and such only, are Gissing's devotees. Now, it is quite true that many of the quarter-educated at whom Gissing himself so often scoffed are drawn to that literary naturalism which in part descends from Gissing; but these people—many of them young and only commencing a general acquaintance with literature—do not today seek out Gissing. Indeed, they have not heard of him at all; they sport about the feet of Wolfe and Farrell and Dreiser or some other idol, writers for them more attractive precisely because, whatever their merits, the Wolfes and Dreisers and Farrells of our time have themselves been ill-educated and egoistic. Gissing, on the contrary, was educated all too thoroughly, if such a thing be possible, supported throughout life by the classical discipline; and if egoism means self-conceit, he had hardly any of it. A realistic novelist who does not blame circumstance or environment or heredity for his failures hardly seems conceivable, here in the middle of the twentieth century. But Gissing did not. He blamed his own character.

I am inclined to think that most people who still read Gissing, far from being ill-educated egoists, are generous, contemplative, conservative, liberal (for the latter two terms need not exclude one another). Most of them had their attention first drawn to him by being told of *Henry Ryecroft*, and having passed beyond that noble little book into the somber depths of the novels, never managed to forget him. I may be in error concerning Gissing-readers, not having interviewed a truly random sample, to employ a phrase repugnant to the Gissing tradition; for although I have talked with some hundreds of people who read books, I have met with very few who know George Gissing.

One reason why so few make his acquaintance lies in the fitting circumstance that Gissing, unfortunate in his choice of occupations and women, seems often to have been no more fortunate in his choice of friends. The principal accounts of his private life come from two literary men who were close to Gissing while he lived, but who dealt with him chiefly in superior pity once he was dead: Morley Roberts and H. G. Wells. Compare Gissing's treatment of Wells in *Ryecroft* ("G. H. Rivers," you may remember) with Wells's treatment of Gissing in *Experiment in Autobiography* (1934), and you shiver at the thought of what can be done to you once you are fled from this vile world. Another reason is that Mrs. Grundy, whom Gissing more than once defied by name and defeated (in Pyrrhic style), exults over him now that he is dead, and fear of what that woman might say has induced people who loved him to lock up letters and choose their phrases. Gissing ought to be indemnified for both injuries.

II

Known to fewer than he ought to be, George Gissing; but known, still. What has saved him from the abyss into which slipped the welter of late-Victorian and Edwardian novelists? Not the mere distinction of having been the first man to write accurately of the nether world. His soul saved him; and his expression of modern pessimism; besides his modern version of the consolations of Epicurus; and certain rare merits as a literary artist. These properties have kept him afloat on the literary sea and may suffice to buoy him up even after certain reputations of his generation still prominent have gone under.

He has kept afloat; he has continued to interest critics of high talents; but somehow his admirers always write of him half apologetically, as if it were necessary to dampen their own praise. This trait begins with Gissing's obituary in the London *Times* in 1903: "The result was a series of books which, if they cannot justly be called great, were at least the work of a very able and conscientious artist, whose purity and solidity may win him a better chance of being read a hundred years hence than many writers of greater grace and more deliberately sought charm." Paul Elmer More, in 1918: "Gissing has his devotees, of whom, to a certain extent, I count myself one. But none of us, I think, would place him quite on a level with Thackeray and Trollope." Granville

Hicks, in 1939: "Gissing's achievement . . . though it was repeatedly marred by defects of an uncommon grossness, was substantial."

The confirmed Gissing-reader knows what these critics mean. Gissing, compelled to pay homage to the publishers' three-volume novel, often was prolix; sometimes he was oddly stiff in his beginning chapter; now and then, the strong effect he achieves near the middle of his story trickles away before *finis*. One feels these things sorrowfully. But then, perhaps, a reaction commences in the judgment of the Gissing-reader, who proceeds to ask himself just why he experienced this dissatisfaction. Could it have been because Gissing came so near to creating the illusion of reality that his failure to accomplish the whole of the sorcery told the more painfully? We do not expect from most important English novelists a complete reproduction of life—certainly not from Hardy or Meredith, Gissing's contemporaries. We do expect it from Gissing, because it is the goal he set himself. Prolix, stiff, uneven he is, on occasion. But is not Trollope more digressive? Hardy sometimes more formal? Dickens less balanced? The Gissing-reader is tempted to remark to himself, "Gissing may not be in the first rank of novelists. But who is?"

A Gissing-reader often has difficulty in determining whether he is attracted by Gissing's books or by Gissing's soul. In the Christian sense, Gissing—metempsychosed Epicurean that he was—hardly would have acknowledged the possession of a soul; but, tormented, it bobs up before us. The interesting characteristic of this soul is its defiance of circumstance. Plunged among the poorest of the poor, he rises to scoff at equality and social revolution; subjected to repeated injuries at the hands of women, he idealizes Woman; engulfed by industrialism, he finds his home in Greece and Rome; reared in materialism, he becomes a partisan of morality. Whatever his misadventures, the man who possessed this soul was either strong or perverse.

His was a soul aching with the pessimism of our time. In the dreariness of modern life, in the melancholy expression of alarm at the death of old ways, in the wail of the inhabitants of the metropolitan nether world, in the self-probing inspection of the vanity of human wishes, in the preoccupation with amorous passion and with the problems of marriage that are so much with us now—in these themes of Gissing's is contained an analysis of our miseries no writer since has surpassed. The artist of misery can never be popular; but, having genius, neither can he be forgotten.

III

Unlike many another realistic novelist, Gissing was a true artist. He began as a pamphleteer; but soon abandoning the crusade for social reform, he made artistic beauty his life's aim—the beauty of truth barren, perhaps, yet always dignified by literary style of a high order. His Harold Biffen stalks after a butcher and his girl, alert to record their every phrase; but such was not really Gissing's own method. The fascination with trivia, the gloating over physiological detail, the sobersided imitation of sociology that have come to be identified with realism are not found in Gissing; Stephen Crane is a cataloguer beside him, Frank Norris a dust-sifter. Reality he was determined to reproduce, but reality chiefly of human character, delineated against a sketchy background of the commonplace details of life. To accomplish his purpose he possessed a tool denied his twentieth-century inheritors: the discipline of classical thought and letters. Few other Englishmen have been so much in love with the books and traditions of Greece and Rome as was this poverty-spurred young man from industrial Yorkshire; what few pounds he could save during his literary slaving were spent to take him to Italy and Athens. With the classical tradition he combined a minute knowledge of English authors, so that the models for his style were Scott and Thackeray and Dickens, not Turgenev and Dostoevski and Balzac, admirer of the Continental realists though he became; he presents no parallel with George Moore's imitation of Zola. His school of literary realism was of his own foundation, a growth out of his early miseries in the depths of London.

Accordingly, in these remorseless tales of his is a literary beauty—a union that has come to be thought anomalous in naturalistic fiction. Take a single passage of description from *Thyrza* (1887) (chosen not because it is markedly striking, but because it is a good sample of Gissing's pace)—realism unadulterated, but the realism of a man with taste and discrimination:

> Caledonian Road is a great channel of traffic running directly north from King's Cross to Holloway. It is doubtful whether London can show any thoroughfare of importance more offensive to eye and ear and nostril. You stand at the entrance to it, and gaze into a region of supreme ugliness; every house front is marked with meanness and inveterate grime; every shop seems breaking forth with mould or dry-rot; the people who walk here appear one and all to be employed in labour that soils body and mind. Journey on the top of a tram-car from King's Cross to Holloway, and civilization has taught you its ultimate achievement in ignoble hideousness.

> You look off into narrow side-channels where unconscious degradation has made its inexpugnable home, and sits veiled with refuse. You pass above lines of railway, which cleave the region with black-breathing fissures. You see the pavements half occupied with the paltriest and most sordid wares; the sign of the pawnbroker is on every hand; the public-houses look and reek more intolerably than in other places. The population is dense, the poverty is undisguised. All this northward bearing tract, between Camden Town on the one hand and Islington on the other, is the valley of the shadow of the vilest servitude. Its public monument is a cyclopean prison; save for the desert ground around the Great Northern Goods Depot, its only open ground is a malodorous cattle-market. In comparison, Lambeth is picturesque and venerable, St. Giles is romantic, Hoxton is clean and suggestive of domesticity, Whitechapel is full of poetry, Limehouse is sweet with sea-breathings.

This is only a species of aside in a tale of the slums; to find Gissing at his stylistic best, one reads *Ryecroft* or the books on Dickens, work that came easily to him. Yet it is not in description or narration that his chief talent lay, but in the gradual revelation of the minds and hearts of his characters. He is not fertile in his invention of men and women—and, indeed, while he has a powerful intellect, he has small creative imagination. His best depictions are of a few types of humanity, reproduced with variations in most of his novels: the young man in solitude (Waymark in *The Unclassed,* Peak in *Born in Exile* [1892]); the woman fiercely weak (Emma in *A Lodger in Maze Pond,* Carrie in *Workers in the Dawn* [1880]); the grim old man (Alfred Yule in *The New Grub Street,* Lord in *In the Year of Jubilee* [1894]); the unworldly lover of books (Christopherson in the story of that name, Grail in *Thyrza*); and a dozen others, each of which, perhaps, had his prototype in Gissing's personal history. The girl of noble sincerity, the intellectual charlatan, the domineering woman of position, the discontented workingman, the predestined spinster, the meditative clergyman, the naive reformer—these nearly complete his roster. The better ones stick in your memory. Deliberately abandoning the depiction of eccentricity (which Dickens so loved) because Gissing believed eccentricity to be dying under modern standardization, confining himself to scenes and incidents common enough, he succeeds all the same in putting living beings into our imagination. An attentive reader of *The New Grub Street* probably will retain a permanent impression of five characters—Reardon, Biffen, Amy, Alfred Yule, Jasper Milvain. There are not many writers who can do as much with the images of substantially normal people.

What makes Gissing's power of fastening upon our memory more remarkable, it is accomplished without true plot. In the novels he wrote at the height of his abilities, very little happens—little, that is, which the reader was not sure would happen after he had got through the second chapter. Violence is rare, there is no exaggeration of the picturesque, events move relentlessly toward that baffling of hopes which we know from the first to be inevitable. Much of the ruddy color of Morrison's stories of the East End is avoided deliberately. What Gissing does, he achieves by the power of the word and the appeal to universal experience. The half-chapter which describes the interview at a coffee-stand between sour old Alfred Yule and the beggar, once a surgeon, who tells him that he is doomed to blindness—this is perhaps the best instance, in *The New Grub Street* or elsewhere, of Gissing's faculty for transmuting the ingredients of realism into something unexcelled in its kind. The conversation is done; Yule gives the pauper a five-shilling fee and walks home; it is the end for the two of them. This grim restraint, this "minor key" as Gissing calls it, requires a disciplined style. Style Gissing has.

IV

A tormented soul, a pessimistic view, a memorable style—these only would not suffice to keep the grass green on Gissing's grave. But conjoined to them is the fact that Gissing was a moralist. His literary course was a search for moral purpose. If the aim of literature be to prove that there is purpose in nothing, it follows that there can be little purpose in books. Such a dilemma most pessimistic realists confront; but Gissing escapes by his belief in a Good. It is not the good of Christianity, nor yet the good of the materialistic reformer, but a pagan good—the good of Epicurus. Gissing refers only once to that philosopher, and then in a diary-entry remarking that a bust of Epicurus, in Rome, has a long nose. True Epicureanism permeated Gissing, all the same—the real Epicurean spirit of quiet resignation, retirement from ambition, the simple pleasure of contemplation, a gentleman's morality of peace and moderation, a pervading determination to live with dignity. It is easy to forget that Epicurus was a lofty moralist. But there were Right and Wrong for the Greek; and they were as real for Gissing. No divine justice rules Gissing's world; virtue has no certain desert, vice no sure penalty; but there lies behind Gissing's books the premise that one follows the good because it is beautiful and wise. This moral element won for Gissing in America the praise of Paul Elmer More and other humanists.

From half the hints one receives concerning Gissing, the reader approaching this realist for the first time might think him hardly a fit teacher of morals. Mutterings about "morbid theories of sex," ominous phrases concerning a wasted life, rest in actuality upon only two little dark spots in a career of hardship. When young and enthusiastic, Gissing filched some coins to assist a girl of the streets, and paid for it with a prison sentence; and when a lonely man nearing his end, he committed adultery by going off to France with a woman not his wife—an offense much mitigated, perhaps, by the fact that Edith Gissing had for years been in a madhouse. Otherwise, his was a remarkably conscientious life, full of diligence, affection, and fidelity to principle—a life not unworthy of some philosopher out of Diogenes Laertius.

In Gissing's books is no assurance that virtue has its material reward; indeed, it often encounters disaster; but neither is there any suggestion that a man should live otherwise than honorably. Godwin Peak, tired of life that meant loneliness, ends miserably somewhere in Italy, and Bruno Chilvers has a fashionable parish; but who would be Chilvers? Here is that brave defiance of adversity, that manliness, already remarked in Gissing. On the other hand, neither is roguery triumphant: Glazzard, his jealous revenge done, knows to what he has shrivelled in the process; Dyce Lashmar, the charlatan, disastrously overreaches himself. Ecclesiastes, from which Gissing liked to quote, was branded upon his heart.

To break with the modern world, to live as a man of gentle instincts and sound sense should, in such retirement as he can seek out—this is the only hope and consolation Gissing offers those who read him: this, and life lighted by truth. But then, Epicurus himself could do no more, and Epicurus left us no book like *Ryecroft*.

> Life is done—and what matter? Whether it has been, in sum, painful or enjoyable, even now I cannot say—a fact which in itself should prevent me from taking the loss too seriously. What does it matter? Destiny with the hidden face decreed that I should come into being, play my little part, and pass again into silence; is it mine either to approve or to rebel? Let me be grateful that I have suffered no intolerable wrong, no terrible woe of flesh and spirit, such as others—alas! alas!—have found in their lot. Is it not much to have accomplished so large a part of the mortal journey with so much ease? If I find myself astonished at its brevity and small significance, why, that is my own fault; the voices of those gone before had sufficiently warned me. Better to see the truth now, and accept it, than to fall into dread surprise on some day of weakness, and foolishly to cry against fate. I will be glad rather than sorry, and think of the thing no more.

Thus *The Private Papers of Henry Ryecroft*. "I am inclined to think he died of congestion," writes Norman Douglas, in *Siren Land* (1911), "for there was that within him—some macrocosmic utterance—which vainly endeavoured to pierce the gathering mists of introspection: the Ryecroft litany, beloved of weaker brethren, marks the parabola into the unfolding gloom. The old, old story: inefficient equipment, not of intellectuality but of outlook and attitude, and likewise of *bête humaine*; of that tough, cheerful attitude which, sanely regarded, is but sanity itself."

The measure of justice in this judgment on Gissing, like so many other criticisms from men he influenced somehow against their will, needs review. But whatever his flaws, fifty years have not effaced him; he is current. And a man who knows George Gissing has come a good way toward knowing the spirit of our age.

["Who Knows George Gissing?" Western Humanities Review, *Vol. 4 (Summer 1950), 213–22.]*

❖

Wyndham Lewis's First Principles

Wyndham Lewis (1882–1957) was an English novelist, essayist, and painter whose importance placed him with Ezra Pound, T. S. Eliot, and James Joyce among the "Men of 1914." Since his death, his reputation has been in eclipse, even though no evaluation of modernism can afford to ignore him. In the essay below, Kirk measures Lewis's significance as novelist, satirist, and social critic. Left-leaning critics view Lewis in the tradition of "the anti-democratic intelligentsia." Kirk's estimate of the principles governing Lewis's contribution to arts and letters refutes this view. Among Lewis's "first principles" Kirk emphasizes private liberty and private judgment, free will and free human rationality. The disintegration of these principles, as Kirk shows, is mirrored in novels such as The Revenge for Love *(1937) and* Self Condemned *(1954). That this essay appeared in* The Yale Review *in June 1955, when Lewis was still alive, points to Kirk's prescient qualities as a critic of literature.*

In the course of a criticism of American liberalism published in *Partisan Review*, Mr. Irving Howe made the following curious remark: "This prevalence of liberalism yields, to be sure, some substantial benefits. It makes us properly skeptical of the excessive claims and fanaticisms that accompany ideologies. It makes implausible those 'aristocratic' rantings against democracy which were fashionable in some literary circles a few years ago. (So that when a charlatan like Wyndham Lewis is revived and praised for his wisdom, it is done, predictably, by a Hugh Kenner in the *Hudson Review*.)" I read these sentences three or four times. What did Mr. Howe mean? I share with him his dislike of ideology, which old John Adams called "the science of Idiocy"; I agree with Mr. Howe's subsequent observation that American liberalism today is itself become an ideology, and in proportion has lost the appetite for freedom. But however does Mr. Wyndham Lewis come into all this? Mr. Lewis, true enough, has been a severe critic of American life and of "democracy," if by "democracy" is meant the modern mass-age, in which vague sense too many people use the word. Yet how anyone who has read Lewis's books attentively (particularly *The Apes of God* [1930], *The Art of Being Ruled* [1926], *America and Cosmic Man* [1948], and *The Writer and the Absolute* [1952]) can think of Mr. Lewis as a writer of "aristocratic" proclivities, passes my understanding. (I should not object in the least to his being aristocratic; I am merely stating a fact.) And why Mr. Howe should have referred to him as a charlatan puzzled me considerably. A charlatan, surely, is a person who deals in shams: Mr. Lewis has spent his life denouncing shams. Could it be that Mr. Howe thought of him as a charlatan because he writes upon serious subjects without being a professor, or even a doctor of philosophy? But Mr. Lewis's learning is genuine, whether or not one agrees with his deductions from premise and fact. (I myself, probably, disagree with Mr. Lewis's conclusions as often as Mr. Howe does, though not always for the same reasons.) And as Mr. Robert Hutchins, who enjoys an extensive acquaintance among professors, wrote recently, "One of the most striking things about the works that have made the minds of various ages is that almost none of them were written by professors." I am inclined to think, then, that Mr. Irving Howe, like many other people with some pretensions to a knowledge of twentieth-century letters, has misunderstood the character of Mr. Lewis's work and the character of Mr. Lewis himself.

Now Mr. Lewis is a man of mark and a writer of power; he is one of the few English men of letters in our time whose books probably will be remembered, if books are remembered at all, a century from now. Therefore I think it worthwhile to examine here his four recent books (*Self Condemned, Rotting Hill* [1951], *The Writer and the Absolute,* and *Rude Assignment* [1950]) and his best novel (*The Revenge for Love,* recently republished in England, and published for the first time in America) with the aim of describing Mr. Lewis's significance as a novelist and as a critic of society.

Wyndham Lewis lives today almost wholly in the realm of the mind, for he is blind, and can paint no more; he sits sardonically among his books and papers in his Notting Hill flat, contemptuous of the dreary sprawling city and the mechanized sprawling society around him. Unlike old Coleridge, at Highgate, he cannot gaze prophetically over "London and its smoke-tumult, . . . attracting towards him the thoughts of innumerable brave souls still engaged there." (These are Carlyle's words.) "A sublime man; who, alone in those dark days, had saved his crown of spiritual manhood; escaping from the black materialisms and revolutionary deluges, with 'God, Freedom, and Immortality' still his; a king of men." No, the rising generation will not rally round Wyndham Lewis, even though, like Coleridge, the constant gist of his discourse is lamentation over the sunk condition of the world. The dark days lie as heavy on Wyndham Lewis as upon any of us, and far heavier than they lie upon most. God, Freedom, and Immortality are not his; yet there in Notting Hill still sits (in this time of buckram masks and literary phantasms) a man.

Now Mr. Lewis (though he confesses to having poured the molten iron of satire but once, and that in *The Apes of God*) stands out as a man and a writer because he is a satirist. Unlike Evelyn Waugh and Aldous Huxley, he rarely employs exaggeration to bring his satire to perfection; in his later books, especially, in *The Revenge for Love* and *Rotting Hill* and *Self Condemned*, he prefers to scourge the naked follies of the time by the method of relentless naturalism. Percy Hardcaster, the professional Communist revolutionary, is real and drawn to scale, in every part; the socialist parson called "The Bishop's Fool," in *Rotting Hill*, in his pathos and his futility, is taken from the life; the very minor and evanescent characters, like Dr. Gratton-Brock in *Self Condemned*, are perfect reproductions, executed with a loathing fascination, of twentieth-century sham and pomposity. And the art of satire, as Lewis argues in *Rude Assignment,* can endure only while the satirist stands firm upon a ground of moral principle, from which he can assail his victims with confidence: satire will be written, and read, and applauded, only when writers and the public acknowledge the existence of abiding moral standards. If no values exist, then follies and crimes are not follies and crimes at all, but merely phenomena of meaningless life; and no one will appreciate satire because no one will believe that the satirist is attacking anything of importance.

Under precisely this terrible difficulty the satirist labors in our time; satire commonly is regarded as mere malice, or bad form, because "everything is relative," and it is cruel to reproach people for doing no more than following their humor. How, for instance, could one write a satire on adulterers calculated to move the disciples of Dr. Alfred Kinsey? In an age when men and women do not perceive the purpose of satire, the satirist will be detested, as a spoil-sport—and, if possible, suppressed. Mr. Lewis has had to contend against the spirit of the age in this, as in much else. "Where there is truth to life there is satire," Lewis writes; in this sense, he has always been a satirist, though not in the narrower sense (approved by himself) of a writer who describes "not people such as ourselves, but a symbolic company." W. B. Yeats told the young Lewis that, as a satirist, he would be *stopped*—for that is what always happens in England to satirists. People have been trying to stop Wyndham Lewis for some decades now. They have denounced him at times, and ignored his books at other times, but they have never quite succeeded in stopping him; and I think that soon he is going to be heard by the people who need him, and who will not forget him.

If Mr. Lewis has been a genuine satirist, and not a charlatan, by his own definition he must have adhered to certain articles of faith, certain enduring values, certitudes from which, secure, he would strike out at folly and vice in his time. What, precisely, are Mr. Lewis's first principles? From what philosophical redoubt can he defy cant and popular passion, and fire his volleys at the sophister and the calculator, the art-fraud, the mawkish sentimentalist, the devotee of violence, the public-school collectivist, the counterfeiting cosmopolitan, the Welwyn Garden City snob, the envious proletarian university-student, the art-tart county-family girl, the logical positivist from Cambridge who had "whittled himself away to a colourless abstraction which hardly constituted even a target," the ruined and lying doctor of medicine, the malignant and godless vicar? Swift, for all his loathing of fallen human nature, was a Christian and a Tory, and so stood for certain things very old and high; Flaubert, as Lewis observes, indulged in "the satire of nihilism," since for him "human life in its entirety is composed of folly and crime in one degree or another," and stood for nothing whatsoever. Now Wyndham Lewis is neither Swift nor Flaubert; he is neither a Christian nor a nihilist. Though he shares Swift's disgust with the flesh, he has been cudgelling the nihilists for half a century. Lewis stands for something.

Like Tarr, however, the central character in his first novel (1918), Lewis has always rather tried to stand for nothing but a Stoic apathy, an almost Olympian indifference, a detachment from life, an ironical and disconcerting reasonableness. From such a position, Tarr regards the mad German Kreisler and his own fiancé Bertha with an impersonal, if not uncharitable, self-sufficiency; from such a position, Mr. Park, in Lewis's short story, "The Rebellious Patient" (*Shenandoah*, Summer–Autumn, 1953), regards Dr. Musgrave with a brooding contempt. When Lewis's characters descend from this detachment into the contests of humanity (as Tarr does with Anastasya, "swagger sex"), ordinarily the consequences are unpleasant. That has been true of Lewis's own career. Lewis's detestation of cant, and his half-reluctant concern for the future of the human race, have drawn him repeatedly into the arena of controversy, where he has been as hacked and battered as any old gladiator, though he has given as good as he got. To be theoretically in favor of apathy, and yet congenitally drawn to the defense of forlorn causes, does not sweeten a man's temper. Mr. Wyndham Lewis, at seventy, is a very crusty customer, and a very courageous one. I repeat that he stands for something.

Mr. T. S. Eliot wrote in 1937 that Lewis, in *The Lion and the Fox* (1927), is defending the detached observer, which makes him unpopular with majorities:

> The detached observer, by the way, is likely to be anything but a dispassionate observer; he probably suffers more acutely than the various apostles of immediate action. The detached observers are in theory the philosophers, the scientists, the artists, and the Christians. But most of the people who profess to represent one or another of these categories, are more or less implicated in the politics of their time and place. Philosophy has long since been suspect; and the kind that makes the most voluble pretensions to impartiality may be the most dangerous. The future of the detached observer does not seem to be very bright.

Wyndham Lewis certainly does not expect his own future to be bright, or anyone else's. We languish in an age of ideologies, so that detachment is denounced as treason. For many people, it has become impossible to conceive that anyone should not be an ideologist. Mr. Lewis, not being a Marxist, was attacked as a Fascist; his critics did not admit the possibility of his detesting all forms of collectivism and fanaticism. Because he never conformed to any ideology, Wyndham Lewis never enjoyed the praise of any influential coterie; just as Professor Harding, in *Self Condemned*, is driven first out of the universities and then into a life-in-death because he will not teach ideology. In his chapter "Absolute Utopias," in *The Writer and the Absolute*, Lewis quotes Burke at length, approving Burke's denunciation of "doctrine and theoretic dogma." Mr. Howe's juxtaposition of "the excessive claims and fanaticisms that accompany ideologies" with the name of Wyndham Lewis therefore perplexes me. Does he really think that Mr. Lewis is given to "excessive claims and fanaticisms"? Just what ideology is Mr. Lewis supposed to have espoused, and in what literary circles is he supposed to have been fashionable? He seems to me to have fought against the current the whole of his life; the impulse to contradict cant is in the man's nature; and if the Benthamite ideology, say, had been popular between 1909 and 1949, Wyndham Lewis would have exerted himself as strongly against Benthamism as he has against Communism, impressionism, existentialism, and three or four other popular notions in the world of politics and the world of art. Mr. Hugh Kenner's perceptive little crucial study, *Wyndham Lewis* (1954) gives us a glimpse of a proud, cross-grained, subtle man, as obsessed with ideas as he is scornful of ideology, standing quite alone in the midst of all the winds of doctrine.

Mr. Lewis, in fine, has always been detached, never dispassionate; and though never an ideologist, he has always subscribed to a set of principles, some of which he frankly acknowledges, others of which he himself may not even recognize as the foundation for his satirical intrepidity. Principle, as Burke declared, is a very different thing from abstraction. Principle ordinarily comes to a man from the wisdom of his ancestors; abstraction is the product of a man's own puny little private stock of reason. And Mr. Lewis—although true human reason has few better defenders than he in our time—derives his principles, in considerable part, from prescription. He speaks, however eccentrically at times, for the wisdom of our ancestors. More specifically, however, he speaks for a set of principles which are not particularly ancient. These are the principles of liberalism: not twentieth-century liberalism, which has become an ideology, but the confident and robust liberalism of nineteenth-century England, with all its virtues and all its faults. Wyndham Lewis, private character and artistic talents aside, is the possessor of a mind rather like John Morley's. Such a mind detests cant and slices through humbug and sentimentality; such a mind also suffers, sometimes, from an excessive desire for self-reliance and an excessive confidence in rationality.

The older Mr. Lewis grows, the more clearly apparent do his liberal proclivities become, and the more nearly certain does it seem that he lives in the tradition of English liberal thought and letters since Locke. I do not mean that Mr. Lewis is a Manchesterian economist, or a Benthamite reformer of laws, or a Gladstonian opponent of empire. I do mean that he believes in the highest degree of private liberty, as opposed to the claims of the group; that he has a profound trust in the powers of the private judgment, if only men would consent to be reasonable; that he dislikes the centralized political authority of the state; that he (as Leslie Stephen said of the Whigs) is "invincibly suspicious of parsons"; that he distrusts both the aristocracy and the masses; that he defends the great English middle classes, of which he is a member; that he has an aversion to ideology, whether the sentimental sympathy of Rousseau or the corrosive envy of Marx; that he adheres, at least practically, to the theory of free will, abjuring historical determinism; that he has very little taste for mystery or flights of pure imagination. I do not say that he has never deviated in the slightest from this set of principles; not one of the great Victorian liberals, after all, consistently kept every article in this catechism at all times. At present, for instance, Mr. Lewis believes that we must establish a Leviathan world-state, if we are to save ourselves from catastrophe, which is not a liberal idea in the sense that Lord Acton understood liberalism; but the same idea is espoused with greater enthusiasm by one of the present chief representatives of the American school of liberalism, Mr. Robert Hutchins.

I believe, then, that Mr. Lewis is rather an old-fashioned man, Vorticism and *The Caliph's Design* (1919), notwithstanding. Old-fashioned ideas very frequently are sound and true ideas. In some ways, however, he may not be old-fashioned enough: liberalism is a fresh and tender growth in comparison with certain older systems of thought that still live among us. I think that the error of judgment which led Mr. Lewis to hope, in 1931, that some good might come out of Adolph Hitler's projects (an error which he quickly recognized and acknowledged, the following year) was in considerable part a product of Lewis's liberal optimism and liberal individualism, impatient at the cant and the muddling of those years. The liberal, throughout modern history, has tended to forget that a regime of feeble reason may give way not to sweetness and light, but to a regime of unreason.

Free human rationality is the principal end in life, in Mr. Lewis's opinion. He makes this point in his chapter "Intuition versus the Intellect," in *Rude Assignment*:

> The subtitle of this chapter reads: "Is there such a thing as an Intellectual?" So let me, in concluding, summarize my answer to that question.—If you, for the purpose of belittling him, affix the term "intellectual" (or more familiarly "highbrow") to any man of conspicuous intelligence, or whose standards notoriously are not those of the market-place, then there is such a thing only in your stupid mind, or on your foolish lips. But there is another and more serious sense, in which such a term may be admitted, and even serve a useful purpose.
>
> The definition of "intellectual" would be no easy task, as this chapter has proved. Julien Benda—deliberately ignoring all who did not fit in—would have defined it as a learned man prostituting his high function and inciting others to violence. His polemical opposites would say (scowling at Benda) that it denoted a democrat in an Ivory Tower, preaching peace and plenty—in contrast to war and want. All I need say, as my final word on this subject, is that few intellectuals are to be found who are prepared to oppose the Zeitgeist. The latter is committed to courses which, if pursued to their logical ends, will wipe out all that the human intellect has contrived, distinguishing us from cattle and pigs, and still more from bees and centipedes.

This treason of the intellectuals, submitting tamely to a process of social alteration which would make an end of intellect, submerging individuality in a collective dreariness, is the principal theme of Lewis's fiction since 1937. *The Revenge for Love*, for which Spain on the eve of explosion is the backdrop, has most of its principal scenes in the Communist and literary-radical circles of London, exposed with a fierce energy and accuracy by Lewis as repellent combinations of inverted snobbery, appetite for power, muddled humanitarianism, private interest, and conspiratorial malice; I know of no other novel which touches on such matters and such people with equal discernment except Conrad's *Under Western Eyes* (1911). The only decent people in the book are dupes, Victor and Margot Stamp, a poverty-stricken painter of small talents and his dreamy wife; they are used as bait by the London Communists, and go over a cliff in the Pyrenees. Margot, who reads Ruskin, sees the whole set for what they are—though, in the end, this does not save her; she senses the inhumanity of these reformers, sufficiently represented by Gillian Phipps, the young woman with the boarding-school accent who likes to be kissed by men of the lower orders:

> Margot understood that no bridge existed across which she could pass to commune as an equal with this Communist "lady"—living in a rat-infested cellar out of swank (as it appeared to her from her painfully constructed gimcrack pagoda of gentility). Nor did she wish to very much, because—for Victor's sake—she dreaded and disliked all these false politics, of the sham underdogs (as she felt them to be), politics which made such a lavish use of the poor and the unfortunate, of the "proletariat"—as they called her class—to advertise injustice to the profit of a predatory Party, of sham underdogs athirst for power: whose doctrine was a universal Sicilian Vespers, and which yet treated the real poor, when they were encountered, with such overweening contempt, and even derision.

This betrayal of reason by its guardians does not always take so active and conscious a form as that committed by the "intellectuals" of these left-wing conspiratorial circles; commonly, indeed, the betrayers remain unaware of the grand tendency of their notions, and sometimes they may act with the greatest good will. The vicar in "The Bishop's Fool," the most powerful story in *Rotting Hill* and one of the most memorable and terrible short stories of this century, is a truly good man, a Christian socialist, an Anglo-Catholic, bearing up under an oppressive poverty that is crushing the Church of England, wearing patched clothes so that he may buy books and an occasional picture, generous, humble, open-minded; his only trouble is that, though an educated man, he is a fool. His ritualism so alienates his parishioners that no one comes to church; but he does not complain, for he is sure that praying at home does them quite as much good. (They do *not* pray at home.) His amorphous social radicalism alienates the principal farmer of the parish, a brute who has replaced the absentee squire as the man of influence in the country round—and who presently will be replaced by a commissar, Lewis suggests. When attacked physically by the drunken farmer in a pub, the parson is too charitable even to defend himself—and so is beaten and fearfully injured while his parishioners mock him. This is the new order of things, giving the quietus to the shadow of the old; and the old is kicked and broken because of a failure of reason.

Mr. Lewis's latest novel, *Self Condemned*—his first long work of fiction since 1941—is a story of personal and social disintegration, coming very close in its implications to Flaubert's satirical nihilism, and yet redeemed from that catastrophe by Wyndham Lewis's sense of what has been in the world of reason, and of what ought to be. Professor René Harding—who has a great deal in common with his creator—resigns his chair of history at the University of London because he cannot endure cant and hypocrisy: his influential book, "The Secret History of World War II," has been the product of his growing conviction that conventional history is a mischievous sham. A friendly review summarizes his opinions:

> The wars, civil massacres which should be treated as police court news, provide the basis for the story of mankind we encounter in history books. The explanation of this terrible paradox, that the state should always be in the hands of ruffians or of feeble-minded persons, is that the enormous majority of men are barbarians, philistines, and mentally inhabit an "heroic" age, if not a peculiarly violent Stone Age. And upon that popular plane the political world has its being. A number of creative "sports" are born into every successive generation of uncreative gang-rule. Though frowned on or even hated by the majority, these individuals nevertheless introduce into the dull and sodden stream of the average a series of startling innovations. . . .
>
> The history of our century would not be one mainly of personalities (though, alas, they are there as ever). What we should see would be big, ideologic currents, gaudily coloured, converging, dissolving, combining or contending. It would look like a chart of the ocean rather than a Madame Tussaud's Waxworks; though there would be faces (one with a tooth-brush moustache), like labels of one or other of the big currents of ideas. Then there would be the mountainous blocks of all kinds, as though raised up by an earthquake: there would be the piling up of tremendous inventions, their instant conversion to highly unsuitable uses: the criminality of man rioting in the midst of these unnumbered gadgets. Then there would be the growth, in every society, of the huge canker of Debt. In more and more insane proportions, the Credit System would be apparent, developing its destructive bulk. One would sense nebulous spiders, at the heart of wider and wider webs of abstract simulacras of wealth, suspended over everything: hordes of men engaged for years in meaningless homicide: and vast social revolutions

> as the culmination of a century of plots, and propaganda of brotherly love at the point of a pistol, and *la haine créatrice*. So there would be arabesques of creation and of destruction, the personal factor unimportant, the incarnations of ideas, the gigantic coloured effigies of a Hitler or a Stalin, no more than the remains of monster advertisement.

Convinced that no university could long tolerate the teaching of history upon this pattern, Harding, just before the outbreak of war, goes to Canada with his wife, leaving behind him a London sinking into the soddenness of Rotting Hill. But Canada, for the Hardings, turns out to be no better than a debased and exaggerated caricature of European decay. They subsist through the winter in dismaying poverty, living in one room in a disreputable hotel; Harding is beaten in the beverage-room by a criminal pugilist from the United States who dislikes Harding's English accent. The only friend of letters whom they meet is an owl-like pathic named Furber, on whose advances of cash Harding comes to depend. Hester Harding, longing for the England of her youth, is driven to desperation by this life; and when, presently, Harding gives way to necessity and accepts a professorship at Momaco University, she throws herself under a truck. Her suicide drives Harding to the verge of madness: he is nursed back to a kind of health at a Catholic retreat, and contemplates becoming a Catholic; but when his powers have returned to him, his overweening rationality makes him despise such an act of faith. Thus he languishes on at Momaco, his abilities as thinker and writer deteriorating, until an invitation comes from an American university, and he accepts, and goes to the United States to linger out his life without purpose and without hope. An impulse toward self-destruction, a defiance of the whole hum-drum world of dreary facts, had been mingled with his philosophical repudiation of modern ideology, from the first, and he knew it. That character-dissolving influence now triumphs, leaving Harding to a life in death: "and the Faculty had no idea that it was a glacial shell of a man who had come to live among them, mainly because they were themselves unfilled with anything more than a little academic stuffing."

Harding is beaten down by the insensate forces of social disintegration which he had himself described in his book; and even his inner will to disaster, probably, is the reaction of a high and austere nature to an age of sensuality and unreason. His dislike of existence extends to the act of procreation, for which he despises himself even while he indulges his lust. Hester Harding is described by Mr. Kenner as "vacuously libidinous," but this is unfair. It is Harding who is libidinous, and we are allowed to see his wife only through

Harding's eyes. Hester has love in her, and Harding has none. René Harding, indeed, is defecated rationality; and so, in his writings, with very few exceptions—the devotion of Margot to Victor Stamp, in *The Revenge for Love,* is the chief one—Wyndham Lewis himself seems. It was one of the cardinal faults of the old liberalism that the heart was denied its claims.

Self Condemned is a description of a world that unreason has mastered, even in its sanctuaries of learning. Almost nowhere does Harding find understanding of his principles and scruples—the malice and stupidity of his associates enrage him. The one man who feels sympathy, his friend Rotter, is a specimen of a dying breed, the scholar of modest private means, whom taxation and inflation soon will annihilate. Not in England, or in Canada, or the United States, in times to come, will there be any place for Harding or for Rotter; the critics of thought and society will be crushed into the mold of an unreasoning conformity; and man will be even as the bee and the centipede, if he does not destroy himself. The higher natures, like Harding's, will be the first to perish.

Now what redeems this fierce indictment of modern life from the satire of nihilism is Lewis's staunch liberal prejudice. The triumph of unreason and brutality is not an inevitable consequence of irresistible historical forces, but the result of a betrayal of human reason, a deliberate repudiation of the works of the mind. Man has within him the power to be something better than a Hardcaster or a Furber. The instrument for his salvation is his reason; yet, engulfed in a confusion of humanitarianism that really is inhumane, of collectivism that masquerades as sympathy, of fallacious notions concerning human nature and the state, of uniformity under the name of justice, modern man is denying his reason. The nineteenth-century world, whatever it lacked, was a world of energy, variety, a considerable degree of justice, private security, and free expression. Those inestimable benefits of modern civilization, the work of Professor Harding's creative men, are now being undone by the destructive men. Lewis himself, speaking through Rotter, recognizes the vanity of expecting that these gains would continue or even endure:

> In the nineteenth century in England and America, and even elsewhere, it was universally thought that a new age of tolerance and intelligence, of "decency" and humaneness, had begun; and just as a great number of practices belonging to the bad old times of the unenlightened past, such as slavery, duelling, hanging and quartering, public executions, imprisonment for debt, child-labour, cruel sports, ill-treatment of animals and so forth, had been discountenanced and abolished (for ever, it was supposed), so gradually all

> such odious survivals would disappear, and "The world's great age begin anew, the golden years return." The time when nations would recognize the wickedness and wastefulness of war was near at hand. This belief was unchallenged in the English-speaking countries at the beginning of the century, and such feeling lingered even as late as Woodrow Wilson's Paris peacemaking, or the Kellogg Pact. But actually the world-war gave the deathblow to this belief, and the happenings of the last two decades have done nothing to reinstate it. The optimistic idealism of the Nineteenth Century, although it is not identical with, inherited something from the Enlightenment of the Eighteenth Century.

Human reason, in fine, was not enough to persuade men to safeguard even their own material advantages. Wyndham Lewis's own first principles, liberal in origin, founded upon the assumption that an unflinching rationality might suffice to master the evil and the stupidity in human nature, have carried their author only to Rotting Hill and to the cliff in Spain and to the hotel-room in Momaco. The violence of Europe at war has its microcosm in the Hotel Blundell, where the janitor is a lascivious imbecile and the proprietor is a dapper murderer. The London house where the Hardings had lived goes downhill during the war: ". . . the cellar was full of dead leaves and a wild cat had established its home there, a brood of wild kittens sprang about among the leaves. This wild cat so terrorized the tenants that they dared not go down to their trash bins just outside the cellar-door."

Wyndham Lewis is a true satirist, and no charlatan; he is also a man of powerful mind. From his set of liberal principles of a vanished age, he has every justification for scourging the vices and crimes and follies of an age of reason. Yet upon principles of pure rationality, I think, there is no more hope of reviving the liberal world of stability and variety and private rights than there was hope for Harding after his pure rationality returned to him and he rejected religious consolation. Enlightened self-interest, the slogan of nineteenth-century liberalism, leaves love and faith out of its calculations. Love lacking, the inner life of Lewis's characters is dry and sardonic; faith lacking, the civil social order which Lewis describes with such a ruthless precision dissolves into its constituent atoms.

The rising generation will not look to Wyndham Lewis at Notting Hill as once they looked to Coleridge at Highgate, for Notting Hill is much farther down toward the river, and the dry rot works there nowadays with a malignant cunning. It would do them no harm to go to Mr. Wyndham Lewis: he would tell them some hard truths, of which we all stand in need. I think that a good many of them are going to read Lewis, these next few years, but that they will have to look elsewhere for some consolation or guidance. Lewis points the way to nothing; yet he stands for something manly and free, and for the cold scorn of the real satirist. As Harding found Momaco only a debased Notting Hill, so we in our generation have nowhere to take refuge from the Hardcasters and the Furbers, the symbols of conspiratorial violence and heartless degeneracy. Plato and Euclid could shelter within the walls of Megara; no Megaras are left to us. We shall be driven at last, I suspect, to aspire once more to love and faith, if only out of dread of the wild cat in the cellar.

["Wyndham Lewis's First Principles," The Yale Review, *Vol. 44 (June 1955), 520–34. Also published in* Beyond the Dreams of Avarice: Essays of a Social Critic *(Chicago: Henry Regnery Company, 1956), 311–25.]*

❖

T. S. Eliot's *The Waste Land*

T. S. Eliot's "strange great poem," The Waste Land *(1922), was "to turn the literary world upside down." Kirk's discussion of the poem is found in* Eliot and His Age: T. S. Eliot's Moral Imagination in the Twentieth Century *(1971), among his finest accomplishments.* "The Waste Land," *he writes, "is the endeavor of a philosophical poet to examine the life we live, relating the timeless to the temporal." Kirk's interpretation attests to the chief strength of his book as a whole: interweaving the history of an era with close critical analysis. What further enhances Kirk's approach is his effort to fathom the meaning of* The Waste Land *as a narrative poem without falling into the traps of obscure literary theory and abstraction. Steadfastly he strives to make as clear "the general meaning of* The Waste Land *. . . as its particular lines are dark." Kirk's elucidation of the poem's complexity saves a reader from being stranded in Eliot's use of ancient myths and symbols in a modern setting.*

For a man like Eliot, imbued with the idea of the contract of eternal society, the prospect of Europe in the autumn of 1921 was dismal enough. The Hapsburg system had been torn apart, and the impoverished succession-states, riven by faction and ideology and ethnic rivalries, clearly could achieve no enduring order. Ruined Germany, the Weimar Republic feeble from the first, was hard pressed to withstand Communist insurrection. The face and the spirit of France were ravaged. In Italy, Communist and Fascist bands, terrible simplifiers, struggled for power; Mussolini would triumph a year later. The Bear, now Red, glowered upon the West. Ireland was lost to the United Kingdom, as Sinn Fein and the Black and Tans competed in terror. Lloyd George's inflation was followed by an abrupt deflation; two million men were unemployed in Britain. "The glory of Europe is extinguished forever," Burke had declared in 1789; if the indictment had been hyperbole then, it seemed accurate enough in 1921.

This decay of order and justice and freedom within the old European community was paralleled by the decadence of the old moral order, the Church falling into disrepute and the governing motive of many eminent men being merely "put money in thy purse." For the charlatan and the cheat, large opportunities were opened everywhere; while the old motives to integrity were fearfully shaken. Out of the War's brutality had emerged gross appetites and violent ambitions, and everywhere egoism swaggered. A mind disciplined by a classical education thought of the Roman decadence. One heard endless prating about democracy, but the actual tendency of the time seemed to be toward the servitude to desire in private life, and the servitude to ideology in public affairs. It was a loveless prospect, and the community of souls was stricken.

Were *The Waste Land* only the poetic lament of a man whose marriage had not fulfilled his hopes, and who had worked himself to the bone, it would remain interesting—but it could not have spoken as a conscience to a multitude of other consciences. A widespread decay of love is no accident: causes may be discerned, and remedies—however difficult—may be suggested. In short, Eliot has described in *The Waste Land* not merely his ephemeral state of mind; much more important, he has penetrated to causes of a common disorder in the soul of the twentieth century.

Disdaining the Romantic lyric poet's exaltation of the ego, Eliot subordinated private emotion to the expression of general truths. A few brief passages from "Tradition and the Individual Talent"—published only two years earlier—may suggest his determination to rise above personal comment on the universe:

"The progress of an artist," Eliot had reasoned,

> is a continual self-sacrifice, a continual extinction of personality . . . the more perfect the artist, the more completely separate in him will be the man who suffers and the mind which creates; the more perfectly will the mind digest and transmute the passions which are its material. . . . Impressions and experiences which are important for the man may take no place in the poetry, and those which become important in the poetry may play quite a negligible part in the man, the personality. . . . It is not in his personal emotions, the emotions provoked by particular events in his life, that the poet is in any way remarkable or interesting. . . . Poetry is not a turning loose of emotion, but an escape from emotion; it is not the expression of personality, but an escape from personality.[3]

So *The Waste Land* ought not to be read as a sublimation of Eliot's emotions in 1921—which, whether or not complex, certainly were not unusual. It is Eliot's thought and expression that matter. He was troubled in 1921, privately; but he knew that most men have been troubled, and that many have endured troubles with resignation and fortitude. Not his private misgiving, but his concern with the condition of modern man, is what gives *The Waste*

Land an enduring force. Before him sprawled a prospect of private and public disorder. Although he suffered under this general distemper, it is anything but a private perplexity that Eliot sets before us.

Confronted with this scene, Eliot is not "disillusioned" (for when had he been the dupe of illusion?) or despairing, though gloomy enough. The first necessity, he implies, is to ask the right questions. How have we come to this pass? The "protagonist" (as the critics generally call him) really is the Seeker; and he is searching for the springs of love.

The Waste Land might have been more coherent and less puzzling had Ezra Pound let it alone—although then it would have stirred up less of a sensation. Eliot, in part recovered from his collapse, brought to Pound at Paris, near the end of 1921, a poem twice as long as *The Waste Land* we know; moreover, Eliot proposed to publish it with "Gerontion" as a prologue. There were lyrics that Pound excised; they appeared later as portions of "The Hollow Men" and as "Dream Songs" in Eliot's *Minor Poems*. Eliot had strained his hand while rowing, and so gave Pound a draft typewritten, for the most part; Pound crossed out his large deletions and wrote in his amendments.

"Pound was, in fact, a dominating director," Eliot would write in 1946. "He has always had a passion to teach. In some ways, I can think of no one whom he resembled more than Irving Babbitt—a comparison neither man would have relished." Babbitt's influence upon himself was evident, Eliot went on; and he suggested that Pound, like Babbitt, was one of those "men so devoted to ideas, that they cannot engage in profitable discussion with those whose ideas differ from their own." But Eliot accepted Pound's authority, and the manuscript (or typescript, rather) of *The Waste Land* shrank. "I should like to think that the manuscript, with the suppressed passages, has disappeared irrecoverably; yet, on the other hand, I should wish the blue pencilling on it to be preserved as irrefutable evidence of Pound's critical genius.[4]

So the seeming discontinuity and the abrupt—often jarring—succession of images and evocations and incorporated quotations that we encounter in *The Waste Land* result in considerable part from Pound's advice; these aspects seem to have disconcerted, at first, even Eliot himself. It had not been his intention, while writing at Margate and Lausanne, to employ these kaleidoscopic or cinematographic devices to such an extent: he had in mind a more smoothly flowing monologue. Had he not yielded to Pound's energy, we might have had a long poem less magical, yet better fulfilling Eliot's intention: the Great Refusal of Gerontion, followed by the delineation of sterility in the Waste Land, and incorporating the picture of the Hollow Men's vacuity—altogether, with transitional and elucidatory passages, a more coherent denunciation of modern disorder, more fully representative of Eliot's own intellect and method. In the long run, this might have been better teaching. Beyond any doubt, nevertheless, the enthusiasm and the scandal that resulted from publication of the Pound-revised poem would have been less if Eliot had withstood Pound.

When first I read *The Waste Land*, in my student days, I was annoyed by the seeming pedantry—ineffectual pedantry, at that—of Eliot's Notes, which explain little enough and have misled many readers and critics. The Notes to *The Waste Land* were in part an endeavor to compensate for Pound's merciless deletions, and some of them carry a hint of Eliot's whimsy and self-mockery; he was no lover of a heavy ostentatious apparatus of scholarship. But chiefly the Notes were improvised to satisfy the printer: there were sixty-four pages, altogether, to be filled in the little book, and the poem itself was too short for that compass, so padding must be provided. Eliot did not fall into that folly ever again.

The Notes may be ignored; so may some of the criticism of *The Waste Land*. Certain critics have offered theories about the poem so openly in conflict with Eliot's own literary principles and with his later writings that one wonders whether those commentators ever read the poem itself with a desire to understand; they have read the Notes and have read earlier critics—whom they imitate or denounce. But the poem may be read appreciatively without the possession of a doctoral degree in literature; and it is no allegory, but rather after its fashion a narrative poem, as the *Aeneid* and *The Divine Comedy* are narrative and philosophical.

In October, 1922, this poem was published in *The Criterion*, Eliot's own new review, without notes; it appeared in *The Dial*, across the Atlantic, in November—again without notes, because *The Dial's* editors declined to print them. The first edition of the book was published in New York (a thousand copies, with the Notes) by Boni and Liveright, that December; the first English edition (less than five hundred copies) was brought out by the Woolfs in September, 1923. The Age of Eliot had arrived with a clap of thunder.

For with *The Waste Land*, Eliot completed the success he had commenced with *Prufrock*: he won over, horse, foot, and dragoons, the rising generation of aspiring literary talents.[5] With a certain disrelish, E. M. Forster was to acknowledge Eliot's ascendancy over the young:

> For Mr. Eliot's work, particularly *The Waste Land*, has made a profound impression on them, and given them precisely the food they needed. And by "the young" I mean those men and women between the ages of eighteen and

> thirty whose opinions one most respects, and whose reactions one most admires. He is the most important author of their day, his influence is enormous, they are inside his idiom as the young of 1900 were inside George Meredith's, they are far better qualified than their elders to expound him, and in certain directions they do expound him.[6]

True, *The Waste Land* suggested better than had Eliot's earlier poems the way the "Invisible Poet" was steering—and so waked the justified suspicions of those young neoterists who had taken up with ideology, the inversion of religious dogma. Malcolm Cowley has described the mixed feelings of the young progressivists and levelers who were enchanted by the novelty of *The Waste Land*, but uneasy with its moral and social implications. "Strangeness, abstractness, simplifications, respect for literature as an art with traditions—it had all the qualities demanded in our slogans." They would defend the poem against the old entrenched schools of criticism, and against popular misunderstanding; but at heart they did not like it:

> When *The Waste Land* first appeared, it made visible a social division among writers that was not a division between capitalist and proletarians. . . . But slowly it became evident that writers and their theories were moving toward two extremes (though few would reach one or the other). The first extreme was that of authority and divinely inspired tradition as represented by the Catholic Church; the second was Communism. In Paris, in the year 1922, we were forced by Eliot to make a preliminary choice. Though we did not see our own path, we instinctively rejected his.[7]

From the publication of *The Waste Land*, indeed, men of the Left would begin to fulminate against Eliot—as presently they would complain of Robert Frost; for those two poets became defenders of the moral imagination, with its roots in religious insights and in the continuity of civilization. This the intelligent ideologue could not abide, committed as he was to mechanism and futurism.

Nearly half a century after the arrival of *The Waste Land*, it still remains desirable to inquire—for the common reader, and for a good many uncommon readers—just what Eliot was saying in that startling poem. Although merely to list the commendable critical essays about *The Waste Land* would require the equivalent of a chapter of this book, mystery and mystification continue to shroud Eliot's intentions. Some critics descend so deep into a line-by-line analysis (often in the flickering light of the befuddling Notes) that they are themselves lost, like their readers, in contrived corridors. A close examination of Eliot's sources and allusions is all to the good; but that has been accomplished already by several competent hands.[8]

My own summary analysis, which follows, is an endeavor to penetrate to the heart of this poem, necessarily refraining from comment upon Eliot's technique, and avoiding most excursions into his evocation of prophets, saints, poets, potentates, and anthropologists. Now that we may read at our leisure the whole body of Eliot's work, it is possible to see *The Waste Land* in the perspective of Eliot's later poetry and prose, and so to emancipate ourselves from the understandable limitations of those critics who wrote only a few years after the poem burst upon them. This verb "burst" I employ deliberately, upon the authority of William Carlos Williams, whose school of poetry was undone by Eliot: "Then out of the blue *The Dial* brought out *The Waste Land* and all our hilarity ended. It wiped out our world as if an atom bomb had been dropped upon it and our brave sallies into the unknown were turned to dust."[9]

At the heart of this poem of exploration lies the legend of the Grail, and more especially the symbol of the Chapel Perilous. (Eliot, not expecting *The Waste Land* to achieve so surprising a popularity, assumed that those who might read him would know tolerably well the Chapel Perilous and many other allusions and symbols in his lines. But already the decline of the old humane schooling, in classroom and home, had diminished in his audience the thrill of recognition; already the American college, as Babbitt had said, was turning out more pedants and more dilettantes, but fewer young people of truly liberal learning.)

How may a man be born again and a blasted land made to bloom anew? Why, screw your courage to the sticking-place: dare to ask terrifying questions, and you may be answered.

In some versions of the Grail legend, questing knights who entered the Chapel Perilous—ringed about with tombs—beheld the cup, the lance, the sword, the stone. If they found the hardihood to inquire, they would be answered: they would be told the meaning of these things; told at once, perhaps, or perhaps later. And of that questioning great good would come: the Fisher King's wound would be healed, and the desolate land would be watered again. "So in a civilization reduced to 'a heap of broken images' all that is requisite is sufficient curiosity," Hugh Kenner comments keenly; "the man who asks what one or another of these fragments means . . . may be the agent of regeneration. The past exists in fragments precisely because nobody cares what it meant; it will unite itself and come alive in the mind of anyone who succeeds in caring, . . . in a world where 'we know too much, and are convinced of too little.'"[10]

Knowing that past and present really are one, Eliot draws upon the myths and the symbols of several cultures to find the questions that we moderns ought to ask. Myth is not falsehood; instead, it is the symbolic representation of reality. From ancient theological and poetical and historical sources, burningly relevant to our present private and public condition, we summon up the moral imagination. We must essay the adventure of the Chapel Perilous if we would not die of thirst; we must confront the Black Hand and the dead Wizard-Knight, there in the ruinous Chapel; if we face down the horror, and dare to ask the questions, we may be heard.[11]

The most superficial adverse criticism of *The Waste Land*, advanced chiefly by doctrinaire progressivists and humanitarians or by grimmer ideologues, is this: "Eliot," they say, "is snobbishly contrasting the alleged glory and dignity of the Past with what he takes for the degradation of the democratic and industrialized Present. This is historically false, and ought to be repudiated by all Advanced Thinkers."

But that is not at all Eliot's intention. The Present, Eliot knew, is only a thin film upon the deep well of the Past; the Present was ceasing to exist even as he wrote at Margate or at Lausanne; the Present evaporates swiftly into the cloud of the Future; and that Future, too, soon will be the Past. The ideological cult of Modernism is philosophically ridiculous, for the modernity of 1971, say, is very different from the modernity of 1921. One cannot order his soul, or participate in a public order, merely by applauding the will-o'-the-wisp Present. Our present private condition and knowledge depend upon what we were yesterday, a year ago, a decade gone; if we reject the lessons of our personal past, we cannot subsist for another hour. Just so it is with the commonwealth, sustained by a community of souls: if the community rejects its past—if it ignores both the insights and the errors of earlier generations—then soon it comes to repeat the worst blunders of past times. Whether or not Time is a human convention merely (on which point, Eliot had not made up his mind as he wrote *The Waste Land*), the Past is not dead, but lives in us; and the Future is not a foreordained Elysium, but the product of our own decisions in this vanishing moment that we enjoy or endure.

The Waste Land, then, is no glorification of the Past. What the reader should find in this poem, rather, is Eliot's understanding that, by definition, human nature is a constant; the same vices and the same virtues are at work in every age; and our present discontents, personal and public, can be apprehended only if we are able to contrast our present circumstances with the challenges and the responses of other times. Aside from this, Eliot's glimpses and hints of a grander style and a purer vision in other centuries are chiefly the established device of the satirist, who awakes men to their parlous condition of abnormity by contrasting living dogs with dead lions.

Lost, we must ask for directions; and those directions do not come from living men only.[12] For authoritative guidance, Eliot turned especially, in this poem, to Saint Augustine, the Buddha, and the Upanishads. "The unexamined life is not worth living," as Socrates told his disciples. *The Waste Land* is the endeavor of a philosophical poet to examine the life we live, relating the timeless to the temporal. A Seeker explores the modern Waste Land, putting questions into our heads, and though the answers we obtain may not please us, he has roused us from our death-in-life. For just that is the Waste Land: the realm of beings who think themselves quick, but who exist only in a condition subhuman and sub-natural, prisoners in Plato's cave.

In *The Waste Land*, tremendous questions echo round the Chapel Perilous. In the progress of a terrifying quest, some wisdom is regained, though no assurance of salvation. We end by knowing our peril, which is better than fatuity: before a man may be healed, he must recognize his sickness.

Regeneration is a cruel process: so commences "The Burial of the Dead," the first of the four parts of *The Waste Land*: the half-life underground seems preferable to many. No sooner is this said than there breaks in the querulous voice of a woman, Marie—encountered in an Alpine hotel, perhaps overheard in chance conversation: she is a displaced or stateless person from the wreck of the Austro-Hungarian structure, with memories of staying at the archduke's, her cousin's; the mountains conceal her, and she takes that for freedom; her roots withered, she drinks coffee in the Hofgarten, and drifts. Such is the condition of Europe in 1921, for Heartbreak House is roofless in the Continent, too.[13]

As she falls silent, a voice is heard, prophetic or ghostly, inviting the son of man to take shelter under a red rock, where he will be shown fear in a handful of dust. (In Hadrian's villa, the subterranean mock Hell could be entered from any building of that sprawling expanse; just so, it is easy to pass from a café by the Starnbergersee, in one moment, to the Waste Land, where "the dead tree gives no shelter, the cricket no relief.")

The next moment, memory and desire have wafted in the hyacinth girl, the image of lost love; four lines from *Tristan und Isolde* summon her up from the dead, in this month of lilac and hyacinth and illusory spring. The episode in the hyacinth garden had been like the trance of those who sought the Grail but were unworthy. The hyacinth is withered now, and the girl vanished, amid stony rubbish. Aye, that episode's done for: will the future bring consolation?

So we come to Madame Sosostris, with her Tarot cards, decadent sibyl misreading her own pack. Fear death by water, she says—to people perishing of thirst. Her counsels would deny us rebirth through grace in death, the fertilizing power of water; she does not find the Hanged Man—Christ, or the Dying God—in the fortune she tells. But perhaps, unwittingly, this witch has conjured up a ghost: Stetson, who died a coward at Mylae—which might have been the Dardanelles, these wars having much of a likeness.

Thus "The Burial of the Dead" concludes with the Searcher's reproach to dead Stetson, not far from London Bridge:

"That corpse you planted last year in your garden,
"Has it begun to sprout? Will it bloom this year?
"Or has the sudden frost disturbed its bed?
"O keep the Dog far hence, that's friend to men,
"Or with his nails he'll dig it up again!"

This is a play upon Webster's lines in *The White Devil* (1612):

But keep the wolf far hence, that's foe to man,
For with his nails he'll dig them up again.

An aside concerning the Dog is excusable here, for these particular lines of *The Waste Land* illustrate admirably the wide variety of interpretations of Eliot possible and even plausible. (Some critics abstain altogether from comment upon this particular passage.) Consider three glossators of good reputation, far apart.

First George Williamson, in his *Reader's Guide to T. S. Eliot:*[14] "If Dog involves Sirius—as in 'Sweeney among the Nightingales'—he becomes a sign of the rising of the waters and is friendly to growth. But Dog may also involve Anubis, guardian of the dead, who helped to embalm the broken Osiris. By his ambiguity the Dog presents an ironical aspect, and this irony centers in the intent of the planting . . . "

Second, D. E. S. Maxwell, in his *Poetry of T. S. Eliot*:[15] "The Dog may be spiritual awareness or conscience, which Stetson makes no attempt to arouse, in the fear that it might force him to recognize his spiritual failings, to attempt to redeem himself—this none of the people of the waste land wishes to do, for it requires effort and positive action."

Third, Cleanth Brooks, in his *Modern Poetry and the Tradition*:[16] "I am inclined to take the Dog . . . as Humanitarianism and the related theories which, in their concern for man, extirpate the supernatural—dig up the corpse of the buried god and thus prevent the rebirth of life." He adds a footnote: "The reference is perhaps more general still: it may include Naturalism, and Science in the popular conception as the new magic which will enable man to conquer his environment completely."

Would it have been well to be disinterred by the Dog, or not well? Eliot never explained, and such controversies may continue so long as English poetry is criticized. This catacomb, layer upon layer, of evocation and suggestion in *The Waste Land* makes this poem subtle and strange and ambiguous as the Revelations of Saint John. Many lines are puzzling as the characters written by the sibyl on the leaves she scattered. Yet the general meaning of *The Waste Land* is as clear as its particular lines are dark.

So the Seeker clambers over the heap of broken images, leaving "The Burial of the Dead," to enter upon "A Game of Chess," the second part of the poem—and he stumbles into a boudoir. At first this room is mistaken for Cleopatra's; but really this is no chamber of grand passion and queenly power; it is only the retreat of a modern woman, rich, bored, and neurotic. On a wall, the picture of the metamorphosis of Philomel is a symbol of the reduction of woman to a commodity—often a sterile or stale commodity—in modern times. (The levelers would bring us down, Burke had said, to the doctrine that "a woman is but a woman; a woman is but an animal, and an animal not of the highest order.") Modern woman is ravished, but nowadays she is transformed into no sweet nightingale.

In this boudoir the woman is haunted, starting at noises on the stair, seeking in empty talk the quieting of a subtle dread; no diversion satisfies her—surely not "OOOO that Shakespeherian Rag." "Think," she tells the Seeker; and indeed he does:

> *I think we are in rats' alley*
> *Where the dead men lost their bones.*

So it is with the woman of fashion—and not otherwise with the woman of the ladies' lounge of the London public house, talking of adultery and abortion. The game of chess that modern woman plays is her undoing; sexual power is atrophied to the parched attempt at gratification of an appetite which cannot be satisfied by flesh only; love becomes an empty word. And the bartender calls out repeatedly, "HURRY UP PLEASE IT'S TIME": like the woman of the boudoir, the woman of the pub idles away the hours and days and years until death knocks.

Leaving the pub, the Seeker drifts down the Thames: we hear the Fire Sermon, the third part of this poem. The polluted river does not cleanse; dull lusts, sexual or acquisitive, hang about it now; the Seeker finds no gaiety and no glory. He becomes hermaphrodite Tiresias, impotently witnessing copulation without ardor and loss of chastity without either pleasure or remorse:

When lovely woman stoops to folly and
Paces about her room again, alone,
She smoothes her hair with automatic hand,
And puts a record on the gramophone.

Against this degradation, the Seeker appeals to the true City of love and gaiety, with music upon the waters. One hears as a distant echo, the voices of children singing of the Grail. But the Fisher King himself, perhaps the wounded Fisher of Men, casts his lines in a dull canal behind the gashouse, even the romantic memory of his crumbling castle departed. Here the dead do not rise to the surface, their bones being cast into a dry garret and "rattled by the rat's foot only, year to year." From Highbury down to Margate Sands, this river—once life-bestowing—has turned sinister. The varieties of concupiscence have driven out love. Those who amuse themselves beside the river or drift down it (to their undoing) fancy that they are safe enough:

But at my back in a cold blast I hear
The rattle of the bones, and chuckle spread from ear to ear.

Infatuation with transitory impulses, the Buddha had said in his Fire Sermon, oppresses man; abjure desire. And as Augustine sought redemption from the unholy loves of Carthage, so the Seeker prays that the Lord may pluck him as a brand from the burning.

Out to sea the Thames carries us—and to the ten enigmatic lines of the fourth part of this poem, "Death by Water." Passing beyond profit and loss, Phlebas the drowned Phoenician entered the whirlpool. In time, we all are swallowed by the whirlpool; yet what we have taken for "life" may be worse than death; and perhaps through dying we come to the life eternal. Madame Sosostris had predicted death by water. Yet is this "dying" really annihilation? May it not be rebirth, as by baptism? However that may be, a surrender to the element of water is better than endless torment in the fire of lust.

It is not in the ocean depths that the Seeker ends his quest. In the concluding part of this poem, "What the Thunder Said," he ascends into the mountains—once the source of life-giving water—Gethsemane and the slaying of God in his mind. The "red sullen faces" that sneer upon him from "doors of mudcracked houses" are God-forsaken; the thunder is dry and sterile. Someone walks beside him: the Fisher King, perhaps, who once guarded the Grail; and a mysterious third being, hooded. Is this the Christ, or the Tempter of the

Wilderness, or some Hollow Man? In this delusory desert, the traveler can be certain of nothing.

This upland desolation, ravaged by hooded hordes, is the waterless expanse of Sinai for lost peoples—of this century and of many centuries—who wander aimlessly, uprooted by terrible events; it is the eastern Europe of 1921, and also the "Hell or Connaught" of all the vanquished. "Cracks and reforms and bursts in the violet air" of twilight work the ruin of cities: Athens and Alexandria and Vienna and London become as the Cities of the Plain; the terrible simplifiers contend against one another in the Last Days.

Here the landscape is by Bosch or Breughel, and woman's sexuality, sunk into witchcraft, engenders a brood of monsters, "bats with baby faces." The world is turned upside down: voices call from dry cisterns and wells. Threading his way upward through this horror, the Seeker arrives at the Chapel Perilous, dry bones and tumbled graves.

Empty and forgotten the Chapel stands, "the wind's home." Yet the Seeker has arrived at the place where, even now, questions are answered in the moonlight for those who dare to ask in earnest. At a cock's crow from the rooftree, the diabolical powers round about are dispersed for the moment. A damp gust brings rain, and the thunder speaks.

That thunder is the voice of revealed wisdom: it is the Indo-European "DA," a root from which have sprung up many trunks; it is, if you will, the "I am that am" from the Burning Bush. And the thunder of DA utters three sounds that are the answers—sibylline indeed—to the Seeker's questions. They are "datta," "dayadhvam," and "damyata," from the Brihadaranyake-Upanishad. And they signify "give," "sympathize," and "control."

So saith the Lord: give, sympathize, control. But though the Seeker had found courage to carry him to the Chapel Perilous and to ask the dread question, has he resolution and faith sufficient to induce him to obey the thunder? Some rain has fallen; but the sacred river wants a flood; mind and flesh are feeble. For lack of human daring, the Waste Land may remain ghastly dry.

Give? That means surrender—yielding to something outside one's self. If sexual union is to be fertile, there must occur surrender of self in some degree, momentary self-effacement in another. Lust, too true, may produce progeny; but those are the bats with baby faces. Larger even than procreation, giving or surrender means the subordination of the self (as of the arrogant private rationality) to an Authority long derided and neglected. Can modern man humble himself enough to surrender unconditionally to the thunder from on high?

Sympathize? That means love and loyalty, and the diminishing of private claims. We all lie in the prison-house of self-pity; and to recognize the reality of other selves—more, to act upon that reality—must require unusual strength: the virtue of *caritas*. The overweening modern ego has grown fat on the doctrine of self-admiration; the community of souls has been falling apart for some centuries now.

Control? That, as Babbitt had said, is to place restraints upon will and appetite. True control is exerted not through force and a master, but by self-discipline and persuasion of others. But can the strutting will restrain itself by its own act? Can modern appetites, so long unchecked—so long gorged on blood and foulness, as during the War—be confined once more to their proper place? We have indulged the *libido*; now can we return to the other kind of freedom, *voluntas*—to Cicero's ordered and willed freedom? Our desires are insatiable, and the thunder is distant.

So the thunder has answered the questions that were put in the Chapel Perilous. It was painful to seek for those answers; it will be agony to obey. Still the Seeker hesitates, though now the arid plain is behind him. He casts his lines upon the waters. London Bridge is falling down: the outer order of civilization disintegrates. But may not ruins be shored up? And should not a man commence the work of renewal, spiritual and material, by setting his lands in order: by recovering order within his own soul? The world may deride as folly such aspirations; but this is a mad world, my masters. Play Quixote. Give, sympathize, control; and the peace that passes all understanding be upon you.

"This seemed a new voice, revealing ancient things in a new way," Rose Macaulay recollects concerning the mark made at once by *The Waste Land* among other seekers:

> the dark corridors where dreams lurk, where primeval history hides, were furnished with what seemed at times (but was not) a haphazard, inconsequent juxtaposition of images, and with fragments of social dialogue at tea parties, in streets, in pubs, fragments thrown up out of what mysterious context of experience? They drifted by, slipping again into the mist; their echoes disturbed. . . . The known landscape sprang to life: the stony waste, the decayed hole among the mountains, the empty chapel, the wind's home. All this we know by nature, it is our heritage. But it is not left as we leave it; into it break thunder and voices and talk, turning the scene upside down; one has to think, to understand and follow. . . .[17]

Eliot had asked the great questions; and in the Waste Land, here and there, blades of grass had begun to sprout.

["The Inner Waste Land and the Outer," Eliot and His Age: T. S. Eliot's Moral Imagination in the Twentieth Century *(La Salle, IL: Sherwood Sugden & Company, 1984), 73–91.]*

V.

PLACES AND PEOPLE

Reflections of a Gothic Mind ❖ Eigg, in the Hebrides
❖ A House in Mountjoy Square ❖
The Architecture of Servitude and Boredom ❖
Criminal Character and Mercy

When Russell Kirk writes of the places and the people in his life and in his travels, he reveals a deep human sympathy and intuitive reverence that go beyond, and replenish, the intellectual and critical qualities that distinguish his writings as a moral historian and philosopher. No less present in his impressions of the people he meets, and the places in which he happens to be living, or is visiting, is his imaginative power in painting the human scene, wherever it happens to be and in whatever season, clime, or time. He calls up his memories with the powers of a gifted storyteller, and with an abundant love of variety, mystery, tradition—of "immemorial ways, old morals, old customs, old loves, the wisdom of the species, the life of rural regions and little communities," as Kirk expressed it at the end of his life. The things that are especially venerable for him—sights, sounds, houses, associations, relationships, even silences—come to vivid life in his writings in which storytelling, autobiographical reflections, moral contemplations, and social criticism (and reality) are richly integrated.

Faith in the human spirit is renewed by Kirk, and where and when he sees it as being lost, or forgotten, he remains strong in his belief that its recovery is not impossible—his "cheerfulness keeps breaking in," he confesses. But by no means does Kirk romanticize the human condition or overestimate its possibilities. Whether he is writing about places or people his discriminations and judgments hew closely to the stark, hard truths of reality. What he sees and reports—whether about the insidious ways in which modern machine-civilization overwhelms the rural pattern of existence, or the growing decay of urban living, or the risk of ugly architecture, or the problem of human boredom, or human criminality that defies the possibility of rehabilitation—emerges from the depths of both his historical imagination and his moral sense. Gently but firmly, Kirk prods his reader to make the great journey from "the ruins of fallen orders" to the kingdom of the highest things.

Reflections of a Gothic Mind

The following selection, which serves as the introductory part of Kirk's Confessions of a Bohemian Tory *(1963), provides autobiographical insights into his formative experiences and perceptions of the places and the people in his life. Here he paints the scenes of his early life in Michigan; speaks of his Scottish and New England roots; expresses his loyalty to his ancestors for helping him to mold his moral and historical sense. These words from "Reflections of a Gothic Mind" herald his calling as a man of letters who possesses a Gothic rather than an Enlightenment mind: "I did not love cold harmony and perfect regularity of organization; what I sought was variety, mystery, tradition, the venerable, the awful. I despised sophisters and calculators; I was groping for faith, honor, and prescriptive loyalties. I would have given any number of neo-classical pediments for one poor battered gargoyle."*

A connoisseur of slums and strange corners, I have dwelt in more garrets and cellars, forest cabins and island hovels, than I can recall. These random memoirs, vignettes, and meditations are occasional fruits of a frugal and often picturesque solitude.

I have thriven upon a diet of crackers and peanut-butter during nine years of college and university; I have been content with ducks' eggs and goats' milk in the Hebrides. Conversely, I have spent dreamy weeks and months in Italian palaces and in the great country houses of Scotland. Few men, I fancy, have seen more of the extremes of society. Always celibate and generally cheerful, I have known the Skid Rows of Detroit and Los Angeles, the literary circles of London and Madrid, the backwoods from Beaver Island to Morocco. As I write these lines, I am a healthy bohemian, old style, forty-four years in age, with miles to go before I sleep.

A Tory, according to Samuel Johnson, is a man attached to orthodoxy in church and state. A bohemian is a wandering and often impecunious man of letters or arts, indifferent to the demands of bourgeois fad and foible. Such a one has your servant been. Tory and bohemian go not ill together: it is quite possible to abide by the norms of civilized existence, what Mr. T. S. Eliot calls "the permanent things": and yet to set at defiance the soft securities and sham conventionalities of twentieth-century sociability.

If any reader, on picking up this book, has expected to encounter between its covers those adolescent attitudes which certain recent scribblers have substituted for style and wit, he must be disappointed. I offer no true narrations of first encounters with women of easy virtue, nor any history of Freudian obsession. Though I have heard most of the foul words in several tongues, I vex you with none of them. While the bohemian may burn his candle at both ends, he leaves the ungirt loin to the debauché who does not light his lamp at all. The genuine bohemian is too busy, and too much taken with life, to sink into decadence—which is the loss of an object. And if the bohemian is of a Tory cast, he may even abjure license, drunkenness, and dirt. I have enjoyed most of the wines of Latin lands, but—like Hawthorne's Yankee tavern drinkers—have been besotted by none.

These occasional pieces of mine are fragments of autobiography, in part reworked and reprinted from periodicals; observations on men of mark, travel, education, politics, and the spirit of the age, chiefly selected from my newspaper column (called, whatever you may think, "To the Point") and from my page, "From the Academy," in *National Review*: and a congeries (with perhaps a certain subtle coherence) of *pensées* written, often, at the back of the North Wind. If the reader finds in this book any faint echo of Charles Lamb or George Gissing or Robert Louis Stevenson, this writer will be infinitely gratified.

So between these covers you will not find the escapades of Rimbaud, Toulouse-Lautrec, or Van Gogh: Hollywood, anyway, tore those passions to tatters long ago. You will not encounter the perversity of Wilde, nor even the deliquescence (virtuoso of the uncanny though I have aspired to be) that was Poe. These confessions, however erratic, are not neurotic. And any occasional eccentricity, I forewarn you, may be vulpine.

I commence with a brief account of my manner of existence before I became—considerably to my own astonishment—a subject for *Current Biography* and the *Celebrity Register*. Without design or strong exertion, I have fallen into the best of lives, that of the independent men of letters—a dying breed, but one capable still of a shrewd cut or thrust before twilight.

❖

As the chronology of civilization runs in Michigan, the town of Plymouth is old, settled by New Englanders in the 1820s: and the oldest part of that town is the north end, where the grist-mill stood by the little River Rouge, and the forgotten Lutheran graveyard huddles still by the railroad tracks. Near the railway station stands a bungalow, of a scale almost majestic, built in 1913 by my grandfather, Frank Pierce, the leading spirit of the North End, or Lower Town: and here, late in 1918, I was born.

My young father, a railroad engineer, came of a line of Scottish farmers pushed off the land in Michigan by the gasoline-engine revolution that Henry Ford (himself born in this plain to the northwest of Detroit) had set in motion a decade earlier. My Old-Testament second name, Amos, came from the Pierces, my mother's family, New England stock of whom the first, Abraham, had landed at Plymouth in Massachusetts in 1623: of their family before the Atlantic was crossed, the Pierces—like John Adams in this—knew nothing.

Among the clannish Pierces I was reared. What the Adamses had been in a great way, the Pierces had been in a small. A volunteer in King Philip's War, a judge or two, a Revolutionary veteran, a launcher of privateers, an adventurer in the California goldfields, a Civil War colonel, builders of log cabins and clearers of wilderness farms from Massachusetts, through New Hampshire and New York, to the heart of Michigan—such the Pierces had been.

Their Puritanism had mellowed early (Abraham Pierce being brought to trial, in 1625, for indolence on the Sabbath); yet they continued good-naturedly virtuous. Only one case of bastardy, in any branch of the family, had been recorded in the course of three centuries: they had a reputation for openhandedness, though they were unrelenting toward scoundrels: and from the middle of the seventeenth century the heads of the family had been men of some local influence. If, then, the family history—written by the Union colonel, though he lost his right arm at the head of his brigade—scarcely was Gray's "short and simple annals of the poor," still it remained a record of lives obscure enough, and often hard enough, through ten American generations.

The elder Russell Kirk, my father, a man of considerable physical strength, born on a farm, looked back to the old rural tranquillity of brick farmhouses and horses and apple orchards and maple groves from which he was swept away by the tide of industrialism. If he did not lead a life of quiet desperation, still he felt an enduring dissatisfaction with the age of the machine; and from very early years I shared his hostility toward assembly-line civilization. My mother, a tiny, tender, romantic woman endowed with fortitude, read to me Lewis Carroll and Stevenson and Scott and Grimm and the adventures of the noble company of the Table Round, so that my imagination lapped up the fabulous and chivalrous, a mighty prop to health of mind in children. As an immediate practical consequence, the quality of fancy gave me some ascendancy over the other boys of the neighborhood, whose games I devised and whose forces I marshalled. Even today, one can hear in the alleys and the railroad yards of Plymouth, of an evening, the shouts of rival bands at a game of Prisoner's Base, which pastime I dug out of a book: best played in the dark, to the accompaniment of croaking frogs and puffing switch-engines.

In the 1920s, the old Tom Sawyer sort of life still persisted, little altered, among American boys in places like Plymouth. But I shared none of Huckleberry Finn's rebellion against things established. I felt a strong suspicion of change, and a longing for continuity. To lie with my father beneath an oak on the hill above the mill-pond (we lived for a time in the miller's rambling house, with its Greek Revival grace), or to walk with my grandfather in search of fossils and arrowheads upon the terminal moraine four miles north of the town—in such occupations, even when I was too young to criticize my own prejudices, I felt a deep satisfaction, having joined past and present.

Though bookish from the beginning, I never liked school: it took me away from my books, my walks, and my mother and grandfather. Yet the public schools of Plymouth were sound, directed by an old-fashioned superintendent, my grandfather's friend: the old literary and mathematical disciplines were not then much enervated by "instrumentalism" and sociability. I learnt much history and humane literature, and thought my teachers finished scholars, and my schoolfellows a decent lot. Discipline was expected in school: but industrial life, the decay of family, and doctrinaire Deweyism changed all that, even while I was growing up. Throughout much of my life, I have contrived to scurry into the castle just before the portcullis fell. Only a few years after I left grade-school, the temper of students and the tone of public instruction changed for the worse: the radio, the speed of the dawning age, and the fancy-deadening influence of modern technology were making their mark upon the rising generation.

In my education, family mattered more than school. On both paternal and maternal sides, my family remained little diminished by the times as a power for love, teaching, and economic security. Through my father I was endowed with rural uncles and aunts and cousins, a jolly and generous lot, Kirks and Simmonses; over them presided my grandfather John Kirk, a humorous old farmer with tremendous white eyebrows, still much the Scot, though two generations had elapsed since the family left the Lothians. He lived, however, against a background of moribund farms and empty barns sagging to their ruin, of fields surrendered to burdock and milkweed, of sons and nephews turning perforce to Detroit and the factories. Thus the economic unity of the family was dissolving, and the state—though I could not then perceive these things—was covetous of the family's other functions.

My father's folk lived in the south-eastern corner of Michigan. My mother's family lived, most of them, nearly two hundred miles to the north and west, in Mecosta County; and about them stretched, to the horizon and beyond, the stump country—the cut-over lands that the lumbermen of the 'seventies and 'eighties had left desolate behind them. Often I went there in summer; from my earliest recollection of the region, I loved its bleak ridges and its scrubby second-growth woods, its remote lakes and its sand trails, its poverty-racked farmsteads and the silent village of Mecosta itself, shrunk to a tenth of its early population, where no one seemed to stir except on Saturday night, and then only feebly—a village of one great broad street a mile long, white clapboard shops with false fronts scattered along it. The village would have suited Wyoming or Colorado well enough; the country round it, however, belonged peculiarly to the lake states. Glaciated and ravaged, Mecosta County was like the empty land that peers out of the pages of the *Mabinogion*. Here I came to know the world of silence.

On the rise of ground at the western end of the village stand two white houses in the bracketed style, imposing for that stony country. The larger of these, built by my great-great-great-uncle Giles Gilbert, a lumber baron, had passed out of the family's possession long before. The other house, with a stiff angular grace to it, had been built by my great-grandfather, Amos Johnson; and when Giles Gilbert, having swept away the forests of Mecosta, strode westward to denude Oregon, his nephew Amos remained behind, having sent down roots into this poor country. He became village president and county judge, a power in all the affairs of Mecosta: a tall and majestic man with a red beard and brooding eyes. His wife, Estella, was a Russell, from New York; and she lived a great while, so that I knew her for years, and sat at her feet, and she told me of the old forest-days, and the great fires, and Indians now swept away by tuberculosis and fever, and the storms of years forgot by everyone else. There she sat in her high-buttoned black shoes and immaculate old-fashioned dress, a dignified and even haughty little figure; she owned a respectable library, and was fond of Willa Cather's novels; and at nighttime—so I was told in later years—she used to retire to her room to talk with the dead.

Among the Johnsons, though they were men of action—several of my great-grandfather's brothers died by violence—a vein of spirituality was strong. In the remoteness of Mecosta, to which only the more enthusiastic Christian sects then penetrated, this spiritual yearning had been diverted into the Dead Sea of Spiritualism. Once upon a time Mecosta even had a Spiritualist Church, of which the Johnsons had been pillars; and in the tall white house above the town had taken place glimpses into the abyss little short of necromancy. My Gothic imagination, delighted by such reminiscences, detected about the old house a peculiar genius; and the atmosphere of the place was augmented by the fact that nothing had been changed since 1893. The Panic of that year had fallen heavily upon Amos Johnson, breaking the bank he owned, and taking most of his land; and before he could fight his way back, he died. His widow kept the house and its contents unaltered, she and my great-aunts living hospitably in the white house, with its plush sofas and marble-topped tables. For my part, I would not have changed one square inch of the enchanted world of Mecosta. The old house was stuffed with curiosities: my great-grandfather's silver-mounted pistol, carried in the vanished lumber-camps; enormous earrings made of '49 gold; antique toys; glass slippers; a music-box that had been to the Klondike. Over everything brooded an air, by no means oppressive, of faded splendors, vanished lands, and baffled expectations. The vanity of human wishes being writ large at Mecosta, I learnt that lesson early.

At Mecosta my great-grandfather Isaac Pierce, too, had lived, with his wife Caroline—Isaac Pierce the hunter for California gold and Wyoming rancher, later president of Mecosta Village. These great-grandparents had died long before I was born; but their only son, Frank Pierce, had spent his youth in Mecosta, and there married Eva Johnson, a strong-willed and indefatigable woman. Frank Pierce, who had been born in a log cabin in southwestern Michigan, in time left Mecosta, for lack of occupation in that decayed place, and became a man of business in Plymouth; and that accounted for me. Upon me as a child, Frank Pierce exerted more influence than anyone else except my mother, his daughter Marjorie.

Frank Pierce was a small-town banker; but that description gives only a hint of the man. A village Hampden, the champion of the North End in the affairs of Plymouth, adviser to everyone in Lower Town who sought his counsel, a village commissioner, president of the school board, he was a wise man, much-read in books and life; and although he had many admirers, he had no intimates of his own generation, nor did he seem to desire them. Of an evening he sat solitary in his parlor, reading his Dickens or Mark Twain or John Clark Ridpath's *History of the World* (1901); until I came to display some glimmerings of sense, Frank Pierce never expected his tastes to be shared by anyone. Though affable and even witty, he lived principally within himself, and his dignity was respected. He was rather a little man, and rotund; yet he could walk down Mill Street, bare-headed and in his shirt sleeves, and remain dignified. He had a way of lending money out of his private purse, without security or interest, to young people who needed it; and a man who does that does not grow rich.

On our long walks, Mr. Frank Pierce and I talked of the idea of progress, the character of Richard III, the nature of immortality, the significance of dreams, the style of Poe, and why the sea is boiling hot, and whether pigs have wings.

The old gentleman was fearless. His bank in the North End had been essayed three times by bandits: once by a crazy farmer whom my grandfather outwitted, but the second time by two accomplished criminals. (Machine-gun Kelly, serving a life sentence years later, is said to have confessed that this was his job.) This pair kidnapped Mr. Pierce as he walked down Mill Street in the morning, forced him at pistol-point to open the safe, apologized for their rudeness, and marooned him in a barn some miles from town. He never forgave himself for having opened the safe, though presumably he would have been shot if he had refused; and when the next robbers came, he fought them off. Washington, Lincoln, and Theodore Roosevelt were his exemplars: he applauded loudly in a motion-picture which showed their faces, careless of the stares of his neighbors. In his cash-drawer at the bank he kept a heavy revolver, and in the breast pocket of his coat, a tear-gas fountain pen. Thus I was initiated into the violence of Michigan in the 'twenties, and learned how anarchy lies just under the skin of civilization.

By the autumn of 1929, when I was eleven years old, I had begun to read newspapers. I was annoyed at the emphasis the papers gave to the flurry in Wall Street: what I wanted was news of capitals and diplomats. Early the next year, I began to learn my error, as the Great Depression engulfed Kirks and Pierces. Frank Pierce, mercifully, died suddenly at the summit of a good life, before the banks fell to their ruin.

Late in 1932, I heard members of my own family saying, gloomily, "If something isn't done, there'll be a revolution." At the age of fourteen, being a complete Jeffersonian, I was puzzled as to how there might be a democratic insurrection against a government chosen by universal suffrage. None of the people who talked of revolution had any intention of participating in rebellion, nor did they desire it: they simply were dismayed at the deflation of the American economy, the collapse of which my grandfather had thought to be imminent, though nearly everyone else, worshipping Progress, had been confident that American industrialism would swagger on without impediment. What seemed more dangerous, even then, to me, was talk of the need for a Strong Man to sweep away the stupid politicians who, it was fashionable to say, were responsible for the Depression. A few years later, I observed that some of the people who in 1932 had been insistent upon the necessity for a Strong Man were become most zealous advocates of "economic democracy"; and I came to reflect upon the possibility that democracy might assume a despotic form, as against the old Jeffersonian Republic, and upon the fact that some people, loving change for its own sake, can embrace Communism or Fascism with equal ardor, according to the slogans of the hour. A sinister book appeared, made into a sinister motion-picture: *Gabriel Over the White House* (1933). Accepting the journalists' denunciations of Mr. Hoover at face value, I thought that Mr. Hoover ought to go; but I perceived that it would be better to make Mr. Hoover president for life than to surrender the Republic to some ruthless *protégé* of Gabriel.

The Depression sat lightly enough upon me; after all, there was plenty to eat in the house, and my only diversions were reading and walking, which cost nothing. A time came when my mother (who was in the habit of tucking the family's cash among the pages of books, after the Bank Moratorium swept away bank accounts) drew out one twenty-dollar bill from Kipling's *The Light That Failed* (1891) and said that only this stood between us and want. Twenty dollars, however, seemed riches to a boy; and, besides, I was certain that the economy, already at nadir, soon would begin to creak upward. I now detested President Roosevelt as cordially as I had rejoiced in his election, for I took it that he would cheerfully sweep away the whole of the Constitution, if he found it would make him popular. Besides, I now had become a sworn adherent to the doctrines of Manchester. But the opinions of a boy of fourteen are worth no more than a passing observation. The plaster fell from the ceilings of our house; an apathy descended upon most of us; yet the Kirks and the Pierces made their way through the Depression and the Roosevelt Recession with family unity unimpaired, even keeping up an undismayed jollity, at the Fourth of July and Hallowe'en and Christmas and New Year's Day.

These were my high-school years. Like my grandfather before me, I had companions, but few friends. Being full of high-flying romantic ideals, I adored my Dulcineas del Toboso principally from afar, doubtless to the preservation of my Quixotic principles and the improvement of my studies. The current "social activities" of young people bored me. I thought the music at dances hideous and modern ballroom dancing a perversion of an ancient art. I disliked speed and automobiles. Thus left to my own devices, I came into young manhood with leisure enough to reflect upon the larger meanings of existence. I read Gibbon and Macaulay and Prescott, and all the novelists. I read H. G. Wells, resolving to refute him one day. When I was sixteen, an essay of mine was published in a magazine; but, having no high opinion of my deserts, I felt that I would be satisfied with fortune if I could contrive somehow to creep through life with a bowl of bread and milk a day, and time enough to read—as Lucy Ashton sang, in my favorite romance,

Vacant heart, and hand, and eye
Easy live and quiet die.

I explored the north woods of Michigan, and picked fruit or berries in the summers for pocket money, and was well taught at the high school.

Also, I became a perfect mechanist and atheist. No member of my family had been baptized since time out of mind, nor did any of them go to church. Theirs was not the irreligion of the proletariat, but rather a piety divorced from institutional Christianity, Quaker-like in its reliance upon the dictates of conscience and private judgment. They encouraged my little sister and me to attend Sunday School; but, having made the attempt at the nearest evangelical chapel, I considered this well-meaning atmosphere (to my supercilious young mind) to be deficient in taste, imagination, and learning; I took it to be a microcosm of all religion; and I would have none of it. The Bible, indeed, I had been taught by my mother from early years, and the family, shrugging tolerantly, presumed this would suffice. In point of fact, the Kirks' and Pierces' piety, being the residue of a distant institutional Christianity, needs must trickle away, once separated from its springs, becoming feebler as generation succeeded generation; Abraham Pierce's indolence on the Sabbath had pointed the way. Yet, until my parents' generation, they had no doubt of an Omniscience governing this world, or of a morality ordained by that Power, or of an immortality that was His gift. It remained for me, as a boy, to carry dissent to its logical conclusion—denial even of these premises. Thinking I understood "science" (of which, like most mechanists of our time, I had only the barest smattering), I was convinced that I understood life and death and the infinite, and that they were trifles. Though not much heartened by these conclusions, I clung to them, upholding atheism against grandmother and great-aunts with a Scottish or Puritanical tendentiousness. The family, difficult to shock, predicted that I would shed these notions as I grew older; I hotly denied the possibility; nevertheless, as the years passed, by the grace of God I came to do precisely what they had said I would do.

What would become of this boy? My family had little idea, and I had none. By 1936, employment was nearly as difficult to find as it had been in 1930; and I, about to be graduated from high school, expected only to walk in the obscure ways of life, as Burke had said most men must, and to try to be content with my lot. Chance, or one of those curious combinations of small causes which we call chance, took a hand here: a kindly high-school principal suggested that I apply for a scholarship at the State College. For lack of anything better to seek, apply I did; my application was successful, rather to my astonishment. Off to the College that autumn I went, leaving home reluctantly; and, with no tuition to pay, and perhaps two hundred dollars to last me through the nine-months' session, I settled in a rooming house and began to marvel at that Leviathan called a State College.

The principal end of a state educational system—whether all of its admirers confess this truth or not—always has been to impose a uniform character upon the rising generation, rendering young people obedient to the state from habit and prejudice, even when the state has dissolved the ancient loyalties that bound man to man. With this aim, in its higher reaches, at the State College, were mingled the utilitarian object of imparting technical skills and an impulse toward worldly advancement. Toward these several aims, I felt hostile. Devoted to the old literary disciplines, I found myself at an institution where humane learning was barely tolerated, as a kind of superficial adornment to society; and the administrators of the place probably felt some dim animosity toward liberal education, suspecting that the classical disciplines teach a man to form his own opinions and to respect those of dead generations—while what the masters of a state educational system desire is the inculcation of conformity to present state policy, "group awareness," not independent or traditional judgment. I was grateful, nevertheless, to the alumni of the College for sending me there to be schooled; and, on the whole, my four years in the dull and tidy town of East Lansing passed pleasantly enough. The place was then conservative in the sense that Bagehot describes the middle classes of France as conservative: utterly satisfied with its own nature, and fearful of any change which might endanger material possessions. During my first college year, the great sit-down strikes occurred in the automobile factories of Michigan, and a desultory fight was waged in the road leading to the College, between union zealots marching on the place from Lansing and students (most of them from small towns and farms) who detested unionism; the students won, tossing their adversaries in the little river that flows through the campus. Unlike most students in the great city universities or the Eastern colleges during the 'thirties, then, I found myself (though a Tory, or at least an Old Whig, by instinct) almost an advanced thinker in the midst of folk convinced that whatever is, is right.

As David Hume took pleasure in living upon sixpence a day, so I wrapped my poverty about me like a cloak, ate peanut-butter and crackers with relish in my rooms, delighted in every privation, violated the American tradition of Working Your Way Through College, and was the Gissing of East Lansing. I found it much easier to contract my wants than to expend time as a base mechanical; thus I contrived to read extensively in fields my proper studies never touched upon—old books of travel, forgotten corners of belles-lettres, African history, Samuel Johnson's essays. *Simplicitas* and *frugalitas*, I found, were the virtues dearest to my heart. Having discovered Epictetus and Seneca and Marcus Aurelius, I turned Stoic, feeling infinitely elevated above my old mechanistic metaphysics. I was even able to buy books—Aristotle and Polybius for instance, and a set of Conrad—and in my third year, I made friends. There were then six thousand students at the College—about five thousand, five hundred too many for true education, though this host has quintupled since my student days—and among them I found a half dozen young men of a sort I had not known before, hearty and sensible, fond of good talk and much coffee, football players and dilettantes and readers of good books, and a sentimental Communist. What mattered more to me in the long run, I made friends among the professors; for state educational systems have not yet contrived any wholly efficient method for extirpating individuality and traditional character from the ranks of their servants. Professors of history and of literature were kind to me; some of them I came to know intimately; and one of them encouraged me in my writing, until presently I surprised myself by being published in the sober quarterlies—high-flying essays on tragedy and republican virtue.

But now the prospect of being made a bachelor of arts was hard upon me: and what then? The degree-snobbery of twentieth-century America seemed to dictate that I must be something more than a bachelor, if I wished to live a life that would not be quiet desperation; so I looked for university fellowships; and Duke University, in North Carolina, gave me one. I came thus to know the South, which had captured my imagination years before, in books; and what remained to be seen of the Old South, I saw, then or in my army years: Richmond and Charleston and Savannah, cities that had not yet surrendered incontinent to the new order of American life: and quiet corners like Petersburg, in Virginia, and Hillsborough, in North Carolina, and Fernandina Island, in Florida. I wandered through the Negro slums of New Orleans and the Cracker shanties beside the Florida swamps. Here was a conservative society struck a fearful blow eighty years before, and still dazed: decrepit though it was, I liked it better than the life of certain northern cities I knew. I confronted the fact of the Negro in America, too, reflecting that the most important "problems" of human existence never are solved, unless by letting Providence work. I read of the old planter life, and poked into its ashes; and presently I wrote a dissertation about the politics of John Randolph of Roanoke, the most interesting man in American history, and the most neglected. Years later, this was published as a little book, more praised than it deserved to be.

The eccentric genius of the planter-orator helped to form my mind and style; and about the same time, I began to apprehend a greater thinker and statesman, who remained thereafter my guide in much: Edmund Burke. The fire of his *Reflections* (1790) did for me what it had done for Randolph and for so many others—even for my old Gibbon: it converted prejudice into principle, and a confused love of the past into an apprehension of the wisdom of our ancestors. But even as I began to know the genius of Burke, the fountains of the great deep broke up: the conflagration of fanatic nationalism and voracious appetite, which for the preceding two years had been consuming the remnant of the traditional order in Europe, now licked at the United States. By the day of Pearl Harbor, I was twenty-two years old, a master of arts, and the spectator of a prospect more terrible even than that which Burke had contemplated.

For some months I marked time in the sprawling Rouge plant of the Ford Motor Company, where modern mass-production had achieved its first triumph. I had worked for Mr. Henry Ford earlier, during my summers, and knew the great industrialist to talk with, and thought I understood him well enough, that tall old man who had swept away nearly every vestige of the rural society of Wayne County in which he had his own roots, and now wandered restlessly amid the evidences of his own irrevocable revolution, trying to save within the high brick walls of his museum in Dearborn some scraps of the old simplicities. In a lodging-house in Dearborn I sank rapidly into an apathy which the modern industrial system induces, sleeping long, ignoring the future, reading nothing but Charles Lamb in the course of six months, and filled with a sense of the disjointedness of the time. From this condition the United States Army rescued me in the summer of 1942, so that presently I found myself a sergeant in the Chemical Warfare Service.

Of my four years in the army, I spent three in the heart of the Great Salt Lake Desert, surely one of the most desolate and most healthful spots in all the world; so while millions of men were slaughtering one another upon the Ukrainian steppes or in the Papuan jungles, I lay enchanted, like Merlin in the oak, in a desert so long dead that it seemed nothing was allowed to die there any longer. Now and then I was blistered with mustard gas, or choked with phosgene, by some small mishap; but these diversions aside, the Great Salt Lake Desert (once the initial shock of its emptiness was forgot) became a wholesome place for body and soul. Away out at Granite Peak, true, in the midst of the salt flats, we were experimenting with "biological warfare"; and at another spot in our Gehenna, we were building replicas of German and Japanese apartment-houses and then burning them down with incendiary bombs; but we committed our atrocities in the abstract, as if they were childish games. So long as our post remained small in numbers, it kept a certain homeliness, we being kind to one another, out of a common pity; but before long the American lust for aggrandizement was set to work, and we crowded a thousand men into our barracks, as if we were trying to copy Dachau, keeping them busy at occupations rather like taking in one another's laundry.

Great dunes surrounded our camp; when I had leisure, which was most of the time, I sat upon the sand reading *Hamlet,* or Ibsen, or Sophocles, in order not to mar the scenery. That strange mountain, the Camel's Back, stared down at me: it was a thing drowned and then washed up from the ocean of time, for on its sides were the successive bench-marks made by waves of seas that dried a million years ago. If I sank into sleep—an easy thing to do in the sun, for the nearest tree, a scrubby juniper, was miles distant—the little lizards slid across my face. One looked across the salt and alkali, where nothing at all lived, into Nevada on the horizon. This was a region almost devoid of human history: a few naked Gosiutes had lurked on its fringes, a hundred years gone, and Jed Smith had staggered across it once, and now a few shepherds occasionally made their way round it; that was all. The Great Salt Lake Desert was barren beyond belief, but not, I think, God-forsaken.

Here it was that I commenced, very languidly, to move from my Stoicism toward something more. It was not toward pantheism that I moved, for the rattlesnake, the lizard, the gray sagebrush, and the bitter juniper-berry do not inspire Wordsworth's love of divine handiwork. Yet the consciousness of a brooding Presence stirred in me something of the desert prophet whose name I bore—rather, as Chesterton says in another context, like rousing "a great wild forest passion in a little Cockney heart." The desert knew no benevolence; it was terrible; but awe and veneration being close allied, truly the fear of God is the beginning of wisdom. Something made me inquire within myself by what authority I presumed to doubt—though I had not yet read Newman's observation that it is better to believe all things than to doubt all things. Upon authority all revealed religion rests; and the authority which lies behind Christian doctrine is massive. By what alternative authority did I question it? Why, chiefly upon the promptings of people like H. G. Wells and Leonard Woolf, with whose other opinions I did not agree in the least. Why should I prefer their negations to the affirmations of men whose precepts I took for gospel: the principles of Johnson and Burke, of Coleridge and More? If their minds gave credence to revealed religion, must not I, in mere toleration, open my mind to the possibility of its truth? So, by slow degrees, the heart is moved; and if I was now scarcely better than a skeptic, still that was a far cry from the positivism of my 'teens. In the Great Salt Lake Desert—whether or not the awfulness of the place worked some change in me—I began to perceive that pure reason has its frontiers, and that to deny realms beyond them is puerility. Yet even within the realm of reason, once disbelief in a supernatural order is suspended, evidences of every sort begin to pour in—evidences drawn from the natural sciences, from psychology, from history, from physics—demonstrating that we are part of some grand and mysterious scheme, which works upon us through Providence. This granted, one must turn for elucidation of those mysteries to a different science, theology; and then—but I got no further than this, in the desert. Knowledge of this sort comes through illation; it is borne in upon the mind, in hints and fragments, not systematically; and my illative sense began to stir in the stony shadow of the Camel's Back.

If I came some way toward an apprehension of Divine nature, there upon the dunes that were the beaches of a forgotten sea, I moved further toward a proper understanding of my own nature. I had told myself, ever since I had begun to think about such matters, that I admired the intellect of the Enlightenment of the seventeenth and eighteenth centuries; and now I came to realize that this was false. Those were splendid centuries, but I did not in truth sympathize with the currents of thought and feeling in those ages; what I respected in the Enlightenment was the men who stood against the whole tendency of their epoch, men like Johnson and Burke.

Mine was not an Enlightened mind, I now was aware: it was a Gothic mind, medieval in its temper and structure. I did not love cold harmony and perfect regularity of organization; what I sought was variety, mystery, tradition, the venerable, the awful. I despised sophisters and calculators; I was groping for faith, honor, and prescriptive loyalties. I would have given any number of neo-classical pediments for one poor battered gargoyle. The men of the Enlightenment had cold hearts and smug heads; now their successors were in the process of imposing a dreary conformity upon all the world, with Efficiency and Progress and Equality for their watchwords—abstractions preferred to all those fascinating and lovable peculiarities of human nature and human society which are the products of prescription and tradition. This desert of salt would be a cheerful place by comparison with the desolation of the human heart, if the remains of Gothic faith and Gothic variety should be crushed out of civilization.

While I stared across the desert, the greatest of all wars passed me by; I scarcely had heard a voice raised in anger. Like Sinbad transported by his roc, I was discharged as impersonally and insignificantly as I had been conscripted, and found myself back in Plymouth and Mecosta, cognizant of a good deal more about my fellow-men, something more about myself, and a little about Omniscience, but otherwise unaltered. Where should I turn now? I still lacked any discernible bent or purpose; with some trepidation, I thought of entering the foreign service; then, to my surprise, I was offered a post as instructor in the history of civilization at my old State College. Though flattered to be mentioned in the same breath with Guizot and Buckle, I seriously doubted my competence to undertake anything of that nature; but the State College, growing mushroomlike, was almost as eager for more professors as it was for more students; so, taking the College's shilling, I steeled myself to play a Cyclops leading the blind. I might succeed in teaching myself something, in any event; and being then twenty-eight years old, I thought I had best make some such endeavor.

The higher learning in America is fallen upon evil days. In part, this is the fault of the students: most of them come for entertainment, or for some fancied enhancement of their social status, or for Mammon; and they come in such great numbers that it is almost impossible for the remnant who are interested in the higher learning to accomplish anything; besides, the majority resent the presence of the minority who read books, and so the majority do their worst to compel the application of Gresham's Law to matters of the mind.

In part, this is the fault of the administration of the colleges and universities. For many of these men, mere aggrandizement, in enrollments and buildings and course-catalogs and football victories, is the chief end of universities. They have not read Newman, nor anyone else worth reading, and do not intend to. They pander to the silliest impulses in state legislatures and associations of alumni, and endeavor to stir up interest in costly and useless "educational" fripperies when even legislatures and alumni-associations have no taste for them. They would establish colleges of necromancy if they thought anyone would enroll. Next to aggrandizement, they love incessant change, laboring to destroy that continuity of purpose and accumulation of knowledge and method which have been the mark of the great universities of the past.

Most of all, perhaps, the professors are at fault. Having become proletarians, they think as proletarians. In all American society, which generally is mobile to the point of nausea, the professors are the most thoroughly rootless class. Their families, if they have any, are mere households; they own almost no property; they move from one college to another as if they were gypsies; they live only in the present, and talk chiefly of petty promotions and increases of pay; they are bullied by educationists of John Dewey's school who verge on feeble-mindedness, and can be duped by such people more easily than any simple savage. They are indolent, many of them, and envious. Some, declining to profess anything, believe only in negations, and lack the intellectual power of the old-fashioned dominie.

Among them, nevertheless, endure a good many scholars of liberal minds and loyal hearts, resolute amid the shadows of the Petrified Forest of Academe: and for the sake of this Remnant, the class of professors is worth saving. As a body, moreover, they and the clergy (what Coleridge called the Clerisy) are the bearers of the Word; and civilization could not endure without them, nor the higher order of religion.

Because I had happened to be sent to college, and because I had been made a professor myself, I was burdened with a purpose at last. It seemed that I was meant to labor for a time in this vineyard, whether or not I cared for the place: the hand of Providence may have been in the business. I liked farmers better than professors; I even preferred the company of men of business, or sometimes the inhabitants of the slums which I had come to know in the course of my vagrant existence; but perhaps my mission was to the classes, rather than to the masses, and that particular class among whom I was meant to do my best seemed to be the body of professors. And here and there were good and learned men whose approbation made the labor seem worthwhile. For long periods of time, I might seem to be sowing the salt sea; yet every now and then I would hear a voice, or receive a letter, that told me a conscience had spoken to a conscience. Professors and priests are meant to be the conservators of mankind, to which end they are set among men, reminding us that we are not the flies of a summer. Their labor is to tell men that certain truths endure, that upon human nature a peculiar character has been stamped by the Creator with which we tamper at our peril, and that the complex of ideas and methods which we call civilization cannot subsist without moral sanctions. Priest and professor are meant to show men the mysterious coherence and continuity which binds all things in their places.

I resolved to do what I could, in my feeble way, to restore this sense of their conservative function among professors. I wrote; and nearly a hundred of my articles were printed; and the object of all my writings was the conservation of the moral and social heritage of the ages. I taught; and there were some students who would listen. In the end, the educationists and the utilitarians and the charlatans were more than I could bear with, and, recollecting the precept of Archilochus, I beat a retreat that I might fight another day. Two years after I had left the profession, I published a book, *Academic Freedom* (1955) which dealt with these matters; and, to my surprise, it made its influence felt.

While I still was one of the class of professors, I had written other books. I had made up my mind to write a book in memory of the principal conservative thinkers of America and Britain, so that their ideas might help us professors in our sad hour. I thought, too, that the book might be of some interest to another class of persons whose talents are much atrophied in our time, yet whose potentialities for good or evil are vast: journalists. And despite the decline of the Common Reader and the old middle-class public that bought books, there might be found some others who would look into this projected volume.

To write that book—which I came to call *The Conservative Mind* (1953)—I went to Scotland. My Scottish name, my discipleship to Sir Walter, and the quality of *frugalitas* all drew me there; besides, half the book was to be concerned with the ideas of Englishmen and Scots. Thus I settled at the ghostly ancient gray town of St. Andrews, which I loved as better men before me had; and, as Dr. Johnson had said, St. Andrews was eminently suitable for studies. The little, dignified, medieval university of St. Andrews made me a doctor of letters, and after I had returned to Michigan I wrote another book, about St. Andrews town and St. Andrews University, with bishops and chancellors and wraiths and men of blood. The past walks in the thick St. Andrews fog: for a man with a Gothic mind, few places on earth could have done more to quicken the imagination.

In Scotland and England I found, as Hawthorne had found a hundred years before, the metaphysical principle of continuity given visible reality. British society and the face of Britain were for me the expression (as they had been the inspiration) of Burke's principles of social immortality and of social reform: the past ever blending with the present, so that the fabric continually renews itself, like some great oak, being never either wholly old or wholly young. But I perceived that this whole elaborate structure of sentiment and social organization was in great danger from Benthamism, Marxism, and all the forces of consolidation and uniformity which threaten to crush mankind into one iron mold, reckless of human individuality—in this, defying the biological truth that the strongest impulse of all living things, stronger than the fear of death or the instinct for reproduction, is the preservation of distinctive individuality. And I perceived that all Britain was living upon capital, moral and physical capital: the rising rate of crime and the falling rate of energy were evidence enough.

But these were good years for me. I was abroad much of the time between 1948 and 1955; I came to know the Low Countries, and walked through Switzerland and Styria, and slept in the slums of Dublin, and sat hours and days in the piazzas of the Italian cities, and visited the last of the Caetani in their Prosperpine's Garden at the dead town of Ninfa. So far as it still could be done, I did what Belloc had done half a century before me, learning history by seeing the things and the men. I sat with blind old Wyndham Lewis in his studio at Notting Hill Gate, "Rotting Hill"; with T. S. Eliot, at the Garrick Club, I talked of the sunk condition of the universe; Roy Campbell and I drank our beer in pubs full of Irish laborers; high in the ancient decayed tenement of James's Court, below Edinburgh Castle, I munched pickled walnuts with George Scott-Moncrieff where David Hume had eaten his porridge. I knew the little Kingdom of Fife best of all, with its great houses—Kellie Castle, built by Fenton after he dirked the Earl of Gowrie on the stairs of Gowrie House; Balcarres, with its magnificent library of early books, its Italian primitives, and its rolling park; Durie, where ghosts walk in the garden. Here the unbought grace of life, despite a multitude of burdens, lives still.

My tall book *The Conservative Mind* was published; it was received with courtesy and understanding, in most quarters, and was read by more people than my publisher or I had expected, and went into many printings and foreign editions. I followed it with another book, *A Program for Conservatives* (1954), which also made its way in the world, although it seemed to bewilder a good many people; for the program I commended was not a neat system of positive law, but a change of heart, by which order and justice and freedom may find some chance of survival in these dark days. Somehow I found myself a leader of an intellectual movement, without having intended to be anything of the sort.

For the past decade, in consequence, I have spoken in nearly every state of the Union—sometimes a hundred and fifty lectures in a year; and I have spent much time in international conferences in Britain, Belgium, Switzerland, Spain, Italy, and remoter places. Sketches and little essays . . . are fragments of these hurrying years. In 1962, I found myself writing a daily newspaper column, "To the Point," which mysteriously found several million readers. By way of diversion, I published a Gothic romance and a collection of my short stories, too. And from time to time, succumbing to academic inclinations, I have been research professor of politics, or visiting professor of American studies, or some other sort of academic grandee, at universities and colleges on either coast.

But I am best content when planting little trees at Mecosta. To plant a tree, in our age when the expectation of change commonly seems greater than the expectation of continuity, is an act of faith. Also it is an act of historical penance, restoring the fairness of the land. At Mecosta, where the heron flaps over the swamp and the beaver splashes in his pond, community and a sense of continuity are not dead. In the corrida, the bull, after every charge, returns to a certain stamping-ground he has made for himself, as if to renew his strength. So it ought to be with bohemians, and especially those of a Tory cast. According to John Henry Newman, Toryism is loyalty to persons. I venture to add that also it is loyalty to places. In fancy, I can see myself settled in a strange old house in the windy Orkneys, or established in some little palazzo near the cathedral of Orvieto, above the Umbrian plain. But only in fancy: for, no matter how far a man strays, it is well that his home should remain a place where his ancestors lie buried. In the phrase of Burke, we learn to love the little platoon we belong to in society. . . .

Publishing a book of episodes and reflections, nowadays, is almost as impractical a venture as it has become to cast a slim volume of verses into the cauldron of modern taste. Yet possibly some readers may find in these vagrant pages an occasional amusement—or even hear, at rare intervals, the faint whisper of a conscience to a conscience.

["Reflections of a Gothic Mind," Confessions of a Bohemian Tory: Episodes and Reflections of a Vagrant Career *(New York: Fleet Publishing Corporation, 1963), 3–30.]*

Eigg, in the Hebrides

Kirk is an evocator of spirit of place. Poetry of feeling and expression characterizes his impressions of Eigg, chief among the Isles of the Hebrides, with its dwindling number of inhabitants, half of them crofters. These crofters lived in the highlands and islands of Scotland and owned five or six acres of arable land attached to a house and with rights of pasturage. Kirk mourns the growing extinction of the peasants' rustic way of life, of which Eigg is "the last of an old song," as he traces the legendary history of the island back to the missionary Saint Donan, who was martyred in 618. His depiction of the cruel devolution of an older order and rural tradition is at times heartrending. Nostalgic for the simple tastes and agrarian character of Eigg's "heirs of the old clansfolk," this lyrical essay also is completely realistic in discerning the rising menace of machine-civilization.

When you come to the silver sands below the straggling village of Arisaig, near the tip of the remote and empty peninsula of Morar in the Scottish Highlands, a sharp black peak rises to the west, seven miles out at sea. This grim sickle-like pinnacle is the Sgurr of Eigg. In Eigg, chief among the Small Isles of the Hebrides, still live a hundred people, half of them crofters—a fast-diminishing remnant of the old island peasantry. Gaelic-speaking crofters have inhabited Eigg these thousand years and more. But if society continues to drift along the course it has been following in recent decades, the crofters will not last out our century.

Only five miles long, from the crag at its northern extremity to the little harbor on its southern shore, this Isle of Eigg, and less than half as wide. Early in the eighteenth century, more than five hundred persons, mostly MacDonalds of Clanranald, managed to exist upon their fertile plots in the shelter of the precipices; but the disastrous results of the Jacobite uprising of 1745, the extinction of the old clan life and of the chiefs of Clanranald themselves, and the "clearances" which for a century swept off the population of the Highlands and islands—these things nearly destroyed the Gaelic-speaking, Catholic peasantry of Eigg. In some of the islands, not only the old society but the entire population was obliterated. Eigg, more fortunate or more hardy, escaped the worst, and in the sprinkling of old white cottages called Cleadale, with a cataract-streaked wall of rock at their back and the Sound of Rum booming at their feet, the crofters kept body and soul together until the Crofting Acts of the 1880s guaranteed their tenure and partially checked the ruin of their simple economy. They are in Cleadale still. Seventeen crofts or cottage-plots of arable land, generally comprising five to seven acres each, were laid out in 1810; they all still remain in a legal sense, but only eight are cultivated now, although most of the cottages are inhabited. Once another community of such peasant proprietors existed on the western shore, but the fifteen families there were expelled by the farmer of Laig, the greater of the two farms in Eigg, and they migrated to America in the 1850s.

For the rest, the present population of Eigg consists of the factor and his family; the farm tenants and their servants (distinct from the independent crofters) at the two farms; the servants about the lodge of the island's English laird Lord Runciman; the Catholic priest, who cultivates his own croft; the Church of Scotland missionary, Mr. Macaskill, who keeps goats in the garden of his eerie manse; the doctor, who drives a jeep; the schoolteacher to seventeen children; Ann and Angie, the pretty twin sisters who keep the cooperative store; and George Scott-Moncrieff, the Scottish writer, whose children scramble barefoot up the scowling cliffs. In July and August some cash income straggles in from the summer visitors, nearly a hundred all told, who put up at the manse or one of the farms (there being no hotel or even tavern) or are guests at the lodge or in the cottages. The animal population consists of one pink pig, a few of those noisy oceanic birds called shearwaters, the missionary's half-dozen goats, some horses, a herd of wild-eyed Highland cattle and an equal number of their more familiar cousins, several hundred sheep, and one million rabbits. The rabbits are shot incessantly for supper and systematically trapped for sale on the mainland; but they continue to multiply, although a frightening species of tapeworm is beginning to provide a check upon their numbers.

A vegetable menace is more formidable than the rabbit-plague: bracken. This tall weed—higher than a man's head, where it grows unchecked—encroaches on land which formerly was grazing-range for cattle. Cattle can eat bracken in small quantities, and keep it down; but when cattle are replaced by sheep, the bracken spreads rapidly along the slopes, exterminating the heather and grasses and so destroying the pasturage, for sheep refuse to touch it. Throughout the Highlands and islands, the sheep are pushed farther and farther down the glens as bracken spreads; and cattle cannot be reintroduced to check the weed, because large amounts of it are poisonous to them. If cut, the indomitable thickets grow up once more in no time. Only one method of attack destroys this plant: pulling. But effective pulling requires a great many hands, and the glens of the mainland and the five hundred islands of the Hebrides, once so densely populated, can no longer muster enough men to keep weeds at bay. In Eigg, the green bracken engulfs the sheepwalks, forms jungles along the beds of streams, and creeps avariciously towards the little crofts. By the end of this century, it may have conquered the land all the way down to the tide.

A rutted track, almost always muddy from the showers of the misty Western Isles, twists sharply up from the little old harbor (where the Clanranald pier still can be seen) past the manse and the Church of Scotland and the school and the shop and the cottage-post office, and follows a ridge until it descends dramatically into Cleadale and dwindles away somewhere along the cliff-flank to the north. Except for a couple of farm trucks and the doctor's jeep and a cart or two, it bears only foot traffic. At its highest point, where the wind usually tears at your hat, a curious stone is set on end: they tell you this marks the spot where coffins were rested, in forgotten years, when people carried their dead to the weed-grown graveyard on the braes back of Kildonan, but probably it is commemorative only of one such funeral-march, the burial of a priest about 1870.

Resting by that stone, you look across the desolate beauty of this high, lonely, somnolent island to the rough sea which separates it from the deserted and broken coast of the mainland, with the great peaks of the western Highlands, Ben Nevis among them, crowding one another back of Morar and Knoidart. You glimpse the tiles of the low-pitched roof at Kildonan farmhouse, down a sort of glen, and perhaps make out the whitewashed walls of a cottage or two, built, like all Hebridean cottages, of rubble. Not much thatch remains in Eigg, for the "black houses" of the islands, low huts of loose stones without chimney or regular window, are disused or converted into byres in Eigg, although you may still see men and women living in them (comfortably enough, after all) in South Uist or Barra or some other of the Outer Isles.

But in many ways Eigg is the last of an old song. Planes now make regular flights to the Outer Isles, steamers call beyond the Minch several times a week, even buses are in use out there, and tourists patronize the hotels at Castlebay and Lochboisdale and Stornoway; yet Eigg, so much closer to the mainland, is a placid backwater, with only the tin roofs of its houses to distinguish it, in the eye of a man climbing the Sgurr, from an eighteenth-century community.

Water runs everywhere in Eigg. From the cliffs upon which the shearwaters nest, a half-dozen waterfalls break perpetually, converted into white torrents after a rain. The summer of 1949 was considered one of the driest seasons Scotland ever endured, but every day of August rain came to Eigg, usually all day. Towards the end of the month the rain slackened, but a mist like cotton candy descended massively, as if lowered from heaven, and settled at a point some fifty feet above the valley floor, ringing the cliffs. Cleadale was imprisoned, the air perfectly clear and everything visible down at ground level, but that immense blanket suspended just above, shutting out the world for a week. At night the shearwaters, circling from the precipices, screamed like devils from above the barrier.

All August fires burned on the hearths or in the primitive iron stoves of Eigg; at the damp manse, on its wind-tormented knoll, the missionary piled turfs on the fire in the parlor for his guests, going out every two hours for more fuel (peat, of some quality, can be got for the digging almost everywhere in the islands). The missionary and his family rattle about in the deserted rooms of this vast empty house and so confine themselves chiefly to the long kitchen. When Samuel Johnson was in the Isles, the minister of the Kirk lived here, to tend his cure of souls in the Parish of the Small Isles, but in Eigg itself he had not a single parishioner: the natives were all Roman Catholics.

They are Catholic still, half of them; the others, chiefly of later stock brought into the island by the proprietors and the farmers, are communicants of the Kirk. The Reformation never came effectively to Eigg, nor, until the wireless and the penny press forced their way in during the last generation, did any other great innovation, not even the English tongue. Priest and missionary still preach one sermon in English and another in Gaelic. But the Gaelic is withering, says Mr. Macaskill, old words being forgotten and modern English terms penetrating to occupy a void which an ancient and static language, almost without a literature, cannot fill. The people of Eigg speak to you in a careful and correct modern English, the English of the state schools, a world away from the Lowland Scots. Among themselves they use Gaelic regularly, but they read the English press, they hear the British Broadcasting Company. All the same, decay of the old tongue and the old ways is retarded in Eigg by the absence of the cinema and of much communication with modernity. To reach even the little mainland port of Mallaig is inconvenient and expensive; to buy a ticket on the West Highland railway, the only public transportation to the rest of the world, is beyond the means of most folk in Eigg except on extraordinary occasions.

The islanders of Eigg are poor; but they are comfortable, and probably they are better off, materially, than they have previously been in all history. Few are left to share the land, for one thing; but let the process of depopulation be carried a little further, as it has been in many of the islands, and the result will be very different. Now, however, their cottages are sound and tidy, their work is not exhausting, and they dine as well, certainly, as most British people. Chickens and ducks, on many crofts a cow, a good-sized garden, watercress from the brook, rabbits easily shot, and fish from the Sound of Rum—these supply a healthy diet for most of the crofters. Meat has to be ordered especially from a butcher in Mallaig, and bread, too, comes from there. During the late war, when they were virtually cut off from civilization, the people of Eigg managed to exist on such Hebridean provender as whelks gathered on the tidal rocks and a species of pudding made from seaweed. The cottages seldom need repair, rough clothing is all anyone really requires, and there is nowhere to buy a drink—the people at the lodge, and the priest, possibly have the only whisky in the island. Incidentally, Eigg has no policeman.

Cash, however, is as hard to come by as a subsistence is easy to get. The income of one of the poorer sharecroppers of Georgia would greatly exceed the currency that these families see from one year's end to another. Though the farmers do well enough by raising cattle for export, the crofter has almost nothing but what he makes from occasional lobster-fishing, from small services to the summer visitors, or some other modest windfall. The fisheries upon which the Outer Isles depended never were an important element in the economy of agricultural Eigg, which is just as well, because the decay of the herring fisheries has ruined places like Barra.

The islanders do not seem to miss money very much. One elderly but muscular crofter, who smiles eternally, came into a tiny competence when he was young. He at once retired, to spend his years fishing and resting, until very recently, when he married; and now he has to work for his family. But he assumes the new burden without complaint. Englishmen and many Lowlanders say the crofters of the island are lazy; they suspect they sleep until noon. Often these strictures are the consequence of misunderstanding the schedules of a very simple rural and piscatorial life, but no crofter is a devotee of efficiency. Crofting inescapably is inefficient, in the view of a machine-civilization, and it requires some degree of frugality and prudence; not many Americans could support a household on five or six acres of land. In many respects, the crofters of Eigg are fortunate people, even though the basis of their life is dissolving. Probably they reserve good fortune in this era of calamity, for their ancestors' lives generally were rough, dangerous, meager, and short.

Regular chronology is of very recent adoption in Eigg. Lacking—as all the Gaelic Highlands and islands lacked—a written literature, a juridical organization, and all but the simplest commerce, the people kept no ledgers or journals or calendars, but spoke of events as preceding or following some catastrophe; and now one cannot be sure, even within a century or two, of the date at which most things happened. No one knows quite when Eigg was settled, but presumably that elusive missionary St. Donan found someone to baptize when he landed here in the early days of Culdee Christianity. He had raced the redoubtable St. Columba to the island (for ruthless competition prevailed in the saving of souls during that age) and had won; in dudgeon, it is said, Columba cursed him. The curse was efficacious, for presently Vikings ravaged Eigg, and Viking women—this must have been during the Norse colonizing of the Hebrides—martyred Donan after the fashion of St. Sebastian. You find his grave in the midst of a dense plantation. During the seventeenth century it was opened, and a number of skeletons were found within, all headless.

Close by is the island's graveyard, most of it a tangle of briars and bracken. The graves of nameless sailors of the Royal Navy, cast up at Laig in the middle of the last war, are the latest interments. At one side stands a roofless seventeenth-century Catholic chapel built by a Clanranald, something of a curiosity even in a country so crowded with ruins as Scotland, because post-Reformation Catholic churches were a defiance of the Establishment. As you cross the threshold of this chapel, a sepulchral stone face, very crudely but disturbingly carved, stares from the rough wall. A sea wind sighs through the ruined Scots vaulting, bracken catches at one's ankles, and the fine Celtic cross glows pink among the gravestones. This is the solitude of a thousand years of defeat.

Probably there was once a monastic community in Eigg; certainly a primitive nunnery, complete with miniature water mill, existed in Canna—tucked right into a cliff-wall. Until the last century, the glebe attached to the Kirk manse was of great extent for this island, more than two hundred acres, and possibly it had been church land from the very beginning of Hebridean society. It is alienated and uncultivated now, and even the stone barn by Mr. Macaskill's manse now is empty.

If authority in Eigg first was churchly, presently the book of judges was followed by the book of kings, and the chieftains of Clanranald, with their extensive territories in the Outer Isles, the Inner Isles, and the mainland, established a patriarchal supremacy in Eigg. Very little trace remains of their time, and the site of the house of their tacksmen—for the chief did not reside here—is occupied by the Catholic presbytery. Clanranald had a house down by the quay in neighboring Canna, however, part of which still is habitable. There the last Clanranald was taken by the Devil, late in the eighteenth century.

The priest tells you the story. Old and avaricious, the last Clanranald had ordered great clearances in South Uist, but perhaps the sight of his clansmen mercilessly thrust out upon the beach or packed into emigrant-ships touched his conscience, for he was seized with an inexplicable fear. Sick in body and soul, he entered his boat and sailed for the mainland, two of his tacksmen with him. But once the boat put out of Uist, an indescribable sea beast, fittingly prodigious, appeared in its wake and followed all the way to Canna. There Clanranald, in agony, had himself put ashore into the house by the harbor, and the sea beast waited in the mouth of the anchorage. While Clanranald lay in bed, spent, with the tacksmen attentive at his side, a piercing whistle sounded, and he tried to leap up, but the clansmen held him. It came a second time, and he fought with them like a madman; and when the third stentorian whistle sounded, he fell back dead into their arms, and the sea beast vanished. Eigg has had no true chief or laird since, only proprietors, many of them not Scots, and no vestige remains of the clan spirit.

Bogles and apparitions of several sorts have always been frequent in Eigg, tucked away in the Celtic Fringe. "Aye," Mr. Macaskill may remark abruptly, his strong face a study in solemnity, "It's a fearsome thing to be all alone at night in this manse." Yet despite the presence of fairies, invisible coffins, cattle-vexing monsters, and visions of the future, the great deed of blood which is the only famous episode in Eigg's history—the Massacre—seems to have left no supernatural trace. No one has any precise notion of when it took place, although the Massacre is the principal anchor in the chronology of the island. Sir Walter Scott, who landed here in 1814, carried off from the cave of the Massacre a skull that had been a young woman's, but even his antiquarian researches gave him no ground for computing the time of this atrocity. It seems to have occurred within the sixteenth century, when the Hebrides still were not far removed from a kind of savagery, and all during the eighteenth and nineteenth centuries it was considered an episode of horror almost unparalleled. The refinements of our era, however, make the affair seem rather commonplace.

All the MacDonalds of Eigg died simultaneously by violence in a cave under the island. At that time only one family not named MacDonald lived in Eigg—the descendants of a shipwrecked MacLeod, who surreptitiously got a young woman of Eigg with child and whose isolated household was barely tolerated. Only these MacLeods, who were forced to hide apart from the MacDonalds during the trouble, survived the Massacre. The initial offense was given by the powerful MacLeods of Syke, some of whose fishermen or rovers landed suddenly in Eigg and ravished MacDonald girls; but they were caught, tied hand and foot by the MacDonalds, and set adrift to die in an open boat. They drifted back to Skye, however, and the clan of MacLeod promptly raised what was for the Hebrides a great invasion fleet to take vengeance. The people of Eigg saw the ships approaching, and hid in a cave over two hundred feet long, with a deceptively narrow mouth, close by the sea. The MacLeods, landing, found no one and assumed that all the two hundred MacDonalds had managed to escape to another island. But shortly after they set sail, their lookouts, glancing back towards the Sgurr, saw a man high on the hill—a scout rashly sent out too soon by the MacDonalds in the cave. MacLeod turned round, followed the spy's tracks in the snow to the cave mouth, and called upon the MacDonalds to surrender. They did not dare. Among the trapped MacDonalds was a woman who had done some favor to MacLeod, so that the besiegers told her to come out and be spared. She would come, she replied, if they let her bring along, scot-free, a man for each finger on her hands. Fearing treachery, the MacLeods refused, and so the woman stuck with her clan. Then the MacLeods kindled a great fire directly before the mouth of the cave, and all the MacDonalds were stifled. For centuries after, their bones were strewed over the cave's floor, but now one finds only the skeleton of some stray sheep. Clanranald's people recolonized Eigg, and life in the black houses went on unchanged.

The days of the Reformation, so terrible elsewhere in Scotland, seem to have been mild by contrast in the Small Isles; indeed, there was no Reformation. For a time, after the '45, the Catholic islanders were forced to attend Mass secretly in a great, naturally-vaulted, open-mouthed sea cave, with a ledge for altar and pulpit; but though the Kirk was officially established and endowed in Eigg, no one attended its services. Doctor Johnson was particularly anxious to visit Eigg and Canna, consistently Catholic, because "religion is a great preservative of custom," yet he did not manage the trip.

Jacobite disaster after 1745 was a calamity for Eigg second only to the Massacre. Clanranald had been out for Prince Charlie, and for some time after Culloden the chief skulked in Eigg, but subsequently got away. Some of Clanranald's principal followers were less fortunate, however, since an English warship appeared in the harbor and her captain demanded the arrest of all Jacobites who had been with the Pretender and the surrender of all weapons in Eigg, on pain of ravaging the island. To avert a sack, the priest persuaded the people to obey, and the men who possessed arms came down to the pier to give them up; but once disarmed, they were put in irons, herded aboard a vessel, and transported to the West Indies. None ever returned. Then the English abused Eigg at will for some weeks, burning cottages and slaughtering cattle, demanding extortionate quantities of provender for the supply of their brig; they went so far, legend relates, as to plow the Sinking Sands at Laig, destroying the razor-fish (a species of clam) formerly gathered there; and thus this creature, generally plentiful in the islands, is unknown at Cleadale. When the English at last departed, the surviving MacDonalds commenced wearily to patch together what they could of their old communal life.

Though so much of Hebridean culture was swept away after the '45, storytelling and Gaelic songs lingered on until a much later date. In Eigg, a population in part illiterate and without any very elaborate means of entertainment would gather round the peat fires in the evenings and recite old tales. These stories were considered narrative history, not works of imagination; they were sincere attempts to preserve a record of interesting occurrences in the island. "You have come thirty years too late to learn them," says Hugh Mackinnon, who cultivates two crofts. For the generation of islanders who did not know the pleasures of the state school, the wireless, and the penny press is extinct; the *Sunday Mirror* and *Reynolds' News* have swept the ancient legends clean out of the mind of Eigg. But despite his modesty, Mr. Mackinnon himself has retained a remarkably large number of these stories, more than anyone else in the Small Isles, perhaps, for an old man in Canna who was renowned for his stories and songs, the last of the old blood in that island, died four years ago. One sits in Hugh Mackinnon's neat parlor, with its sturdy furniture, drinking milk from his cows and munching biscuits, and he summons one story after another out of his memory; he would have ten times as many, twenty times, he declares, if he had paid decent attention to old folk in his parents' generation.

Hearing these stories, one realizes how very recent is the assimilation of Eigg to the rationalism and standardization of modern life. There were fairies in the last generation, and Hugh Mackinnon speculates on the relationship between belief and actuality. Over towards the narrow strip of cliff-hemmed land called Struldh, a fairy knoll still can be seen. Here it was that the fairies took the minister's wife, near the end of the eighteenth century. She really existed, this Mrs. Macaskill (for the minister's name, then as now, was Macaskill), sister to MacLean of Col, the friend of Boswell and Johnson. A dreamy girl, the minister's wife used to wander past Kildonian Braes, and sit musing in this solitude. One day, here upon the cliffs, she saw a mysterious ship offshore, and a small boat put out from it. The minister's wife composed a song about the apparition, which Mr. Mackinnon (who thinks his legends in Gaelic but speaks them in English) vainly tries to translate for one; and the next day she returned to the same spot. No one ever saw her again. Though they searched every nook of the rugged island, she was gone, for the fairies had claimed her.

The fairies of Eigg appear to have been malevolent. Mr. Mackinnon's father, indeed, was nearly concerned with one of them. An old couple who lived up beyond Cleadale, on land now deserted, came to the elder Mackinnon (then a young man) in fright and dismay. A fairy, they told him, was milking their cows. He went with them to the hill-pasture, and as they approached the cattle, a great creature like a lizard slipped away and was enveloped by the mist. Mackinnon went home, where he doubled up a sixpence to make a silver bullet for shooting the fairy, but his parents dissuaded him from interfering in such occult matters; and at last the old couple afflicted by these visitations, hopeless, left Eigg.

Witches, so abundant throughout most of Presbyterian Scotland until well into the eighteenth century, never seem to have plagued Eigg. Coming events, particularly woes, cast their shadows before them, however. In Eigg, as generally in Hebrides, the spectral funeral procession occasionally manifests itself, and Hugh Mackinnon has had personal experience of this. Walking along the road between manse and harbor one night, he found himself suddenly prevented from going forward; although no visible obstacle intervened, his body seemed to be pressing against some substance indefinable yet impenetrable. Hugh stepped into the ditch and made his way carefully along the side of the road for a little distance, after which he was able to proceeed normally. A few days later, an old man in a cottage by this track died, and his corpse was borne along precisely that route. This, in substance, is the usual experience of men who stumble into such a foreshadowing of death; it is thought that the phantom coffin itself blocks their path.

These legends are told with an ingenuousness and occasional inconsequentiality which is strong evidence of their validity; the people of Eigg appear never to have attempted embroidering their narratives (there are a great many more) or remolding them into significance if they lacked meaning. The peat smokes, a bit of it flares and is reduced to ash, the night mists convert all Eigg outdoors into a black cellar; and these fragmentary chronicles drift sleepily through the low room—"I saw pale kings and princes too, pale warriors, death-pale were they all. . . ." By the twenty-first century, perhaps, they will be obliterated as thoroughly as the traditions of the Picts.

Some of the Hebrides are completely desolate already. St. Kilda, away out in the Atlantic, is the most notorious example of this depopulation, for every inhabitant was removed by the government during the 1920s and resettled unhappily on the mainland, so that only sea birds now inhabit a land which men had possessed since the dawn of society. But there are many other instances, a melancholy catalogue. In an age when over-population and lack of foodstuffs loom so terribly, this abandoning of inhospitable regions (where, all the same, men have existed uncomplainingly for more than a millennium) is one of the most alarming symptoms of social decadence. The causes of such a retreat are complex, among them a popular appetite for luxury and novelty, a misplaced humanitarianism, a concentration on "efficient production" of sheep to the exclusion of human beings, and the iron regulations of government. A scanty rural population away up at the end of nowhere gets small consideration in an age of great cities. Take the regulation of fish prices, for instance. Herring from the Western Isles formerly brought a price somewhat higher than that of other herring, because of their superior quality. But the government, in fixing food prices, set a general maximum price for all herring. Therefore the herring fisheries of the North Sea have captured most of the market, no price-differential being allowed, and the herring industry at Castlebay in Barra is an utter wreck. There were other factors, but this blow was decisive. The state doles out various subsidies to Highlands and islands, but they do not compensate for the blunders of paternalism, and the population sinks closer and closer to the vanishing point.

One is inclined to believe, now and then, that the modern state does not want remnants and minorities to exist. Industrialism and government may be almost unconscious in their opposition, but its effect upon an older order is frightening. The insistence upon conformity, the assumption of the state and of urban society that only the suburban ideal of life is desirable—why, presently such assumptions are expressed in legislation, ours being an age of omnicompetent statute. Survival of people like the crofters is a standing criticism, however feeble, of centralized and industrialized society. And few epochs have been less tolerant of criticism than ours. First St. Kilda goes and then greater islands, and soon whatever remains of rural tradition elsewhere, and only one sort of man is left: the city man, standardized and unpropertied and subservient to a government, a corporation, or a union. Once the city man is deprived of the admonitory contrast which remnants of an earlier rural civilization provide, he sinks deep into self-complacency, materialism, and social boredom.

Well, Eigg and other Small Isles suffer from the acceleration of this vast economic and political drift. Young people, infected with the spirit of the age, want to live in towns and go to movies and own motorcycles. Desires of which earlier islanders knew nothing have become necessities and are increasingly difficult to satisfy. Cash must now be got, consequently. Eigg imports coal, instead of cutting and carrying peat; she buys her bread from the mainland; she has to pay taxes which, however slight in comparison with metropolitan burdens, still require cash. Social insurance, rather paradoxically, is a heavy expense to the crofters, for they are in the category of "self-employed" and must pay into state funds not only a worker's contribution, but an employer's share besides. Both inclination and the demands of the intolerant outside world compel a subsistence-producer to become in some degree a cash-earner. Yet how are they to get money? The outside world often proves uncooperative. After the late war, for instance, a number of young men who had been in the forces were anxious to return to Eigg, if only they could manage to find a living. They proposed to go into tweed-weaving. The state was obdurate; not only was there an absence of positive encouragement, but officialdom would allow no temporary exemption from the purchase-tax and a host of regulations, the hampering effect of which made the scheme impracticable. The young men went to sea or to Glasgow.

Big government prefers to deal with big enterprise, not with small, independent, possibly cantankerous units; and socialism being a bigger form of big government, its dislike of exceptions and minuteness is the stronger. The Seven Men of Knoidart found this out. Knoidart is a broad and wild mainland peninsula, visible from Eigg, on which the original crofting population has shrunk appallingly. The present proprietor manifested an increasing hostility towards the remaining crofters, and they felt themselves threatened with economic strangulation. Therefore, several families—the Seven Men—retaliated by a "land raid," fencing and endeavoring to cultivate a large part of the peninsula.

Now the rights of crofters have always been difficult to define. Highland and island crofters are the heirs of the old clansfolk, whose patriarchal economy was vastly different from English and Lowland legal and economic organization. As the military function of the chieftains atrophied, particularly after the '45, those leaders began to imitate the tastes, habits, and prerogatives of English and Scottish nobility and gentry, and to deal with the territories under their hereditary chieftainship, which had been a species of trust, as a private estate. Thus came the clearances, the Highland equivalent of enclosures, in which the Highland and island peasants were treated by their former protectors as mere squatters or tenants at will, rather than as members of the same family with communal rights. By that kind of historical retribution in which men used to see the hand of Providence, presently the majority of the chiefs lost their money and their authority. In the islands, particularly, the rights which the old chieftains had enjoyed were purchased by ordinary proprietors, often Lowlanders or Englishmen.

Resistance by the crofting peasantry to this highhanded procedure became effectual only in the 1870s. The subsequent Crofting Acts made all crofts still in existence permanent tenures. Crofters pay a statutory rent to the proprietor, but he has no other power over them, and the rents fixed in the 1880s are only nominal today, of course: the priest in Eigg pays a mere three pounds a year for his seven acres, and the proprietor of Canna gets altogether from his tenants the sum of thirty pounds annually. (In these times, island lairds dependent chiefly on their rents, whether of farms or crofts, are in a bad plight, what with rates, income taxes, unearned-income taxes, death duties, and prices.)

But do the crofters have other traditionary, prescriptive rights as well? Do they have a right to more land, for instance, if their crofts are insufficient to support them? This question has never been properly settled, and for many decades there have been land raids by the crofters, especially in the Outer Isles, either to protect themselves from what they consider the cupidity of proprietors or for aggrandizement. Government has rarely ventured to intervene against the crofters, for a considerable body of public opinion has upheld them.

The hardy Seven Men of Knoidart, however, acted in a world increasingly collectivized after a new fashion. The proprietor of Knoidart appealed to government for an act of interdict against them. The Socialist Secretary of State for Scotland appointed a commission to look into the affair, and the commission declared it was expedient not only to restrain the crofters, but to award the proprietor a large cash subsidy so that he could run thousands of additional sheep on what used to be crofting land; one is told he was even more surprised than gratified. An interdict was put in force against the Seven Men; they have no adequate communication with the rest of the world, and probably their cause is lost. It is interesting that the decision was made by socialist humanitarians on the ground of the expediency of efficient food production (a socialism which owes more to Bentham than to Morris), and that public opinion, once so interested in the crofters, remained apathetic. True, some Glasgow trades-union members voted for a sympathetic strike in aid of the Seven Men, a gesture as pathetically generous as it was ineffectual and ill-advised. The dismal Glasgow slums still retain a lingering tenderness for the crofters, since it was the Highland clearances that filled the Glasgow factories and tenements to bursting.

Eigg is not troubled by land raids, but the crofters of Eigg, too, are menaced by this modern temper which demands "production" and despises independence. In the other Small Isles, the problem of depopulation must be solved in this decade, or it will solve itself forever. Little Muck is reduced to twelve or fifteen people. Canna, once prosperous, has only some forty persons despite the energies of its erudite laird, John Lorne Campbell. "And they're mostly old people in Canna," says Father MacLean. "Old bachelors and old maids. They've seen too much of each other, and don't care about marrying now." As for Rum, which suffered two merciless clearances, it has no one at all except a handful of domestic servants and gamekeepers about Kinloch Castle. The proprietress, a very old Frenchwoman, wants no settlers, trespassers, or poachers on the island, which is one pile of fierce mountains; she in her Victorian castle, and her husband in his tomb on the other side of the island, brood over this desolation. No one but the priest and the minister (for Sunday services) is permitted to land.

Eigg has not come to this pass. But how will matters end? Almost all communal spirit is lost already; only the two churches keep a spark of it glowing. A dance or two in summer at the lodge provide the only occasions for a general gathering. On August 1949, a remarkable event occurred: an old man in the southern end of the island went to visit his sister, whom he had not seen for a full generation. She lived four miles away, up north. This sort of isolation and apathy drive young blood out of a place. In most of the United States, some kind of bond would be provided by the form, however attenuated, of township government. But such places as Eigg have no local government, not even a school board; all such affairs are handled at the county level, and Inverness-shire is an enormous area which stretches right across Scotland from sea to sea. Subsidies, social planning from above, and any amount of condescending pity cannot fill the void left when the true spirit of local association has been starved to death.

Such remedies as might be applied can hardly be discussed here. The stimulation, or rather toleration, of genuine domestic industries; the suiting of governmental framework to men rather than of men to framework; the praise, rather than ridicule, of simple tastes and rural character—these measures require both high imagination and enormous patience. We moderns are deficient in both qualities. But the problem of the soul of Eigg is the microcosmic problem of the soul of our world. If places like Eigg die, one must diagnose modern society as infected by a virus probably incurable.

Perched atop the Sgurr, one giddily sees a green island beneath his feet. This greenness is deceptive, for a great part of it is lush bracken. Gulls flap screaming past you, the steamer *Lochearn* is a speck up the Sound of Sleat, the wreck of a crofter's cottage is gray against the earth in Grulin. You have a noble vista of the world, if you dare to climb the Sgurr: the view of a world which, neglecting the particular, may discover that it forfeits the general.

["Eigg, in the Hebrides," Beyond the Dreams of Avarice: Essays of a Social Critic *(Chicago: Henry Regnery Company, 1956), 280–97.]*

❖

A House in Mountjoy Square

*In July 1952 Kirk was granted the D. Litt. (*litterarum doctorem*), the highest arts degree of St. Andrews, the senior Scottish university, where he had studied since September 1948. During these years he visited Ireland frequently; his essay "A House in Mountjoy Square," an elegant slum in Dublin, was published in 1949. In it he describes his week's stay in Mountjoy Square, laid out about the middle of the eighteenth century, with the high brick mansions still standing, their "eerie beauty shining out of decay." Kirk graphically pictures the poverty and squalor smirching the old squares of Dublin: "The portico-columns are hacked and the fanlights smashed, in fifteen out of twenty of these houses; the plaster falls, the knocker is ripped away, the slum-urchins caper and scream upon the steps, Mick lounges by the window—and they are legion, the dusty, ragged, impudent, shrewd, good-natured little brats of Dublin." Kirk's talent for social criticism and storytelling infuses this early essay.*

Guinness and Catholic fervor make up the spirit of Dublin. The eighteenth-century capital on the Liffey is an amusing place for a week's visit—but not, perhaps, for a lifetime.

"The distressing thing about Dublin, as about all Irish towns," writes A. E. Coppard, "is its domestic architecture. It doesn't merely decay, it is smitten by a disease from which there seems to be no recovery. The walls fall in—let them fall. Is there a conflagration—well, then we go, and the ashes are triumphant. If a window is broken, it is like the vow of a bad woman—broken forever. Calamity here is progressive." It was three decades and more gone that Coppard made his observation, and the pace of calamity in Dublin has not slackened.

Mountjoy Square, north Dublin, was laid out about the middle of the eighteenth century. The houses stand yet: high brick mansions, of three stories and a half, masterfully designed, each with its delicate pillared doorway and fanlight, its iron railing just separating it from the sidewalk. The American will be reminded of Beacon Hill, the Englishman perhaps of Chelsea. You can get into one of these aristocratic houses, for it is a youth-hostel; and although the happy-go-lucky poverty that is Dublin's mingled curse and blessing has crept into the wide corridor and lies in the thick dust on the stairs and the grime on the floor, you still can look at the eerie beauty shining out of decay, that sort of beauty our age knows too well. Your glance runs up the sweep of the staircase, over the proportions of the rooms (built for grandeur, not for comfort), especially across these ceilings, picked out in blue-and-red geometrical designs or adorned with Grecian nymphs in moulded plaster; you cannot fail to notice the fireplaces, marbles carved to gratify men dead these two centuries.

Mountjoy Square is broad, and all about it, street on street, stand houses much like this; and elsewhere in Dublin, mile on mile, the elegant skeleton of the eighteenth century smiles upon you with a macabre coquetry. But old Dublin, dear dirty Dublin, is dead, dead, dead—buried and mouldered and left to ghouls. The portico-columns are hacked and the fanlights smashed, in fifteen out of twenty of these houses; the plaster falls, the knocker is ripped away, the slum-urchins caper and scream upon the steps, Mick lounges by the window—and they are legion, the dusty, ragged, impudent, shrewd, good-natured little brats of Dublin. Walk a block north or south of Dame Street, east or west of O'Connell or Grafton, and you are among the poorest of the poor. You may be looking through the plate-glass at a blackthorn stick that costs two guineas; and then you swing about to find at your elbow a lad right out of Sean O'Casey's play, *The Shadow of a Gunman* (1923), bedraggled overcoat and all, endeavoring to sell you a penny newspaper.

For Ireland, despite gains since the Second World War, remains poor—poor as any mouse that lingers in the cobwebbed Church of Ireland after his cousins have crossed the green to seek the crumbs of the Papists. Dublin is poor, and drinks her Guinness, and thinks now of New York, now of Rome—enamored of them both.

In the argot of the Black and Tans, the quarter of the old city round about St. Patrick's Cathedral (Swift is dust there, and Stella) was "the passage of the Dardanelles"; every other high house held a sniper, in those days when men and boys in the tattered overcoats swarmed out of the Coombe and out of the streets by St. Michan's out of Ringsend and out of Mountjoy Square, urged on by their women, to burn the Custom House and blow up the Four Courts and die in the flames of the Post Office.

Where are those terrible fellows now? Why, at your elbow, crossing themselves as they pass the Augustinian church, asking you for a match, keeping an eye on the babies who roll marbles into the sidewalk-traps. They remain as poor as they were then, as pious, as fond of poteen and oratory. But they are not Jacobins any longer, and one suspects that even the half-plaintive fuss about ending Partition heats few of them. Transplant this grinding, grimy poverty, this swaying on the verge of mendicity, to Brussels or Copenhagen, and you might be in the grip of a Terror within a year. Yet these people are cheerful, chaste, and (to write in generalizations) honest; I do not think the Garda has an intolerably difficult job.

"Saints preserve us!" cried a middle-class Dublin woman to a friend of mine, upon learning that I lodged in Mountjoy Square. "However does the poor boy get in there at night? Why, he'll find himself with his throat cut." The bourgeoisie of Dublin have trickled away to the southern suburbs, for the most part abandoning the old squares to other orders of society; and the illusions entertained by middle-class Dublin folk concerning the mysterious proletariat differ little from those of middle-class people in Manchester or New Orleans. For all that, in a week of poking about dark streets I was accosted only by one woman with a whiskey-cough and by one boy, aged six, who wanted "the time, please, sir."

Original sin scarcely is eradicated in the Green Isle; yet at least religion is a living influence, the consolation and compulsion of the masses, the chief guardian of social order. No other place in the Western world is so devout, unless it be Quebec, where the cassock is even more nearly omnipresent. And this brand of Catholicism still is exported in strong concentrations to America. A Michigan friend recently told me,

> My cousin has a mother who is of the Irish-Puritan breed of Catholic. Pat made a few disparaging remarks about the Church in Italy (he has been not far from the part Levi writes of in *Christ Stopped at Eboli* [1945]). She jumped to her feet, hollered in a loud voice that she was Irish Catholic and she'd have none of it, marched to the piano and played with gusto and great volume "Peter Street, Dublin," so that nobody could carry on a conversation in anything lower than a scream. After a time, without taking her hands from the keyboard, her grey hair standing out from her head, she peered about—her blue eyes like wild horses—and seeing everyone silent, wheeled and remarked, "For real music, there's none like the Irish!"

So much for the blending of national vanity with religious passion among the Irish of Dublin or far corners. But for an idea of how strongly impressed upon the Irish character must be the Christian understanding of resignation, one ought to stroll through the very oldest lanes of Dublin, down Winetavern Street and Bridge Street, where not even ruins stand: no, a desolation of demolition in the heart of the medieval town, leveled as if by thousand-pound bombs—though cleared actually by prosaic decree of government. One passes by the roofless wreck of St. Audoen's church with its battlemented tower, through St. Audoen's Arch that was built to withstand Edward Bruce, and comes upon a nomad camp right in the forum—that is, a cluster of gypsy caravans, placidly established, dogs and all, where once the city wall stood. ("We raze our ancient edifices to clear the ground where the hordes of the future will encamp in their mechanized caravans," Mr. T. S. Eliot writes.) All about, *les miserables* in crumbling tenements or dingy modern "artisans' dwellings."

How does Dublin, in a world of ideological passion, remain so gaunt and yet so placid? Why, because the Irish now have no government to rise against except their very own; and because the Catholic Church in Ireland has come close to fulfilling Edmund Burke's ideal of a church that is the embodiment of a nation's spirit; and because truly the Irishman is conservative to the bone.

To the Englishman, this last remark may seem eccentric; and the innovations of modern Ireland—peasant proprietorship, state railways, pensions without end—have changed the face of things, certainly. Irish politicians play with the taxing-power in the interesting ways of all modern politicians—including the alteration of the landscape. Walking through the twisting old village of Castletown Roche, in the Blackwater valley where Burke spent his boyhood, I saw the roofs of the pleasant cottages tumbling in; while on the town's fringe, long rows of half-finished dwellings of poured concrete, uniform, dismal, set in humorless rows like so many badly-designed little prisons, show the hand of the modern state. The smashed castle (Cromwell did for it) still is on the hill, and the Church of Ireland on a knoll, and these monstrosities beside to represent the spirit of our age. Admitted, all this: and then the Irishman is conservative.

The little cells of communists that once tried to burrow their way into Irish revolutionary organizations have withered in such infertile soil; even the Labour party is impotent. As the embers of nationalism cool, possibly new ideological appetites may be whetted. But I doubt it. Ireland does not look up toward the red dawn.

For Ireland still is wrapped, comfortably swaddled, in native tradition. The traditional Irish whimsicality and eccentricity, despite the spread of Americanization, remain reasonably healthy. And the tradition of Irish rural life has only begun to give a little before post-war industrialization. The Irish cottager has his land now; it may be a poor thing, but his own; and so he has that tangible share in the commonwealth which is the surest guarantee of social permanence.

This allegiance of the peasant was won at a great price—the cost of breaking the Irish gentry, that class to which Ireland owes her name for valor, genius, and wit, as well as folly. The aristocracy is nearly gone; and without an aristocracy of some sort, a country is in danger of intellectual sterility, a state worse than physical poverty. Be that as it may, Castle Rackrent was burnt during the Troubles, and the thatched cottage survives the Palladian mansion. Though the price was high, the reward has been popular assent to a stable society.

Near the end of a day of walking, I found myself at the antipodes from Mountjoy Square, in another and older Ireland—the village of Newcastle, fifteen miles west of Dublin, a little to the south of the anachronistic Grand Canal that still points toward Limerick. An old, old alehouse, tidy and decent; a string of sound old cottages, saffron-washed, with their thatch dry and warm; a ponderous ancient church, the tower broken, mouldering in a tangled graveyard, and by it a ruin out of which the rooks fled cawing; great beeches and limes draped with the Irish ivy; and round them the glistening Irish fields, and over them the soft Irish sun setting.

This may be bucolic sentimentality; yet I fancy that the traditional life of such a place is a sounder existence than a scheme of co-ordinated happiness sent express from Dublin or London or Washington or Moscow.

["A House in Mountjoy Square: Notes of a Wandering Scholar," College Echoes *(St. Andrews Committee of the Students' Representative Council), Vol. 60 (May 1949), 29–31. Subsequently published in* Confessions of a Bohemian Tory: Episodes and Reflections of a Vagrant Career *(New York: Fleet Publishing Corporation), 1963, 69–74.]*

The Architecture of Servitude and Boredom

Disregard of the imagination and the human scale is reflected, Kirk says in this essay, in the "architecture of sham." Our cities repudiate "old truths about form, symbol, and pattern in architecture and in urban planning"; contemporary architecture fails to "wake the imagination or satisfy the memory." A short walk on the streets of an American city will confirm Kirk's criticisms, as one is derailed by grimy and amorphous buildings, and by marks of servitude and boredom on the faces of the people. Who can forget a once beautiful church lying in ruins, the victim of a bored youngster's match? Refusing to surrender to "the city of destruction," Kirk offers these "general principles of urban restoration": adapt architectural reform to "the human scale"; nurture roots in the community called a city; proclaim that the criterion of urban planning should be the common good, not commercial gain; base civic restoration on customs and traditions found in "the architectural well of the past."

Britain's urban riots of July 1981 came to Edinburgh somewhat tardily, but they arrived. Being there at the time, I asked a knowledgeable Scottish engineer, who builds roads but is an architect too, what had caused the Edinburgh troubles.

"Bad architecture," he told me. He meant that the Edinburgh riot arose in one of the ugliest and most boring of the county-council public housing schemes, afflicted by a ghastly monotony. He did not suggest that the rioters were endowed with good architectural taste; it was rather that the people who dwell in this Edinburgh housing-scheme are perpetually discontented, without quite knowing why—and spoiling for a fight.

It would not be difficult to show that the dreariness of life in "working-class" quarters of English and Scottish towns was a principal cause of the burning and the looting and the stoning of police which came to pass in Liverpool and London and other places. It was not that the districts where the riots occurred were architectural survivals from the Bleak Age: no, those quarters were built or rebuilt after the Second World War. But everything in them, including the police stations, was shoddy and badly designed. It has been said that mankind can endure anything except boredom. With great buildings or with small, the architecture of our mass-age, in this latter half of the twentieth century, has been wondrously boring. Also it has been an architecture of sham: the outward symbol of a society which, despite all its protestations of being "free" and "democratic," rapidly sinks into servility.

What Sir Osbert Sitwell has called "the modern proletarian cosmopolis" has been sliding, politically and architecturally, toward general boredom and general servitude. Talking vaguely of egalitarianism and an "international style," the "renewers" of our cities have been creating vistas of boredom. Amidst this monotony, the natives are restless. With every month that passes, the rate of serious crimes increases. And what is done to alleviate such discontents? Why, not infrequently the public authorities are moved to relieve the barrenness of their urban landscapes by commissioning somebody to design (for a delightful fee) another piece of "junk" sculpture, product of the blow-torch, to be erected in some place of public assembly. Public funds have been made available lavishly to encourage such artistic frauds. Yet somehow these contributions to a city's amenities do not restore civic virtue: the rates of murder, rape, and arson continue to rise.

❖

Two decades ago, when Jane Jacobs published her detailed and convincing study *The Death and Life of Great American Cities* (1961), I naively assumed that the tide had turned; that our hideous blunders in urban planning were repented by the leaders of business and industry; that we might discern the beginnings of a recovery of the humane scale in our urban life and conceivably in our architecture. Seventeen years ago, when I addressed at St. Louis (then the most decayed city in America) the National Conference of the American Institute of Planners, I fancied that I discerned among some urban planners glimmerings of sense and taste. But I was mistaken.

For the policies of the Johnson administration, in the name of urban "renewal," created urban deserts and jungles on a scale previously unparalleled in time of peace. George Romney, in his last address as governor of Michigan, declared that the great Detroit riots had been provoked by "urban renewal and federal highway building." He was accurate; and nobody paid any attention.

Dr. Martin Anderson's book *The Federal Bulldozer* (1964) described the Johnsonian folly, and suggested remedies; but only some minor checks upon the process were effected. We continued to dehumanize our cities; if the pace of destruction is somewhat slowed nowadays, that is chiefly for lack of funds. Quite literally, as T. S. Eliot observed concerning education in his *Notes Towards the Definition of Culture* (1948), we are "destroying our ancient edifices to make ready the ground upon which the barbarian nomads of the future will encamp in their mechanized caravans."

❖

As I endeavored to remind the American Institute of Planners, successful planning must be concerned primarily with the person, and how he thrives under a large plan; with the republic (or the public interest), and what sort of society arises from grand designs. I quote Eliot once more: "One thing to avoid is a *universalized* planning; one thing to ascertain is the limits of the plannable."

Assuming, however, that urban planning has no limits, the breed of urban planners have given us the architecture of servitude and boredom. Over the past quarter of a century and more, anarchy and desolation have been the consequences of grandiose pseudo-planning. One is a good deal safer in Palermo, or Tunis, or Fez, than in New York, or Chicago, or Los Angeles. For those ancient towns, whatever their difficulties and their poverty, remain genuine communities, in which the townsman still is a person, not wholly lost in the faceless crowd; and in which, whatever the degree of civic corruption, still the public authority can maintain a tolerable order. Our urban planners have lost those civic advantages.

Some years ago I received a letter from a young man in Oklahoma, conservatively inclined, who had dropped out of college because his university, like the American urban behemoth, possessed neither imagination nor humane apprehension. I offer you some of his observations on urban planning and architecture.

> First, the quality of the architecture. Organic architecture is being ignored, for the most part, because of its personal and individual quality. Planning for the individual must entail an individual architecture, not international style *à la* the current mode of Paul Rudolph, Louis I. Kahn, Gordon Bunshaft, and the Eastern boys.
>
> Second, the sheer size of our cities will kill humane culture. You are acquainted with the Brave New Worlds that our latest periodicals display, such as Paulo Soleri's "City on the Mesa." Frightful, but it is coming—the mob loves it; togetherness.
>
> Third, the automobile is obsolete. It is time we recognized this before the auto makes civilization obsolete. . . . The Highway Commissioner must be stopped—or, better, overruled.

> Fourth, the land speculators are the great makers of slumurbia, responsible for the concentration of skyscrapers. All too often they are defended as part of a free economy.
>
> . . . It seems to me that we can plan the functional requirements of a city, but the more we plan the *culture* of cities, meaning especially the architecture of cities, the worse it will get. In other words, plan part of the city, and include as part of the plan a great deal that is unplanned.

Just so; this seeming paradox is what Eliot meant in his remarks on the limits of planning. In American society, urban planning has tended to reflect the talent of Americans for technological success, but also to reflect their frequent deficiency in the realm of imagination, remarked by Tocqueville a century and a half ago. So we find ourselves in our air-conditioned urban jungle.

❖

I venture to suggest just now some general principles of urban restoration which might help to redeem this country from boredom and servitude.

First, the architecture of a city and a countryside ought to be adapted to the humane scale. A city is not simply a collectivity; it is a vital continuity, composed of a great many distinct individuals, most of whom have no desire to be precisely like everybody else. Society is not a machine: on the contrary, it is a kind of spiritual corporation; and if treated as a machine, people rebel, politically or personally.

Second, the community called a city must nurture roots, not hack through them. Neighborhoods, voluntary associations, old landmarks, historic monuments—such elements make men and women feel at home. They bind together a community with what Gabriel Marcel calls "diffused gratitude." Restoration and rehabilitation almost always are preferable to grand reconstitution—even when more expensive, which repair rarely is.

Third, the measure of urban planning should be not commercial gain primarily, but the common good. In miscalled "urban renewal," the Johnson administration's "war on poverty" actually was war against the poor, for the advantage of the speculator and the contractor. Once I spoke to an association of Jewish charities in a large meeting-room at the top of Boston's museum of science. From the windows, we looked across the bay to a district covered by immense high-rise and high-rent apartments, or even more costly condominiums. Only three years earlier, I was told by the rabbi who chaired our meeting, this had been a low-rent district inhabited by poor Jews. The area had not been a slum, he said; and he mused, looking out the window. "Where are they now?" he murmured. "Why, dead, or swept under the rug." Those words would have been as true in a hundred other American cities.

Fourth, civic restoration must be founded upon the long-established customs, habits, and political institutions of a community. Most convictions and institutions are products of a long historical process of winnowing and filtering. No planner, however ingenious, can make humanity happy by being stretched upon a Procrustean bed of social innovation. And among the deepest longings of humankind is the desire for permanence and security of territory, "a place of one's own."

These four very general principles, generally disregarded by the typical planner of the twentieth century, slowly obtain a hearing once more. We may see them at work practically in the successful restoration, for instance, of an eighteenth-century city of high interest—Savannah. But these beneficent concepts have not yet entered the heads of the run-of the-mill city politician and urban administrator.

❖

Consider Detroit, the city I used to know best. Nobody can take pleasure in knowing Detroit well nowadays. That city's publicists boast of the Renaissance Center, a group of glittering colossal towers near the river, including a hotel, offices, and a shopping complex—the whole constructed very like a fortress, with redoubts, doubtless in anticipation of a storm by the nearby proletariat, one of these days. From the restaurant at the summit of the Detroit Plaza Hotel, one can behold mile upon mile of decay and obliteration of a city founded at the beginning of the eighteenth century. Nearly all the old neighborhoods and districts of Detroit that I used to explore during my college days have been effaced. Even the old high-domed City Hall has vanished without trace. The central block of the Wayne County Courthouse, with its quadriga and elaborate baroque decoration, still stands—overshadowed by the Renaissance Center; but those in Detroit's seats of the mighty mean to pull it down, another job for the wrecking contractors.

From the Renaissance Center, one may stroll in relative safety to the cafes of Greektown, less than a hundred yards distant. Beyond that little old quarter only the unwary venture: a glance at a map showing the incidence of violent crimes in Detroit will explain why.

Greektown is safe because the streets are thronged with people day and night; because its two- or three-story buildings are fully inhabited, with old women watching the streets from upper windows; because it is not much afflicted by vacant lots where predators lurk; because a social (and ethnic) community survives there. The humane scale has not been wiped out of existence by civic "planners."

But the boasted Renaissance Center, externally and internally a triumph of extravagantly bad taste, is a besieged island amidst the swamps of urban savagery. It is designed vertically, not horizontally: so its tenants meet chiefly in elevators, not knowing one another. Certain happy persons, true, have been mightily enriched by this Detroit development—persons with large political influence, which obtained abundant federal funds for the project. One wonders whether, twenty years from now, the Renaissance Center will not have been demolished in its turn.

A few miles north of the Renaissance Center—on a clear day, one can see the district with the naked eye from the top of the Renaissance Center's towers—there used to lay the old district of Poletown, inhabited by people of eastern European stock. That whole neighborhood was pulled down, every brick, stone, and stick of it, to supply a site (mostly parking lots) for a General Motors plant. Thousands of people, many of them elderly, nearly all of them in narrow circumstances, were abruptly uprooted. They protested vehemently, to no avail. Where did they go? Some doubled up in slums—though they were not slum-folk before. Others presumably settled in new low-income housing developments, commonly uglier and more dangerous than the older slums. Two Catholic churches were demolished, despite the resistance of pastors and congregations. One protesting pastor died, a few months later, of a broken heart; newspapers and their writers to the editor praised him—after his funeral.

This scandalous "clearance," widely and unfavorably publicized, was made possible by an unholy alliance. The chief powers in this league were former Detroit Mayor Coleman Young; General Motors planners, said to have been bullied by Mayor Young; and the late Cardinal Dearden, archbishop of Detroit, who was given to much talk about injustice toward the poor (that is, the abstract poor at large, not the poor of Poletown), and all that. When General Motors tardily offered to move one of Poletown's churches to a new site, the Cardinal rejected the offer and insisted upon demolition—to the astonishment and rage of pastor and parishioners.

It is rather a nasty story, deserving of a short sardonic book. So Poletown is gone; and the decent folk of small means who lived there were shuffled off to the architecture of boredom and servitude. We may be sure they'll not spend their declining years in any Renaissance Center. Again, the power of eminent domain and plenty of public money were employed in this successful assault on community and the humane scale of living. Are people treated more arbitrarily, with greater disregard of their rights in property, in a socialist dictatorship?

After this fashion, even in these United States, there takes form the future collectivism, like one of H. G. Wells's utopias or Aldous Huxley's dystopia: the countryside almost wholly depopulated; the great bulk of the population packed into smart, shoddy, comfortless, impersonal "housing developments"; and looming above this landscape and manscape, the blank-walled towers of the administrative class. The architecture of this future domination—or, rather, this emerging domination—retains nothing whatsoever that wakes the imagination or satisfies the memory. One may predict that in this domination of utilitarianism, life will be unsafe increasingly, as well as unsatisfying; and that despite an outward appearance of material accomplishment, real incomes will diminish steadily: architectural impoverishment and general impoverishment are joined historically. Jacquetta Hawkes's fable "The Unites" represents the final degradation of such a collectivism.

In that tale, Miss Hawkes (Mrs. J. B. Priestley) describes a future society from which all privacy, all art (except degraded vestiges), all beauty of architecture, and all symbols have been stripped away, together with all belief in the divine. Production and consumption—though reduced to bare subsistence levels—are the obsessions of the folk who call themselves the Unites. I quote a passage from this fable:

> Perhaps it was this utilitarianism more than anything else which made Unite existence fall so far below the worst of human life in former days. Peasants of old had lived from birth to death almost as helplessly, with almost as little hope of escape, but their life's course had been decked with fantasy and symbol, with simple art and ritual, with very many things that were of no use in daily life except to make it human and significant. Now utilitarianism itself was at its most base, for needs and expectations had been so much reduced that all were perfectly satisfied. To have no desire is far more dreadful than for desire to remain unfulfilled.

The population of our cities is not very far from that condition. When all interesting architecture has fallen into the limbo of lost things, presumably the rising generation will raise no objection to the architecture of servility and boredom, because they will know no alternative. Desire will have starved to death. As Jacquetta Hawkes implies, architecture, like all art and all science, arises originally out of the religious impulse; and when a culture's religious quest and yearning have expired, then architecture, like all the other aspects of a culture, falls into decadence. Thus the total condition of our urban life and the dreariness of our architecture are not separate phenomena.

❖

But I must permit some cheerfulness to break in, at this point. Here and there in this land, effective resistance is offered to the evangels of architectural boredom. Two decades ago, it was proposed to sweep away the old streets of Galena, Illinois—one of our surviving historic towns with a good deal of interesting architecture—in order to build supermarkets and "modernize" generally. After a hard fight, in which I took some hand, the "developers" were defeated.

Through years of protest and litigation, we succeeded in one major contest against utilitarian city planners, in a really big city: the defeat of the Riverfront Expressway at New Orleans, which would have blighted the French Quarter and done other mischief. You can read about that fight in a book by Richard Baumbach and William Borah, *The Second Battle of New Orleans* (1981). The advocates of preservation of our architectural patrimony do obtain some hearing today—after most of that patrimony has been flattened.

Preservation of good buildings, good streets, and good districts is only one aspect of our struggle against the architecture of servility and boredom. New construction, whether downtown or in the suburbs, looms larger. High costs of all building unite with the sorry limitations of most architects to produce barren public buildings, office towers, and "motor hotels"; while the condominiums and the tract-houses employ third-rate materials and fourth-rate interior decoration. Ever since the Second World War, the old arts of building have lain in the sere and yellow leaf. Facile apologies for shoddy and dreary work are offered—as, in Waugh's novel *Helena* (1950), the architects and sculptors of the Emperor Constantine offer him excuses for not building a triumphal arch in the old grand style: "That is not the function of the feature, sire," and similar jargon. At length Constantine demands of them, "Can you do it?" And those architects are compelled to answer, "No." So it is in our age: a principal reason why our buildings are ugly is that our architects and craftsmen have quite forgotten how to construct handsome buildings. Incidentally, I commend to everyone interested in the relationships between social decay and the decline of architecture and the arts a slim book published in 1952 by Bernard Berenson: *The Arch of Constantine, or The Decline of Form.*

About all that can be said of most recent building, on every scale, in this country is this: American building is not quite so wretched as building today in most of the rest of the world. Recently I spent a few hours—as much time as I could endure—in the City of London, once dominated by St. Paul's and the Tower. Here Julius Caesar built his fortress on the Thames, and the hideous new museum of the City of London is full of Roman artifacts. The City, for centuries past the financial center of British Empire and Commonwealth, was badly smashed by German bombs; strange to say, some of the damage still has not been cleared up. But the City has been rebuilt, of really nasty gray concrete, already badly streaked, obscuring the great dome of Wren's cathedral, elbowing aside the Tower, supplanting the old picturesque confusion of the streets by a new ugly confusion worse confounded. This "Barbican Scheme" betrays the failure of intellect and imagination throughout Britain since the Second World War. What has been done in the neighborhood of the Barbican is a disgrace to England so embarrassing that few people mention it. Even in a Communist state, such an architectural atrocity would not be permitted, and the engulfing of a famous cathedral by dismal office-buildings would be rejected. Surely it is not from Britain today that a revival of architectural imagination can be expected. Nor do we encounter imaginative building in Germany, France, Italy, or Scandinavia. Everywhere it is the architecture of the mass-age, so far as "lodging" goes; and the architecture of the Bureaucrat's Epoch, so far as public buildings are in question.

Well, do I give you naught for your comfort? Do we descend steadily, and now somewhat speedily, toward a colossal architecture of unparalleled dreariness, and a colossal state of unparalleled uniformity—at best Tocqueville's "democratic despotism"? Will all of us labor under a profound depression of spirits (in part conscious, in part below the level of consciousness) because of the boring and servile architecture about us? And will the society now taking form in America resign itself to a parallel barrenness of soul and mind, under a political domination of unimaginative and complacent bureaucrats and managers?

No, not necessarily. Let us leave historical determinism to the Marxists and other ideologues. The courses of nations depend upon the energy and the talents of particular individuals—and upon Providence, always inscrutable. It remains true even in this mass-age of ours that individual genius and courage—or, at least, the imagination and boldness of a handful of men and women—may leaven the lump of dullness and apathy, all across the land. In practical politics, something of that sort has begun to occur among us.

From causes which at present no one guesses, conceivably there may come about a reinvigoration of urban planning and of architecture and of the humane scale. Rather as the current discoveries about the Shroud of Turin conceivably may work a widespread renewal of belief in the literal resurrection of the body, so people at the end of the twentieth century may discover afresh old truths about form, symbol, and pattern in architecture and in urban living.

The architectural and artistic charlatan, leagued with the spoilsman and the bureaucrat, may be thrust aside, abruptly, by a new breed of architects and artists endowed with the moral imagination. There have occurred ages when an architecture of vigor and freedom flourished, nurtured by myth and symbol and human confidence. Given faith and hope, it is yet imaginable that we may draw upon the architectural well of the past to bring into being an architecture (in the larger sense of that word) strong and humane. I have endeavored to diagnose the architectural malady; others must prescribe the remedies.

["The Architecture of Servitude and Boredom," Redeeming the Time, *edited with an introduction by Jeffrey O. Nelson (Wilmington, DE: Intercollegiate Studies Institute, 1996), 87–99.]*

❖

Criminal Character and Mercy

In this essay Kirk reflects on crime and punishment, and on the capital penalty as a compassionate measure. He makes it plain that the subject of criminal character and mercy must be separated from abstract humanitarian presuppositions and theories that easily, if conveniently, crumble into a sentimentalism ruled by emotion and not reason. To illustrate his case he gives the examples of two personal acquaintances, a convicted larcenist and an armed robber, who freely admitted, in the light of their own crimes and incarceration, that the death penalty needed to be imposed to protect the less from the more guilty. Kirk also describes how the misadventure of his grandfather, a bank manager kidnapped by two hardened bank robbers, early on instilled in him "a certain healthy prejudice in favor of stern deterrents." Sentimentalism and meliorism, he concludes, ultimately flounder on the reefs of illusion. Death is the final mercy for a slayer.

To perceive truth, we require images. As G. K. Chesterton put it, all life is an allegory, and we can understand it only in parable. I am about to offer some observations concerning mercy: that is, mercy toward deadly criminals. I believe that the capital penalty has a compassionate function. I propose to make my point through presenting a series of images—some of them drawn from perceptive works of fiction, others taken from my own experience and acquaintance in the course of a wandering life.

My introductory image is extracted from a memorable novelette by the German writer Stefan Andres, *We Are God's Utopia* (1955). This is a realistic episode from the Spanish Civil War, and it takes place in a desolated convent in a deserted walled town. One faction—the Reds, apparently—have confined two hundred prisoners of the opposing faction in the cells of a convent. These prisoners will be executed if the battle goes against the faction to which the jailers belong.

The captors are commanded by a lieutenant, Don Pedro, who already has committed indescribable atrocities. The memory of the worst of these acts will not permit the lieutenant to sleep—not in this very convent where he tortured the nuns to death.

Among the prisoners here is a former priest, Paco, taken in arms. Don Pedro implores Paco to hear his confession, so that he may sleep again. Although no enthusiast himself for the rite of confession, Paco consents to receive this dreadful penitent. In the course of the lieutenant's confession, Paco learns that Pedro, when a boy, had tortured cats hideously; that he had beheaded the puppets in his own puppet-theater; that he had flung to his death the kindest man Paco ever had known; that he had kept the nuns screaming in agony all night long. Yet Teniente Pedro has taken no real pleasure in these acts; they have made him sad, at the time of their commission and thereafter. He says to Paco, "I dwell in myself as though in a grave!"

The sometime priest absolves Pedro, for at the moment of absolution he is contrite. (Half an hour later, nevertheless, he will direct the massacre of the prisoners.) But before granting absolution, the confessor instructs his penitent, who kneels before him:

> "I tell you, it would be good for you if you were to die in the war." The voice was silent; after a pause it went on. "Yes, pray to God for death. According to the laws of man—but no, you know that!—no sin can separate you from God if you want to come back to Him, but it can separate you from life. For this reason, the death penalty for certain crimes has a decidedly compassionate character. You are a criminal of this sort. Pray to God for death!"

To Don Pedro, death would bring relief from his ghastly sadness and the moral solitude in which he had suffered since childhood; relief from the tormenting memory of his atrocious crimes; relief from the depravity of his own nature. Like most murderers, Pedro is not totally corrupt: he is capable of some kindly acts and of gratitude. But there is no way in which he can be redeemed or relieved of the torment of being what he is, in the flesh—except through death. To such a one, capital punishment would be an order of release. Sin already has separated the atrocious homicide from true life; yet through grace in death, even the slayer's soul may be redeemed. Death is not the greatest of evils. In the language of orthodoxy, indeed, death is no evil at all.

At this point, it may be objected that I have offered merely a fictitious instance. But great works of fiction are more true than particular incidents of the actual: that is why they are recognized as great. Andres gives us in this story a kind of distillation from mankind's experience of spirit. Those of us who have knocked about the world have encountered our real Teniente Pedros. It is not pleasant to meet them in confined quarters. A friend of mine spent much of his life in the company of conspicuous specimens of such unregenerate humanity. Permit me to offer you, then, a different sort of image: that of my friend the late Clinton Wallace, very much flesh and blood.

Clinton was the most heartfelt advocate of capital punishment that ever I have met. At the age of fourteen, Clinton had run away from a brutal father. Thereafter, until he came to live in my house, Clinton spent his life either on the roads or in prisons. His convictions were for petty offenses against property—usually the pilfering of church poor-boxes—or for endeavoring to escape from prisons. He was a giant in size and strength, and an innocent.

I do not mean that Clinton was a fool: the prison psychiatrists wrote him down as "dull normal," but Clinton was neither dull nor normal. He did not drink, except for one glass of beer on especially convivial occasions; did not smoke; did not curse; did not offend against women or children. His only vice, aside from petty larceny in time of necessity, was indolence. (Like Don Pedro, though, Clinton dwelt in himself, as in a grave.)

Clinton could recite a vast deal of good poetry, could make himself amusing, loved children, and prided himself upon being nonviolent. The worst aspect of life in prison, Clinton told me once, was not the boredom, or even the loss of liberty, but the foul language of the convicts—their every other word an obscenity. In recent years, Clinton added, prison conversation had grown monotonous—everybody discussing interminably the pleas of Miranda and Escobedo.

My wife once asked Clinton—who lived with us for six years near the end of his tether—how many of the men in prison are innocent.

"They're all innocent," Clinton replied. "You only have to ask them." He chuckled briefly. "They're all guilty, really, guilty as sin. Many of them are animals, brutes that ought to be put out of their misery."

From the worst forms of degradation at the hands of fellow prisoners, Clinton had been saved by his size, strength, and stentorian power of lung. But he had not been spared the company of the depraved. For some months, in one prison, Clinton's cellmate had been a man who had taken off his wife's head. That missing head never had been discovered. Clinton (who, like Don Pedro, had trouble getting to sleep) used to lie awake in his bunk at night, watching his cell-mate in the opposite bunk and stroking his own throat to reassure himself.

Clinton went on, in his kitchen-table conversations with us, to talk of the horror and the danger of existence in company with such men. Any tolerably decent person who had been sentenced to confinement might find himself at their mercy. "They're lower than beasts." Out of compassion for the other prisoners and for the guards, Clinton argued, the death penalty ought to be imposed upon men who had committed deliberately those crimes once called capital.

"Nobody can reform you," Clinton would continue. "There's no such thing as a 'reformatory' or a 'correctional facility.' The only person who can reform you is yourself. You have to begin by admitting to yourself that you did wrong. Then you may begin to improve a little."

Clinton Wallace had concluded from much observation and painful experience that very few deadly criminals possess either the ability or the intention to reform themselves. It is their nature, outside of prison, to prey beast-like upon whomever they may devour; and if confined within prison, these human predators are impelled by their very nature to ruin the other inmates. From the time he first was imprisoned—for truancy, at the age of fourteen—Clinton had been flung behind bars with such men. To make a swift lawful end of them, he declared, would be a work of mercy for all concerned.

My acquaintance with convicts is not confined to Clinton Wallace. For armed robbery, my friend Eddie was sentenced to three to thirty years imprisonment. (It was his first offense, committed under the influence of a kinsman and perhaps of drugs.) Within the walls, Eddie's religious yearnings of earlier years returned to him, and he grew almost saintly amidst the general corruption. As a reward for his good conduct, the warden was ready to assign him to an open-air work detail in the Upper Peninsula of Michigan. "For God's sake," Eddie cried, "don't do that to me! Put me in solitary if you have to, but keep me behind these walls! In a camp like that, I wouldn't have a chance against the gangs."

Eddie was a rough-and-ready young man, a seaman by trade, courageous to the point of recklessness. He did not labor under any illusions concerning the character of the dominant spirits within prison walls. He knew that no adequate punishment could be imposed upon any "lifer" who might take it into his head to do Eddie a mischief—including as "mischief" a knife between Eddie's ribs. So Eddie was no advocate of gentleness with the brutally violent.

Both Clinton and Eddie, flesh and blood though they were, have appeared as characters in short stories of mine—Clinton in my best-known tale, "There's a Long, Long Trail a-Winding"[1]; Eddie in my story, "Lex Talionis."[2] I drew them with affection from life. The final penalty called capital punishment does something to protect those men behind bars, like Clinton and Eddie, who may yet redeem themselves.

I have been suggesting through these incidents and images that captial punishment possesses certain merciful aspects. It may be merciful, first, in that it may relieve a depraved criminal of the horror of being what he is. It may be merciful, second, in that it can help to protect the less guilty from the more guilty. And in a third way, which I am about to touch upon, capital punishment may mercifully protect the guiltless from the more extreme forms of violence.

❖

Here the arguments concerning "deterrence," already widely discussed, may emerge afresh. But let me assure you that I have no intention of returning to the theoretical and statistical considerations advanced so often. Instead I offer you now another image which strongly impressed itself upon my consciousness, early. It is an image formed out of a real happening—the kidnapping of my grandfather.

Although that abduction occurred when I was a small boy, I recollect all the details clearly. As noted elsewhere in this volume, Frank Pierce, my grandfather, was a bank manager, a well-read man, kindly and charitable, the leading spirit of our Lower Town by the great railway yards outside Detroit. During the 1920s he repelled several attempts at robbery of his bank. (He carried a tear-gas fountain pen and kept a pistol handy in a drawer, but always had succeeded in baffling the robbers without using either instrument.) On one occasion, for all that, my grandfather lost the contest.

As he walked from his house toward his bank, very early in the summer morning, an automobile drew up alongside him, a submachine gun was pointed at him, and he was persuaded to enter the car. His captors were two: a vigorous voluble man and an armed thing muffled in women's clothes which never spoke—possibly a disguised man.

They took my grandfather to his bank, long before any customers would appear, and ordered him at gunpoint to open the safe. He would not do so. The two robbers sat down to converse with Mr. Pierce; there was plenty of time yet. The voluble robber, in rather friendly fashion, recounted the story of his own life. He had been a victim of circumstances, he said; but he had transcended them by taking up the robbing of banks. He held a theory of law and society rather like that of Thrasymachus, it seemed to my historically-minded grandfather: that is, the robber maintained that might is right, and that he was by nature one of the strong, which truth he was presently demonstrating. He then requested Mr. Pierce, once more, to open the safe. My grandfather still refused.

"Then, Mr. Pierce, though I've come to like you, I'm going to have to kill you." The voluble robber explained that for the sake of his very reputation and livelihood, it was regrettably necessary for him to shoot bankers who set him at defiance. How otherwise could he subsist at his trade? So, if you really won't. . . .

Convinced of his companion's sincerity, my grandfather opened the safe. The robbers took the money and drove away with my grandfather to an isolated barn. They left him inside, very loosely tied about his wrists, with the admonition that if he should come out within ten minutes, he would be shot. But my grandfather emerged as soon as he heard the robbers' car roar away. It had been his one defeat.

Years later, in an Illinois prison, a police officer who had known my grandfather happened to talk with Machine-gun Kelly, generally believed to have been the author of the St. Valentine's Massacre in Chicago. According to my grandfather's acquaintance, Kelly told him that the Plymouth bank-robbery had been one of his jobs, and that he had taken a liking to Mr. Pierce, the banker. Whether or not there was truth in this confession, certainly the man who kidnapped my grandfather was an accomplished professional criminal without scruples. Against him my grandfather could have been a convincing and convicting witness. Then why did he let my grandfather live? Perhaps because this robber was a highly rational criminal who calculated chances and weighed penalties. Pursuit for a murder is more intense than for a mere robbery, and penalties are heavier.

As others have suggested, the degree of deterrence provided by any severe penalty depends in part upon the calculating intelligence of the criminal—or the lack of reckonings and calculations on his part. From what I have observed, systematic bank robbers and safecrackers commonly are cold, egoistic, calculating persons who rank Number One very high indeed, look out carefully for Number One, and therefore weigh disadvantages and penalties. Fairly often they, like my grandfather's kidnapper, develop ideological apologies for their actions. Upon such mentalities, the final penalty of death may exercise a prudent restraint.

I have digressed at this length to suggest that the death penalty may be merciful toward the victims of certain types of crimes, committed by certain types of persons. In such cases, heavy penalties—and capital punishment especially—tend to deter a rational offender from covering up one crime by committing a worse. The instance of my grandfather's misadventure early fixed in my mind, at least, a certain healthy prejudice in favor of stern deterrents.

Doubtless many people could tell us of more dreadful cases of criminality, within their personal experience, than these three vignettes drawn from my own past which I have just presented. The breakers of violence sweep ever higher up the beaches of our civilization. We have supped long on horrors. About four years ago, my wife was kidnapped—though she escaped, chiefly through her gift of persuasion. (That episode also has gone into a short story of mine, "The Princess of All Lands.")[3] Everyone knows how the previous exemptions from criminal depredations have been cancelled. That, I suppose, is why we are discussing the possible restoration of capital punishment.

❖

The meliorists of the nineteenth century took it for granted that by a century after their time—by the year 1980, say—violent criminality would be virtually extinguished through universal schooling, better housing, better diet, general prosperity, improved measures for public health, and the like. They assumed that capital punishment was a relic of a barbarous and superstitious age. Capital punishment, they thought, was merciless; and they were themselves evangels of mercy. Their intellectual descendents did succeed, by the 1950s, in abolishing the death penalty throughout most of the civilized world.

But they did not succeed in abolishing hideous crimes of the sort formerly labelled "capital." In the most affluent of great countries, the United States, the rate of serious crimes rose most steadily and rapidly. At a time when the need for restraints upon criminality appeared to be greater than before, penalties were diminished. All this was done in the name of mercy.

Yet to whom was this mercy extended? Was it mercy toward the criminals? The recent insistence of a murderer in this country upon being executed according to sentence is no peculiar phenomenon. Doubtless many of the unfortunates being worked slowly to death in the prison-camps of the Soviet Arctic would find a firing-squad far more merciful than the pretended mercy of a thirty-year sentence. But we need not turn to totalist lands.

Is it not refined cruelty to keep alive, in self-loathing, a man who is a grave danger to the innocent and a grisly horror to himself? And to do such a thing in countries long admired for the justice of their laws? Once, walking Dartmoor, I came within sight of Dartmoor Prison, celebrated in so many English detective-yarns, but abandoned since I strolled nearby. At that time there was immured in Dartmoor Prison a little man with a talent for escaping. Although serving a life term there, he had managed to get out four or five times. And every time he contrived to elude his pursuers long enough to find, ravish, and kill a small girl. That done, he would submit in apathy to arrest and return to Dartmoor Prison.

This pitiable, loathsome being, after recapture, would be overwhelmed by remorse and would beg for death—which would be denied him, although yet another sentence of imprisonment for life would be imposed. For what purpose was his life so carefully preserved? His continued existence here below was of benefit only to the gutter press of London, which regaled the public with details of his atrocities. To whom was this policy merciful? To the other inmates of Dartmoor, compelled to associate with this creature? To the rural population of Devonshire, among whom the creature repeatedly committed his depredations? What sort of human dignity was this abstinence from capital punishment upholding?

Georgia's most talented writer of this century, the late Flannery O'Connor, once read aloud to me the most famous of her short stories, "A Good Man Is Hard to Find" (1955). Flannery was no sentimentalist and no meliorist; blameless herself, she nevertheless perceived the whole depravity of our fallen nature. In her art, she agreed with T.S. Eliot (who never read her stories) that the essential advantage for a poet "is to be able to see beneath both beauty and ugliness; to see the boredom, and the horror, and the glory."

In "A Good Man Is Hard to Find," Miss O'Connor describes the roadside murder of a whole family by an escaped convict called The Misfit, and his chums. (Flannery told me that she got The Misfit's sobriquet from Georgia newspapers—their appellation for a real-life fugitive from justice quite as alarming as Flannery's character.) The Misfit, like Teniente Pedro in *We Are God's Utopia,* is not without his amiable qualities: he apologizes to the grandmother (whom he kills a few minutes later) for not having a shirt to his back. He is a psychopath who had been "buried alive" in the penitentiary. Like many others of his dreadful nature, he has drifted through existence:

> "I was a gospel singer for a while," The Misfit said. "I been most everything. Been the arm service, both land and sea, at home and abroad, been twice married, been an undertaker, been with the railroads, plowed Mother Earth, been in a tornado, seen a man burnt alive once," and he looked up at the children's mother and the little girl who were sitting close together, their faces white and their eyes glassy; "I even seen a woman flogged," he said.

After a nightmare conversation about how "Jesus thown everything off balance," the grandmother impulsively touches The Misfit; and he shoots her three times. His helpers return from disposing of the other members of the helpless family.

> "She would of been a good woman," The Misfit said, "if it had been somebody there to shoot her every minute of her life."
>
> "Some fun!" Bobby Lee said.
>
> "Shut up, Bobby Lee," The Misfit said. "It's no real pleasure in life."

Aye, a good man is hard to find; in Adam's fall we sinned all; yet the depth and extent of our depravity varies from one person to another; and for the safety—perhaps the survival—of our species, it was found necessary in all previous ages to put out of their misery such criminals as The Misfit. Their physical presence among us cannot well be tolerated; the ultimate mysterious judgment upon their souls—so Flannery O'Connor implies—we leave to God.

To the Dartmoor child-ravager or the Jesus-accusing Misfit, what sort of mercy was burial alive in a penitentiary? Why, such preservation at public expense is merciful only if the mere prolongation of life here on earth is viewed as the chief purpose of existence; it is merciful only if one assumes that death brings annihilation—in Eliot's lines,

> *whirled*
> *Beyond the circuit of the shuddering Bear*
> *In fractured atoms.*

The abolition of capital punishment, I mean, is one of the products of humanitarianism—that is, of the belief that man's cleverness will suffice for all purposes, without need for knowledge of the transcendent and the divine.

Yet humanitarianism is now a decayed creed, worthless as a defense against the ideologues and the terrorists of our age, insufficient even to induce men and women to perform the ordinary duties which are supposed to bring the rewards of ordinary integrity. In a world that has denied God the Father, God the Son, and God the Holy Ghost—why, today the Savage God lays down his new commandments. The gods of the copybook headings with fire and slaughter return. The humanitarian who finds nothing sacred except (mysteriously) human life (so long as it is a criminal's life, not the life of an unborn infant) soon goes to the wall, throughout most of the world, in our time. Flannery O'Connor, a woman of humane letters, was no humanitarian. She was aware that this brief existence of ours—in her case, a brief life of physical suffering—is not the be-all and end-all. She did not mistake physical death for spiritual destruction.

❖

One of the many consequences of the widespread decay of belief in the resurrection of the flesh and the life everlasting has been the revulsion against capital punishment. But our understanding of the human soul begins to revive—encouraged, strange though it may seem to some people, by the speculations of physicists. No longer does it seem absurd to deny the suppositions of materialists and mechanists; no longer is it a mark of ignorance to declare that man is made for eternity. For a popular treatment of this renewed awareness of the realm of spirit, I refer those interested to Morton T. Kelsey's book *Afterlife: The Other Side of Dying* (1979); I might cite also a score of other serious books, among them certain studies of what time is and of what energy is.

The rejection of capital punishment in any circumstances thus is becoming an attitude which belongs to the intellectual and moral era that is passing. If the deprivation of life by human agency amounts only to opening the gate of another realm of existence—why, Death has lost his sting.

Why do some people retain so extreme an aversion to capital punishment that they would deny the death penalty even to condemned murderers who desire to be executed? Because of the fear of death—the dread of the void, of annihilation. Their dread of extinction—even if repressed in their conversation—for themselves is so powerful that they cannot abide the terminating of others' lives, not even the lives of Don Pedros and Misfits. It is an illogical dread, this terror of the inevitable: for we all die, just the same. John Strachey, as the Labour Party was about to push the Churchill government out of power, promised the electorate that under socialism the ministry of health would work such wonders that human life itself would be prolonged indefinitely. This did not come to pass. No statutes can assure immortality, except perhaps for corporations.

Yet why is death so dreadful? On my recommendation, the American Book Awards people chose as one of the five best religious books of 1979 Peter J. Kreeft's *Love Is Stronger Than Death*. "Death makes the question of God an empirically testable question," Kreeft writes. "Death makes the abstract God-question concrete. Instead of 'Is there a God?' the question becomes 'Will I see God?'" Death may give life to much, Peter Kreeft tells us:

> We have lost all our absolutes today except one. Once, we had God, truth, morality, family, fidelity, work, country, common sense, and many others—perhaps too many others. Now, in the age of absolute relativism, one absolute is left: death. Death is the one pathway through which all people at all times raise the question of the absolute, the question of God. The last excuse for not raising the God-question is Thoreau's "one world at a time." Death removes this last excuse.

The zealots against capital punishment fear to raise the God-question. Yet death, as Peter Kreeft tells us, can be a friend, a mother, a lover. Those who do not fear to clasp darkness as a bride die well, and are not extinguished. For all of us, in the end, death is the ultimate mercy. I do not understand why we should deny that mercy to slayers whose earthly existence is a grave; nor why we should deny a merciful protection to the guiltless whose purpose in this world may be undone by those guilty slayers.

["Criminal Character and Mercy," Redeeming the Time, *edited with an introduction by Jeffrey O. Nelson (Wilmington, DE: Intercollegiate Studies Institute, 1996), 240–53.]*

❖

VI.

THE DRUG OF IDEOLOGY

The Drug of Ideology ❖ The Errors of Ideology ❖
Libertarians: Chirping Sectaries ❖
Can Virtue Be Taught?

Throughout his writings Russell Kirk was to decry "Demon Ideology," which he associated with modern political fanaticism and utopian schemes found both on the Left and on the Right. In ideology he detected a hunger for revolutionary action that would transform society and human nature itself. With Edmund Burke, he viewed ideology as an "armed doctrine," as the enemy of religion, metaphysics, tradition, custom, convention, prescription, and old constitutions.

Communism, fascism, and Nazism personified for Kirk totalitarian ideological movements, intent on imposing their theories of power and social order. Their goals were brutally transparent: to foment, in Kirk's own words, "a dogmatic political theory which is an endeavor to substitute secular goals and doctrines for religious goals and doctrines"; in short, to bring about the omnipotence of the state that restricts freedom, dictates allegiances, and captures the mind.

Kirk is equally alert to insidious forms of ideology, including the "democratic ideology" that he detects in its American character and that he believes to be a formula for civil religion; this "ideology of Americanism," he warns, needs to be carefully watched for the dangers it poses to a free and humane society. He is especially apprehensive that some conservatives might adopt a narrow ideology in the absence of intelligent leadership and moral imagination. In this respect, Kirk singles out libertarianism as a simplistic ideology that is a radical and doctrinaire version of philosophical anarchy.

For Kirk, the conceptions of modern ideologues are in essence those of "the terrible simplifiers," to apply here Jacob Burckhardt's phrase to the architecture of a New Social Order. Ideology, in form and function, stands for the repudiation of the ethical life, the replacement of the moral virtues, and the extinction of the permanent things. In a word, ideology magnifies the semblances of vice.

The Drug of Ideology

"We are not at an end of our struggle, nor near it. Let us not deceive ourselves; we are at the beginning of great troubles." Burke goes on in the same prophetic passage, found in his Letters on a Regicide Peace *(1796), to say that "[i]t is with an* armed doctrine *that we are at war." Like Burke, Kirk never wavered in censuring the inroads of armed doctrines in the modern state. In "The Drug of Ideology," he strives to help the reader to apprehend the duplicitous features of ideology, its sham abstractions and promises, its conditions of "intellectual servitude." Here he identifies rigid forms of ideology since the last years of the eighteenth century—Jacobinism, communism, fascism, Nazism. In twentieth-century ideologists ("after the manner of Robespierre") Kirk adduces evidence of a zealous rebellion against God and man that epitomizes abnormity in its most deformed energies and aspects.*

In our age, most of the world has fallen into profound political disorder; and while the United States may seem an island of tranquillity, comparatively speaking, in a sea of troubles, nevertheless we are not secure. In politics, as in letters, abnormity gains ground. . . .

One may discern the principal causes of social disorder. Some of them are the consequences of swift economic and technological change, and those cannot be examined at any length here. But also a social order begins to disintegrate—or is supplanted by a very different domination—when political custom and political theory are overwhelmed by ideology; and when established political institutions are abandoned or permitted to decline, out of popular indifference and ignorance. . . . I am concerned with the desertion from political theory and tradition, and what may be done about it; with the neglect of institutions that maintain order and justice and freedom, and with the results of such dereliction. The permanent things of the commonwealth stand in peril, throughout the world. Our first necessity is to understand the nature of ideology.

"Ideology" does not mean political theory or principle, even though many journalists and some professors commonly employ the term in that sense. Ideology really means political fanaticism—and, more precisely, the belief that this world of ours may be converted into the Terrestrial Paradise through the operation of positive law and positive planning. The ideologue—Communist or Nazi or of whatever affiliation—maintains that human nature and society may be perfected by mundane, secular means, though these means ordinarily involve violent social revolution. The ideologue immanentizes religious symbols and inverts religious doctrines.

What religion promises to the believer in a realm beyond time and space, ideology promises to everyone—except those who have been "liquidated" in the process—in society. Salvation becomes collective and political. "When the intellectual feels no longer attached either to the community or the religion of his forbears," Raymond Aron writes in *The Opium of the Intellectuals* (1957), "he looks to progressive ideology to fill the vacuum. The main difference between the progressivism of the disciple of Harold Laski or Bertrand Russell and the Communism of the disciple of Lenin concerns not so much the content as the style of the ideologies and the allegiance they demand."

As a term of modern politics and sociology, "ideology" may be defined tentatively. It is an alleged science of politics, dogmatic and often utopian, closely allied with the interests of a particular social class or political sect. Several powerful ideologies or quasi-ideologies have been at work in the nineteenth and twentieth centuries. This word has passed through complicated changes of meaning, however, and often is misapplied.

In France, at the close of the eighteenth century, the term was employed by the disciples of Condillac, particularly Destutt de Tracy, whose *Les éléments d'idéologie* appeared in five volumes between 1801 and 1815. The original "ideologists" or "ideologues" believed that all knowledge is derived from sensation, and that a science of ideas could be developed upon this basis, describing the history and evolution of thought, and applicable to politics, ethics, and pedagogy. Thus originally "ideology" was a kind of climax of the rationalism of the Enlightenment, an attempt to systematize and apply knowledge obtained from sensory perception. The intellectual origins of ideology are described by a number of writers, perhaps most recently in two books by Thomas Molnar, *The Decline of the Intellectual* (1961) and *Utopia, the Perennial Heresy* (1967).

Napoleon, in 1812, looking with disfavor upon the ideological school, ridiculed Destutt de Tracy and his associates as "ideologists," men of hopelessly abstract and fanciful views, unacquainted with the realities of the civil social order. From an early date, accordingly, "ideology" and "ideologist" or "ideologue" became terms of derogation, implying misguided intellectuality as banefully applied to social concerns. Thus John Adams, in 1813, wrote of ideology:

> Our English words, Idiocy or Idiotism, express not the force or meaning of it. It is presumed its proper definition is the science of Idiocy. And a very profound, abstruse, and mysterious science it is. You must descend deeper than the divers in the *Dunciad* to make any discoveries, and after all you will find no bottom. It is the bathos, the theory, the art, the skill of diving and sinking in government. It was taught in the school of folly; but alas! Franklin, Turgot, Rochefoucauld, and Condorcet, under Tom Paine, were the great masters of that academy!

The chief political thinkers of the English speaking world, at least, have abjured ideology. In his *Logic* (1843), John Stuart Mill declares, "I would willingly have . . . persevered to the end in the same abstinence which I have hitherto observed from ideological discussions." In America and Britain, long hostile toward what Burke called "the abstract metaphysician" in politics, the concept of ideology always has been unpopular—at least until quite recently.

About the middle of the nineteenth century, Karl Marx and his disciples considerably altered the meaning of "ideology." According to Marx—particularly in his *Poverty of Philosophy* (1900)—ideology is a cloak for class interests, an outwardly rational instrument of propaganda, a veil of argument produced to disguise and defend an established social order. In Marx's phrases, "The same men who establish social relations conformably with their material productivity, produce also the principles, the ideas, the categories, conformable with their social relations." Thus Marx attacked the social theories of his own time and of earlier ages as ideologies meant to maintain capitalism, feudalism, imperialism, and other systems. Marxism itself, however, rapidly developed into an ideology, or dogmatic system of politics professing to found its structure upon a "reality" ascertained by sensory perception alone.

In the present century, Karl Mannheim distinguished between the "particular" and the "total" meanings of ideology. "The former," Mannheim wrote, "assumes that this or that interest is the cause of a given lie or deception. The latter presupposes that there is a correspondence between a given social situation and a given perspective, point of view, or apperception mass." In general, Mannheim takes the view that ideology is irrational, and in modern times merges with utopianism.

Since the Second World War, in serious discussions, "ideology" usually has meant a dogmatic political theory which endeavors to substitute secular doctrines and goals for religious doctrines and goals—what J. L. Talmon calls "political messianism." The ideologue promises social, rather than personal, salvation; and this salvation, occurring in time, is to be achieved through a radical transformation of social institutions, involving the destruction of existing law and institutions, and probably requiring violence against the present possessors of power. On principles allegedly rational and scientific, ideology is meant to reconstruct and perfect society and human nature.

It follows that the various ideologies which have arisen since the concluding years of the eighteenth century—Jacobinism, socialism, communism, anarchism, syndicalism, fascism, Naziism, and others—all are opposed by conservatism, which is founded upon the concept that politics is the art of the possible, and the concept that the old and tried is preferable to the new and untried. In the aphorism of H. Stuart Hughes, "Conservatism is the negation of ideology."

Yet, as I remarked earlier, today "ideology" frequently is used as if the term were synonymous with "political philosophy" or "political theory." Tacitly, this assumption suggests that any theoretical foundation for politics or sociology must be involved either with social utopianism (often fanatical) or with veiled class interests, or with both. This corruption of the term, produced in part by a vulgarizing of the concepts of Marx and Mannheim, makes sober examination of social first principles more difficult, particularly in a time when ideological passions and prejudices retain power throughout most of the world.

Real thinking is a painful process; and the ideologue resorts to the anaesthetic of social utopianism, escaping the tragedy and grandeur of true human existence by giving his adherence to a perfect dream-world of the future. Reality he stretches or chops away to conform to his dream-pattern of human nature and society. For the concepts of salvation and damnation, he substitutes abstractly virtuous "progressives" and abstractly vicious "reactionaries."

The twentieth-century ideologue, after the manner of Robespierre, thinks that his secular dogmas are sustained by the Goddess Reason; he prides himself inordinately upon being "scientific" and "rational"; and he is convinced that all opposition to his particular wave of the future is selfish obscurantism, when it is not direct vested interest. One may add that ever since the modern scholar began to call himself an "intellectual," he has tended to fall addict to the opiate of ideology; for the word "intellectual" itself, used as a noun of persons, implies an overweening confidence in Reason with a capital R, to the exclusion of faith, custom, consensus, humility, and sacred mystery.

The ideologue, in brief, is one of Orwell's new-style men "who think in slogans and talk in bullets." For the ideologue, humankind may be divided into two classes: the comrades of Progress, and the foes attached to reactionary interests. All human actions may be judged in terms of ideological motive, the ideologue is convinced. An African leader who wishes to settle for the practicable and to maintain amicable relationships with Europeans, for instance, must be a tool of "colonialists" or in the pay of a sinister capitalistic cartel; it is inconceivable that such a leader should be sincere in his course of action. On the other hand, a revolutionary, in Africa or elsewhere, always is right: just conceivably he may be over-zealous on occasion, but the purity of his motives is beyond question. The ideologues are Burckhardt's "terrible simplifiers." They reduce politics to catch-phrases; and because they will tolerate no stopping-place short of heaven upon earth, they deliver us up to men possessed by devils.

Ideology, Objectivity, and Scientism

"Ideology is existence in rebellion against God and man," Eric Voegelin writes. "It is the violation of the First and Tenth Commandments, if we want to use the language of Israelite order; it is the *nosos*, the disease of the spirit, if we want to use the language of Aeschylus and Plato. Philosophy is the love of being through love of divine Being as the source of its order." For a great while, Voegelin continues, ideology has held a mortgage upon science—that is, upon systematic thought.

But the ideologue does not think of himself as a simplifier or a sloganizer. He believes that he is objective and scientific, even dispassionate. An anti-collectivist ideologue (rather a rare breed, in this century), Miss Ayn Rand, even concocts a rigorous ideology called "Objectivism." All faithful followers of systematized ideologies believe themselves to be objective; their adversaries, to a man, are subjective.

So permit me to digress here concerning "objectivity," a word as much abused as "ideology." The modern devotee of objectivity prides himself upon being a realist, a man who perceives the world as it truly is, without being deluded by visions, personal interests, or irrational emotions. But no man is more unphilosophical than one who fancies that he is totally objective.

Objectivity means the property or state of being objective. The word now implies absorption in, or concern with, external objects, as opposed to "subjectivity," or concern with self and the interior life.

Yet historically considered, the terms "objectivity" and "objective" meant to medieval and Renaissance scholars quite the contrary of their twentieth-century connotations. From about 1300, when Duns Scotus defined the term, until late in the eighteenth century, "objectivity" and "objective" were generally understood to refer to things perceived or thought, intentional, or representative; while "subjective," during those centuries, meant things in their own form. This earlier usage is suggested by Bishop Berkeley (1709): "Natural phenomena are only natural appearances. They are, therefore, such as we see and perceive them. Their real and objective nature are therefore the same."

For the past two centuries, however, "objectivity" has connoted real" objects, as opposed to "subjectivity," or concern with the subject of cognition, the mind. In addition, "objectivity" has come to imply concentration upon external objects of thought—things or other persons—as against attention to one's self, one's own ways, one's own sensations. In this sense, the "objective" man is one who concerns himself with external facts or what he believes to be "objective" reality, rather than with his own emotions, personality, and thoughts. The rationalistic, nineteenth-century usage is exemplified by a remark of John Fiske: "The only healthful activity of the mind is an objective activity, in which there is as little brooding over self as is possible." Fiske is echoed by another enthusiast for this sort of objectivity, John Dewey, in *Democracy and Education* (1916): "The idea of perfecting an 'inner' personality is a sure sign of social division. What is called 'inner' is simply that which does not connect with others—which is not capable of free and full communication. What is termed spiritual culture has usually been futile, with something rotten about it, just because it has been conceived as a thing which a man might have internally—and therefore exclusively."

In the "objective" paradise of Dewey and his disciples, as in Huxley's *Brave New World* (1932), everybody belongs to everybody else—and not one's body merely, but one's mind, becomes public domain. Dewey was bent, though perhaps only half consciously, on creating an impersonal society: that is, a society in which strong personalities would be eliminated. For there is no personality, really, except inner personality, subjective personality; if, then, its perfection is denounced as rotten, human beings are expected to efface personality altogether. They become "other-directed men." Lacking belief, loyalty, and self-reliance, dependent upon an unattainable perfect objectivity, they are moved only by fad and foible, and are blown about by every wind of doctrine. Objectivity of this sort terminates in pusillanimity.

Many twentieth-century writers and scholars praise "objectivity" as impartial and accurate; and they disparage "subjectivity" as sliding toward illusion, partisanship, and emotional disturbance. Thus most sociologists, say, profess devotion to objectivity; while poets, concerned with personal experience, are allegedly immersed in subjectivity. It remains most doubtful, nevertheless, whether any man may so wholly divest himself of prejudice, early opinions, and private experience as to manifest a thoroughgoing objectivity.

In the social studies, for instance, not a few doctors of philosophy call "objectivity" what really is their own ideology. Thus they praise to the skies a book that advocates a positivistic view of man and society; if that book espouses the cause of centralized planning, the omnicompetent state, and the progressive standardizing of all aspects of life, it is "objective"—that is, the book conforms to reality, or to what should be reality. If a book takes another tack, holding by religious conceptions of man and prescriptive opinions of the free and just society—why, the authors of so disagreeable a work must be nasty subjectivists.

For in an age of strong ideological tendencies, many people who profess devotion to "objectivity" may be self-deluding victims of a curiously inverted "subjectivity," indulging an intolerant zeal for "tolerance," a passionate attack on passion, a bigoted denunciation of bigotry. In such circumstances, "objectivity" is confounded with ideological preference, and the "objective" ideologue demands conformity to his notion of reality—or of what ought to be the state of society.

In actuality, "objective" and "subjective" approaches to true perception are not inimical, but rather co-ordinate, and even symbiotic. Accurate understanding of external objects, distinct from consideration of self, is the essential method of modern science; but the knowledge gained from personal experience and meditation is necessary for the classification and ordering of phenomena. Thus poetic insight, if "subjective," nevertheless broadens and deepens the vision; while scientific examination, if "objective," confirms or corrects the private judgment.

To resume, nevertheless the typical ideologue thinks of himself as perfectly objective. The core of his belief is that human nature and human society may be improved infinitely—nay, perfected—by the application of the techniques of the physical and biological sciences to the governance of men. Nearly all nineteenth and twentieth-century radical movements drew their inspiration in considerable part from this positivistic assumption; Marxism is only one of the more systematic products of this view of life and thought. For the convinced positivist-ideologue, traditional religion has been a nuisance and a curse, because it impedes the designs of the ideological planner. Science, with a Roman S, should supplant God. The religious teacher would give way to the "scientific" manager of the new society.

This rather vague claim that society ought to be regulated on "scientific" principles has held an appeal for some physical and biological scientists; and the less such scientists have known of humane letters, history, and political theory, the more enthusiastic they have tended to be for a new order which would sweep away all the errors and follies of mankind by a rational application of scientific theory and method. The high achievements of physical and biological science in the nineteenth century gave powerful reinforcement to the advocates of "scientism" in sociology and politics. Religion, moral tradition, and the complex of established political institutions were irrational and unscientific and subjective, it seemed; surely the scientists must show the preachers and politicians the way to a better world. H. G. Wells was the ablest vulgarizer of scientistic ideology.

But since the middle of the twentieth century, a good many intelligent people have been taking a second look at the claims of pure science, of the "science of society," and of religion. Fresh scientific speculation has called into question the soundness of many of the assumptions of the mechanistic physics and the Darwinian biology of the nineteenth century; while a revival of serious theology and a renewed interest in political theory have strengthened the positions of people who think that they were not born yesterday. The catastrophic social events of our century, moreover, have caused some of us to inquire whether there is not something fundamentally wrong with philosophical and scientific and sociological postulates which promise us the terrestrial paradise but promptly deliver us at the gates of a terrestrial hell. Fascism, Naziism, and communism all have claimed to be scientific.

A good representative of reformed scientific opinion is Dr. Edmund W. Sinnott, dean of the graduate school of Yale University, writing in *The Bulletin of the Atomic Scientists* (December 1956). After presenting very fairly and even evangelically the case for scientific positivism and objectivity, he proceeds to demolish it. With Aristotle, Sinnott recognizes final causes: he is a teleologist. What animates every organism, what constitutes its nature, is *purpose*: "If it be accepted, the idea of purpose, of intention, of the motive power of a goal or ideal rather than of an organic 'drive,' changes the orientation of our psychical lives." Man, he argues, is drawn toward a goal; and that goal often cannot be perceived or apprehended through the methods of exact science. "The closest contact with reality for many people is through this unexplained, mysterious urgency in life experienced in flashes of insight, for these carry with them a great weight of authority." So here an eminent professor of science has stood up for subjectivity, for the man of vision, for Carlyle in Leith Walk or Pascal murmuring "Fire, fire, fire!"

"The days of the evolutionary optimists are gone," Sinnott continues, "who believed that progress is inherent in the nature of things and that man is bound to grow better almost automatically. If we are to find a way out of our troubles, we must appeal not only to the rational attitudes and methods of the scientist but also to man's inner spiritual motivation. Love may turn out to be a more valuable resource than logic."

For Sinnott, science cannot supplant religion; both science and religion "have indispensable contributions to make to the great task of building a society in which men will not only be safe and wise and happy and loving but will gain the serene confidence that their lives are in harmony with the universe itself."

So scientism—the facile application of the teachings of natural science to the affairs of mankind—is on boggy ground today: social "objectivity," like social Darwinism, is parting company with much present scientific theory. The representative ideologue is unaware how very old-fangled he is becoming in his notion of what pure science teaches.

Yet it would be foolish optimism to mistake the speculations of some leading philosophers of science for the convictions of the whole body of teachers of science, researchers, and scientific technicians. A professed man of science still may remain as much an ideologue as any agent of the Chinese "Cultural Revolution."

At the convention in 1956 of the American Association for the Advancement of Science, for instance—meeting only a short time after Professor Sinnott wrote—there still were exhibited (together with more encouraging opinions) certain depressing examples of the influence which scientistic ideology still exerts upon American society. Consider a research-project in "intellectual potential" described to the Association by its authors, an associate professor of psychiatry and an associate professor of pediatrics at Ohio State University.

The purpose of this research-project was to discover whether heredity determines individual intelligence to any marked degree. These two professors studied the behavior of a thousand infants in Baltimore, all about forty weeks old, excluding babies with damaged brains from consideration in their general conclusions. Upon the "developmental score" employed in this study, ninety per cent of the infants scored between 90 and 120, with 100 as the norm. Race, economic status, and education of parents seemed to have no discernible effect upon the scores of particular babies. Therefore, the professors announced, one baby seems to be as intelligent as another; and undeniable variation of children at a later age must be "wholly a result of education and environment."

"Intelligence," an educationist said once, "is simply what our tests test." This particular research project appears to me a tolerable example of an ideological mortgage upon the work of science. Leaving aside certain logical and statistical fallacies involved in this project, still the range between 90 and 120 indicates a very considerable difference in infant minds. But the principal foolishness of such a survey is its claim to measure human intelligence at a stage when the human creatures concerned could not yet be called rational human beings. One might as well try to determine the swiftness of a fawn by examining the creature in embryo, as to try to determine the power of the human intellect by observing the behavior of a baby a few months old. Man's rationality is made possible by his mastery of words and his employment of his hands. A little baby knows no words, and therefore no general concepts; he can use his hands to little purpose, and therefore is not yet even a tool-using animal. Of course all small babies seem much the same in intelligence; for none of them has, at that stage, much intelligence distinctively human; they are almost identical in their poverty. If a thousand forty-weeks-old baboons or chimpanzees had been observed and tested alongside the human infants, doubtless the apes would have come out much better on the development-score, for their nature matures much more rapidly than does the human. Therefore, one supposes, we ought to conclude that the differences between baboon baby and human baby are matters of education and environment, and baboons should be entitled to the privileges and immunities of the United Nations' Universal Declaration of Human Rights.

This latter-day *tabula rasa* doctrine of the psychiatrist and the teacher of pediatrics, I suspect—though I do not know the professors in question—is ideologically inspired. It is "democratic," in the Jacobin meaning of that word. All people *ought* to be equal, the egalitarian ideologue commences; but if persons are unequal in intelligence from a very early age, then it may be difficult to establish among them equality of condition; so the "scientific" dogma must be made to fit the ideological dogma, and Jonathan Edwards and Sam Jukes will be demonstrated, by "development-scores," to be naturally as much alike as two peas in a pod. Intelligence is what our tests test; and if tests reveal disconcerting individual differences—why, back to your development-scores, men. Having arrived at a tentative conclusion about certain infants by scientifically dubious means, then the ideologue hastily tacks on to his structure grand generalizations, quite unsupported even by his own evidence, concerning the native intelligence of adults. This is scientism in its worst sense: science enslaved by ideological prejudice.

In genetics, as in other sciences, the ideologue recoils from his own conclusions only when the results indubitably are ruinous—as in the notorious affair, in Soviet Russia, of Lysenko's theories about corn, faithful to Marxism but false to nature and productive of monstrous crop-failures. The ideologue, I am saying, is not genuinely objective and not genuinely scientific. In essence, ideology is a passionate endeavor to overthrow the spiritual and moral order, as well as the social order; and scientific doctrine is no better than a tool for the ideologue. Raymond Aron makes this point:

> Communism developed from an economic and political doctrine at a time when the spiritual vitality and the authority of the Churches was in decline. Passions which in other times might have expressed themselves in strictly religious beliefs were channelled into political action. Socialism appeared not so much a technique applicable to the management of enterprises or to the functioning of the economy, as a means of curing once and for all the age-old misery of mankind.
>
> The ideologies of the Right and of the Left, Fascism as well as Communism, are inspired by the modern philosophy of immanence. They are atheist, even when they do not deny the existence of God, to the extent that they conceive the human world without reference to the transcendental.

Ideology is intellectual servitude. And emancipation from ideology can be achieved only by belief in an enduring order of which the sanction, and the end, are more than objective, more than scientistic, more than human, and more than natural.

Ideology and American Society

The American soil is not well prepared for pure ideology. Half a century ago, Santayana wrote that "it will take some hammering to drive a coddling socialism into America." The hammering of ideology has been heard since then, but political religion has not yet triumphed. Though, as Aron knows, the United States has its political illusions, these are not precisely identical with the illusions of the French intellectual of the Left:

"The 'American way of life' is the negation of what the European intellectual means by the word ideology," Aron remarks.

> Americanism does not formulate itself as a system of concepts or propositions; it knows nothing of the "collective savior," the end of history, the determining cause of historical "becoming," or the dogmatic negation of

> religion; it combines respect for the constitution, homage for individual initiative, a humanitarianism inspired by strong but vague beliefs which are fairly indifferent to the rivalries between the churches (only Catholic "totalitarianism" is considered disquieting), the worship of science and efficiency. It does not involve any detailed orthodoxy or official doctrine. It is learned at school, and society enforces it. Conformism if you like, but a conformism which is rarely felt to be tyrannical, since it does not forbid free discussion in matters of religion, economics, or politics.

Yet a hankering after ideology has existed since early times in America, though never well satisfied; and at moments, during the past forty or fifty years, it seemed as if ideology were about to capture the American mind. That ideology, if it had come to exercise an hegemony over American thought, would have borne the name of Liberalism. Communism, though it contrived to entrench itself in some high places among American intellectuals, never attracted so great a share of them as went over to Marxism in France or Germany or Italy or even Britain; while Fascism took no root here at all.

Something called Liberalism, nevertheless, became very nearly a secular orthodoxy among American writers and (more especially) American professors. No one was quite sure what Liberalism amounted to—which kept it from becoming a full-grown ideology. To some, Liberalism meant anti-religious opinions; to others, socialism, or a managed economy; to a different set, absolute liberty of private conduct, untrammeled by law or tradition; to a number, perpetual doubt for the sake of doubting; to one lot, old-fangled Benthamism.

This Liberal secular orthodoxy is decaying now, to the alarm of its principal champions, some of whom defend it with the zeal of genuine ideologues, although they are not quite sure just what they are defending. Nowadays these champions, confronted with the revival of conservative ideas, alternate between the argument that conservatism is getting nowhere at all, and the contention that conservatism is so dreadfully powerful as to drive persecuted liberals into holes and corners.

As a matter of fact, the precepts of Liberalism still dominate a great many American writers and professors, who sometimes are intolerant in the name of liberal toleration; but the odds are that this Liberal orthodoxy cannot now harden into a true ideology. The fantastics of the New Left dearly would love to embrace a rigorous ideology; but they fall out so much among themselves, and within themselves, that no body of secular dogmas takes form.

America needs nothing less than it needs ideology. Not abstractions, but prudence, prescription, custom, tradition, and constitution have governed the American people. We have been saved from ideology by political tradition. We still subscribe, however confusedly, to the norms of politics; we still cherish the permanent things.

For nearly two centuries, the outward forms of government in this nation have altered little. Although during the past four decades, and particularly during the past ten years, the actual functioning of our political system has changed rapidly, still the facade of the political edifice looks much as it used to. Within, nevertheless, the house is being transformed—even if few desire a radical transformation. No system of laws and institutions is immutable. Can the American Republic direct such change into actions which will reconcile with our historical experience and our prescriptive institutions that spirit of the age which now shakes the house?

Change, as Burke said, is the means of our preservation: as the human body exhausts old tissues and takes on new, so must any vigorous society. Yet rash and mindless change, striking to the heart of society, may destroy the continuity which invigorates a nation. The character of change in America probably will be determined, for good or ill, within the next few years.

Whatever our civil discontents at present, we stand in little peril of a political revolution which would destroy our national foundations. The American people remain, in some ways, the most conservative in the world—even though their conservatism is not so much the product of reflection as it is of habit, custom, material interests, and attachment to certain documents, most notably the Declaration of Independence and the Constitution of the United States. Our difficulty, indeed, is not just now the clutch of ideology, but rather complacency—the smug general assumption that the civil social order, in essence, always will be for our sons what it was for our fathers.

"With conservative populations," Brooks Adams wrote, "slaughter is nature's remedy." He referred to a complacent democratic conservatism of the crowd. If American order, justice, and freedom are to endure, some of us must look into the first principles of politics and apply the wisdom of our ancestors to the troubles of our time. To preserve all the benefits of American society—which may be lost not through revolution, but perhaps in a fit of absence of mind—we must turn political philosophers, as did our ancestors in the last quarter of the eighteenth century.

Like the English, the Americans usually have been reluctant to embark upon abstract political speculation. Except for the period just before, during, and after the Revolution, and—to a lesser extent—the years before and immediately after the Civil War, we have produced little political philosophy; we have trusted, instead, to constitution, custom, convention, consensus, and the wisdom of the species.

Indeed, the Declaration and the Constitution, though drawn up by men of philosophical knowledge and power, are not in themselves manuals of political philosophy. The Declaration of 1776 is simply a declaration—and a highly successful piece of immediate political propaganda; such philosophical concepts as find expression therein are so mistily expressed as to mean all things to all men, then and now. The Constitution is not a tract at all, but a practical instrument of government, molded in part by necessary practical compromises.

We will not repudiate the Declaration, nor much alter the formal Constitution. Yet no society can be bound by parchment. With vertiginous speed, the character of American society is being altered. Can a people whose modes of living, economy, and diversions differ radically from those of the eighteenth century continue to live in harmony and prosperity under a political system developed in very different circumstances? Can a people of whom the immense majority now dwell in megalopolis, for instance, govern themselves on the old principles of American territorial democracy?

For my part, I do not think that we could construct a brand-new constitution better calculated to reconcile the claims of order and the claims of freedom than does our old Constitution—whatever its anomalies and difficulties today. If that is true, then we will do well to seek means for reinvigorating the Constitution and making sure it deals adequately with the conditions of the twentieth century; otherwise it may be altered out of recognition by an extravagant "judicial reinterpretation," unsupported either by precedent or by public consensus—or, in the long run, it may be discarded altogether by an impatient Executive Force, Congress, and people.

And we must remind ourselves that beneath any formal constitution—even beneath our Constitution, the most enduringly successful of such formal documents—lies an unwritten constitution much more difficult to define, but really more powerful: the body of institutions, customs, manners, conventions, and voluntary associations which may not even be mentioned in the formal constitution, but which nevertheless form the fabric of social reality and sustain the formal constitution.

So the examination of our present discontents cannot be confined to an exercise in formal constitutional law. To discuss the future of American politics, we must confess that, vastly important though they are, the Declaration and the Constitution do not constitute the be-all and end-all of political wisdom; and that, when the file affords no precedent, we must turn from the legal brief to political philosophy.

Recourse to political first principles is attended by risks. Scarcely anything could be more ruinous than to turn the American people into a set of half-schooled coffee-house philosophers, ideologues bent upon gaining Utopia instanter, terrible simplifiers in politics. Yet in the exigencies of our decade, a people cannot govern themselves wholly by the decisions and the rhetoric of 1776 and 1787. The intellectual and political leaders of our age have the duty of guiding public opinion into prudent consideration of the means for harmonizing our prescriptive politics with modern conditions that require some tolerable action. I am saying that there exists real danger of our drifting mindlessly into the mass-age, unaware that order and justice and freedom are fragile; and that today, as much as in 1776 or 1787, we need to discuss questions concerning the vitality of the good civil social order.

Ever since the Civil War, political thought has languished in the United States. For important political theory almost always is developed out of a time of troubles, when thinking men, forced to examine their first principles, seek means to avert the imminent collapse of order, so as to restore some measure of justice and security to a wounded society. The political writings of Plato and Aristotle came out of such an age. So did Cicero's works, and Dante's, and Hobbes's, and Machiavelli's, and Hooker's, and Locke's, and Burke's, and Marx's. The nature of the confusion which provokes the exposition of political theory may be the inadequacy of an old order, morally and administratively, as it was in the society of Calvin and of Rousseau; or the confusion may be the consequence of a new order's search for sanction, as it was in the society of Bodin or of Bentham. Doubt and violence are the parents of social speculation. Prescription, legal precedent, and muddling through suffice for ages or nations that experience no serious threat to things established.

Thus the political ideas of Adams, Hamilton, Madison, and Jefferson, though rooted in English and colonial experience and mightily influenced by the legacy of English political philosophy, took form as prudent endeavors to restore order and justice to a commonwealth distressed by revolution. Thus the ideas of John Randolph and Calhoun were expressed as a defense of established institutions in the Old South. Once the triumph of the Union, however, had put an end to the debate between North and South, and once the swelling prosperity of the United States after the Civil War combined with the nation's comparative isolation to make any foreign menace trifling, American political speculation sank to a lower level.

No political philosopher of remarkable stature appeared during the closing third of the nineteenth century, and the bulk of what passed for political thought in this country was simply the reflection of various English and German liberal ideas, adapted to the American climate of opinion. There seemed to be no need for reference to first principles; Things were in the saddle, and most men were content to let Things ride mankind. Warning voices like those of Henry and Brooks Adams were rather despairing protests than expressions of political philosophy. As the First World War approached, and as the economic and moral problems of the post-war era became pressing, ideas were granted some small hearing, it is true, so that Irving Babbitt and Paul Elmer More and George Santayana asked the right questions. Yet Things galloped on; the New Deal, fortunately perhaps, was the expression of vague humanitarian aspirations and positive grievances, not of any coherent "liberal" or "radical" system of thought. Nor was America's participation in the Second World War governed by any body of general ideas: caused by the combination of moral indignation with fear of Germany and Japan, American intervention stood bewildered for want of first principle when the problems of the peace had to be confronted.

The genius of American politics, as Daniel Boorstin suggests, consists in an innocence of abstract doctrine and theoretic dogma; and this is quite as true of the genius of English politics. Yet possibly the immunity of these nations from the curse of ideology has resulted not so much from a deliberate contempt for theory, as from two peculiar advantages that today are much diminished: first, a comparative physical isolation from other powers that made possible the postponement of grave decisions; second, an underlying set of moral and political assumptions, common to nearly everyone in these societies, which were the products of a venerable historic experience, and which served the purpose that political dogmas serve in nations less governed by general prejudice, prescription, and custom.

Yet a time may come in the history of nations when the previous security against foreign intervention is destroyed, and when tradition and established usage are so weakened that they cannot stand unbuttressed against the assaults of ideology. Such an era is America's near the close of the sixties. The dissolution of America's old political and military isolation requires no comment; we survived by a single generation the end of Britain's comparative isolation. The breaking of the cake of custom is the subject of many books, though all its intricacies have not yet been explored. It must suffice to say here that with the triumph of modern technology, the ascendancy of general literacy and secularized schooling, the extreme mobility and fluidity of twentieth-century American society, the disappearance of many elements of authority and class, and the diffusion of positivistic ideas—why, tradition and custom in the United States, though by no means effaced, have lost much of their old power. We live, then, in an insecure society, doubtful of its future, an island of comparative but temporary sanctuary in a sea of revolution; and neither the old isolation nor the old received opinions of the mass of men seem calculated to hold out unassisted against the physical force of revolutionary powers and the moral innovations of modern ideologies. This is just such a time as has required and produced, repeatedly in the course of history, a reexamination of first principles and a considered political philosophy. . . .

["The Drug of Ideology," Enemies of the Permanent Things: Observations of Abnormity in Literature and Politics, *Rev. ed. (La Salle, IL: Sherwood Sugden & Company, 1984), 153–71.]*

❖

The Errors of Ideology

This essay appears first in The Politics of Prudence *(1993). In it Kirk warns that it is necessary to resist ideological politics. "In his march towards Utopia," he writes, "the ideologue is merciless." Kirk predicts that the twenty-first century, no less than the twentieth, will see the birth of new forms of ideology, each promoting a political formula, each promising earthly happiness, each preoccupied with economic and material interests, each promulgating a new religion of progress and change that wipes out the norms of order, justice, freedom. All ideologies, Kirk argues, emerge from dreams of culture and society in which the man-god has built the indestructible city and tower of Babel. The visionary schemes of ideologues are in reality, he is suggesting, new Babels and new hells. Ideologues are present-day Titans who, as we are reminded by G. K. Chesterton, the conservative English writer admired by Kirk, do not scale heavens but lay waste the world.*

The word *ideology* was coined in Napoleonic times. Destutt de Tracy, the author of *Les éléments d'idéologie* (five volumes, 1801–15), was an abstract intellectual of the sort since grown familiar on the Left Bank of the Seine, the haunt of all budding ideologues, among them in recent decades the famous liberator of Democratic Kampuchea, Pol Pot. Tracy and his disciples intended a widespread reform of education, to be founded upon an alleged science of ideas; they drew heavily upon the psychology of Condillac and more remotely upon that of John Locke.

Rejecting religion and metaphysics, these original ideologues believed that they could discover a system of natural laws—which system, if conformed to, could become the foundation of universal harmony and contentment. Doctrines of self-interest, economic productivity, and personal liberty were bound up with these notions. Late-born children of the dying Enlightenment, the Ideologues assumed that systematized knowledge derived from sensation could perfect society through ethical and educational methods and by well-organized political direction.

Napoleon dismissed the Ideologues with the remark that the world is governed not by abstract ideas, but by imagination. John Adams called this newfangled *ideology* "the science of idiocy." Nevertheless, during the nineteenth century ideologues sprang up as if someone, like Jason, had sown dragons' teeth that turned into armed men. These ideologues generally have been enemies to religion, tradition, custom, convention, prescription, and old constitutions.

The concept of ideology was altered considerably in the middle of the nineteenth century, by Karl Marx and his school. Ideas, Marx argued, are nothing better than expressions of class interests, as related to economic production. Ideology, the alleged science of ideas, thus becomes a systematic apology for the claims of a class—nothing more.

Or, to put this argument in Marx's own blunt and malicious terms, what has been called political philosophy is merely a mask for the economic self-seeking of oppressors—so the Marxists declared. Ruling ideas and norms constitute a delusory mask upon the face of the dominant class, shown to the exploited "as a standard of conduct, partly to varnish, partly to provide moral support for, domination." So Marx wrote to Engels.

Yet the exploited too, Marx says, develop systems of ideas to advance their revolutionary designs. So what we call Marxism is an ideology intended to achieve revolution, the triumph of the proletariat, and eventually communism. To the consistent Marxist, ideas have no value in themselves: they, like all art, are worthwhile only as a means to achieve equality of condition and economic satisfaction. While deriding the ideologies of all other persuasions, the Marxist builds with patient cunning his own ideology.

Although it has been the most powerful of ideologies, Marxism—very recently diminished in strength—has competitors: various forms of nationalism, negritude, feminism, fascism (a quasi-ideology never fully fleshed out in Italy), naziism (an ideology in embryo, Hannah Arendt wrote), syndicalism, anarchism, social democracy, and Lord knows what all. Doubtless yet more forms of ideology will be concocted during the twenty-first century.

Kenneth Minogue, in his recent book *Alien Powers: The Pure Theory of Ideology* (1985), uses the word "to denote any doctrine which presents the hidden and saving truth about the world in the form of social analysis. It is a feature of all such doctrines to incorporate a general theory of the mistakes of everybody else." That "hidden and saving truth" is a fraud—a complex of contrived falsifying "myths," disguised as history, about the society we have inherited. Raymond Aron, in *The Opium of the Intellectuals*, analyzes the three myths that have seduced Parisian intellectuals: the myths of the Left, of the Revolution, of the Proletariat.

To summarize the analysis of ideology undertaken by such scholars as Minogue, Aron, J. L. Talmon, Thomas Molnar, Lewis Feuer, and Hans Barth, this word *ideology*, since the Second World War, usually has signified a dogmatic political theory which is an endeavor to substitute secular goals and doctrines for religious goals and doctrines; and which promises to overthrow present dominations so that the oppressed may be liberated. Ideology's promises are what Talmon calls "political messianism." The ideologue promises salvation in this world, hotly declaring that there exists no other realm of being. Eric Voegelin, Gerhart Niemeyer, and other writers have emphasized that ideologues "immanentize the symbols of transcendence"—that is, corrupt the vision of salvation through grace in death into false promises of complete happiness in this mundane realm.

Ideology, in short, is a political formula that promises mankind an earthly paradise; but in cruel fact what ideology has created is a series of terrestrial hells. I set down below some of the vices of ideology.

> 1) Ideology is inverted religion, denying the Christian doctrine of salvation through grace in death, and substituting collective salvation here on earth through violent revolution. Ideology inherits the fanaticism that sometimes has afflicted religious faith, and applies that intolerant belief to concerns secular.
>
> 2) Ideology makes political compromise impossible: the ideologue will accept no deviation from the Absolute Truth of his secular revelation. This narrow vision brings about civil war, extirpation of "reactionaries," and the destruction of beneficial functioning social institutions.
>
> 3) Ideologues vie one with another in fancied fidelity to their Absolute Truth; and they are quick to denounce deviationists or defectors from their party orthodoxy. Thus fierce factions are raised up among the ideologues themselves, and they war mercilessly and endlessly upon one another, as did Trotskyites and Stalinists.

The evidence of ideological ruin lies all about us. How then can it be that the allurements of ideology retain great power in much of the world?

❖

The answer to that question is given in part by this observation from Raymond Aron: "When the intellectual feels no longer attached either to the community or the religion of his forebears, he looks to progressive ideology to fill the vacuum. The main difference between the progressivism of the disciple of Harold Laski or Bertrand Russell and the Communism of the disciple of Lenin concerns not so much the *content* as the *style* of the ideologies and the allegiance they demand."

Ideology provides sham religion and sham philosophy, comforting in its way to those who have lost or never have known genuine religious faith, and to those not sufficiently intelligent to apprehend real philosophy. The fundamental reason why we must set our faces against ideology—so wrote the wise Swiss editor Hans Barth—is that ideology is opposed to truth: it denies the possibility of truth in politics or in anything else, substituting economic motive and class interest for abiding norms. Ideology even denies human consciousness and power of choice. In Barth's words, "The disastrous effect of ideological thinking in its radical form is not only to cast doubt on the quality and structure of the mind that constitute man's distinguishing characteristic but also to undermine the foundation of his social life."

Ideology may attract the bored man of the Knowledge Class who has cut himself off from religion and community, and who desires to exercise power. Ideology may enchant young people, wretchedly schooled, who in their loneliness stand ready to cast their latent enthusiasm into any exciting and violent cause. And ideologues' promises may win a following among social groups that feel pushed to the wall—even though such recruits may not understand much of anything about the ideologues' doctrines. The early composition of the Nazi party is sufficient illustration of an ideology's power to attract disparate elements of this sort.

On the first page of this introductory chapter I suggested that some Americans, conservatively inclined ones among them, might embrace an ideology of Democratic Capitalism, or New World Order, or International Democratism. Yet most Americans with a sneaking fondness for the word *ideology* are not seeking to sweep away violently all existing dominations and powers. What such people really mean when they call for a "democratic ideology" is a formula for a civil religion, an ideology of Americanism, or perhaps of the Free World. A trouble with this civil-religion notion is that the large majority of Americans think they already have a religion of their own, not one cobbled up by some department in Washington. If the approved civil religion, or mild ideology, should be designed, by some subtle process, to supplant the congeries of creeds at present flourishing in this land—why, such hostility toward belief in the transcendent, such contempt for the "higher religions," is precisely the most bitter article in the creed of those ideologies which have ravaged the world for the past eight decades.

Yet possibly all that is intended by enthusiasts for this proposed new anti-communist ideology is a declaration of political principles and economic concepts, to be widely promulgated, legislatively approved as a guide to public policy, and taught in public schools. If this is all, then why insist upon labelling the notion an ideology? An innocent ideology is as unlikely a contraption as Christian Diabolism; to attach the sinister tag "ideology" would be like inviting friends to a harmless Hallowe'en bonfire, but announcing the party as the new Holocaust.

If this "democratic ideology" should turn out, in practice, to be nothing worse than a national civics program for public schools, still it would require being watched jealously. Cloying praise in every classroom of the beauties of democratic capitalism would bore most pupils and provoke revulsion among the more intelligent. And it is not civics courses, primarily, that form minds and consciences of the rising generation: rather, it is the study of humane letters. I should not wish to see what remains of literary studies in the typical public school supplanted by an official propaganda about the holiness of the American Way or of the Free World Way or of the Democratic Capitalist Way.

I am not of the opinion that it would be well to pour the heady wine of a new ideology down the throats of the American young. If one summons spirits from the vasty deep, can they be conjured back again? What we need to impart is political prudence, not political belligerence. Ideology is the disease, not the cure. All ideologies, including the ideology of *vox populi vox dei*, are hostile to enduring order and justice and freedom. For ideology is the politics of passionate unreason.

❖

Permit me, then, to set down here, in a few paragraphs, some reflections on political prudence, as opposed to ideology.

To be "prudent" means to be judicious, cautious, sagacious. Plato, and later Burke, instruct us that in the statesman, prudence is the first of the virtues. A prudent statesman is one who looks before he leaps; who takes long views; who knows that politics is the art of the possible.

A few pages ago I specified three profound errors of the ideological politician. Now I contrast with those three failings certain principles of the politics of prudence.

> 1) As I put it earlier, ideology is inverted religion. But the prudential politician knows that "Utopia" means "Nowhere"; that we cannot march to an earthly Zion; that human nature and human institutions are imperfectible; that aggressive "righteousness" in politics ends in slaughter. True religion is a discipline for the soul, not for the state.

> 2) Ideology makes political compromise impossible, I pointed out. The prudential politician, *au contraire*, is well aware that the primary purpose of the state is to keep the peace. This can be achieved only by maintaining a tolerable balance among great interests in society. Parties, interests, and social classes and groups must arrive at compromises, if bowie-knives are to be kept from throats. When ideological fanaticism rejects any compromise, the weak go to the wall. The ideological atrocities of the "Third World" in recent decades illustrate this point: the political massacres of the Congo, Timor, Equatorial Guinea, Chad, Cambodia, Uganda, Yemen, Salvador, Afghanistan, and Somalia. Prudential politics strives for conciliation, not extirpation.
>
> 3) Ideologies are plagued by ferocious factionalism, on the principle of brotherhood—or death. Revolutions devour their children. But prudential politicians, rejecting the illusion of an Absolute Political Truth before which every citizen must abase himself, understand that political and economic structures are not mere products of theory, to be erected one day and demolished the next; rather, social institutions develop over centuries, almost as if they were organic. The radical reformer, proclaiming himself omniscient, strikes down every rival, to arrive at the Terrestrial Paradise more swiftly. Conservatives, in striking contrast, have the habit of dining with the opposition.

In the preceding sentence, I employed deliberately the word *conservative* as synonymous, virtually, with the expression "prudential politician." For it is the conservative leader who, setting his face against all ideologies, is guided by what Patrick Henry called "the lamp of experience." In this twentieth century, it has been the body of opinion generally called "conservative" that has defended the Permanent Things from ideologues' assaults.

Ever since the end of the Second World War, the American public has looked with increasing favor upon the term *conservative*. Public-opinion polls suggest that in politics, the majority of voters regard themselves as conservatives. Whether they well understand conservatives' political principles may be another matter.

Halfway through the second administration of President Reagan, an undergraduate of my acquaintance was conversing in Washington with a young man who had secured a political appointment in the general government. That fledgling public man commenced to talk of a "conservative ideology." The college student somewhat sharply reminded him of the sinister signification of that word "Ideology." "Well, you know what I mean," the youthful politician replied, somewhat lamely.

Yet it is doubtful if the officeholder himself knew precisely what he had meant. Did he fancy that *ideology* signifies a body of well-reasoned political principles? Did he desire to discover a set of simplistic formulas by which capitalism might be extended over all the world? Or did he indeed wish to overthrow by violent action our existing social order and to substitute an artificial society nearer to his heart's desire?

We live in a time when the signification of old words, like much else, has become insecure. "Words strain, / Crack and sometimes break, under the burden," as T. S. Eliot puts it. In the beginning was the Word. But nowadays the Word is confronted by Giant Ideology, which perverts the word, spoken and written.

It is not merely the rising political talents of our age that fail to apprehend the proper employment of important words—and particularly misunderstand the usage of *ideology*. An elderly lady writes to me in defense of yesteryear's movement called Moral Rearmament, which three decades ago claimed to provide America with an ideology. "Perhaps I am wrong, but it has always seemed to me that Ideology means the power of ideas," this correspondent states. "The world is run by ideas, good ones or bad ones. We need a great idea or ideal to replace the false ideas that dominate today. How long can we survive as a free nation when the word *freedom* has been corrupted?"

This lady's concluding point is a keen one. But I must add, "How long can we survive as a free nation when the word *ideology*, with its corrupting power, is mistaken for a guardian of ordered liberty?"

I do not mean to mock; for I encounter this confusion among people whom I know well and respect heartily. One such, a woman who is an able writer and a bold spirit, retorts that her dictionaries—Webster and Oxford—disagree with Russell Kirk's more lengthy definition of *ideology*. "If Oxford is right and ideology means 'the science of ideas,' could they not be good ideas? I quite agree that many ideologies do great harm, but surely not all? In any event, I'm a congenital pragmatist," she concludes, "and semantics are not my strong point."

Nay, madam, *all* ideologies work mischief. I am fortified by a letter from an influential and seasoned conservative publicist, who applauds my excoriation of young ideologues fancying themselves to be conservatives, and of young conservatives fondly hoping to convert themselves into ideologues. This latter correspondent agrees with me that ideology is founded merely upon "ideas"—that is, upon abstractions, fancies, for the most part unrelated to personal and social reality; while conservative views are founded upon custom, convention, the long experience of the human species. He finds himself confronted, from time to time, by young people, calling themselves conservative, who have no notion of prudence, temperance, compromise, the traditions of civility, or cultural patrimony.

"The woods are full of these creatures," this gentleman writes. "The conservative 'movement' seems to have reared up a new generation of rigid ideologists. It distresses me to find them as numerous and in so many institutions. Of course, many are libertarians, not conservatives. Whatever they call themselves, they are bad for the country and our civilization. Theirs is a cold-blooded, brutal view of life."

Amen to that. Is conservatism an ideology? Only if, with Humpty Dumpty, we claim the prerogative of forcing words to mean whatever we desire them to signify, so that "It's a question of who's to be master, that's all." Let us conservatives conserve the English language, along with many other surviving good things. Let us raise up the banner of honest and accurate vocabulary. Let us venture, whatever the odds, to contend against ideologues' Newspeak.

The triumph of ideology would be the triumph of what Edmund Burke called "the antagonist world"—the world of disorder; while what the conservative seeks to conserve is the world of order that we have inherited, if in a damaged condition, from our ancestors. The conservative mind and the ideological mind stand at opposite poles. And the contest between those two mentalities may be no less strenuous in the twenty-first century than it has been during the twentieth. Possibly this book of mine may be of help to those of the rising generation who have the courage to oppose ideological zealots.

["The Errors of Ideology," The Politics of Prudence, *1st ed. (Bryn Mawr, PA: Intercollegiate Studies Institute, 1993), 1–14.]*

❖

Libertarians: Chirping Sectaries

Beyond general agreement on the evils of the totalist state, conservatives and libertarians have nothing else in common, Kirk concludes in this essay. In the libertarian he detects a "fanatic attachment to a simple solitary principle:— that is, to the notion of personal freedom as the whole end of the civil social order, and indeed of human existence." The libertarian, Kirk argues, dreads "obedience to the dictates of customs." The defiance of authority, in the name of being absolutely free in morals as in politics, is an integral principle of the libertarian ideologue who would eliminate limits and restraints. Among "the more conspicuous insufficiencies of libertarianism as a credible moral and political mode of belief," Kirk lists the rejection of transcendent moral order, the indiscriminating allegiance to self-interest, the failure to comprehend the human condition as being both good and evil, the adoption of egoistic attitudes that scorn the virtue of humility.

Any discussion of the relationships between conservatives (who now, to judge by public-opinion polls, are a majority among American citizens) and libertarians (who, as tested by recent elections, remain a tiny though unproscribed minority) naturally commences with an inquiry into what these disparate groups hold in common. These two bodies of opinion share a detestation of collectivism. They set their faces against the totalist state and the heavy hand of bureaucracy. That much is obvious enough. What else do conservatives and libertarians profess in common? The answer to that question is simple: nothing. Nor will they ever. To talk of forming a league or coalition between these two is like advocating a union of ice and fire.

The ruinous failing of the ideologues who call themselves libertarians is their fanatic attachment to a simple solitary principle—that is, to the notion of personal freedom as the whole end of the civil social order, and indeed of human existence. The libertarians are old-fangled folk, in the sense that they live by certain abstractions of the nineteenth century. They carry to absurdity the doctrines of John Stuart Mill (before Mill's wife converted him to socialism, that is). To understand the mentality of the libertarians, it may be useful to remind ourselves of a little book published more than a hundred and forty years ago: John Stuart Mill's *On Liberty*. Arguments that were flimsy in 1859 (and were soundly refuted by James Fitzjames Stephen) have become farcical today. So permit me to digress concerning Mill's famous essay. Some books tend to form the character of their age; others to reflect it; and Mill's *Liberty* is of the latter order.

That tract is a product of the peacefulness and optimism of Victorian England; written at the summit of what Bagehot calls the Age of Discussion, it is a voice from out the vanished past of nineteenth-century meliorism. The future, it turned out, was not to the school of Mill. As Mill himself was the last of the line of British empiricists, so his *Liberty*, with its foreboding remarks on the despotism of the masses, was more an epilogue to middle-class liberalism than a rallying-cry.

James Mill, John Stuart Mill's austere doctrinaire father (what sour folk many of these zealots for liberty turn themselves into!) subjected his son to a rigorous course of private study. By the time he was eight years old, J. S. Mill knew nearly everything that a doctor of philosophy is supposed to know nowadays; but his intellect was untouched by the higher imagination, and for that Mill groped in vain all his life long. J. S. Mill became all head and no heart, in which character he represents Jeremy Bentham; yet in truth, it was Mill himself, rather than Bentham, who turned into defecated intellect.

Mill exhibited but one failing, so far as emotions go, and that not an uncommon one—being too fond of another man's wife. F. A. Hayek has discussed this association and its consequences for Mill and his followers. Mill eventually married this dismaying blue-stocking, Harriet Taylor, the forerunner of today's feminist militant. He was devoted to her, and she to humanitarian abstractions. It was under her tutelage that he wrote *On Liberty*. The intellectual ancestors of today's libertarians were no very jolly crew.

"By slaying all his animal spirits," Ruth Borchard writes of Mill, "he was utterly cut off from his instincts—instinct for life, instinctive understanding of nature, of human nature in general and of his own in particular." It might be interesting to examine how these deficiencies in Mill characterized and vitiated the whole liberal movement in English and American thought; and how they affect the vestigial form of nineteenth-century liberalism that now styles itself "libertarianism." But we must pass on, remarking only that this imperfect apprehension of human nature is readily discerned in the pages of Mill's essay *On Liberty*.

Now the younger Mill, in his essays on Coleridge and Bentham, had remarked truly that the cardinal error of Bentham was his supposition that the affairs of men may be reduced to a few simple formulas, to be applied universally and inflexibly—when actually the great mysterious incorporation of the human race is infinitely subtle and complex, not to be dominated by neat little abstractions. Yet into precisely this same pit Mill falls in his *Liberty*. In his introductory chapter, he declares his object to be the assertion of

> one very simple principle, as entitled to govern absolutely the dealings of society with the individual in the way of compulsion and control, whether the means used by physical force in the form of legal penalties, or the moral coercion of public opinion. That principle is, that the sole end for which mankind are warranted, individually or collectively, in interfering with the liberty of action of any of their number, is self-protection. That the only purpose for which power can be rightfully exercised over any member of a civilized community, against his will, is to prevent harm to others.

This seems an attractive solitary simple principle. It sufficiently defines the convictions of twentieth-century libertarians, I believe. But the trouble with it is that solitary simple principles, however tidy, really do not describe human behavior, and certainly cannot govern it.

James Fitzjames Stephen, a forthright man of affairs and a scholar in the law, perceived with irritation that fallacy which makes Mill's *Liberty* a frail reed in troubled times; and in *Liberty*, *Equality, Fraternity*, which Stephen published in 1873, he set upon Mill with a whip of scorpions. John Stuart Mill, in Stephen's eyes, was hopelessly naive:

> To me the question whether liberty is a good or a bad thing [Stephen wrote] appears as irrational as the question whether fire is a good or a bad thing? It is both good and bad according to time, place, and circumstance, and a complete answer to the question, in what cases is liberty good and in what is it bad? would involve not merely a universal history of mankind, but a complete solution of the problems which such a history would offer. I do not believe that the state of our knowledge is such as to enable us to enunciate any "very simple principle as entitled to govern absolutely the dealings of society with the individual in the way of compulsion and control." We must proceed in a far more cautious way, and confine ourselves to such remarks as experience suggests about the advantages and disadvantages of compulsion and liberty respectively in particular cases.

In every principal premise of his argument, Stephen declared, Mill suffered from an inadequate understanding of human nature and history. All the great movements of humankind, Stephen said, have been achieved by force, not by free discussion; and if we leave force out of our calculations, very soon we will be subject to the intolerant wills of men who know no scruples about employing force against us. (So, one may remark, many twentieth-century libertarians would have had us stand defenseless before the Soviet Russians.) It is consummate folly to tolerate every variety of opinion, on every topic, out of devotion to an abstract "liberty"; for opinion soon finds its expression in action, and the fanatics whom we tolerated will not tolerate us when they have power.

The fierce current of events, in our century, has supplied the proof for Stephen's case. Was the world improved by free discussion of the Nazis' thesis that Jews ought to be treated as less than human? Just this subject was presented to the population of one of the most advanced and most thoroughly schooled nations of the modern world; and then the crew of adventurers who had contrived to win the argument proceeded to act after the fashion with which we now are dreadfully familiar. We have come to understand, to our cost, what Burke meant by a "licentious toleration." An incessant zeal for repression is not the answer to the complex difficulties of liberty and order, either. What Stephen was saying, however, and what we recognize now, is that liberty cannot be maintained or extended by an abstract appeal to free discussion, sweet reasonableness, and solitary simple principle.

Since Mill, the libertarians have forgotten nothing and learned nothing. Mill dreaded, and they dread today, obedience to the dictates of custom. In our time, the real danger is that custom and prescription and tradition may be overthrown utterly among us—for has not that occurred already in most of the world?—by neoterism, the lust for novelty; and that men will be no better than the flies of a summer, oblivious to the wisdom of their ancestors, and forming every opinion merely under the pressure of the fad, the foible, the passion of the hour.

It may be objected that libertarian notions extend back beyond the time of Mill. Indeed they do; and they had been refuted before Stephen wrote, as John Adams refuted them in his exchange of letters with Thomas Jefferson and with John Taylor of Caroline. The first Whig was the devil, Samuel Johnson informs us; it might be truer to say that the devil was the original libertarian. "Lo, I am proud!" The perennial libertarian, like Satan, can bear no authority temporal or spiritual. He desires to be different, in morals as in politics. In a highly tolerant society like that of America today, such defiance of authority on principle may lead to perversity on principle, for lack of anything more startling to do; there is no great gulf fixed between libertarianism and libertinism.

Thus the typical libertarian of our day delights in eccentricity—including, often, sexual eccentricity (a point observed by that mordant psychologist Dr. Ernest van den Haag). Did not John Stuart Mill himself commend eccentricity as a defense against deadening democratic conformity? He rejoices, our representative libertarian, in strutting political eccentricity, as in strutting moral eccentricity. But, as Stephen commented on Mill, "Eccentricity is far more often a mark of weakness than a mark of strength. Weakness wishes, as a rule, to attract attention by trifling distinctions, and strength wishes to avoid it."

Amen to that. Passing from the nineteenth century to the twentieth, by 1929 we encounter a writer very unlike Mill exposing the absurdities of affected eccentricity and of doctrinaire libertarianism: G. K. Chesterton. Gabriel Gale, the intuitive hero of Chesterton's collection of stories entitled *The Poet and the Lunatics* (1955), speaks up for centricity: "Genius oughtn't to be eccentric! It ought to be the core of the cosmos, not on the revolving edges. People seem to think it a compliment to accuse one of being an outsider, and to talk about the eccentricities of genius. What would they think if I said I only wish to God I had the centricities of genius?"

No one ever has accused libertarians of being afflicted with the centricities of genius: for the dream of an absolute private freedom is one of those visions which issue from between the gates of ivory; and the dreadful speed with which society moves today flings the libertarians outward through centrifugal force, even to the outer darkness, where there is wailing and gnashing of teeth. The final emancipation from religion, convention, and custom; and order is annihilation—"whirled / Beyond the circuit of the shuddering bear / In fractured atoms."

In *The Poet and the Lunatics*, Chesterton offers us a parable of such licentious freedom: a story called "The Yellow Bird." To an English country house comes Professor Ivanhov, a Russian scholar who has published *The Psychology of Liberty*. He is a zealot for emancipation, expansion, the elimination of limits. He begins by liberating a canary from its cage—to be torn to pieces in the forest. He proceeds to liberate the goldfish by smashing their bowl. He ends by blowing up himself and the beautiful old house where he has been a guest.

"What exactly is liberty?" inquires a spectator of this series of events—Gabriel Gale, Chesterton's mouthpiece. "First and foremost, surely, it is the power of a thing to be itself. In some ways the yellow bird was free in the cage. It was free to be alone. It was free to sing. In the forest its feathers would be torn to pieces and its voice choked forever. Then I began to think that being oneself, which is liberty, is itself limitation. We are limited by our brains and bodies; and if we break out, we cease to be ourselves, and, perhaps, to be anything."

The Russian psychologist could not endure the necessary conditions of human existence; he must eliminate all limits; he could not endure the "round prison" of the overarching sky. But his alternative was annihilation for himself and his lodging; and he took that alternative. He ceased to be anything but fractured atoms. That is the ultimate freedom of the devoted libertarian. If, *par impossible*, American society should accept the leadership of libertarian ideologues.

❖

Notwithstanding, there is something to be said for the distintegrated Professor Ivanhov—relatively speaking. With reference to some remarks of mine, there writes to me Mr. Marion Montgomery, the Georgia novelist and critic: "The libertarians give me the willies. I much prefer the Russian anarchists, who at least have a deeply disturbed moral sensibility (that Dostoevsky makes good use of), to the libertarian anarchists. There is a decadent fervor amongst some of the latter which makes them an unwelcome cross for conservatism to bear."

Just so. The representative libertarian of this decade is humorless, intolerant, self-righteous, badly schooled, and dull. At least the old-fangled Russian anarchist was bold, lively, and knew which sex he belonged to.

But surely, surely I must be misrepresenting the breed? Don't I know self-proclaimed libertarians who are kindly old gentlemen, God-fearing, patriotic, chaste, well endowed with the goods of fortune? Yes, I do know such. They are the people who through misapprehension put up the cash for the fantastics. Such gentlemen call themselves "libertarians" merely because they believe in personal freedom, and do not understand to what extravagance they lend their names by subsidizing doctrinaire "libertarian" causes and publications. If a person describes himself as "libertarian" because he believes in an enduring moral order, the Constitution of the United States, free enterprise, and old American ways of life—why, actually he is a conservative with imperfect understanding of the general terms of politics.

It is not such well-intentioned but mislabeled men whom I am holding up to obloquy here. Rather, I am exposing the pretensions of the narrow doctrinaires who have imprisoned themselves within a "libertarian" ideology as confining and as unreal as Marxism—if less persuasive than that fell delusion.

Why are these doctrinaire libertarians, with a few exceptions, such very odd people—the sort who give hearty folk like Marion Montgomery the willies? Why do genuine conservatives feel an aversion to close association with them? (Incidentally, now and again one reads of two camps of alleged conservatives: "traditionalist conservatives and libertarian conservatives." This is as if a newspaperman were to classify Christians as "Protestant Christians and Muslim Christians.") Why is an alliance between conservatives and libertarians inconceivable? Why, indeed, would such articles of confederation undo whatever gains conservatives have made in this United States?

Because genuine libertarians are mad—metaphysically mad. Lunacy repels, and political lunacy especially. I do not mean that they are dangerous; they are repellent merely, like certain unfortunate inmates of "mental homes." They do not endanger our country and our civilization, because they are few, and seem likely to become fewer. (I refer here, of course, to our homegrown American libertarians, and not to those political sects, among them the Red Brigades of Italy, which have carried libertarian notions to grander and bolder lengths.) There exists no peril that American national policy, foreign or domestic, will be in the least affected by libertarian arguments; the good old causes of Bimetallism, Single Tax, or Prohibition enjoy a better prospect of success than do the programs of libertarianism. But one does not choose as a partner even a harmless political lunatic.

I mean that the libertarians make up what T. S. Eliot called a "chirping sect," an ideological clique forever splitting into sects still smaller and odder, but rarely conjugating. Such petty political sectaries Edmund Burke pictured as "the insects of the hour," as noisy as they are ineffectual against the conservative power of the browsing cattle in an English pasture. If one has chirping sectaries for friends, one doesn't need any enemies.

What do I mean when I say that today's American libertarians are metaphysically mad, and so repellent? Why, the dogmas of libertarianism have been refuted so often, both dialectically and by the hard knocks of experience, that it would be dull work to rehearse here the whole tale of folly. Space wanting, I set down below merely a few of the more conspicuous insufficiencies of libertarianism as a credible moral and political mode of belief. It is such differences from the conservatives' understanding of the human condition that make inconceivable any coalition of conservatives and libertarians.

1. The great line of division in modern politics—as Eric Voegelin reminds us—is not between totalitarians on the one hand and liberals (or libertarians) on the other; rather, it lies between all those who believe in some sort of transcendent moral order, on one side, and on the other side all those who take this ephemeral existence of ours for the be-all and end-all-to be devoted chiefly to producing and consuming. In this discrimination between

the sheep and the goats, the libertarians must be classified with the goats—that is, as utilitarians admitting no transcendent sanctions for conduct. In effect, they are converts to Marx's dialectical materialism; so conservatives draw back from them on the first principle of all.

2. In any society, order is the first need of all. Liberty and justice may be established only after order is tolerably secure. But the libertarians give primacy to an abstract liberty. Conservatives, knowing that "liberty inheres in some sensible object," are aware that true freedom can be found only within the framework of a social order, such as the constitutional order of these United States. In exalting an absolute and indefinable "liberty" at the expense of order, the libertarians imperil the very freedoms they praise.

3. What binds society together? The libertarians reply that the cement of society (so far as they will endure any binding at all) is self-interest, closely joined to the nexus of cash payment. But the conservatives declare that society is a community of souls, joining the dead, the living, and those yet unborn; and that it coheres through what Aristotle called friendship and Christians call love of neighbor.

4. Libertarians (like anarchists and Marxists) generally believe that human nature is good, though damaged by certain social institutions. Conservatives, on the contrary, hold that "in Adam's fall we sinned all": human nature, though compounded of both good and evil, is irremediably flawed; so the perfection of society is impossible, all human beings being imperfect. Thus the libertarian pursues his illusory way to Utopia, and the conservative knows that for the path to Avernus.

5. The libertarian takes the state for the great oppressor. But the conservative finds that the state is ordained of God. In Burke's phrases, "He who gave us our nature to be perfected by our virtue, willed also the necessary means of its perfection. He willed therefore the state—its connexion with the source and original archetype of all perfection." Without the state, man's condition is poor, nasty, brutish, and short—as Augustine argued, many centuries before Hobbes. The libertarians confound the state with government. But government—as Burke continued—"is a contrivance of human wisdom to provide for human *wants*." Among the more important of those human wants is "a sufficient restraint upon their passions. Society requires not only that the passions of individuals should be subjected, but that even in the mass and body, as well as in the individual, the inclinations of men should frequently be thwarted, their will controlled, and their passions brought into subjection. This can be done only *by a power out of themselves*; and not, in the exercise of its function, subject to that will and to those passions which it is its

office to bridle and subdue." In short, a primary function of government is restraint; and that is anathema to libertarians, though an article of faith to conservatives.

6. The libertarian thinks that this world is chiefly a stage for the swaggering ego; the conservative finds himself instead a pilgrim in a realm of mystery and wonder, where duty, discipline, and sacrifice are required—and where the reward is that love which passeth all understanding. The conservative regards the libertarian as impious, in the sense of the old Roman *pietas*: that is, the libertarian does not venerate ancient beliefs and customs, or the natural world, or his country, or the immortal spark in his fellow men. The cosmos of the libertarian is an arid loveless realm, a "round prison." "I am, and none else beside me," says the libertarian. "We are made for cooperation, like the hands, like the feet," replies the conservative, in the phrases of Marcus Aurelius.

Why multiply these profound differences? Those I have expressed already will suffice to demonstrate the utter incompatibility of the two positions. If one were to content himself simply with contrasting the beliefs of conservatives and libertarians as to the nature of liberty, still we could arrive at no compromise. There is the liberty of the wolf, John Adams wrote to John Taylor; and there is the liberty of civilized man. The conservative will not tolerate ravening liberty; with Dostoevski, he knows that those who commence with absolute liberty will end with absolute tyranny. He maintains, rather, what Burke called "chartered rights," developed slowly and painfully in the civil social order, sanctioned by prescription.

Yet even if libertarian and conservative can affirm nothing in common, may they not agree upon a negative? May they not take common ground against the pretensions of the modern state to omnicompetence? Certainly both bodies of opinion find that modern governments, even in such constitutional orders as the United States, seem afflicted by the *libido dominandi*. The primary function of government, the conservatives say, is to keep the peace: by repelling foreign enemies, by maintaining the bed of justice domestically. When government goes much beyond this end, it falls into difficulty, not being contrived for the management of the whole of life. Thus far, indeed libertarian and conservative hold something in common. But the libertarians, rashly hurrying to an opposite extreme, would deprive government of effective power to undertake the common defense or to restrain the passionate and the unjust. With the libertarians in mind, conservatives repeat Burke's aphorism: "Men of intemperate mind never can be free. Their passions forge their fetters."

So in the nature of things conservatives and libertarians can conclude no friendly pact. Conservatives have no intention of compromising with socialists; but even such an alliance, ridiculous though it would be, is more nearly conceivable than the coalition of conservatives and libertarians. The socialists at least declare the existence of some sort of moral order; the libertarians are quite bottomless.

It is of high importance, indeed, that American conservatives dissociate themselves altogether from the little sour remnant called libertarians. In a time requiring long views and self-denial, alliance with a faction founded upon doctrinaire selfishness would be absurd—and practically damaging. It is not merely that cooperation with a tiny chirping sect would be valueless politically; more, such an association would tend to discredit the conservatives, giving aid and comfort to the collective adversaries of ordered freedom. When heaven and earth have passed away, perhaps the conservative mind and the libertarian mind may be joined in synthesis—but not until then. Meanwhile, I venture to predict, the more intelligent and conscientious persons within the libertarian remnant will tend to settle for politics as the art of the possible, so shifting into the conservative camp.

["Libertarians: Chirping Sectaries," Redeeming the Time *(Wilmington, DE: Intercollegiate Studies Institute, 1996), 271–83.]*

❖

Can Virtue Be Taught?

This reflective essay addresses the problem of how men and women are to preserve "the virtue of moral worth." Virtue, Kirk stresses, is an "old word" closely tied to the inherited wisdom of the ages as embodied in common acceptations and affirmations. "For virtue, we should remember, is energy of soul employed for the general good." It is a word, and also a concept, that has been deprived of values that traditionally reside in moral goodness, moral duties, moral laws. Kirk concurs with Plato and Aristotle that moral virtue grows out of habit and that intellectual virtue develops through systematic instruction. The "sprig of virtue is nurtured in the soil of sound prejudice; healthful and valorous habits are formed; and, in the phrase of Burke, 'a man's habit becomes his virtue.'" Americans have not bothered to think about virtues as distinct forms of moral life, even as established moral teachings have become casualties of ideology.

Are there men and women in America today possessed of virtue sufficient to withstand and repel the forces of disorder? Or have we, as a people, grown too fond of creature-comforts and a fancied security to venture our lives, our fortunes, and our sacred honor in any cause at all? "The superior man thinks always of virtue," Confucius told his disciples; "the common man thinks of comfort." Such considerations in recent years have raised up again that old word "virtue," which in the first half of this century had sunk almost out of sight.

I venture first to offer you a renewed apprehension of what "virtue" means; and then to suggest how far it may be possible to restore an active virtue in our public and our private life. If we lack virtue, we will not long continue to enjoy comfort—not in an age when Giant Ideology and Giant Envy swagger balefully about the world.

The concept of virtue, like most other concepts that have endured and remain worthy of praise, has come down to us from the Greeks and the Hebrews. In its classical signification, "virtue" means the power of anything to accomplish its specific function; a property capable of producing certain effects; strength, force, potency. Thus one refers to the "deadly virtue" of the hemlock. Thus also the word "virtue" implies a mysterious energetic power, as in the Gospel According to Saint Mark: "Jesus, immediately knowing that virtue had gone out of him, turned him about in the press, and said, 'Who touched my clothes?'" Was it, we may ask, that virtue of Jesus which left its mark upon the Shroud of Turin?

Virtue, then, meant in the beginning some extraordinary power. The word was applied to the sort of person we might now call "the charismatic leader." By extension, "virtue" came to imply the qualities of full humanity: strength, courage, capacity, worth, manliness, moral excellence. And presently "virtue" came to signify, as well, moral goodness: the practice of moral duties and the conformity of life to the moral law; uprightness; rectitude.

In recent decades, many folk seemingly grew embarrassed by this word virtue; perhaps for them it had too stern a Roman ring. They made the word "integrity" do duty for the discarded "virtue." Now "integrity" signifies wholeness or completeness; freedom from corruption; soundness of principle and character. You will gather that "integrity" is chiefly a passive quality, somewhat deficient in the vigor of "virtue." People of integrity may be the salt of the earth; yet a rough age requires some people possessed of an energetic virtue.

When we say that a man or a woman is virtuous, what do we mean? Plato declared that there are four chief virtues of the soul: justice, prudence, temperance, and fortitude. (Of these, the virtue most required in a statesman is prudence, Plato remarked.) To these classical virtues, Saint Paul added the theological virtues: faith, hope, and charity. These constitute the Seven Virtues of the Schoolmen. Against them are set the Seven Deadly Sins: pride, avarice, lust, anger, gluttony, envy, and sloth. Incidentally, there was a more specific medieval list of "the sins that cry out to heaven for vengeance": oppression of the poor, willful murder, sodomy, and defrauding a laborer of his wages.

Such formulas of the cardinal and the theological virtues have been fixed in the minds of many of us, either through church teachings or through humane letters. Yet virtue is something more than the sum of its seven parts. From the sixth century before Christ down to the twentieth century, this word "virtue" carried with it the strong suggestion of public leadership. The truly virtuous man would assume public duties, the ancients believed. Take these words from Cicero's *Republic*:

> What can be more noble than the government of the state by virtue? For then the man who rules others is not himself a slave to any passion, but has already acquired for himself all those qualities to which he is training and summoning his fellows. Such a man imposes no laws upon the people that he does not obey himself, but puts his own life before his fellow-citizens as their law.

By the "virtuous man," that is, the classical writers meant a leader in statecraft and in war, one who towered above his fellow citizens, a person in whom courage, wisdom, self-restraint, and just dealing were conspicuous. They meant a being of energy and force, moved almost by a power out of himself.

How was this virtue, this conspicuous merit and talent to lead, acquired by men and women? That question provoked the famous debate between Socrates and Aristophanes. Socrates argued that virtue and wisdom at bottom are one. When first I read Socrates' argument, I being then a college freshman, this seemed to me an insupportable thesis; for we all have known human beings of much intelligence and cleverness whose light is as darkness. After considerable experience of the world and the passage of more than four decades, to me Socrates' argument seems yet more feeble.

And so it seemed to Aristophanes. The sophists—that is, the teachers of rhetoric and prudence, Socrates among them—professed that they could teach virtue to the rising generation. Through development of the private rationality, those teachers declared, they could form talented leaders within the state: men of virtue, or charismatic power, endowed with the talents required for private and public success.

To the great comic poet, this notion seemed a dangerous absurdity. Greatness of soul and good character are not formed by hired tutors, Aristophanes maintained: virtue is natural, not an artificial development. Who possesses virtue? Why, not some presumptuous elite of young men trailing effeminately after some sophist or other. The true possessors of virtue are the men of the old families, reared to righteousness and courage, brought up in good moral habits, from their earliest years accustomed to discipline and duty. Their prudence and their daring defend the state. Just how far the hero-poet Aristophanes believed virtue to be inherited, and how far he took it to be nurtured by family example and tradition, we do not know at this remove. But it is clear that Aristophanes laughed to scorn the thesis that virtue may be imparted by schoolmasters.

The Greek teachers of philosophy, nevertheless, Plato and Aristotle eminent among them, refused to abandon their attempt to impart virtue through appeal to reason. A kind of compromise was reached in Aristotle's *Ethics*. There Aristotle argues that virtue is of two kinds: moral, and intellectual. Moral virtue grows out of habit (*ethos*); it is not natural, but neither is moral virtue opposed to nature. Intellectual virtue, on the other hand, may be developed and improved through systematic instruction—which requires time. In other words, moral virtue appears to be the product of habits formed early in family, class, neighborhood; while intellectual virtue may be taught through instruction in philosophy, literature, history, and related disciplines.

The experience of the Romans during their republican centuries may serve to delineate the two different kinds of virtue. So late as the period of Polybius, the Roman citizens retained their "high old Roman virtue," the product of tradition and deference to example, of habits acquired within the family. They maintained the virtues of reverence, seriousness, equitableness, firmness of purpose, tenacity, hard work, steadiness, frugality, unselfishness, self-restraint—and other virtues besides. All these were habits that grew into virtues.

Then came to Rome the Greek philosophers, with much abstract talk of virtue. But the more the sophists praised an abstract virtue, the more did the *mores maiorum*, the ancient manners or habits of Rome, sink into neglect. Ancestral ways diminished in power; ethical speculation spread. Although the high old Roman virtue was not altogether extinguished until the final collapse of *Romanitas* before the barbarian wanderers, by the time of Nero and Seneca there had come to exist, side by side, a fashionable array of ethical teachings, derived from Greek sources—and a general decay of public and private morals, from the highest social classes to the lowest.

This Roman experience seems to justify the argument of Aristophanes that virtue cannot be taught in schools. Rather, the sprig of virtue is nurtured in the soil of sound prejudice; healthful and valorous habits are formed; and, in the phrase of Burke, "a man's habit becomes his virtue." A resolute and daring character, dutiful and just, may be formed accordingly.

During the Korean war, only one American soldier taken prisoner and confined in North Korea succeeded in escaping and making his way back to his own lines—a sergeant named Pate, set down in his captors' records as a "reactionary." Sergeant Pate, an unlettered man, was possessed of the Roman virtues of *discipline*, *firmitas*, *constantia*, and *frugalitas*. His father, Pate remarked, had taught him only two principles: first, if a man calls you a liar, knock him down; if he calls you a son of a bitch, kill him. Ethical instruction in casuistry might have made Sergeant Pate less resistant to Communist indoctrination and less resolute in his daring escape: that is, less virtuous. For virtue, we should remember, is energy of soul employed for the general good.

Intellectual virtue divorced from moral virtue may wither into a loathsome thing. Robespierre (1758–94) was called by his admirers "the voice of virtue"; certainly Robespierre (who justified the slaughter of his opponents by coining the aphorism that one can't make an omelet without breaking eggs) was forever prating of virtue. "Virtue was always in a minority on the earth," said that murderous prig, the "Sea-Green Incorruptible." That sort of intellectual virtue, an aspect of what I have called defecated rationality, still rises up perennially in Paris, and is exported to Ethiopia, to Cambodia, to any national soil that seems ready-furrowed for this poisonous seed. Intellectual virtue, genus Robespierre, is a kind of delusory ethical snobbery, ferocious and malicious, annihilating ordinary human beings because they are not angels.

The abstract intellectual virtue of the Parisian coffee-house intellectual, I am suggesting, is a world away from the habitual high old Roman virtue. The virtues of the statesmen and soldiers of the early American Republic were not at all allied to the bloody fanatical "virtue" that was to arise during the French Revolution. So if we aspire to renew American virtue near the close of the twentieth century, surely we will do well to look with skepticism upon proposals for some sort of abstract "civil religion." An arid virtue that is intellectual only must be unreliable at best, and dangerous often. From time to time in recent years, various educational instrumentalists and progressivists have advocated the public teaching of a "religion of democracy"—that is, a public ethic founded upon ideological premises. Such an artificial intellectual contraption, with no better footing, would be mischievous in its consequences.

A false, carping, malicious "virtue" is worse than no virtue at all. The urgent need of the United States of America, near the end of the twentieth century, is for a virtue arising from habit and affection, rather than from ideological preaching. Without such a renewed true virtue, our commonwealth may not endure. I think of the words of Simone Weil concerning our era, in her "Reflections on Quantum Theory":

> It is as though we had returned to the age of Protagoras and the Sophists, the age when the art of persuasion—whose modern equivalent is advertising slogans, publicity, propaganda meetings, the press, the cinema, and radio—took the place of thought and controlled the fate of cities and accomplished coups d'etat. So the ninth book of Plato's *Republic* reads like a description of contemporary events. Only today it is not the fate of Greece but of the entire world that is at stake. And we have no Socrates or Plato or Eudoxus, no Pythagorean tradition, and no teaching of the Mysteries. We have the Christian tradition, but it can do nothing for us unless it comes alive in us again.

Just so. It is not propaganda nor productivity nor intellectuality that has power to invigorate America at the crisis of the nation's fate. By virtue are nations defended. But virtue in this land of ours seemingly never lay at a lower ebb. The instruments of false persuasion listed by Simone Weil (1909–43)—the tools of the philodoxers, the purveyors of delusory opinion—have been increased in cleverness since she wrote, by the triumph of television. In no previous age have family influence, sound early prejudice, and good early habits been so broken in upon by outside force as in our own time. Moral virtue among the rising generation is mocked by the inanity of television, by pornographic films, by the twentieth-century cult of the "peer group." By example and precept, until quite recently, grandparents and parents conveyed to young people—or a considerable part of them—some notion of virtue, even if the word itself was not well understood. The decay of family, worked by modern affluence and modern mobility, has mightily diminished all that. As for the influence of the churches—why, more is left of it in the United States than in most countries; but in the typical "main line" church an amorphous humanitarianism has supplanted the emphasis upon virtue that runs through the Christian tradition.

And so we return, finding ourselves in circumstances very like those of the Greeks of the fifth century, to the ancient question, "Can virtue be taught?"

Let me confess at once my inability to provide any simple formula, promptly applicable, for the widespread renewal of the pursuit of virtue. Some people fancy that if only schools would turn their attention systematically and earnestly to this problem, relief soon would follow. But it will not do to become so sanguine.

For Aristophanes was right, I believe, in proclaiming (in *The Clouds* and elsewhere) that moral virtue is not learnt in schools. If good moral habits are acquired at all, they are got ordinarily within the family, within the neighborhood, within the circle of close associates in youth; often good moral habits, or bad ones, are fixed by the age of seven, little more than a year after school has begun for the typical child. The early life of the household and the early life of the streets count for immensely much; and I need not try your patience by expatiating mightily on the sort of character (or lack thereof) formed by the childhood associations and impressions of a large part of our urban population—or, for that matter, our suburban population. I do not refer to the ADC slums merely. In the affluent household too, when parents' opinions and tastes are shaped by incessant watching of television, we need not wonder that children learn the price of everything and the value of nothing.

Boys and girls will model themselves, if they can, upon exemplars. But what sort of exemplars? Rock stars, and the fancied personalities of the heroes and heroines of the soap operas, have become the exemplars for a multitude of American young people in their most formative years. Rarely are such persons, or pseudopersons, admirable mentors.

Enjoying the good fortune to grow up before television did, I found, when a boy, another sort of exemplar, who taught me of virtue by example, and to a lesser extent by precept: my grandfather, who died at my own present age. He was a generous and popular bank manager and local public man, who had a short way (several times) with bank robbers. Also he possessed important books, and read them and good periodicals, and helped to develop my own relish for reading. My grandfather was endowed with the cardinal and the theological virtues (if the latter in a form somewhat skeptical and heterodox). By conversing with him and watching him (he all unaware, probably, of the power of his influence upon me), I learned what it is to be a man.

At no time could every family provide such an exemplar; yet time was when emulation within the family amounted to more than it does nowadays. My relationship with my grandfather made it easy for me to understand Aristophanes' implicit argument that virtue arises easily, if mysteriously, among families. My grandfather had many virtues and no vices. I assumed then, somewhat naively, that the Republic had sufficient such leaders and molders of opinion as my grandfather, and would have enough such always.

But I digress. My point is this: the recovery of virtue in America depends in great part upon the reinvigoration of family. It would be vain for us to pretend that schools and colleges somehow could make amends for all the neglect of character resulting from the inadequacies of the American family of the eighties. With some few exceptions, men and women have acquired their virtues or their vices quite outside the classroom. (There comes into my mind's eye a glimpse of Catholic young men, at a Jesuit university, diligently cheating during an examination concerning Aquinas's "On Truth.")

If the family continues to decay in its functions, so will virtue continue to decline in our society. I offer no placebo, in either the liturgical or the medicinal signification of that word. *Placebo Domino in regione vivorum*? Nay, but the man or woman brought up without moral virtue shall not be acceptable to the Lord in the land of the living.

Having turned liturgical for the moment, I venture a few words about the churches. Rather as some people expect too much from the schools concerning virtue, so other people count overly upon churches and clergymen as molders of virtuous character.

For Jeremy Bentham (1748–1832) notwithstanding, the Church is not a moral police force. What the Church always has been meant to do, really, is to offer a pattern for ordering the soul of the believer; and to open a window upon the transcendent realm of being. It is true that mastery of the theological virtues ought to follow upon sincere belief, and that sometimes it does so follow. Certainly there would be little virtue in our civilization, and quite possibly there would exist no modern civilization at all, were it not for Christian preaching of the theological virtues. From the discipline of the theological virtues issue saints from time to time, as from the discipline of the cardinal virtues issue heroes. Yet it will not do to expect priest or minister to fill the vacuum left by the disappearance of family exemplar or mentor.

Now the churches of America, nevertheless, ought to do far more good work toward the renewal of virtue among persons than they actually are performing nowadays. I do not mean that the Church should become censorious as it was in Scotland in Knox's day, or as it was in New England in my great-great-great-great-great-great-great-great-grandfather's years at Plymouth. I do mean that the Church ought to address itself less to prudential considerations of the hour's politics—at which business the Church usually demonstrates its incompetence—and much more to showing the pertinence of the theological virtues to our present discontents, private and public. Certain developments within theological colleges, here and there, encourage me to think that such an alteration of approach has commenced. And it is altogether possible that a general widespread renewal of faith in the supernatural and transcendent character of Christian belief may come to pass within the next few years—a phenomenon more tremendous than the Great Awakening ushered in by Wesley and others two centuries ago. But to pursue that possibility here would lead me to the mysteries of the Shroud of Turin; I must stick to my last.

However that may be, the present influence of the Christian churches is not calculated to bring about much revival of the concept or the practice of the virtues, theological or cardinal. Most graduates of seminaries seem incapable today of discussing virtue, or particular virtues, with much historical or philosophical insight. For the moment, we must not look to institutional Christianity for rousing moral virtue; as Simone Weil suggests in the passage I quoted earlier, the Christian moral tradition lies dormant (at best) in modern hearts; if it is to come alive again, probably it must be revivified by some outer power.

The moral virtue which grows out of habit being difficult of attainment in our era, people turn their attention to intellectual virtue. It was so in the fifth and fourth centuries before Christ. The whole great philosophical achievement of Socrates, Plato, and Aristotle, indeed, was an endeavor to impart intellectual virtue to the rising generation, moral virtue having shrivelled in an age when "the rude son may strike the father dead." Far from having much immediate practical effect upon the young people of their time, the effort of Socrates, Plato, and Aristotle was a failure. (The fact that Aristotle schooled in philosophy a future great king did not produce any general alteration of minds and hearts.) Finding the old Greek religion and morality enfeebled, and moral habits much impaired, Socrates endeavored to substitute for habitual moral virtue the identification of virtue with wisdom: intellectual virtue. The immediate benefits of this venture were not obvious: Alcibiades and Critias were among Socrates' more successful disciples. Virtue of a sort was theirs; but not the virtue of moral worth.

Yet there have been times when intellectual virtue has been imparted successfully. Such, in British North America, was the second half of the eighteenth century, when there was developed a class of able persons (enduring as a class so late as the 1830s) who knew the meaning of virtue. Theirs was the schooling of English gentlemen of the age, deliberately intended to bring home the idea and the reality of virtue to those members of the rising generation presumably destined to be leading men of their society—whether (in Burke's phrases) "men of actual virtue" or "men of presumptive virtue." (This distinction is one between "enterprising talents" and inherited rank and wealth.)

And how were such young persons schooled in virtue? They were required to read carefully, in the classical languages (chiefly in Latin), certain enduring books that dealt much with virtue. In particular, they studied Cicero, Vergil, and Plutarch, among the ancients. They memorized Cicero's praise of virtuous Romans; they came to understand Vergil's *labor, pietas, fatum*; they immersed themselves in the lives of Plutarch's Greeks and Romans "of excellent virtue"—men in whom the energy of virtue had flamed up fiercely.

It does not follow that we, in our time, could produce such a generation of leaders as signed the Declaration and wrote the Constitution, were we suddenly to sweep all rubbish and boondoggle and driver training out of the typical American school curriculum, and install instead the required reading of 1787, say. For that study and reflection necessary for the attainment of intellectual virtue cannot unaided put flesh upon virtue's dry bones. For intellectual virtue to become active virtue—whether after the fashion of Washington or the fashion of Robespierre—favorable circumstances must occur. In the Thirteen Colonies, the altered relationships between Britain's Crown-in-Parliament and the dominant classes in America provided opportunity for the Americans schooled in virtue—particularly, though by no means exclusively, the men of actual virtue—to take power into their hands. And by 1832, the last survivors from America's intellectual-virtue school of earlier decades

(John Quincy Adams, in particular) were being thrust aside by men of another pattern.

It is possible for schools of intellectual virtue to endure a great while, and to exert a very strong practical influence. In essence, the famous public schools (together with many good "private" boarding schools) of England have been for centuries centers for imparting intellectual virtue to boys who presumably have obtained (most of them, anyway) a good deal of moral virtue within their own families. Such, at least, has been the aspiration of the British public schools, represented at their best by the ideas and methods of Dr. Thomas Arnold (1795–1842). Probably the days of the public schools and the boarding schools generally are numbered in Britain now. But the long history of those schools suggests that intellectual virtue was better imparted in England than in Greece. At the English schools, until recent decades, the core of the discipline of intellectual virtue was the study of Cicero, Vergil, Plutarch, and classical literature generally.

In these United States, scarcely a school remains, I suppose, where the notion of intellectual virtue still is entertained. A fair amount of the content of such studies, nevertheless, used to be conveyed by literary and historical courses in American intermediate and secondary schooling. That remnant has been trickling away—and not in America only. C. S. Lewis, four decades ago, assailed the corruption of school courses in humane letters in England; he found the new textbooks sneering at virtue of any sort. Great literature used to train the emotions, Lewis wrote:

> Without the aid of trained emotions the intellect is powerless against the animal organism. I had sooner play cards against a man who was quite skeptical about ethics, but bred to believe that "a gentleman does not cheat," than against an irreproachable moral philosopher who had been brought up among sharpers. In battle it is not syllogisms that will keep the reluctant nerves and muscles to their post in the third hour of the bombardment. . . . And all this time—such is the tragi-comedy of our situation—we continue to clamour for those very qualities we are rendering impossible. You can hardly open a periodical without coming across the statement that what our civilization needs is more "drive," or dynamics, or self-sacrifice, or "creativity." In a sort of ghastly simplicity we remove the organ and demand the function. We make men without chests and expect of them virtue and enterprise. We laugh at honour and are shocked to find traitors in our midst. We castrate and bid the geldings be fruitful.

We are worse off still, in the eighties. So far, what attempts we have made in America to impart virtue once more have been confined principally to "research projects" (usually with plenty of public funds behind them) in that hideous sham called "values clarification." But I am descending into bathos.

Can virtue be taught? Why, it can be learnt, though more through a kind of illative process than as a formal program of study. Surely it cannot be taught by those incompetent and chameleon-like intellectuals whom Solzhenitsyn calls "the Smatterers." Few seem competent to teach virtue in our Republic nowadays; and relatively few hungry sheep look up to be fed.

Yet adversity, which we Americans seem liable to experience sharply and suddenly in this present decade, frequently opens the way for the impulse toward virtue. The terrible adversity endured by decent folk in Soviet Russia forged the virtue of Solzhenitsyn, a hero for our age. Only rags and tatters of the old moral virtue survived in Russia after the triumphs of Lenin and of Stalin; Solzhenitsyn and some other Russians of moral vision found it necessary to raise up intellectual virtue from the ashes of revolution. They have succeeded, in the sense that Socrates and Plato succeeded; whether their reconstruction of virtue will take on flesh more swiftly than did the Greek reconstitution, we do not yet know.

"Feed men, and then ask them of virtue" is the slogan upon the banners of the Anti-Christ, in Solovyov's romance. We have done just that in this Republic, since the Second World War. We Americans have grown very well fed, very much starved for virtue. Nowhere is this more amply illustrated than in Washington. Whether or not virtue can be taught, we have not troubled our heads with it, nor our hearts. When the Rough Beast slouches upon us, what Theseus or Perseus, incandescent with the energy of virtue, will draw his sword?

["Can Virtue Be Taught?" The Wise Men Know What Wicked Things Are Written on the Sky *(Washington, DC: Regnery Gateway, 1987), 66–78.]*

❖

VII.

DECADENCE AND RENEWAL IN EDUCATION

The Conservative Purpose of a Liberal Education ❖ The American Scholar and the American Intellectual ❖ The Intemperate Professor ❖ Teaching Humane Literature in High Schools

Russell Kirk wrote hundreds of essays, articles, newspaper columns, and three books on American education. From 1946 to 1953, he was an assistant professor of history at Michigan State College, but he left his teaching post following a dispute with college authorities over academic standards. Though he never again settled on any campus, he lectured and taught for various durations in many American colleges and universities.

Steadfastly, Kirk criticized higher education for lowering standards, especially after World War II. In the 1960s and 1970s, in particular, he worried over the many disruptions resulting from campus radicalism. He came to associate the deterioration in the educational system with the growing stress on vocationalism, specialization, life-adjustment, heightened by the ideological agenda of American academics. The consequence of this decline not only in higher but also in secondary and elementary education was the erosion of the values and virtues of liberal education. In a large sense, Kirk was continuing the earlier battles that Irving Babbitt (1865–1933), the great American critic and teacher, waged against utilitarian educational ideas of "training for service and training for power."

How can we turn back the tide of the leveling process of doctrinaire educationists in positions of authority who water down standards? How can we save true liberal education from drifting into the "'hollow dark'"? How can we restore the main function of humane education: "to conserve a body of received knowledge and to impart an apprehension of order to the rising generation"? These, for Kirk, were crucial questions with which he wrestled vigorously in his lifetime.

To be sure, Kirk's views on education were not always accepted even by friendly critics who recognized the truth of Kirk's charges of decadence in higher education, but who also questioned whether his concepts of educational improvement were attainable, given the academic-bureaucratic power-structure of the educational system as a whole. No doubt Kirk was deeply aware of the difficulty of implementing his educational remedies. Yet, to the very end, he remained loyal to his vision of renewal in education. Both his critique of and his remedies for our educational problems continue to remain pertinent and challenging.

❖

The Conservative Purpose of a Liberal Education

"Liberal education" is a term often confused with "political liberalism," as well as with professional and technical education, as Kirk attempts to show in this essay. The true mission of education, he feels, must be clearly defined and distinguished from sociopolitical and material interests. For Kirk, liberal education has to be essentially conservative in character since its primary function "is to conserve a body of received knowledge and to impart an apprehension of order" in young people. Wisdom and virtue should be its dominant concerns. He is acutely aware, however, that American education generally scoffs at these concerns, choosing instead to train "an 'elite' of presumptuous specialists." Kirk is unflinching in his criticism of utilitarian-sentimental educational philosophy that weakens the values of humane learning and that, in consequence, leads to confusion and chaos in the modern educational world.

Our term "liberal education" is far older than the use of the word "liberal" as a term of politics. What we now call "liberal studies" go back to classical times; while political liberalism commences only in the first decade of the nineteenth century. By "liberal education" we mean an ordering and integrating of knowledge for the benefit of the free person—as contrasted with technical or professional schooling, now somewhat vaingloriously called "career education."

The idea of a liberal education is suggested by two passages I am about to quote to you. The first of these is extracted from Sir William Hamilton's *Metaphysics* (1859):

> Now the perfection of man as an end and the perfection of man as a mean or instrument are not only not the same, they are in reality generally opposed. And as these two perfections are different, so the training requisite for their acquisition is not identical, and has, accordingly, been distinguished by different names. The one is styled liberal, the other professional education—the branches of knowledge cultivated for these purposes being called respectively liberal and professional, or liberal and lucrative, sciences.

Hamilton, you will observe, informs us that one must not expect to make money out of proficiency in the liberal arts. The higher aim of "man as an end," he tells us, is the object of liberal learning. This is a salutary admonition in our time, when more and more parents fondly thrust their offspring, male and female, into schools of business administration. What did Sir William Hamilton mean by "man as an end"? Why, to put the matter another way, he meant that the function of liberal learning is to order the human soul.

Now for my second quotation, which I take from James Russell Lowell. The study of the classics, Lowell writes, "is fitly called a liberal education, because it emancipates the mind from every narrow provincialism, whether of egoism or tradition, and is the apprenticeship that every one must serve before becoming a free brother of the guild which passes the torch of life from age to age."

To put this truth after another fashion, Lowell tells us that a liberal education is intended to free us from captivity to time and place: to enable us to take long views, to understand what it is to be fully human—and to be able to pass on to generations yet unborn our common patrimony of culture. T. S. Eliot, in his lectures on "The Aims of Education"[1] and elsewhere made the same argument not many years ago. Neither Lowell nor Eliot labored under the illusion that the liberal discipline of the intellect would open the way to affluence.

So you will perceive that when I speak of the "conservative purpose" of liberal education, I do not mean that such a schooling is intended to be a prop somehow to business, industry, and established material interests. Neither, on the other hand, is a liberal education supposed to be a means for pulling down the economy and the state itself. No, liberal education goes about its work of conservation in a different fashion.

I mean that liberal education is conservative in this way: it defends order against disorder. In its practical effects, liberal education works for order in the soul, and order in the republic. Liberal learning enables those who benefit from its discipline to achieve some degree of harmony within themselves. As John Henry Newman put it, in Discourse V of his *Idea of a University* (1873), by a liberal intellectual discipline, "a habit of mind is formed which lasts through life, of which the attributes are freedom, equitableness, calmness, moderation, and wisdom; of what . . . I have ventured to call the philosophical habit of mind."

The primary purpose of a liberal education, then, is the cultivation of the person's own intellect and imagination, for the person's own sake. It ought not to be forgotten, in this mass-age when the state aspires to be all in all, that genuine education is something higher than an instrument of public policy. True education is meant to develop the individual human being, the person, rather than to serve the state. In all our talk about "serving national goals" and "citizenship education"—phrases that originated with John Dewey and his disciples—we tend to ignore the fact that schooling was not originated by the modern nation-state. Formal schooling actually commenced as an endeavor to acquaint the rising generation with religious knowledge: with awareness of the transcendent and with moral truths. Its purpose was not to indoctrinate a young person in civics, but rather to teach what it is to be a true human being, living within a moral order. The person has primacy in liberal education.

Yet a system of liberal education has a social purpose, or at least a social result, as well. It helps to provide a society with a body of people who become leaders in many walks of life, on a large scale or a small. It was the expectation of the founders of the early American colleges that there would be graduated from those little institutions young men, soundly schooled in old intellectual disciplines, who would nurture in the New World the intellectual and moral patrimony received from the Old World. And for generation upon generation, the American liberal-arts colleges (peculiar to North America) and later the liberal-arts schools and programs of American universities, did graduate young men and women who leavened the lump of the rough expanding nation, having acquired some degree of a philosophical habit of mind.

You will have gathered already that I do not believe it to be the primary function of formal schooling to "prepare boys and girls for jobs." If all schools, colleges, and universities were abolished tomorrow, still most young people would find lucrative employment, and means would exist, or would be developed, for training them for their particular types of work. Rather, I believe it to be the conservative mission of liberal learning to develop right reason among young people.

Not a few members of the staffs of liberal-arts colleges, it is true, resent being told that theirs is a conservative mission of any sort. When once I was invited to give a series of lectures on conservative thought at a long-established college, a certain professor objected indignantly, "Why, we can't have that sort of thing here: this is a *liberal* arts college!" He thought, doubtless sincerely, that the word "liberal" implied allegiance to some dim political orthodoxy, related somehow to the New Deal and its succeeding programs. Such was the extent of *his* liberal education. Nevertheless, whatever the private political prejudices of professors, the function of liberal education is to conserve a body of received knowledge and to impart an apprehension of order to the rising generation.

Nor do I think it the function of genuine schooling to create a kind of tapioca-pudding society in which everybody would be just like everybody else—every young person, perhaps, to be the recipient eventually of a doctoral degree, even if quite innocent of philosophy. Instead, a highly beneficial result of liberal education, conservative again, is that it gives to society a body of young people, introduced in some degree to wisdom and virtue, who may become honest leaders in many walks of life.

At this point in my remarks, someone at this friendly gathering may mutter, knowingly, "An elitist!" Living as we do in an age of ideology, nearly all of us are tempted to believe that if we have clapped a quasi-political label to an expression of opinion, we have blessed or damned it; we need not examine the expression on its own merits. In educationist circles, "elitism" is a devil-term, for isn't everybody just like everybody else, except for undeserved privilege?

Yet actually I am an anti-elitist. I share T. S. Eliot's objections to Karl Mannheim's theory of modern elites. I object particularly to schemes for the governance of society by formally trained specialized and technological elites. One of my principal criticisms of current tendencies in the higher learning is that, despite much cant about democratic campuses, really our educational apparatus has been rearing up not a class of liberally educated young people of humane outlook, but instead a series of degree-dignified elites, an alleged meritocracy of confined views and dubious intellectual and moral credentials, puffed up by that little learning which is most truly described by that mordant Tory Alexander Pope as a dangerous thing. We see such elites at their worst in "emergent" Africa and Asia, where the ignorant are oppressed by the quarterschooled; increasingly, if less ferociously, comparable elites govern us even in America—through the political structure, through the public-school empire, through the very churches.

Such folk were in George Orwell's mind when he described the ruling elite of *Nineteen Eighty-Four* (1949): ". . . made up for the most part of bureaucrats, scientists, technicians, trade-union organizers, publicity experts, sociologists, teachers, journalists, and professional politicians. These people, whose origins lay in the salaried middle class and the upper grades of the working class, had been shaped and brought together by the barren world of monopoly industry and centralized government."

Now it is not at all my desire that university and college should train up such elites. When I say that we experience an increased need for truly liberal learning, I am recommending something to leaven the lump of modern civilization—something that would give us a tolerable number of people in many walks of life who would possess some share of right reason and moral imagination; who would not shout the price of everything, but would know the value of something; who would be schooled in wisdom and virtue.

I am suggesting that college and university ought not to be degree-mills: they ought to be centers for genuinely humane and genuinely scientific studies, attended by young people of healthy intellectual curiosity who actually show some interest in mind and conscience. I am saying that the higher learning is meant to develop order in the soul, for the human person's own sake. I am saying that the higher learning is meant to develop order in the commonwealth, for the republic's sake. I am arguing that a system of higher education which has forgotten these ends is decadent; but that decay may be arrested, and that reform and renewal still are conceivable. I am declaring that the task of the liberal educator, in essence, is a conservative labor.

The more people who are humanely educated, the better. But the more people we have who are half-educated or quarter-educated, the worse for them and for the republic. Really educated people, rather than forming presumptuous elites, will permeate society, leavening the lump through their professions, their teaching, their preaching, their participation in commerce and industry, their public offices at every level of the commonwealth. And being educated, they will know that they do not know everything; and that there exist objects in life besides power and money and sensual gratification; they will take long views; they will look forward to posterity and backward toward their ancestors. For them, education will not terminate on commencement day.

Not long ago I spoke at a reputable liberal-arts college on the subject of the order and integration of knowledge. There came up to me after my lecture two well-spoken, well-dressed, civil graduating seniors of that college; probably they were "A" students, perhaps *summa cum laude*. They told me that until they had heard my talk, they had been unable to discover any pattern or purpose in the college education that they had endured for four years. Late had they found me! Where might they learn more?

I suggested that they turn, first of all, to C. S. Lewis's little book *The Abolition of Man* (1947); then to Michael Polanyi's *Personal Knowledge* (1958), and to William Oliver Martin's *Order and Integration of Knowledge* (1957). Were I speaking with them today, I should add an important book I have read since then, Stanley Jaki's *The Road of Science and the Ways to God.*

Those two young men went off in quest of wisdom and virtue, of which they had heard little at their college, and I have not beheld them since. I trust that they have read those good books and have become members of that unknowable Remnant (obscure, but influential as Dicey's real shapers of public opinion) which scourges the educational follies of our time.

If college and university do nothing better than act as pretentious trade-schools; if their chief service to the person and the republic is to act as employment agencies—why, such institutions will have dehumanized themselves. They will have ceased to give us young people with reason and imagination who leaven the lump of any civilization. They will give us instead a narrow elite governing a monotonous declining society, rejoicing in a devil's sabbath of whirling machinery. If we linger smug and apathetic in a bent world, leaving the works of reason and imagination to molder, we will come to know servitude of mind and body. The alternative to a liberal education is a servile schooling. And when the flood-waters of the world are out . . . , it will not suffice to be borne along by the current, singing hallelujah to the river god.

Some of you may have seen the edition of Irving Babbitt's *Literature and the American College* which I brought out recently, and the edition of Babbitt's *Democracy and Leadership* which I brought out through Liberty Press in 1980. Babbitt's warning, in 1908, about the decay of liberal education has taken on grimmer significance since he wrote. Permit me to quote here the concluding sentences of his *Literature and the American College:*

"Our colleges and universities could render no greater service than to oppose to the worship of energy and the frantic eagerness for action an atmosphere of leisure and reflection," Babbitt insisted.

> We should make large allowance in our lives for "the eventual element of calm," if they are not to degenerate into the furious and feverish pursuit of mechanical efficiency. . . . The tendency of an industrial democracy that took joy in work alone would be to live in a perpetual devil's sabbath of whirling machinery and call it progress. . . . The present situation especially is not one that will be saved—if it is to be saved at all—by what we have called humanitarian hustling. . . . If we ourselves ventured on an exhortation to the American people, it would be rather that of Demosthenes to the Athenians: "In God's name, I beg of you to *think*." Of action we shall have plenty in any case; but it is only by a more humane reflection that we can escape the penalties sure to be exacted from any country that tries to dispense in its national life with the principle of leisure.

By "leisure," Babbitt meant opportunity for serious contemplation and discussion. On the typical campus of 1987—particularly the vast confused campus of what I call Behemoth University—there is opportunity aplenty for hustling or for idleness, but the claims of true academic leisure are neglected. Much more has been forgotten, too, especially the notion of the philosophical habit of mind.

Perhaps I have been addressing you somewhat abstractly. Permit me, then, to suggest briefly the relevance of liberal education, in its conservative function, to our present discontents.

Nowadays I frequently visit Washington—this city of which Joseph de Maistre said that it never could become a capital. In one sense, de Maistre is vindicated: Washington remains a dormitory town rather than a true national capital, no center for right reason and imagination, a confused and confusing locus of administration, rather than of decision. A good many friends of mine—some about my own age, but most of them a generation younger—have taken office recently; they profess their eagerness for guidance.

They find themselves struggling to act decisively within a vast proliferating bureaucracy, interested seemingly in its own power and preferment. There is urgent need for great decisions; but thought is painful; and the bureaucracy prefers boondoggles and stagnation. Great decisions cannot be long postponed, for the foreign and domestic concerns of the United States will not stay long for an answer.

You may recall the medieval legend of Friar Bacon and Friar Bungay. Bacon had constructed a head of brass, which he expected to speak and reveal the secret of defending England against England's enemies. But exhausted by his labors, Friar Bacon found it necessary to nap while waiting for the brazen lips to part; so he appointed his apprentice, Friar Bungay, to wake him the moment the Head should utter a word.

As the great scientist slept, the brazen oracle commenced to function. "Time will be!" it pronounced. Friar Bungay, terrified, addressed the Head foolishly. "Time is!" the head proclaimed. Still Bungay babbled. Then the Head exclaimed "Time was!"—and burst into a thousand fragments. When Bacon awoke, the opportunity was lost forever.

So matters stand in Washington nowadays. Irrevocable decisions must be reached before that tide in the affairs of men has begun to ebb. Those of my friends who are possessed of a liberal education have the sort of reason and imagination calculated to provide us with prudent and far-reaching decisions. But they stand a small minority among the specialists and technicians, the elite, who dominate the operation of the enormous federal machinery. And sooner than we expect, the Brazen Head may thunder, "Time was!"

Some years ago, President Nixon, in the course of an hour's conversation, asked me, "What one book should I read?" He added that he had put that inquiry, more than once, to Daniel Patrick Moynihan and Henry Kissinger; but they had given him lists of a dozen books, and the President, under the pressures of his office, could find time for only one seminal book. What should it be?

"Read T. S. Eliot's *Notes Towards the Definition of Culture*" (1948), I told Mr. Nixon. He wanted to know why.

"Because Eliot discusses the ultimate social questions," I replied. "He deals with the relationships that should exist between men of power and men of ideas. And he distinguishes better than anyone else between a 'class' of truly educated persons and an 'elite' of presumptuous specialists—remarking how dangerous the latter may become."

President Nixon discovered not long later that the elite of his administration were deficient in that wisdom and that virtue so much needed in America. A liberally educated man learns from Plato and from Burke that in a statesman the highest virtue is prudence. The sort of high prudence required in great affairs of state has not frequently been encountered in Washington during the past several decades. One reason for this deficiency has been our American neglect of liberal education, as defined by John Henry Newman. I remind you now of Newman's definition:

> This process of training, by which the intellect, instead of being formed or sacrificed to some particular or accidental purpose, some specific trade or profession or study or science, is disciplined for its own sake, for the perception of its own object, and for its own highest culture, is called Liberal Education; and though there is no one in whom it is carried as far as is conceivable, yet there is scarcely any one but may gain an idea of what real training is, and at least look toward it, and make its true scope, not something else, his standard of excellence.

True liberal education, that standard of excellence, that conservator of civilization, is required not in Washington alone, but everywhere in our society. Most possessors of a liberal education never come to sit in the seats of the mighty. Yet they leaven the lump of the nation, in many stations and occupations; we never hear the names of most of them, but they do their conservative work quietly and well.

In my lecture "Can Virtue Be Taught?" I mentioned my grandfather, Frank Pierce, a bank-manager. Although he spent only one term at college—studying music at Valparaiso University—he was a liberally educated gentleman; for liberal education may be acquired in solitude, if necessary. On the village council and the school board, he was a pillar of probity and intelligence. From his example I came to understand the nature of wisdom and virtue.

Frank Pierce, possessing four tall cases of good books—chiefly humane letters and historical works—was able to reflect upon the splendor and the tragedy of the human condition. He was no prisoner of the provinciality of place and circumstance, nor of time.

Such conservative people, endowed with a liberal understanding, have taken a large part in giving coherence and direction to our American society. I do not know what we Americans might have become, had we not such men and women among us. I do not know what we will do if they vanish from our midst. Perhaps then we will be left to celebrate "a devil's sabbath of whirling machinery," supervised by specialists—an elite without moral imagination, and deficient in their understanding of order, justice, and freedom. And after that, chaos.

Much needs to be conserved in these closing decades of the twentieth century, when often it seems as if "Whirl is king, having overthrown Zeus." One benefit of a liberal education is an understanding of what Aristophanes meant by that line—and of how Aristophanes, and Socrates, retain high significance for us. If you have studied Thucydides and Plutarch, you will apprehend much about our present time of troubles; and if you cannot order the state, at least a liberal education may teach you how to order your own soul in the twentieth century after Christ, so like the fifth century before him.

If, in a way that is at once conservative and radical and reactionary, we address ourselves to the renewal of liberal learning, conceivably we may yet live a life of order and justice and freedom. But if we linger smug and apathetic in a bent world, increasingly dominated by squalid oligarchs, we shall come to know servitude of mind and body. If our patrimony is cast aside, Edmund Burke reminded his age, "The law is broken, nature is disobeyed, and the rebellious are outlawed, cast forth, and exiled from this world of reason, and order, and peace, and virtue, and fruitful penitence, into the antagonist world of madness, discord, vice, confusion, and unavailing sorrow."

When liberal education is forgotten, we grope our way into that antagonist world—if you will, from space to anti-space, into Milton's "hollow dark." In such an antagonist world there would be no pleasant speculative gatherings like ours this day, for no liberal learning would remain to be conserved.

["The Conservative Purpose of a Liberal Education," The Wise Men Know What Wicked Things Are Written on the Sky *(Washington, DC: Regnery Gateway, 1987), 79–89.]*

❖

The American Scholar and the American Intellectual

In this essay, Kirk points out how the term "intellectual" originally had "a disparaging signification," and how it became in the twentieth century "a distinct term of commendation." He himself is not comfortable with intellectual as a word or as a concept, even as he does not like to see any scholar, bookman, or man of letters falling into the nets of ideology. Hence, Kirk neither accepts nor condones American intellectuals who "proceed to discard the wisdom of our ancestors and to try to remould human nature and society after an image contrived from their own petty stock of private rationality." And he goes on to insist that it is the scholar's task to promote moral aims and aspirations, and also to identify "our real duties and our real limitations." This assiduously argued essay enables a reader to distinguish between the responsibility of the scholar and the agenda of the intellectual.

We hear a great deal nowadays about the lamentable plight of the American intellectual. I think that the American educated man, or at least the American who has submitted to a certain amount of formal instruction, is indeed in an unhappy situation; and part of his unhappiness is the consequence of his calling himself an "intellectual." That term implies defecated rationality, the exaltation of pure logic, presumptuous human reason unassisted by religious humility and traditional wisdom, above veneration and conscience. I do not think that we are going to effect much improvement in education until we confess to ourselves that there is something greater than pure individual reason. That higher wisdom is religious truth.

Until a very few generations ago, men took it for granted that the essence of true education was religious knowledge. Theology was queen of the sciences; professors and teachers, Catholic or Protestant, were men in holy orders, or at least men thoroughly schooled in theology, apologetics, Biblical studies, and the wealth of Christian thought. A learned man was a clerk, a cleric. Nor was this true simply of the Christian nations: Judaism, Mohammedanism, Buddhism, Brahmanism, and all the higher religions had in their charge the education of the people. As philosophy, art, law, and all the more important elements of civilization developed out of religious principle and faith, so formal schooling was the creation of the church, and instruction in religious truth remained until very late the primary aim of schools and universities. Here in America, the whole tone and temper of learning and society was immeasurably influenced by our church-founded universities and colleges.

Yet in America, as in most of the rest of the world, a divorce between religion and education began to take effect about the middle of the nineteenth century, with the rise of scientific materialism, aggressive secularism, state educational institutions, and the triumph of technology. Knowledge, simple secular instruction, might teach a man all that he needs to know in this life, the zealots of the new order insisted. Religion, these reformers maintained, was unscientific, irrational: at best, it was a personal, private, mystical experience, not fit to be discussed in schools. The clerisy—the body of preachers and teachers imbued with a sense of religious consecration—gave way to the intellectuals. And from the consequences of this neglect of religious wisdom, we have suffered terribly, and we are destined to suffer for a great while yet. Newman, more than a century ago, prophesied these consequences:

> In morals, as in physics, the stream cannot rise higher than its source. Christianity raises men from earth, for it comes from heaven; but human morality creeps, struts, or frets upon the earth's level, without wings to rise. The Knowledge School does not contemplate raising man above himself; it merely aims at disposing of his existing powers and tastes, as is most convenient, or is practicable under circumstances. It finds him, like the victims of the French Tyrant, doubled up in a cage in which he can neither lie, stand, sit, nor kneel, and its highest desire is to find an attitude in which his unrest may be least.

Now the unrest and the ill repute of the American intellectual, I think, are caused primarily by this divorce of knowledge from religious truth; and I propose to say a little about defecated intellectuality.

Not long ago someone wrote to Bertrand Russell inquiring after his definition of an "intellectual." Lord Russell replied most forthrightly:

"I have never called myself an intellectual, and nobody has ever dared to call me one in my presence.

"I think an intellectual may be defined as a person who pretends to have more intellect than he has, and I hope that this definition does not fit me."

Earl Russell, being well acquainted with the signification of words, spoke with some authority on the modern usage of "intellectual." The word has had rather an interesting history. In the seventeenth century, it was indeed employed as a noun, chiefly to describe a person who holds that all knowledge is derived from pure reason. It had even then, and earlier, a denigratory implication. The more common term for this concept was "intellectualist." Bacon writes critically, in the *Advancement of Learning* (1605), of the intellectualist as an abstract metaphysician: "Upon these intellectualists, which are, notwithstanding, commonly taken for the most sublime and divine philosophers, Heraclitus gave a just censure." Bishop Parker remarks how "These pure and seraphic intellectualists forsooth despise all sensible knowledge as too grosse and material for their nice and curious faculties." Hume demolished the eighteenth-century intellectuals, or intellectualists, who took Reason for their guide to the whole nature of man; they were the *a priori* reasoners, upon the model of Locke; Hume does not employ the word "intellectual," however. Coleridge—again, however, not using the word—attacked them as the devotees of the mere Understanding, "the mere reflective faculty," as distinguished from the Reason, or organ of the supersensuous.

As a noun descriptive of persons, "intellectual" scarcely appeared at all in nineteenth-century dictionaries. So far as the term was employed, it meant the "sophisters and calculators" whom Burke had denounced, the abstract *philosophes*; it was a category despised equally, though for different reasons, by Romantics and Utilitarians. It is scarcely surprising, then, that the word retains a disparaging signification. It was closely linked with an unimaginative secularism: Newman attacked Sir Robert Peel for embracing it. All in all, "intellectual" meant just what Bacon meant by it, a person who overrates the understanding. By implication, an intellectual neglected the imagination, the power of wonder and awe, and the whole great realm of being which is beyond mere rational perception.

Fairly early in the twentieth century, however, a group of persons began to describe themselves as intellectuals. Throughout the nineteenth century, a man no more would have thought of calling himself an intellectual than a woman would have thought of calling herself a bluestocking. The words used to describe persons possessed of what Burke called "a liberal understanding" were varied, and none of them wholly satisfactory: scholar, bookman, philosopher, university man. Coleridge coined a new word to describe the teachers and preceptors of society, including the clergy and the lay scholars: the clerisy. A principal reason why no one word adequately described such a class of persons was that, in most of Europe and America, and especially in Britain and the United States, intellectuality was not the particular property of any class or order. A banker, like Grote, might possess the liberal understanding; or a politician, like Disraeli or Franklin Pierce; or a judge, like Tocqueville or Chancellor Kent; or a wine-merchant's son, like Ruskin; or an engraver and printer, like Blake. Thus it was reserved to the twentieth century to try to make "intellectual" a distinct term of commendation.

The current employment of "intellectual" appears to be derived from the jargon of Marxism. It is directly linked with the notion of a body of schooled and highly rational persons bitterly opposed to established social institutions—outcasts in a sense, men who go out to the Cave of Adullam, uprooted, rootless, radical folk, what Gissing called "the unclassed." *Les intellectuels* was the term of contempt employed by the factions of the Right, during the Dreyfus controversy, to describe the café revolutionaries, the men who had broken with tradition, the enemies of patriotism, order, and the wisdom of the ages. It implied an opposition between the life of the mind and the life of society—or, at least, an inimicality between "advanced social thinkers" and the possessors of property and power. It also implied, commonly, a contempt for religious ideas and establishments. In the definition of the twentieth-century dictionaries, an intellectual is "a person of a class or group professing or supposed to possess enlightened judgment with respect to public or political questions." The link with social and political action is significant of the aims and limitations of the twentieth-century intellectuals. A "liberal understanding" in Burke's sense, Newman's "liberal education," the world of contemplation and silence, was not what they were after: they wanted to mould society nearer to their hearts' desire, not to adhere to traditional humanism by improving private mind and character.

The Marxists seem to have been the first body of "intellectuals" to call themselves just that. In their sense, "intellectuals" was the Anglicized form of the Russian *intelligentia,* more awkwardly if more literally translated as "intelligentsia." In nineteenth- and twentieth-century Russia, the *intelligentia* were the emancipated and revolutionary body of educated or half-educated people, university students and graduates, who felt that the old Russia was hopelessly reactionary and mindless—and that, indeed, it held no place for them. They considered themselves enemies of established society and the church, opposed both to convention and to the state, self-liberated from prejudice and prescription. In all charity, it must be said that though they thought of themselves as emancipated, in fact often they merely were unbuttoned. Out of this *intelligentia* came the Nihilists—and, in the fullness of time, the Narodniks and the Mensheviks and the Bolsheviks. This curious class, a kind of intellectual proletariat, is described by Dostoievski, in its earlier stages; Conrad's *Under Western Eyes* (1911) examines these people, too, particularly through the character of Razumov—who, though unsuccessfully reacting against the emancipated *intelligentia,* cannot free himself from their temper and society.

The *intelligentia* were displaced persons, schooled beyond their proper expectations in life, severed from tradition but unable to find comfortable niches in the world of modernity.

An intelligentsia of this description increased rapidly in numbers throughout much of Europe in the latter half of the nineteenth century, and began to be a force in all sorts of odd corners of the world; its lineaments may be discerned now in nearly every Latin-American state, and in India, Indonesia, and even the modern towns of Africa. It never has attained to corresponding influence in the English-speaking states, however, in part because of the traditional liberal learning there (closely joined to the old religious and humanistic disciplines and the concept of free and dignified personality in all walks of life), in part because representative government and social mobility have provided safety-valves.

What Dr. Albert Salomon, in *The Tyranny of Progress* (1955), calls the "coffeehouse intellectual," then, so subversive in the Continent, represented no real threat to things established in the English-speaking states. Pitt and Liverpool might find it prudent to keep an eye upon the radical journalist and pamphleteer; but as the mob was Tory, so was the great majority of scholars and writers. Burke, when he exposed the designs of Dr. Price and the "constitutional societies," found the clergy—dissenting or Anglican—actually more radical than Grub Street was. Oxford and Cambridge, Harvard and Yale, throughout the eighteenth and nineteenth centuries, scarcely were seedbeds of revolt; while the newspaper office and the publishers' string of writers did not turn out Trotskys. Café society (in the French or German sense, not the gossip-column signification) did not dominate the realm of scholarship and authorship and political speculation in Britain and America. "Mr. Trotsky of the Central Cafe," in Vienna, could walk into the street and make a revolution; but he had no Anglo-Saxon counterpart.

Until recent years, London and New York knew little of this atmosphere. The scholar and the writer were not alienated men. Not until the 1920s, in Britain and America, was there much talk of the treason of the intellectuals; and that was because the word "Intellectual" was seldom employed, for lack of any distinct class to which it might be attached. Only as Britain and America lost their comparative isolation from European ideology, and only as there began to grow up in these nations a body of persons educated beyond their expectations in life, opposed to established social institutions, did the word "intellectual" obtain currency and the place of the intellectual in English and American society begin to be argued about. And it remains true, as Lord Russell's sardonic remark suggests, that not many people in these nations want to be called intellectuals—and that some of the more intelligent and best-educated Englishmen and Americans are most hostile to what I have called "defecated intellectuality." Burke could imagine nothing more wicked than the heart of a thoroughbred metaphysician—that is, presumptuous rationality, the cult of Reason, divorced from religion, tradition, honor, and duties. This remained almost the universal Anglo-American attitude until recent years.

Emerson did not write about the "American intellectual"; he wrote of the American Scholar; indeed, he disliked the concept of "a sort of Third Estate with the world and the soul," a body of persons claiming to speak exclusively for the intellect, and for the intellect only. The aversion to defecated intellectuality may be observed not only among our statesmen—Washington, John Adams, Webster, Lincoln, Theodore Roosevelt—but among our men of letters and speculation: take Hawthorne, Melville, Lowell, Henry Adams, and George Santayana, to speak almost at random. Some of our writers and critics might remark sadly the deficiency of contemplation and the higher imagination in America, but they did not aspire to set up the "Intellectuals" as a distinct caste. Had not the New England farmer who read good books as much a right to be considered an intellectual being as any coffeehouse Bohemian? Was Calhoun, reading in his solitary way at Fort Hill, any less a thinking man than an Amherst professor? Who was the "Intellectual"—Clarence King or William Graham Sumner? Schooling was easily enough available to almost anyone that wanted it; the domination of higher education in America by church-founded colleges tended to prevent any opposition between tradition and intellectuality; while popular government made it difficult for the intellectually alienated to maintain that he was kept under by some iron political domination. Thus we hear next to nothing about "the role of the intellectual," as a distinct breed, until the alteration of American character and the triumph of urbanization, within this century, bring to the United States conditions in some degree analogous to those of Europe.

I have suggested that the concept of the "intellectual" is closely joined to class antagonism and radical political alteration. The thinking man in America generally has not spoken of himself as a member of a distinct order, precisely because class has been so amorphous in this country. He was not excluded by the nobility or the church or the central bureaucracy: there existed no nobility, and no church establishment, and no bureaucracy in the European sense, to exclude him. He might be lonely, but he was not oppressed; if he felt himself neglected or almost friendless, still he attributed his condition to the ancient preoccupation of the mass of men with material ends, not to organized obscurantism in high places. Only when a doctrinaire hostility toward traditional religion, "capitalism," and established political forms began to make itself felt in America, particularly with the growing influence of Marxism and other European ideologies in the 1920s and the vague discontents of the Depression, did a number of educated Americans commence to call themselves intellectuals.

So the American Intellectuals were identified from the first with a political and social movement loosely called "Liberalism"—very different in some respects from the English liberalism it thought it emulated, and ranging all the way from a mild secularism to outspoken sympathy with Communist Russia. Often it was linked, philosophically, with Pragmatism, and with various experimental undertakings in education and practical morality. It tended rapidly to become an ideology, as Mr. David Riesman and others have suggested recently, with its secular dogmas and its slogans. Mr. Lionel Trilling and Mr. William J. Newman have stated that they use the terms "liberal" and "intellectual" almost synonymously. The "progressive" assumption in America (with some justification, during the 'twenties and 'thirties) has been that if a man thinks, he must vote for "liberal" candidates.

One may add that there were reasons for this desertion of many educated Americans to ideology. The disquietude of reflective persons in a country apparently given over to getting and spending; the condition of the underpaid professor or teacher in an acquisitive environment; the decay of the old American respect for learning—a decay which seemed actually to grow more alarming in direct ratio to the ease with which high school diplomas and college degrees were obtained, on the principle that whatever is cheap is correspondingly little valued—all these influences tended to produce an alienation of the scholar and the writer from established American society, including religious tradition. "Intellectuals" appeared in America when the works of the mind began to lose ground in public esteem.

Probably I have made it clear that I am fond neither of the word nor of the concept "Intellectual." But if by "Intellectual" (however unsuitable that word may be, historically) is meant the thinking man, the philosopher, the true scholar, the person who believes that the life of the mind is more important than the acquisitive instinct, then I am all in favor of the intellectual. My point is that I do not like to see the scholar, the member of the clerisy, consider himself a rootless Bohemian, an enemy of tradition, a revolutionary, a participant in a Jacobin elite. I do not like to see him fall victim to ideology; for ideology is inimical to real intellectual attainment. I do not want to see him range himself against the American people, or against our social and political institutions, or—worse still—against our religious understanding: for the ensuing struggle would be disastrous both to the intellectual and the nation, and probably would be decided against the intellectual. I do not like to see the American scholar and bookman and intelligent man of action forced into the mould cast, say, by *Partisan Review*. When Mr. Wyndham Lewis, in *Rude Assignment* (1950), defends the "intellectual" in the cant usage of that word (and Mr. Lewis is well aware that the strict usage is something else), I am on his side: "If you, for the purpose of belittling him, affix the term 'intellectual' (or more familiarly, 'highbrow') to any man of conspicuous intelligence, or whose standards notoriously are not those of the market-place, then there is such a thing only in your stupid mind, or on your foolish lips."

It is, then, a case of serious misunderstanding when Mr. Arthur Schlesinger, Jr., writing in *The Reporter*, declares that I am devoted to vexing "all those who can read without moving their lips." To the "Intellectual" as a rootless Bohemian, an alienated man, a Jacobin, a presumptuous innovator, a person who makes excessive claims for defecated rationality without allowing any place for veneration or tradition or moral worth, I am profoundly opposed. But to the real works of the mind, elevated power of intellect, the scholar, the philosopher, the bookman, the clerisy, the union of right reason with humility and duty, I am humbly dedicated. It is because I do not want the thinking American to sink into the condition of an ideologue that I venture to criticize the drift of the American intellectual.

Mr. Leslie Fiedler, in his *An End to Innocence* (1955), repeatedly remarks how badly the American intellectual erred during the past two decades, and suggests that he needs now to move in a different direction. Mr. David Riesman has some valuable observations to the same effect. Our intellectuals, he says, "need to be defended, not attacked, if they are to succor their 'nerve of failure.'" This is true. Yet I feel that the role which Mr. Riesman himself has in mind for the intellectual is far from satisfactory. An experimenter in morals and in "consumption," an "autonomous man" cut off from religion and tradition, a species of dilettante who prides himself on being different, for no particular reason and with no particular duties—this, after all, is not so very much better than naïve adherence to ideology, although possibly less dangerous.

I confess, in short, to being one of those scholars whom John Dewey detested, endeavoring as I do (in Dewey's words) "to justify rationally the religious-tribal beliefs, moral preoccupations and privileges of their noble masters." (What Dewey meant by this disagreeable description was any educated man who might be inclined to believe that there was light in the world before John Dewey lit his torch.) It is precisely because I respect the scholar, the professor, the scientist, and the lonely thinker that I am hostile toward the clique of "We Happy Few," the closed corporation of the half-educated who call themselves intellectuals—and who then proceed to discard the wisdom of our ancestors and to try to remould human nature and society after an image contrived from their own petty stock of private rationality. I think that a man who believes we wandered in darkness, until Marx and Freud and Dewey took us by the hand, is doing everything in his puny power to injure the mind of our civilization—however humanitarian his intention may be. My model for the scholar is that described by Orestes Brownson in his address "The Scholar's Mission," at Dartmouth College, in 1843:

> I understand by the scholar no mere pedant, dilettante, literary epicure or dandy; but a serious, robust, full-grown man; who feels that life is a serious affair, and that he has a serious part to act in its eventful drama; and must therefore do his best to act well his part, so as to leave behind him, in the good he has done, a grateful remembrance of his having been. He may be a theologian, a politician, a naturalist, a poet, a moralist, or a metaphysician; but whichever or whatever he is, he is it with all his heart and soul, with high, noble,—in one word, religious aims and aspirations.

The scholar of religious aims and aspirations is a man of true freedom of mind. Much of what is said and written nowadays about academic freedom is so much cant. Too often the defenders of the liberties of the Academy take for their motto that of Rabelais' Abbey of Thélème, "Do as you will." This anarchic freedom never really existed in any university, and never can. The Christian knows that true freedom is not simply to "do as you will." For the Christian, freedom is submission to the will of God; and this is no paradox. We are free in proportion as we recognize our real duties and our real limitations. Then we may act within the just confines of our nature, and act with courage. But if we claim an anarchic freedom, we all become so many Cains. The scholar who claims an anarchic freedom may become a sour, conspiratorial, envious creature, like Professor Mulcahey, in Miss Mary McCarthy's novel *The Groves of Academe* (1952).

And a second description of freedom runs through Christian thought, as it ran through the Stoic philosophy and through Indian tradition: freedom is the absence of desire. Exalt the Self, the solitary human atom, above authority, tradition, and conscience, and you make yourself, in the name of freedom, the victim of *hubris*.

Real intellectual freedom must be in accord with submission to the will of God and with subjection of desires. And every right is married to some duty. Academic freedom is married to the duty to seek and to teach the truth. The scholar is protected in his right to think and to say things which might not be tolerated in the marketplace because of the assumption that he is a man devoted to the conservation and the advancement of Truth. If, deserting Truth, he lusts after Power, then he loses his claim to the special freedom of the Academy. And as a friend of mine says who has had much experience of American universities, when some professors nowadays talk about academic freedom, language has lost its meaning for them. They really are not talking about academic freedom, but only about academic power. They are very little interested in conserving or advancing Truth, and are still less interested in securing intellectual or academic freedom for others. What they mean, when they say "academic freedom," is power to dominate the wills of their colleagues and to force the minds of their students into an ideology that they happen to fancy. It is because of these persons that academic freedom is endangered today. No order falls except from its own weakness; and if academic freedom is lost, it will be because the scholar has forgotten that he is a Bearer of the Word. He will have become an intellectual in the root-meaning of that term.

In this time of equalitarian conformity, boredom, and mechanization, when Things are in the saddle and the triumph of technology threatens to suppress the truly human person, we require intellectual power and virtue more than ever before—and courage to resist popular infatuations. "The scholar is not one who stands above the people," Brownson says, "and looks down on the people with contempt. He has no contempt for the people; but a deep and all-enduring love for them, which commands him to live and labor, and, if need be, to suffer and die, for their redemption; but he never forgets that he is their instructor, their guide, their chief, not their echo, their slave, their tool." We now need a genuine clerisy as never before we needed such in America. But I do not believe we are going to obtain anything of the sort if we endeavor to create an intelligentsia, a rootless class of half-educated persons after the European model. The reflective and conscientious American needs to do his duty as an intellectual leader; but he needs to remember that in such a society as ours, the restriction of intellectuality to a presumptuous caste may be disastrous. We may turn out some millions of intellectuals, but we may simultaneously do our worst to stifle the wise man and the truly liberal understanding.

["The American Scholar and the American Intellectual," Beyond the Dreams of Avarice: Essays of a Social Critic *(Chicago: Henry Regnery Company, 1956), 3–15.]*

❖

The Intemperate Professor

Throughout his career Kirk was deeply concerned with educational problems facing the United States. Books like Academic Freedom: An Essay in Definition *(1955),* The Intemperate Professor and Other Cultural Splenetics *(1965), and* Decadence and Renewal in the Higher Learning *(1978) outline his concerns with vigor and indignation. As one distinguished university president, Henry M. Wriston, wrote of Kirk, "in criticism he is a precisionist. But when he has a point to make he writes with his fist." In the following selection Kirk is unsparing in what he says about the radical agenda of ideologues in the academy. For some professors the mission of the university is to convert wisdom into power, thus nullifying the axiom "that the aim of education is the improvement of human reason and imagination, for the individual's sake." Though this essay appeared in 1965, it has even greater relevance today as "secular indoctrinators" spawn new "educational wastelands."*

At a well-reputed private university, a faculty committee was selecting the people to be invited as guest lecturers during the next year. One member of the faculty suggested a famous professor of philosophy, Dr. Y—. This scholar, a forthright Marxian socialist, has long been associated with "liberal" and "progressive" causes. But Dr. Y— also happens to be a courageous anticommunist, opposing the presence of communist teachers in the colleges—not merely because he disagrees with them, but because they are conspiratorial agents, discrediting the Academy and deliberately violating professional ethics.

Yet the dean of the faculty angrily vetoed the name of Dr. Y—. "What?" demanded the dean. "Y—? That Fascist reactionary? Why, he's against academic freedom." Not himself a Communist, the dean was all in favor of academic freedom: liberty, that is, for anyone not deviating from the dean's private convictions. There are no real enemies to the Left, the dean holds, and anyone who thinks otherwise ought to be considered an anathema.

College trustees, and even journalists, are often startled at the pugnacity of some professors when certain political or economic questions are raised. Frequently the social opinions of numerous American college and university teachers seem to be held with a defiant rigidity. Though these scholars may praise complete freedom of opinion in the abstract, still if someone advances an argument running counter to their political prejudices, they reach for bell, book, and candle. Having known some hundreds of professors on fifty or sixty campuses, I venture first to describe this professional intemperance and then to suggest its causes.

Writing to me about a certain "liberal" conformity in textbooks for courses in American history, Professor Stephen Graubard, a historian of science observes, "Someone ought to analyze the reasons why an entire class of scholars, teachers, and workers in the field of American history should think so much alike. The situation resembles unpleasantly the pre-revolutionary conditions at the Russian universities of Tsarist days, where faculty and students formed a hostile falange against the regime. That our American government should seem in the same position as the Tsar, is very depressing." My correspondent, born in eastern Europe, once was a Communist, and knows American campuses thoroughly. Though there is some measure of exaggeration in his comparison, it remains certain that many professors are profoundly discontented with modern American life, and endeavor to arouse a similar dissatisfaction among their students.

"He that lives in a college, after his mind is sufficiently stocked with learning," Edmund Burke wrote while he was still a young man, "is like a man who, having built and rigged a ship, should lock her up in a dry dock." Now I submit that the principal threat to academic freedom in the United States comes from dry-docked minds: the minds of "ideologues" within the walls of the Academy. Some men who spend their lives within the Academy grow mellow; but others turn sour.

One form that such sourness takes is an incessant assertion of one's rights and a perpetual neglect of one's duties. So it comes to pass that certain of the professors, in nearly every college, who cry out most fiercely against alleged external threats to academic freedom, are in reality themselves more hostile to the liberties of the mind than is any Philistine without.

I am in the habit of calling such soured professors "the sp'iled praist" and "the stickit minister." Among the Irish, the "sp'iled praist" is a person who, having once entertained ambitions to be enrolled among the clergy, is disappointed—and so turns against all things established. Among the Scots, the "stickit minister" is a person who has lumbered halfway along the road to ordination, but has got bogged down for life, and so labors discontentedly as a dominie. Sp'iled praists and stickit ministers seldom are cheerful company. Their minds have been dry-docked; and that in rather a mean and ruinous dry dock. They put one in mind of Wordsworth's lines:

The good die first;
And they whose hearts are dry as summer dust
Burn to the socket.

In university and college, especially here in America, the sp'iled praist and the stickit minister, if they turn professors, tend to become secular indoctrinators. Theirs is the glory of Cyrus P. Whittle, the Yankee schoolmaster in Santayana's novel, *The Last Puritan* (1936): to demolish famous reputations and to expose as shams the most cherished traditions of our culture. Too many professors feel that they have been invested with the prophetic afflatus; and, having discarded theology and morals like so much antiquated rubbish, they are thrown back upon the dreary resources of twentieth-century nihilism. To feel one's self a prophet, but at the same time to insist "I am, and none else beside me," is to indulge a dangerous mood. A prophet without a gospel is worse off than a rebel without a cause. For lack of anything better, such a professor often turns to some "political religion," some ideology, as a substitute for the traditions of civility and right reason.

Most faculty members, according to Dr. George N. Shuster, president emeritus of Hunter College, have been sincerely dedicated to their profession. But their taste for a kind of secular religion also has tended sometimes toward intolerance. As Dr. Shuster writes, "Many have been or are sons of rabbis or ministers of the Gospel who have preferred secular learning to the lore of Scripture. These have given to the universities and colleges they have served a very special impulse to achieve innovation and even reform. Perhaps they are primarily responsible for a quality which no one can dissociate from the American campus and which is virtually unknown in Europe—a characteristic to be defined on the one hand as an almost bellicose addiction to freedom and on the other as a commitment to a 'liberal position,' not quite a dogma but almost one, which assays the Devil according to the degree of his 'conservatism.'"

Nowadays, the liberal or radical quasi-dogma of the bellicose professor usually is some variety of socialism, though often called "liberalism"; sometimes it goes so far as communism. But this choice of allegiance is almost accidental, dictated only by the climate of opinion in our time. In another age or country, the secular preacher in the college, the professor whose mind is in the sour dry dock, might turn to fascism, or anarchism, or Lord knows what.

The disease of our time, Edmund Burke said of his own era, is an intemperance of intellect. . . . An intemperance of intellect, which Burke called "the cause of all our other diseases," provokes the present controversy over academic freedom. Zealots of various persuasions have been attempting, sometimes with the best of intentions, to convert higher learning into an instrument for "social reconstruction," or for instilling "100% Americanism," or for "remaking human nature." Usually their endeavors are intemperate; for it is intoxicating to try to transmute Wisdom into Power. So far as academic freedom is endangered today, that freedom can be preserved only if we hold fast to an old principle: that the aim of education is the improvement of the human reason and imagination, for the individual's own sake. The Academy gained its peculiar freedom because the Academy was temperate. If the Academy becomes tipsy, blown about in every wind of doctrine, filled with professors who prefer power to wisdom, people eager to adore the idols of the marketplace, then the Academy will have lost its principle of temperance, and soon will lose its freedom.

Nearly everyone in the United States favors academic freedom—in the abstract. But the tendency of democracies to seek virtual unanimity of opinion, at every level of society, which Tocqueville saw at work long ago, continues to operate in America. For many people nowadays, among them professors, "academic freedom" means perfect liberty to agree with *their* opinions. So long as the alleged violation of academic freedom is against a latter-day "liberal," a number of these gentlemen are ready to protest vehemently. But if the unfortunate is a conservative, or an old-fangled liberal, or even an anti-communist Marxist—why, what do deviationists like that need freedom for?

A certain college teacher of German, for instance, has been hounded out of one institution after another, by anonymous accusers, and by some of his colleagues. He had been so misguided as to become an obscure member of the Nazi party, in Germany—the land of his birth—in the last year of the Second World War. No one accuses him of teaching Nazi doctrines in his classes, nor even of entertaining privately, nowadays, totalitarian notions. But having once erred—though in another land, and under some compulsion—he may never be forgiven.

A case may be drawn up, of course, in defense of such severity. But *severitas* ought not to be partisan. This persecution contrasts interestingly with the impassioned defense which certain ritualistic liberals have made of former—or even present—Communists among their academic colleagues. Only one variety of totalism, we are to conclude, must be punished by exclusion from the Academy.

Real academic freedom is a right or privilege enjoyed by scholars in institutions of higher learning. The theory of academic freedom is that the search after Truth involves certain risks: for Truth is not always popular in the marketplace, and there are opinions and fields of speculation that cannot prudently be discussed in the daily press, or in public meetings. Academic freedom is intended to give the scholar a measure of security against arbitrary interference with his study and teaching—though such security never can be perfect. Now every right we enjoy has some corresponding duty. The obligation which corresponds to the right of academic freedom is this: the scholar must be dedicated to the conservation and the advancement of the Truth. He must be the guardian of the wisdom of our ancestors, and the active thinker who reconciles permanence and change in his generation. If, failing to fulfill these responsibilities, he becomes a propagandist, a secular indoctrinator, a man in love with power, then he falls derelict in his duty, losing his sanction for the peculiar freedom of the Academy. He ought, in short, to be a man of temperate intellect.

In American colleges today, some of the people who talk most loudly about the "menace to liberal values" are themselves intolerant of other people's opinions. According to the poet and scholar Ludwig Lewisohn, it is the "conservative professor and student, the religious professor and student" who today are a forlorn and persecuted remnant. Dr. Morton Cronin, writing in the *New Republic*, ironically says that *some* conservatives are tolerated on American campuses—so long as they are quiet, not vexing faculty meetings with their opinions. These gentlemen, Mr. Cronin adds, are the Uncle Toms of Academe; they must content themselves with saying that "they're not ashamed of being black."

One liberal professor, Dr. Ralph Gilbert Ross of the University of Minnesota, has been somewhat disquieted by the intolerance of colleagues. Writing in *Commentary*, he says that a faculty committee, of which he was a member, refused to promote a professor on the ground that he once had said something in favor of Senator Joseph McCarthy. Himself no admirer of the late Joseph McCarthy, Mr. Ross adds uneasily that perhaps this discrimination might be justified by the argument that anyone who sympathized with Senator McCarthy was stupid. But the episode affected him disagreeably, as it well might.

At a municipal college, a professor with many publications to his credit was due to receive permanent tenure of his post. A faculty committee objected to his receiving tenure. (Few of the committee members having published much, one is tempted to think of the fable of the fox and the grapes. But their charge against their colleague amounted to an accusation of personal immorality.) Pressed to be more specific, they replied that the candidate was "against democracy." What did they mean? Well, said the committee sourly, the professor had written some unkind things about that democratic educator John Dewey. Their premise seems to have been that academic freedom means the liberty to agree with Dewey. In this case, despite the efforts of the faculty committee, the college's president sustained and promoted the "immoral" professor. Some twentieth-century liberals are ready to defend to the death their monopoly of the classroom. At the same time, they declare that Voltaire was a great fellow.

Their discrimination against the academic dissenter is not purely political: it extends to questions of religious belief. In many colleges, the established professorial orthodoxy is quite as intolerant of religious conviction as the medieval Church was intolerant of heresy. The Roman Catholic scholar is the worst bugaboo of such professors, but in diminished degree this hostility may extend to every variety of Christianity, excepting—and then grudgingly—only the more enthusiastic advocates of the "Social Gospel." A liberal professor of this stamp frequently equates communism and catholicism as "totalitarian movements," arguing that the Catholic scholar ought not to be admitted to the Academy because he is "committed to dogmas," and is "not his own master," and is "not free to pursue the truth wherever it may lead." (All truth, you know, leads to secularized "liberalism.") A priest in Detroit, for instance, though attached to a municipal university, was rebuffed by a professor of sociology, who refused even to argue with him in print, "because Father M— lacks the necessary scholarly disciplines." That the priest happened also to be a doctor of philosophy of a secular university was brushed aside as an irrelevant fact: every priest, the implication ran, is by nature an ignorant obscurant.

And sometimes this discrimination is sectional, or regional, in character. The seaboard states of the Northeast, in the view of some orthodox twentieth-century liberals, are the repository of learning and enlightenment, while the wicked South is the pit of blackest ignorance and reaction. If the doctrinaire liberal never has been south of Mason and Dixon's line, his righteous prejudice is so much the stronger. He doesn't need to *see* the South; to go there would turn his stomach, he knows. He has read about the South in Mr. Erskine Caldwell's novels and has seen it depicted on Broadway; and that's evidence enough. If someone interjects that the most flourishing school of American writing today is Southern—why, the impertinent heretic must be a Fascist and a racist. An English friend of mine, new to this country, suggested to Northern liberal acquaintances that he might enroll at Duke University in North Carolina. "What?" they murmured, scandalized. "Duke? That's a *Southern* university." Such contempt sometimes extends, though not so strongly, to the Middle West. Those states, an Eastern ritualistic liberal knows, are the Bible Belt, the abode of the late Joseph McCarthy, and a cultural wasteland. Even scholars of outwardly tolerable views, if they come from this desolation, may be suspect as corrupted by prairie bigotry, until they have demonstrated the contrary.

But above and beyond politics and religion and region, the all-embracing conformity exacted by the ritualistic liberals is conformity to the doctrine of "non-commitment." A scholar, these gentlemen argue, ought to be committed to no firm point of view about anything. Though he ought to pursue Truth, he must never embrace her. His mind, like that of John Locke's infant, ought to be a blank tablet, so far as first principles of morals and politics and taste are concerned. He should doubt all things, for the sake of doubting; he should break down old prejudices in students' minds. Nothing is settled, or ought to be; the function of the university is to "destroy all barriers to the questing spirit of man." At a state college in Michigan, certain professors of education, sociology, and psychology—dedicated liberals all—drew up an elaborate set of tests to be administered to all entering freshmen and all graduating seniors, for determining their "value preferences" and "environmental prejudices," and how efficaciously the college does its good work of eradicating stubborn convictions acquired from tradition and family instruction.

One of these tests included a question as to whether the student believed that "it is wrong for a brother to have sexual relations with his sister." The student who replied "yes" was classified, so far as this question went, as inclined toward irrational prejudices. Not that the liberal professors were in favor of incest on principle; they said they were in favor of nothing on principle; they simply aspired to "give the student an open mind" and "set free the inquiring rationality." When the tests were analyzed, they found, presumably to their sorrow, that graduating seniors left college with the very prejudices they had entertained as freshmen: the college had failed in its mission.

Whether the liberal professors really act upon this absolute relativism is another matter. At an Ohio university, a decade ago, some of these scholars proposed that all members of the faculty be required to vow that they would teach only by "the empirical method." This, it turned out, meant the philosophical and social principles of John Dewey. Only after heated debate was the proposal defeated. In politics, the ritualistic liberals affirm, a scholar ought to have no commitments—except, that is, to democracy and liberalism. Strong affirmation of faith in democracy and liberalism isn't commitment; it's merely the Truth. And who defines democracy and liberalism? A faculty committee of latter-day liberals. Who else could?

At one great university, a conservative scholar was proposed for an appointment. No, never, said the doctrinaire liberals: he's committed to a "point of view." They wouldn't for the world think of depriving him of his right to express that point of view—except at their university. Some brave soul suggested, at this moment, that the faculty already included several eminent men of the Left. "Nonsense!" said the majority; commitment in *that* direction—well, it's harmless anyway.

Here I have set down some fragmentary evidence of the malady of the intemperate professor. Upon many American campuses, the prevailing climate of opinion remains—if modified—still a quasi-collectivistic liberalism, among faculty politicians and those energetic persons who push themselves to the headships of lecture committees and tenure committees. Theirs is a wondrously illiberal liberalism. The most charitable view a dispassionate observer can take of these gentlemen is that they do not understand the meaning of their own favorite word "liberal." At a Wisconsin college, some young instructors objected to having any known conservative speak on the campus, because "this is a liberal arts college." Conceivably they really were ignorant that political liberalism is much younger than the liberal arts—unaware that the liberal education which John Henry Newman praised is quite different from the partisan social liberalism which Newman detested.

A gentleman with considerable experience of our universities observes to me that many professors really are not interested in academic freedom, however great an outcry they make about alleged threats to their right to free expression. What some professors really mean when they say "academic freedom" is academic power. They do not truly desire to conserve or extend the realm of Truth, or to teach a body of knowledge to intelligent students. What they really desire is authority to bend their colleagues and their students to their own will. They seek to compel colleagues, students, and society to submit to some ideology; and even that ideology is not so important to them as the sense of power which accompanies this opportunity to propagandize, to indoctrinate, to alter society and human nature radically. Men generally are too fond of power. Harder to repress than lechery or gluttony or avarice, this lust for power is the strongest of vices. But the scholar professes to have given up his claim to power in favor of the service of Truth. And so a professor lusting after power, under the cloak of academic freedom, converts liberty into license. He is not truly seeking freedom either for himself or for others, such a power-tipsy professor; he really wishes to impose his own will and opinions, without much scruple, upon whoever happens to fall within his influence.

I am not saying that this fault of intemperance afflicts *most* American professors. The majority of them are tolerant enough, interested in their discipline rather than in power. Nor am I saying that intemperance and power-lust are peculiar to *American* professors; as Raymond Aron suggests in his book *The Opium of the Intellectuals* (1957), this situation has been at least as bad in the French universities; and I have met at Oxford colleges certain influential professors who are quite as politically dogmatic and impatient of contradiction as are their American counterparts. I am saying only that on many of our campuses the belligerent political radical or anti-religious zealot has an influence out of proportion to the numerical strength of his clique. And I am trying to analyze the reasons for this intemperance of intellect.

A well-known economist, Professor Ludwig von Mises, tells us that American intellectuals have an "anti-capitalist mentality." Living in a competitive society, which offers large rewards to practical abilities, we Americans pay the professor less well, in money and status, than certain other societies have rewarded him. In the United States, Dr. Mises suggests, the intellectual rarely is invited to mingle with the rich, famous, and powerful; feeling neglected, he develops a deep resentment against "capitalism," attributing to free enterprise his own unprosperous condition. Though his own mentality is distinctly procapitalist, Professor Mises sees no remedy for this prejudice on the part of American professors; he implies only that we ought to keep these envious folk from exercising power. "To understand the intellectual's abhorrence of capitalism," Mises writes, "one must realize that in his mind this system is incarnated in a definite number of compeers whose success he resents and whom he makes responsible for the frustration of his own farflung ambitions. His passionate dislike of capitalism is a mere blind for his hatred of some successful 'colleagues.'"

Envy being part of original sin, it is perhaps inevitable that a twentieth-century professor of envious disposition should attribute his discontent to the workings of the profit motive, quite as it was tempting for an envious scholar of the Dark Ages to attribute his comparative failure to the workings of Satan. Every age has its devils and its whipping boys. Yet, though unconscious or half-conscious envy certainly is a factor in the mentality of the Academy's sp'iled praists and stickit ministers, I think there are other causes for their attitude; and there may be remedies.

Among the tangle of causes for sour discontent in the Academy, four seem especially powerful. These may be described as Frozen Liberalism, the Chaotic Campus, the Depression Mentality, and the Utopian Delusion.

By Frozen Liberalism, I mean that many college teachers formed their opinions—or got them ready-made—thirty or forty years ago, and have refused to alter them since. Thinking always is painful, and why should a professor be expected to suffer? A European intellectual who often lectures in America, Dr. Erik von Kuebnelt-Leddihn, speaks ironically of a "Holy Liberal Inquisition" which dominates a great many American campuses: every scholar is expected by the Inquisitors of One-Hundred-Per-Cent Liberalism to subscribe to their secular catechism, or else be anathema. Recently, for instance, Dr. Glenn Campbell was appointed to the headship of the Hoover Institution at Stanford University. No sooner had he arrived than the local liberal inquisitors asked if he had any sympathy with the political and economic views of Mr. Herbert Hoover, founder of the institution. When they discovered him so heretical as to express substantial agreement with Mr. Hoover, they persuaded the Stanford faculty senate to pass a resolution—by a narrow majority—denouncing the appointment of Dr. Campbell.

These Inquisitors—many less courteous than the monks who interrogated Galileo—often are gentlemen who read the *Nation* and the *New Republic* from cover to cover in the twenties and thirties—and have read little since. For them, liberalism is a closed and immutable system, easily expressed in journalists' phrases. Franco-Spain is Hell, and the Chinese communists still are simple agrarian reformers. In such attitudes, they have much in common with the Depression Mentality I describe below; but the distinguishing characteristic of these Frozen Liberals is their inverted conservatism. They seem resolved that no doctrine of an origin more recent than their own graduate school years should be discussed on an American campus. The revival of conservative political and economic ideas is especially shocking to them, but they have their own conservatism.

This conservatism of mental indolence and jealous self-interest is no new phenomenon; in one form or another, it has existed among institutionalized scholars ever since the schools of Plato and Aristotle arose. Nowadays, because the dominant orthodoxy of a generation ago was Ritualistic Liberalism, the inverted conservatism of these professors is Frozen Liberalism. Though they profess to be haters of all things established, these scholars actually detest any change in their own disciplines or in the social opinions they acquired in youth. Mr. Arthur Koestler, in his recent book, *The Sleepwalkers* (1959), describes the trial of Galileo and observes, in passing, that "professionals with a vested interest in tradition and in the monopoly of learning" always tend to block the development of new concepts. So the Aristotelian scholars in the seventeenth-century universities dealt intolerantly with Galileo. "Innovation is a twofold threat to academic mediocrities: it endangers their oracular authority, and it evokes the deeper fear that their whole laboriously constructed intellectual edifice might collapse. The academic backwoodsmen have been the curse of genius from Aristarchus to Darwin and Freud. . . ." The intemperate Frozen Liberals of the American campus in 1965 are just such academic backwoodsmen.

By the Chaotic Campus, I mean the mass scale, the confusion, and the lowering of standards which afflict most American campuses nowadays. Swollen by the "rising tide" of enrollments since the Second World War, American universities and colleges are bursting with prosperity—of a sort. Whatever the benefit of conferring degrees upon a proportion of the population three times as large as used to attend college, this process of sudden expansion has tended to dehumanize the college. All activity—except at such liberal arts colleges as mean to hold the line against mass growth—is more and more standardized, but not more and more orderly. The businesslike administrative officers of the college increase in importance; the scholarly professor slides toward the status of a hired hand. Many students enroll only for a snob degree, urged on by parents, or for four years of dating and sports cars. Some are incapable of real college study; others are unwilling to make the effort genuine study exacts. Although I cannot enter here into the complex ills of the college boom, I suggest that this partial collapse of order and discipline in our colleges, this break with the quiet life which used to be general on American campuses, distresses and alienates some able teachers.

For the professor by nature is attached to order. He professes a regular discipline. He believes in intellectual standards. When the time is out of joint, especially on his campus, he is badly disquieted. He never expected to grow rich by teaching; but he did expect a fairly leisurely, retired, respected profession. He did not contract to be ordered about by a college administrative bureaucracy, or to put up with insolent, indolent, and sometimes fraudulent students. All about him he sees confusion nowadays; and sometimes he attributes this confusion, this loss of his old status, to the political system and the economy which govern our modern nation. He protests against this chaotic change by appealing to a "liberal" ideology, perhaps—even though triumph of the sort of liberalism he adores might aggravate, really, the campus confusion.

This Chaotic Campus is an affliction of the past fifteen years, mainly, though its roots go back to the beginning of this century. Some intelligent people are already doing what they can to remedy its worst aspects. In his essay on "Academic Leisure," more than fifty years ago, Irving Babbitt of

Harvard gloomily described the "humanitarian hustling" in American colleges: the passion for attempting everything, hurriedly and superficially; the tendency for the college to try to be all things to all men—and to deprive the scholar of his rightful and necessary intellectual leisure. "Of action we shall have enough in any case," Babbitt concluded, "but it is only by a more humane reflection that we can escape the penalties sure to be exacted from any country that tries to dispense in its national life with the principle of leisure."

Here I suggest only that the sourness and resentment of some American professors nowadays is in consequence of this "humanitarian bustling" on the campus—our swollen enrollments, our disregard of real standards, our indifference to the claims of the scholar. And I put the question that an extending of higher schooling to many more young people may become a national injury, rather than a general improvement, if those young people are taught superficially by professors who have been alienated from our society by the very process of rapid expansion on the campus.

One instructor in English literature whom I know has his students read the books of Mickey Spillane, as principal examples of twentieth-century writing. It isn't that the professor admires *Kiss Me, Deadly* (1952) or its author: no, he says that "Spillane is a Fascist." Yet Mickey Spillane, my acquaintance declares, is a typical specimen of the modern America—decadently tough, loveless, aimless, seeking escape in violence. Spillane represents disorder; therefore the professor—very much a dry-docked mind—orders his students to read Spillane, as "contemporary literature," presumably that they may learn how evil our society has become and how it ought to be supplanted by a "new order." When I hear well-meaning people argue that simple quantitative growth of enrollments is bound to improve American culture and politics, I think of this professor and his influence. No small amount of professors' intemperance is provoked by the disorderly campus of 1965.

By the Depression Mentality, I mean that the majority of today's college teachers—the professors in their forties—attended high school and college during the era of the Great Depression; and some of them cling fondly to the slogans and attitudes of those turbulent years. The New Deal, the Popular Front, the leagues against war and fascism, the bewildering kaleidoscope of proposals for radical social change which were brought forward as early as 1929 and endured into the forties—with these, the present generation of professors grew up intellectually. And not a few of them grew up, also, with a haunting sense of economic and psychological insecurity, conscious of the "underprivileged" and the "malefactors of great wealth" and all that—sometimes identifying themselves with the idealized Common Man.

As in that penetrating but short-lived Broadway play, *The Egghead* (1958), many a professor of this day is fixed emotionally to the political and intellectual commitments of his undergraduate days. "Prevailing opinions," Disraeli wrote more than a century ago, "generally are the opinions of the generation that is passing." The problems of 1965 are not precisely the problems of 1932; but some college teachers grow vexed when their students decline to share their enthusiasms for the causes of yesteryear. In practical politics, a goodly number of professors think we still are fighting the battles of the Hoover and Roosevelt administrations; though they fancy themselves a daring *avant-garde*, in actuality they are tearfully nostalgic. Looking for a second Franklin Roosevelt to lead them to Zion, some long for positions of authority in Washington, another rally of brain trusters. For a time, many saw such a leader in Adlai Stevenson; later, they turned to Senator Hubert Humphrey, who had been a professor himself. I know of private and state colleges in which the whole faculty of certain departments swore by Humphrey, urging their students to campaign for him. They not only wanted Mr. Humphrey for president, but were thoroughly convinced that the Common Man would nominate and elect him. Their chagrin after the West Virginia primary in 1960 was not pretty to look upon.

Professor Moses Hadas, an elderly classicist, laments the fact that his students have turned conservative. Years ago, he says, he used to tell his classes about Agis and Cleomenes, the radical reforming kings of Sparta who came to a miserable end for the sake of a dream; but his students of today—unlike students of a generation gone, who desired to emulate the Spartans—think Agis and Cleomenes were fools. Certainly radicalism does not thrive among college students as it did in the confused and ideologue-plagued thirties; and this student hostility to radical innovation disturbs and sometimes infuriates nostalgic professors. "Why, these youngsters think we're old fogies," the chairman of a department of English said to me. "They just don't go for the causes that used to excite us." If you have thought you were leading a triumphal march toward a Brave New World, with the students at your back, and then glance around to find that, instead, you have turned your back on the students; if you find yourself middle-aged and rather lonely, and unable to understand the rising generation that was supposed to require your leadership—why, you may have some excuse for a jaundiced disposition.

This source of alienation among professors will work its own cure, for the graduate students of the sixties—the professors of the seventies and eighties—will have their roots in the Eisenhower era; and whatever their deficiencies, they are unlikely to hold many illusions about Soviet Russia, or to cherish the memory of Harry Hopkins and Henry Wallace. But the ill feeling of certain professors against an era which failed to become the Century of the Common Man will persist until they add emeritus to their titles. Marx and Freud, names dear to the young intellectuals of the twenties, will yield pride of place to other seminal minds. That is the way of the world, but the dry-docked professor resents the nature of things.

By the Utopian Delusion, I mean the notion that somehow human existence ought to be perfectly happy, and since it is not nowadays, the System or perhaps "wicked reactionaries" are to blame. This doctrine of the perfectibility of man and society is derived from the Enlightenment of the eighteenth century; it is at loggerheads with the Christian belief that human nature necessarily is flawed and that perfect happiness cannot be attained in this world, man being incurably restless and insatiable here below. To enjoy Heaven here and now, to create the Terrestrial Paradise—this is the ambition of the Utopian intellectual.

Modern society is riddled with imperfections; so all societies have ever been. But modern society also has certain considerable merits, and these the Utopian professor among us usually has ignored. In economics, for instance, he has behaved as if wealth were somehow the gift of nature, and if we could arrange for the government to distribute it equally, human perfection would be at hand. Though the terrible events of the twentieth century have disconcerted many scholars who formerly believed in the march of Progress with a capital P, something of their hope for the earthly paradise lingers on—and something, also, of their anger with the vested interests who, they think, are bent upon thwarting the aspirations of the Common Man.

Since the Russian Revolution, this Utopian impulse usually has taken the form of sympathy with communism. Not more than 5 percent of American college teachers ever were Communists, though the number of fellow travelers was considerably greater; and since the Second World War, the hard core of Communists has shrivelled. Yet there endures on the campus a kind of sneaking sympathy with revolutionaries who profess doctrines of total equality, so that gentlemen like Dr. Castro still have their panegyrists.

If one is to believe a certain survey of academic opinion,[2] nearly one quarter of our teachers of social science in college appear to be determined radicals. The percentage of radicalism also runs fairly high in departments of English, to judge from my own observations. I am not sure why, though it is conceivably because many professors of English literature permit a vague sentimentality to do duty for a serious understanding of politics.

Although the primary function of the professor is to pass on to the rising generation a body of knowledge, it is true that the professor has the right, and even the duty, to criticize his age. Colleges ought not to be centers for smugness. But from lively criticism to indoctrination for revolutionary change may be a dangerous leap. Our civil social order, with its high degree of justice and freedom, with its guarantees of human dignity, has been slowly and painfully created by thousands of years of historical experience, trial and error. The imprudent Utopian professor can do great mischief to enthusiastic and impressionable young people by inculcating among them a sneering and sullen mood, by setting for them social goals impossible to attain. Burke called the Jacobin radicalism of the French Revolution "the revolt of the enterprising talents of a nation against its property." The thoroughgoing Utopian professor would like to do just that—to make of his students sullen or rash rebels against everything established. To live with a gnawing grudge against one's own civilization is the way to a personal Hell, not to the Terrestrial Paradise.

Personally, indeed, some of the Utopian intellectuals are markedly unattractive. One professor of my acquaintance is given to long discourses in praise of universal brotherhood and the welfare state. But when some unlucky student presents him with note cards incorrectly arranged, the humanitarian scholar flings the lot of them on the classroom floor, contemptuously, and watches the student pick them up. This professor says he detests "the authoritarian personality" and desires complete democracy, economic as well as political. Yet he might not have done badly as a commissar or a gauleiter; for some of those gentleman, too, commenced as Utopian intellectuals.

During the next few decades, I suspect, there will be less talk in the Academy about marching to the earthly Zion and more attention to the norms of morals and politics and taste, from which we derive order in personality and justice in society. I think we are going to see more intelligently conservative professors. The Academy is beginning to regain its balance, to revive the pagan virtue of temperance.

The degree of academic freedom which any educational system can sustain always depends upon the general soundness and thoroughness of that educational system. If the professor is a half-educated man, intoxicated by a little learning and convinced that, out of his omniscience, he has the duty to impose his convictions upon his students; if the student is ill-grounded and unable even to read critically—why, then the free exchange of opinions, founded upon the assumption that professors are servants of truth and that students are competent to distinguish between falsity and right reason, becomes almost impossible. The intemperate professor, the presumptuous "intellectual," becomes the secular indoctrinator; and the student becomes his dupe. In America, this problem of academic freedom will be solved only by a restoration of real learning, at every level of schooling.

The sp'iled praist and the stickit minister in the Academy are inhumane: that is, they have forgotten the purposes of the Academy. For the truth of ethical and intellectual attainment, they have substituted the illusion of Utopian social reconstruction. What example a teacher sets is quite as important as what he teaches. While a temperate and generous mind can wake the best in the rising generation, a sour and carping view of life can warp the character of college students.

Such, down to our time, is the ancient contest between philosopher and philodoxer. Gradual disillusion with ideology may be the salvation of the Academy's temperance. "Intelligence will tell in the long run," a Harvard colleague said once to Irving Babbitt, "even in a university." Aye, intelligence—with a dash of humility.

["The Intemperate Professor," The Intemperate Professor and Other Cultural Splenetics *(Baton Rouge, LA: Louisiana State University Press, 1965), 3–20.]*

❖

Teaching Humane Literature in High Schools

The teaching of literature in American high schools, Kirk says, is in a state of confusion. A misguided concern for relevance and the notion that literature has no real purpose afflict literary studies. There are no standards or norms, progressivist educationists claim, as they proceed to dismiss the belief that the aim of literature is to awaken us to truth and beauty through the imagination. Here Kirk presents a program of reading rooted in English language and literature. He includes work in prose and poetry ranging from John Bunyan's prose allegory The Pilgrim's Progress, *in the ninth grade, to William Shakespeare's historical play* Henry V, *in the tenth grade, to Herman Melville's novel* Moby Dick, *in the eleventh grade, to Joseph Conrad's novel* Lord Jim, *in the twelfth grade. Literature as the pursuit of wisdom undergirds Kirk's corrective syllabus. His recommendations deserve consideration at a time when many American educators refuse to answer this critical question: Must mediocrity be compulsory?*

In many American high schools, the teaching of literature is in the sere and yellow leaf. One reason for this decay is the unsatisfactory quality of many programs of reading; another is the limited knowledge of humane letters possessed by some well-intentioned teachers, uncertain of what books they ought to select for their students to digest well.

In this brief essay, I propose to suggest, first, the sort of literature which ought to be taught; and then to list certain works of imaginative letters—poetry, novels,plays, philosophical studies, and other branches of letters not embraced by the natural sciences or by social studies—especially commendable for this purpose. T. S. Eliot remarked that it is not so important what books we read as that we should read the same books. He meant that a principal purpose of studying literature is to give us all a common culture, ethical and intellectual, so that a people may share a general heritage and be united through the works of the mind. There exist a great many good books, Eliot knew: of these many commendable books, we need to select for general study a certain elevated few for particular attention, that nearly everyone may share in our cultural patrimony. This is my purpose here—though I claim no sovereign authority, and stand ready to have other people substitute books of equal merit for some or many of the titles I suggest.

What is wrong with the typical high-school anthology or program of literature nowadays? I am of the considered opinion that the usual courses in literature, from the ninth grade through the twelfth (also, generally, in lower grades), suffer from two chief afflictions. The first of these is a misplaced eagerness for "relevance." The second of these is a kind of sullen purposelessness—a notion that literature, if it has any end at all, is meant either to stir up discontents, or else merely to amuse. Let me touch briefly here on both troubles.

Literature certainly ought to be relevant to something. But to what? Too many anthologists and teachers fancy that humane letters ought to be relevant simply to questions of the hour—the latest political troubles, the fads and foibles of the era, the concerns of commercial television or of the daily newspaper. Such shallow relevance to the trivial and the ephemeral must leave young people prisoners of what Eliot called the provinciality of time: that is, such training in literature is useless to its recipients within a few years, and leaves them ignorant of the enduring truths of human nature and of society.

Genuine relevance in literature, on the contrary, is relatedness to what Eliot described as "the permanent things": to the splendor and tragedy of the human condition, to constant moral insights, to the spectacle of human history, to love of community and country, to the achievements of right reason. Such a literary relevance confers upon the rising generation a sense of what it is to be fully human, and a knowledge of what great men and women of imagination have imparted to our civilization over the centuries. Let us be relevant in our teaching of literature, by all means—but relevant to the genuine ends of the literary discipline, not relevant merely to what will be thoroughly irrelevant tomorrow.

As for the second affliction, purposelessness, the study of literature would not have been the principal content of formal schooling for many centuries, had humane letters seemed to offer only a kind of safety-valve for personal discontents, or else merely a form of time-killing—the filling of idle hours. In every civilized land, literary studies were taken very seriously indeed until recent decades. Literature and its related arts usually were called "rhetoric," in times past; and this word "rhetoric" means "the art of persuasion, beautiful and just." Literature, in short, was and is intended to persuade people of the truth of certain standards or norms. Literature has been regarded as the peer of theology and philosophy because literature's real purpose is quite as serious as the purposes of theology and philosophy. But literature's proper method differs from the methods of theology and philosophy. Unlike those disciplines, literature is supposed to wake us to truth through the imagination, rather than through the discursive reason. Humane letters rouse us to the beautiful and the just through symbol, parable, image, simile, allegory, fantasy, and lively example. The purpose of literature is to develop the moral imagination. If human beings do not feel the touch of the moral imagination, they are as the beasts that perish.

Or, to put it another way, the aim of humane letters, of our courses in "lit" or (hideous phrase) "communications skills," is to form the normative consciousness. That I may make myself clear, indulge me here in a digression directly related to this general topic of what books to study in literature courses.

❖

Until very recent years, civilized folk took it for granted that literature exists to form the normative consciousness: that is, to teach human beings their true nature, their dignity, and their rightful place in the scheme of things. Such has been the end of poetry—in the larger sense of that word—ever since Job and Homer.

The very phrase "humane letters" implies that literature is meant to teach us the character of human normality. This is an ethical discipline, intended to develop the qualities of manliness, or *humanitas*, through the study of important imaginative books. The literature of nihilism, of pornography, and of sensationalism, arising in the eighteenth century and stronger still in our time, because of the decay of the religious understanding of life and of the Great Tradition in philosophy, is a recent development. Or rather, it is a recent disease.

This normative end of letters has been particularly powerful in English literature, which never succumbed to the egoism that came to dominate French letters at the end of the eighteenth century. The names of Milton, Bunyan, Dryden, and Johnson—or, in America, of Hawthorne, Emerson, Melville, and Henry Adams—may be sufficient illustrations of this point. The great popular novelists of the nineteenth century—Scott, Dickens, Thackeray, Trollope—all assumed that the writer lies under a moral obligation to normality: that is, explicitly or implicitly, he is bound by certain enduring standards of private and public conduct.

Now I do not mean that the great writer incessantly utters homilies. With Ben Jonson, he may scourge the follies of the time, but he does not often murmur, "Be good, sweet maid, and let who will be clever." Rather, the man of letters teaches the norms of our existence, often rowing with muffled oars. Like William Faulkner, the writer may write much more about what is evil than about what is good; and yet, exhibiting the depravity of human nature, he establishes in his reader's mind the awareness that there endure standards from which we may fall away; and that fallen nature is an ugly sight. Or the writer may deal chiefly, as did J. P. Marquand, with the triviality and emptiness of a smug society which has forgotten norms. The better the artist, one almost may say, the more subtle the preacher. Imaginative persuasion, not blunt exhortation, commonly is the strategy of the literary champion of norms.

This principle prevailed almost until the end of the eighteenth century. Since then, the egoism of one school of the Romantics has obscured the primary purpose of humane letters. And many of the Realists have written of man as if he were brute only—or, at best, brutalized by institutions. In our own time, and especially in America, we have seen the rise to popularity of a school of writers more nihilistic than ever were the Russian nihilists: the literature of *merde*, of disgust and denunciation, sufficiently described in Edmund Fuller's mordant study *Man in Modern Fiction* (1958). To the members of this school, the writer is no defender or expositor of norms; for he fancies that there are no standards to explain or defend; a writer merely registers, unreservedly, his disgust with humanity and with himself—and makes money by it. (This is a world away from Jonathan Swift, who, despite his loathing of most human beings, detested them only because they fell short of what they were meant to be.)

Yet the names of our twentieth-century nihilists will be forgotten in less than a generation, I suspect, while there will endure from our age the works of a few men and women of letters whose appeal is to the enduring things, and therefore to posterity. I think, for instance, of Gironella's novel *The Cypresses Believe in God* (1951). The gentle novice who trims the hair and washes the bodies of the poorest of the poor in old Gerona, though he dies by Communist bullets, will live a long space in the realm of letters; while the scantily disguised personalities of our nihilistic authors, swaggering nastily as characters in the best-sellers, will be extinguished the moment when the public's fancy veers toward some newer sensation. For as the normative consciousness breathes life into the soul and into the social order, so the normative understanding gives an author lasting fame.

Malcolm Cowley, writing a few years ago about the recent crop of first-novelists, observed that the several writers he had discussed scarcely had heard of the Seven Cardinal Virtues or of the Seven Deadly Sins. To these young novelists, crimes and sins are merely mischances; real love and real hatred are absent from their books. To this rising generation of writers, the world seems purposeless, and human action meaningless. And Cowley suggested that these young men and women, introduced to no norms in childhood and youth except the vague attitude that one is entitled to do as one likes, so long as it doesn't injure someone else, are devoid of spiritual and intellectual discipline—are empty, indeed, of true desire for anything but notoriety.

This sort of aimless and unhappy writer is the product of a time in which the normative function of letters has been badly neglected. Ignorant of his own mission, such a writer tends to think of his occupation as a mere skill, possibly lucrative, sometimes satisfying to one's vanity, but dedicated to no end. Even the "proletarian" writing of the twenties and thirties acknowledged an end; but that has died of disillusion and inanition. If writers are in this plight, in consequence of the prevailing "permissive" climate of opinion, what of their readers? Comparatively few book-readers nowadays seek normative knowledge. They are after amusement, sometimes of a vicariously gross character, or else pursue a vague "awareness" of current affairs and superficial intellectual currents, suitable for cocktail-party conversation. Nature abhorring a vacuum, into minds vacant of norms must come some force—sometimes force of diabolical bent.

Literature can corrupt; and it is possible, too, to be corrupted by an ignorance of humane letters, much of our normative knowledge necessarily being derived from our reading. The person who reads bad books instead of good may be subtly corrupted; the person who reads nothing at all may be forever adrift in life, unless he lives in a community still powerfully influenced by what Gustave Thibon calls "moral habits" and by oral tradition. And absolute abstinence from printed matter has become rare. If a small boy does not read *Treasure Island* (1883), odds are that he will read *Mad Ghoul Comics*.

So I think it worthwhile to suggest the outlines of the literary discipline which induces some understanding of enduring standards. For centuries, such a program of reading—though never called a program—existed in Western nations. It strongly influenced the minds and actions of the leaders of the infant American Republic, for instance. If one pokes into what books were read by the leaders of the Revolution, the Framers of the Constitution, and the principal men of America before 1800, one finds that nearly all of them were acquainted with a few important books: the King James version of the Bible, *Pilgrim's Progress* (1678–84), Plutarch's *Lives of the Noble Greeks and Romans*, something of Cicero, something of Virgil, perhaps the *Book of Common Prayer*. This was a body of literature highly normative. The founders of this Republic thought of their new commonwealth as a blending of the Roman

Republic with prescriptive English institutions; and they took for their models in leadership the prophets and kings and apostles of the Bible, and the great Greeks and Romans of antiquity. Cato's stubborn virtue, Demosthenes' eloquent vaticinations, Cleomenes' rash reforming impulse—these were in their minds' eyes; and they tempered their conduct accordingly. "But nowadays," Chateaubriand wrote in nineteenth century, "statesmen understand only the stock-market—and that badly."

Of course the understanding of the Framers of the Constitution was formed by more than books. They learnt the nature of reality in the business of life, as well as in family, church, and school. Yet great books counted for much with them.

For we cannot apprehend enduring standards of conduct or of taste if we rely only on personal experience. Private experiment with first principles frequently is ruinous, and at best time-consuming; while, as John Henry Newman wrote, "Life is for action." Therefore we turn to the bank and capital of the ages, the normative wisdom found in literature, if we seek guidance in great concerns. Ever since the invention of printing, the printed page has had a large part in molding opinions. Sometimes this is no better than what D. H. Lawrence called "chewing the newspapers." Courses in literature are supposed to lift us above mere newspaper-chewing.

For some fifty years, in America, we have been failing to develop the normative consciousness of young people through the systematic and careful study of great literature. We have talked about "education for life" and "training for life-adjustment"; yet many of us seem to have forgotten that literary disciplines are a princpal means for learning to accept the conditions of existence. Moreover, unless the life to which we are urged to adjust ourselves is governed by norms, it must be a wretched life for everyone.

One of the faults of the typical "life-adjustment" curriculum has been the substitution of "real-life situation" reading for the study of truly imaginative literature. A young teacher of high-school English tells me that her tenth-grade pupils do not take to the stories of virtuous basketball players, dutiful student nurses, and other "real-life" idols thrust upon them. These pupils turn, instead, to what they may procure at the corner drugstore: Ian Fleming, Mickey Spillane, or worse. If we deprive young people of imagination, adventure, and heroism, they are not likely to embrace Good Approved Real-Life Tales for Good Approved Real-Life Boys and Girls. On the contrary, they will resort to the dregs of letters, rather than be bored. And the consequences will be felt not only in their failure of taste, but in their misapprehension of human nature, lifelong; and, eventually, in the whole temper of a people.

Nowadays the advocates of life-adjustment education give a little ground sullenly, before their critics. The intellectual ancestor of their doctrines was Rousseau. Although I am no warm admirer of the notions of Rousseau, I relish still less the doctrines of Gradgrind, in Dickens's *Hard Times* (1845). So I hope that life-adjustment methods of teaching may not be supplanted by something yet worse. A mistaken zeal for vocational training in place of normative instruction; an emphasis upon the physical and biological sciences that would push literature into a dusty corner of the curriculum; an attempt to secure spoken competence in foreign languages at the expense of the great works of our own language—these might be changes in schooling as hostile toward the imparting of norms through literature as anything which the life-adjustment folk have perpetrated.

❖

What I have written here ought to be commonplace. Yet these ideas seem to have been forgetten in many quarters. This normative endeavor ought to be the joint work of family and church and school. As the art of reading often is better taught by parents than it can be taught in a large schoolroom, so a knowledge of good books comes from the home at least as frequently as from the classroom.

Whether one's reading-tastes are developed in the school, the public library, or the family, there are certain patterns of reading by which a normative consciousness is developed. These patterns or levels persist throughout one's education (whether it is school-learning or self-instruction). We may call these patterns fantasy; narrative history and biography; imaginative creations in prose or verse; and philosophical writing (in which I include theology).

With these levels or patterns in mind, I have arranged a sample program of reading for the concluding four years of secondary schooling. I list only works in the English language (or translations which have become part and parcel of English literature) both because my space is limited and because really "foreign" literature should be taught in classes in French, German, Spanish, and the like.

I repeat that I do not insist upon the particular books suggested below, although I think them excellent ones; all I am trying to do here is to suggest the general tone and quality of a good program in humane letters. I have included some old school favorites because their merit and importance have not diminished; on the other hand, I have excluded some old chestnuts (like George Eliot's *Silas Marner* [1861]), because they were never first rate.

Because style and wisdom did not expire with the nineteenth century, among my selections are a number of our better recent authors. Students between the ages of thirteen and eighteen ought to be treated as young adults, actually or potentially capable of serious thought; therefore this is not a list of "children's books." But neither is it an exercise in pop culture and contemporaneity.

These are books calculated to wake the imagination and challenge the reason. None ought to be too difficult for young people to apprehend well enough—provided that they are functionally literate.

Ninth-grade Level

For this year I emphasize *fantasy*, in the larger sense of that abused word. If young people are to begin to understand themselves, and to understand other people, and to know the laws which govern our nature, they ought to be encouraged to read allegory, fable, myth, and parable. All things begin and end in mystery. Out of tales of wonder comes awe—and the beginnings of philosophy. The images of fantasy move us lifelong. Sir Osbert Sitwell, when asked what lines of poetry had most moved him in all his life, replied candidly, "Froggie would a-wooing go, whether his mother would let him or no." So here are my fantastic recommendations—

John Bunyan, *The Pilgrim's Progress* (1678–84) (This is the most influential allegory in the English language.)

William Shakespeare, *A Midsummer Night's Dream* (1595–96)

Nathaniel Hawthorne, *The House of the Seven Gables* (1851) or (perhaps preferably) *The Marble Faun* (1860)

Robert Louis Stevenson, *Kidnapped* (1886) or one of his volumes of short stories

Ray Bradbury, *Something Wicked This Way Comes* (1962) or *Dandelion Wine* (1957) (Bradbury is something far better than an accomplished "science-fiction writer"; he is a man of remarkable ethical insights and great power of style.)

Walter Scott, *Old Mortality* (1816) *or The Heart of Midlothian* (1818) (These are much more important romances than is *Ivanhoe* [1819], so commonly taught.)

Select poems of Spenser, Burns, Coleridge, Wordsworth, Shelley, Tennyson, Whittier, Longfellow, Chesterton, Kipling, Masefield, Yeats, Frost, and others—selected with an eye to the marvellous and the mysterious.

(It will be noted that for this grade, as for later ones, all recommended books are available in inexpensive paperback editions; it is unnecessary, except with incompetent teachers, to employ a fat and rather repellent anthology; besides, most high-school anthologies nowadays are shoddy.)

Tenth-grade Level

Here our vehicle for rousing the moral imagination is narrative history and biography (including autobiography). Reading of great lives does something to form decent lives. I draw upon both "actual" and "imaginary" sources for this branch of literature.

Daniel Defoe, *Robinson Crusoe* (1719–20)
William Shakespeare, *Antony and Cleopatra* (1607–8) or *Henry V* (1509–99)
Francis Parkman, *The Oregon Trail* (1847) or *The History of the Conspiracy of Pontiac* (1851)
Mark Twain, *Huckleberry Finn* (1884) or *Life on the Mississippi* (1883)
Plutarch, select *Lives of the Noble Greeks and Romans* (1914–28) (probably in the Dryden-Clough translation)
William Makepeace Thackeray, *Henry Esmond* (1852)
Benjamin Franklin, *Autobiography* (1771–90)

(These choices, like those for ninth-grade students, range widely in time and approach; but all are very readable. They offer something to every educable student.)

Eleventh-grade Level

Here, as "imaginative creations," I recommend for the third year of high school certain books which require serious interpretation and discussion.

John Milton, *Paradise Lost* (1667)

Jonathan Swift, *Gulliver's Travels* (1726) (only two or three voyages thereof) (Need it be remarked that Gulliver was not intended for the amusement of children?)
Herman Melville, *Moby Dick* (1851) or selected short stories
Charles Dickens, *Great Expectations* (1860–61) or *Bleak House* (1852)
T. S. Eliot, *Murder in the Cathedral* (1935) (No drama is more relevant to the conflict of loyalties in the twentieth century.)
George Orwell, *Animal Farm* (1945)
Select poems of a philosophical cast—George Herbert, Richard Crashaw, Andrew Marvell, Samuel Johnson, Oliver Goldsmith, Alexander Pope, and others chiefly of the seventeenth and eighteenth centuries.

(Fiction is truer than fact: I mean that in great fiction we obtain the distilled judgments of writers of remarkable perceptions—views of human nature and society which we could get, if unaided by books, only at the end of life, if then.)

Twelfth-grade Level

This is the year for developing a philosophic habit of mind through close attention to humane letters. "Scientific" truth, or what is popularly taken for scientific truth, alters from year to year—with accelerating speed in our time. But poetic and moral truths change little with the elapse of centuries; and the norms of politics are fairly constant.

Select *Epistles* of St. Paul (King James version), taught as literature (I assure you that this is quite constitutional, even in public schools.)
William Shakespeare, *King Lear* (1605–6) or *Coriolanus* (1608–9)
Samuel Johnson, *Rasselas* (1759)
Marcus Aurelius, *Meditations* (preferably in Long's translation)
C. S. Lewis, *The Screwtape Letters* (1942) or *The Great Divorce* (1946)
Christopher Marlowe, *Dr. Faustus* (1604)
Joseph Conrad, *Lord Jim* (1900) or *Nostromo* (1904)

(It might be useful to add to these a little book of reflections or essays—George Gissing's *Private Papers of Henry Ryecroft* [1903], say, or Alexander Smith's *Dreamthorp* [1863] or selections from Hawthorne's letters, or Kempis's *Imitation of Christ* [1426]).

Tentative though the preceding recommendations are, I think them calculated to rouse the moral imagination of many students, and not to bore the average pupil. They pay close attention to the greater poets in the English language since the beginning of the seventeenth century; they include three years' study of the most powerful creative writer, Shakespeare; they touch upon both the classical and the Christian roots of humane letters; they introduce students to a dozen major novels; and—unlike most existing programs in literature at the typical high school—they give some place to history and biography.

Quite possibly these suggested lists may not please teachers who merely accept whatever they happen to find in anthologies, nor yet teachers who attempt to convert courses in literature into courses in current social problems. Certainly they will not please teachers who find thinking painful. I have a simple test of teacher-competence, which any instructor in high school literature might do well to apply to himself. It is this: can you understand, and explain to a class, two very direct and memorable poems—Kipling's *The Gods of the Copybook Headings* (1919) and Chesterton's *The Ballad of the White Horse* (1911)? If you cannot, you have chosen the wrong vocation.

Certainly many of the folk who edit high-school anthologies have chosen the wrong vocation. They think of classes in literature as a kind of adolescent-sitting, or at best an opportunity to impart Approved Social Attitudes. They despair of competing with Demon Television. They seem strongly prejudiced against anything published before 1920, say. One way to escape from the clutches of this breed of "educator" is to abjure anthologies altogether and turn instead to the original works of literature, not to the anthology-snippets. And today the price of all the cheap reprints for a semester's study may be less than the price of the bulky and unloveable anthology.

How many favorites of my own have I omitted from this list! Where are Chaucer, Ben Jonson, John Dryden, Edmund Burke, Lord Macaulay, John Henry Newman, Benjamin Disraeli, Oliver Goldsmith, John Ruskin, Washington Irving, William Morris, Fenimore Cooper, George Gissing, George Bernard Shaw, Roy Campbell, William Faulkner? I would not be wounded if someone should substitute Trollope for Thackeray, or Tolkien for Bradbury. What I am offering here is not a dogmatic syllabus, but rather an approach to the study of humane letters by young people—an approach meant to induce them to ask themselves and one another and their teachers certain ultimate questions; also meant to help them learn the difference between praiseworthy writing and wretched writing.

Of course I do not mean that the books listed above, for those four grades, are the Great Books, exclusively, of English letters. They are some of the great books; all of them are important books; those who read these books will be led to many other important books, in school or out of it. We are embarrassed by the riches of English literature, nearly eight centuries of it.

Readers of this inadequate essay who are interested in other lists of the books we ought to know would do well to take up Sir Arthur Quiller-Couch's slim volume *The Art of Reading* (1920) (hard to obtain in America nowadays), or more recent books about great books by John Erskine, Montgomery Belgion, and others. To know what is wrong with the typical school program in literature (on either side of the Atlantic), read C. S. Lewis's essay *The Abolition of Man* (1947). And to the teacher who seeks to learn how to make dead books come alive—why, I commend particularly Gilbert Highet's *The Art of Teaching* (1950).

The survival or the revival of sound study of literature is bound up with the survival of civilization itself. Literary culture will endure through these dark days if enough men and women are aware that the purpose of literature is not simple amusement, nor sullen negation, but rather the guarding and advancement of the permanent things, through the power of the word.

If literature has no object, it does not deserve to survive. Many writers and publishers and reviewers clearly are of the opinion that literature exists only to fill their pockets and tickle their vanity. Any honest physical labor is more edifying than that. But perhaps we will see the beginning of a reaction against such decadence in letters, if only from mankind's primal instinct for the perpetuation of the species.

The rejection of humane letters is an act of childish impatience and arrogance. The consequences of that rejection are not restricted to juvenile years, but may endure to the end of life. When the great books are forgotten or burnt—why, as George Orwell reminds us in *Nineteen Eighty-Four* (1949), "Here comes a chopper to chop off your head."

["Humane Literature in High Schools," Textbook Evaluation Report, *No. 665 (New Rochelle, NY: America's Future, 1977), 1–10.]*

VIII.

THE AMERICAN REPUBLIC

The Declaration of Independence and the Constitution of the United States, Kirk believed, express the American understanding of order; and "the American Republic still asserts the validity of the old moral principles and the practicality of its established institutions." Order, freedom, and justice, he said, were fundamental virtues binding American society. The Framers of the Constitution, he pointed out, took it for granted that a moral order, founded upon religious truths, supports and parallels the political order.

Americans, Kirk noted, looked for guidance not just to their own historical past, but to the "remembered past" of Western civilization, to a long and vindicated continuity of law and institutions prior to American history. In especial Kirk's view of history and tradition in relation to the American republic revolves around the Hebraic understanding of God, the literary and philosophical concepts of ancient Greece and Rome, and ideas and mores derived from Britain.

In the last years of the twentieth century, Kirk saw signs of the weakening of our inheritance of order; this weakening he connected with the adoption of a multiculturalist ideology that could "pull down the whole elaborate existing culture of this country in order to make everybody culturally equal." A liberal mindset in the judiciary, Kirk also found, undermined general legal principles affecting not only the obligations and responsibility of each citizen, but also ethical norms for the human being. "The expectation of change," he felt, seemed greater than "the expectation of continuity."

"Americans are part of a great continuity and essence," Kirk always insisted, and he cited such figures as the planter-statesman John Randolph of Roanoke, the political and religious thinker Orestes Brownson, and the sixteenth president of the United States, Abraham Lincoln, as sturdy protectors of a just society in which divine justice and human justice cohered. For Kirk the problem of political constitutions was that of reconciling liberty with law. His lifelong concern with American character and institutions is best expressed in *Rights and Duties: Reflections on Our Conservative Constitution* (1990; 1997), when he cautions that "the alternative to a politics of elevation is a politics of degradation."

❖

THE FRAMERS: NOT PHILOSOPHES BUT GENTLEMEN

In Kirk's book The Conservative Constitution *(1990), writes American historian Forrest McDonald, readers will find a "special combination of learning, common sense, and literary eloquence." "The Framers: Not Philosophes but Gentlemen," the title of the third chapter, pays tribute to the fifty-five delegates who gathered in Philadelphia in the summer of 1787 to frame the Constitution. In the Framers Kirk sees "gentlemen-politicians" whose perceptions of the human condition came from the Bible and the Book of Common Prayer. The wisdom of the past inspired their ideas and informed their decisions. Kirk provides a striking contrast between the Framers at the Constitutional Convention, who recognized "the old traditions of civility," and the French* philosophes, *drunk on theory, who contributed directly to the Revolution of 1789 and were so arrogant in their presumptions that they created "a new calendar in which the Year One would record . . . [their] own accession to power."*

If the leading patriots of 1776 were no flaming radicals when they signed the Declaration of Independence, the delegates who framed the Constitution in 1787 were pillars of order. To understand that Constitution, it is well to know something of the minds and the manners of the fifty-five politicians who gathered at Philadelphia to "form a more perfect Union."

Now and again one encounters allusions to "the philosophy of the Framers of the Constitution." Indeed there were lovers of wisdom among the Framers; yet the delegates to the Constitutional Convention were anything but abstract metaphysicians.

Three years after the Constitutional Convention had concluded its deliberations, Edmund Burke wrote that nothing was more consummately wicked than the heart of an abstract metaphysician, who should attempt to govern nations by speculative political dogmas. He had in mind the Parisian *philosophes* who had brought on the French Revolution. The men of Philadelphia—some of Burke's admirers among them—had not at all resembled those *philosophes*.

So it will not do to attribute to the Framers some peculiar "philosophy." With only three or four exceptions, they were Christians of one profession or another: that is, they took their primary assumptions about the human condition, consciously or unconsciously, from the Bible and (many of them) from the Book of Common Prayer. Probably nearly all of them had been affected early by *The Pilgrim's Progress* (1678, 1684). Scarcely any of them had been influenced by the French Enlighteners. They were not political theorists, but men of much experience of the world, assembled not in hope of creating the Terrestrial Paradise, but rather to contrive a tolerable practical plan of general government: a plan for survival.

Those Framers of 1787 were not bent upon grand alterations in morals and manners. Perhaps the most ludicrous thing ever uttered about them was a sentence from Rexford Guy Tugwell, in 1970. In Tugwell's judgment, the delegates at Philadelphia had assembled to undo the existing religion and the established mores of the United States. In Tugwell's words, "The framers, meeting in Philadelphia in the summer of 1787, were there because neither the Ten Commandments nor the going rules for social behavior were any longer adequate."

Well! Not one word was uttered, during the Convention's four months, about the Decalogue; and in the seven articles adopted, nothing whatever was said about religion except that no religious test should be required for holding federal office. This does not signify that the delegates aspired to establish some civil religion as an alternative to Judaism and Christianity; it is simply that their constitution was to be a practical instrument of government, not a work of politico-religious dogmata. As for the subversion of "going rules of social behavior"—why, those fifty-five gentlemen politicians were themselves the arbiters of behavior, if not of morals, in their generation. Being no Jacobins, they and their class entertained not the slightest notion of undoing the received mores and manners.

No, the Framers were not abstract metaphysicians. It was the most speculative man among them, Dr. Franklin, who suggested that their crucial sessions should be opened with prayer. The names of Diderot, of Helvetius, of Voltaire, of Rousseau, were not heard at the Convention. Of political philosophers, only Montesquieu was mentioned repeatedly, and he chiefly because of his praise for the old Constitution of England.

Sometimes the Constitution of the United States is commended as if it had been created out of whole cloth, overnight, from the glowing imagination of the Framers. That notion is far from the truth. Sometimes the Framers themselves are spoken of with a veneration like that accorded to the Hebrew prophets or the mythical founders of Greek cities. But actually the Constitution grew out of centuries of practical political experience on either side of the Atlantic, rather than springing from ingenious fine-spun innovating theory. Truly the Constitution is a bundle of compromises, although it is much else besides. Any tolerable order in politics necessarily is a bundle of compromises among interests and classes: a principal merit of the Framers was their ready recognition of this ineluctable fact. As Burke said of government generally, it is a contrivance of human wisdom to supply human wants. In the sagacious observation of Daniel Boorstin, "The American future was never to be contained in a theory."

The politicians who framed the Constitution were not an elite of theorists, but an assembly of governors, in the old signification of that word *governor*. They were representatives of a class, in every former colony, that had exercised authority almost from the very early years of British settlement in North America; they were drawn from a natural aristocracy. Experience, education, and wealth, passed on from generation to generation of Americans, tended to develop a continuity of public influence within leading families; while the relatively broad franchises that came to pass in most colonies nevertheless gave provincial and local government a democratic cast.

Broadly speaking, it was the body of men familiar with America's provincial and local governments who made both the Revolution and the Constitution. This was the class that, far from intending any subversion of the social and moral order in America, took alarm at Shays' Rebellion and so forged a strong Constitution.

Long participation in provincial and local public affairs shaped this American natural aristocracy; while the French Revolutionaries, for the most part, were men previously excluded from any effective exercise of power, and so naive in great questions of public policy. The Americans were men of political experience; the French, men of political theory, and that theory untested. The French Revolutionaries rejected the historical and political inheritance of their country, while the Americans declared that their revolution was fought to preserve their British heritage. The members of America's natural aristocracy, or most of them, thought of themselves as restorers of what was being lost—not as adversaries of the past.

Members of this natural aristocracy governed the Republic of the United States for almost precisely half a century, 1775 to 1825. Let us have a look at the breed.

❖

Four years after the Great Convention, in the course of opposing the sentiments of "the insane Socrates of the National Assembly," Edmund Burke would describe the natural aristocracy that makes possible the existence of a nation; his sentences applied nearly as well to the leading class in America, at that hour, as to the gentry of England, Scotland, and Ireland.

"A true natural aristocracy is not a separate interest in the state, or separable from it," Burke wrote in his *Appeal from the New to the Old Whigs*.

> It is an essential integrant part of any large body rightly constituted. It is formed out of a class of legitimate presumptions, which, taken as generalities, must be admitted for actual truths. To be bred in a place of estimation; to see nothing low and sordid from one's infancy; to be taught to respect one's self; to be habituated to the censorial inspection of the public eye; to look early to public opinion; to stand upon such elevated ground as to be enabled to take a large view of the wide-spread and infinitely diversified combinations of men and affairs in a large society; to have leisure to read, to reflect, to converse; to be enabled to draw the court and attention of the wise and learned wherever they are to be found;—to be habituated in armies to command and to obey; to be taught to despise danger in the pursuit of honour and duty; to be formed to the highest degree of vigilance, foresight, and circumspection, in a state of things in which no fault is committed with impunity, and the slightest mistakes draw on the most ruinous consequences—to be led to a guarded and regulated conduct, from a sense that you are considered as an instructor of your fellow-citizens in their highest concerns, and that you act as a reconciler between God and man—to be employed as an administrator of law and justice, and to be thereby amongst the first benefactors to mankind—to be a professor of high science, or of liberal and ingenuous art—to be amongst rich traders, who from their success are presumed to have sharp and vigorous understandings, and to possess the virtues of diligence, order, constancy, and regularity, and to have cultivated an habitual regard to commutative justice—these are the circumstances of men, that form what I should call a *natural* aristocracy, without which there is no nation.[1]

This description comprehends both the men of presumptive virtue and the men of actual virtue. In one way or another, every delegate to the Constitutional Convention rightfully might have claimed to be numbered among the American natural aristocracy, according to Burke's categories of qualification.

John Adams, in his correspondence with John Taylor of Caroline, defined an aristocrat as any person who could command two or more votes—his own, and at least one other person's. But in employing the phrase "natural aristocracy" I signify something more coherent and demanding than Adams's simple test. From Maine to Georgia, along the Atlantic seaboard especially, there flourished a mode of breeding, schooling, and involvement in public affairs that produced what Edmund Burke would call a natural aristocracy. Many of the members of that body were men who rose to ascendancy principally through their own talents: such leading men Burke referred to as "the men of actual virtue." Other members of that natural aristocracy, in Burke's description, were the men of presumptive virtue—those endowed by birth with the unbought grace of life, the heirs to old families and broad lands.

Even though no peer of the United Kingdom ever took up permanent residence in North America, and very few Americans were knighted during the colonial era; even though no bishops were consecrated for North America by the Church of England—nevertheless, a ruling class, an aristocracy, had grown up quite naturally in the Thirteen Colonies; that class had fought and won the War of Independence; that class framed the Constitution of the United States.

Four decades after the Great Convention, Fenimore Cooper upheld the premises upon which the concept of a gentleman rested. "The word 'gentleman' has a positive and limited signification," Cooper wrote in *The American Democrat*. "It means one elevated above the mass of society by his birth, manners, attainments, character, and social condition. As no civilized society can exist without these social differences, nothing is gained by denying the use of the term."[2] Fifty-five men so elevated, in one fashion or another, made up the body of delegates of 1787: gentlemen politicians.

Charles A. Beard, in 1913, ruffled the dovecotes of complacent Americanism by pointing out that the Framers, almost without exception, were men of property desirous of obtaining more property. It surprises me that anyone was startled by this revelation: property and power are wedded eternally, and if the one is transferred to new hands, the other will follow. It was family possession of property—in land, chiefly—that had given a fair number of the Framers their early advantages in life: private property, as everybody in the Colonies knew, makes possible independence of action. To this should be added that with a few exceptions, notably that of James Wilson, the Framers were not notorious for avarice: that grasping appetite for the world's goods, that democratic materialism reproached by Tocqueville in the 1830s, was not so powerful in 1787 as it would become later. One recalls Henry Adams's survey of the United States in 1800, the population indolent rather than energetic, many Americans content with mere subsistence. In 1787, moved by hopeful speculation and great economic expectations though many of the Framers were, they could not honestly be regarded as grinders of the faces of the poor: they were unlike the merciless Frenchmen of the Directory, a decade later, who enriched themselves out of the revenues; unlike, too, the British crew of politicians described by Stanley Baldwin as "hard-faced men who looked as if they had done well out of the War." Nearly all of the Framers, true, did well out of their war, or at least out of the peace that followed; even the delegate least endowed with fortune in 1787, William Few, a Georgia frontiersman, ended his days as the rich president of the City Bank in New York. (The two delegates who in 1787 were the richest Framers, Robert Morris and James Wilson, would fall to their financial ruin a few years later, through the besetting vice of speculation.) But the mere acquisition of wealth does not bring political sagacity; often it has quite the contrary effect. If the Framers generally had inherited or piled up ample means, still their participation in America's natural aristocracy was founded on more than Burke's "sharp and vigorous understandings" of rich traders.

Several of the more influential Framers indeed had been "bred in a place of estimation," some great family house and estate; had been taught "to respect one's self"; had enjoyed "leisure to read, to reflect, to converse." These gentlemen were at once persons of presumptive virtue and of actual virtue. Consider John Dickinson, heir to a property six miles square, in Maryland; George Mason, of Gunston Hall, one of northern Virginia's great planters, the fourth proprietor bearing the name of George Mason; John Rutledge, of the old Charleston family, who had been dictator of South Carolina during the Revolution; Gouverneur Morris, of Morrisiana, a man of means from New York; and of course George Washington.

As for being "habituated in armies to command and to obey" or taught "to despise danger in the pursuit of honour and duty," a good many of the Framers had been under arms during the War of Independence, supplying that "cheap defense of nations" of which Burke was to write in 1790: that is, the martial obligation of gentlemen, rooted in the chivalric tradition. Alexander Hamilton, Charles Cotesworth Pinckney, John Dickinson, John Francis Mercer, Alexander Martin, John Langdon, David Brearly, William Few, Thomas Mifflin, and Richard Dobbs Spaight had commanded regiments; some Framers had held still higher commissions; and the Convention was presided over by the gentleman who had been commander-in-chief.

Administrators of law and justice may be said to have dominated the Convention, for more than half the Framers had been lawyers or judges; George Wythe of Williamsburg had been the most eminent of them. All were much read in Blackstone (a Tory, incidentally) and earlier authorities on the law. Rufus King and Gouverneur Morris, immensely successful lawyers, were perhaps the most conservative of all the Framers. James Wilson was to write the first American work on jurisprudence; Luther Martin was the energetic and almost perpetual attorney general of Maryland.

Men of "high science, or of liberal and ingenuous art" were not absent from the Convention, Benjamin Franklin the most famous among them. A good many Framers had been teachers at one time or another. James Madison seemed to be the most scholarly of the delegates, but many of them had studied profitably at the American colleges, at Oxford or Cambridge, or at the Scottish and Irish universities. Several—Hamilton in particular—wrote admirable prose; and rhetoric, "the art of persuasion, beautiful and just," was a discipline most of them had acquired systematically. Madison's mind, more than any other man's, gave shape to the Constitution, and Madison cited great writers more frequently than did any other delegate. He was more a man of theory than were most of the Framers; but Madison too, like David Hume, usually was empirical. With Burke, the well-read Framers who had been liberally educated were averse, most of them, to political metaphysics.

"Rich traders" possessing "the virtues of diligence, order, constancy, and regularity" had their considerable part in the convention, from Robert Morris, the Revolution's financier, to Elbridge Gerry, of Marblehead's "codfish aristocracy." No great differences of manners, schooling, or dress distinguished the men of commerce at the Convention from the landed men.

Thus the elements of natural aristocracy which Burke discerned in English society existed also in the United States; and from that aristocracy of nature every delegate to the Great Convention came. Factions, sectional and economic, developed to some extent at the Convention; the advocates of a strong general government and the defenders of states' powers had much to dispute about; yet the civility of the debates and the reasonable acceptance of compromises set off the Great Convention from nearly all other endeavors, ancient or modern, to establish a fundamental political compact. In an era of duelling, no delegate at Philadelphia called out any other delegate. Formal manners happily prevailed; gentlemen most civilly spoke with gentlemen; no marked class rivalries could be discerned in the proceedings; the four months of discussion passed as if friends engaged in an enterprise of common benefit, friends reared in a common culture who understood one another very well, were settling amicably the details of their venture. That, in fact, on a grand scale, was what the Convention amounted to. Although the beginning of the Deluge, the French Revolution, lay only two years in the future, in the United States the men of prescriptive virtue and the men of actual virtue had no falling out: they settled for security and good order, but set limits to the power of the general government—so effecting a very high achievement in the history of politics, the maintaining of a healthy tension between the claims of authority and the claims of liberty.

The spirit of religion and the spirit of a gentleman, Burke would write in 1790, had sustained European manners and civilization. What was the religion of the American natural aristocracy that drew up the Constitution? One might call it the gentleman's religion. At least fifty of the Framers would have subscribed to the Apostles' Creed; no atheist raised his voice at the Convention; but neither was religious enthusiasm (in the eighteenth-century sense of the term) much in evidence. By 1787, Deism had nearly trickled away in North America, but the natural aristocracy was tolerant and temperate in faith. Sectarian distinctions often were blurred: one might be half Quaker and half Episcopalian; half Presbyterian, half Methodist. It would have been politically imprudent, and ungentlemanly besides, to raise questions of religious differences when political consensus was being sought.[3]

Such were the common elements among the fifty-five Framers—who, all things considered, got on uncommonly well one with another. Despite their differences upon this or that prudential question, the Framers formed almost a club of gentlemen united to secure an enduring social order. It remains to inquire how this natural aristocracy of the Convention was shaped, and why it differed so strikingly from the circle of revolutionary victors who would seize power in France only a few years later, and by what means those Framers were able to construct a Constitution that would endure for two centuries, during which era nearly all other national constitutions would be overthrown.

❖

Except for the expulsion or subjugation of what had been the "Tory" interest in the Thirteen Colonies, a class of "gentlemen freeholders" (as they were called in Virginia) effectively had remained dominant from 1775 to 1787, preventing or modifying any large radical alterations of the social structure and the customary ways of life in what had been the Thirteen Colonies. Burke would declare that the French Revolution had been worked by a parcel of hack attorneys in the provinces. It had been otherwise in America: the American revolution and the American restoration of order had been accomplished earlier by experienced public men who had known themselves entitled to the "chartered rights" of Englishmen; who were steeped in knowledge of British constitutionalism, law, and history; whose interest lay in maintaining a political and social continuity. That is one reason why the Constitutional Convention may be called a gathering of friends.

Another reason why it was possible for the delegates to work out a political consensus was their sharing of an inherited literary culture. American schooling and college education in the latter half of the eighteenth century had helped to prepare this natural aristocracy for high public responsibilities. Theirs had been the schooling of English gentlemen of their age, deliberately contrived to rear the rising generation in piety and manliness.

Most of the Framers, twenty or thirty years earlier, had been required to study certain enduring books that were intended to develop a sense of order in the person and in the commonwealth. Among the ancients, they studied Cicero, Plutarch, and Vergil especially. They had memorized Cicero's praise of Roman *mores*, the high old Roman virtue; their imagination had been roused by the lives of Plutarch's heroes; they had come to understand Vergil's *labor, pietas, fatum.*[4]

Instruction in classical history and humane letters did not necessarily incline the rising generation toward respecting the wisdom of their own national ancestors: a classical education did not have that salutary effect upon the Jacobins of France. But in America the classical models were reconciled with, and supplemented by, instruction in British political history and the wealth of English literature. The schooled American was aware of participating in a long continuity and essence of culture, even though he dwelt on the western extremity of that civilization; unlike the French visionary, the schooled American did not presume to draw up a new calendar in which the Year One would record his own accession to power.

But as is true in most eras, books published in their own time, and pamphlet literature, influenced the American natural aristocracy more than did writings of an earlier age. The Framers had read attentively Montesquieu (*The*

Spirit of Laws being first published in English translation in 1750), David Hume, Samuel Johnson, Adam Smith, Edmund Burke (whose *Annual Register* had been for them a principal reliable source of knowledge of events during their own years). Few of them had been much affected by French thought published during their own formative years; indeed, for that matter, even Thomas Jefferson did not read Rousseau (Gilbert Chinard has shown) until well after 1776. Thus to their common heritage of practical political experience, what Patrick Henry had called "the lamp of experience," was joined a common literary culture. And in the English language, those important writers of their own time whom most of the Framers admired certainly were no social revolutionaries. Of course they had read Tom Paine, too; but Paine went back to England in 1787, his influence upon American opinion already much diminished.

A third influence that made the Constitutional Convention a gathering of friends, rather than an assembly of political fanatics, was the concept of a gentleman. The first article of the Constitution would provide that the United States might grant no title of nobility, and that no office-holder should accept a foreign title without the consent of the Congress; but the delegates at Philadelphia, quite unlike the French constitution makers a few years later, had no intention of putting down gentlemen. Presumably every Framer thought of himself as a gentleman, and desired to be so regarded. Gentility, by the eighteenth century, did not require that a man or a woman be high-born; rather, it signified outwardly manners and dress and speech; inwardly, a sense of honor and duty.

The English model of a gentleman did not cease to influence Americans with the British defeat at Yorktown. In 1787, Sansculottism, "many-headed, fire-breathing," had not yet inquired, "What think ye of me?" There were ragged men in America, true, and Shays had led some of them against courts of justice; but it was not partisans of Daniel Shays who deliberated at Philadelphia. Under the influence of the canons of gentle manners, the Convention was conducted with a decorum not since encountered in these United States, and Framers of divergent views observed with one another the old traditions of civility. Temperate speech led to temperate agreement and to permanence of the Convention's product.

Some of the Framers, especially the Episcopalians among them, had read Thomas Fuller's essays on the True Gentleman and on the Degenerous Gentleman, published in Fuller's quarto *The Holy State and the Profane State* (1642). "He is courteous and affable to his neighbors," Fuller wrote of the True Gentleman. "As the sword of the best tempered metal is most flexible, so the truly generous are the most pliant and courteous in their behavior to their inferiors."[5] Aye, the gentleman must be a man of good breeding; also he must be a man of honor who would not lie or cheat; a man of valor, who would not flee before enemies; a man of duty, who would serve the commonwealth as magistrate or member of an assembly; a man of charity, spiritual and material. Undoubtedly some of the Founders were what Fuller called Degenerous Gentlemen, selfish and cunning opportunists; but most lived as best they might by gentlemen's rules. And some of them—Washington, Dickinson, Mason, Rutledge, Gouverneur Morris, others—had fulfilled all their lives the gentleman's obligations of manners, honor, valor, duty, and charity; and so would live to the end.

Politics, we cannot too often remind ourselves, is the art of the possible. The Framers were not a club of speculative *philosophes*. They had a remarkably clear understanding of what might be possible and of what was improbable; perhaps some of them had altogether too keen an eye to the main chance, but they did not err in any visionary fashion.

Their aristocratic realism made possible the survival of the American democracy. Near the close of the twentieth century, in most of the world, natural aristocracy has been destroyed, suppressed, or perverted to ideological servitude. Therefore the nations, particularly the "emergent" ones, are governed by squalid oligarchs, or else are reduced to anarchy. We will not look again upon the like of the Framers of 1787. So we will do well, I think, to refrain from discarding the parchment of 1787 in favor of a plastic modernist constitution.

There come to my mind certain remarks by John Randolph of Roanoke, very much an aristocrat, at the Virginia Convention in 1829:

> Dr. Franklin, who, in shrewdness, especially in all that related to domestic life, was never excelled, used to say, that two movings were equal to one. So to any people, two constitutions are worse than a fire . . . . I am willing to lend my aid to any very small and moderate reforms, which I can be made to believe that this our ancient government requires. But, far better would it be that they were never made, and that our constitution remained unchangeable like that of Lycurgus, than that we should break in upon the main pillars of the edifice.[6]

Like much else that Randolph told his contempories, those sentences regain significance in the year 1990.

["The Framers: Not Philosophes but Gentlemen," The Conservative Constitution *(Washington, DC: Regnery Gateway, 1990), 35–48.]*

The Constitution and the Antagonist World

Although Kirk believes that neither the written Constitution of the United States nor the unwritten constitution has been significantly transformed, he refuses to be complacent in estimating the future prospects of the Constitution. He sees no clear and present danger of altering "the old Constitution," but he is bothered by some of the ominous decisions of the Supreme Court during the past forty years: "Possessing powers not conferred upon the judicial body of any country, the Supreme Court has made itself into a reforming council, politicized." He fears that a second national Convention could endanger that "long continuity of law and political institutions that runs back beyond the beginning of American history." And he is particularly troubled by what he sees as the tendency of the Supreme Court's majority, and of federal and state judges, to hold that religion of any sort is suspect. Such an attitude will lead to the loss of belief in a transcendent order and to intensified political and constitutional drifting.

Once upon a time it was the assumption of most of the people in the world that the fundamental constitution of their society would endure to the end of time, or at least for a very great while, or certainly for the lifetime of those who recently had become adults. But events since 1914 have destroyed that expectation, mercilessly, in country upon country, culture after culture.

Whole peoples have been uprooted or transplanted, or perhaps extirpated; complex patterns of life have been devastated or totally supplanted; political systems have vanished almost without trace; classes have been effaced, ancient rights abolished, the cake of custom ground to powder. Constitutions written and unwritten have been subverted almost overnight by conventions of political fanatics, and innovating substitute constitutions in their turn have been expunged within a few years, making way for yet more novel political structures—no less evanescent. Even Britain has experienced much constitutional alteration during the past quarter of a century, especially in local government.

Among great powers, only the American Republic has not deliberately altered its general frame of government—neither the formal written Constitution of the United States nor the unwritten constitution that, in the phrase of Orestes Brownson, "is the real or actual constitution of the people as a state or sovereign community and constituting them such or such a state." I say "deliberately," implying that the American people, as represented in the Congress and in the state legislatures, has not approved very large changes in the political structure. Nor have they, as people, endorsed large innovations in the complex of customs, conventions, and prescriptions that compose the unwritten constitution. It is true that several amendments to the federal Constitution have been ratified, but none of these, not even the two extending the franchise, greatly altered the general political structure. Many state constitutions have been revised, and of course technological, economic, demographic, and moral alterations outside the strictly political pattern have produced large social consequences. Nevertheless, the formal federal Constitution framed in 1787 still functions for the most part, and the large majority of American citizens still take for granted the mass of customs, conventions, mores, and social beliefs that amount to an unwritten constitution, and which generally are older than the written Constitution of 1787. In short, Americans have known no political revolution, either violent or accomplished without bloodshed, for two centuries; nor have we consciously swept away old ways of living in community so that we might conform to some brave new ideological design.

Americans stand politically strongly attached to old ways of managing public affairs, rejecting all proposals for thoroughgoing constitutional revision, holding inviolate documentary and even architectural symbols of the national experience. Probably the considerable majority of Americans today assume that our national constitutions will endure for time out of mind, that the political order, at least, which the present generation knows will be known also by their grandchildren and great-grandchildren, that in time past other nations may have fallen low even as Nineveh and Tyre, but that the United States of America, as a system of order and justice and freedom, is immutable.

This is a natural presumption, the power and prosperity of this nation in the closing years of the twentieth century considered. Not since 1814 has the continental United States had to repel foreign troops. There has not occurred any catastrophic interruption of domestic tranquillity since 1865, and the American economy has become a cornucopia, with only infrequent, occasional, and partial interruptions of its bounty. How could this constitutional order ever come to an end?

Such, no doubt, were the sentiments of the inhabitants of the Roman empire near the end of the Antonine age, although already Marcus Aurelius had great difficulty in raising revenue sufficient to defend the northern frontiers and greater difficulty still in repelling, sword in hand, the barbarian hosts. Roman history no longer being taught in American schools, the public is unaware of such parallels. There are few readers of such studies as Freya Stark's *Rome on the Euphrates* (1966), which traces convincingly the fashion in which a great power decayed for lack of imagination.

In my seemingly complacent account of America's conservative ways, then, I have omitted something important: the strong tendency of our courts of law, the Supreme Court of the United States in particular, to remold our political and social institutions nearer to the judges' hearts' desires. The courts, joined by the Congress, the state legislatures, and the executive branch, busily have conferred new rights, entitlements, and privileges upon large classes of citizens. New constitutional rights are discovered or proposed annually; next to nothing is said about constitutional duties. Most professors and publicists still appear to fancy that more emancipation from old-fangled moral restraints, not to mention more generous public largesse—so like the old Roman liturgies—would relieve us of worry and work. Yet just now we perhaps perceive a reaction against large scale constitutional alteration by a judicial aristocracy or council of elders—the Ephors of Washington.

But I lack time to cry O tempora! O mores! adequately. Kipling's lines must suffice, a single stanza:

On the first Feminian Sandstones we were promised the Fuller Life
(Which started by loving our neighbour and ended by loving his wife)
Till our women had no more children and the men lost reason and faith,
And the Gods of the Copybook Headings said: "The Wages of Sin is Death."

No civilization endures forever; no national constitution can of itself sustain a people bent upon private pleasures, asking not what they can do for the country, but what the country can do for them. So I venture upon some speculations concerning the future of American politics—signifying by the word *politics* not partisan controversies, but constitutional establishments, custom and convention, political principles.

❖

I speculate in the manner of Edmund Burke, at once the most imaginative and most practical of writers and doers in our political tradition of the English-speaking peoples: Burke, the philosopher in action. I do not mean that you and I can peer through dead men's eyes. Rather I am asking you to put on the mind of Burke with me, to look at the future of American politics as he looked at the future of European politics in his day—with wonderful prescience, as affairs turned out.

I choose Burke as our guide for this time travel because, in the words of Harold Laski, "Burke has endured as the permanent manual of political wisdom without which statesmen are as sailors on an uncharted sea." Or, to quote Woodrow Wilson, "Burke makes as deep an impression upon our hearts as upon our minds. We are taken captive, not so much by his reasoning, strongly as that moves to its conquest, as by the generous warmth that steals out of him into our hearts."

In his *Reflections on the Revolution in France* (1790), his *Appeal from the New to the Old Whigs* (1791), his *Thoughts on the Cause of the Present Discontents* (1770), and other writings and speeches, Burke has much to say about constitutions, the British Constitution in particular—though not one word, friendly or hostile, about the American Constitution of 1787. Very succinctly, though I hope not superficially, I offer you some observations of Burke upon healthy and unhealthy constitutions of government. We will confine ourselves to four of Burke's constitutional arguments; then let us try to apply these reflections, so far as they are pertinent to our own age, to prospects for the constitution (in its larger sense) of the United States.

Burke's first constitutional principle is that a good constitution grows out of the common experience of a people over a considerable elapse of time. It is not possible to create an improved constitution out of whole cloth. As he declared in his "Speech on the Reform of Representation" (1782), "I look with filial reverence on the constitution of my country, and never will cut it in pieces and put it into the kettle of any magician, in order to boil it, with the puddle of their compounds, into youth and vigor. On the contrary, I will drive away such pretenders; I will nurse its venerable age, and with lenient arts extend a parent's breath."[7] An enduring constitution is the product of a nation's struggles. Here Burke is echoed by one of his more eminent American disciples, John C. Calhoun, in his *Disquisition on Government*.

> A constitution, to succeed, must spring from the bosom of the community, and be adapted to the intelligence and character of the people, and all the multifarious relations, internal and external, which distinguish one people from another. If it does not, it will prove, in practice, to be, not a constitution, but a cumbrous and useless machine, which must be speedily superseded and laid aside, for some other more simple, and better suited to their condition.[8]

A truth that Burke emphasizes almost equally with the preceding "organic" concept of constitutions is the necessity of religious faith to a constitutional order. "We know, and, what is better, we feel inwardly, that religion is the basis of civil society, and the source of all good, and of all comfort," he writes in *Reflections on the Revolution in France*. "We know, and it is our pride to know, that man is by his constitution a religious animal; that atheism is against, not only our reason, but our instincts; and that it cannot prevail long." An established church is required—parallel with "an established monarchy, an established aristocracy, and an established democracy. . . . All persons possessing any portion of power ought to be strongly and awfully impressed with an idea that they act in trust, and that they are to account for their conduct in that trust to the one great Master, Author, and Founder of society."[9] The first clause of the First Amendment to the Constitution, and the American circumstances which produced that clause—Burke's "dissidence of dissent, and the Protestantism of the Protestant religion"—had forestalled any established national church in the United States, three years before Burke published his *Reflections*. But the First Amendment, and curious interpretations of its first clause by the Supreme Court in this century, leave us today in some perplexity.

A third point in Burke's constitutional principles which needs to be noted here is his emphasis upon the function of a natural aristocracy, in which mingle both "men of actual virtue" (the "new" men of enterprising talents) and "men of presumptive virtue" (gentlemen of old families and adequate means). It is this aristocracy, "the cheap defense of nations," that supplies a people's leadership. (In a more grudging fashion, a similar apology for aristocracy is advanced by John Adams.) Burke asserts also the necessity for an "establishment of democracy"; he is the most practical eighteenth-century advocate, indeed, of popular government. Nevertheless, "A true natural aristocracy is not a separate interest in the state, or separable from it," Burke writes in his *Appeal from the New Whigs*. "It is an essential integrant part of any large body rightly constituted."[10]

Fourth, Burke contends that the good constitution maintains a balance or tension between the claims of freedom and the claims of order. Natural law is a reality, and from natural law flow certain natural rights. But government does not exist merely to defend claims of personal liberty. The Rights of Man claimed by the French revolutionaries are impossible to realize, unlimited, in any civil social order. "By having a right to everything they want everything," Burke writes in his *Reflections*:

> Government is a contrivance of human wisdom to provide for human wants. Men have a right that these wants should be provided for by this wisdom. Among these wants is to be reckoned the want, out of civil society, of a sufficient restraint upon their passions. Society requires not only that the passions of individuals should be subjected, but that even in the mass and body, as well as in the individuals, the inclinations of men should frequently be thwarted, their will controlled, and their passions brought into subjection. . . . In this sense the restraints on men, as well as their liberties, are to be reckoned among their rights.[11]

On no point of political theory in America does greater confusion exist than upon this question of "human rights" as set against the need for restraints upon will and appetite.

So much for four principles of constitutional order that recur in Burke's speeches and writings over three decades. Let us now see how far the American constitution, both written and unwritten, accords with these principles, and how strongly prepared the American constitutional order may be to withstand powerful challenges in the dawning years.

❖

Consider first Burke's conviction—well sustained by the painful experience of Europe after the two World Wars and by the emergent nations of Africa and Asia—that any sound national constitution must be the fruit of long experience, tried and tested, that "paper constitutions" are not worth the paper they have been written upon, and that sudden, sweeping, large scale alterations of an old constitution almost certainly must destroy its ancient virtues rather than lopping off its acquired vices. May we apply these admonitions to the written Constitution of the United States in our present circumstances?

There exists today no popular demand for abrogating the Constitution of 1787 in general and substituting some new fundamental law. But there do exist strong movements to make specific important changes in the Constitution—changes or amendments, however, the intention of which is to return interpretation of the Constitution to what was the common understanding or usage until recent decades. Thus the pressure for formal alteration of the Constitution is conservative, not innovative. The principal constitutional amendments proposed at present are designed to compel Congress to balance the federal budget, to make abortion unlawful (reversing Supreme Court decisions of recent years), to permit prayer in public schools (so reversing other Supreme Court decisions), to return to legislative bodies jurisdiction over the apportionment and boundaries of legislative districts (which until 1962 remained a "political question" outside the jurisdictions of federal courts). The popular movement is therefore not for striking down old constitutional provisions or interpretations, but for returning to precedents only very recently overthrown by federal judges. In short, there exists no clear and present danger of a discarding of the old Constitution by the people, by the Congress, or by the executive branch.

Innovative alteration of the Constitution has been the work, instead, of a majority of the justices of the Supreme Court within the past forty years, chiefly. Possessing powers not conferred upon the chief judicial body of any other country, the Supreme Court has made itself into a reforming council, politicized. The phrase "Judicial usurpation," nowadays employed by opponents of certain Supreme Court decisions, almost certainly would have been employed similarly by Burke in his time had the British judiciary then possessed authority sufficient to undo acts of Parliament—which of course the British judges did not have, and do not possess today.[12] In his "Speech on the Economical Reform," in 1780, Burke remarked that "the judges are, or ought to be, of a reserved and retired character, and wholly unconnected with the political world." Twenty-two years ago, my friend C. P. Ives commented on this passage from Burke, "What Burke would have thought when justices of the highest court felt compelled to campaign, at least quasi-politically, in defense of their own prior decisions as judges, it is not hard to infer."

A second constitutional convention could be called, but a second convention would possess arbitrary power to amend the old Constitution as the delegates might think fit or to sweep the Constitution altogether away, supplanting it by a new creation—which is precisely what the delegates to the Convention of 1787 did to the Articles of Confederation. Should a new convention be summoned, grandiose proposals for constitutional innovation might be put forward forcefully by persons and interests whose intellectual mentors would be not Edmund Burke or John Adams, but Jean-Jacques Rousseau or Jeremy Bentham, given to abstraction and levelling innovation. Sentimental egalitarianism on the one hand, dull utilitarianism on the other, might undo the prudent work of the Federalists, breaking that long continuity of law and political institutions that runs back beyond the beginning of American history. Thus men and women respectful of the established Constitution should be in mind that a second national convention, even though brought by a conservative impulse, might have radical consequences—of a populist cast, or of a centralizing cast, or of both afflictions blended.

Second, what of the religious basis of the American order? Joseph Story and James Kent, the great early commentators upon American constitutional law, pointed out that although America has no national establishment of religion, American laws and social institutions rest upon the moral postulates of the Christian religion. Sometimes, since the 1940s, the Supreme Court's majority, and a good many other federal and state judges, have seemed to hold that religion of any sort is suspect and should be excluded from public life.

If the latter understanding prevails in the interpretation of the written Constitution and works changes in our unwritten constitution of custom and convention, then very grave consequences are liable to develop. One of them would be the steady increase of fraud and violent crime, not to be adequately held in check by police powers, for religious belief is sufficiently enfeebled in our time already, with ineluctable moral consequences, and disapprobation by the state would work yet more mischief. Another consequence would be an increased danger from virulent ideology of one sort or another, for ideology rushes in to fill the vacuum left by the decay of religion. In foreign affairs, the decline of Americans' religious belief would mean an increase of the appeals of Marxism and of Marxist powers. A third consequence, intended to diminish the effects of the two afflictions just described, might be the systematic development of a "civil religion" of Americanism, a kind of Americanist ideology built of bricks from the yard of John Dewey and his disciples—dull, unimaginative, materialistic, and in the long run destined to ignominious failure.

In a time when telephone companies look forward to profits to be made from "dial-a-porn" services (within federal regulations, of course), and when all the police powers of federal and state and local governments do not suffice to put down an enormous traffic in narcotics, some freethinking spirits may begin to apprehend the truth in Burke's declaration that the state is built upon religious consensus. If we inquire whether the constitutions of government in the United States will endure a hundred years now, the speculative answer must depend in no small part on whether there still will subsist, a century from now, widespread belief in a transcendent order. It may not be in the power of the political authority to renew the religious understanding, but at least the political authority can refrain from accelerating the decay of religious learning.

Third, what are we doing in America to develop people of virtue and wisdom sufficient to lead the democracy and sustain our old constitutional order of justice and freedom? The alternative to an aristocracy (the leadership of the best in the public interest) is an oligarchy (the leadership of the rich in their own interest). It is inane merely to chant, with Carl Sandburg,

"The People, yes!" A people deprived of honest, able, and imaginative leadership will come to ruin.

The popular and journalistic response, in 1983, to the United States Commission on Excellence in Education did hearten some of us, for temporarily it overcame the educationists' denunciations of "elitism" and showed that a considerable part of the public has become aware of our American failure to develop right reason and moral imagination, scientific understanding and political knowledge, among the rising generation; our failure to provide, if you will, sufficient opportunity for the healthful growth of a natural aristocracy, which is essential to the survival of a democracy. But the administration of proposed educational reforms has fallen back into the hands of the very foundation bureaucrats, accrediting agencies, departments of public instruction, pillars of the National Education Association, and all those dull dogs of Holy Educationism who prate endlessly of "equity" (meaning enforced educational mediocrity) and shudder internally at the mention of "excellence" (which would eliminate the oligarchs of the educationist empire, should excellence actually be achieved). We may make some improvements in schooling at every level, but they will be small ameliorations, as matters drift at present.

The principal purpose of what has been called liberal education was to develop a considerable body of young people who would become molders of public opinion and leaders of community—the natural aristocracy, which is something different from the "meritocracy" and specialized elite that grow in the twentieth-century welfare state.

But how much truly liberal education do we undertake nowadays? We still go through the motions—and then a large proportion of young people who have been endowed with the degree of bachelor of arts go on to work toward the degree of MBA, as if liberal learning were irrelevant to the real world. What we require more urgently than we do routine business skills is young men and women of courage and imagination, who know that life is for something more than consumption.

The Constitution is not sustained by intellectual mediocrity, obsession with creature comforts, and "four legs good, two legs bad" praise of an abstract democracy. If we neglect the talents of the ablest of the rising generation, we are left in the long run with what Tocqueville called democratic despotism—a regime of stagnation and dull uniformity—if not with something still worse than that.

Finally, it is even truer today than it was in Burke's time that those who begin by claiming everything will end with nothing at all—not even a Republic. An effectual "welfare rights" lobby piles up incredible federal deficits and national debts, as if wealth were a mere matter of printing presses and new debt ceilings. Presently such claims of entitlements make it difficult to maintain the common defense. The Bill of Rights is invoked as if it really were a suicide pact—from those who would defend to the death the inalienable right of a mugger to buy a "Saturday night special," to those humanitarians who insist that even imminent peril to public health must not be permitted to impede exercise of the inalienable right to engage in sexual perversions.

Great states with good constitutions develop when most people think of their duties and restrain their appetites. Great states sink toward their dissolution when most people think of their privileges and indulge their appetites freely. This rule is as true of democracies as it is of autocracies. And no matter how admirable a constitution may look upon paper, it will be ineffectual unless the unwritten constitution, the web of custom and convention, affirms an enduring moral order of obligation and personal responsibility.

❖

The ruin or the recovery of America's constitutions, and the general future of American politics, will be determined more by choices than by circumstances. Here I have done no more than to suggest what some of those choices must be. "Not to lose ourselves in the infinite void of the conjectural world," Burke wrote near the end of his life in the *First Letter of the Regicide Peace* (1796), "our business is with what is likely to be affected for the better or the worse by the wisdom or weakness of our plans." To shape the American political future through prudent and courageous choices is yet within the realm of possibility. "I despair neither of the public fortune nor of the public mind," Burke continued. "There is much to be done undoubtedly, and much to be retrieved. We must walk in new ways, or we can never encounter our enemy in his devious march. We are not at an end of our struggle, nor near it. Let us not deceive ourselves; we are at the beginning of great troubles."[13]

As it was with Britain in the closing years of the eighteenth century, so is it with America in the closing years of the twentieth. As did the British then, we confront an armed doctrine and are divided in our own counsels. And yet our own general complacency scarcely is shaken: most of us behave as if nothing very disagreeable ever could happen to the Constitution of the United States, and as if the political future of this nation would be a mere alternation of Republican and Democratic presidential victories, somewhat less interesting than professional baseball and football.

The crash of empires and the collapse of constitutions have blinded and deafened most of the world since 1914. Only American territories and American laws have stood little touched amidst the general ruin. It is not accident that will preserve them for posterity. Of those Americans who dabble in politics at all, many think of such activities chiefly as a game, membership on a team, with minor prizes to be passed out after the latest victory. Yet a few men and women, like Burke, engage in politics not because they love the game, but because they know that the alternative to a politics of elevation is a politics of degradation. Let us try to be of their number.

["The Constitution and the Antagonist World," Rights and Duties: Reflections on Our Conservative Constitution*, edited by Mitchell S. Muncy (Dallas, TX: Spence Publishing Company, 1997). Also published in* The Conservative Constitution *(Washington, DC: Regnery Gateway, 1990), 216–29.]*

❖

John Randolph of Roanoke: The Planter-Statesman

Kirk's account of John Randolph (1773–1833) as a planter-statesman was originally a part of his thesis submitted for the degree of master of arts at Duke University in 1941. In 1951 this work, under the title Randolph of Roanoke: A Study in Conservative Thought, *was published by the University of Chicago Press. Born in Crawsons, Virginia, Randolph served in Congress and briefly in the Senate from 1799 to 1829. One "great cardinal principle," he declared at the Virginia Constitutional Convention of 1829, "should govern all wise statesmen—never without the strongest necessity to disturb that which was at rest." Randolph knew from his own experience "the sordid cares of a planter," but he also believed that man gains real liberty on his own land, free of debt. His vision of the benefits of an agrarian society was doomed by "'new men and new doctrines,'" but his principles of politics, statecraft, and economics, Kirk asserts, deserve emulation.*

I

John Taylor of Caroline declared that land is the basis of all wealth and that therefore land deserves power in government.[14] Whether Randolph of Roanoke, the admirer of Smith, Ricardo, and Say, admitted the truth of the first part of this physiocratic contention is doubtful; something more modern is implied in Randolph's political economy; and, indeed, old John Taylor belonged to the generation which preceded Randolph's. But whatever opinion the man of Roanoke held concerning the economic preeminence of land, no ambiguity shrouded his conviction that the agricultural life is the best state of society man can ask. Randolph was one of the greatest of the planter-statesmen who filled so large a role in the history of the southern states, from the time of Washington to the time of Davis; and among all those memorable names, the agrarian society had no more consistent, shrewd, and fierce defender than John Randolph.

"Defender" is a word chosen deliberately here; for the agricultural interest almost always was reeling before the assault of other interests, and, too often, agriculture lost ground, for all the illustrious muster-roll of its partisans. Probably the successive defeats of the farm and the plantation in national political contests were a result neither of any innate weakness of rural people nor yet of timidity on the part of their leaders; the cause lay in the conservative nature of the agricultural interests, which had little to gain from change, while the commercial, financial, and industrial interests were full of youthful vigor and rapacity; agriculture could hardly encroach upon them, but they could extort tribute from agriculture. The agrarian party was generous enough at times, moreover—upon the plea of national security—to sacrifice its own advantage to embargo and tariff, while the other economic interests rarely made such concessions.[15] In the West, it is true, the agricultural interest was so linked with expanding industrial forces, and so heartily in accord with that speculative spirit which has always been a danger to American farming and agricultural life—Tocqueville remarks that an American clears a farm only with the intention of selling it for a profit—that for years the western states remained the political allies of the industrial and financial North. Before 1824 the rural party was self-conscious and articulate only in the southeastern states, notably Virginia.

Between 1800 and 1828, between Jefferson and Jackson, the planters and farmers pressingly required a champion in Congress; for although the Virginia dynasty, theoretically fond of the rural ideal, and the Republican party, professedly representative of the agricultural interest, maintained control of national politics during the greater portion of this era, still the agricultural economy was exposed to a series of distressing blows all during these years. The farmer always tends to be weaker politically than his numbers seem to indicate. "It is the choicest bounty to the ox," said Randolph, "that he cannot play the fox or the tiger; so it is to one of the body of agriculturalists that he cannot skip into a coffeehouse and shave a note with one hand, while with the other he signs a petition to Congress portraying the wrongs and grievances and sufferings he endures, and begging them to relieve him."[16] Lacking the collective cunning and proximity to adminstration which commercial and industrial forces possessed, the country population was badly prepared to make a stand in Congress. Who was to be their spokesman at Washington? Old John Taylor, that indefatigable writer of treatises, entered Congress with reluctance and departed with alacrity, for he was no popular orator; Jefferson and his successors, however much they praised the life of the farmer, found themselves compelled to pursue policies which left that farmer in a state nearly as disastrous as that in which Jefferson was to find his own lands; Nathaniel Macon and other planter-legislators, great and small, had the requisite devotion but not the requisite genius. The duty fell to John Randolph.

Acerbity of temper and indifference to popularity were flaws which kept Randolph from being a really successful leader of the opposition; but in some other ways he was admirably qualified to maintain the responsibility. He could command public attention—like a necromancer fascinating a snake—in a way no other man of his time could. He could join to the agricultural party other factions which, for a time, had the same objectives: the slavery interest, the states' rights thinkers, and on occasion even the commercial classes of New England. He was himself a successful planter, supervising the cultivation of his thousands of acres; he lived like a pre-Revolutionary Virginia gentleman, bumping over the wretched roads in his old-fashioned English coach, and his slaves rode blooded horses; but he inhabited a simple cabin and spent the greater part of each year in the oppressive routines of growing tobacco and grains. More, he was devoted by inheritance and principle to the society of the country gentleman and the Virginia landlord. The agricultural ideal occupied as important a place in his system as in Jefferson's, though Randolph's ideal was the old Tidewater life and Jefferson's a yeoman population destined never really to develop as the President hoped.

In some ways a very practical man, Randolph was a severe critic of the rural life he defended, just as he criticized all that he loved. To Josiah Quincy he wrote of "the sordid cares of a planter," to which he was condemned every long and dreary winter: "They remind me of Cromwell, when he turned farmer at St. Ives; for without vanity I may compare myself to what Oliver was *then,* and may with truth declare, that my 'mind, superior to the low occupations to which I am condemned, preys upon itself.'"[17] Randolph's solitary and half-mysterious existence as a Roanoke planter must have had its effect upon his delicate temperament; even while he was still living at Bizarre, away from the shadows of Roanoke, his half-brother, Henry St. George Tucker, wrote to James M. Garnett of Randolph's brooding bitterness: "It is manifest that his solitude has great influence upon his feelings."[18] Yet probably Randolph could have endured no other life; certainly his detestation of towns, his revolt against social mediocrity, and his devotion to field sports would have made Tucker's life as a successful Winchester lawyer anathema to him. In the view of Randolph, Macon, Stanford, and William Leigh, of southern Virginia and northern North Carolina, only in the country, on his own land and free from debt, did a man experience real liberty; and only such men, as a class, were competent to determine the policies of the state.

What did Randolph believe to be the model agricultural economy? We have remarked that he found his model in the image of pre-Revolutionary Virginia; Jefferson sought for his in the visions of an egalitarian future.

Jefferson's successful campaign for the abolition of entail and primogeniture was intended to equalize landholding, to establish upon a broad base a state—perhaps a nation—of freeholders, small farmers, each nearly self-sufficient economically, producing their foodstuffs and the bulk of their other necessities. Labor on these holdings was to be chiefly that of freemen, the possessors. Such an economy never did come to prevail in Virginia; and, while the radical revision of the laws of descent did indeed greatly diminish the prosperity and influence of the old families that had led the Old Dominion, still it failed signally to produce a general equalization of landowning. Tocqueville attributes to the American abolition of entail and primogeniture a very great share in the restlessness, cupidity, and wistful materialism of the American people; it destroyed one of those artifices which, in Burke's phrase, enable "generation to link with generation" and distinguish men from "the flies of a summer."

John Randolph, for his part, roundly damned this alteration of the laws of descent; that act of innovation had enervated the great families which contributed, in previous generations, so much to Virginia's glory. Frequently he referred to this topic and once wrote, while in Europe, to Brockenbrough, that he had no hope for a restoration of the ancient Virginian spirit,

> the state of society and manners which existed in Virginia half a century ago; I should as soon expect to see the Nelsons, and Pages, and Byrds, and Fairfaxes, living in their palaces, and driving their coaches and sixes; or the good old Virginia gentlemen in the assembly, drinking their twenty and forty bowls of rack punches, and madeira, and claret, in lieu of a knot of deputy sheriffs and hack attorneys, each with his cruet of whiskey before him, and puddle of tobacco-spittle between his legs.[19]

Yet he fought for the old ways toward which he was already looking back with a nostalgia so many Virginians later were to share.

The old Virginian life Randolph praised had not been simply a society dominated by great slaveholding landlords. He spoke contemptuously of Wade Hampton and his fellows as "cotton barons" and declared the real substance of society to be the independent planters and farmers of small freeholds, which class he eulogized in the Virginia Convention of 1829, speaking of "the good old Virginia planter—the man who lived by hard work, and who paid his debts."[20] That which Randolph desired was a society with a great number of small freeholders to furnish the bulk of the governing class and a scattering of wealthier and better-educated great planters to furnish suitable leadership for the commonwealth. Indeed, his own congressional district was made up of such a society, with a few great landholders like Randolph, the Carringtons, and the Leighs, and a numerous class of less wealthy landowners who, like the Bouldins, sometimes achieved important political office. Randolph, like Jefferson, believed in an aristocracy of nature, not of station; but he thought that aristocracy of nature largely determined by the gifts of good family and of possession of property.

Jefferson apparently held that his agricultural class should devote its energies principally to the raising of foodstuffs for their own consumption rather than to a money crop like tobacco. While Randolph raised the greater part of the food for his slaves on his own lands, still tobacco was his chief crop, and he was the foremost advocate of the old trade with England, exchanging Virginian agricultural staples for British manufactures.[21] Although Jefferson wrote his famous phrase comparing cities to the sores of the body and recommended an economy strictly agricultural, trading with the "workshops of Europe," this stand of his was altered after the embargo days, and he came to recommend the encouragement of American factories. This, Randolph could not tolerate; he would not buy from the North, out of resentment at protective tariffs, and he even sent his books to England to be bound. As in Jefferson's literary taste, a certain old-fashioned element lingered in Jefferson's economic thought; the President spoke of the advantage in international trade as lying in the disposal of "national surpluses," in his letters to Du Pont de Nemours and others.[22] Randolph, much read in Smith and Ricardo, perceived more distinctly the nature of specialization and the economic advantages of unrestricted international commerce, and contended that America was as unsuited for really profitable manufacturing as England was for really profitable agriculture.[23]

Such, then, was Randolph's specific for a satisfactory agricultural society—concepts shared by the Old Republicans. Randolph failed to gain the restoration or perpetuation of his system; but so did Jefferson fail to achieve his agrarian ideal. The Old Republicans failed because they were in an irremediable political minority; because they could not rid themselves of the burden of negro slavery; and because, very possibly, Malthus's geometrical increase of population was against them—overpopulation, the problem of problems. Their system of landholding was suited to a static population but hardly to a swelling one; and even the rapid advance of the agricultural frontier could not preserve their nation from the necessity of adopting a complicated economy of large-scale manufactures, intricate finance, rapid transportation, and urban life. The Republicans might have retorted that the swelling of population, through immigration and commerce, was deliberately encouraged by the classes and regions which stood to gain by change; but it was too much to expect mankind not to fill a void as rapidly as air fills a vacuum. Desperately the successors of the Old Republicans endeavored to maintain their position by the acquisition of western territories to be amalgamated with the southern agricultural system; and the very endeavor brought closer the war which was to strike down their society. Time and space were against the planter-statesmen. But in many ways the life they sought to perpetuate was good; not a few men would think it a better state of society than that our age must accept; and they are hardly to be censured for standing like men for the old ways. For Cato to stand against Caesar and the forces that Caesar represented was hopeless; but it was not ridiculous. No fatal weakness existed in the Old Republicans' economy *per se*; but for them the time was out of joint. Their principles of public and private conduct are not invalidated by time's annihilation of the economic system in which their ideas developed. On the management of government, the conduct of foreign relations, and the commercial policy of the state, Randolph and his fellows spoke out boldly to defend the plantation. Although the plantation is gone, there remains a need for honest politics, intelligent statecraft, and sound public economics. In Randolph's career is exhibited the doomed course of the plantation-politicians, and in his principles are elements still worth attention in this very different epoch.

II

Their most consistent spokesman, Randolph, permanently defined the platform of the planter-statesmen when he told the House of Representatives, early in 1813:

> Is it necessary for men at this time of day to make a declaration of the principles of the Republican party? Is it possible that such a declaration could be deemed orthodox when proceeding from lips so unholy as those of an excommunicant from that church? It is not necessary. These principles are on record; they are engraved upon it indelibly by the press and will live as long as the art of printing is suffered to exist. It is not for any man at this day to undertake to change them; it is not for any men, who then professed them, by any guise or circumlocution to conceal apostasy from them, for they are there—there in the book. . . . What are they? Love of peace, hatred of offensive war, jealousy of the state governments toward the general government; a dread of standing armies; a loathing of public debt, taxes, and excises; tenderness for the liberty of the citizen; jealousy, Argus-eyed jealousy, of the patronage of the President.[24]

From the advocacy of these principles, Randolph and his faction did not retreat. They had been the principles of Jefferson and his devotees in 1800, Randolph declared; they remained the principles of true Republicans. A simple, economical, limited, peaceful government was the only government consistent with the society they represented—a government fit for a stable, rural nation. But there remains a great deal of room for increase of these virtues in the state in our own more complex society.

Always prominent in the Old Republican creed was a demand for purity and simplicity in public affairs, retrenchment and reform. The sincerity of Randolph's long campaign against profligacy, corruption, and time-serving in governmental affairs never has been successfully impeached, even by his most hostile critics. From his fiery Yazoo speeches to his duel with Clay, Randolph was the dread of every self-seeker in Congress; and although some writers have believed Randolph's ideals of purity impossible of attainment and his stand as a political St. Michael too top-lofty, few have condemned his general course of action. Randolph and the other Old Republicans were men of private honesty, of economical and self-sufficient habits; they saw no reason why private morals should not be public morals or why the government should plunder, or be plundered, when the citizen should not. Out of their very nature they were opposed to regular party organization, to all intricacies of party machinery, to caucus and convention. Their dislike for practical politics, then, was another obstacle between them and success.

Although they were resolute supporters of the rights of private property, they did not hold that private property dishonestly obtained had a clear title against government; as John Taylor wrote, "If Jugurtha had been rich enough to buy Rome, ought the nation to have submitted to the sale, because the bargain was made with the government?"[25] Thus it was that Randolph denounced the Yazoo land companies and prevented, until 1818, any compensation of those associations. That Jefferson did not take a firm stand against the Yazoo speculators helped provoke John Randolph's initial opposition to his administration, and the Roanoke orator detested Madison in the belief that he was a "Yazoo man." Yazoo left a rift between Jefferson and his congressional leader which never could be bridged. Speculative land companies had obtained immense grants of territory from a Georgia legislature they had corrupted by shameless bribery; a well-purged legislature indignantly repealed the land grants; and those companies of speculators in lands along the Yazoo River appealed to Congress to compensate them for their losses. The same measures toward persuasion which had been exercised in Georgia now appeared in Washington, the notorious Gideon Granger, postmaster general, presuming to lobby for the bill on the floor of the House—until Randolph denounced him as one accustomed to "buy and sell corruption in the gross." Jefferson and the northern Republicans winked at the affair, out of expediency (indeed, in later years Jefferson actually would have liked to appoint Granger to the Supreme Court); but Randolph and the Old Republicans now began to take shape as a faction, outraged at this violation of the purity of the Republican party. They never would compromise with great selfish interests; they had a terror of what has since come to be known as the "pressure group."

This was barefaced corruption; but the Old Republicans dreaded scarcely less that double-dealing, secrecy, and pretense in public affairs which come with governmental meddling in economic concerns. "I was not born into this order of things, and I will never consent, voluntarily, to become the vassal of a privileged order of military and monied men, by whom, as by a swarm of locusts, the produce of my land is to be devoured, and its possessor consigned to indigence and scorn. He who will not assert his place in society deserves to be trampled under foot."[26]

Faithful to Randolph's declaration, the Old Republicans asserted their place with great wrath and did their best to prevent the devouring of the produce of their lands; even when the government was in their own hands, they did not trust it. In 1803, when he exerted high influence upon the course of the federal administration, Randolph wrote to Nicholson: "To me the tendency of the power of appointment to office (no matter to what individual it may be trusted) to debauch the nation and to create a low, dirty, time-serving spirit is a . . . serious evil."[27]

Going beyond their assault on the abuse of public funds, the Old Republicans demanded strict economy in lawful and necessary expenditures. Randolph's opposition to the proposal of a sword for the adventurer Eaton and to a mausoleum for Washington, while in these days they may seem petty wrangling, were matters of principle; for Randolph believed that if governmental appropriations for baubles were not checked at the outset, they never would be halted. One of his chief objections to the program of internal improvements was that it would require funds which should be used instead to pay the federal debt, which he considered a drain upon the public for the benefit of special interests: "Let us leave the profits of labor in the pockets of the people, to rid them of that private embarrassment under which they so extensively suffer, and apply every shilling of the revenue, not indispensable to the exigencies of the government, to the faithful discharge of the public debt, before we engage in any new schemes of lavish expenditure."[28] From an early period, the Old Republicans foresaw that progressive inflation of credit and currency which has been a prominent characteristic of the American economy since the foundation of the Republic. Financial inflation means instability and the ruin of old ways; the innate conservatism of the Old Republicans, agrarian reformers though they were, revolted at the prospect of a society forever in flux and change.

Debt, Randolph maintained, was slavery; and once he startled the House by crying out, "Mr. Speaker, I have discovered the philosopher's stone. It is this, sir—Pay as you go! Pay as you go!"[29] In 1828 Macon, who was lodging with Randolph in Washington, wrote to a friend an expression of his and Randolph's view of the course of Congress:

> Almost every bill reported is to take money out of the Treasury or taxes from the U. S. It must be thought by some, I wish not by too many, that a public debt is a public blessing and all who live on the public, no doubt think, the more taxes the better, and that every tax adds to industry, and the harder people are put to it, the more easy they will be to govern; from such I wish to be delivered and hope the country may be free from them.[30]

Something of a late-twentieth-century flavor is in this paragraph. Randolph might have expressed such an opinion more elegantly than did his old friend from North Carolina, but he would have put it no less energetically.

Yet he was not so fanatically devoted to economy that he neglected stability in government; for when it was suggested at the Virginia Convention that the number of state representatives be reduced in order to cut legislative expenses, he opposed this false saving: "These savings made by paring down the legislature, and lopping off the council, may not prove to be true economy. Remember the fable—if the sheep will not spare enough of their fleece to feed the dogs, they may have to spare the whole of it, and the carcass to boot, to the wolf.[31]

And at this same constitutional convention of 1829, Randolph aptly expressed his whole distrust of government, with its passion for positive law, innovation, and regulation, with its powers of corruption and exploitation, with its demand for haste and uniformity:

> I am much opposed, Mr. R., except in a great emergency—and then the legislative machine is always sure to work with sufficient rapidity—the steam is then up—I am much opposed to this "dispatch of business."The principles of free government in this country (and if they fail—if they should be cast away—here—they are lost forever, I fear, to the world) have more to fear

> from armies of legislators, and armies of judges, than from any other, or from all other causes. Besides the great manufactory at Washington, we have twenty-four laboratories more at work, all making laws. In Virginia we have now two in operation, one engaged in making ordinary legislation, and another *hammering* at the fundamental law. Among all these lawyers, judges, and legislators, there is a great oppression on the people, who are neither lawyers, judges, nor legislators, nor ever expect to be—an oppression barely more tolerable than any which is felt under the European governments. Sir, I never can forget, that in the great and good book to which I look for all truth and all wisdom, the Book of Kings succeeds the Book of Judges.[32]

This attitude it is which, in large degree, clears the Old Republicans from any imputation of seeking advantage for themselves or their class in their stand against power in the state. They fought for the planter life, for the life they thought best; but they did not ask special advantage for that agricultural society, unlike the farm bloc of a later day. They asked only to be left unmolested, allowed to buy and sell in a free market, not to be taxed for the benefit of other interests, not to be forced into another mode of life. All government, said Randolph, was menacing; the only safety for every interest and class and section lay in limitation of the power of governments, in jealous supervision of governmental operation. Let government leave men to their own concerns and be economical, equitable, and honest. Randolph's principles of political, purity and social organization gave way to a different order of things chiefly because other great interests, reckless of such concepts, found it advantageous to conduct government along very different lines; and although the Old Republicans experienced temporary victories in their struggle for honesty and simplicity, their campaign was a stubborn retreat. From 1805 onward, Randolph's school of the agricultural interest and the earlier Republican idealism was hopelessly outnumbered.

III

In order to flourish, or even to exist, the society of the planters was dependent upon the guarantees of a strictly construed Constitution, upon a reasonably free trade with the world, upon simple and austere government, and upon lasting peace. From all these motives, and also because men of the sturdy conservative convictions held by the Old Republicans were naturally lovers of tranquillity and foes of aggression, Randolph's faction stood opposed to war and foreign alliances. They resisted as best they could the approach of the

War of 1812; and, when apparently the struggle had become inevitable, John Randolph, Stanford, and a few other congressmen struggled almost unaided against the tide. Randolph experienced his sole defeat for a seat in the House in consequence of his opposition; but events seemed to vindicate his conduct, and he was returned by his constituents, in the following election, to continue for the remainder of his career the advocacy of diplomatic isolation and economic internationalism for America.

From his Jacobin days in 1797, when Randolph opposed war with France, until the days of the Panama Congress in 1826, Randolph was foe of all proposals for hostilities or foreign entanglement—if one excepts some remarks of his recommending retaliation against England, after the "Chesapeake" affair. From the inception of the embargo until the last echoes of the second war with England had died, the danger of war, together with denunciations of the American restrictive commercial policy, was the great theme of his speeches. His remarks—some of them nearly as pertinent now as then—are worth sampling with a view toward their relation to his planter society.

In John Adams's administration Randolph called the federal troops "ragamuffins," and in Jackson's administration he sneered at them as "mercenaries." He declared them a threat to the powers of the states, for he placed his reliance for state sovereignty chiefly in the physical superiority of the states to the federal government and not in parchment guarantees; moreover, they were a drain upon the public purse. His own plan for efficiently arming the militia, and substituting flying trains of artillery for permanent harbor fortifications and Jefferson's gunboats, never was adopted; but it had merit, John Taylor writing of it: "Mr. Randolph's proposal . . . is the most effectual, principled, and grand measure, which has been introduced since the government has been in operation. He ought to nurse his popularity in Congress, if for no other end, but to carry the one point."[33]

Nursing popularity was a talent in which Randolph was totally deficient; instead, sarcasm and terror were his weapons. He opposed the increase of the national army with great bitterness; his speeches from 1807 until the close of hostilities with Britain expound his views with a thoroughness that cannot be imitated here.[34] On November 21, 1812, he delivered one of his most significant speeches on the question of military establishments and preparations for war, holding that he derived his principles from the old and true doctrines of the Republican party and that he would not yield them for the sake of popularity.[35] He declared that Britain was our shield against Napoleonic tyranny; he exposed the "agrarian cupidity" of the West, which sought war in order to provide markets for its hemp and foodstuffs; and he proclaimed that the Republicans were following the path disastrously trodden by the Federalists:

> There is a fatality, sir, attending plenitude of power. Soon or late, some mania seizes upon its possessors; they fall from the dizzy height, through the giddiness of their own heads. Like a vast estate, heaped up by the labor and industry of one man, which seldom survives the third generation, power gained by patient assiduity, by a faithful and regular discharge of its attendant duties, soon gets above its own origin. Intoxicated by their own greatness, the Federal party fell. Will not the same causes produce the same effects now as then? Sir, you may raise this army, you may build up this vast structure of patronage, this mighty apparatus of favoritism; but—"lay not the flattering unction to your souls"—you will never live to enjoy the succession. You sign your political death warrant. . . .
>
> He was not surprised at the war spirit which is manifesting itself in gentlemen from the South. In the year 1805–06, in a struggle for the carrying-trade of belligerent colonial produce, this country was most unwisely brought into collision with the great powers of Europe. By a series of most impolitic and ruinous measures, utterly incomprehensible to every rational sober-minded man, the Southern planters, by their own votes, succeeded in knocking down the price of cotton to seven cents, and of tobacco (a few crops excepted) to nothing, and in raising the price of blankets (of which a few would not be amiss in a Canadian campaign), coarse woollens, and every article of first necessity, three or four hundred percent. And, now that by our own acts we have brought ourselves into this unprecedented condition, we must get out of it in any way but by an acknowledgement of our own want of wisdom and forecast. But is that the true remedy? Who will profit by it? Speculators; a few lucky merchants who draw prizes in the lottery; commissaries and contractors. Who must suffer by it? The people. It is their blood, their taxes, that must flow to support it. . . .[36]

In speech after speech, Randolph demonstrated how ruinous the war was for his own Virginia—more ruinous even than the nonimportation and embargo acts. And the young men of Virginia, he added, their prospects of employment and independence ruined, drift away to Washington, there "dancing attendance for a commission." War and an omnipotent administration breed similar servility in politicians of all parties, who begin to sink into "very good courtiers"; thus effective opposition withers, and free government with it.[37]

There is evident here Randolph's dread of the corrupting power of government in general and the federal government in particular. The greatest danger did not come from abroad, maintained Randolph; it was domestic and a real threat to liberty. As he replied to Calhoun in 1816:

> The gentleman had represented this country as contending with Great Britain for existence. Could the honorable gentleman, or any other man, Mr. R. asked, believe that we would ever have a contest with any nation for existence? No, said Mr. R., we hold our existence by charter from the great God who made this world; we hold it in contempt of Great Britain—I speak of civil freedom—I am addressing myself to one who understands these distinctions. We do not hold our right to physical being or political freedom by any tenure from Europe; yet we hold our tenure of civil liberty by a precarious tie, which must be broken; for, from the disposition to follow the phantom of honor, or from another cause, this country is fairly embarked on a course of policy like that which is pursued by other governments in Europe.[38]

Randolph's unyielding opposition to war and expansion and his advocacy of the most unpopular of courses at that time brought general condemnation upon him; the town of Randolph, in Georgia, named in his honor, was renamed Jasper, in wrath;[39] and even the poets assailed him. Referring to his habit of sucking stick candy in the House chamber, one wrote of Randolph:

> *When* bitter *Randolph* candy *ate,*
> *We wondered, one and All!*
> *But, see the strange decree of fate*
> *Turn* Candy *into* Gall*!*[40]

Randolph endured the storm, and the disasters of the war with England proved him a true prophet and restored him to a measure of favor; thereafter he pursued relentlessly his attacks on intervention in foreign quarrels. Such intervention would disrupt the finances of the country, he knew; it would divert attention from disturbed and pressing domestic affairs; it would endanger, by the possible exercise of the treaty power, the guarantees of the Constitution and the authority of the House. In the debate on the Greek question and in that on the Panama Congress, he delivered particularly important speeches, and, since it is not possible to review his whole course of defense of American political isolation, we may obtain a fair picture of his stand by glancing at a part of one of his speeches on the former subject. The passion for intervening in the concerns of Europe and Latin America led, he maintained, to unconstitutional projects and policies, to ends and means never contemplated by the framers of the Constitution; he, who before 1812 had declared, "We will come out of this war without a Constitution," believed this would be the result of foreign meddling short of war, as well.

> It has once been said, of the dominions of the king of Spain—thank God! it can no longer be said—that the sun never set upon them. Sir, the sun never sets on ambition like this; they who have once felt its scorpion sting are never satisfied with a limit less than the circle of our planet. I have heard, sir, the late coruscation in the heavens attempted to be accounted for by the return of the lunar cycle, the moon having got back into the same relative position in which she was nineteen years ago. However this may be, I am afraid, sir, that she exerts too potent an influence over our legislation. . . .
>
> Let us, said Mr. R., adhere to the policy laid down by the second, as well as the first founder of our Republic—by the Camillus, as well as Romulus, of the infant state—to the policy of peace, commerce, and honest friendship with all nations, entangling alliances with none; for to entangling alliances you must go, if you once embark in such projects as this. And with all his British predilections, Mr. R. said, he suspected he should, whenever that question should present itself, resist as strongly an alliance with Great Britain as with any other power. We are sent here, said he, to attend to the preservation of the peace of this country, and not to be ready, on all occasions, to go to war whenever anything like what in common parlance is termed a *turn up* takes place in Europe.
>
> I can, however, assure the committee, for one, that the public burdens on those whom I represent here (though they are certainly better off than those to the North and the West of them: that is till you come to the favored states, where the interest of the public debt is paid and where almost all the public moneys are disbursed)—their burdens, sir, are as great as they can bear, because their private engagements are greater than they can discharge—and if this is not a self-evident proposition, I am at a loss to know what can be such. And this universal distress in the country has been the effect of freaks of legislation in the past. I do not deny but there may be some who have drawn great prizes in the lottery, but that is not the case with the great mass of the nation. And what is this scheme but a lottery? If it should end in war, there will be more great prizes to be drawn, but it will be for me, for those whom I represent, to pay them. . . .
>
> For my part, I would sooner put the shirt of Nessus on my back than sanction these doctrines—such as I never heard from my boyhood until

> now. They go the whole length. If they prevail, there are no longer any Pyrenees—every bulwark and barrier of the Constitution is broken down; it is become a *tabula rasa*, a *carte blanche*, for every one to scribble on it what he pleases.[41]

Randolph always could sum up his own views more concisely and more eloquently than another could hope to do; and this speech expressed the dislike of the Old Republicans for governmental measures which went beyond the boundaries of the United States, containing within the space of a few thousand words probably the most able refutation of imperialism that has been heard in Congress. War and imperialism meant the undermining of the society and the constitution for which Randolph and his friends stood; they meant the economic ruin of their institutions; and they meant that spirit of managing other men's affairs which was so repugnant to these lovers of freedom. It was the War of 1812 which struck an awful blow at their cause, and it was a later war which crushed them to earth.

IV

In 1808 John Brockenbrough wrote to Randolph: "Patriotism is a mighty precious thing when it costs nothing, but the mass of mankind consider it a very foolish thing when it curtails their self-indulgence."[42] This was during the days of Jefferson's embargo. The Old Republicans, in whom there was little of self-indulgence and a great deal of true patriotism, opposed with all their strength what they considered the ruinous stifling of their economy; and not long after Brockenbrough wrote, the mass of the people, long faithful to the Jeffersonian program, began to turn toward repeal of the prohibition of commerce. For once the Old Republican school triumphed, and they were to win other victories of this sort—in the South, at least. Essential in the Old Republican program was opposition to all regulation of commerce and finance by the federal government—opposition of the embargo and its kindred measures, to the tariff, to the Bank of the United States. Gradually the Old Republicans and their political inheritors brought the majority of the electorate in the southern states to adopt this hostility toward federal control of trade and industry.

The fear and hatred of restrictive measures and special legislative privilege to economic interests, which had been perhaps the chief characteristics of the Republican party in the first Congress, were kept alive from the second administration of Jefferson to the first administration of Jackson principally by the Old Republicans. The Virginia dynasty and the National Republicans came to look with a most favorable eye upon the protective tariff, the neomercantile system, and even the federally chartered Bank. The Old Republicans saw the doom of their institutions in such establishments, for they knew that wealth, and power with it, would flow to other classes and other regions than their own were those policies to continue; and they thought such a society far inferior to theirs. Not only would there be these economic consequences, but the constitutional precedents set by such a loose interpretation of federal authority would demolish utterly strict construction; and strict construction was an end in itself with these lovers of liberty. John Taylor expressed their viewpoint at great length and with admirable strength in his books; but it is worth our time to see what Randolph's more eloquent tongue had to say.

John Randolph's great speech, in 1806, against Gregg's Resolution commenced his onslaught upon those restrictions on exports and taxes on imports which would ruin his Old Virginia. Randolph's economics were the doctrines of the classical school, and their consistency was unassailable. Calhoun opposed them, in his earlier years, because he considered domestic manufacturing necessary for national strength in war; but he did not deny that Randolph's premises were economically sound, laying aside questions of political expediency. No one could successfully deny the fact; and certainly no one could successfully meet Randolph in a debate on the question. The argument on Gregg's Resolution, however, was not so much a question of economic principle as it was of the constitutionality of restraint of trade and of its possible effect upon the matter of war or peace. Said Randolph:

> As in 1798 I was opposed to this species of warfare, because I believed it would raze the constitution to its very foundation—so, in 1806, 1 am opposed to it, and on the same grounds. No sooner do you put the constitution to this use—to a test which it is by no means calculated to endure—than its incompetency becomes manifest, and apparent to all. I fear, if you go into a foreign war for a circuitous, unfair carrying-trade, you will come out without your constitution. Have you not contractors enough yet in this House? Or do you want to be overrun and devoured by commissaries and all the vermin of contract? I fear, sir, that what are called the "energy men" will rise up again; men who will burn the parchment. We shall be told that our government is too free; or, as they would say, weak and inefficient. Much virtue, Sir, in terms! That we must give the President power to call forth the resources of the nations. That is to filch the last shilling from our pockets—to drain the last drop of blood from our veins.[43]

Yet Gregg's Resolution to forbid importation from Great Britain and her possessions was as nothing in comparison with Jefferson's embargo, soon to follow. Randolph supported the embargo when it first was introduced in the House, but, after realizing its purpose, voted against it; he had thought it designed only as a temporary measure, which he previously had recommended, for securing American shipping in American harbors before undertaking retaliation against Britain or France. But an indefinite suspension of commerce was wholly another matter; Randolph thought the first form of embargo to be a simple regulation of commerce and therefore constitutional; the second, however, amounted to a prohibition or destruction of commerce and did not accord with the spirit of the commerce clause in the Constitution. For its duration, Randolph assailed the embargo; in its comparatively short span of existence, it did incalculable harm to the agrarian cause, since it ruined half of Virginia and stimulated the manufacturers of New England and the Middle Atlantic States, which demanded tariff protection once the embargo vanished.

Randolph's assaults on the embargo and that greater evil, the war which followed it, are matters of political history; both events hastened the decline of his Virginia and led to the establishment of that national mercantile policy he so deplored—the protective tariff. He proclaimed that "the embargo, like Achilles' wrath, was the source of our Iliad of woes!"[44] To Brockenbrough he wrote of "the exploded mercantile system, revived and fastened, like the Old Man of the Sea, around our necks." In 1816 he delivered one of the most searching criticisms of that policy, during the discussion of the tariff bill. It was nothing more than a system of bounties to manufacturers, he said with passion, "to encourage them to do that which, if it be advantageous to do at all, they will do, of course, for their own sakes." The productive labor of the country would be distorted and molded into a thousand fantastic shapes to suit the intent and the profit of these special interests. It was simply a question of whether a planter would consent to be taxed to enable another man to set up a spinning jenny. Randolph would sell in the best market and buy in the cheapest and never would agree to this intricate neomercantilism of bounties, even though the proponents of protection should agree to establish bounties for the raising of tobacco, too. The agriculturalist bore the brunt of the war and taxation. The agriculturalist, that great stable element of society, was to be pillaged for the benefit of a class of speculators and note-shavers:

> The agriculturalist has his property, his lands, his all, his household goods to defend; and like that meek drudge, the ox, who does the labor and plows the ground, and then, for his reward, takes the refuse of the farmyard, the

> blighted blades and the mouldy straw, and the mildewed shocks of corn for his support—while the commercial speculators live in opulence, whirling in coaches and indulging in palaces; to use the words of Dr. Johnson, coaches which fly like meteors and palaces which rise like exhalations. Even without your aid, the agriculturalists are no match for them. Alert, vigilant, enterprising and active, the manufacturing interest are collected in masses and ready to associate at a moment's warning for any purpose of general interest to their body. . . . The cultivators, the patient drudges of other orders of society, are now waiting for your resolution; for on you it depends whether they shall be left further unhurt or be, like those in Europe, reduced, *gradatim*, and subjected to another squeeze from the hard grasp of power.[45]

Despite all its passion, this defense of the agrarian society was as unavailing as most such pleas since Randolph's time. His remarks upon the tariff of 1824, already quoted partially in a previous chapter, were similar in vein: England, he said, possessed a natural advantage in manufacturing; she was welcome to it, for that condition of society meant only misery for the bulk of her inhabitants."[46] He fought the tariff throughout the last year of his congressional career, at the time his colleague Macon wrote to Edwards: "I have heard that the tariff would be taken up today or tomorrow in the H. of R. We must wear old clothes, and put patch on patch, and not be ashamed, provided we owe nothing, though we may not be dressed in the fashion, there is no better fashion, than to be out of debt."[47] Such was the simplicity of these Old Republicans, whom northerners sometimes described as luxurious proprietors supported by the labor of slaves.

Linked with their opposition to restrictions upon commerce was the hatred of the Old Republicans for the federally chartered Bank of the United States. Their opposition (or, at least, that of many of them) was not limited to that great institution; they disliked the state banks, as well. There was nothing fundamentally ridiculous in their position. They were opposed to borrowing and debt; they were advocates of a simple agricultural economy; they were "hard-money men"; and the states, or the colonies, had prospered earlier without banks. Had they been able to perpetuate the society they loved, banks might not have been a necessity, though they might have been a convenience. But many of the Old Republicans thought such convenience outweighed by the evils of concentration of economic power, complication of the economy, and encouragement to extravagance the banks brought with them. The federal Bank was unconstitutional, moreover, they contended; and, in time, the people were to accept the latter contention of the Old Republicans.

Randolph wrote to Brockenbrough, president of the Bank of Virginia, that a banking house was a house of ill fame."[48] He saw the Bank of the United States as an unconstitutional monster, created for the benefit of an avaricious class and serving as a tool of the centralizers. His chief assault on the Bank came in 1816, during the debate over rechartering the institution. Randolph agreed that the circulating currency of the day was in a deplorable state of fluctuation, but he saw no remedy in the Bank—and, most certainly, no remedy worthy of the price that would have to be paid. True payments never can be made solely by credit and paper; precious metals, or paper bottomed on them, are indispensable. He foresaw a consequent management of the national economy by the federal executive to suit the will and discretion of politicians. The banks had become so powerful, such an influence upon almost all men of consequence, that "we are tied hand and foot to this great Mammon, which is set up to worship in this Christian land"; and the government, while denouncing religious hierarchy, establishes a new economic hierarchy:

> The stuff uttered on all hands, and absolutely got by rote by the haberdashers' boys behind the counters in the shops, [is] that paper now in circulation would buy anything you want as well as gold and silver. . . .
>
> He despaired, he said, almost of remedying the evil when he saw so many men of respectability directors, stockholders, debtors of the banks. To pass this bill, he said, would be like getting rid of the rats by setting fire to the house; whether any other remedy could be devised, he did not now undertake to pronounce. The banks, he said, had lost all shame, and exemplified a beautiful and very just observation of one of the finest writers, that men banded together in a common cause, will collectively do that at which every individual of the combination would spurn.[49]
>
> And Randolph declared, several days later, that he was the holder of no stock whatever, except live stock, and had determined never to own any; but if this bill passed, he would not only be a stockholder to the utmost of his power, but would advise every man, over whom he had any influence, to do the same, because it was the creation of a great privileged order of the most hateful kind to his feelings, and because he would rather be the master than the slave. If he must have a master, let him be one with epaulettes, something that he could fear and respect, something that he could look up to—but not a master with a quill behind his ear.[50]

The Bank was chartered; but Randolph was to triumph in death, for Jackson, whom he first supported and then cursed, carried on, in this respect at least, the Old Republican tradition. Nevertheless, time has brought the complicated credit economy Randolph dreaded, with finance the master of man. "Who can bind posterity?" Randolph exclaimed despairingly.

V

As early as 1811 John Randolph said of the Republicans of true principles:

> He feared, if a writ were to issue against that old party—as had been facetiously said of another body, of our valiant army—it would be found impossible for a constable with a search warrant to find it. There must be a return *non est inventus*. Death, resignation, and desertion had thinned their ranks. They had disappeared. New men and new doctrines had succeeded.[51]

The Republican principles of 1800 were indeed deserted by most of their champions, out of necessity or inclination; but Randolph and his allies were constant. Right or wrong, they were faithful, and such fidelity in politics merits a high reward which the Old Republicans never did receive. True, their principles coincided with the measures which would best protect their class, and in that they may be said to have yielded to self-interest; but Randolph, with his abhorrence of natural-rights doctrine, would have admitted freely the impeachment. He sought to safeguard himself and his society; that, and not abstract theory, he would have maintained, was the whole basis of politics. Randolph and his friends fought for the agricultural life. They were vanquished.

Yet those doctrines of 1800 did not perish; they were guarded, battered but obdurate, by the Old Jacobins and were passed on to a later generation of southern thought (and, in a measure, of northern thought) which gave them a more hearty welcome than they had long experienced. Those principles of a society of freeholders have in them an attraction for some natures which does not perish with the times. Those political standards, in part the product and in part the corollary of this school of thought, have been sorely trampled, but they have not been refuted. Purity and economy in government, peace and prudence in foreign relations, and freedom from economic oppression by special interests are ideals which, if remote of achievement, still are worth striving toward.

["The Planter-Statesman," John Randolph of Roanoke: A Study in American Politics, *4th ed. (Indianapolis: Liberty Fund, 1997), 123–53.]*

Orestes Brownson and the Just Society

Kirk admired and wrote frequently on Orestes Brownson (1803–76), a restless, versatile, and fiercely independent political philosopher who moved from a strict Puritanism to an ardent Roman Catholicism. In this essay, published in The Month *(December 1954), Kirk views Brownson as an "American exponent of the venerable principle of Justice at once Christian and classical, religious and humane." Brownson, he believes, helps us not only to find ways of reconciling orthodoxy with Americanism but also to learn how justice requires the authority of religious truth abiding in moral standards of judgment. A major feature in this essay is Kirk's generous use of quotations from Brownson's writings, which eloquently attest to Brownson's ability to transcend politics and sectarianism and to attain principles that establish "the meaning of justice, and the nature of the enemies of justice."*

A few months after the murder of Lincoln, Orestes Brownson published a systematic treatise on American order, *The American Republic* (1866). Brownson (who disliked Lincoln, but disliked the Secessionists even more) is intellectually one of the most interesting of all Americans, and his examination of order in the United States is an original work—though it is a kind of summary of what he had been writing in periodicals for the preceding quarter of a century. Although long neglected by most historians of American politics and thought, in recent years Brownson and his writings have received considerable attention, and *The American Republic* has been reprinted. There is good reason for this: late in the twentieth century, Americans confront the fundamental problems of personal and social order in which Brownson was passionately interested.

Lord Acton, who possessed one of the best intellects of nineteenth-century England, thought that Orestes Brownson was the most penetrating American thinker of his day; and that is a high compliment, for it was the day of Hawthorne, Melville, Emerson, and a half-dozen other men of the first rank in the works of the mind. The versatility of the man has made it difficult to fit him into any convenient category. He was a considerable political philosopher, a seminal essayist on religion, a literary critic of discernment, a serious journalist of fighting vigor, and one of the shrewder observers of American character and institutions. The long span of Brownson's career, too—

for, born in 1803, he was engaged in controversy all the while from 1827 to his death in 1876—prevents his being classified within any conventional literary era. Nor was he a regional writer: a New Englander by birth, he spent much of his life in New York and Detroit, and died in Michigan; he is buried in the chapel of the University of Notre Dame, in Indiana. Midway in his life, Brownson became a Catholic, so departing from what the typical historian of culture likes to call the "mainstream" of American intellectual development; this deviation accounts in part for the neglect of Orestes Brownson in most books about American intellectual history. Yet he called himself "a true-born Yankee," and so he was—with the forthrightness, energy, and intellectual belligerence of his kind.

Brownson's course in partisan politics was intricate, from the time of Jackson to the time of Hayes; the course of his political and religous thought was equally perplexed, until 1844. Born into poverty, and chiefly self-educated, Brownson had to grope his way through the sects and factions of New England until he reached that understanding of things sacred and secular for which he had been seeking. He was a Bible-reader from early childhood; his quest for religious certitude led him from the Congregationalism of his boyhood successively to Presbyterianism, Universalism, humanitarianism, Unitarianism, and Transcendentalism. He was a Universalist minister at one time, and a Unitarian minister later; he was active in the socialistic undertakings of Robert Owen and Fanny Wright; for a year he was a militant atheist and revolutionary conspirator. But in none of these movements did he find intellectual or emotional satisfaction. Somewhere, Brownson believed, there must exist a source of religious authority, without which men are at sea; he found that in the Catholic faith, being baptized and confirmed in 1844.

His social ideas went through a succession of changes closely parallel to those in his religious convictions. Brownson was a socialist long before the name of Marx was known, and in several respects anticipated Marx's thought—which made him the more formidable as an opponent of socialism in his maturity. He was besides, in his early years, a complete democrat, taking equality of condition for a natural right—the principle upon which the civil social existence ought to be ordered.

Brownson always believed that if a principle were sound, there could be no danger in pushing it to its logical consequences. This he did with the principle of democratic equality, in his "Essay on the Laboring Classes," published in 1840. Equality of civil rights, he argued, must lead to equality of condition—to economic equality. The inheritance of private property, the system of bank credit, and all other principal features of what Marx would call "capitalism" must be abolished, then, so that equality of condition might triumph. Brownson defended this thesis stoutly; it did much mischief to the cause of the Democratic party, which he then supported. Ironically enough, the election of 1840 disillusioned this unequivocal egalitarian. The "Tippecanoe and Tyler Too" campaign, with its gross demagoguery, compelled Brownson to ask himself whether a republic could endure without recognizing clear principles of moral authority. When the American people elected a President on the strength of the assertions that General William Henry Harrison had been born in a log cabin (which was not strictly accurate) and drank hard cider, something was lacking in the social order. "We for one confess," Brownson wrote later, "that what we saw during the presidential election of 1840 shook, nay, gave to the winds all our remaining confidence in the popular democratic doctrines."

So after 1840 Brownson defended the permanent things. He had concluded from close observation of the American people that pure democracy and economic equality were miserable shams, which could lead only to the destruction of liberty and justice in any country. But if the idea of equality of condition was false, upon what principle ought an intelligent man to found his politics? Brownson came to perceive that somewhere there must reside an authority, in the original Latin meaning of that word—a source of moral knowledge, a sanction for justice and order.

Brownson did not become the defender of everything that existed in American society about the middle of the nineteenth century: he remained a mordant critic of many aspects of that society, but stood up for the principles of order which (however much obscured) made possible the American Republic. His politics were the politics of a religious man, not of a Benthamite who looks upon the Church as a moral police-force. Brownson understood that we cannot separate the world of spirit and the world of society into distinct entities; but he had no intention of using the Church to advance his political beliefs, or of using his political convictions to advance the interests of the Church. Religion and politics are forever joined in this: mundane justice and order require a moral sanction; and that sanction cannot be found outside religious principle. He courted no man's favor, and was as fierce against the Utilitarian intellectual and the money-obsessed entrepreneur as against the Marxist fanatic and the revolutionary.

Brownson was more than a vigorous controversalist: he was a political philosopher, something rare in the United States. Before Brownson wrote, only two important American books could be considered treatises on political philosophy—Adams's *Defense of the Constitutions* (1787–88) and *The Feder-*

alist (1787–88)—and even those were apologies for a political situation and a particular set of circumstances, rather than analyses of the essence of political order. In Brownson's own time, his friend John C. Calhoun would write two logical political dissertations of a philosophical character, in defense of the South's stand. Yet in general Brownson's essays and his *American Republic* retain more meaning for our time than do Calhoun's works.

Brownson told Americans how even they, in their seemingly triumphant materialism and swaggering individualism, could not long endure without knowing the meaning of justice. In reminding Americans of this, Brownson did not make himself popular. Ordinarily he was on the losing side at national elections. He had a following, but he strove against the current in his day. Yet the subtle influence of Brownson's writings, though it may be difficult to trace down to our time, has done something to chasten American impulsiveness and materialism. Today he can be read with interest and sympathy, which is more than can be said for most polemicists of yesteryear, popular though they may have been at the height of reputation.

Brownson waged intellectual battle upon several fronts. First, he had to contend against the radical doctrine of the Rights of Man—not those natural rights of which the Church long had spoken, but instead the arrogant abstract rights of Paine and Priestley and the French revolutionaries, divorced from duties and shorn of religious sanctions. Second, he had to deal with the delusion that "the voice of the people is the voice of God," which in America was put forward as an excuse for majorities to alter all law as they might choose, regardless of justice toward minorities and individuals. Third, he was confronted by aggressive individualism—in part an American growth, in part the spirit of the age—which often sacrificed the common good in public affairs to immediate money-getting and private advantage. Fourth, he struggled against a sentimentality like that of Jean Jacques Rousseau, which mistook a misty-eyed compassion for Justice. Fifth, he defended Justice against a smug secularism, which looked upon Sin as merely a vestigial survival from barbarous times, sure to disappear with the march of progress. Sixth, he had to stand fast against the disintegrating competition of sectarianism, a chaos of cults which diminished the teaching authority of the Christian Church.

Brownson's was a lonely labor. For generations, the New England conscience had been some support for a just social order; but in Brownson's day, the old puritanical uprightness of New England was awash in a sea of innovating doctrines—later-day Congregationalism, Unitarianism, Universalism, Transcendentalism, and the rest. Brownson knew all these well, and found them unable to bear the weight of Justice. At the same time, the old planter-society of the South, resentful and fearful, was struggling against the North's new industrialism; saddled with its Peculiar Institution, slavery, the South moved toward violence. In the North, the zealots for Abolition, bent upon the destruction of one evil at the risk of aggravating other social afflictions, mistook social surgery for Justice. And beyond these American difficulties, Brownson discerned the rise of the "labor question" and the approach of socialism—an ideology that confounded Justice with absolute equality of condition.

Yet Brownson did not lose heart. Tireless, he labored to persuade his fellow-Americans of their common need for a principle of authority. Justice, he said, requires Authority—not the authority of soldier or policeman, but the authority of religious truth. No people can enjoy a just society without some standard of judgment superior to the mood of the moment; and this is especially true in democratic states, which have no hereditary class of magistrates to sustain the laws. Now this abiding standard of righteousness, or principle of authority, must be ethical in its nature; and to receive habitual assent from the people, that ethical system must refer to religious sanctions. This standard must be interpreted authoritatively by some body fitted for that function: the Church is required. Simple popular opinion never can maintain Justice:

> But we are told, once more, that practically it can make no difference whether we say the will of God is sovereign, or the will of the people; for the will of the people is the will of God. . . . We deny it. The will of God is eternal and immutable justice, which the will of the people is not. The people may do and often actually do wrong. We have no more confidence in the assertion, "The people can do no wrong," than we have in its brother fiction, "The king can do no wrong." . . . For very shame's sake, after denying, as most of you do, the possibility of an infallible church immediately constituted and assisted by infinite wisdom, do not stultify yourselves by coming forward now to assert the infallibility of the people.

So Brownson wrote in his essay on "Legitimism and Revolution" in 1848, the year of the *Communist Manifesto*. "In most cases," Brownson continued, "the sufferings of a people spring from moral causes beyond the reach of civil government, and they are rarely the best patriots who paint them in the most vivid colors, and rouse up popular indignation against the civil authorities. Much more effectual service could be rendered in a more quiet and peaceful way, by each one seeking, in his own immediate sphere, to remove the moral causes of the evils endured."[52]

Without Authority vested somewhere, without regular moral principles that may be consulted confidently, Justice cannot long endure anywhere. Yet modern liberalism and democracy are contemptuous of the whole concept of moral authority; if not checked in their assaults upon habitual reverence and prescriptive morality, the liberals and democrats will destroy Justice not only for their enemies, but for themselves. *Under God*, the will of the people ought to prevail; but many liberals and democrats ignore that prefatory clause. In America, particularly since 1825, there had been distressingly obvious a tendency to make over the government into a pure and simple democracy, centralized and intolerant of local rights and powers, upon the model of Rousseau. That "pure" democracy, if triumphant, would destroy the beneficent "territorial democracy" (a phrase Brownson borrowed from Disraeli) of the United States, with its roots in place. This would be a change from a civilized constitution to a barbaric one. The Civil War, said Brownson, had accelerated the process.

"But the humanitarian democracy, which scorns all geographical lines, effaces all individualities, and professes to plant itself on humanity alone, has acquired by the war new strength, and is not without menace to your future. . . . " The humanitarian presently will attack distinctions between the sexes; he will assail private property, as unequally distributed.

> Nor can our humanitarian stop there. Individuals are, and as long as there are individuals will be, unequal: some are handsomer and some are uglier, some wiser or sillier, more or less gifted, stronger or weaker, taller and shorter, stouter or thinner than others, and therefore some have natural advantages which others have not. There is inequality, therefore injustice, which can be remedied only by the abolition of all individualities, and the reduction of all individuals to the race, or humanity, man in general. He can find no limit to his agitation this side of vague generality, which is no reality, but a pure nullity, for he respects no territorial or individual circumscriptions, and must regard creation itself as a blunder.[53]

The humanitarian, or social democrat (here Brownson uses those terms almost interchangeably), is by definition a person who denies that any divine order exists. Having rejected the supernatural order and the possibility of a Justice more than human, the humanitarian tends to erect Envy into a pseudo-moral principle. It leads him, this principle of Envy, straight toward a dreary tableland of featureless social equality—toward Tocqueville's democratic despotism, from which not only God seems to have disappeared, but even old-fangled individual man is lacking.

Yet the social democrat is not the only enemy of Justice and Authority in our time. The disciples of Bentham, with their moral calculus, their exalting of self-interest, and their social atomism, are the other side of the coin. Their principle of universal competition, and their fallacy that political constitutions can be created overnight, damage Justice in society as much as do the illusions of the socialistic leveller: because some men are more able and energetic than others, we cannot leave justice to pure competition in society. For then

> they in whom selfishness is the strongest will gain the preponderance, and, having the power, must, being governed only by selfishness, wield the government for their own private ends. And this is precisely what has happened, and which a little reflection might have enabled anyone to have foretold. The attempt to obtain wise and equitable government by means of universal competition, then, must always fail. But this is not the worst. It, being a direct appeal to selfishness, promotes the growth of selfishness, and therefore increases the very evil from which government is primarily needed to protect us.

Both the socialist and the enthusiast for perfect competition, then, would undo Justice. But this descent of modern society into injustice may be arrested, Brownson argues: roused to their peril, men may renew true Justice. Suppose that modern men return to their belief in a Justice divinely ordained: what will be the shape of a just society, when the character of true human wants is better understood?

The just society will seek to give unto each man his due: not through the release of selfish impulse, not through a sentimental and enervating socialism, but by recognizing both the Christian virtue of charity and the profound natural differences that distinguish one human being from another. The just society will not repudiate democracy, properly understood, though it will turn away from both the atomistic "Jacksonian" democracy and the oppressive humanitarian democracy:

"Democracy, understood not as a form of government, but as the end government is to seek, to wit, the common good, the advance in civilization of the people, the poorer and more numerous, as well as the richer and less numerous, classes, not of a privileged caste or class, is a good thing, and a tendency toward it is really an evidence of social progress."[54] Such a democracy, if it is to remain just, must be restrained by solemn and prudent constitutions and by an enlightened faith. Nevertheless, its government will not hesitate to conduct itself with courage or to undertake large projects. It is shallow sophistry to say that government is a necessary evil: government is no evil, but a device of divine wisdom to supply human wants. The function of government is not repressive merely:

> Its office is positive as well as negative. It is needed to render effective the solidarity of the individuals of a nation, and to render the nation an organism, not a mere organization—to combine men in one living body, and to strengthen all with the strength of each, and each with the strength of all—to develop, strengthen, and sustain individual liberty, and to utilize and direct it to the promotion of the common weal—to be a social providence, imitating in its order and degree the action of divine providence itself, and, while it provides for the common good of all, to protect each, the lowest and meanest, with the whole force and majesty of society. . . . Next after religion, it is man's greatest good; and even religion without it can do only a small portion of her work. They wrong it who call it a necessary evil; it is a great good, and instead of being distrusted, hated, or resisted, except in its abuses, it should be loved, respected, obeyed, and, if need be, defended at the cost of all earthly goods, and even of life.[55]

The government justly may perform all those labors which surpass the reach of individual abilities; and justly may do all that can be done to secure every man in his natural liberty, and to advance the culture of society. But the success of this just government will be dependent upon those men of superior abilities who alone can provide for the progress of humanity and the preservation of the wisdom of our ancestors. Out of a solemn concern for the operation of Justice, Brownson argues, society ought to take every care that superior abilities should not be disparaged or positively repressed, that superior energies be not denied their reward, that learning be not trodden down by men without imagination. To each his own: to the natural entrepreneur, the fruits of industry; to the natural scholar, the contemplative leisure which is his need and his reward.

In any particular country, Brownson maintains, the form of government must be suited to the traditions and the organic experience of the people: in some lands that will be monarchy, in others aristocracy, in America republicanism, or democracy *under God*. It will not stoop to the degradation of the democratic dogma; it will not contest the sovereignty of God, which is absolute over all of us. It will secure to every man his freedom. And that freedom obtains the justice of which Plato wrote in his *Republic*, and Cicero in his *On Duty*: the right of every man to do his work, free of the meddling of others; the right of every man to what is his due.

Such is the nature of true social justice, Brownson declares: not the selfish loneliness of the Benthamite philosophy, nor the mean equality of the Socialists, but a liberation of every man, under God, to do the best that is in him. Poverty is no evil, in itself; obscurity is no evil; labor is no evil; even physical pain may be no evil, as it was no evil to the martyrs. This world is a place of trial and struggle, so that we may find our higher nature in right response to challenge.

To the Socialist, says Brownson, poverty, obscurity, and physical suffering are positive evils, because the Socialist does not perceive that these challenges are put into the world to save us from apathy and sloth and indifference. The Socialist would condemn humanity to a condition of permanent injustice, in which no man could hope for what is his due, the right to exercise his talents given him by God; the Socialist would keep us all in perpetual childhood:

> Veiling itself under Christian forms, attempting to distinguish between Christianity and the Church, claiming for itself the authority and immense popularity of the Gospel, denouncing Christianity in the name of Christianity, discarding the Bible in the name of the Bible, and defying God in the name of God, Socialism conceals from the undiscriminating multitude its true character, and, appealing to the dominant sentiment of the age and to some of our strongest natural inclinations and passions, it asserts itself with terrific power, and rolls on its career of devastation and death with a force that human beings, in themselves, are impotent to resist. Men are assimilated to it by all the power of their own nature, and by all their reverence for religion. Their very faith and charity are perverted, and their noblest sympathies and their sublimest hopes are made subservient to their basest passions and their most grovelling propensities. Here is the secret of the strength of Socialism, and here is the principal source of its danger.[56]

Those lines were written only a few months after the proclaiming of the Communist Manifesto. At that early date, Orestes Brownson had seen the dread strength of the Marxist heresy, an attempt at total destruction of the old order of human existence.

The United States was not brought into being to accomplish the work of Socialism. For every living nation, Brownson wrote in *The American Republic*, "has an idea given it by Providence to realize, and whose realization is its special work, mission, or destiny." The Jews were chosen to preserve traditions, and so that the Messiah might arise; the Greeks were chosen for the realizing of art, science, and philosophy; the Romans were chosen for the developing of the state, law, and jurisprudence. And the Americans, too, have been appointed to a providential mission, continuing the work of Greece and Rome, but accomplishing yet more. The American Republic is to reconcile liberty with law:

> Yet its mission is not so much the realization of liberty as the realization of the true idea of the state, which secures at once the authority of the public and the freedom of the individual—the sovereignty of the people without social despotism, and individual freedom without anarchy. In other words, its mission is to bring out in its life the dialectic union of authority and liberty, of the natural rights of man and those of society. The Greek and Roman republics asserted the state to the detriment of individual freedom; modern republics either do the same, or assert individual freedom to the detriment of the state. The American republic has been instituted by Providence to realize the freedom of each with advantage to the other.[57]

The reconciling of authority and liberty, so that justice might be realized in the good state: that mission for America is not accomplished, a century later, but is not forgotten. During the blighted years of "Reconstruction" in the South (a failure anticipated by Brownson, who despised the Radical Republicans), that mission of ordered freedom would seem infinitely remote from fulfillment.

Yet Brownson labored on, an old man in Detroit, exhorting Americans to vigor. *Under God*, said Brownson in his emphatic way, the American Republic may grow in virtue and justice. A century later, the words "under God" would be added to the American pledge of allegiance. Brownson's principles of justice, after all, expressed those American moral habits of thought and action that Tocqueville had found strong. The violence and confusion of Brownson's time would diminish somewhat; Marxism would make little headway in the United States. So thoroughly American himself, Orestes Brownson knew that there was more to America's great expectations than the almighty dollar.

["Brownson and a Just Society," The Month, *Vol. 12 (December 1954), 348–65. Also published as "Brownson and the Just Society,"* The Roots of American Order *(La Salle, IL: Open Court, 1974), 457–68.]*

Woodrow Wilson and the Antagonist World

In his analysis of Woodrow Wilson (1856–1924), the twenty-eighth president of the United States, Kirk focuses on some of his paradoxes. "Wilson the natural conservative became the rhetorical liberal," Kirk says, and this transposition led to inconsistency. Yet Wilson also sought to emulate Burke's model of a statesman and was "the last of our literary statesmen, bringing to the presidential office the humane and juridical disciplines." During World War I and the making of the peace, he embraced the illusion of "liberal universalism" antithetical to "the facts of European political reality." By believing in a political dreamworld of "a world safe for democracy" and "a world safe from war," he betrayed the classical virtue of prudence. Kirk's guiding principle of critique and judgment in this essay is rooted in these words: "A statesman deserves to be recollected not simply for what he did, but also for what he refrained from doing."

Few great names have gone out of favor more rapidly than that of Wilson. The reason is not far to seek. Wilson's fervent admirers, in the twenties and thirties, were progressives and liberals; they it was who enshrined him in that curious pantheon honoring Jefferson, Jackson, Wilson, and Franklin Roosevelt as the deities of American liberalism. But now the liberals have discovered that Wilson never really was one of their number; he had feet of clay; he was a natural conservative. And therefore Wilson has been cast into the outer darkness.

It seems surprising, looking back at Wilson and his era, how the liberals ever blundered into this embarrassing error. For Wilson openly proclaimed himself a disciple of redoubtable American and English conservative thinkers; the aim of his practical politics was to preserve traditional America and, if possible, to restore some things that were passing out of American society. Whenever he did adopt a policy unmistakably liberal, it was more or less against his will, and out of force of circumstance: the income tax, for instance, was thrust upon him—as upon Gladstone—by financial exigencies, but he abhorred it.

Accident has much to do with careers. Wilson the natural conservative became almost by chance the presidential candidate of the liberals, and found himself head of a party which barely knew him. Politicians, even the best of them, to some extent must speak the language of their followers: Wilson did so, but more from the exigencies of the situation than from any voluntary commitment. Interesting parallels have been drawn between Wilson and Gladstone—who, of course, at one time was the leading light of Toryism, but through rivalry with Disraeli found himself at the head of Liberalism.

Yet the superficial conjunction of Wilson with Progressivism deceived liberals in the years following Wilson's death; they took the natural and philosophical conservative for the liberal ideologue, endowing the sober Princeton professor with their own aspirations. Only now are they undeceived, when the real distinctions between conservative and liberal thought have become clearer than at any time since the Civil War. And it should be remarked, in justice to Wilson's liberal admirers and critics, that Wilson's language and action, during the War and the making of the Peace, provided some excuse for this confusion. It is difficult for a public man to escape becoming what his associates insist he is. Moreover, the climate of liberal opinion was powerful then; in office, Wilson experienced the seductions of that liberal climate of opinion—as did John F. Kennedy, much later—and to some extent abandoned his conservative principles for liberal abstractions.

When I was a schoolboy, we were told to write essays on how President Wilson would have made this sad old world into a terrestrial paradise, if only he had not been hampered (transiently, we were to trust) by a few Wicked Men in France and Massachusetts and Idaho. In all innocence, I wrote an essay about Wilson which deviated from this view, and was reproved by the teacher. That attitude of unquestioning admiration has passed now. One cannot read without a smile such sentences as this of Harold B. Howland (in his *Theodore Roosevelt and his Times*, published in 1921) concerning the presidential contest of 1912: "One thing was clear from the beginning: the day of conservatism and reaction was over; the people of the United States had definitely crossed their Rubicon and had committed themselves to spiritual and moral progress." Whatever sort of progress we have experienced since 1912, and no matter how many Rubicons we have crossed, we have not known Wilson's New Freedom, and it is difficult to discern the marks of our predicted spiritual and moral elevation.

Surely Wilson, despite the phrase "The New Freedom," by 1912 had shown few signs of being anything but a prudent conservative reformer, desirous of keeping America what she had been. He put no faith in schemes for altering profoundly the political and economic structure. At a time when there was talk of modelling the federal administration after the British Parliament, with cabinet responsibility and Congress put in the role of a body of critics, Wilson was prompt to declare the imprudence and impossibility of any such importation of parliamentary institutions grown up from roots quite different from those of American federalism. This is but an example; in many other matters, by 1912, Wilson had written and acted as a reflecting conservative.

Nowadays, adulation of Wilson is confined chiefly to circles of old-fangled doctrinaire liberals unlike Wilson himself; their fondness for the political absolute has gone far beyond him. His name is muttered occasionally as an incantation to sanction proposals for a World State quite contrary to his idea of national self-determination, or to endorse egalitarian schemes which would have been anathema to him. I speak here of the bewildered breed called the ritualistic liberal; the attitude of the younger revisionist liberals among us is different. So we return to Richard Hofstadter and Louis Hartz.

"His hard doctrinaire mind," Hartz writes about Wilson, "taken as a whole, was not of the American type." And Hartz continues, in *The Liberal Tradition in America* (1955):

> The policy of Wilson in peace, so striking a contrast to the realpolitik of the Old World and ultimately so abject a victim before it, was shot through and through with the absolute "Americanism" on the basis of which the war was fought. His central dilemma, what Walter Lippmann called "the inner contradiction" of his thought, is by now a commonplace: the attempt to apply to a world in crying need of integration and on the brink of capitalist decline the political formulas of nationalism and free trade that the nineteenth century evolved. But to say merely this, to classify Wilson as a decadent disciple of Gladstone, is not only to miss the American contribution to his perspective, but actually to obscure it. Wilson's blindness was not only philosophic, it was empirical as well, the product of a peculiar historic experience. . . .

Hofstadter is harder still upon Wilson, because Wilson really was old-fashioned, a believer in free enterprise, unwilling to usher in the "corporate and consolidated society" which Mr. Hofstadter takes to be the wave of the future. "Wilson's speeches," Hofstadter observes, "the best parts of which are printed in *The New Freedom*, sound like the collective wail of the American middle class." Wilson did not strike to the heart of things; he ought to have removed the causes of national antagonism: "It had always been Wilson's aim to preserve the essentials of the *status quo* by reforming it; but failing essentially to reform, he was unable in the end to preserve."

Coming from an historical determinist like Hofstadter, this complaint that Wilson did not single-handedly turn the world inside out is amusing. But Hofstadter's indictment is thoroughgoing:

> He appealed for neutrality in thought and deed, and launched upon a diplomatic policy that is classic for its partisanship. He said that American entrance into the war would be a world calamity, and led the nation in. He said that only a peace between equals would last, and participated in the *Diktat* of Versailles. He said that the future security of the world depended on removing the economic causes of war, and did not attempt even to discuss these causes at the Peace Conference. He declared his belief in the future of government ownership, and allowed his administration to close in a riot of reaction. He wanted desperately to bring the United States into the League, and launched on a course of action that made American participation impossible. No wonder that in one of his moments of apprehension he should have confessed to George Creel: "What I seem to see—with all my heart I hope that I am wrong—is a tragedy of disappointment."

This verdict on Wilson is true enough; and yet there was more to Wilson than inconsistency, ineffectuality, and failure. I think that there is something better in failing as Wilson failed than in sitting in the scorner's seat. Such judgments by Hofstadter and Hartz illustrate the realism and the destructive power of the revisionist liberal; but also they reveal the prudential liberal's inability to offer any alternative to tradition, short of totalist ideology.

Still, Wilson failed. He talked of a war to end war; but his policies, at the end of that war, had a terrible part in breaking up the old international order and precipitating our civilization into that "antagonist world" (Burke's phrase), in sundering the bands of established community "on speculations of a contingent improvement," and condemning the world to "madness, discord, vice, confusion, and unavailing sorrow." Now Wilson was a good man, a strong man, a learned man, an intelligent man, a religious man. It seems worthwhile to inquire into the causes of this consequential failure.

Hartz and Hofstadter imply that Wilson failed because he was not a radical; he did not tear up the old order by the roots and supplant it by a Grand Design. "The Conservative as Liberal," Hofstadter calls Wilson, accurately. The bent of Wilson's nature was conservative; and Hartz and Hofstadter cannot forgive him for that. But he was born into a liberal era; the political vocabulary of his time was that of the liberals; and, perhaps more than in most eras, the conservatives of the time seemed to be the Stupid Party. Wilson the natural conservative became the rhetorical liberal. A man's words can master him; phrases can intoxicate; and, uttering the slogans of liberalism that were fashionable in his generation, Wilson presently came to act upon liberal abstractions. Out of that conflict between conservative impulse and liberal phrase grew much of Wilson's inconsistency when he had practical decisions to make; and the inconsistency attained its grim culmination when the Peace was to be made.

Before recounting what Wilson lacked, we ought to recall what he possessed. He was pious and courageous, well educated, honest, devoted to duty. He knew much of history and political theory. He tried always to emulate Burke's model of a statesman, combining a disposition to preserve with an ability to reform. There was little of the demagogue in Wilson. As things are going, he may be recorded as the last of our literary statesmen, bringing to the presidential office the humane and juridical disciplines. He did not merely drift with events: he perceived some of the deeper issues of this century better than anyone else among successful politicians, and much of *The New Freedom* remains worth reading. He was the sort of leader who makes possible the existence of democratic republics.

Wilson stood in the line of two strong schools of political wisdom: the constitutional writings of the founders of the American Republic, and the Christian doctrines and English experience that found their best expression in Burke. "Ever since I had independent judgments of my own, I have been a Federalist," Wilson said once. From an early age, too, he had been a disciple of Burke. His essay on "Edmund Burke and the French Revolution" shows a better understanding of Burke's principles than was possessed by most English scholars of his generation; it is, indeed, one of the better essays ever written on Burke. "Burke was himself, and was right," Wilson says, when Burke set his face against the French Revolution. And in that essay occurs a passage which cast its shadow upon Wilson's future career: "There is often to be found in the life of a great man some point of eminence at which his powers culminate and his character stands best revealed, his characteristic gifts brought to light and illustrated with a sort of dramatic force. Generally it is a moment of success that reveals him, when his will has had its way and his genius its triumph." Wilson's own moment came with the making of the Peace, in an hour of triumph; but all of Wilson's weaknesses stood revealed in that moment, and the apparent success sank abruptly into the bitterness and frustration of his final months.

Hartz and Hofstadter believe that this failure resulted from Wilson's innate conservatism, which prevented him from getting at the real causes of national rivalry and war. But is it not more true to say that Wilson's failing was rather that he was insufficiently conservative? The political wisdom of the Federalists and Burke was diluted, in Wilson, by a dose of doctrinaire liberalism. In the hour of crisis, liberal abstraction prevailed over conservative prudence. Wilson's failure was not that he declined to reconstitute the whole complex fabric of European and American society, warp and woof. Had he undertaken any grand design of this sort, his failure would have been more catastrophic. For it was not in Wilson's power, nor in any other man's, to accomplish anything of that sort. Even supposing this undertaking to have been desirable, neither Wilson nor anyone else possessed the knowledge, the force, and the following even to contemplate such a scheme. Wilson knew that such an attempt must provoke impassioned resistance, and that this resistance could be broken only by means which would corrupt the reformers. Seeing such an attempt being made in Russia, and recognizing the Russian Revolution as the grimmer brother of the French Revolution, he strove to check that Revolution. Like Burke, he was right, though it has taken some people nearly half a century to learn to agree with him. It is silly to reproach Wilson for not undertaking what he could not even have thought of undertaking; and he would have been wicked, knowing history as he did, to have set his hand to such a task.

Wilson resigned himself to the possible: he did what he could to establish a better order among nations. His principles were confused, the times moved too fast for him (particularly in the ruins of the Austro-Hungarian system), and he proved far too thoroughly convinced of his own wisdom, too unyielding, to achieve anything which might endure. Yet the errors into which he fell were not the errors of conservative policy; they were the errors of liberalism; they were errors of the sort which Gladstone made in diplomacy. The climate of opinion in 1918 and 1919 was liberal, and it is hard to say who might have done better in Wilson's place. It is vain to imagine John Adams or John Quincy Adams, Disraeli or Salisbury, dominating the meetings of the Big Four. Wilson, then, was no unworthy spokesman for America. His failure was the failure of the nation's political imagination in those years, a normative failure. We may have learned something since then; but often I doubt it.

Certain liberal abstractions concerning the nature of political order and the nature of man lay behind Wilson's doctrine of national self-determination, behind his assumption that leagues of nations and paper constitutions and treaties might of themselves bring peace and contentment, behind his insistence upon fitting the map of Europe into his ideal design. He had learned much from the Federalists and Burke; but he had not learned prudence, which Burke considered the highest virtue in a statesman. His attachment to Burke's politics was similar to that of the English Liberal school, best exemplified by Gladstone and Morley. That aspect of Burke's thought which defends prescription and prejudice, which perceives how dangerous it is to disturb anything that is at rest, which is prepared to tolerate an old evil lest the cure prove worse than the disease, he understood imperfectly. Burke, respecting the ancient political communities of Europe, seeing in them Gothic edifices whose grotesqueness masked a mighty strength for good, never would have thought of approving a doctrinaire and wholesale shifting of boundaries, a vast abolition of governments and substitution of new ones, an overthrow of historical and natural groupings in favor of simple language-affinity. Burke would have perceived at once the consequence of abolishing the power which held together the heart of Europe and checked German and Russian ambition, the Austrian system. But it was Bentham or Mill, not Burke, whose pupil Wilson became in the making of the Peace.

To the conservative of Burke's school, the world is at best a tolerable place, kept in order chiefly through respect for custom and precedent. It may be patched and pruned here and there; but the nature of man remains flawed, ambition always aspires to domination, and states are kept at peace only by a balancing of power, a recognition of the traditions of civility, and a concern for real interests. Parchment and declarations of the rights of man cannot restrain private or national concupiscence. To the liberal, on the other hand, the world is infinitely improvable, and so is man himself; experiment and emancipation will lead to peace; and what ought to be, shall be. So Wilson thought and acted through the War and the making of the Peace.

The idea that power may be checked only by countervailing power always has been distasteful to the liberal. Wilson's concept of national self-determination, his championship of the League, and much of the rest of his program reflected that distaste. A vague confidence in Progress, Equality, and the People overcame the cautionary precepts of Burke and the Federalists. "You are a Liberal," the Duke of Omnium says to Phineas Finn, in one of Trollope's parliamentary novels, "because you know that it is not all as it ought to be, and because you would still march on to some nearer approach to equality; though the thing itself is so great, so glorious, so god-like,—nay so absolutely divine,—that you have been disgusted by the very promise of it, because its perfection is unattainable."

Trollope knew his Liberals. This yearning to march on toward some future universal condition of democracy and equality got the better of Wilson, when authority was his. Despite his earlier declarations that the American Republic—though a model for other states—could not be transplanted, he called upon America to make the world safe for democracy; and this same liberal universalism marked his arguments in the shaping of the evanescent Peace. They were arguments not from prudence, not from principle as Burke had described principle, but from abstraction; and the states upon which he bestowed his blessing collapsed in less than two decades, because they were constructed in defiance of history, of real interests, and of the hard facts of power.

Ortega, in the year Wilson died, already was writing of "decadent democracy," betrayed by its own fallacies and mediocrity. Wilson did not make the world safe for democracy: in Europe, he succeeded only in clearing away the old forms and loyalties which might have withstood the totalitarians. He helped to bring to a transitory ascendancy democratic governments which were modelled upon France (whatever institutions they may have borrowed superficially from Britain and America) with all the weaknesses which the abstractions of the French Revolution inflicted upon political administration and popular opinion. The task was impossible to achieve. American political features that were the peculiar products of a peculiar historical experience could not be transported to Europe. No American, probably, was better qualified for the work than Wilson, for he knew history, and he had been much abroad; yet, in the haste and confusion which preceded the Versailles conference, he made arbitrary decision after arbitrary decision which ran counter to the simple facts of European political reality. His naive acceptance of Benes's claim that the Sudeten Germans were few and feeble is only one of many errors. And, disastrous though these decisions were in the immediate sense, they have done even greater harm in encouraging among many Americans, ever since, the notion that somehow American "experts," given rein, possess knowledge and energy sufficient to resolve happily, in short order, the quarrels which have plagued the Old World these weary centuries. That mood of optimism brooded over Yalta; it is not gone from among us yet. Like faith without works, faith without insight can work infinite mischief; and optimism without a chastening humility can undo the practical, patient accomplishment of dutiful men over many centuries.

To argue whether Wilson, in these matters, was a "true liberal" or a false liberal is to waste time and to ignore the regular progression through which the liberal creed has gone since the beginning of the nineteenth century. The germ of what liberalism affirms today was present in the theories of Bentham, and even in the orations of Charles James Fox. The augmented role of positive law, the sweeping away of prescriptive institutions, an egalitarianism progressing from equality of franchises to equality of condition: these doctrines the liberals simply have extended logically. And the triumph of their doctrine has left them feeble before the totalists, who claim the right to inherit the liberal hegemony; there is nothing surprising in the canonization of Tom Paine by the Soviets. So far as Wilson was swept along by the liberal climate of opinion in his generation, he was as true a liberal as any in that camp. Not long before he died, he uttered some kind words about socialism. But so did Acton; so did John Stuart Mill; so did even old John Bright.

It is the liberal veneer upon Wilson's mind and action which has diminished his reputation among us, and it is no longer possible to defend him successfully in his liberal aspect—those mordant latter-day liberals Hartz and Hofstadter have seen to that. Yet I think that we should remember how Wilson was more than a doctrinaire liberal. A statesman deserves to be recollected not simply for what he did, but also for what he refrained from doing. Burke and Adams lingered always at the back of Wilson's mind: if he indulged in radical political alteration abroad, still he refused to countenance radical social alteration; and it is difficult to imagine him sanctioning the blunders and fallacies of Yalta, or singing the praise of the Universal Declaration of Human Rights.

If, on speculations of a contingent improvement, he confounded abstraction with principle and unwittingly opened a way unto that antagonist world of discord and unavailing sorrow which now is ours, still he stood by his God, his country, and his civilization. Woodrow Wilson knew what was worth conserving, though unhappily he vacillated at the crisis of his fate. . . .

["Woodrow Wilson and the Antagonist World," Enemies of the Permanent Things: Observations of Abnormity in Literature and Politics, *Rev. ed. (La Salle, IL: Sherwood Sugden & Company, 1984), 182–91.]*

❖

IX.

CONSERVATORS OF CIVILIZATION

The Conservative Humanism of Irving Babbitt ❖
Paul Elmer More on Justice and Faith ❖
George Santayana Buries Liberalism ❖
The Humane Economy of Wilhelm Röpke ❖
Max Picard: A Man of Vision in Our Time

We require principles of order if humane society is to survive, Kirk never tired of stressing. But principles also require guardians of standards and truths that decide the destiny of mankind. In his writings Kirk devotes considerable attention to great thinkers who convey wisdom and insight and whose reflections help deepen our understanding of the human condition and the organization of life. Thinkers of themselves, Kirk reminds us, are not nearly great enough without also being contemplators, even prophets, who discern the eternal nature of things in the process of transcending the flux of time and history.

What Kirk's exemplars have most in common is a plenary moral vision that absorbs the meaning of existence at all levels and in all of its dynamics and consequences. Indeed, what makes them unique is their pursuit of virtue as the highest good and their humility in the consonant recognition of a greatness of power beyond the purely temporal, the personal, or the local. Their historical understanding, at its depth and magnitude, is inclusive in its capacity not only to connect noetic, moral, and spiritual elements, but also to interfuse the economic, political, philosophical, and religious dimensions. Their intrinsic greatness is measured by an added capacity to soar beyond diagnostic discriminations and to envision the possibilities of renewal, regeneration, and redemption of the individual and the community, of both personal and public order.

Those whom Kirk counts among great modern thinkers are seers and sages, teachers and critics, who grasp the deformations of existence that mirror the crisis of civilization in the twentieth century. And as the philosopher Eric Voegelin observed, himself one of Kirk's great thinkers, once the massive process of deformation imposes itself on a man, "he conforms to it and consequently deforms himself by making deformed existence the model of true existence."

Kirk's great men are great thinkers. He searches after them not as he would for heroes, or for geniuses, but for their wisdom of thought, and for the paradigms of character and soul, of social and moral order, that they generously impart. His is an instinctive reverence for thinkers who give constant witness to the function of guidance, who honor and conserve the idea of value and who give voice to the discrimination of value, which is their special and sacred responsibility.

To save civilization from sliding into the abyss of barbarism and brutality, and of spiritual ruin, was a concern that was never to leave Russell Kirk's mind and thought.

❖

THE CONSERVATIVE HUMANISM OF IRVING BABBITT

Irving Babbitt (1865–1933), renowned American humanist and moralist critic, holds a preeminent place in Kirk's work and thought. From 1948 to 1963, he undertook knapsack travels abroad, sometimes walking forty miles a day. Among the writers he read every evening during these walks was Irving Babbitt. Eventually Kirk was to publish major writings on Babbitt; the first appeared in The Conservative Mind *(1953) and is included here. For Kirk, Babbitt's achievement is of supreme importance: "He joined the broken links between politics and morals, and that is a work of genius." Kirk singles out these teachings from Babbitt's legacy: one's highest self is ruled by "the law for man" and not "the law for thing"; prejudice and prescription must be defended against naturalistic assumptions; sentimentalism, humanitarianism, and what Babbitt termed "the myth of man's natural goodness" erode the roots of civilized life; the virtues of order and proportion sustain character and culture in a world of change and confusion.*

As if they recognized in him their most formidable adversary, writers of the Left have attacked Irving Babbitt with a vituperation somewhat startling when one remembers that this abuse is directed against a contemplative

Harvard professor of comparative literature. Oscar Cargill, in his *Intellectual America* (1948), exclaims furiously, "We know not in what superstitious eighteenth century sectarianism Babbitt was reared, but his lack of salivary control at the mere mention of *science* or *democracy* suggests the rural hymn singer and sermon note-taker, rather than the cosmopolitan." Harold Laski, in *The American Democracy* (1948), declares that Babbitt won no pupils. Ernest Hemingway, fuming at Babbit's faith in human dignity, says he wants to know how genteel Babbit will be when he dies. As a matter of fact, Babbitt was a big, earnest Ohioan who worked on a Western ranch in his youth, studied at Harvard and at Paris, wandered afoot in Spain, fought against the currents other men rode to success, and died with remarkable fortitude, working to the last to convince America that man cannot remain human unless he restrains his appetites. Although friendly to religion, he remained suspicious of all churches; if he detested the corruption of American principles, still he is one of the most thoroughly native of American writers. Aristotle, Burke, and John Adams were his mentors in social thought. Founding the school of American philosophy which he called humanism, he left behind him an influence which may endure long after Laski has been nearly forgotten at the London School of Economics. In him, American conservatism attains maturity.

The heart and essence of Babbitt's intellectual system, says his ally Paul Elmer More, is contained in a footnote to Babbitt's criticism of Rousseau in *Literature and the American College* (1908), his first book:

> The greatest of vices according to Buddha is the lazy yielding to the impulses of temperament (*pamâda*); the greatest virtue (*appamâda*) is the opposite of this, the awakening from the sloth and lethargy of the senses, the constant exercise of the active will. The last words of the dying Buddha to his disciples were an exhortation to practice this virtue unremittingly.

The disciplinary arts of *humanitas*—that exercise of Will which distinguishes man from beast—are dying of neglect in this era; contemptuous of the realm of spirit which Buddha and Plato alike describe, modern man is corrupted by a gross naturalism, reducing all things to a single sensate level. If man forgets the dual nature of existence, he stifles his higher self, which is ruled by the law for man, as contrasted with the law for thing which governs the senses; thus he commits suicide. Having destroyed his higher self, a man dooms his lower self too, for without the directing power of Will, he tumbles into the anarchy of the beasts. In our time the task for the humanist is to remind society of its spiritual reality. Babbitt and his colleagues are merciless toward the humanitarian, as distinguished from the true humanist. Humanitarians in the tradition of Bacon and Rousseau are sentimentalists who think that all human problems may be resolved by the application of physical remedies. The humanitarian's indiscriminate utilitarian method engenders hostility toward that hierarchy of values which erects distinctions between saint and sinner, scholar and barbarian. Intent upon an egalitarian condition for society, the humanitarian tries to extirpate those spiritual essences in man which make possible truly *human* life.

Irving Babbitt's enemies promptly labelled this advocacy of spiritual self-discipline and subordination of the senses "Puritanism," as if that were *per se* its condemnation. And it is Puritanical, the creed of humanism—in the sense that Plato and Augustine were Puritans. Babbitt and More rejected Calvinism with abhorrence as a system corrosively deterministic; their faith rested upon the premise of free will; and yet it remains true enough that something of the old New England austerity lived in both these Middle Westerners and gave them the iron resolution to speak up for dualism and the life of spirit in an era dedicated to the senses and sentimentality. The humanist, wrote Babbitt in his first book, "believes that the man of to-day, if he does not, like the man of the past, take on the yoke of a definite doctrine and discipline, must at least do inner obeisance to something higher than his ordinary self, whether he calls this something God, or, like the man of the Far East, calls it his higher Self, or simply the Law. Without this inner principle of restraint man can only oscillate violently between opposite extremes, like Rousseau, who said that for him there was 'no intermediary term between everything and nothing.'"[1] The saving of civilization is contingent upon the revival of something like the doctrine of original sin.

For a student of social conservatism, the most important book among Babbitt's seven volumes is *Democracy and Leadership* (1924); and since (as More observes) Babbitt was a "rotary" writer, touching upon the essentials of his system in each of his books rather than developing his ideas in sequence, a close examination of this courageous essay provides a tolerable view of the whole of his humanistic system. It was published in 1924, when American millionaires pushed up like mushrooms; and Babbitt was as contemptuous of millionaires as he was of Jacobins. "A few more Harrimans and we are done," he had written sixteen years earlier. For he knew that the Rockefellers and Harrimans represented the same forces as did John Dewey: they stood for the delusion that men can be improved upon utilitarian principles. If, as Lloyd George said, the future will be taken up even more than is the present with economic problems—why, the future will be superficial. That naturalism which began at least as early as the Renaissance, was made "scientific" by Bacon, and was popularized by Rousseau, now has progressed to a degree which imperils the structure of social life. The old bulwarks of prejudice and prescription have been demolished by the popularization of naturalistic ideas in every segment of society; and the humanist can counter this radicalism only by winning men to an alternative system of ideas. "Progress according to the natural law has been so rapid since the rise of the Baconian movement that it has quite captivated man's imagination and stimulated him to still further concentration and effort along naturalistic lines. The very magic of the word progress seems to blind him to the failure of progress according to the human law," Babbitt had written in 1919.[2] Humanists now must remind the world that there is law for man and law for thing, or resign themselves to catastrophe. Forms and restrictions will not keep society from destroying itself, if ideas are lacking: "The attempt to oppose external and mechanical barriers to the freedom of the spirit will create in the long run an atmosphere of stuffiness and smugness, and nothing is more intolerable than smugness. Men were guillotined in the French Revolution, as Bagehot suggests, simply because either they or their ancestors had been smug. Inert acceptance of tradition and routine will be met sooner or later by the cry of Faust: *Hinaus ins Freie!*"[3] Perhaps no generation ever was more smug than Babbitt's; and the very radicals among his audience, enveloped in their own interesting unconscious smugness, quite certain of evolutionary proletarian bliss, called Professor Babbitt an obscurant because he predicted the coming of chaos.

Rousseau, first among the theorists of radical democracy, the most eminent contemner of civilization, gave the wrong answers to the right questions. He denied the duality of human experience, and relied upon the régime of the senses as the means to general happiness. Rousseau's (and Whitman's) sentimental dream of democratic fraternity is, like utilitarian theories, a particular aspect of humanitarianism, or the naturalistic movement. Humanitarianism omits the keystone of the arch of humanity, which is Will. "As against expansionists of every kind, I do not hesitate to affirm that what is specifically human in man and ultimately divine is a certain quality of will, a will that is felt in its relation to his ordinary self as a will to refrain."[4] This power, peculiar to man, of invoking a check upon the impulses of sense, even upon the impulses of reason, is what makes him *human*. The surrender of Rousseau to desire, the surrender of the Utilitarians to avarice, end in the dehumanization of our race. If social reform is substituted for self-reform, emotional anarchy presently undoes every project of the humanitarian. In *Literature and the American College*, Babbitt had distinguished between humanist and humanitarian; in *The Masters of Modern French Criticism* (1912), he had analyzed the decay of standards and the rise of relativism; in *The New Laokoon* (1910), he had examined the anarchy in literature and art that is consequent upon decline in standards; in *Rousseau and Romanticism*, he had said that the imagination holds the balance of power between the higher and lower natures of man, and that Rousseau's idyllic imagination corrupted the aspirations of modern man. Now, in *Democracy and Leadership*, he was endeavoring "to show that genuine leadership, good or bad, there will always be, and that democracy becomes a menace to civilization when it seeks to evade the truth. . . . On the appearance of leaders who have recovered in some form the truths of the inner life and repudiated the errors of naturalism may depend the very survival of Western civilization." *Democracy and Leadership* is perhaps the most penetrating work on politics ever written by an American—and this precisely because it is not properly a political treatise, but really a work of moral philosophy. "When studied with any degree of thoroughness," Babbitt wrote in his first paragraph, "the economic problem will be found to run into the political problem, the political problem into the philosophical problem, and the philosophical problem itself to be almost indissolubly bound up at last with the religious problem." Many political scientists have paid small attention to this book. But if science is more than the accumulation and classification of physical data, Babbitt's view of politics is science upon a high plane.

Modern politics, like modern civilization in general, says Babbitt, long has been exposed to the disintegrating influence of the naturalist. "The naturalist no longer looks on man as subject to a law of his own distinct from that of the material order—a law, the acceptance of which leads, on the religious level, to the miracles of other-worldliness that one finds in Christians and Buddhists at their best, and the acceptance of which, in this world, leads to the subduing of the ordinary self and its spontaneous impulses to the law of measure that one finds in Confucianists and Aristotelians." In politics, the father of this modern denial of a higher will—i.e., a moral system to which man can appeal from his own lower nature—is Machiavelli, who, with the aversion all naturalists display for dualism, would not allow men to possess a divided allegiance, fealty to both a mundane state and the City of God. Yet Machiavelli and his followers are not true realists: "The Nemesis, or divine judgment, or whatever one may term it, that sooner or later overtakes those who transgress the moral law, is not something that one has to take on authority, either Greek or Hebraic; it is a matter of keen observation." With Hobbes, this negation of morality enters English political thought, and we continue to suffer from its poison. "If one is to refute Machiavelli and Hobbes, one must show that there is some universal principle that tends to unite men even across national frontiers, a principle that continues to act even when their egoistic impulses are no longer controlled by the laws of some particular state supported by its organized force."The utilitarian temper encouraged by Locke further degraded the venerable concept of public office as a consecrated trust, and "if the aristocratic principle continues to give way to the equalitarian denial of the need of leadership, parliamentary government may ultimately become impossible."

Upon the ruins of the medieval idea of government which Machiavelli and his followers undermined, Rousseau erected a kind of quasi-religious political contrivance, supplied with its own myths from his idyllic imagination, inspired by the notion that pity has primacy among human emotions. The sentimental doctrine of the General Will, which Rousseau produced to mortar this system together, from the beginning was full of menace. "By this device Rousseau gets rid of the problem that has chiefly preoccupied political thinkers in the English tradition—how, namely, to safeguard the freedom of the individual or of minorities against a triumphant and despotic majority." Rousseau's fallacious new dualism, that which postulates the citizen in his private capacity and the citizen as a member of the community, may provide the apology for a tyranny more crushing than anything Rousseau himself denounced.

Burke, continues Babbitt, perceived all this; and Burke knew, better than anyone else, that the only kind of conservatism which can survive is an imaginative conservatism. But the strong tendency of the times impaired his appeal to the traditional conservative symbols of the imagination: Baconian love of novelty and change, discovery piled on discovery, the hope that we are moving toward some "far-off divine event," undid the defenses of prejudice and prescription and "a wisdom above reflection" upon which Burke relied to save true liberalism. Modern conservatives, or liberals, must find other instruments and methods.

These new instruments of conservation will need to be ingenious; for they must be employed against the tremendous imperialistic instinct of modern democracy. It is an error (as Mirabeau said) to suppose that democracy and imperialism are inimical; they will hunt together in our time, as they did in Periclean Athens and Revolutionary France. Japan, if converted to democracy, will be many times more dangerous than when governed by a conservative aristocracy, content with the present arrangement of things. Eight years later, Babbitt returned to this theme in *On Being Creative* (1932), taking note of André Siegfried's dread of the American's "consciousness, still more dangerous, of his 'duties' toward humanity."[5] Imperialism is one aspect of man's ancient expansive conceit, which the Greeks knew would bring hubris, and then blindness, and finally nemesis. "Man never rushes forward so confidently, it would sometimes seem, as when he is on the very brink of the abyss." Humility, which Burke ranked high among the virtues, is the only effectual restraint upon this congenital vanity; yet our world has nearly forgotten the nature of humility. Submission to the dictates of humility formerly was made palatable to man by the doctrine of grace; that elaborate doctrine has been overwhelmed by modern presumption, the self-reliance which radiates from Rousseau and Emerson; "and it is not as clear as one might wish that European civilization can survive the collapse of this doctrine." Babbitt himself never embraced the idea of grace; but he perceived its transcendent importance, as had Pascal and the Jansenists, and his frequent return to this topic foreshadows the fascination of Christian novelists and apologists with the doctrine of grace during recent decades.

With the decline of the doctrine of grace and with the theological confusion that the Reformation admitted, a doctrine of work began to take its place—but a concept almost wholly divorced from its old theological namesake. Francis Bacon expounded this exaltation of labor above piety and contemplation; Locke carried it to its utilitarian extreme in his Second Treatise; Adam Smith echoed him, Ricardo enlarged upon the idea, Marx reduced "work" to the purely quantitative view. "The attempt to apply the utilitarian-sentimental conception of work and at the same time to eliminate competition has resulted in Russia in a ruthless despotism, on the one hand, and in a degrading servitude, on the other." How are we to escape from this fallacious concept of the nature of work? The humanitarians are guilty of participation in this error: "Even when they do not fall into the cruder quantitative fallacies, they conceive of work in terms of the natural law and of the outer world and not in terms of the inner life."

But "work" really is a thing very different from this; and Babbitt appeals to Buddha and Plato for his definition. True work, the higher work, is labor of the spirit, self-reform; and this brings us to the nature of Justice. "The Platonic definition of justice as doing one's own work or minding one's own business has perhaps never been surpassed." The only true freedom, Babbitt adds, is the freedom to work. "It is in fact the quality of a man's work that should determine his place in the hierarchy that every civilized society requires." They who work with their minds should rank above those who work with their hands; but men engaged in a genuinely ethical working are higher still. Any real civilization must relieve certain individuals of the necessity for working with their hands, so that they may participate in that leisure which is an indispensable preparation for leadership.

These leaders in spirit and mind must be taught to rise superior to material possessions; and this cannot be accomplished without a genuinely ethical or humanistic working.

> To proclaim equality on some basis that requires no such working will result ironically. For example, this country committed itself in the Declaration of Independence to the doctrine of natural equality. The type of individualism that was thus encouraged has led to monstrous inequalities and, with the decline of traditional standards, to the rise of a raw plutocracy. . . . The remedy for such a failure of the man at the top does not lie, as the agitator would have us believe, in inflaming the desires of the man at the bottom; nor again in substituting for real justice some phantasmagoria of social justice.

Such substitution generally brings fanatical attacks on property itself, and presently upon thrift and industry; provokes suppression of competition, which is necessary to rouse man from his native indolence. From the confusion of decreeing an absolute equality without any properly understood ethical basis, America never has recovered: "It is not yet clear that it is going to be possible to combine universal suffrage with the degree of safety for the institution of property that genuine justice and genuine civilization both require." Inflation of the currency will be the most common and subtle form of this peril.

Every man must find his happiness in work or not at all. Yet in our time the mass of men are bored with their labor—a consequence, partially, of the humanitarians' misunderstanding of the essence of work. Their inability to define love and liberty has brought us to similar bafflement in these vast matters. In substance, the humanitarians' failure is the product of their ignorance of man's ethical will, of the fact that his only real peace is spiritual peace. In our pupilage to the humanitarians, we have lost sight of standards; upon the restoration of standards depends the preservation of our civilized life and our humanity.

> Commercialism is laying its great greasy paw upon everything (including the irresponsible quest of thrills); so that, whatever democracy may be theoretically, one is sometimes tempted to define it practically as standardized and commercialized melodrama. . . . One is inclined, indeed, to ask, in certain moods, whether the net result of the movement that has been sweeping the Occident for several generations may not be a huge mass of standardized mediocrity; and whether in this country in particular we are not in danger of producing in the name of democracy one of the most trifling brands of the human species that the world has yet seen.

What is it that has persuaded America to accept the quantitative test in all things, so that "the American reading his Sunday paper in a state of lazy collapse is perhaps the most perfect symbol of the triumph of quantity over quality that the world has yet seen"? The loss of true leadership is both cause and effect of our deficiency in standards. "One should, therefore, in the interests of democracy itself seek to substitute the doctrine of the right man for the doctrine of the rights of man." Frequently democracy has been no more than an attempt to eliminate the qualitative and selective principles in favor of abstract theories of the general will. In the United States, this struggle between true and false liberalism, qualitative and quantitative democracy, has been substantially the contest between Washington's liberty and Jefferson's liberty. Jefferson wished to emancipate men from external control; but he never understood, as Burke knew, how power without and power within always must remain in ratio; so that every diminution of power on the part of the state, unless it is to result in injury to society, should be accompanied by an increase of self-control in individuals. The Epicurean and speculative Jefferson disliked the whole idea of rigid self-discipline, to which the house of Adams was devoted; and Jefferson's example encouraged the expansive and coarsely individualistic tendencies of Americans. Judicial control, uncongenial to Jefferson in either its political or its ethical form, remains a chief guarantee of our liberty; but it has been terribly injured by our proclivity toward imperialism and quantitative judgment.

The Federal Constitution and the Supreme Court and other checks upon immediate popular impulse are to the nation what the higher will is to the individual. Where our society succeeds, usually it is in consequence of this restraining influence in our thought and political structure; where it fails, often it is in consequence of our sentimental humanitarianism: "We are trying to make, not the Ten Commandments, but humanitarianism work—and it is not working. If our courts are so ineffective in punishing crime, a chief reason is that they do not have the support of public opinion, and this is because the public is so largely composed of people who have set up sympathy for the underdog as a substitute for all the other virtues." The utilitarian energumen, with his emphasis on "outer working," moves further and further toward a dehumanized society: "The type of efficiency that our master commercialists pursue requires that a multitude of men should be deprived of their specifically human attributes, and become mere cogs in some vast machine. At the present rate even the grocer in a remote country town will soon not be left so much initiative as is needed to fix the price of a pound of butter."

Where are we to discover the leaders who may redeem us from all this? Their great merit must be humility; nothing else will serve. Thus the scientist is disqualified, for we know his presumption; and the artist-aristocrat would be quite as disagreeable. To trust in the divinity of the average, dispensing with leadership altogether—a popular notion—is worse folly still; and the fickleness of the public has made even the radical reformer lose faith in this dream. No, in this hour when our need for leadership is desperate, when our power extends across oceans and gropes blindly for lack of direction, it will not save us to "evolve under the guidance of Mr. H. L. Mencken into second rate Nietzscheans." Leadership can be restored only by the slow and painful process of developing moral gravity and intellectual seriousness, turning back to the strength of traditional doctrines—the honesty with which they face the fact of evil. Our spiritual indolence can be overcome only by a re-examination of first principles. "The basis on which the whole structure of the new ethics has been reared is, as we have seen, the assumption that the significant struggle between good and evil is not in the individual but in society. If we wish once more to build securely, we may have to recover in some form the idea of 'the civil war in the cave.'"

We need to examine our definition of work—which depends upon our definition of nature. What we mean by "liberty," in turn, depends upon our meaning for "work." Our regeneration is contingent, then, upon resort to Socratic methods, involving these definitions and those of "justice" and "peace." This is no mere question of the Schools. "The time may come, if indeed it has not come already, when men will be justified in asserting true freedom, even, it may be, at the cost of their lives, against the monstrous encroachments of the materialistic state." We must purge ourselves of the notion that pure equality is consonant with liberty and humility. The need for restoration of standards in our life means that we shall have to ascertain some ethical centre. The ethical state is possible, human nature being susceptible to right example. But our ethical centre must be more than our current adulation of "service." The real leader is no mere humanitarian; his sanctions come from will and conscience.

When all is said, we are brought back to the question of Will. The "idealist" and "realist" schools of political thought, both rooted in naturalism, will not do for our time. Anyone who transcends naturalism "ceases in about the same measure to be either a humanitarian idealist or Machiavellian realist. He becomes aware of a quality of will that distinguishes man from physical nature and is yet natural in the sense that it is a matter of immediate perception and not of outer authority." Is there not a power independent of our senses, independent even of our ordinary reason, to which we may appeal against our very selves? In sober fact, do men have souls, or do they not? Upon one's solution of this inquiry rests the basis of politics; for if men do not possess souls, if there is no higher will, then they may as well be treated as parts of a machine—indeed, they cannot be treated otherwise. Babbitt contemplates politics upon a height too giddy for many men to ascend; but his postulates granted, politics cannot be discussed satisfactorily upon any other level.

One plane is higher still, Babbitt remarks at the end of his desultory but noble book: and that is the plane of grace. "Traditionally the Christian has associated his liberty and his faith in a higher will with grace." But Babbitt cannot persuade himself to clamber to that crag; he is not really sure it exists; and he endeavors to express his system in "terms of work," ethical work, the activity of the higher nature of man, as distinguished from communion with God. He stops short of Burke, therefore, and Hooker, and the Schoolmen. Paul Elmer More came to believe that one dare not halt at the level of work, but must press on for security to religious faith.

Justice has not been done here to Babbitt. His great erudition is only suggested; his intricate mind is obscured by the curtness of this summary. He joined the broken links between politics and morals, and that is a work of genius. He knew that the conservation of the old things we love must be founded upon valid ideas of the highest order, if conservatism is to withstand naturalism and its political progeny. "The conservative nowadays," he observes in one of his numerous moments of sharpshooting prescience, "is interested in conserving property for its own sake, and not, like Burke, in conserving it because it is an almost indispensable support of personal liberty, a genuinely spiritual thing." Babbitt's teachings already have had some influence in guiding American conservative thinkers to positions more tenable. His influence may grow, attracting to the austere cause of Work and Will a succession of the men whom a nation economically mature must find if that nation is to be something more than a machine.

["The Conservative Humanism of Irving Babbitt," Prairie Schooner, *Vol. 26 (Fall 1952), 245–55. Also found under the title "Irving Babbitt's Humanism: The Higher Will in a Democracy," Chapter 12, Section 2,* The Conservative Mind: From Burke to Eliot, *7th rev. ed. (Washington, DC: Regnery Publishing, Inc., 1999, c1953), 419–32.]*

Paul Elmer More on Justice and Faith

Paul Elmer More (1864–1937), who joined Irving Babbitt in the neohumanist cause to promote classicism and restraint, was another American critic whose writings Kirk read during his travels. A master of English prose style and a probing critic of ideas, More declared war on the pragmatism of William James, the naturalism of John Dewey, and the sentimentality of the socialists. More is best known for his Shelburne Essays, *published in eleven volumes between 1904 and 1921. In his writings, Kirk says, there runs "a stern continuity": "the insistence that for our salvation in this world and the other, we must look to things of the spirit, accept the duality of human nature, remind ourselves that the present moment is of small consequence in the mysterious system of being." In especial Kirk focuses on More's* Aristocracy and Justice *(1915) for its powerful indictment of the philosophy of flux and the "New Morality of drifting."*

On North Avenue in Cambridge, once, Babbitt suddenly clenched his hands and exclaimed to Paul Elmer More, "Great God, man, are you a Jesuit in disguise?" Babbitt endeavored all his life to teach himself tolerance toward churches; but it was otherwise with More; and that far-ranging critic remarks, with something like a smile, "I have never been able to answer the question satisfactorily."[6]

Though he was born in Missouri, More stands conspicuous in the tradition of New England thought—as, indeed, so much that is called "Middle Western" today is really the New England mind and character transplanted. With a sense of dedication rare in his generation, while still a young man he retired to the hamlet of Shelburne, in New Hampshire, so that he might find the leisure and the detachment necessary for contending intelligently with our modern complexity; and then returning into the world, intellectually armored, very like a prophet, he struggled as lecturer and essayist and editor of the *Nation* against the pragmatism of James, the naturalism of Dewey, the sentimentality of the socialists, the presumption of a people who had forgotten the truth of dualism. He disciplined himself into mastery of English prose style; and as a critic of ideas, perhaps there has not been his peer in England or America since Coleridge. "All differences of opinion," Cardinal Manning once observed, "are at bottom theological." More's adherence to this principle became his great strength; commencing as a thorough skeptic, he ended as the most eminent Anglican thinker in the history of the United States, possibly the most learned American theologian of any communion.

The first of the eleven volumes of More's *Shelburne Essays* was published in 1904. Through this glowing critical series, through the five volumes of *The Greek Tradition* (1921–31), through the *New Shelburne* Essays (1928–36) that were published in the last decade of his life, runs a stern continuity: the insistence that for our salvation in this world and the other, we must look to things of the spirit, accept the duality of human nature, remind ourselves that the present moment is of small consequence in the mysterious system of being. If, with William James, we resign ourselves to the stream of time and change, we invite inner and outer catastrophe:

> Sometimes as I consider with myself how this illusion daily more and more enthralls and impoverishes our mental life by cutting off from it all the rich experience of the past, it is as though we were at sea in a vessel, while a fog thickened, closing in upon our vision with ever narrower circle, blotting out the far-flashing lights of the horizon and the depths of the sky, throwing a pall upon the very waves about us, until we move forward through a sullen obscurity, unaware of any other traveller upon that sea, save when through the fog the sound of a threatening alarm beats upon the ear.[7]

Much read in Burke and Newman, More understood that when generation thus ceases to link spiritually with generation, first civilization and then human existence itself must shrivel. And men will ignore the past and the future, he came to believe, without a pervasive belief in the reality of the transcendent. Man must lead a double life, More wrote in concluding the first volume of *Shelburne Essays*, balancing between law for man and law for thing, never losing the distinction between his public and his private duty. Our modern social confusion, intellectually considered, is the consequence of confounding the sphere of private morality with the sphere of public activity. This is the enormous error of the humanitarians. When the religious impulse is contracted to mere "brotherhood of man," fratricide is not far distant. Near the end of the third volume of the *New Shelburne Essays* (1936), More repeated this declaration: "The one effective weapon of the Church in her campaign against the unnecessary evils of society, her one available instrument for bringing into play some measure of true justice as distinct from the ruthless law of competition and from the equally ruthless will to power of the proletariat, is through the restoration in the individual human soul of a sense of responsibility extending beyond the grave."[8] *Pleonexia*, the "perpetual and restless desire of power after power, that ceaseth only in death," can be restrained by no force in this world—solely by an inner human check which is of supernatural origin.

Its religious instincts suppressed or bewildered, our society must find its way back to permanence, or die. Modern romanticism and modern science, though superficially inimical, share a disastrous impressionism; for both have surrendered to the theory of ceaseless flux, with no principle of judgment except the shifting pleasure of the individual. This is Pragmatism, the cancer of our intellect. In such times, the man of conscience must declare boldly that he is a reactionary; otherwise formlessness in philosophy and letters will become formlessness in society, impotent acceptance of change, leading to the individualism of Cobden or the collectivism of Marx—in either case, the stifling of civilization by material forces; or, this bulwark failing in turn, then anarchy. "The saying has gone abroad that strength means joy in change and that he who would question change is reactionary and effeminate." Yet is a reactionary nothing more than a coward before innovation, no more than a slave of the Past? "Reaction may be, and in the true sense is, something utterly different from this futile dreaming; it is essentially to answer action with action, to oppose to the welter of circumstance the force of discrimination and selection, to direct the aimless tide of change by reference to the co-existing law of the immutable fact, to carry the experiences of the past into the diverse impulses of the present, and so to move forward in an orderly progression. If any young man, feeling now within himself the power of accomplishment, hesitates to be called a reactionary, in the better use of this term, because of the charge of effeminacy, let him take courage."[9]

A manual to candid and intelligent reaction against the philosophy of flux is *Aristocracy and Justice*, the ninth volume of the *Shelburne Essays* (1915). How are men to be saved from themselves? How are they to be saved from their drifting lassitude, the product of a facile evolutionary philosophy, which must end (if not arrested) in a catastrophe of which the war that began in 1914 is merely a foreshadowing? In the realm of society, men require an aristocracy to lead them aright. To acknowledge this aristocracy, we must be frankly and nobly reactionary. "We have the naked question to answer: How shall a society, newly shaking itself free from a disguised plutocratic régime, be guided to suffer the persuasion of a natural aristocracy which has none of the insignia of an old prescription to impose its authority?"[10] To persuade victorious democracy that it must resurrect aristocracy: this is the tremendous practical problem in our politics.

The cant phrase that "the cure of democracy is more democracy" lies; the real cure must be not more, but *better* democracy. Improvement never can come from the mass itself; it must be the work of natural aristocracy, which "does not demand the restoration of inherited privilege or a relapse into the crude dominion of money; it is not synonymous with oligarchy or plutocracy. It calls rather for some machinery or some social consciousness which shall ensure both the selection from among the community at large of the 'best' and the bestowal on them of 'power'; it is the true consummation of democracy." Our first step toward the creation or resuscitation of natural aristocracy ought to be a reform of our institutions of higher learning.

Like a great old tree, our society has been dying at the top. The educated classes are in danger of turning traitors to the civilization which sustains them—deluded by humanitarianism, perhaps ignorant of their own proper duties.

> At other times the apprehension has been lest the combined forces of order might not be strong enough to withstand the ever-threatening inroads of those who envy barbarously or desire recklessly; whereas today the doubt is whether the natural champions of order themselves shall be found loyal to their trust, for they seem no longer to remember clearly the word of command that should unite them in leadership.
>
> Idealists like G. Lowes Dickinson count upon a "slow, half-conscious detachment of all of them [the leaders of modern society] who have intelligence and moral force from the interest and active support of their class."[11] (The Harrimans whom Babbitt contemned in one generation as the unabashed exemplars of utilitarian avarice become in the next generation zealots for the welfare state.) That decay of the venerable humanistic intellectual discipline in higher education, of which decadence President Eliot's innovations at Harvard are a symptom, is a chief cause of this bewilderment or treason of the clerisy. We have forgotten the Magna Carta of our education—Sir Thomas Elyot's *Boke Named the Governour* (1531).
>
> The scheme of the humanist might be described in a word as a disciplining of the higher faculty of the imagination to the end that the student may behold, as it were in one sublime vision, the whole scale of being in its range from the lowest to the highest under the divine decree of order and subordination, without losing sight of the immutable veracity at the heart of all development, which "is only the praise and surname of virtue." This was no new vision, nor has it ever been quite forgotten. It was the whole meaning of religion to Hooker, from whom it passed into all that is best and least

> ephemeral in the Anglican Church. It was the basis, more modestly expressed, of Blackstone's conception of the British Constitution and of liberty under law. It was the kernel of Burke's theory of statecraft. It is the inspiration of the sublimer science, which accepts the hypothesis of evolution as taught by Darwin and Spencer, yet bows in reverence before the unnamed and incommensurate force lodged as a mystical purpose within the unfolding universe.[12]

Lacking such an education, men have no hold upon the past; they are at the mercy of every wind of doctrine.

For real liberty—the liberty of true distinction, not the fierce levelling freedom of envy—the leaders of society require a liberal education. With such a discipline, they can serve as a true natural aristocracy, mediating between plutocracy and egalitarian democracy. The soul of this humanistic discipline is study of the classics; they teach man the meaning of Time, and "confirm him in his better judgment against the ephemeral and vulgarizing solicitations of the hour." When our universities and colleges devote themselves to turning out specialists and technicians and businessmen, they deprive society of its intellectual aristocracy and, presently, undermine the very social tranquillity upon which modern specialization and technical achievement are founded.

Yet the precise means of ensuring the life of a natural aristocracy is not so important a question as the principle upon which a true aristocracy will manage the affairs of mankind. That principle is Justice, and the existence of civilization hangs on this. But how may Justice be defined? More offers a series of definitions, with the aim of demolishing the sentimental term "social justice" which has been so useful an instrument to radicalism. Put very simply, justice is "the act of right distribution, the giving to each man his due"; but that, to have real meaning, requires further definition of *right* and *due*. When we examine more closely the impulse called justice, we find that it is "the inner state of the soul when, under the command of the will to righteousness, reason guides and the desires obey"—or, briefly, "Justice is happiness, happiness is justice." What, then, is social justice? More condemns impartially Nietzsche's "will to power" and its opposite, the humanitarian, socialistic ideal of absolute equality. Social justice, instead, is "such a distribution of power and privilege, and of property as the symbol and instrument of these, as at once will satisfy the distinctions of reason among the superior, and will not outrage the feelings of the inferior." No absolute rule exists for striking this balance, no more than there is any absolute code of morals for individual conduct; but the same criterion applies to it that is our means of approaching individual justice: "Social justice and personal justice both are measured by happiness."The legislator must distinguish nicely between superiority and egotism, special merit and public contentment. It is a work of mediation, of compromise, and we must resign ourselves to the fact that along with justice there always must remain some individual deprivation or scarcity, which we are too prone to call "injustice."We are not perfect or perfectible creatures; and if we would be in harmony with Nature, we must not damn the nature of things (like Porson trying to blow out the mirrored image of a candle-flame) and demand that absolute Justice which does not reside in this world.

Property, without which civilization cannot endure, is really "the magnifying of that natural injustice [the initial inequality of men] into that which you may deplore as unnatural injustice, but which is a fatal necessity, nevertheless. This is the truth, hideous if you choose to make it so to yourself, not without its benevolent aspect to those, whether the favorites of fortune or not, who are themselves true—ineluctable at least." Unless we call civilization a mistake, any attempt to ignore natural inequality and propertied inequality is sure to cause general unhappiness. "Security of property is the first and all-essential duty of a civilized community." Life is a primitive thing; we share it with the beasts; but property is the mark of man alone, the means of civilization; therefore, says More in a bold phrase which has infuriated his humanitarian opponents, "To the civilized man the *rights of property are more important than the right to life*."

He goes farther still. So important is property to truly human existence, that even if men rob under cover of the laws (for no set of laws can be perfect), "It is better that legal robbery should exist along with the maintenance of law, than that legal robbery should be suppressed at the expense of law." For the worst thing which can happen to law is its over-extension, its expansion to fields in which it cannot be competent; then disrespect for law in all its capacities will become general. If you deny a fact, the fact will control you. This is true of property. "You may to a certain extent control it and make it subservient to the ideal nature of man; but the moment you deny its rights, or undertake to legislate in defiance of them, you may for a time unsettle the very foundations of society, you will certainly in the end render property your despot instead of your servant, and so produce a materialized and debased civilization."

When property is insecure, the spirit of materialism flourishes. In such times of want, intellectual leisure is denounced popularly as abnormal and anti-social; the scholar is detested. "There is something at once comical and vicious in the spectacle of those men of property who take advantage of their leisure to dream out vast benevolent schemes which would render their own self-satisfied career impossible." Private ownership, production, and distribution are indispensable to the progress of society; and we need to strengthen ourselves "against the insidious charms of a misapplied idealism." Transfer the ancient prerogatives of property to the labor which produces property, and our venerable institutions, the Church and the University most of all, are in terrible peril. "For if property is secure, it may be the means to an end, whereas if it is insecure it will be the end itself."

In a century when the aristocratic principle, the classical idea of justice, and the institution of property all are menaced, what effective stand can conservatives take? Great advantages are with the radicals—the seductions of flattery, the opportunism which deals with immediate material needs to the exclusion of distant considerations, the force of humanitarian sympathies. "It is not strange, therefore, that the history of England since the Revolution of 1688, with intervals of timid delay, has been the record of a gradual yielding to the steady thrust of opportunism." The conservative can appeal to the imagination of men; but he must be sure his own imagination is sound and true. The conservative must make certain of the rectitude of his own morality. He has now to contend against the New Morality, that vague but virulent social passion which, if it means anything, "means the reconstruction of life at the level of the gutter." Humanitarianism, usurping the place of the Church, endeavors to ignore the existence of Sin and to erect sympathy into a social theory, leaving individual responsibility out of account. Sympathy and justice are confounded.

Confronted with such disheartening odds, the conservative must retire into himself for a space, so that he will remember "that his nature is not simple and single, but dual," a reflection of incalculable ethical value. Within him is a truer self, an inner check, "unchanged amid continual change, of everlasting validity above the shifting values of the moment." Guided by this intuition, "he will know that the obligation to society is not the primal law and is not the source of personal integrity, but is secondary to personal integrity. He will believe that social justice is in itself desirable, but he will hold that it is far more important to preach first the responsibility of each man to himself for his own character." Abjuring cant, he will discover a fortitude which may yet suffice to defend the old morality against a collective and sentimental humanitarianism that, without conservative opposition, would devour its own sustenance incontinently.

And by way of conclusion, More undertakes a final definition of justice: "the Everlasting Morality of distinctions and of voluntary direction opposed to the so-called New Morality of drifting." Aristocratic leadership and a voluntary society are allied naturally; the morality of flux rapidly sweeps through the stage of humanitarianism into the stage of collective compulsion. Politics leads to morals.

Morals, in turn, must lead to religious faith. In the last volume of the *Shelburne Essays*, More suggests that fear is an inevitable factor in human conduct; and, religious fear absent, men soon become subject to fears of a description more immediate and more difficult to alleviate, the fear of class war, or of destitution, or of subjugation to the machine.

> As we contemplate the world converted into a huge machine and managed by engineers, we gradually grow aware of its lack of meaning, of its emptiness of human value; the soul is stifled in this glorification of mechanical efficiency. And then we begin to feel the weakness of such a creed when confronted by the real problems of life; we discover its inability to impose any restraint on the passions of men, or to supply any government which can appeal to the loyalty of the spirit. And seeing these things we understand the fear that is gnawing at the vitals of society.

Humanitarians, having dissolved the old loyalties and prescriptions, find themselves defenseless before the boss, the union-leader, the political policeman, the very pitiless machine-society they had welcomed. Fear, like injustice and sin, will not be eradicated from the world; but the fear of modern civilization is a terror peculiarly hideous. What is to be done? "It looks as if, first of all, we needed somehow or other to get the fear of God back into society."[13]

This said, Paul Elmer More turned to the second great phase of his contribution to American philosophy and letters, that study of Platonism and Christianity he called *The Greek Tradition*. In *Platonism* (1928) and in *The Religion of Plato* (1921), he analyzed Platonic dualism, with its distinct realms of idea and matter, recognizing in the constitution of man the existence of a power beyond himself. More traced the revolt of Stoic and Epicurean monistic systems against this dualism in *Hellenistic Philosophies* (1921). Next, in *The Christ of the New Testament*, he wrote the greatest American work of Christian apologetics, assailing the modernists with all the weight of his erudition and all the majesty of his style. Belief in the Incarnation is in conformity to reason: for the supernatural, if it is to be apprehended clearly by man, must make itself felt in natural forms; and historical evidences for the powers of Christ carry overwhelming conviction. "At least of Christianity, whatever may be said of other forms of faith," he wrote later, in *The Catholic Faith*, "one thing is certain, that it depends upon revelation, that without revelation the belief of the Christian is a baseless assumption.[14] With *Christ the Word* (1927), More completed his vindication of orthodoxy; and though these books cannot be properly discussed here, they dealt a most serious blow to the theological modernism of the twentieth century, establishing strongly that premise of metaphysical dualism upon which More's critical and social ideas were built. An heir to the Puritan mind, More had perceived that Puritanism, with all its dogged power, still remained only a courageous negation; and he returned to an affirmation as bold in the twentieth century as Puritanical dissent had been in the seventeenth.

"The *Shelburne Essays* and the five volumes of *The Greek Tradition*," Walter Lippmann once wrote,

> are more than the monumental work of a literary critic. They are a record of continuous religious discovery within a nature that combines in exquisite proportions a delicate sensibility with a hard-headed instinct for reality. It makes no particular difference whether one agrees with all his particular judgements; to read him is to enter an austere and elevated realm of ideas and to know a man who, in the guise of a critic, is authentically concerned with the first and last things of human experience.[15]

Nothing else in American letters, for union of constancy with power of execution, equals More's intricate countermine to radical naturalism in philosophy and radical humanitarianism in social controversy. More resolved to counteract the influence of men like John Dewey, "with a precious panacea for the calamities of history," infatuated of neoterism, the itch for change; and certainly the pragmatists seem unhappily simple by the side of More. For him, sin and redemption, justice and grace, were realities which the naturalists can ignore only at the cost of brutalizing society; and, after eight decades of controversy, the tide appears to be turning slowly in More's favor.

He knew that a high conservatism requires imagination; he knew that it requires something even rarer and nobler, consecration. "It is true that religion, or religious philosophy, as its friends and foes have seen from the beginning, is an alleviator of discontent and a brake upon innovation," More said in 1921; "but the content it offers from the world of immaterial values is a necessary counterpoise to the mutual envy and materialistic greed of the natural man, and the conservatism it inculcates is not the ally of sullen and predatory privilege but of orderly amelioration."[16] These are the sentiments of a reactionary philosopher who dignified reaction, who reminded a hurrying generation that the American and the English and the Christian and the Greek pasts are not dead, and that the stream of being in which the pragmatists splash may be tumbling down to a Dead Sea. Between the pessimism of Henry Adams and the strong faith of More is a chasm, and its presence suggests that both the deterministic theories of the Adams brothers and the naturalistic confidence of Positivism in "some far-off divine event" may retreat before a revived theism. With Babbitt and More, American conservative ideas experienced a reinvigoration attesting the coquetry of History and the mystery of Providence.

["Paul Elmer More on Justice and Faith," The Conservative Mind: From Burke to Eliot, *7th rev. ed. (Washington, DC: Regnery Publishing, Inc., 1986, c1953), 432–43. This selection is from Chapter 12, Section 3.]*

❖

George Santayana Buries Liberalism

George Santayana (1863–1952), the Spanish-born American philosopher, is for Kirk representative of "the American conservative impulse after 1918." Utilitarian utopianism and liberal doctrines, Santayana insisted, subordinate individuality to the forces of efficiency and uniformity, and push Americans towards an industrial socialistic future and the tyranny of the majority. Kirk quotes this sentence from Dominations and Powers *(1951) as an example of Santayana's prophetic recognition of "the turbid confusion of American society": "'If one political tendency kindled my wrath, it was precisely the tendency of industrial liberalism to level down all civilizations to a single cheap and dreary pattern.'" Such a liberalism produces an "empty atomic individuality" and places character and tradition at the mercy of social reformers. Santayana spent his last years in a Catholic convent in Rome. Here, Kirk observes, he "wrote on, nobly sane in a generation of frenzy; and surely the civilization which possessed a Santayana retains some chance for regeneration."*

He feared me," George Santayana writes of his friend Andrew Green. "I was a Mephistopheles masquerading as a conservative. I defended the past because once it had been victorious and had brought something beautiful to light; but I had no clear expectation of better things in the future. He saw looming behind me the dreadful spectres of death and of truth."[17] Like Green, the educated public of America often has been charmed and perturbed simultaneously by the dispassionate and versatile Santayana—who, though exerting so strong an influence upon American thought, rarely confessed himself to be an American; forty years of American association were insufficient to wash away the Spanish birth he cherished and the cosmopolitan position—a blend of aesthetic Catholicism with skepticism—from which he viewed American and English ideas with a quizzical urbanity. In that amusing, discursive, and melancholy novel *The Last Puritan* (1935), one perceives how deeply he penetrated into Anglo-American character and institutions, and how he never really was assimilated to them. As a conservative thinker, he has illuminated British and American society with an exotic light; yet his discipline was English and New English; Burke, for instance, strides through Santayana's books (*Winds of Doctrine* [1926] being a title extracted from Burke and St. Paul), and even the Genteel Tradition of New England letters which Santayana dissected was woven into his education. If not part of American society, still he was inside that society in a way Tocqueville never could attain.

After the theistic humanism of Babbitt and More, the materialism of Santayana may seem a weakening of the conservative fibre, a postscript to Henry Adams. Yet Santayana's metaphysics, though at odds with dualism, repudiates the common sort of mechanism, exposes the egoism of the Idealists, and, with a good-natured nudge, consigns James's pragmatism to the nursery. "The intellectual world of my time alienated me intellectually. It was a Babel of false principles and blind cravings, a zoological garden of the mind, and I had no desire to be one of the beasts."[18] Something Hellenistic suffuses the thought of Santayana, who agrees with Plato that only the knowledge of ideas can be literal and exact, while practical knowledge necessarily is mythical in form; but, like the Hellenistic moralists, he cannot accept a thoroughgoing dualism.

> To double the world would unspiritualize the spiritual sphere; to double the truth would make both truths halting and false. There is one only world, the natural world, and only one truth about it; but this world has a spiritual life possible in it, which looks not to another world but to the beauty and perfection that this world suggests, approaches, and misses.[19]

Spirit lives only through matter; divine purpose, which we delineate in our myths, is real, but manifested only in natural ways; nothing is immortal, not even the forms of beauty to which Santayana's books are devoted. His naturalism is not irreligious, he says; religion and the poetry of mythology are not mere childish science, but endure as "subtle creations of hope, tenderness, and ignorance," true in a lofty sense which grubby isolated facts never can attain; Christianity, productive of so much virtue and beauty, has no enemy in him. But he cannot subscribe with his reason to these venerable orthodoxies. All things perish, the most ancient opinions among them, and the philosopher will smile tolerantly at progress and decay, content with the immense variety of character and phenomena. If this cosmic urbanity diminishes Santayana's consistency and his will, still only an heroic thinker can resign himself cheerfully to contemplation of the flux, too terrible even for Heraclitus or Empedocles. Often the imperturbable Santayana, in Boston, Berlin, London, Avila, or Rome, is very like Stilbo (described by Seneca), tranquil amid the sack of Megara, indifferent to catastrophe, indifferent to the conquering Demetrius who, enthroned, wonders at the philosopher. What has he lost? Goods, daughters, his house? All these are nothing, only "the adventitious things that follow the beck of fortune"; permanence is nothing; he retains his self, and all the consolations of natural beauties and mysteries.

Such grand placidity colors Santayana's social thought.

> For myself, even if I could live to see it, I should not be afraid of the future domination, whatever it may be. One has to live in some age, under some fashion; I have found, in different times and places, the liberal, the Catholic, and the German air quite possible to breathe; nor, I am sure, would communism be without its advantages to a free mind, and its splendid emotions. Fanatics, as Tacitus said of the Jews or Christians, are consumed with hatred of the human race, which offends them; yet they are themselves human; and nature in them takes its revenge, and something reasonable and sweet bubbles up out of the very fountain of their madness.[20]

Beneath this generous tolerance, however, Santayana adheres to a firm and haughty standard for judging dominations and powers: a good society is beautiful, a bad society ugly. Upon this ground, he builds his conservatism and his condemnation of the direction modern life has taken.

In the course of a conversation with John D. Rockefeller, Santayana mentioned Spain's population; and the millionaire, after a pause, murmured, "I must tell them at the office that they don't sell enough oil in Spain." Here in one sentence leered the ugliness and barrenness of the modern age. "I saw in my mind's eye," adds Santayana, "the ideal of the monopolist. All nations must consume the same things, in proportion to their population. All mankind will then form a perfect democracy, supplied with rations from a single centre of administration, as is for their benefit; since they will then secure everything assigned to them at the lowest possible price."[21] This utilitarian utopia, prophesied by Henry and Brooks Adams as the triumph of the cheapest, starves the realm of spirit and the realm of art as no other domination can. The culmination of liberalism, the fulfillment of the aspirations of Bentham and Mill, and of the French and American democratic spokesmen, it is also the completion of capitalism. It is communism. Rockefeller and Marx were merely two agents of the same social force—an appetite cruelly inimical to human individuation, by which man has struggled up to reason and art.

Through half a century, from his early *Reason in Society* (1905) to his late *Dominations and Powers* (1951), Santayana was consistently contemptuous of the innovation which despoils the world in the name of efficiency and uniformity, consistently quick to defend the conservation of social harmony and tradition. "A reformer hewing so near to the tree's root never knows how much he may be felling," he wrote in 1905. "Possibly his own ideal would lose its secret support if what it condemns had wholly disappeared." Individualism is the only ideal possible; and if individuals are subordinated to the state, it is only that they may fulfill their devotion to things rational and impersonal, a higher individualism. For a time, democracy and individualism exhibit a parallel growth; but presently democratic legislation presumes to regulate all things, and industrial liberalism, supported by democracy, aspires to replace individuality by efficient standardization; thus the man who loves beauty and variety will endeavor (like Socrates in *Dialogues in Limbo*) to puncture the bubbles of social planners who have forgotten the real aim of society, the life of mind and art.

"It is unfortunate to have been born at a time when the force of human character was ebbing, when the tide of material activity and material knowledge was rising so high as to drown all moral independence," says Peter Alden in *The Last Puritan*. This ebbing of real humanity has been accelerated by the whole "liberal" movement, Santayana wrote in 1926: "That comfortable liberal world was like a great tree with the trunk already sawed quite through, but still standing with all its leaves quietly rustling, and with us dozing under its shade. We were inexpressibly surprised when it fell and half crushed us; some of us are talking of setting it up again safely on its severed roots."[22] But the shell of Christendom has been broken, and a new spirit, that of emancipated, atheistic, international democracy, is dragging us toward an industrial socialistic future. Liberalism, once professing to advocate liberty, now is a movement for control over property, trade, work, amusements, education, and religion; only the marriage bond is relaxed by modern liberals. "The philanthropists are now preparing an absolute subjection of the individual, in soul and body, to the instincts of the majority—the most cruel and unprogressive of masters; and I am not sure that the liberal maxim, 'the greatest happiness of the greatest number,' has not lost whatever was just or generous in its intent and come to mean the greatest idleness of the largest possible population."

This is no perversion of liberalism, but simply its natural progression. Liberalism (fortunately) has been always a secondary state, living like a saprophyte on the tissue of the previous age, inheriting its monuments, feelings, and social hierarchy. "Liberalism does not go very deep; it is an adventitious principle, a mere loosening of an older structure."[23] Manifestly, in our time, it is simply a transition from Christendom, aristocracy, and family economy to an overwhelming utilitarian collectivism. By the horrors of competition and the trial of war have the liberals been discredited. Santayana's essay "The Irony of Liberalism," included in *Soliloquies in England* (1922), is a funeral sermon over the aspirations of Bentham and Cobden and J. S. Mill. Modern liberalism—though the ancients knew better—wanted to enjoy both liberty and prosperity simultaneously. Prosperity involving subjection to things, however; soon it appears that the real love of the liberals is not for liberty, but for progress; and by "progress" the liberals mean expansion. "If you refuse to move in the prescribed direction, you are not simply different, you are arrested and perverse. The savage must not remain a savage, nor the nun a nun, and China must not keep its wall." Tradition is suspect to the liberal; he insists upon reform, revision, restatement: "A man without traditions, if he could only be materially well equipped, would be purer, more rational, more virtuous than if he had been an heir to anything. *Weh dir, dass du ein Enkel bist!* Blessed are the orphans, for they shall deserve to have children; blessed the American!" But logically, the application of liberal doctrines would lead to a Nietzschean world, if anywhere, and no one who has tasted the actual liberal system seems to like it; for if it represses its Nietzschean squint, it turns out dismally hollow. Even for the rich, a liberal system is an agony of doubt and hesitation. "I find no sense of moral security among them, no happy freedom, no mastery over anything. Yet this is the very cream of liberal life, the brilliant success for the sake of which Christendom was overturned, and the dull peasantry elevated into factory-hands, shopkeepers, and chauffeurs."

When the aim of life is to imitate the rich, and "opportunity" is made generally available, general discouragement is the consequence. No paradox, this: the average man, formerly content in his special craft or his old simplicities, is hopelessly out of the running in the race for wealth, and exhausts himself very early, and lingers on only in boredom. Despite its pretenses, the liberal system has degraded the masses. The mediocre man "then becomes a denizen of those slimy quarters, under the shadow of railway bridges, breweries, and gasworks, where the blear lights of a public house peer through the rain at every corner, and offer him the one joy remaining in life." Nominally literate, this populace is manipulated by the press, dosed with every variety of superstition, bullied by the advertiser and the propagandist. "Liberalism has merely cleared a field in which every soul and every corporate interest may fight with every other for domination. Whoever is victorious in this struggle will make an end of liberalism; and the new order, which will deem itself saved, will have to defend itself in the following age against a new crop of rebels." The present-day liberal, become an advocate of the tyranny of the state in every field, offers as an apology his intention of freeing the people. "But of freeing the people from what? From the consequences of freedom."

In the preface to *Dominations and Powers*, Santayana wrote from his Roman convent, "If one political tendency kindled my wrath, it was precisely the tendency of industrial liberalism to level down all civilizations to a single cheap and dreary pattern." Even material well-being, in the long run, is jeopardized by material development of this description; the best we can hope for is a gradual slackening of economic pace. An empty atomic individuality replaces real individual character: "When all are uniform the individuality of each unit is numerical only." Men have then indeed become Burke's flies of a summer. In this ponderous organized blindness, chivalry (which Santayana praises nearly in the tone of Burke) is dead, supplanted by a cringing anxiety to be safe. The banners of liberalism are snatched by the communists, for the liberals have failed in both their aspirations, material comfort and moral liberty. Liberalism

> had enabled mankind to grow far more numerous and more exacting in its standard of living; it had multiplied instruments for saving time and labour; but paradoxically had rendered life more hurried than ever before and labour more monotonous and in itself less rewarding. The people had been freed politically and nominally by being given the vote, and enslaved economically in being herded in droves under anonymous employers and self-imposing labour leaders. Meanwhile the liberal rich, who had expected to grow richer and did so when individually enterprising, became poorer and idler as a class, and more obviously withdrawn from the aristocratic leisure,

> sports, and benevolent social and intellectual leadership which they had supposed themselves fitted for. Nothing was rationalized by the liberal régime except the mechanism of production. Society meantime had been unhinged, and rendered desperate, and governments had been either incapacitated by intellectual impotence or turned into party tyrannies.[24]

Acting under the illusion that graceful yielding would ensure general peace, the liberals relaxed the traditional order. "When we have conceded everything that anybody clamours for," they thought, "everyone will be satisfied; and then if any picturesque remnant of the traditional order is left standing, we shall at last be able to enjoy it safely and with a good conscience." But the liberal's dearest friend and ally, the reformer, had a Will of his own to satisfy, a secret and consuming intolerance of the old order or anything out of harmony with his own ingenious schemes. While any opposition exists to the consummation of his ego, he will allow no peace in society. And can that ego ever rest? The first half of the twentieth century has shown the liberals that their own wealth, taste, and intellectual liberty are intended to vanish in the next reformation. "The concupiscence of the flesh, the concupiscence of the eyes, and the pride of life exhaust and kill the sweets they feed upon; and a lava-wave of primitive blindness and violence must perhaps rise from below to lay the foundations for something differently human and similarly transient."

The conceit of the present generation of reformers is the "freedom" of uniformity, Russian style or American style, in which man feels himself content because personal opinion is eradicated and he knows no other condition. Whether educated "to be like Stalin" or to "adjust to the group" after the notion of John Dewey, the tendency of these gigantic states is toward a sheep-population, though achieved in Russia by harsh compulsion, in America by contagion and attraction. A militant demand for unanimity leads to a society hypnotized by the statistical psychologist, the strings and wires of the human psyche in his hands, and he commissioned to pull them. His subjects are the proletariat, "an ugly modern word for an ugly thing," a vast crowd of exiles in their own country, who have nothing in common but the mere physical and vital powers of man, whatever traces of civilization linger among them rapidly dying in their nondescript and unsettled society. They have no art, no religion, no friends, no prospects; work for them is an evil, so that their chief effort is to diminish work and increase wages. This endeavor failing in the long run (for they multiply like wild animals), proletarians become equal in one thing, certainly: in their misery. How long can an elite of administrators and statisticians, themselves starved of imagination by an education grossly acquisitive and presumptuous, hold together such a society? Santayana hints at some hope for converting this body of administrators into a timocracy; but, neglecting the means, he slips rapidly into another topic.

The schoolmaster Cyrus P. Whittle, in *The Last Puritan*, is a type of the bitter reforming zealot who is bringing this proletarian planners' society closer. His joy is to vilify all distinguished men; but he has his secret devotion, his species of religion.

> Not only was America the biggest thing on earth, but it was soon going to wipe out everything else; and in the delirious dazzling joy of that consummation, he forgot to ask what would happen afterwards. He gloried in the momentum of sheer process, in the mounting wave of events; but minds and their purposes were only the foam of the breaking crest; and he took an ironical pleasure in showing how all that happened, and was credited to the efforts of great and good men, really happened against their will and expectation.

Affection and dread run mingled through Santayana's analysis of America, especially in *Character and Opinion in the United States* (1920). A new type of American, foreign to the sour uprightness of the old Yankee, has made his appearance—"the untrained, pushing, cosmopolitan orphan, cock-sure in manner but not too sure in his morality." Social radicalism is in the American's blood, although because of his individualism and rough comradeship, "it will take some hammering to drive a coddling socialism into America." The American's preoccupation with quantitative standards, his insistence upon conformity, are ominous for the future. "America is all one prairie, swept by a universal tornado. Although it has always thought itself in an eminent sense the land of freedom, even when it was covered with slaves, there is no country in which people live under more overpowering compulsions." Is civilization indeed to be remoulded by this overweeningly confident nation, the Cyrus P. Whittles bringing down everything not incontestably American?

The tradition of English and American liberties (which are a world away from "absolute liberty") now struggles against "an international democracy of the disinherited many, led by the disinherited few," that "would abolish those private interests which are the factors in any cooperation, and would reduce everybody to forced membership and forced service in one universal flock, without property, family, country, or religion."[25] A society led by "Niebelungen who toil underground over a gold they will never use," creatures of the narrow utilitarianism that liberals approved, threatens to make proletarianism universal. Occidental civilization has abused the whole concept of production, complicating life without ennobling the mind; and this is especially true in America. Materialism, confused with tradition, is turned into a sort of religion, and more and more America inclines toward a universal crusade on behalf of this credo of mechanized production and mass consumption. Americans seldom perceive the terror just underfoot: "A barbaric civilization, built on blind impulse and ambition, should fear to awaken a deeper detestation than could ever be aroused by those more beautiful tyrannies, chivalrous or religious, against which past revolutions have been directed."[26]

What hope remains for saving the life of reason and the tradition of liberties? Santayana, who is inclined to believe that material forces are the real agent in historical change, reproves our "attributing events to the conscious ideals and free will of individuals."[27] Yet it is not always futile to defy the times: when Charles I had the choice of dying as a traitor for resisting the apparent will of his people, or of leading them to their moral ruin, his sacrifice did achieve its aim in part, sheltering the deep roots of Church and monarchy, preserving a refinement in English life and feeling.[28] The lover of reason and beauty will contend against a brutal mechanized monotony with all his powers; and conceivably he may so modify any domination that in some measure nobility of mind will endure under the yoke.

Santayana left America in 1912; he abandoned London and Oxford, too, after some years, withdrawing from this vertiginous world, a very old man, to that most conservative of all places, Rome: Rome, where nothing dies but of extreme caducity, where Nero's ghost, metamorphosed to a monstrous crow, roosted on a bough for a millennium, and where the last of the Stuarts languishes in Canova's marble under the dome of St. Peter's. There the agony of a blind society, burning in its own furnaces, pursued him, so that St. Benedict's abbey upon Monte Cassino was smashed to powder while he wrote in his cloister, and Nuremburg, the great medieval center of craftsmanship, was erased by modern techniques. He wrote on, nobly sane in a generation of frenzy; and surely the civilization which possessed a Santayana retains some chance for regeneration.

["George Santayana Buries Liberalism," The Conservative Mind: From Burke to Eliot, *7th rev. ed. (Washington, DC: Regnery Publishing, Inc., 1986, c1953), 443–52. This selection is from Chapter 12, Section 4.]*

The Humane Economy of Wilhelm Röpke

Wilhelm Röpke (1899–1966), a much-respected social thinker and architect of Germany's economic recovery after World War II, was admired by Kirk as an economist and a friend. German by birth, he had settled in Switzerland during the war years, serving as professor of economics at the University of Geneva's Graduate Institute of International Affairs. He strongly opposed both Nazism and communism. In his books Röpke was critical of both socialist economic theories and "unthinking" capitalism; humanizing modern industrial political economy became his central aim. Big government, bureaucracy, collectivism, monopolization, and, above all, proletarianization constituted, in Röpke's eyes, economic maladies that take us "along the wrong road." Kirk goes on to caution that "unless we begin to think of humanizing our American economy, our cities will continue to disintegrate, and the American people increasingly will grow bored and violent"—precisely the symptoms and the consequences of what Röpke saw as a political economy that lacked an ethical base.

Permit me to offer you some observations concerning Wilhelm Röpke, a principal social thinker of the twentieth century—and, incidentally, the principal architect of Germany's economic recovery at the end of the Second World War. His books are out of print in this country at present, except for *The Social Crisis of Our Time* (1950), of which I brought out a new edition recently. And to my remarks on Professor Röpke I shall add certain related reflections of my own.

Röpke was the confident champion of a humane economy: that is, an economic system suited to human nature and to a humane scale in society, as opposed to systems bent upon mass production regardless of counterproductive personal and social consequences. He was a formidable opponent of socialist and other "command" economies; also a fearless perceptive critic of an unthinking "capitalism." Although German by birth, during the Second World War Roepke settled in Geneva, where he became professor of economics at the Graduate Institute of International Affairs. There he wrote *Civitas Humana* (1944); *The Social Crisis of Our Time* (1950); *Economics of the Free Society* (1942); *The Solution of the German Problem* (1937); the essays included in the volumes *Against the Tide* (1947); and *Welfare, Freedom, and Inflation* (1957). The title of his last book published in America, *A Humane Economy* (1960), was suggested by me.

A gentleman of high courage and a sincere Christian, Röpke set his face against both the Nazis and the Communists. He was intellectually and physically vigorous: an accomplished skier, he always climbed back up the mountainside, rather than riding a chair-lift. Knowing that man is more than producer and consumer, Röpke detested Jeremy Bentham's Utilitarianism, and found that most of his fellow-economists perceived human existence very imperfectly, being blinkered by utilitarian dogmata.

Before turning to Röpke's arguments, I venture to offer some background of his thought, during the disorderly period that followed upon the Second World War, a time during which the idea of grand-scale social planning exercised a malign power. Roepke was the most effective opponent of that *Planwirtschaft*.

That highly speculative division of knowledge which our age calls "economics" took shape in the eighteenth century as an instrument for attaining individual freedom, as well as increased efficiency of production. But many twentieth-century teachers and speciaists in economics became converts to a neo-Jacobinism. (Burke defines Jacobinism as "the revolt of the enterprising talents of a nation against its property.") Such doctrines of confidence in the omnicompetence of the state in economic concerns came to predominate in state polytechnic institutes and state universities especially. Quite as eighteenth-century optimism, materialism, and humanitarianism were fitted by Marx into a system which might have surprised a good many of the *philosophes*, so nineteenth-century utilitarian and Manchesterian concepts were the ancestors (perhaps with a bend sinister) of mechanistic social planning. The old Jacobins scarcely realized that their centralizing tendencies were imitative of the policies of the Old Regime; so it is not surprising that recent humanitarian and collectivistic thinkers forget their debt to Jeremy Bentham. Yet the abstractions of Bentham, reducing human beings to social atoms, are the principal source of modern designs for social alteration by fiat.

At the end of the Second World War, centralizers and coercive planners were mightily influential in western Europe and in Britain, and were not missing in the United States. The modern nation-state enjoys effective powers of coercion previously unknown in political structures. But the increase of coercion frustrates the natural course of development; economic theory as a basis for state coercion has repeatedly proved fallible; "planning" destroys the voluntary community and tries to substitute an ineffectual master plan (as, most ruinously, in Iran under the Shah); the goals of state action should be judicial rather than economic; and thus the whole perspective of "social planners" is distorted. In opposition to the dominant school of economic theory just after the Second World War, such economists as Röpke, W. A. Orton, F. A. Hayek, and a handful of others strove to restrain the economic collectivists.

Although he proved himself very competent to deal with the vast post-war economic difficulties of Germany, a major industrial country, nevertheless Roepke much preferred the social and economic patterns of Switzerland, where he lived from the triumph of Hitler until the end of his life. His model for an humane economy can be perceived by an observant traveller in Switzerland.

❖

Professor Röpke seemed to have read everything. He was familiar, for instance, with the social ideas of Calhoun and Fenimore Cooper, concerning which most American professors of economics are densely ignorant. Wilhelm Roepke knew the insights of religion and poetry, the problems of continuity and morality. His book *The Social Crisis of Our Time* is at heart an analysis of the menace that Röpke called "the cult of the colossal." Social equilibrium has been overthrown in our age, Röpke knew. Here are some moving sentences of his concerning that grim subject:

> Men, having to a great extent lost the use of their innate sense of proportion, thus stagger from one extreme to the other, now trying out this, now that, now following this fashionable belief, now that, responding now to this external attraction, now to the other, but listening least of all to the voice of their own heart. It is particularly characteristic of the general loss of a natural sense of direction—a loss which is jeopardizing the wisdom gained through countless centuries—that the age of immaturity, of restless experiment, of youth, has in our time become the object of the most preposterous overestimation.

Of all our afflictions, Röpke continues, the fruits of moral decay, of consolidation, and of the worship of bigness, the worst is proletarianization. Capitalism may have introduced the modern proletariat, but socialism enlarges that class to include nearly the whole of humanity. Our salvation, Röpke argues, lies in a third choice, something different from either ideological socialism or doctrinaire capitalism.

"Socialism, collectivism, and their political and cultural appendages are, after all, only the last consequence of our yesterday; they are the last convulsions of the nineteenth century and only in them do we reach the lowest point of a century-old development along the wrong road; these are the hopeless final state toward which we drift unless we act," Röpke writes. "The new path is precisely the one that will lead us out of the dilemma of 'capitalism' and collectivism. It consists of the economic humanism of the 'Third Way.'"

That same infatuation with "rationalism" which terribly damages communal existence also produces an unquestioning confidence in the competitive market economy and leads to a heartless individualism which, in Röpke's words, "in the end has proved to be a menace to society and has so discredited a fundamentally sound idea as to further the rise of the far more dangerous collectivism." In such a world, where old landmarks have been swept away, old loyalties ridiculed, and human beings reduced to economic atoms, "men finally grasp at everything that is offered to them, and here they may easily and understandably suffer the same fate as the frogs in the fable who asked for a king and got a crane."

In his chapter "The Splendor and Misery of Capitalism," Röpke examines succinctly the maladies of our present economy and observes that the same economic disharmonies become chronic under socialism. Then he turns to the second part of *The Social Crisis of Our Time*, entitled "Action."

"Socialism—helped by the uprooted proletarian existence of large numbers of the working class and made palatable for them by just as rootless intellectuals, who will have to bear the responsibility for this—is less concerned with the interests of these masses than with the interests of those intellectuals, who may indeed see their desire for an abundant choice of positions of power fulfilled by the socialist state," Röpke instructs us.

Röpke relishes this class of persons as masters of society even less than he does the monopolists and the managers. His object is to restore liberty to men by promoting economic independence. The best type of peasants, artisans, small traders, small and medium-sized businessmen, members of the free professions and trusty officials and servants of the community—these are the objects of his solicitude, for among them traditional human nature still has its healthiest roots, and throughout most of the world they are being ground between "capitalistic" specialization and "socialistic" consolidation. They need not vanish from society; once more they may constitute the masters of society; for Switzerland, in any case, "refutes by its mere existence any cynical doubt regarding the possibility of realizing our program."

Loathing "doctrinaire rationalism," Röpke is careful not to propound an arbitrary scheme of alteration and renovation. Yet his suggestions for deproletarianizing are forthright. Family farms, farmers' cooperatives for marketing, encouragement of artisans and small traders, the technical and administrative possibilities of industrial decentralization, the diminution of the average size of factories, the gradual substitution for the "old-style welfare policy" of an intelligent trend toward self-sufficiency—none of these projects is novel, but they are commended by an economist possessing both grand reputation and sound common sense. To cushion society against the fluctuations of the business cycle, for instance, the better remedy is not increased centralization, a most dubious palliative, but instead the stimulating of men to get a part of their sustenance from outside the immediate realm of financial disturbance. Specialization often works mischief, he says:

"The most extreme examples of this tendency are perhaps some American farmers who had become so specialized and so dependent on their current money incomes that when the crisis came they were as near starvation as the industrial worker. At the other, more fortunate end we see the industrial worker in Switzerland who, if necessary, can find his lunch in the garden, his supper in the lake, and can earn his potato supply in the fall by helping his brother clear his land." Humanizing of economic structure was the kernel of Röpke's proposals. For him, political economy had an ethical foundation.

Röpke was no apologist for an abstraction called "capitalism"—a Marxist term, incidentally, foolishly pinned to themselves by numerous vainglorious champions of economic competition. He knew that the worship of Mammon is damnable.

He spoke always of the human condition, and how we might win our way back to a humane economy. Three decades after Röpke's death, we have lost ground in that endeavor. Washington, London, Tokyo, and Moscow are even more obsessed by the Gross National Product than they were in the fifties, although the paper statistics of the GNP have not produced stability or contentment, and the terrorist walks abroad. There comes to mind the legend inscribed on a chateau's sundial, in 1789: "It is later than you think." The nexus of cash payment, never a strong social link, does not suffice to keep down fanatic ideology, nor even to assure prosperity.

❖

An economy obsessed by an alleged Gross National Product—no matter what is produced, or how—becomes inhumane. A society that thinks only of alleged Efficiency, regardless the consequences to human beings, works its own ruin. Here there comes to my mind a passage from the writings of W. A. Orton, an American conservative economist, a contemporary of Röpke. In his book *The Economic Role of the State* (1950), Orton ironically describes the cult of Efficiency:

"Let us therefore praise the great god Efficiency," Orton writes.

> All he demands is that we make straight his path through the desert and purge the opposition. . . . How much more mastery is evident in the controls of a supersonic plane than in the clumsy splendor of some medieval shrine! How much higher a peak of human achievement! Human? Let us not be too particular about that, for this is where science plays the joker. . . . We arrive at "justice" without mercy, "liberation" without liberty, "victory" without peace, "efficiency" without effort, "power" without potency—because the means we collectively employ lie on a plane so different from that of the ends we humanly desire that, the more they succeed, the more they fail. That is the nemesis of all "great powers" and the end of all who put their trust in them. God knows, this is not a new story.

Detroit, the city I have known best, has worshipped the great god Efficiency. During my own lifetime, Detroit has produced tremendous wealth in goods and services. But the city has been a social failure, and so have most of America's other cities. Once called "the arsenal of democracy," nowadays Detroit, become ruinous and ungovernable, more frequently has been referred to as "the murder capital of America." In Celine's famous novel *Journey to the End of Night* (1934), the journey terminates at Detroit.

In the shocking decay of that great city, one beholds the consequences of an inhumane economy—bent upon maximum productive efficiency, but heedless of personal order and public order. Of course the automobile manufacturers of Detroit, in the early years of their operation, had no notion of what might be the personal and social effects of their highly successful industrial establishment; nor had anyone else. But they seem still to be ignorant of such unhappy consequences, or else indifferent to the consequences, so long as profits continue to be made. . . .

My argument is this: unless we begin to think of humanizing our American economy, our cities will continue to disintegrate, and the American people increasingly will grow bored and violent. Some folk in authority are beginning to apprehend that human nature may revolt at having an inhumane scale thrust upon mankind. The failure of high-rise public housing, in city after city, is an illustration of this hard truth. In Newark, New Jersey—a city worse decayed than Detroit, if that be conceivable—the Scudder Homes, a monolith of "housing" thirteen stories high, was demolished by high explosives, life having become intolerable there for the low-income tenants. Town-houses of two or three stories are being built as replacement: a healthy reaction against public housing's anonymous collectivism. New Jersey's manager of the federal Department of Housing and Urban Development, just before the destruction of Scudder Homes, delivered a public address. In his words, "Sophocles said, 'Though a man be wise, it is no shame for him to live and learn.' It is no shame for us to learn from this experience."

Is it so difficult, after all, to convince Americans that simplicity may be preferable to complexity, modest contentment to unrestrained sensation, decent frugality to torpid satiety? If material aggrandizement is the chief object of a people, there remains no moral check upon the means employed to acquire wealth: violence and fraud become common practices. And presently the material production of such a society commences to decline, from causes too obvious for digression here. Our industrial economy, of all economic systems man ever created, is the most delicately dependent upon public energy, private virtue, fertility of imagination. If we continue to fancy that Efficiency and Affluence are the chief aims of human existence, presently we must find ourselves remarkably unprosperous—and wondrously miserable.

Röpke, Orton, Colin Clark, and a few other political economists have been so instructing us for the past half-century. President Bush spoke of bringing about "a kinder, gentler America." That consummation, so much to be desired, requires the humane imagination. And study of the thought of Wilhelm Röpke may nurture that imagination.

["The Humane Economy of Wilhelm Röpke," The Politics of Prudence, *1st ed. (Bryn Mawr, PA: Intercollegiate Studies Institute, 1993), 114–24.]*

❖

Max Picard: A Man of Vision in Our Time

Max Picard (1888–1965), who came from a Jewish-Swiss family, was born in Schopfheim, in the Grand Duchy of Baden. Abandoning a promising medical career because he found the profession mechanical and positivistic, he turned to philosophy and religious studies, and eventually became a Roman Catholic. In the early 1920s he settled in southern Switzerland and lived in a little Alpine chalet overlooking Lake Lugano. Here he wrote such books as Hitler in Our Selves *(1948),* The Flight from God *(1951),* The World of Silence *(1952), and* Man and Language *(1963). Kirk praises Picard as a seer, a sage, a "eulogist of silent dignity," and a critic of the errors of modernity: discontinuity, fragmentation, disorder, "verbal noise." He devoted himself "to the contemplation of divine wisdom" and to a life of piety. At the end, Kirk writes, "in a hospital bed, Picard was penniless. But the trace of God's smile did not depart from him."*

Max Picard's World of Silence

Not all minds are captive. The service of God being perfect freedom, the philosopher and the writer who do not live under totalist dominations, and who do not shut their eyes to a reality which transcends the ordinary senses, are able to enjoy even in our century a liberty far removed from license. I have known some such men of letters and thought; and one of the wiser among them was Max Picard.

He was such a man of vision—a seer, a sage—as perceives the permanent things with a clarity unknown to most of us. With wonderful simplicity, Picard—who was born a Jew, became a Christian, and on his deathbed returned to the faith of his fathers—wrote of our blindness in the modern era; and hope never forsook him, and abnormality never touched him. A few more Picards, and twentieth-century letters would be redeemed.

Cribbed in institutions, battening on linguistic analysis, twentieth-century philosophy—which, today, might better be called philodoxy—seems afflicted with a death-wish. Logical positivism, dominant in American and British universities, is suicidally bent upon establishing the impossibility of knowing anything. (As Wyndham Lewis suggested in *Self Condemned* [1954], the neo-positivist pedant reduces himself to a mosquito, able to wound, nearly invulnerable to counter-assault—but only an insect, not a man.)

Much as the red squirrel retreats before the merciless gray squirrel, so the philosopher, lover of wisdom, has retired from the stricken field; today we know the conquering philodoxer, the lover of opinion or arid doctrine. The sage has succumbed to the ideologue or the "scientific" nihilist. Yet here or there endures a wise man of the stamp of Pascal or Samuel Johnson, abiding in a tradition, still employing the power of the Word to scourge the follies of the time. Such a man was Max Picard, who lived upon a mountain high above Lugano. There in his Ticino village he was nearly as poor in the world's goods as Diogenes, but a better man and a happier man than Diogenes.

In his devotion to the poetic and the intuitive as paths to wisdom, Picard was almost a pre-Socratic. His books are slim, evocative, and unforgettable. Several of them have been done into English: *The Flight from God* (1951), *The World of Silence* (1952), *Man and Language (1963), Hitler in Our Selves* (1947), *The Disintegration of Forms in Modern Art* (1954), *The Atomizing of the Person* (1958). Picard set his face not only against logical positivism, but against pragmatism, rationalism, and skepticism. Though his every reflection has for its premise the existence of God and a transcendent order, in his temper and style one encounters no suggestion of neo-Thomism. His simplicity and directness, studded with aphorisms, make him one of the few recent writers on first principles who may be read with pleasure and quick apprehension. Yet Picard never beckoned to the vulgar.

He was a hard hater of noise and an ardent lover of silence. But noise, with a diabolical power, followed Picard up from modernity, even to his little Alpine chalet. For the automobile, that mechanical Jacobin, now pants its way up the wooded slopes of the mountains; and trucks shift gears ferociously as they round the bends of the road across the valley from Picard's house, their squeal and screech and grate echoing to the cool terrace where he used to sit. As Picard wrote, modern noise was bent upon the utter conquest of silence in all its forms—the silence which has nurtured contemplation, and even the silence of God.

As eulogist of silent dignity, Picard admired old Spain. In his chapter "History and Silence," in *The World of Silence*, one finds this passage:

> There are nations that seem to slumber in silence for long centuries: such are the Spaniards during the last three centuries. The silence in which they live is not an emptiness, nor is it a symptom of sterility. It is rather a sign of the importance and value of silence for the Spaniards. Spain has been con-

> sidered backward and old-fashioned because it did not join in the universal noise and mobility of the modern age by industrializing its economy. But Spain is no more backward than a child that wants to stay with its mother, or that comes back to its mother, and to silence.

It was well for Picard, nevertheless, that he—who rarely travelled—did not visit Spain in his later years. For Zurich, a city which Picard despised as the apotheosis of modern avarice and innovation, is quiet and restrained in comparison with modern Madrid, where the blare of radios with their flamenco or pseudo-flamenco wails, the blast of motorcycle exhausts, and all the din of a modern proletarian cosmopolis have tortured silence to death. Once noise breaks in triumphantly upon an ancient citadel of silence, it gives no quarter. Even Toledo, once famous for its almost deathly stillness, now is a place where one has difficulty sleeping o' nights: the nocturnal Spaniard, given electric lights and mechanical noisemakers, goes at the destruction of silence more enthusiastically than the Swiss. In ruinous and impoverished Avila, true enough, the spirits of Saint Teresa and of Saint John of the Cross still brood over the town within the walls, and silence has a respite from torment; there Soledad, Solitude, that beautiful woman's name, is not forgotten.

Modern relish for clatter and jabber, however, has done its work in Spain wherever prosperity has reared its head. Once I lunched in the hills of Mallorca, at an inn set upon the lip of a gorge. On the ridge opposite our windows I saw a big monastic-like building amid the mist, and I asked my friends what it was. "That's the headquarters of the Spanish League of Silence," my friends told me. "Many Spaniards gather there to talk at great length about the virtues of silence."

At this moment, there burst into the inn a well-dressed man who sat himself down and cried to the landlord, "Do you have a radio here? I don't have one at my place." Indeed there was a radio, which the gentleman tuned in, full blast, and proceeded to enjoy by tapping time with his feet.

"That gentlemen is the head of the Spanish League of Silence," my friends remarked. Presently he was joined by two colleagues, and the three of them, ordering lunch, proceeded to talk at the top of their lungs about the wonders of silence. "Silence! That's what we need in Spain! More silence, more silence!"

As frequently occurs in Latin lands, their conversation soon turned to politics. In Palma lives my friend Camilo Cela, who (with Gironella) is one of the two best living Spanish writers. The head of the League of Silence did not like Cela.

"That Cela! He pretends to be against the regime, but he fought for Franco last time, and when the test comes, he'll be on that side again. But then it will be *our* turn; and bam bam bam bam bam bam bam!" The members of the League of Silence simulated the rattle of a machine gun. Don Quixote does forever ride a dusty road in Castile; yet now, as then, he is one of a forlorn and proscribed minority. The world belongs to the vulgar—including the vulgar intellectuals.

Picard detested the radio as much as he did the machine gun. "Radio has occupied the whole space of silence," he wrote. "There is no silence any longer. Even when the radio is turned off, the radio-noise is so amorphous that it seems to have no beginning and no end; it is limitless. And the type of man formed by the constant influence of this noise is the same: formless, undecided inwardly and externally, with no definite limits and no standards."

He knew that nature takes vengeance upon her violators; so it seemed altogether possible that modernity, having obliterated noble silence, may find itself self-condemned to one vast ear-splitting explosion—and then the silence, universal and irrevocable, of extinction. The staccato music of the machine gun is a prelude to that last trump.

The discontinuity of modern existence—from which men turn to noise as an anodyne—provokes the machine gun and the men who command it. So Picard writes in *Hitler in Our Selves*:

> Only in a world of total discontinuity could a nullity such as Hitler become Führer, because only where everything is disjointed has comparison fallen into disuse. There was only Hitler, the nullity, before everybody's eyes, and in this instable world wherein everything was changing at every moment one was glad that at least the one nullity, Hitler, remained stable before one's eyes. An orderly world, a hierarchy, would automatically have placed the nullity, Hitler, into nothingness; he could not have been noticed. Hitler was the excrement of a diabolical world; a world of truth in its order would have pushed him aside. . . .
>
> There is no permanence in this world of discontinuity. The ego exists only in the moment and for the moment. The individual, therefore, can have no evolution in the dimension of *time*. Everything has to be done in far too little time; hence, the individual gets restless and nervous. In discontinuity the individual also lacks context with his own personal history; he is lacking in the possibility of joining an experience with the context of previous experiences. Since life is lived solely in the moment and for the moment, the moment must carry all the burden; if the experience of a mo-

> ment is grave, the individual is hit all the harder because the burden cannot be distributed through context with other things. That is what aggravates, exhausts, and unnerves the individual. The ego cries out loud; unable to expand in the dimension of time, the ego in its crying need explodes itself into the dimension of space. Then Hitler came and took over the job of crying into space for all the others, and because his was the loudest cry, he was accepted by all.

At good discourse, Picard was accomplished. Language, divinely implanted, he loved; it was "verbal noise" he condemned. He could talk easily with almost anyone; and when he was in Zurich, his favorite occupation was to converse with market-vendors in the streets. Children understood him readily. In a letter to an American friend, a few years ago, Picard described his visit to a Swiss secondary school:

"A boy stood up and said, 'What are our poets and thinkers for? The statesmen don't bother about them, but behave as though there were no poets and philosophers.'

"I answered that I wouldn't like it, and would be suspicious, if Chancellor Adenauer, for example, should read Sartre or Max Picard. The statesman must derive the practice of his profession from the truth of his profession. I explained to them that at the time of Goethe, the baker and the shoemaker had a more intense relationship to Goethe's poetry, although they never read it, than today when radio and the school stuff Goethe's poetry into everybody. In a real community, as it still existed in Goethe's time, that sort of thing was not necessary. The community joined the individual to everything without his noticing it, and without remark when it happened. All this, strange to say, the students understood."

Such insights the better pupil may grasp from Picard—while the "professional" philosopher might deride them for their very lucidity, much as certain pedants detest Santayana for his felicity of style. To Dr. Dryasdust, now and again Picard will seem platitudinous; but that is because platitudes are true. Though Picard wrote in German, he remained innocent of the ponderous abstraction and obscurity which characterize much of Germanic philosophical discourse. Picard's was more nearly a Latin mind; and, living within sight of Italy, he made cheerful expeditions southward whenever he might.

Though he spoke scarcely more English than I speak German, Picard wrote to me—before we met—that this should be small impediment to our fellowship, for understanding can transcend speech. So, indeed, we found it as we drank wine together on his Alpine terrace. The succinctness of his books was produced by a character that, revering the Word, abhorred wordiness.

"The certainty of self-identification, which man formerly received from his free embrace of language," Picard wrote in *Man and Language*, "is replaced by the merely external duration of verbal noise. The inner, spiritual continuity is replaced by a purely external continuity. Man switches on the radio to make certain that he is still an identifiable person; even the certainty of self-identification is mechanized.

"The language of verbal noise is pervious to everything. 'The earth gives man more self knowledge than all the books, because it offers resistance to him and it is only in conflict with forces outside himself that man finds the way to himself,' writes Antoine de Saint Exupéry. Language is no longer a resisting force. It is pervious to everything, far too pervious. Man is pervious too: he absorbs Negro sculpture and the animal and plant forms of the ninth-century Irish Codex Cenanensis, Toulouse Lautrec and Bavarian folk art, Carpaccio and the moderns, all mixed up together. Man absorbs everything because he has no spiritual continuity. He is no longer committed by anything that comes to him. Everything merely appears and disappears in the verbal noise."

Such loss of intellectual and verbal continuity impoverishes the soul—and destroys the fabric of the civil social order. Words decay into signals for violence. "The word degenerates into the shriek of the moment; by that, it already has sunk to the level of the Hitler shriek." When heart and tongue fall shrieking into disorder, humor perishes.

The ideologue, mistaking abstractions for realities, filled with wrath, forgets how to laugh. In a letter to Henry Regnery, Picard told of an encounter with a gloomy fanatic:

"About fifty years ago, I had a debate on the subject of Communism, with the Communist Frick.

"The Communist: 'In the Communist society, everyone and everything will be equal, everyone will receive the same wage and the same meals, and whoever doesn't work will get neither wages nor anything to eat.'

"I: 'Very well, but what will you do with such people as I, who are completely helpless and impractical? Would I have to go hungry?'

"The Communist: 'No, you will receive wages and something to eat, so that you won't get in the way of others who work!'

"The Communist said this with an even more solemn and sour face than previously, and with no trace of humor. I understood even then that Communism is completely without any human quality, because it has no humor.

"Western capitalism doesn't have any humor either, today, and that comes from the fact that the West has lost its faith. A sense of humor can exist only in a world of faith. For in humor is a trace of the smile with which God observes the mistakes of man. That trace of God's smile, in man, is our sense of humor."

Picard had been a physician early in his life, but he turned to the contemplation of divine wisdom. Therefore he prospered, almost as little under capitalism as he would have prospered under Communism; but at least he was left in peace. An admirer had given him his little house; otherwise, at his end in a hospital bed, Picard was penniless. But the trace of God's smile did not depart from him.

Without humor, Picard would have sunk into despair. He saw just and beautiful rhetoric supplanted by slogan and cant, the dignity of meditation and of silence subjugated by jabber and mechanical noise. The divine, he declared, has been overwhelmed in our time by the demonic, and the demonic never is more powerful than when it appears trivial, as in the discontinuity and banality of the radio. "God, the eternally Continuous," Picard writes in *The World of Silence*, "has been deposed, and continuous radio-noise has been installed in His place. And the fact that although it is a discovery of man, it nevertheless seems to be independent of him, gives it an appearance of twilight mysticism."

Yet we only think that God has been dethroned. Actually, we flee from God, and do not perceive Him because we have turned our backs upon Him. Ours is the world of the Flight.

The Flight from God

In all ages, Picard writes in his book by this title, man is in flight from God; but in our time, the objective world of Faith has been ruined, and the flight immerses nearly everyone. Formerly, man had to separate himself from the world of Faith by an act of decision; today, it is from the Flight that a man must decide to part himself. The Flight has become an organized thing—almost a conscious thing. It shapes its own pseudo-religion, its own economics, its own language, its own art; it destroys nature and community.

Yet amid the terror of the Flight, Picard reminds us that One pursues. The clash of positivism and technology against tradition and moral insight, the upsurge of the demonic disguised as progress, are the principal matters of Picard's meditations. He was a "visionary" not in the sense of a man imprisoned in illusion or ideology, but instead a philosopher whose vision penetrated beyond the ephemeral to a truth which no quantity of "scientific research" could reveal.

"What a mobility of contrivances for endowing man with mobility for the Flight, to hide man and to cause him to vanish!" So Picard writes in his chapter "The Organization of the Flight." "What is terrible is this: it seems that whenever a man or a thing vanishes, God vanishes too. God must be very great, to be present continually, even though he vanishes continually. Once a man paused in the Flight and his heart, too, stopped when he came to understand that God can show himself again as often as he vanishes and that he can show himself everywhere.

> It is love that holds man back from rendering himself mobile for the Flight. A man who loves another, or a thing, contemplates what he loves with care and for a long time, careful to discover in his contemplation if there is a part he has so far neglected to love; and love is long-suffering, waiting until the beloved grows into love. But all this, in the Flight where one must be for ever *en route*, demands too much time. And so the world is being systematically emptied of love. All the relationships within which love can exist—marriage, the family, friendship—are being brought to destruction by the men of the Flight.

In the Flight there are no memories, and manufacture replaces creation. The love, kindness, and fidelity which one finds in the Flight are brummagem products easily discarded on impulse or from convenience: they merely simulate true love, kindness, and fidelity. The Flight itself is a sham-god, and most men mistake the Flight for divinity.

> What the Flight wants is this: to be primal, original, creative, as God is. The category of revolution is used to bring about the original and creative situation. The point of revolutionizing things is not that they may be rendered different, but that they may be returned once again to the beginning. Whatever is primitive is emphasized in culture, in art, in history. Man wants to be present at every beginning, imitating the Creator who is present at every beginning. The Chthonic, that which springs out of the earth, and, in general, whatever is dark, these are popular. Darkness exists before the light of the created; it is the moment prior to creation. Best of all, one would like to enclose the entire Flight in the darkness existing before creation, so that over all there may brood the atmosphere of the beginning, for then, at the beginning, there can be no one but God who creates everything. And so it is, for a world devoid of everything feels itself akin to the beginning where as

> yet nothing exists. In the world of Faith man could not tolerate being so near the true beginning. He not only needs the beginning, even more he needs history, that which follows the beginning, so that there may be a visible gap between himself and the divine beginning.

The Flight, that is, amounts to an inversion of Faith, much as Communism is an inversion of Christianity; it seeks to destroy the past, so that the Flight will seem creator and self-created. The Flight destroys true language and literature, substituting jargon and slogan—after the fashion of Newspeak. . . . For nobility in language is a gift from God, the Pursuer, and therefore cannot be tolerated:

> Whenever in the language of the Flight one reads a sentence, it is as though one leaped across the debris of the word from one part to another, the parts separated by craters. It is no longer as in the world of Faith where the subject is like a pillar from which the sentence begins, passing through the predicate to the object, itself like a pillar. The pillar of the subject is cast down—in the syntax of the Flight one likes to substitute for the massive pillar of the subject some light pronoun; and though in the world of Faith, too, the subject may be replaced by a pronoun, this does not happen so frequently and then with hesitation, for here one feels there is something miraculous about one thing standing for another, the lesser for the greater—the pillar of the subject is cast down and so, too, is the pillar of the object, and both, along with the predicate, lie side by side, the whole a heap of ruins. The erect pillars would arrest the Flight, would stand like a barrier; but now everything lies horizontally, following the line of the Flight.

Thus the Flight from God destroys humane letters. From the Primal Word came our power of language; but we moderns will not acknowledge the Primal Word; therefore we are uncertain, aimlessly wandering, and look upon words as mere counters:

> Those writers who are (in the world of the Flight) judged to be good worry over a word, wondering whether it will keep the meaning they have assigned to it. In thus regarding the word they resemble not a mother looking at her child with love and confidence, but rather a governess whose anxiety, nervousness, and mistrust spring from her profession. In the world of the Flight the poets lose all their strength in patching together the bodies of words as they fall apart and in placing one body of a word beside another and in watching over it lest it should slip away once more. How could any-

> one still have strength enough to give soul and spirit to the body of the word? In the world of Faith the word has not only an intact body endowed with soul and spirit; it also has a world to live in, the world, that is, of Faith. The poet need not begin by creating a world fit for the word; everything is ready, and the poet can use all his strength in being a poet; and this means letting the word strive with the world, that, more clearly than the world itself, the word may declare the name of the Creator.

Sexual powers, and marriage, are distorted in the world of the Flight. Art, too, dies the death: its forms disintegrate. The pseudo-art of the Flight is paraded as a denial of the existence of God. "Man has deliberately isolated Art in such a way that its otherness is manifest. It is as though those in Flight had appointed a few men to fabricate Art in caverns remote from the main road, and then, all of a sudden (that they may give the impression that Art springs from another world), to hold it high above those who are in flight, as though it were a light shining into the world of the Flight from another world." Art exists not for God's sake, but for Art's sake.

So it is with literature, which also is converted into a sham "otherness." Like the Flight's art, the Flight's literature really is produced by the Flight itself, but it is supposed by nearly everybody to have an origin separate from both God and the Flight. It is converted into an instrument of delusion; and the object of this outpouring of books is to destroy Faith by a Babel of opinions.

> In the art and literature of the Flight, things are put out of shape, stunted, crushed, destroyed. One wants only to accustom oneself to the spectacle of annihilation, so one puts that which has been destroyed into the pictures and into literature. . . . This destruction—this extravagance of destruction—this state of being hacked into pieces, this prostration of things in pictures and in literature—all these are, as it were, *final*. It resembles a judgment in that for the man of the Flight it is a substitute for the finality of divine judgment. Once one has beheld the destruction of all things in pictures and in literature, one no longer fears a Last Judgment. One knows that everything that can happen has already happened. What God ought to destroy, man has himself destroyed.

In the Flight, even the faces of men take on a vacant cast; Faith, which animated them, is forgotten. The men of the Flight build cities which are monstrous, and which become the Flight's centers. "The streets resemble pipes into which men are sucked; and a few trees have been dragged along with the men into the city. These stand fearfully on the edge of the street. They no longer know their way back into the countryside, and they try slowly to grow downward through the asphalt and to disappear."

But, all this said, there remains the Pursuer, who says, "You have not chosen Me; I have chosen you." Everything which flees belongs, after all, to God. One still can fling himself back upon the Pursuer, and the Pursuer can arrest and redeem the whole Flight, if He so chooses. The danger is that God may cease to pursue, and those in Flight might circle round him for all eternity, like dead moons. And then comes Picard's final illuminating vision:

> It is unnecessary to doubt when one thinks of God: all doubt is within the Flight. It is unnecessary to fall away from God; it is comic, like a copy—though a clumsy one—of the most monstrous apostasy contained within the Flight. The Flight is designed to be an enormous machine of doubt and apostasy; all doubt, all apostasy, all terror of God, are within the Flight, and one's own morsel of doubt, apostasy, terror, is being torn from one by the machinery of the Flight. Doubts, terrors, uncertainties, are no longer scattered, they are concentrated; one can no longer come across them upon Faith's path; they have been driven together and together they roll onward within the enormous machine of the Flight. There remains only God in his full radiance, his utter clarity; and over against him is the Flight into which all dimness and all ambiguity have been driven. The more the structure of the Flight and the more desperately it plunges onward, the more plainly stands before us the one who is alone: God.

So Max Picard was not dismayed, even though "All that is possible is within the Flight. All that is real is without." Such is the literature of vision, allied to the paintings of William Blake. That these words still may be published in our time, and may be read at least by a few, attests the survival of normality. And, as Isaiah discovered to his surprise, the few may be more numerous than one ever had guessed. The best-seller lists will be crammed with salacity and triviality, no doubt, until television extinguishes altogether the books of the Flight. But the literature of the permanent things, submerged though it may be today, retains a power which defies chthonian darkness.

["A Man of Vision in Our Time," Enemies of the Permanent Things: Observations of Abnormity in Literature and Politics, *Rev. ed. (La Salle, IL: Sherwood Sugden & Company, 1984), 97–108.]*

EPILOGUE

Is Life Worth Living?

Russell Amos Kirk died of congestive heart failure on April 29, 1994, at his home, Piety Hill, in Mecosta, Michigan. The Sword of Imagination: Memoirs of a Half-Century of Literary Conflict *was published posthumously in 1995. "Is Life Worth Living?" the selection which follows, serves as the epilogue to* The Sword of Imagination. *It is his valedictory statement, his farewell. In estimating the value of his life and work Kirk discloses a distinct humility: he is never boastful, or rancorous, or bitter. To the question as to the purpose of human existence, Kirk responds directly and without fear:—". . . to know God, and enjoy Him forever." Nor does he have fear of what lies ahead, for "his worn old knapsack will suffice him for the tramp from corruption to incorruption." Concluding a public lecture, he once assured his listeners: "If you look for the Supernatural, you will find it. I promise you: I have."*

In some ages, what Thoreau says is true: most men lead lives of quiet desperation. They endeavor to evade answering the question "What is the purpose of human existence?" As children, they entertain vague expectations of some future happy condition and achievement; but commonly those hopes are dashed or much diminished once they flap or tumble out of the parental nest. After that, they may live as birds do, from day to day, until they starve or are caught by a cat. Nevertheless, many men and women are haunted by such nagging questions as "What is this all about?" or "Is life worth living?" And a good many, if pressed for an answer, will reply interiorly much as does T. S. Eliot's Sweeney Agonistes: birth and copulation and death; that's all. As to whether such a life, seemingly limited to reproduction and repetition, has significant value—why, some people may shrug, and others shake their heads.

Personal and social decadence, the consequence of the loss of an end or object in existence, come to pass when the shapers of opinion, sophisticated, not philosophers but philodoxers, find nothing worth living for—except sensation. C. E. M. Joad mentions certain characteristics of a decadent society: luxury; skepticism; weariness; superstition; preoccupation with the self and its experiences; a society "promoted by and promoting the subjectivist analysis of moral, aesthetic, metaphysical and theological judgments."

Into such a society Russell Kirk was born—or rather, born in the salad days of such a society, its decay accelerating swiftly as Kirk grew older. His parents did not question whether life was worth living: they lived by tradition merely, growing up decently, marrying when they were about twenty years old, bringing two children into the world, then dying—Kirk's mother giving up the ghost while she still could be called youthful, his father dying blind, sick, and old. Their experiences in the world were unremarkable; they performed their duties patiently, harming no one; they were loving parents. Marjorie Rachel Kirk lived hopeful of great prospects for humankind, but her cheerful spirit was snuffed out by cancer; the elder Russell Kirk accepted his tribulations uncomplaining, though he never had read the Stoics, or for that matter the Book of Job. Had their lives signified something? Does anyone's life signify anything?

Time was when nearly all men and women, believing in some transcendent religion, had taken it that their little lives were bound up with some divine design, which they could not hope to comprehend wholly, but which gave meaning to their existence as persons. Such, at any rate, had been the doctrine imparted to them, and most of them had tried to conform their lives to that eternal purpose.

Russell Kirk's parents had inherited that body of belief, if in a vestigial form. That teaching had led them into honest and kindly lives. But the attenuated tradition that had sustained them was perilously weakened by the middle of the twentieth century. Performance of duties was giving way to eagerness for sensations. And that way lay decadence.

Livy, at the time the Roman republic collapsed, wrote that the Romans of his era seemed to have fallen in love with death. Such a death-urge, interestingly similar to the Roman phenomenon, was at work in America during Kirk's lifetime. (It is grimly amusing to compare Livy's description of the Bacchanalian rites, Book XXXIX of his *History*, with certain cult orgies of the twentieth century; Kirk, in his mystical romance *Lord of the Hollow Dark* [1979], had ventured to picture the diabolic imagination at work in such a cultic initiation of his own time.) From the Second World War onward, the civilization of Europe and the Americas had stumbled into decadence: the moral order seemed to be dissolving. Subconsciously or half consciously, a great many people came to assume that really life was not worth living; the death-urge enticed them, as in Livy's time.

There came to pass a growing general indifference concerning the past and the future of the human species: an echo of the ancient Greek cry of ruthless individuality, "When I am dead, let earth be mixed with fire!" In the name of freedom, modernism had opened the path that leads to dissolution. Indeed, there is terror in a handful of dust. "There is no death," Gregory the Great, in the catacombs, had told his Roman flock. "*Viva la muerte!*" the nihilists of the dying twentieth century seemed to shout.

It was otherwise with Russell Kirk, who in 1993, on the eve of his seventy-fifth birthday, published two more books: *America's British Culture* (1993), a counter-buffet to Demon Multiculturalism; and *The Politics of Prudence* (1993), addressed to the rising generation in search of principles. He was pro-life, although he did not dread his latter end except as it might trouble Annette and the four daughters. To them he could leave little but a handsome house, five acres, a sense of honor, and many happy memories.

At an early age, Kirk had learned from the discourse and the examples of his mother and his grandfather that life is well worth living. He had learned also that life ought to be lived with honor, charity, and prudence. Those and other enduring principles he had accepted on authority: "Believe what all men, everywhere, always have believed." Somewhat to his surprise, his adherence to those precepts brought strength and happiness into his life.

At the age of seventy-five, Kirk had come to understand that he had sought, during his lifetime, three ends or objects.

One had been to defend the Permanent Things, in a world where "Dinos is king, having overthrown Zeus." He had sought to conserve a patrimony of order, justice, and freedom; a tolerable moral order; and an inheritance of culture. Although rowing against a strong tide, in this aspiration he had succeeded somewhat, certainly beyond his early expectation, in reminding people that truth was not born yesterday.

A second had been to lead a life of decent independence, living much as his ancestors had lived, on their land, in circumstances that would enable him to utter the truth and make his voice heard: a life uncluttered and unpolluted, not devoted to getting and spending. In his antique vocation of man of letters, he had achieved that aspiration at Piety Hill.

A third end had been to marry for love and to rear children who would come to know that the service of God is perfect freedom. In his middle years, the splendid Annette had given herself to him and then given him four children, presently endowed with the unbought grace of life. Annette and he helped to sustain the institution of the family by creating a vigorous example.

Thus his three wishes had been granted; he was grateful. Power over others, and much money, he never had desired; he had been spared those responsibilities.

Both on authority and through his own insights and experiences, Kirk had come to understand that there exists a realm of being beyond this temporal world and that a mysterious providence works in human affairs—that man is made for eternity. Such knowledge had been consolation and conpensation for sorrow.

Kirk stood ready to affirm his belief in such knowledge, and to be derided for it, despite his being no Hot Gospeller. Like David Hume, he was more skeptical of Rationalism than of Tradition—a worldly *defensor fidei*. Strongly influenced by Christopher Dawson and Eric Voegelin, Martin D'Arcy and Mircea Eliade, Kirk had come to conclude that a civilization cannot long survive the dying of belief in a transcendent order that brought the culture into being. The ideology of modernism bestrode the intellectual world from 1860 to 1960; after that, its power waned. As Arthur Koestler observed, yesteryear's scientific doctrines of mechanism and materialism ought to be buried with a requiem of electronic music. Once more, in biology as in physics, the scientific disciplines had begun to enter upon the realm of mystery. Kirk had become in his convictions both pre-modern and post-modern.

This Russell Kirk was a canny Scot with a relish for the uncanny. The one high talent with which he had been endowed was imagination, the power of raising up images of truth and terror in the mind; through images, he had come to know something of the world beyond the world. The armed vision, Kirk had discovered, penetrates through the skin of appearances to energetic reality; the unimaginative human being is dully confined to the provinciality of time and to the provinciality of place. His had been a romantic life, conducted on classical lines. Apprehending reality through images, he had succeeded in exhibiting those images of the Permanent Things to a good many people; and after his body was dust, his books would carry on that work.

As his seventy-second birthday had approached, his daughter Cecilia (soon to follow in his steps at St. Andrews University) had told him in her affectionately acerbic way, "You look like a bulldog." He recalled having noticed, at the age of sixteen, his mirrored face, suddenly encountered—innocent and somewhat wistful. Now, the years having swept by giddily, he found himself with a bulldog visage, the veteran of many controversies, mordant on occasion, given to growling, but a good guardian of the threshold and the hearth, kindly with children.

Blessed or cursed with near-total recall, Russell Kirk descried in his kaleidoscopic imagination every scene of every year, almost, in his life. They all had poured by so hastily and tumultuously, and what had been done could not be undone. How very like he had been to Mossy in George MacDonald's tiny book *The Golden Key* (1906), or to John, the latter-day pilgrim in C. S. Lewis's *The Pilgrim's Regress*! Then, too, in his seventh decade Kirk had come to note wryly his resemblance to the Little Pine Tree of Hans Christian Andersen's fable—long eager for the coming of some wondrous event, not apprehending that the splendor of life is here and now.

On the shelves of Kirk's library rest a good many books he never had found time to read through. How many thousands of hours had he wasted in dreamy reverie, after the fashion of the Little Pine Tree? No doctrine is more comforting than the teaching of Purgatory, in part the gift of Gregory the Great to the Church. For purgatorily, one may be granted opportunity to atone for having let some precious life run out like water from a neglected tap into sterile sands. Improving the living moment, Kirk must reform his meandering ways even at this tardy hour. There is the book of children's tales, long in contemplation, that ought to be written; and three more volumes of his integrated essays on various themes, already requested by a publisher, must be compiled; and more volumes for the Library of Conservative Thought (some thirty volumes thereof already published, by late 1994) must be edited. Aristotle instructs us that life is for action; Irving Babbitt, that we must find our happiness in work or not at all. What sort of action, and work for what purpose? The answer is catechetical: to know God, and enjoy Him forever.

This present life here below, Kirk had perceived often in his mind's eye, is an ephemeral existence, precarious, as in an arena rather than upon a stage: some men are meant to be gladiators or knights-errant, not mere strolling players. Swords drawn, they stand on a darkling plain against all comers and all odds; how well they bear themselves in the mortal struggle will determine in what condition they shall put on incorruption. His sins of omission and commission notwithstanding, Kirk had blown his horn and drawn his sword of imagination, in the arena of the blighted twentieth century, that he might assail the follies of the time.

Above the chimneypiece in the drawing room of Piety Hill there hangs an eighteenth-century sword, in its worn leather scabbard, of the Mogul Empire. Kirk obtained it from Count Jas Tarnowski, the great Polish collector of art. This sword was forged in Persia and adorned with silver mountings in France. The head of a leopard, delicately carved in ivory, is its hilt; the creature retains its slender fangs and its ruby eyes. Is it a court sword? Perhaps; yet its edge is jagged and hacked badly, as if this elegant weapon, one grim day, had been passionately employed in desperate battle against a steely adversary. With this pretty, deadly thing, Elrond of Rivendell, master of the Last Homely House, might have hacked at orcs.

Humankind has it on authority that riches cannot well pass through the needle's eye into the world beyond the world. Being unencumbered with pelf, Kirk is not distressed by that difficulty; his worn old knapsack will suffice him for the tramp from corruption to incorruption. In imagination, at least, may he be permitted to carry with him, into another realm of being, beyond time, his Mogul sword? That blade might repel certain Watchers—the old Egyptians dreaded them—at the Strait Gate. Quite conceivably imagination of the right sort may be so redemptive hereafter as here. Forward!

> I am for the house with the narrow gate, which I take to be too little for pomp to enter: some that humble themselves may; but many will be too chill and tender, and they'll be for the flow'ry way that leads to the broad gate and the great fire.
>
> William Shakespeare, *All's Well That Ends Well* (c. 1602), 4:5:46–51

[*"Epilogue: Is Life Worth Living?"* The Sword of Imagination: Memoirs of a Half-Century of Literary Conflict *(Grand Rapids, MI: William B. Eerdmans Publishing Company, 1995), 471–76.]*

❖

BIBLIOGRAPHY

Russell Kirk wrote critical introductions, forewords, and prefaces to sixty-eight books and reprints of scholarly works published in the years 1955–94. For a complete list of these books, see "Section G: Introductions and Forewords to Books," *Russell Kirk: A Bibliography*, compiled by Charles Brown, Mount Pleasant, Michigan: Clarke Historical Library, 1981, 71–74. The updated bibliography, as of 2001, is available in electronic form at the Russell Kirk Center for Cultural Renewal, Piety Hill, Mecosta, Michigan. Dr. Brown's meticulously annotated bibliography is a definitive reference source.

See also the "Selected Bibliography" of both primary and secondary sources included in James E. Person, Jr., *Russell Kirk: A Critical Biography of a Conservative Mind*, Lanham, New York: Madison Books, 1999, 221–27. Person's book, which is essentially a general introduction to Kirk's work and thought, is crafted skillfully and discerningly.

❖

I
Books By Russell Kirk

Academic Freedom: An Essay in Definition. Chicago: Henry Regnery Company, 1955.

The American Cause. Chicago: Henry Regnery Company, 1957. [2nd rev. ed., with a Foreword by John Dos Passos, 1966.]

America's British Culture. New Brunswick, NJ, and London: Transaction Publishers, 1993.

Beyond the Dreams of Avarice: Essays of a Social Critic. Chicago: Henry Regnery Company, 1956. [Rev. ed., Peru, IL: Sherwood Sugden & Company, 1991.]

Confessions of a Bohemian Tory: Episodes and Reflections of a Vagrant Career. New York: Fleet Publishing Corporation, 1963.

The Conservative Constitution. Washington, DC: Regnery Gateway, 1990. [Rev. ed. published under the title *Rights and Duties: Reflections on Our Conservative Constitution*, edited by Mitchell S. Muncy, with an Introduction by Russell Hittinger. Dallas, TX: Spence Publishing Company, 1997.]

The Conservative Mind: From Burke to Santayana. Chicago: Henry Regnery Company, 1953. [3rd rev. ed. published under the title *The Conservative Mind: From Burke to Eliot*, 1960; 7th rev. ed., Chicago and Washington, DC: Regnery Books, 1986.]

A Creature of the Twilight: His Memorials. Being Some Account of Episodes in the Career of His Excellency Manfred Arcano, Minister Without Portfolio to the Hereditary President of the Commonwealth of Hamnegri, and de Facto Field Commander of the Armies of That August Prince. New York: Fleet Press, 1966.

Decadence and Renewal in the Higher Learning. South Bend, IN: Gateway Editions, Ltd., 1978.

Economics: Work and Prosperity. Pensacola, FL: A Beta Book, 1989.

Edmund Burke: A Genius Reconsidered. New Rochelle, NY: Arlington House, 1967. [Rev. and updated ed., with a Foreword by Roger Scruton, Wilmington, DE: Intercollegiate Studies Institute, 1997.]

Eliot and His Age: T. S. Eliot's Moral Imagination in the Twentieth Century. New York: Random House, 1971. [3rd rev. ed., Peru, IL: Sherwood Sugden & Company, 1989.]

Enemies of the Permanent Things: Observations of Abnormity in Literature and Politics. New Rochelle, NY: Arlington House, 1969. [Rev. ed., Peru, IL: Sherwood Sugden & Company, 1984.]

The Intelligent Woman's Guide to Conservatism. New York: Devin–Adair, 1957. [Rev. ed. published under the title *The Intelligent American's Guide to Conservatism*. Dallas, TX: Spence Publishing Company, 1999.]

The Intemperate Professor and Other Cultural Splenetics. Baton Rouge: Louisiana State University Press, 1965. [Rev. ed., Peru, IL: Sherwood Sugden & Company, 1988.]

Lord of the Hollow Dark. New York: St. Martin's Press, 1979. [Reprinted, prefaced with the short story "Balgrummo's Hell," Front Royal, VA: Christendom College Press, 1989.]

Old House of Fear. New York: Fleet Press, 1961. [2nd ed., 1963.]

The Political Principles of Robert A. Taft (with James McClellan). New York: Fleet Press, 1967.

The Politics of Prudence. Bryn Mawr, PA: Intercollegiate Studies Institute, 1993.

The Princess of All Lands. Sauk City, WI: Arkham House, 1979.

A Program for Conservatives. Chicago: Henry Regnery Company, 1954. [Rev. ed., Chicago: Henry Regnery Company, 1962. Also published under the title *Prospects for Conservatives*. Rev., abridged ed., Chicago: Henry Regnery Company, 1956; Rev., enlarged ed., Washington, DC: Regnery Gateway, 1989.]

Randolph of Roanoke: A Study in Conservative Thought. Chicago: University of Chicago Press, 1951. [Rev., enlarged ed. published under the title *John Randolph of Roanoke: A Study in American Politics, With Selected Speeches and Letters*. Chicago: Henry Regnery Company, 1964; 3rd rev. ed., Indianapolis: Liberty Press, 1978; 4th rev. ed., Indianapolis: Liberty Press, 1994.]

Reclaiming a Patrimony: A Collection of Lectures. Washington, DC: The Heritage Foundation, 1982.

Redeeming the Time, edited and with an Introduction by Jeffrey O. Nelson. Wilmington, DE: Intercollegiate Studies Institute, 1996.

The Roots of American Order. La Salle, IL: Open Court, 1974. [2nd rev. ed., Malibu, CA: Pepperdine University Press, 1977; 3rd rev. ed., Washington, DC: Regnery Gateway, 1991.]

St. Andrews. London: B. T. Batsford, 1954.

The Surly Sullen Bell: Ten Stories and Sketches, Uncanny or Uncomfortable, With a Note on the Ghostly Tale. New York: Fleet Press, 1962.

The Sword of Imagination: Memoirs of a Half-Century of Literary Conflict. Grand Rapids, MI: William B. Eerdmans Publishing Company, 1995.

Watchers at the Strait Gate. Sauk City, WI: Arkham House, 1984.

The Wise Men Know What Wicked Things Are Written on the Sky. Washington, DC: Regnery Gateway, 1987.

❖

II
Books Edited

Orestes Brownson: Selected Political Essays, edited and with a new Introduction by Russell Kirk. New Brunswick, NJ, and London: Transaction Publishers, 1990. [Originally published in 1955 by the Henry Regnery Company (Chicago).]

The Portable Conservative Reader, edited with an Introduction and Notes by Russell Kirk. New York: Viking Penguin, Inc., 1982.

❖

III

Books and Articles About Russell Kirk: A Selective List

Attarian, John. "Russell Kirk's Political Economy," *Modern Age: A Quarterly Review*, Vol. 40, No. 1 (Winter 1998), 87–97.

Bliese, John R. E. "Richard Weaver, Russell Kirk, and the Environment," *Modern Age: A Quarterly Review*, Vol. 38, No. 2 (Winter 1996), 148–58.

Boyd, Ian, C. S. B. "Russell Kirk: An Integrated Man," *The Intercollegiate Review: A Journal of Scholarship & Opinion*, Vol. 30, No. 1 (Fall 1994), 18–22.

Bradford, M. E. *A Better Guide Than Reason: Studies in the American Revolution*, 207–217. La Salle, IL: Sherwood Sugden & Company, 1979.

———. "A Proper Patrimony: Russell Kirk and America's Moral Genealogy," in *The Unbought Grace of Life: Essays in Honor of Russell Kirk*, edited by James E. Person, Jr., 70–78. Peru, IL: Sherwood Sugden & Company, 1994.

Campbell, William F. "An Economist's Tribute to Russell Kirk," *The Intercollegiate Review: A Journal of Scholarship & Opinion*, Vol. 30, No. 1 (Fall 1994), 68–71.

Canavan, Francis, S. J. "Kirk and the Burke Revival," *The Intercollegiate Review: A Journal of Scholarship & Opinon*, Vol. 30, No. 1 (Fall 1994), 43–45.

Champ, Robert. "Russell Kirk's Fiction of Entertainment," *The Intercollegiate Review: A Journal of Scholarship & Opinion*, Vol. 30, No. 1 (Fall 1994), 39–42.

Cheney, Brainard. "The Conservative Course by Celestial Navigation," *The Sewanee Review*, Vol. 62, No. 1 (Winter 1954), 151–59.

East, John P. *The American Conservative Movement: The Philosophical Founders*, 17–37. Chicago: Henry Regnery Company, 1986.

Ericson, Edward E., Jr. "Conservatism at Its Highest," *The Intercollegiate Review: A Journal of Scholarship & Opinion*, Vol. 30, No. 1 (Fall 1994), 31–34.

Filler, Louis. "'The Wizard of Mecosta': Russell Kirk of Michigan," *Michigan History*, Vol. 63, No. 5 (September–October 1979), 12–18.

Frohnen, Bruce. "Russell Kirk on Cultivating the Good Life," *The Intercollegiate Review: A Journal of Scholarship & Opinion*, Vol. 30, No 1 (Fall 1994), 63–67.

———. *Virtue and the Promise of Conservatism: The Legacy of Burke and Tocqueville*, 166–75, 196–204 et passim. Lawrence, KS: University Press of Kansas, 1993.

Frum, David. "The Legacy of Russell Kirk," in his *What's Right: The New Conservative Majority and the Making of America*, 159–69. New York: Basic Books, 1996.

Genovese, Eugene D. "Captain Kirk," *The New Republic*, Vol. 213, No. 24 (11 December 1995), 35–38.

Guroian, Vigen. "The Conservative Mind Forty Years Later," *The Intercollegiate Review: A Journal of Scholarship & Opinion*, Vol. 30, No. 1 (Fall 1994), 23–26.

Hart, Jeffrey. "The Varieties of Conservative Thought," in his *The American Dissent: A Decade of Modern Conservatism*, 187–238. Garden City, NY: Doubleday, 1966.

Henrie, Mark C. "Russell Kirk and the Conservative Heart," *The Intercollegiate Review: A Journal of Scholarship & Opinion*, Vo. 38, No. 2 (Spring 2003), 14–23.

———. "Russell Kirk's Unfounded America," *The Intercollegiate Review: A Journal of Scholarship & Opinion*, Vol. 30, No. 1 (Fall 1994), 51–57.

Herron, Don. "Russell Kirk: Ghost Master of Mecosta," in *Discovering Modern Horror Fiction*, edited by Darrell Schweitzer, 21–97. Mercer Island, WA: Starmont House, 1985.

Hittinger, Russell. "Introduction," in *Rights and Duties: Reflections on Our Conservative Constitution*, by Russell Kirk, xiii–xxxi. Dallas, TX: Spence Publishing Company, 1997.

———. "The Unwritten Constitution and the Conservative's Dilemma," *The Intercollegiate Review: A Journal of Scholarship & Opinion*, Vol. 30, No. 1 (Fall 1994), 58–62.

Horowitz, Irving Louis. "Russell Kirk: Past as Prologue," in *The Unbought Grace of Life: Essays in Honor of Russell Kirk*, edited by James E. Person, Jr., 55–58. Peru, IL: Sherwood Sugden & Company, 1994.

Kirk, Cecilia A. "'The Box of Delights': A Literary Patrimony," in *The Unbought Grace of Life: Essays in Honor of Russell Kirk*, edited by James E. Person, Jr., 59–65. Peru, IL: Sherwood Sugden & Company, 1994.

Lora, Ronald. *Conservative Minds in America*, 175–85, 191–94. Chicago: Rand McNally, 1971.

Lukacs, John. "An Exceptional Mind, An Exceptional Friend," in *The Unbought Grace of Life: Essays in Honor of Russell Kirk*, edited by James E. Person, Jr., 51–54. Peru, IL: Sherwood Sugden & Company, 1994.

Lytle, Andrew. "The Terrors of the Soul," in *The Unbought Grace of Life: Essays in Honor of Russell Kirk*, edited by James E. Person, Jr., 87–90. Peru, IL: Sherwood Sugden & Company, 1994.

McDonald, Forrest. "Russell Kirk: The American Cicero," in *The Unbought Grace of Life: Essays in Honor of Russell Kirk*, edited by James E. Person, Jr., 15–18. Peru, IL: Sherwood Sugden & Company, 1994.

McDonald, W. Wesley. "Reason, Natural Law, and Moral Imagination in the Thought of Russell Kirk," *Modern Age: A Quarterly Review*, Vol. 27, No. 1 (Winter 1983), 15–24.

———. *Russell Kirk and the Age of Ideology*. Columbia, MO: University of Missouri Press, 2004.

———. "Russell Kirk on Decadence in an Age of Ideology," *The Hillsdale Review*, Vol. 7 (Winter–Spring 1985), 53–59.

Nash, George H. *The Conservative Intellectual Movement in America Since 1945*, 61–68. Wilmington, DE: Intercollegiate Studies Institute, 1997 [1976].

———. "The Conservative Mind in America," *The Intercollegiate Review: A Journal of Scholarship & Opinion*, Vol. 30, No. 1 (Fall 1994), 27–30.

Newman, R. Andrew. "Pilgrimages and Easter Destinations in The Ghostly Tales of Russell Kirk," *Modern Age: A Quarterly Review*, Vol. 40, No. 3 (Summer 1998), 314–18.

Niemeyer, Gerhart. "Russell Kirk and Ideology," *The Intercollegiate Review: A Journal of Scholarship & Opinion*, Vol. 30, No. 1 (Fall 1994), 35–38.

Panichas, George A. "[Russell Kirk as] Man of Letters," *Growing Wings to Overcome Gravity: Criticism as the Pursuit of Virtue*, 145–56. Macon, GA: Mercer University Press, 1999.

———. "The Moral Imagination," *Growing Wings to Overcome Gravity: Criticism as the Pursuit of Virtue*, 103–9. Macon, GA: Mercer University Press, 1999.

Person, James E., Jr. "The Achievement of Russell Kirk." *Modern Age: A Quarterly Review.* Vol. 47, No. 4 (Fall 2005), 344–49.

———. *Russell Kirk: A Critical Biography of a Conservative Mind*. London, New York, Oxford: Madison Books, 1999.

———. *The Unbought Grace of Life: Essays in Honor of Russell Kirk*. Peru, IL: Sherwood Sugden & Company, 1994.

Phillips, Norman R. "Traditional Humanism: The Views of T. S. Eliot and Russell Kirk," in his *The Quest for Excellence: The Neo-Conservative Critique of Educational Mediocrity*, 51–89. New York: Philosophical Library, 1978.

Ransom, John Crowe. "Empirics in Politics," in his *Poems and Essays*, 135–45. New York: Vintage Books, 1955.

Regnery, Henry. "Russell Kirk: An Appraisal," in *Russell Kirk: A Bibliography*, edited by Charles C. Brown, 127–41. Mount Pleasant, MI: Clarke Historical Society, 1981.

———. "Russell Kirk: A Life Worth Living," *Modern Age: A Quarterly Review*, Vol. 38, No. 3 (Summer 1996), 211–17.

———. "Russell Kirk: Conservatism Becomes a Movement," in his *Memoirs of a Dissident Publisher*, 146–66. New York: Harcourt, Brace, Jovanovich, 1979.

Respinti, Marco. "Kirk and Italy: A Note on the Relevance of Roman Heritage," *The Intercollegiate Review: A Journal of Scholarship & Opinion*, Vol. 30, No. 1 (Fall 1994), 72–75.

Russello, Gerald J. "The Jurisprudence of Russell Kirk," *Modern Age: A Quarterly Review*, Vol. 38, No. 4 (Fall 1996), 354–63.

———. "Time and Timeless: The Historical Imagination of Russell Kirk," *Modern Age: A Quarterly Review*, Vol. 41, No. 3 (Summer 1999), 209–19.

Stanlis, Peter J. "Prophet of American Education," *The Intercollegiate Review: A Journal of Scholarship & Opinion*, Vol. 30, No. 1 (Fall 1994), 76–80.

———. "Russell Kirk: A Memoir of a Friendship," in *The Unbought Grace of Life: Essays in Honor of Russell Kirk*, edited by James E. Person, Jr., 31–50. Peru, IL: Sherwood Sugden & Company, 1994.

Viereck, Peter. *Conservatism Revisited: The Revolt Against Revolt, 1815–1949*. Rev. ed., with the addition of "The New Conservatism: What Went Wrong?," 145–151. New York: Collier Books, 1962.

Wheeler, Harvey. "Russell Kirk and the New Conservatism," *Shenandoah*, Vol. 7, No. 2 (Spring 1956), 20–34.

Whitney, Gleaves. "Seven Things You Should Know About Russell Kirk," *Vital Speeches of the Day*, Vol. 63 (June 1, 1997), 507–11.

———. "The Swords of Imagination: Russell Kirk's Battle With Modernity," *Modern Age: A Quarterly Review*, Vol. 43, No. 4 (Fall 2001), 311–20.

Wilcox, W. Bradford. "Faith in Ruins," *The Intercollegiate Review: A Journal of Scholarship & Opinion*, Vol. 30, No. 1 (Fall 1994), 85–88.

Wilhelmsen, Frederick D. "The Wandering Seer of Mecosta," *The Intercollegiate Review: A Journal of Scholarship & Opinion*, Vol. 30, No. 1 (Fall 1994), 81–84.

Wilson, Clyde N. "Russell Kirk's 'Southern Valor,'" *The Intercollegiate Review: A Journal of Scholarship & Opinion*, Vol. 30, No. 1 (Fall 1994), 46–50.

Wolfe, Gregory. "The Catholic as Conservative: Russell Kirk's Christian Humanism," *Crisis: A Journal of Lay Catholic Opinion*, Vol. 11, No. 9 (October 1993), 25, 27–32.

Zoll, Donald Atwell. "The Social Thought of Russell Kirk," *The Political Science Reviewer*, Vol. 2 (Fall 1972), 112–36.

NOTES

II. Our Sacred Patrimony

The Law and the Prophets (50–79)

1. "A Model of Christian Charity," in *The American Puritans: Their Prose, and Poetry*, edited by Perry Miller (New York, 1956), 78–83. See also *Winthrop's Journal History of New England*, edited by James Kendall Hosmer (New York, 1908 and 1966), Vol. I, 24–50.
2. R. B. Y. Scott, *The Relevance of the Prophets: An Introduction to the Old Testament Prophets and their Message* (New York, 1968), 225.
3. John Adams to F. A. Vanderkemp, February 16, 1809, in *The Life and Works of John Adams*, edited by Charles Francis Adams (Boston, 1854), Vol. IX, 609–10.
4. Roland de Vaux, *Ancient Israel: Its Life and Institutions* (New York, 1961), Vol. I, 99.
5. By definition, the Old Testament is a collection of sacred writings in Hebrew, declared by the Jewish Scribes to have been composed under divine inspiration. "Testament" means "covenant" or "contract" under God. Probably the division and arrangement of the Bible with which most people are familiar was the labor of Stephen Langton, at the University of Paris, about the year 1228 AD. Attempts to make the Bible more easily readable by large deletions and rearrangements often have reflected the editors' preferences and prejudices. Thomas Jefferson made such an attempt at sorting out the sayings of Jesus from the Gospels; but the result was chiefly a calculated reinforcement of Jefferson's own Deism.
6. Here, as usually in these chapters, the English translation is from the King James Bible, the oldest one still in common use. The recent Jerusalem Bible expresses Genesis 8:21 thus: "Never again will I curse the earth because of man, because his heart contrives evil from his infancy." On translations of the Scriptures, see *Translating for King James*, edited by Ward Allen (Nashville, TN, 1969) and Dewey M. Beegle, *God's Word into English* (New York, 1960).
7. See *Ancient Near Eastern Texts Relating to the Old Testament*, edited by James B. Pritchard, 2nd ed. (Princeton, NJ, 1955), 405–7, and Eric Voegelin, *Israel and Revelation* (Baton Rouge, LA, 1956), 98–101.
8. T. R. Glover, *Progress in Religion: An Historial Inquiry* (London, 1922), 143–44.
9. "And this is the writing that was written, MENE, MENE, TEKEL, UPHARSIN. This is the interpretation of the thing: MENE; God hath numbered thy kingdom, and finished it. TEKEL; Thou art weighed in the balances, and art found wanting. PERES; Thy kingdom is divided, and given to the Medes and Persians." Daniel 5:25–28.
10. Moslems proclaim Mohammed as the greatest of the prophets, of course; and the Mormons believe Joseph Smith (1805–44) to have been a latter-day prophet.
11. *The Prophets* (New York, 1971), Vol. II, xvii.

12. Sir Arthur Quiller-Couch ingeniously compared the books of the Bible with works of English literature, suggesting that with the best of intentions, strong impediments have been placed between the common reader and the understanding of sacred literature. Let us imagine—as Quiller-Couch suggested in 1920—"a volume including the great books of our literature all bound together in some such order as this: *Paradise Lost,* Darwin's *Descent of Man, The Anglo-Saxon Chronicle,* Walter Map, Mill's *On Liberty*, Hooker's *Ecclesiastical Polity, The Annual Register,* Froissart, Adam Smith's *Wealth of Nations, Domesday Book*, *Le Morte d'Arthur*, Campbell's *Lives of the Lord Chancellors*, Boswell's *Johnson*, Barbour's *The Bruce*, Hakluyt's *Voyages*, Clarendon, Macaulay, the plays of Shakespeare, Shelley's *Prometheus Unbound, The Faerie Queen*, Palgrave's *Golden Treasury*, Bacon's *Essays*, Swinburne's *Poems and Ballads*, FitzGerald's *Omar Khayyam*, Wordsworth, Browning, *Sartor Resartus*, Burton's *Anatomy of Melancholy*, Burke's *Letters on a Regicide Peace, Ossian, Piers Plowman*, Burke's *Thoughts on the Present Discontents*, Quarles, Newman's *Apologia*, Donne's *Sermons*, Ruskin, Blake, *The Deserted Village, Manfred*, Blair's *Grave, The Complaint of Deor,* Bailey's *Festus,* Thompson's *Hound of Heaven*.

"Will you next imagine that in this volume most of the authors' names are lost; that, of the few that survive, a number have found their way into the wrong places; that Ruskin for example is credited with *Sartor Resartus;* that *Laus Veneris* and *Dolores* are ascribed to Queen Elizabeth, *The Anatomy of Melancholy* to Charles II; and that, as for the titles, these were never invented by the authors, but by a Committee?

"Will you still go on to imagine that all the poetry is printed as prose; while all the long paragraphs of prose are broken up into short verses, so that they resemble the little passages set out for parsing or analysis in an examination paper?" (See Sir Arthur Quiller-Couch, *On the Art of Reading* [Cambridge, 1920], 154–55.)

13. *Hebrew Thought Compared with Greek*, trans. Jules L. Moreau (New York, 1960), 137–38.

14. Gerhart Niemeyer, *Between Nothingness and Paradise* (Baton Rouge, LA, 1971), 166–67.

15. New York, 1947, 51–61.

16. L. M. Nesbitt, *Desert and Forest: The Exploration of Abyssinian Danakil* (London, 1955), 269.

17. Marcion, about the middle of the second century of the Christian era, taught that Christians ought to subscribe only to the "pure gospel" of Saint Paul, and that the Yahweh of the Jews really was not God, but the Demiurge, under whom mankind suffered until the coming of Christ.

18. Daniel Boorstin, *The Americans: The Colonial Experience* (New York, 1958), 19.

19. On the power of Calvinism in early America, see C. Gregg Singer, *A Theological Interpretation of American History* (Nutley, NJ, 1964), particularly the Introduction.

20. *The Democratic Experiment: American Political Theory* (Princeton, NJ, 1967), 35.

21. Clinton Lawrence Rossiter, *Seedtime of the Republic: The Origin of the American Tradition of Political Liberty* (New York, 1953), 55.

What Did Americans Inherit from the Ancients? (80–90)

22. Richard M. Gummere, *The American Colonial Mind and the Classical Tradition: Essays in Comparative Culture* (Cambridge, MA, 1963); *Seven Wise Men of Colonial America* (Cambridge, MA, 1967); *Seneca the Philosopher and His Modern Message* (New York, 1963).

23. For such Tudor translations, see T. S. Eliot, "Seneca in Elizabethan Translation" and "Shakespeare and the Stoicism of Seneca," in his *Selected Essays, 1917–1932* (New York, 1932).

24. See M. E. Bradford, "According to Their Genius: Politics and the Example of Patrick Henry," *A Better Guide Than Reason: Studies in the American Revolution* (La Salle, IL, 1979).

25. Ernest Barker, *Political Thought in England From Spencer to the Present Day* (London, 1938), 167.
26. With a foreword by Russell Kirk (Cumberland, VA, 1987).
27. Letter to Thomas Jefferson, 16 July 1814, in *The Life and Works of John Adams*, edited by Charles Francis Adams (Boston, 1856), Vol. X, 102–3.
28. Facsim. ed. (Clifton, NJ, 1872), 2–3.
29. "The Patristical Idea of Antichrist," *Discussions and Arguments on Various Subjects*, New ed. (London, 1891).

The Light of the Middle Ages (91–106)

30. Steven Runciman, *A History of the Crusades* (Cambridge, 1954), Vol. III, 160.
31. Henry Osborn Taylor, *The Medieval Mind*, 4th ed. (Cambridge, MA, 1950), Vol. II, 536, 586n.
32. Ibid., 409.
33. D'Arcy Thompson, "St. Andrews," in *Science and the Classics* (Oxford, 1940), 240.

The Rarity of the God-Fearing Man (115–23)

34. James Fitzjames Stephen, *Liberty, Equality, Fraternity* (London, 1873), 45–46.
35. London, 1950, 66.

The Necessity for a General Culture (124–34)

36. Christopher Dawson, *Religion and Culture* (London, 1948), 48–49.
37. London, 1949, 2, n. 1.
38. T. S. Eliot, *Notes Towards the Definition of Culture* (London, 1949), 21.
39. Ibid., 26.
40. Ibid., 25.
41. Grand Rapids, 1988, 114–15.
42. Eliot, 23.
43. Address to the American Enterprise Institute, in *The Washington Times*, 28 May 1991, C1, C3.
44. "Toward a Divisive Diversity," *The Wall Street Journal*, 25 June 1991, A18.
45. *The Washington Times*, C3.
46. "Toward a Divisive Diversity," A18.
47. Eliot, 27.

III. Principles of Order

Edmund Burke: A Revolution of Theoretic Dogma (138–53)

1. Henry Crabb Robinson, in 1811, re-read Burke's speeches during the Regency debate. "Their extravagance and intemperance is not less than their splendour. . . . In one of his vehement bursts, after representing the King as hurled from his throne by God, he asserted that the assigning him an establishment was covering his bed with purple, putting a reed in his hand and crown of thorns on his brow, and crying: Hail King of the British! The seeming scorn

of such an allusion, as on other occasions, raised a hostility to the orator quite incompatible with the desired effect of eloquence, to propitiate; yet abstracted from such an impression the image is very happy. Charles Lamb, however, said it was in a vile taste, a little in Mr. Fuller's style." *Henry Crabb Robinson on Books and Their Writers,* edited by Edith J. Morley (London, 1938), Vol. I, 20.

2. "Edmund Burke and the French Revolution," *The Century Magazine*, Vol. LXII (N.S., Vol. XL) (September 1901), 784.

3. Paine certainly wrote one letter to Burke during this period, and perhaps others; also, he may have conversed with him in the autumn of 1789. See Thomas W. Copeland's essay, "Burke, Paine, and Jefferson," in his *Our Eminent Friend Edmund Burke: Six Essays* (New Haven, CT, 1949).

4. *The Heresy of Democracy: A Study in the History of Government* (London, 1954), 188.

5. For a criticism of the rationalistic politics which emerged in the French Revolution and which have exerted considerable power ever since, see Michael Oakeshott, *Rationalism in Politics: And Other Essays* (London, 1962).

6. "Edmund Burke and the French Revolution," 792.

7. Many editions of the *Reflections* exist; that best annotated, the second volume of E. J. Payne's *Burke: Select Works* (Oxford, 1898), unhappily is long out of print. The present writer's introduction appears in the Arlington House edition of the *Reflections* (New Rochelle, NY, 1965).

8. This war of pamphlets may be surveyed by consulting two convenient anthologies: *The Debate on the French Revolution, 1789 1799*, edited by Alfred Cobban (London, 1950) and *The Burke-Paine Controversy: Texts and Criticism*, edited by Ray B. Browne (New York, 1963). The latter volume contains comments by twentieth-century writers.

9. For two brief studies of Burke's influence on American men of politics see James P. McClellan, "Judge Story's Debt to Burke," *The Burke Newsletter*, Vol. VII, No. 3 (Spring 1966), 583–86, and Russell Kirk, "John Randolph of Roanoke on the Genius of Edmund Burke," *The Burke Newsletter*, Vol. IV, No. 1 (Fall 1962), 167–69. For some general remarks on Burke's meaning for Americans see Russell Kirk's review of the second edition of Clinton Rossiter's *Conservatism in America*, in *The Burke Newsletter*, Vol. IV, No. 2 (Winter 1962–63), 190–93.

10. Walter Scott to Henry Francis Scott the younger, of Harden, January 10, 1831, in John Lockhart, *Memoirs of the Life of Sir Walter Scott, Bart.* (Edinburgh, 1853), Vol. X, 32.

11. See Chapter VIII, James T. Boulton, *The Language of Politics in the Age of Wilkes and Burke* (London, 1963).

12. Ibid., 149.

13. See Russell Kirk's "Edmund Burke and Natural Rights," *The Review of Politics*, Vol. 13, No. 4 (October 1951), 441–56, and "Burke and the Philosophy Prescription," *Journal of the History of Ideas*, Vol. XIV, No. 3 (June 1953), 365–89.

14. Boulton, 260–61.

15. November 29, 1793, in Wentworth Woodhouse Papers (Sheffield Central Library), Book I, 945.

16. Louis I. Bredvold, *The Brave New World of Enlightenment* (Ann Arbor, MI, 1961), 134.

17. For Burke's influence on Wordsworth, Coleridge, and others, see Edward Dowden, *The French Revolution and English Literature* (London, 1897) and Basil Willey, *The Eighteenth Century Background* (London, 1949). For Burke's association with literary people of his own generation see the thorough study by Donald Cross Bryant, *Edmund Burke and His Literary Friends* (St. Louis, MO, 1939).

The Prescience of Tocqueville (154–65)

18. Alexis de Tocqueville, *Memoir, Letters, and Remains of Alexis de Tocqueville*, edited by M. C. M. Simpson, trans. Henry Reeve, Vol. II (London, 1862), 384.
19. "Alexis de Tocqueville and Democracy," *The Social and Political Ideas of Some Representative Thinkers of the Victorian Age*, edited by F. J. C. Hearnshaw (London, 1933), 111–12.
20. C. E. M. Joad, *Decadence: A Philosophical Inquiry* (London, 1948), 393.
21. *Democracy in America*, edited by Phillips Bradley (New York, 1948), Vol. II, 261.
22. *Lectures on the French Revolution*, edited by John Neville Figgis and Reginald Vere Laurence (London, 1916), 357.
23. *Memoir, Letters, and Remains,* 64.
24. A distinguished historian recently wrote to me from his native state of New York, "Give *homo novus Americanus* a television set, a frigidaire, a vacuum cleaner, a cocktail shaker, and strip chromium around his kitchen, his bathroom, and his car, and he will boast of the highest standard of living in the world; even though nothing he owns will last much longer than the term in which he has contracted to pay for it."
25. *Democracy in America*, Vol. II, 318.
26. Ibid., Vol. II, 136.
27. Ibid., Vol. II, 228–29.
28. Ibid., Vol. II, 133.
29. Ibid., Vol. II, 145.
30. Ibid., Vol. II, 148.
31. Ibid., Vol. I, 327.
32. Ibid., Vol. I, 236.
33. Ibid, Vol. II, 367–68.
34. *Recollections*, edited by J. P. Mayer (London, 1948), 202.
35. *Democracy in America*, Vol. II, 296.
36. Ibid., Vol. II, 289.
37. Ibid., Vol. II, 282.
38. Ibid., Vol. II, 245–46.
39. Ibid., Vol. I, 10.
40. *Recollections*, 143.
41. *Democracy in America*, Vol. II, 88.
42. September 28, 1853, in *Memoir, Letters, and Remains,* Vol. II, 234–35.
43. A. J. P. Taylor, *From Napoleon to Stalin: Comments on European History* (London, 1950), 66.

T. S. Eliot's Permanent Things (166–75)

44. T. S. Eliot, *Selected Essays*, *1917–1932*, 1st ed. (New York, 1932), 315.
45. Ibid., 6.
46. T. S. Eliot, *On Poetry and Poets* (New York, 1957), 137.
47. *Selected Essays*, 4.
48. T. S. Eliot, *The Idea of a Christian Society* (New York, 1940), 64.
49. *Selected Essays*, 15–16.
50. *Selected Essays*, New ed. (New York, 1964), 351.
51. New York, 1949, 111.

52. *Selected Essays*, 360–61.
53. Ibid., 313.
54. *Selected Essays*, 332.

Eric Voegelin's Normative Labor (176–201)

55. Eric Voegelin, *In Search of Order* (Baton Rouge, LA, and London, 1987).
56. "On Readiness to Rational Discussion," *Freedom and Serfdom*, edited by Albert Hunold (Dordrecht, Holland, 1961), 280.
57. *Journal of the History of Ideas*, Vol. 19 (1958), 444.
58. See "The Man in the Duststorm," in Grene's *Man in His Pride: A Study in the Political Philosophy of Thucydides and Plato* (Chicago, 1950), 95–204.

IV. The Moral Imagination

The Moral Imagination (206–18)

1. Albert Fowler, "Can Literature Corrupt?" *Modern Age: A Quarterly Review,* Vol. 3, No. 2 (Spring 1959), 125–33.

Normative Art and Modern Vices (219–40)

2. See David Riesman, *The Lonely Crowd: A Study of the Changing American Character*, with Nathan Glazer and Reuel Denney, Abridged ed. (New Haven, CT, 1971), 255–56.

T. S. Eliot's The Waste Land *(269–81)*

3. *Selected Essays, 1917–1932*, lst ed. (New York, 1932), 7–10.
4. See T. S. Eliot, "Ezra Pound" (1946), in *Ezra Pound, Collection of Essays . . . on His Sixty-Fifth Birthday*, edited by Peter Russell (London and New York, 1950), 27–28. Actually, Eliot had given the manuscript of *The Waste Land*, in October, 1922, to John Quinn, of New York, to express his thanks for Quinn's many services to him; also he had sold to Quinn, for a hundred and forty dollars, a mass of other early manuscripts of his. This manuscript of *The Waste Land* remained in Quinn's possession and (after 1924) in that of Quinn's sister, until the New York Public Library bought these materials in 1958; this acquisition was kept secret until 1968.

"Criticisms accepted so far as understood, with thanks," Eliot wrote to Pound from London, in January, 1922. Their correspondence at this time contains considerable information as to Pound's changes in the manuscript. See *The Letters of Ezra Pound, 1907–1941*, edited by D. D. Paige (New York, 1950), 167–72.
5. Eliot even captured, as Roy Campbell rejoices, "those who were then the most fervent admirers of J. E. Flecker, Brooke, and Lascelles Abercrombie," that "green and pleasant land" set, who abruptly turned from depreciation of Eliot to adulation, becoming his "most ardent admirers and imitators. . . . From then on the influence of Eliot literally swallowed up many of these minor poets as a blue whale swallows mites of krill." See Roy Campbell, *Light on a Dark Horse* (Chicago, 1952), 203.

6. E. M. Forster, *Abinger Harvest* (London and New York, 1936), 89–96.
7. "Readings from the Lives of the Saints," in his *Exile's Return* (New York, 1934), 123–28.
8. Perhaps the most convincing examination is that of Cleanth Brooks, "*The Waste Land:* Critique of the Myth," in his *Modern Poetry and the Tradition* (Chapel Hill, NC, 1939), 136–72. Another readable and intelligent treatment is that of C. M. Bowra, in his book *The Creative Experiment* (London, 1949), 159–88.
9. *The Autobiography of William Carlos Williams* (New York, 1951), 174.
10. *The Invisible Poet: T. S. Eliot* (New York, 1959), 171.
11. "The horror! The horror!", from Conrad's *Heart of Darkness* (1902), was the epigraph Eliot first chose for *The Waste Land*; Pound persuaded him to supplant it with Petronius's account of the bored sibyl.
12. John Ruskin's name rarely is coupled with Eliot's; yet it was Ruskin who, in the literature of the previous century, gave the best expression of cultural continuity, defended in the twentieth century by Eliot. Take this passage from Ruskin's *Sesame and Lilies* (London, 1865): "We play with the words of the dead that would teach us, and strike them far from us with our bitter, restless will; little thinking that those leaves which the wind scatters had been piled, not only upon a gravestone, but upon the seal of an enchanted vault—nay, the gate of a great city of sleeping kings, who would awake for us, and walk with us, if we knew but how to call them by their names."
13. "Marie" and her murmurs are drawn from the autobiography of Countess Marie Larisch, *My Past* (New York and London, 1916), closely connected with the Archduke Rudolph and Maria Vetsera, who died mysteriously at Mayerling: the suggestion of private and public disorder is obvious. See George L. K. Morris, "Marie, Marie, Hold on Tight," in *Partisan Review*, Vol. XXI (March–April 1954); reprinted in *T. S. Eliot: A Collection of Critical Essays*, edited by Hugh Kenner (Englewood Cliffs, NJ, 1962), 86–88.
14. New York, 1953, 134–35.
15. London, 1952, 39.
16. Chapel Hill, NC, 1939, 145–46.
17. "The First Impact of *The Waste Land*," in *T. S. Eliot: A Symposium for His Seventieth Birthday*, edited by Neville Braybrooke (Freeport, NY, 1968, c1958), 30–31.

V. Places and People

Criminal Character and Mercy (334–44)

1. First published in *Frights: New Stories of Suspense and Supernatural Terror*, edited by McCauley and Kirby (New York, 1976), 5–44. Republished in Russell Kirk's *The Princess of All Lands* (Sauk City, WI, 1979).
2. Published in *Whispers II*, edited by Stuart Schiff (Garden City, NY, 1979), 75–95.
3. Published in Kirk's *Princess of All Lands*.

VII. Decadence and Renewal in Education

The Conservative Purpose of a Liberal Education (398–407)

1. T. S. Eliot, *To Criticize the Critic and Other Writings* (New York, 1965), 61–124.

The Intemperate Professor (418–33)

2. Paul F. Lazarsfeld and Wagner Thielens, Jr., *The Academic Mind* (Glencoe, IL, 1958).

VIII. The American Republic

The Framers: Not Philosophes but Gentlemen (450–60)

1. Edmund Burke, *The Works of the Right Honourable Edmund Burke* (London, 1826), VI, 217–18.
2. With an Introduction by H. L. Mencken (New York, 1931), 112–13.
3. For the religious professions of the Framers, see M. E. Bradford, *A Worthy Company* (Marlborough, NH, 1982).
4. On knowledge of the classics in eighteenth-century America, see Richard M. Gummere, *The American Colonial Mind and the Classical Tradition* (Cambridge, MA, 1963) and his *Seven Wise Men of Colonial America* (Cambridge, MA, 1967).
5. Cambridge, 1648, 138–41.
6. *Proceedings and Debates of the Virginia State Convention of 1829–30* (Richmond, VA, 1830), 312–21; reprinted in Russell Kirk, *John Randolph of Roanoke* (Indianapolis, 1978), 214.

The Constitution and the Antagonist World (461–71)

7. Speech on a motion made in the House of Commons, the 7th of May 1782, for a committee to inquire into the state of the representation of the commons in parliament, *The Works of the Right Honourable Edmund Burke* (London, 1856), VI, 153.
8. *Calhoun: Basic Documents*, edited by John M. Anderson (State College, PA, 1952), 79.
9. *Burke: Select Works*, edited by E. J. Payne (Oxford, 1898), II, 106–10.
10. *Works of the Honourable Edmund Burke*, VI, 217.
11. *Burke: Select Works*, II, 70–71.
12. For analysis and criticism of the Supreme Court's enlargement of its powers, see Raoul Berger, *Government by Judiciary: The Transformation of the Fourteenth Amendment* (Cambridge, MA, 1977); Christopher Wolfe, *The Rise of Modern Judicial Review: From Constitutional Interpretation to Judge-Made Law* (New York, 1986); Carrol D. Kilgore, *Judicial Tyranny* (Nashville, TN, 1977).
13. "Two Letters Addressed to a Member of the Present Parliament on the Proposals for Peace with the Regicide Directory of France," *Burke: Select Works*, III, 4–5, 10.

John Randolph of Roanoke: The Planter-Statesman (472–91)

14. John Taylor, *A Definition of Parties; or the Political Effects of the Paper System Considered* (Philadelphia, 1794), 8.

15. See Henry Adams, *History of the United States of America During the Administrations of Jefferson and Madison* (New York, 1891–98), IV, 281.
16. *Annals of Congress* (14th Cong., 1st sess.), 688.
17. August 30, 1813, in Edmund Quincy, *Life of Josiah Quincy of Massachusetts* (Boston, 1867), 336.
18. July 5, 1811 (Henry St. George Tucker Papers, Duke University).
19. July 24, 1824, in Hugh A. Garland, *The Life of John Randolph of Roanoke* (New York, 1850), II, 225.
20. *Proceedings and Debates of the Virginia State Convention*, 790.
21. See Randolph to Quincy, July 1, 1824, in *Life of Josiah Quincy of Massachusetts*, 353.
22. June 28, 1809, in Thomas Jefferson, *Correspondence Between Thomas Jefferson and Pierre Samuel du Pont de Nemours* (Boston, 1910), 124–27.
23. *Annals of Congress* (18th Cong., 1st sess.), 1, 2362.
24. *Richmond Enquirer*, April 1, 1813.
25. John Taylor, *An Inquiry into the Principles and Policy of the Government of the United States* (New Brunswick, NJ, 1994), 61.
26. See Randolph's letter, signed "Decius," *Richmond Enquirer*, August 15, 1806.
27. October 15, 1803 (Randolph Papers, Virginia State Library).
28. *Annals of Congress* (18th Cong., 1st sess.), I, 1310.
29. Josiah Quincy, *Life of Josiah Quincy of Massachusetts*, 343.
30. Macon to N. W. Edwards, February 17, 1828 (Macon Papers, North Carolina State Department of Archives and History).
31. *Proceedings and Debates of the Virginia State Convention*, 493.
32. Ibid., 802.
33. Taylor to J. M. Garnett, December 17, 1807 (Garnett MSS, Duke University).
34. See especially *Annals of Congress* (10th Cong., 1st sess.), 1904–12.
35. *Richmond Enquirer*, December 5, 1812.
36. *Annals of Congress* (12th Cong., 1st sess.), 442–48.
37. *Richmond Enquirer*, April 1, 1815.
38. *Annals of Congress* (14th Cong., 1st sess.), 845.
39. *Richmond Enquirer*, January 14, 1813.
40. Ibid., January 27, 1816.
41. Ibid., January 31, 1824.
42. Brockenbrough to Randolph, (?) 1808 (?) (copy in Randolph Letters University of North Carolina).
43. *Annals of Congress* (9th Cong., 1st sess.), 560.
44. Hugh A. Garland, *The Life of John Randolph of Roanoke*, I, 213.
45. *Annals of Congress* (14th Cong., 1st sess.), 683–88.
46. Ibid. (18th Cong., 1st sess.), II, 2360.
47. Macon to N. W. Edwards, March 3, 1828 (Macon Papers, North Carolina State Department of Archives and History).
48. William Cabell Bruce, *John Randolph of Roanoke* (New York, 1922), I, 430.
49. *Annals of Congress* (14th Cong., 1st sess.), 1110–13.
50. Ibid., 1339.
51. Ibid. (12th Cong., 1st sess.), 525.

Orestes Brownson and the Just Society (492–501)

52. *The Works of Orestes A. Brownson*, edited by Henry F. Brownson (Detroit, 1882–87), XVI, 68, 81.
53. Orestes A. Brownson, *The American Republic*, facsimile ed. (Clifton, NJ, 1972), 363–64.
54. "Demagoguism," *Works*, XV, 438.
55. "Liberalism and Progress" (1864), *Works*, XX, 354.
56. *The American Republic,* 18–19.
57. Orestes A. Brownson, "Socialism and the Church," *Essays and Reviews, Chiefly on Theology, Politics, and Socialism* (New York, 1852), 499.

IX. CONSERVATORS OF CIVILIZATION

The Conservative Humanism of Irving Babbitt (514–24)

1. Irving Babbitt, *Literature and the American College: Essays in Defense of the Humanities* (Boston and New York, 1908), 60.
2. Irving Babbitt, *Rousseau and Romanticism* (Boston and New York, 1919), 374.
3. Ibid., 25.
4. Irving Babbitt, *Democracy and Leadership* (Boston and New York, 1924), 6.
5.Irving Babbitt, *On Being Creative and Other Essays* (Boston and New York, 1932), 232.

Paul Elmer More on Justice and Faith (525–34)

6. Paul Elmer More, *On Being Human*, in *New Shelburne Essays*, III (Princeton, NJ, 1936), 27.
7. *Shelburne Essays* (Boston, 1904–21), VII, 201–2.
8. *On Being Human*, 158.
9. Ibid., 268–69.
10. *Shelburne Essays*, IX, 21.
11. Ibid., VII, 191.
12. Ibid., IX, 56.
13. Ibid., XI, 256.
14. Princeton, 1931, 170.
15. Quoted in Robert Shafer, *Paul Elmer More and American Criticism* (New Haven, CT, 1935), 271.
16. *On Being Human*, 143.

George Santayana Buries Liberalism (534–42)

17. George Santayana, *Persons and Places, Vol. 2: The Middle Span* (New York, 1945), 149.
18. Ibid., 35–36.
19. George Santayana, *The Realm of Spirit* (New York, 1940), 219.
20. George Santayana, *Soliloquies in England and Later Soliloquies* (New York, 1992), 188.
21. *The Middle Span,* 134.
22. George Santayana, *Winds of Doctrine: Studies in Contemporary Opinion* (New York, 1926), vi.

23. *Soliloquies*, 176.

24. *Dominations and Powers* (New York, 1951), 348.

25. George Santayana, *Character and Opinion in the United States* (New York, 1920), 226.

26. *Reason in Society* (New York, 1948 [1905]), 69.

27. *The Middle Span,* 169.

28. *Dominations and Powers,* 384.

Index

The length of the index reflects the extraordinary range of a visionary man of letters. In its alphabetical arrangement and specificity of detail, the index goes beyond essay titles and the editor's own introductions to the book's nine divisions as well as the headnotes to each selected essay. The main aim of this index is to facilitate a reader's access to the particular ideas, themes, subjects, passages, places, books, and names found in Russell Kirk's essays. Many entries also provide information that augments Kirk's own texts. The multidimensional and interdisciplinary character of his work has been duly integrated to show not only the comparativist orientation of his achievement but also the connectedness of his educational, economic, political, philosophical, and religious interpretations. Even a cursory glance at the index will perhaps challenge a reader to turn to essays in their entirety. If that should in fact happen, it will further confirm the need for an extensive index that finally serves as an index to a preeminent conservative mind.

A

B

C

D

E

F

G

H

I

J

K

L

M

N

O

P

Q

R

S

U

V

W

X

Y

Z

With Gratitude

In undertaking this project nearly a decade ago I had the intention of including in a single volume representative essays of Russell Kirk and, in turn, conveying the thought of an extraordinary man of letters whose value to us increases with the passage of time. My critical intention is at last realized with the publication of *The Essential Russell Kirk: Selected Essays.*

Here I am pleased to record my debt to the following individuals who, through the years, enabled me to prepare and craft the thousand-page manuscript: Mr. Jeffrey O. Nelson, Dr. Kirk's son-in-law and sometime assistant, who from the outset believed in the project and provided me with astute advice regarding the selection and organization of the content; Mrs. Annette Kirk, who unfailingly encouraged me in my daunting task as editor of the anthology and kindly granted me permission to reprint in it writings from her late husband's lifework; Dr. Jeremy Beer, the editor in chief of ISI Books, Jennifer Connolly, Kara Björklund Beer, and John M. Vella, who devoted copious and creative labors to the design and production of the book. Also, I am grateful to T. Kenneth Cribb, Jr., president of the Intercollegiate Studies Institute, for his steady support of my editorial mission.

I want to give especial thanks to my longtime collaborator, Mary E. Slayton, who toiled tirelessly on the manuscript at every stage, from its inception to its final publication. Her work on the Russell Kirk chronology and her compilation of the index exemplify her prodigious endeavors.

This anthology should help remind Kirk's readers of the enduring importance of his vision and introduce a rising generation to the beneficences of a conservative mind that speaks to our time and history. I am confident that those who turn to the pages of this book will be challenged by a thinker who inspires us to transcend the passions and distractions of the hour, and the clamor of opinions.

The Essential Russell Kirk

Designed and typeset by Beer Editorial and Design, Kennett Square, Pennsylvania
Composed in Perpetua, a typeface designed by Eric Gill (1882–1940)
Printed and bound by McNaughton & Gunn, Saline, Michigan
Printed on 50# Natural Offset
Bound in Arrestox Linen